Lecture Notes in Computer Science   8223

Commenced Publication in 1973
Founding and Former Series Editors:
Gerhard Goos, Juris Hartmanis, and Jan van Leeuwen

Mukaddim Pathan   Guiyi Wei
Giancarlo Fortino (Eds.)

Internet and Distributed Computing Systems

6th International Conference, IDCS 2013
Hangzhou, China, October 28-30, 2013
Proceedings

 Springer

Volume Editors

Mukaddim Pathan
Telstra Corporation Limited
Strategic Planning and Investment
Melbourne, VIC 3000, Australia
E-mail: mukaddim.pathan@team.telstra.com

Guiyi Wei
Zhejiang Gongshang University
School of Computer and Information Engineering
Hangzhou 310018, China
E-mail: weigy@zjgsu.edu.cn

Giancarlo Fortino
Università della Calabria
Dipartimento di Informatica, Elettronica e Sistemistica, DEIS
87036 Rende, Italy
E-mail: g.fortino@unical.it

ISSN 0302-9743 e-ISSN 1611-3349
ISBN 978-3-642-41427-5 e-ISBN 978-3-642-41428-2
DOI 10.1007/978-3-642-41428-2
Springer Heidelberg New York Dordrecht London

Library of Congress Control Number: 2013949694

CR Subject Classification (1998): C.2.4, C.2, H.3-4, J.1, D.2, D.4.6, K.6.5

LNCS Sublibrary: SL 3 – Information Systems and Application,
incl. Internet/Web and HCI

Typesetting: Camera-ready by author, data conversion by Scientific Publishing Services, Chennai, India

Printed on acid-free paper

Springer is part of Springer Science+Business Media (www.springer.com)

Preface

Following the previous five successful editions of IDCS – IDCS 2008 in Khulna, Bangladesh, IDCS 2009 in Jeju Island, Korea, IDCS 2010 and IDCS 2011 in Melbourne, Australia, IDCS 2012 in Wu Yi Shan, China – IDCS 2013 was the sixth in the series to promote research in diverse fields related to the Internet and distributed computing systems.

The emergence of the Web as a ubiquitous platform for innovations has laid the foundation for the rapid growth of the Internet. Side-by-side, the use of mobile and wireless devices such as PDAs, laptops, and cell phones for accessing the Internet has paved the ways for related technologies to flourish through recent developments. In addition, the popularity of sensor networks is promoting a better integration of the digital world with the physical environment.

IDCS 2013 received innovative papers on emerging technologies related to the Internet and distributed systems to support the effective design and efficient implementation of high-performance computer networks. The audience included researchers and industry practitioners who are interested in different aspects of the Internet and distributed systems, with a particular focus on practical experiences with the design and implementation of related technologies as well as their theoretical perspectives.

IDCS 2013 received a large number of submissions, from which only 19 regular papers were accepted after a careful review and selection process. This year's conference also featured 12 invited papers from renowned academics and industry practitioners on the conference topics. The contributions to IDCS 2013 covered the topics of ad hoc and sensor networks; Internet and Web technologies; network operations and management; information infrastructure; and resilience, fault tolerance, and availability.

IDCS 2013 was held in the beautiful city of Hangzhou, in the Zhejiang province of China. The conference organization was supported by Zhejiang Gong-Shang University and was held at the Hangzhou Sunday Sunny Resort. The Commonwealth Scientific and Industrial Research Organization (CSIRO), the national government body of scientific research in Australia, was the primary sponsor of the conference. The best paper award of the conference was supported by Daily Positive (D+), a not-for-profit media initiative. The successful organization of IDCS 2013 was possible thanks to the dedication and hard work of a number of individuals. Specifically, we would like to thank Yuxin Mao, Yu Wang, and Jun Shao for their commendable work with the proceedings preparation and conference organization. We also express our gratitude to the honorary chair of IDCS 2013, Prof. Wenzhan Dai, Zhejiang GongShang University, China, and the general chairs Yun Ling, Zhejiang Gongshang University, China, and Dimitrios Georgakopoulos, CSIRO, Australia, for their support of the conference. Last but not the least, we are thankful to all the student volunteers for their effort in the conference organization during 28–30 October 2013.

October 2013   Mukaddim Pathan
                                                              Guiyi Wei
                                                        Giancarlo Fortino

Organization

Honorary Chair

Wenzhan Dai   Zhejiang GongShang University, China

General Chairs

Yun Ling   Zhejiang GongShang University, China
Dimitrios Georgakopoulos   CSIRO, Australia

Program Chairs

Mukaddim Pathan   Telstra Corporation Limited, Australia
Guiyi Wei   Zhejiang GongShang University, China
Giancarlo Fortino   University of Calabria, Italy

Program Committee

Tarem Ahmed	BRAC University, Bangladesh
Hani Alzaid	King Abdulaziz City for Science and Technology, Saudi Arabia
Doina Bein	The Pennsylvania State University, USA
Rajkumar Buyya	The University of Melbourne, Australia
Michael Compton	CSIRO, Australia
Giuseppe Di Fatta	University of Reading, UK
Marcos Dias De Assuncao	IBM Research, Brazil
Abdelkarim Erradi	Qatar University, Qatar
Zongming Fei	University of Kentucky, USA
Joaquin Garcia-Alfaro	Telecom Bretagne, France
Saurabh Kumar Garg	IBM Research, Australia
Chryssis Georgiou	University of Cyprus, Cyprus
Soumya Ghosh	Indian Institute of Technology, Kharagpur, India
Victor Govindaswamy	Texas A&M University-Texarkana, USA
Ragib Hasan	University of Alabama at Birmingham, USA
Mohammad Mehedi Hassan	King Saud University, Saudi Arabia
Dimitrios Katsaros	University of Thessaly, Greece
Hae Young Lee	ETRI, South Korea
Jaime Lloret	Polytechnic University of Valencia, Spain
Rongxing Lu	University of Waterloo, Canada
Carlo Mastroianni	ICAR-CNR, Italy

Table of Contents

A Network-Controlled Approach for the Timely and Reliable Acquisition of Bursty Data in WMSNs*

Phan Van Vinh[1], Je Wook Kim[2], Hoon Oh[1,**], and Levendovszky Janos[3]

[1] School of Computer Engineering and Information Technology
University of Ulsan, Ulsan, Korea
[2] Corporate Research Center of USIS, Ltd, Ulsan, Korea
[3] Faculty of Electrical Engineering and Informatics,
Budapest University of Technology and Economics, Budapest, Hungary
pvvinhbk@gmail.com, jwkim@usis.kr, hoonoh@ulsan.ac.kr,
levendov@hit.bme.hu

Abstract. To build a Safety MOnitoring and Control System (SMOCS) that monitors the safety of the workers and warns them of hazardous situation, many sensor communication devices with different data rates are deployed in the target field. SMOCS collects small scalar data such as temperature, the oxygen content of the air, the occurrence of smoke, gas and/or flame from sensor devices periodically and judges the safety of the working environment primarily. If it perceives a dangerous sign, it acquires still image or video streaming on demand to confirm the situation. Otherwise, the evacuation order by any misjudgment can cause a big loss or annoyance. Since these bursty data have to be delivered to SMOCS reliably and with time constraints, it is challengeable to process those data using a wireless sensor network. A new TDMA-based protocol is designed and is experimented with 30 sensor devices. The results indicate that the new protocol satisfies application requirements well.

Keywords: WMSNs, bursty data, slotted scheduling, energy consumption.

1   Introduction

Wireless Multimedia Sensor Networks (WMSNs) that consist of scalar sensors and multimedia sensors can be used for building a Safety Monitoring and Control System (SMOCS) that monitors the safety of the workers who have to work long in the closed and dangerous working environments and warns them of any hazardous situation. The SMOCS server stores, manages, and analyses data or context information that were sent periodically by every node, and judges whether the target field is safe or not based on the collected context information. If a dangerous situation is perceived, the server sends a request to the workers so that they can take some measures against the danger.

* This research was supported by Basic Science Research Program through the National Research Foundation of Korea (NRF) funded by the Ministry of Education (2013R1A1A2013396).
** Corresponding author.

M. Pathan, G. Wei, and G. Fortino (Eds.): IDCS 2013, LNCS 8223, pp. 1–15, 2013.

In this case, if nodes send scalar data and/or multimedia data periodically without restriction, high data loss and transmission delay or waste of energy consumption will be inevitable due to the limited bandwidth and energy resource. Hence, the efficiency of data processing will degrade sharply, thus paralyzing the network.

In this paper, we discuss the design of a MAC protocol in which a server controls the network in two phases in order to overcome the bandwidth and energy constraints of WMSNs. For example, in case of fire detection, the nodes with temperature sensor, oxygen sensor, gas sensor or flame sensor sends their scalar data to a server periodically. If the server judges that a fire has occurred based on the scalar context information, it sends a command to a node equipped with a multimedia sensor which is located in the spot and requests still image or video data for the confirmation of the fire. If data are processed in two phases, traffic demand will be almost comparable to those in the traditional wireless sensor networks. Accordingly the problem of network efficiency can be overcome to some extent. However, two challenging issues have to be addressed. Firstly, a reliable transmission of the command should be secured since a command is sent in a critical moment. Secondly, the multimedia bursty data have to be delivered to the server reliably and within a specified time bound.

The existing approaches that have been proposed for designing a MAC protocol in WSN can be classified into two types: contention-based MAC protocols and TDMA-based MAC protocols. Contention-based MAC protocols which are based on the CSMA (Carrier Sense Multiple Access) scheme are widely employed in wireless networks due to their simplicity, flexibility, and robustness. Because of energy constraint, most early contention-based MAC protocols focused on low-duty cycle applications to reduce energy consumption. S-MAC [1] with an active-sleep cycle puts nodes to sleep periodically in idle listening period to conserve energy. However, a static active-sleep cycle of S-MAC can cause packet delay and low throughput in case of variable traffic loads. T-MAC [2] can mitigate the drawbacks of S-MAC by using an adaptive active-sleep cycle. B-MAC [3] employs Clear Channel Assessment (CCA) to enhance the utilization of channel and uses Low Power Listening (LPL) scheme to minimize the energy consumption. However, because of using the long preamble mechanism, the latency is gradually accumulated when packet travels through multi-hop path and energy is wasted at both sender and receiver after the receiver has woken up. In general, most of early MAC protocols for low duty applications try to improve energy efficiency, but increase latency as well because they use an active-sleep cycle. In addition, they usually suffer from low transmission reliability because of interference or collision problem. This phenomenon will become worse in the network with high density of nodes. Thus, contention-based MAC protocols may not be appropriate for bursty data acquisition with high load rate and tight bound of loss rate and latency.

On the other hand, TDMA technique can mitigate the interference and collision problem, and reduce packet latency since it can schedule time slots for every node in the network. Thus, several TDMA-based MAC protocols have been proposed recently. TRAMA [4] is an energy-conserving, distributed slot election scheme that is based on traffic information to assign time slots for a particular node. Time interval of LMAC [5] is divided into 32 slots and each node is assigned a slot to transmit a packet in a contention-free manner.

The hybrid MAC protocols which can handle low-rate bursty traffic were also proposed. Z-MAC [6] allocates time slots to every node such that no two nodes within two-hop neighbors are assigned the same time slot in order to prevent interference. Z-MAC also uses CSMA to steal the time slots in case that a node does not use its assigned slots. Z-MAC is efficient with variable traffic, but does not respond to the funneling effect, studied in Funneling-MAC [7], that takes place because nodes close to a sink have to process much more data packets delivered from their descendants. Some tree-based protocols were proposed for wireless ad hoc networks [8-10] and wireless sensor networks [11]. In TreeMAC [11], a node is allocated a different number of slots according to how many descendants the node has and where the node is located.

Recently, some researchers have focused on the design of protocols to support for bursty traffic. ATMA (Advertisement-based Time-division Multiple Access) [12] is a distributed TDMA-based MAC protocol that uses the bursty and/or periodic nature of the traffic to prevent energy waste through advertisements and reservations for data slots. Time in ATMA is divided into frames. Each frame begins with a synchronization period, followed by an advertisement period and ends with a data period. Each node that intends to send data needs to transmit an advertisement packet to reserve a slot for data transmission. ATMA tries to reduce delay and energy consumption; however, it may not be suitable for multi-hop bursty traffic transmission and can also cause high overhead and funneling effect problem if it is applied in a tree topology network. In [13], the MMH-MAC (Mobile Multimode Hybrid MAC) protocol cares the bursty traffic transmission with mobility support. MMH-MAC operates in two modes: an asynchronous mode to synchronize the sender and the receiver; and a synchronous mode in which each node is assigned slots for data transmission. However, the mode transition in MMH-MAC may cause a large overhead and interference which is inevitable due to slot reuse.

Although the existing TDMA-based MAC protocols have their own advantages in application areas, they might not be suitable for bursty data applications in WMSNs because of the following reasons. *First*, the flexibility of slot utilization is low or almost impossible. They assume that every sensor node sends one packet in each cycle and the slot is usually allocated fixedly to a particular sensor node. Thus, the time slot will be wasted in case that the node has no packet to send. On the other hand, if a node has more data packets or bursty data to be transmitted immediately, it is very difficult for that node to utilize the time slots which are already assigned to other nodes. *Second*, the loss of packets or the high delay of packet transmission may be inevitable. In WMSNs for monitoring applications, each node reports the sensed data with very low load rate in a normal state. However, when a critical event occurs, a certain node can be required to send a burst of data urgently to the sink. Without rescheduling slot assignment globally and giving favor of resource allocation for the processing of the bursty data, the bursty data cannot be delivered to a server in a timely manner. *Third*, energy is wasted unnecessary during the processing of bursty data. When a critical event occurs, it may be necessary to limit network operation to the nodes deployed in the particular area and involved in delivering those multimedia data. However, these critical issues were not addressed appropriately in the existing protocols.

In this paper, we propose a new approach, *a network-controlled approach* that addresses the reliable delivery of command, the reliable and timely delivery of bursty data, and also energy efficiency in delivering the bursty data. In this approach, a sufficient number of slots are only reserved for sensor nodes lying on the *hot* path, a path from the sources of bursty traffic to the sink; the other sensor nodes get into sleep state. To deal with the reliability of data transmission, we present a method to build a *b-reliable* tree in which all tree links are reliable bi-directionally to enable reliable peer-to-peer communication. Our experimental results indicate that the proposed approach can handle the critical issues effectively and improve network lifetime significantly.

In what follows, the network model is described in Section 2. We present the formal description of the proposed approach in Section 3. Section 4 covers a performance evaluation. Finally, we make concluding remarks in Section 5.

2   Network Model

A typical network consists of one server (sink) and multiple sensor nodes. A server is wall-powered and acts as a monitoring and control entity while a sensor node equipped with a battery does as a data acquisition device. Typically, there are two types of sensor nodes: *Ordinary node* - a node with compound sensor modules such as motion, heat, light, humidity, etc. and *multimedia node (MN)* - an ordinary node with a camera module which can be turned on or off by a remote command. The camera module remains turned off to conserve the energy until it is requested to capture and transmit bursty data such as a still image or video stream from a server. An *MN* which has an *active camera module* is called an *active multimedia node (AMN)*. An ordinary node senses data from environment and sends it to the server periodically. A server stores the received context data and then analyzes the data to judge whether some critical event has occurred or not. If it perceives a critical event within a spot, it sends a command to an *MN* located at that spot to turn on the camera module and request the bursty data. A typical network model is given in [16].

3   Network-Controlled Multimedia Protocol

3.1   Protocol Structure

The protocol structure begins with the initial contention period (ICP), followed by two repeating periods, the specific MAC protocol period and the bursty data acquisition period (BDAP), as illustrated in Fig. 1. In the ICP, initial time synchronization is performed and then a reliable tree is constructed. In our approach, every sensor node works in two modes: *normal mode and bursty mode*. A node operates in normal mode during the specific MAC protocol period. In this mode, nodes exchange data with each other or report the periodic sensed data to the server using one of existing MAC protocols. Since we only focus on the bursty data delivery, the operation of the specific MAC protocol period is not considered in this paper. A node operates in bursty mode during BDAP which includes the *path reservation period* (PRP) used to establish a *hot* path for the reliable data transmission and the *data acquisition period* (DAP) used to transmit the bursty data. DAP consists of a number of multiple mini-frames where a *mini-frame* is defined as the number of time slots required to send a data packet from *active multimedia nodes* to the server and a *slot* is a time span enough to send one data packet by one hop.

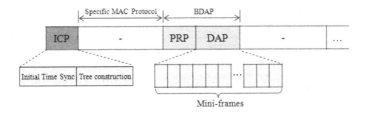

Fig. 1. Protocol Structure

Upon detecting an abnormal situation, a server starts the *PRP* by sending a *multimedia data request* (*MREQ*) message that includes the addresses of the *MNs*. Upon receiving *MREQ*, a target *MN* sends a *resource reservation request* (*RRREQ*) message toward the server to request for transmission resource including the number of demand slots. Based on the information of *RRREQ*, the server calculates the span of DAP and then broadcasts a *resource reservation respond* (*RRRES*) message that includes the calculated time of DAP, and the assigned slots for its descendant nodes. Upon receiving *RRRES*, *AMN* immediately starts sending multimedia data towards the server along the *hot* path. All other nodes which are not involved in the transmission of multimedia data get into sleep state for the DAP.

3.2 Time Synchronization Technique

As a TDMA-based mechanism, our proposed approach also requires network time synchronization to perform its precise operation. Time synchronization is also a common requirement in various protocols and applications. Thus, we employed the Flooding Time Synchronization Protocol (FTSP) [14] which can achieve high precision.

The synchronization message (*SYNC*) contains four fields (*rootID, nodeID, seqNum, globalTime*): *rootID* is the ID of a root node, *nodeID* is the ID of a sender for maintaining neighbor relationship, *seqNum* is the sequence number generated by the root node which is used to handle redundant synchronization messages, and *globalTime* is the current time of the root that is estimated by a transmitter when *SYNC* is broadcast. The sink that has the lowest ID (*nodeID = 0*) becomes a root. *SYNC* is initialed by the sink. Upon receiving *SYNC*, the receiver obtains the local time that refers to the same instant as global time in *SYNC* from the viewpoint of the receiver's local clock. Therefore, *SYNC* provides a pair *<global time, local time>* for synchronization at every receiver. The difference between the local time and the global time of a synchronization point becomes the *time offset* of the receiver and the root. However, the offset is not constant due to clock drift, so to compensate for clock drift, the linear regression technique is used.

Each node maintains the regression table including eight data points where each data point is a pair of the offset and the local time. The regression table is updated upon receiving a new *SYNC* message. Applying the linear regression method for two independent variables, *offset* and local time (*LT*), the linear equation for the regression of *offset* on *LT* is given as follows:

$$offset = \overline{offset} + skew * (LT - \overline{LT})$$
(1)

Where $skew = \dfrac{\sum\limits_{i=1}^{n}(LT_i - \overline{LT})(offset_i - \overline{offset})}{\sum\limits_{i=1}^{n}(LT_i - \overline{LT})^2}$, $\overline{LT} = \dfrac{1}{n}\sum\limits_{i=1}^{n}LT_i$, $\overline{offset} = \dfrac{1}{n}\sum\limits_{i=1}^{n}offset_i$

Given LT, every sensor node can estimate the *global time (GT)* of the root by:

$$GT = LT + offset \tag{2}$$

3.3   Link Quality Estimation and Bi-directional Link Establishment

In tree topology, the successful packet transmission is normally affected by the reliability and goodness of the link between two communication nodes. Therefore, in this work, we take the link quality into consideration in the process of tree construction. Link quality is usually estimated by a *Packet Reception Rate (PRR)* or the physical link quality metrics such as *Received Signal Strength Indicator (RSSI)* and *Link Quality Indication (LQI)* [15] associated with the received packet. These single metrics also have some limitations in the estimate of link quality. PRR requires a large number of observations to obtain usable results. However, PRR cannot classify a good stable link (a link whose quality remains in good state under external effects) and a good unstable link (a link whose quality is easily affected by the minor environmental change). RSSI and LQI can only differentiate between the very good link and the rest one while they are hardly distinguishable between bad, average and good links. To solve the limitation of individual metrics, [16] proposed a method that combines three link quality metrics (RSSI, LQI and PRR) into a consolidated metric, referred to as *linkq* in this paper, which can be determined by

$$linkq = \sqrt{\overline{RSSI_w}^2 + \overline{LQI_w}^2} \tag{3}$$

where: $\overline{RSSI_w} = \dfrac{\sum\limits_{i=1}^{m}(RSSI_i + 100)}{n}$, $\overline{LQI_w} = \dfrac{\sum\limits_{i=1}^{m}LQI_i}{n}$,   m and n is the number of

received and transmitted packets $(0 < m \le n)$. A link is *reliable* if its *linkq* is greater than *a specified threshold*.

Most of researches in WSNs assume that a wireless communication link is bi-directional. However, in the real scenario, it is not always true. A link may not be bidirectional or may not work in a stable manner due to different noise levels on nodes, different transmission powers and antenna gains of nodes, and different environmental factors surrounding each of nodes. Therefore, we propose a new approach to identify the *bi-directionally reliable (B-reliable)* link.

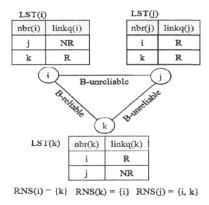

Fig. 2. Example of link state table (LST)

The link (a, b) is said to be *B-reliable* if two directional links from a to b and from b to a are *reliable*. Every node i maintains its *link state table, LST(i)= (nbr(i), linkq(i))*, where *nbr(i)* denotes a neighbor of node i and *linkq(i)* indicates whether link *(nbr(i), i)* is *reliable (R)* or *non-reliable (NR)*. Then, let us define a *reliable neighbor set (RNS(i))* as a set of neighbors who is reliable to node i. Every node i is required to include *RNS(i)* in a control message. Thus, *LST(i)* is updated whenever node i receives or over-hears any control message from its neighbor. Then, a node i that has obtained the *RNS(j)* from node j determines link (i, j) to be *B-reliable* if entry j of *LST(i) is R* and $i \in RNS(j)$. Fig. 2 illustrates the determination of a *B-reliable* link.

3.4   Time Synchronization and Reliable Tree Construction

We describe a new approach to construct a robust tree in which all tree-links are *B-reliable* with time synchronization.

In the ICP, time synchronization is triggered by the *SYNC* message issued periodically by the sink. Upon receiving *SYNC*, every node performs initial time synchronization and rebroadcasts *SYNC* only if it has at least one child [17]. In this process, every node can build an initial *LST*. As soon as the initial time synchronization finishes, tree construction phase is initiated by an *advertisement (ADV)* message issued by the sink which is the only tree member at the beginning. Upon receiving the ADV message, an orphan that has a *reliable link* joins the sink by sending a *join request (JREQ)* message. Note that the ADV or JREQ message includes *RNS*. Upon receiving JREQ, the member sends a *join response* (JRES) message and takes the orphan as its child if the corresponding link between them is *B-reliable*. When the orphan receives JRES, it takes the member as its parent. Another orphan who has overheard JREQ can take the same procedure to become a member if its link is *B-reliable*. If an orphan overhears JREQs from multiple members with *B-reliable* links, it pairs with a member that has the shortest distance to the sink. During the operation time, if a certain node detects the failure of the link to its parent, it tries to find one neighbor that can provide the B-reliable link and shortest distance to the sink and then joins that node by sending JREQ.

3.5   Path Reservation Operation

An ordinary sensor node senses data from environment periodically and transmits the sensed data to the server. When a critical event occurs in a particular area, an *MN* located in that spot is triggered by the server and its camera module is turned on (it becomes an *AMN*). *AMN* sends *RRREQ* toward the sink to request dedicated slots for bursty data delivery. The sink accepts *RRREQ* from *AMN* by broadcasting *RRRES*. These operations are performed during the PRP that is the sub-period of the BDAP.

For convenience of description, we denote $D(i)$ as a set of node i's descendants and let $T(i) = D(i) \cup \{i\}$. Firstly, the sink starts the *PRP* by broadcasting *MREQ = (mIDs)*, where *mIDs* is the list of target address of multimedia nodes, to request for multimedia content. For the purpose of preventing the unnecessary waste of energy, upon receiving *MREQ*, only intermediate node which has the target multimedia node in the descendant list forwards it; the other nodes, simply discard the MREQ message. Upon receiving MREQ, an *MN*, say node i, becomes an *AMN* and then sends *RRREQ = (mID(i), σ_i, η_i)* to its parent where *mID(i)* is the list of *AMNs* that belongs to $T(i)$, σ_i is the number of demand slots that node i needs to process bursty data in one cycle, and η_i is the number of bursty data packets that need to be transmitted. The upstream node, upon receiving *RRREQ*, marks itself as a forwarding node of bursty data transmission and forwards *RRREQ* to its parent node. Then, σ_i can be determined as follows:

$$\sigma_i = \sum_{j=1}^{k} \sigma_{ij} + |mID(i)| \qquad (4)$$

where σ_{ij} is slot demand that node i has received from node j.

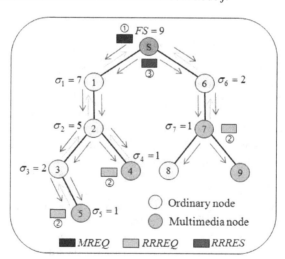

Fig. 3. An example of path reservation operation

Upon receiving *RRREQ*, the sink responds to the request by broadcasting *RRRES*. Every node i, except for the leaf nodes, needs to rebroadcast *RRRES = (mID(i), allocSlot(i), FS, DAP)*, where *mID(i)* is the list of *AMNs*, *allocSlot(i) = (s_{i1}, s_{i2}, ..., s_{ik})*, with $s_{ij} = (ij, startSlot_{ij})$, is the set of dedicated slots that is allocated for the requesting nodes, *frame size* $FS = \sum_{i=1}^{k} \sigma_i$ is the total number of time slots in each mini-frame, and

$DAP = \left(\sum_{i=1}^{k} h_i \eta_i \right) \times slotTime$, where h_i and η_i are the tree depth and the number of bursty data packets of *AMN(i)*, respectively.

An example of the path reservation operation is shown in Fig. 3. There are one sink *S*, four multimedia nodes (node 4, 5, 7, 9) and five ordinary nodes. In this example, node 4, 5 and 7 are the active multimedia nodes that need to transmit multimedia content to the sink.

3.6   Bursty Data Acquisition Operation

Upon receiving *RRRES* from the sink, the corresponding *AMN* starts sending its bursty data packets within the allocated slots, other nodes located on the *hot path* to the sink forwards those data packets, and the others that are not related to those bursty data transmissions get into a sleep state for DAP duration to conserve bandwidth and energy. These operations take place in the DAP sub-period of the BDAP. DAP consists of multiple mini-frames, and the frame size depends on the number of *AMNs* transmitting data concurrently. The number of mini-frames depends on the number of bursty data packets that needs to be sent for each critical event.

When receiving *RRRES*, each node *i* who is located on the *hot path* of bursty data transmission determines the active slot number that it needs to be active to process the packets. The receiving slot (*recvSlot*) and sending slot (*sendSlot*) of node *i* can be determined as follows:

$$recvSlot_i = startSlot_i + \sum_{j=1}^{k} \sigma_{ij} - |mID(i)| \qquad (5)$$

$$sendSlot_i = startSlot_i + \sum_{j=1}^{k} \sigma_{ij} \qquad (6)$$

where σ_{ij} is the number of demanded slots that node *i* received from node *j*.

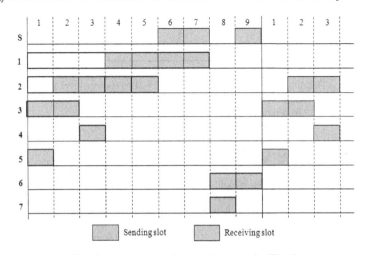

Fig. 4. An example of slot assignment for Fig. 3

Fig. 4 illustrates an example of slot assignment for the bursty data acquisition which has the same topology as shown in Fig. 3. Three *AMNs* (4, 5, 7) send a burst of data packets at slot #3, #1, #8, respectively while node 8, 9 will go to sleep for the *DAP* period. We need 9 slots for three *active multimedia nodes* transmitting data concurrently. It is important to notice that all nodes are only required to be active at its receiving or sending slots and can go to sleep at other slots for energy saving.

Slot reuse can reduce packet latency because two nodes that use the same slot can transmit a packet at the same time. However, the slot reuse is not considered in this paper. The reason is that spatial reuse can reduce the latency but may cause interference since *the radio interference range of a node is always farther than its transmission range.* Any two nodes that use an identical slot may interfere with each other at the parent node that is located in the radio interference range of the other [10].

4   Performance Evaluation

4.1   Experiment Setup

To evaluate performance of our protocol, we conducted experiments in an indoor Testbed that is built with the TelosB motes running TinyOS 2.1. The TelosB mote uses Chipcon CC2420 radio that is compliant with the IEEE 802.15.4 PHY layer standard in the 2.4 GHz ISM band with an 250 kbps data rate [18]. The mote uses an 8 MHz TI MSP430 microcontroller. The current draw of TelosB, excluding the radio, is 1.8 mA in an active mode and 5.1 µA when in a sleep mode. The CC2420 radio consumes 23 mA in a receiving or listening mode, 17.4 mA when transmitting at 0 dBm, 21 µA in an idle mode, and 1 µA in a sleep mode. We can see that the power consumption of the radio when receiving or transmitting is much greater than that when in a sleep mode. Therefore, to extend network lifetime, the radio should be turned on and off according to the duty cycle and the time when a node operates in a receiving, transmitting or listening mode should be kept as less as possible. In CC2420, the transmission power can be programmed at 8 discrete levels between -25 dBm and 0 dBm by setting the *TXCTRL.PA_LEVEL* register values from 3 to 31 in steps of 4. The transmission

Table 1. Experiment parameters

Parameter	Value
Default transmission power	−25 dBm (power level 3)
Channel frequency	2.480 MHz (channel 26)
Radio bandwidth	250 kbps
Sensor model	TelosB
Slot size	12 ms
Frame size (f) (TreeMAC)	3 slots
Cycle size (TreeMAC)	f × n (n = number of nodes)
Data packet length	90 bytes
Normal data rate	0.2 packets/s
Bursty data load (each event)	100 packets
Dimensions	20×30 (m^2)
Number of nodes	1 sink; 30 sensor nodes
Experiment time	3,600 s

channel can be selected from 16 channels available (from channel 11 to channel 26) in the 802.15.4 spectrum. However, since some channels of 802.15.4 may overlap with those of 802.11, we use channel 26 to eliminate interference in the presence of the 802.11 WIFI signal. Some key parameters in the experiment are shown in Table 1.

To evaluate the performance of our proposed protocol (*abbreviated as an RADP protocol*), we compare it with the default IEEE 802.11 CSMA/CA protocol and the TreeMAC protocol [11] which are widely applied in WSNs. TreeMAC is a TDMA-based MAC protocol which has shown the good performance in resolving the funneling effect and hidden terminal problems in WSNs.

In this paper, we consider the performance of bursty data acquisition, so the performance metrics are evaluated based on that activity. Since there are not enough multimedia sensor nodes to generate multimedia data, in this experiment bursty data is generated by the ordinary sensor nodes. A burst of data has 100 packets, each of 90 bytes (the maximum MAC Layer frame of TelosB is 127 bytes), that are generated and queued on multimedia node at the same time. A critical event is generated randomly in the network. It is obvious that the performance is greatly affected by the distance of the multimedia source node from the sink. Thus, we compare the three protocols by varying the position of the source nodes, using the following performance metrics:

- Packet delivery ratio (PDR): The ratio of the average number of successful bursty data packets delivered to the sink to the total number of bursty data packets generated by the source nodes.
- Energy consumption: A total amount of energy that is consumed by every node in the network during the operation period of bursty data acquisition.
- End-to-end delay: An average time elapsed until a bursty data packet from a source node is delivered to the sink.

4.2   Experimental Results

(a) Packet Delivery Ratio

Fig. 5 shows the PDR of the three protocols according to variation of the number of hops from source to a sink (*nHops*). RADP achieves the best PDR over 0.96 overall while CSMA shows a sharply decreasing curve, down to 0.8 as *nHops* increases. The graphs show that the PDR of TreeMAC and CSMA is quite sensitive to *nHops*.

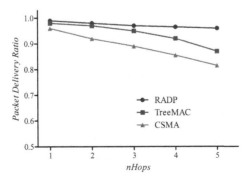

Fig. 5. Packet delivery ratio

Even though the protocol based on a slot scheduling is advantageous, TreeMAC is not free from the interference problem. TreeMAC uses a slot reuse technique with the assumption that two-hop neighbors does not interfere each other. However, this is not true. The theory and measurement about radio propagation [1] have shown that the received signal power P_r decreases with the distance d as $P_r \propto P_t d^{-\beta}$, where P_t is the transmission power and β is an environment-dependent constant normally between 2 and 5. Since the interference range of a radio signal is farther than the transmission range, two nodes with difference of depth 3 that use an identical slot may cause interference at the parent of one node that is located in the radio range of the other. The problem becomes outstanding when tree depth is over 3 and/or node density is high.

Our protocol outperforms the other twos due to two aspects: (1) The reliable tree construction (2) no use of slot reuse technique. However, our protocol fails to achieve 100% of delivery ratio. This is because a packet transmission may be affected by signal attenuation or interference at each link. The probability of the packet loss will obviously increase as a packet travels farther as shown in the figure.

(b) Energy Consumption

The importance of minimizing energy consumption and maximizing network lifetime is second to none in wireless sensor networks. We know that energy is mostly consumed during radio communication. Thus, to measure the energy consumption, we count the amount of time that each node has spent in different operation modes: sleep, idle, receiving or transmitting. The energy consumption in each mode is then calculated by multiplying the cumulative time of each operation and the power consumption amount required to operate the radio in that mode (considering a battery of 3V). In this case, the energy consumption is measured indirectly because of the difficulty in directly observing the current draw on physically small, low power motes.

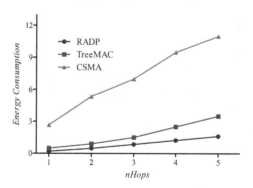

Fig. 6. Energy consumption (J)

Fig. 6 compares the three protocols in terms of energy consumption. Energy consumption was measured for all nodes during the operation period of bursty data acquisition. It is shown that RADP far outperforms CSMA since it allows only nodes on the *hot* path to remain active. TreeMAC also consumes low energy because of the use of the active and sleep cycles. Consequently, for energy efficiency, a node has to turn the radio off if it is not involved in data transmission.

(c) End-to-End Delay

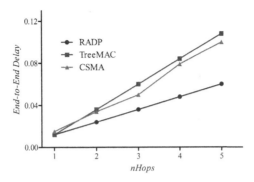

Fig. 7. End-to-End Delay (s)

Fig. 7 compares the three protocols in terms of End-to-End delay according to variation of *nHops*. It is shown that the three protocols have linearly increasing End-to-End delay curves in common as *nHops* increases, and RADP outperforms TreeMAC and CSMA by 35 - 45%.

In RADP, a node at depth h_i takes h_i slots to deliver a data packet to the sink. Meanwhile, TreeMAC shows the highest delay compared with the other two protocols. The reason is that because of using the frame-slot assignment algorithm, each node has to wait until its transmittable slot is ready to forward the packet, upon receiving a packet. The delay becomes severe as *nHops* increases. In TreeMAC, if the transmittable slot of node *i* is *n*, the transmittable slot of its parent is *(n-1), (n+2),* etc. Thus, when receiving a packet, each node has to wait at least 2 slots before forwarding the packet. So, it takes at least delay time $\tau = 1 + 2(h_i - 1) = 2h_i - 1$ (slots) to deliver data packet from a node at depth h_i to a server. Moreover, as shown in Fig. 7, CSMA achieves the lower delay compared with TreeMAC. This is because in CSMA, each node tries to forward a packet with its best effort. However, CSMA experiences more collision and interference as *nHops* increases because of the use of contention-based channel access. Besides the delay when traveling via a multi-hop path, CSMA causes additional delay because of waiting time in exchange of RTS/CTS, channel assessment, back-off period, etc. In addition, the packet latency τ_i of multimedia node *i* can be bounded as follows:

$$h_i \le \tau_i(RADP) < \textstyle\sum_{i=1}^{k} h_i$$
$$2h_i - 1 \le \tau_i(TreeMAC) < 3 \times nNodes \qquad (7)$$
$$h_i(1 + \delta_w) < \tau_i(CSMA)$$

where h_i is tree depth in hops of *AMN(i)* to its sink, k is the number of *AMNs*, *nNodes* is the number of sensor nodes in the network, and δ_w is the waiting time to the exchange of RTS/CTS, back-off, etc.

5   Concluding Remarks

We proposed an efficient sensor network protocol that can not only deliver bursty data reliably, but also can reduce energy consumption. The network operation is controlled by the server. The source node and other corresponding upstream nodes are assigned a number of slots enough for bursty data transmission while the others get into sleep state for saving energy. The experimental results show that our protocol outperforms the other methods significantly in terms of packet delivery, end-to-end delay and energy consumption. Moreover, in practical applications, our method can be easily integrated with another MAC protocol.

References

1. Ye, W., Heidemann, J., Estrin, D.: Medium access control with coordinated adaptive sleeping for wireless sensor networks. IEEE/ACM Trans. Netw. 12, 493–506 (2004)
2. Dam, T.V., Langendoen, K.: An adaptive energy-efficient MAC protocol for wireless sensor networks. In: Proceedings of the 1st International Conference on Embedded Networked Sensor Systems, pp. 171–180. ACM, Los Angeles (2003)
3. Polastre, J., Hill, J., Culler, D.: Versatile low power media access for wireless sensor networks. In: Proceedings of the 2nd International Conference on Embedded Networked Sensor Systems, pp. 95–107. ACM, Baltimore (2004)
4. Rajendran, V., Obraczka, K., Garcia-Luna-Aceves, J.J.: Energy-efficient, collision-free medium access control for wireless sensor networks. Wirel. Netw. 12, 63–78 (2006)
5. Hoesel van, L.F.W., Havinga, P.J.M.: A Lightweight Medium Access Protocol (LMAC) for Wireless Sensor Networks: Reducing Preamble Transmissions and Transceiver State Switches. In: 1st International Workshop on Networked Sensing Systems, INSS 2004, pp. 205–208. Society of Instrument and Control Engineers (SICE), Tokio (2004)
6. Injong, R., Warrier, A., Aia, M., Jeongki, M., Sichitiu, M.L.: Z-MAC: A Hybrid MAC for Wireless Sensor Networks. IEEE/ACM Transactions on Networking 16, 511–524 (2008)
7. Ahn, G.-S., Hong, S.G., Miluzzo, E., Campbell, A.T., Cuomo, F.: Funneling-MAC: a localized, sink-oriented MAC for boosting fidelity in sensor networks. In: Proceedings of the 4th International Conference on Embedded Networked Sensor Systems, pp. 293–306. ACM, Boulder (2006)
8. Han, T.-D., Oh, H.: A Topology Management Routing Protocol for Mobile IP Support of Mobile Ad Hoc Networks. In: Ruiz, P.M., Garcia-Luna-Aceves, J.J. (eds.) ADHOC-NOW 2009. LNCS, vol. 5793, pp. 341–346. Springer, Heidelberg (2009)
9. Oh, H.: A tree-based approach for the Internet connectivity of mobile ad hoc networks. Journal of Communications and Networks 5793, 523–534 (2009)
10. Oh, H., Han, T.-D.: A demand-based slot assignment algorithm for energy-aware reliable data transmission in wireless sensor networks. Wirel. Netw. 18, 523–534 (2012)
11. Wen-Zhan, S., Renjie, H., Shirazi, B., LaHusen, R.: TreeMAC: Localized TDMA MAC protocol for real-time high-data-rate sensor networks. In: IEEE International Conference on Pervasive Computing and Communications, PerCom 2009, pp. 1–10 (2009)
12. Ray, S., Demirkol, I., Heinzelman, W.: ATMA: Advertisement-Based TDMA Protocol for Bursty Traffic in Wireless Sensor Networks. In: 2010 IEEE Global Telecommunications Conference (GLOBECOM 2010), pp. 1–5 (2010)

13. Bernardo, L., Agua, H., Pereira, M., Oliveira, R., Dinis, R., Pinto, P.: A MAC Protocol for Mobile Wireless Sensor Networks with Bursty Traffic. In: 2010 IEEE Wireless Communications and Networking Conference (WCNC), pp. 1–6 (2010)
14. Maroti, M., Kusy, B., Simon, G., Ledeczi, A.: The Flooding Time Synchronization Protocol. In: Proceedings of the 2nd International Conference on Embedded Networked Sensor Systems 2004, pp. 39–49. ACM, Baltimore (2004)
15. Levis, K.S.A.P.: RSSI is under appreciated. In: Proceedings of the Third Workshop on Embedded Networked Sensors, pp. 239–242 (2006)
16. Boano, C.A., Zu, X., x00F, iga, M.A., Voigt, T., Willig, A., Ro, mer, K.: The Triangle Metric: Fast Link Quality Estimation for Mobile Wireless Sensor Networks. In: 2010 Proceedings of 19th International Conference on Computer Communications and Networks (ICCCN), pp. 1–7 (2010)
17. Vinh, P., Oh, H.: RSBP: A Reliable Slotted Broadcast Protocol in Wireless Sensor Networks. Sensors 12, 14630–14646 (2012)
18. TI: CC2420 Datasheet (December 2012)

Minimizing Nested Interrupts
of Secondary Users
in Multi-Priority Cognitive Radio Networks

Ping Zhu[1,*], Tian Ling[1], Guiyi Wei[1], and Bishan Ying[2]

[1] College of Computer and Information Engineering, Zhejiang Gongshang University,
Hangzhou, China
[2] Wasu Media Network Co., Hangzhou, China

Abstract. In cognitive radio networks (CRNs), unpredictable communication interruptions increase data communication delay of secondary users. The QoS of CRNs will dramatically decrease when interruptions are nested. In this paper, we propose a general multiple priority cognitive radio networks (MP-CRNs) model for both single-channel and multi-channel communications. In our MP-CRNs, SUs are divided into multiple categories of different priorities; users with higher priority preemptively interrupt lower ones; interruptions can be nested and all interrupted tasks are resumable. By introducing some extra concepts and terminologies, we first define and model the *nested interrupts*, we then derive and prove the formulas of nested interrupts. We also validate these formulas through mathematical experiments. Using Queuing Theory, we design a *Mutual Minimizing Algorithm* to minimize average *nested interrupts*. We also propose a novel *Turnaround Time Control Algorithm* to minimize SU's turnaround time when considering *nested interrupts*. Simulations and experiments demonstrate the efficiency and effectiveness of the proposed algorithms.

Keywords: cognitive radio networks, multiple priority, nested interrupts, preemptive scheduling, queueing theory.

1 Introduction

Cognitive radio was first introduced by Mitola in [1]. The primary user seizes the spectrum according to their stochastic characteristic; the secondary user leases the spectrum vacancy at the absence of primary user. Such leasing policy is the key idea of cognitive radio, which aims to make most efficient use of precious spectrum resources.

In CRNs, both primary users (PUs) and secondary users (SUs) are FIFO (first-in-first-out) served. An SU will be interrupted by PU during its communication process; the PU communicates without any caution to other users. When

---

* Corresponding author.

M. Pathan, G. Wei, and G. Fortino (Eds.): IDCS 2013, LNCS 8223, pp. 16–29, 2013.

interruption happens, the SU has to hang its working task, wait until PU finishes its service, and then resume the interrupted service. In MP-CRNs (multiple priority cognitive radio networks), the above interrupt process can be nested.

In CRNs [2, 3], users are divided into PUs and SUs. Nevertheless, in real CRNs, SUs are much more complicated than we can imagine. Different SUs differ from each other in arriving/serving processes, QoS requirements [4], etc. Classifying all of them into just one category is not enough. To achieve a preciser model, more user categories are needed. Therefore, we propose the MP-CRNs model to achieve more efficient vacant spectrum allocation, in which SUs are assigned to categories with different priorities. In MP-CRNs, there are n different categories, namely $C_1, C_2, \ldots, C_n$. C_1 represents the highest priority user (PU) and C_i ($i = 2, 3, \cdots, n$) stands for $SU_2, SU_3, \cdots, SU_n$ respectively. Same priority users are FIFO served. A higher priority C_j will interrupt a lower priority C_k, where $k > j$.

As a fundamental element in MP-CRNs, service interruption has been studied over the years. In the area of queueing systems, the queue-length distribution and the waiting time distribution of a single-server queue with service interruption are studied in [5]. Lee [6] discussed the problem of distributed interruption using a semi-Markov method in which the author defines three functions to find the joint probability of queue length, state and sojourn time. Sojourn times of users in M/M/1 queue with processor sharing service discipline and service interruption is detailed through [7]. Recently, Pang [8] established many-server heavy-traffic G/M/n+M model to study the exogenous regenerative service interruptions. However, these previous works only consider interruptions as an additional constraint added to the discussed model. The interruption itself has not been explicitly and theoretically studied ever before.

Besides, current wireless applications in CRNs make the situation even worse. In CRNs with spectrum leasing, the SU's QoS is greatly decreased [9]. In MP-CRNs, where interrupts can be nested, the situation is even worse than in traditional two priority CRNs. A higher priority $C_j(j < i)$ that interrupts C_i may be interrupted by another even higher priority $C_k(k < j)$. The total interrupt overhead in such a three priority MP-CRNs (3MP-CRNs) will be C_i's overhead plus C_j's overhead. However, recent research on CRNs pays little attention to how frequently SUs are interrupted. Although some studies concentrate on the topics of channel switching [10,11], spectrum selection [12,13], multiuser scheduling [4, 14, 15], queue-base control [16, 17], they have not directly investigated interruptions themselves.

In this paper, we propose a general MP-CRNs model. Based on this model, the nested interrupts are derived and proved for the first time, which is further validated by simulations. We also analyze some properties of nested interrupts. Further, we design a *Mutual Minimizing Algorithm* to reduce the average number of MP-CRNs's nested interrupts. We also propose a novel *Turnaround Time Control Algorithm* to minimize SU's turnaround time, through which the nested interrupts and the turnaround time can be mutually minimized.

2 The MP-CRNs Model

2.1 Notations

Before describing the system model, we first list the main notations that are going to be used in this paper for additional clarity.

- C_i : spectrum user of category i, where C_i represents the PU and C_i ($i = 2, 3, \cdots, n$) stands for $\mathrm{SU}_2, \mathrm{SU}_3, \cdots, \mathrm{SU}_n$ respectively.
- λ_i : arrival rate of C_i.
- μ_i : service rate of C_i.
- $E[X_i]$: average service time of C_i, which satisfies $E[X_i] = \frac{1}{\mu_i}$.
- ρ_i : channel utilization factor of C_i, which satisfies $\rho_i = \frac{\lambda_i}{\mu_i}$.
- Γ_i : C_i's non-nested state sequence set.
- γ_i : a possible non-nested state sequence of C_i.
- Γ_i^n : C_i's nested state sequence set.
- γ_i^n : a possible nested state sequence of C_i.
- t_{oh} : unit time consumption per service interruption.
- $\mathfrak{I}_i$: non-nested interrupts of C_i with $t_{oh} = 0$ in M/G/1 queue.
- $\mathfrak{I}_i(t_{oh})$: non-nested interrupts of C_i with $t_{oh} \neq 0$ in M/G/1 queue.
- $\mathfrak{I}_i(k)$: non-nested interrupts of C_i with $t_{oh} = 0$ in M/G/k queue.
- $\mathfrak{I}_i(t_{oh}, k)$: non-nested interrupts of C_i with $t_{oh} \neq 0$ in M/G/k queue.
- $\mathfrak{I}_i^n$: nested interrupts of C_i with $t_{oh} = 0$ in M/G/1 queue.
- $\mathfrak{I}_i^n(t_{oh})$: nested interrupts of C_i with $t_{oh} \neq 0$ in M/G/1 queue.
- $\mathfrak{I}_i^n(k)$: nested interrupts of C_i with $t_{oh} = 0$ in M/G/k queue.
- $\mathfrak{I}_i^n(t_{oh}, k)$: nested interrupts of C_i with $t_{oh} \neq 0$ in M/G/k queue.
- $T_i, i = 1, 2, \ldots, 6$: different time point in example of Figure 2.
- T_i : average effective sojourn time of C_i with $t_{oh} = 0$.
- $T_i(t_{oh})$: average effective sojourn time of C_i with $t_{oh} \neq 0$.
- N_i : average number of arriving users with priority higher than category C_i with $t_{oh} = 0$.
- $N_i(t_{oh})$: average number of arriving users with priority higher than category C_i with $t_{oh} \neq 0$.
- $\mathfrak{I}_{MP-CRNs}^n$: average nested interrupts of MP-CRNs, which is the average of all $\mathfrak{I}_i^n, 2 \leq i \leq n$.
- $\mathfrak{T}_i$: C_i's average turnaround time.
- R_i : C_i's average residential service time.
- $\mathfrak{T}_{MP-CRNs}$: average turnaround time of MP-CRNs, which is the average of all $\mathfrak{T}_i, 2 \leq i \leq n$.
- $g(\mu_i), g'(\mu_j)$: functions that are used to determine monotonicity.

2.2 User Behavior

In MP-CRNs, C_i enters the network according to Poisson distribution with an arrival rate of λ_i and arbitrarily served with service rate μ_i, $i = 1, 2, \ldots, n$. The average service time of C_i is denoted by $E[X_i]$, which is equal to $\frac{1}{\mu_i}$. The ratio of $\frac{\lambda_i}{\mu_i}$ is represented by ρ_i, which stands for the channel utilization factor.

For a given user C_i, $1 < i \leq n$, the sojourn time is comprised of service wait time, service time and interrupt wait time. The service wait time is the time required to serve users whose priorities are not lower than i that are already in the system upon arrival of C_i; the service time is C_i's task duration with average value of $E[X_i]$; the interrupt wait time is the waiting time for users with priority higher than i, whose interrupts arrive when C_i is still in the system.

After waiting for service wait time long, C_i gets into its service/wait cycles. If there are no arrivals of C_j, $j < i$, during its service time, C_i finishes its service and leaves the system; if there are arrivals of C_j, C_i must suspend its service, wait until the accomplishment of each C_j, and then resume its interrupted service.

2.3 Concepts and Definitions

The sojourn time describes the whole time C_i spent in MP-CRNs. However, this time span does not contributes to service interruption at all. C_i's interrupt occurs only after its service wait time. Here we define effective sojourn time:

Definition 1. *effective sojourn time is defined as the time span that starts when the user begins its task and ends when the user leaves the system.*

Definition 2. *non-nested state sequence is defined as non-nested state change serial during user's effective sojourn time.*

We assume that C_i in MP-CRNs is classified into three states: service (S), wait (W) and leave (L). State S means that user is executing its own task; state W indicates that the user is waiting for its order of service; state L represents that the user has finished its task and left the system. According to Definition 2, C_i's non-nested state sequence set can be denoted as:

$$\Gamma_i = \{(S_i W_i)^c S_i L_i | c = 0, 1, \dots\} \qquad (1)$$

Each member in Γ_i is a possible non-nested state sequence of C_i, which is denoted by γ_i. C_i's non-nested state sequence is comprised of c $S_i W_i$ sequences and ends with an $S_i L_i$ sequence. Based on non-nested state sequence, we can define non-nested interrupts as:

Definition 3. C_i's *non-nested interrupts is defined as the total number of non-nested service interruptions by $C_j (j < i)$ during its effective sojourn time.*

According to Definition 3, C_i's non-nested interrupts is the total number of $S_i W_i$ sequences in a non-nested state sequence. Combined with Definition 2, the non-nested interrupts of C_i is equal to the c value in its non-nested state sequence. The average number of C_i's non-nested interrupts are the statistical expectation of c.

As mentioned previously, C_i's non-nested state sequence and non-nested interrupts characterize service interruption only from C_i's individual point of view. The non-nested state sequence describes how often C_i is interrupted during its turnaround time and the non-nested interrupts only measures the overhead that C_i suffers. However, in MP-CRNs, interruptions will possibly be nested. A higher priority $C_j(j < i)$ that interrupts C_i may be interrupted by another even higher priority $C_k(k < j)$, which results in additional overhead. The total interrupts overhead in a nMP-CRNs (n-priority CRNs) will be the sum of all individual overheads.

The non-nested state sequence and non-nested interrupts are sufficient to determine C_i's QoS. However, when we want to analyze the performance from system's point of view, the following nested state sequence and nested interrupts are obligatory:

Definition 4. nested state sequence *is defined as nested state change serial during user's effective sojourn time.*

Denote

$$\Gamma_i^n = \{(S_i W_i \Sigma_j^n)^l S_i L_i | j < i, l = 0, 1, \dots \} \tag{2}$$

as the set of all C_i's nested state sequences. Each member in Γ_i^n is a possible nested state sequence of C_i, which is denoted by γ_i^n. C_i's nested sate sequence is comprised of l recursively defined $S_i W_i \Gamma_j^n$ sequences and an $S_i L_i$ sequence at the end.

Definition 5. C_i's **nested interrupts** *is defined as the total number of nested service interruptions by $C_j(j < i)$ during its effective sojourn time.*

3   Nested Interrupts in MP-CRNs

Denote t_{oh} as unit time consumption per service interruption. In our paper, unit time consumption is assume to be constant with two cases of $t_{oh} = 0$ and $t_{oh} \neq 0$ respectively. The nested interrupts is explored under the M/G/1 and M/G/k queueing models respectively. Thus, four cases altogether will be discussed.

3.1   M/G/1 Model with $t_{oh} = 0$

Theorem 1. C_i's *average nested interrupts in* M/G/1 MP-CRNs *with $t_{oh} = 0$ computes as:*

$$\mathfrak{I}_i^n = \frac{\Sigma_{j=1}^{i-1}\lambda_j}{\mu_i(1 - \Sigma_{t=1}^{i-1}\rho_t)}$$

Proof. Denote T_i as the average effective sojourn time of C_i in M/G/1 MP-CRNs with $t_{oh} = 0$.

T_i satisfies:

$$T_i = E[X_i] + \Sigma_{j=1}^{i-1} E[X_j] \times \lambda_j \times T_i \tag{3}$$

The recursive Eq.(3) is comprised of two parts. The first part is C_i's average service time; the second part is C_i's average interrupt wait time. Calculated in Eq.(3), we get:

$$T_i = \frac{1}{\mu_i(1 - \Sigma_{t=1}^{i-1}\rho_t)} \tag{4}$$

During average effective sojourn time, the average number of arriving users with priority higher than i equals:

$$N_i = \Sigma_{j=1}^{i-1}\lambda_j \times T_i \tag{5}$$

Because each arriving $C_j(j < i)$ will cause an interruption, we have:

$$\mathfrak{I}_i^n = N_i \tag{6}$$

Combining Eq.(4,5,6), the average nested interrupts of C_i in M/G/1 MP-CRNs with $t_{oh} = 0$ is thus:

$$\mathfrak{I}_i^n = \frac{\Sigma_{j=1}^{i-1}\lambda_j}{\mu_i(1 - \Sigma_{t=1}^{i-1}\rho_t)} \tag{7}$$

3.2   M/G/1 Model with $t_{oh} \neq 0$

Theorem 2. C_i's *average nested interrupts in M/G/1 MP-CRNs with* $t_{oh} \neq 0$ *computes as:*

$$\mathfrak{I}_i^n(t_{oh}) = \frac{\Sigma_{j=1}^{i-1}\lambda_j}{\mu_i(1 - \Sigma_{t=1}^{i-1}\rho_t) - t_{oh} \times \mu_i \times \Sigma_{j=1}^{i-1}\lambda_j}$$

Proof. Denote $T_i(t_{oh})$ as the average effective sojourn time of C_i in M/G/1 MP-CRNs with $t_{oh} \neq 0$.

$T_i(t_{oh})$ satisfies:

$$T_i(t_{oh}) = E[X_i] + \Sigma_{j=1}^{i-1}E[X_j] \times \lambda_j \times T_i(t_{oh}) + \mathfrak{I}_i^n(t_{oh}) \times t_{oh} \tag{8}$$

The recursive Eq.(8) is comprised of three parts. The first part is C_i's average service time; the second part is C_i's average interrupt wait time, and the third part is the average overall transition overhead. Calculated in Eq.(8), we get:

$$T_i(t_{oh}) = \frac{\frac{1}{\mu_i} + \mathfrak{I}_i^n(t_{oh}) \times t_{oh}}{1 - \Sigma_{t=1}^{i-1}\rho_t} \tag{9}$$

Notice that $\mathfrak{I}_i^n(t_{oh}) = N_i(t_{oh})$, where $N_i(t_{oh})$ is the average number of arriving users with priority higher than i. The average nested interrupts of C_i in M/G/1 MP-CRNs with $t_{oh} \neq 0$ is thus:

$$\mathfrak{I}_i^n(t_{oh}) = \frac{\Sigma_{j=1}^{i-1}\lambda_j}{\mu_i(1 - \Sigma_{t=1}^{i-1}\rho_t) - t_{oh} \times \mu_i \times \Sigma_{j=1}^{i-1}\lambda_j} \tag{10}$$

3.3   The M/G/k Situations

In our M/G/k models, there are k peer channels in MP-CRNs sharing one exclusive waiting queue. When C_i has its turn to serve, it randomly chooses a channel from the system, each one with equal probability of $\frac{1}{k}$, and then starts its working cycles. The proof of the M/G/k cases are much the same to M/G/1 cases, we only present the result by giving the following two theories.

Theorem 3. C_i's average nested interrupts in M/G/k MP-CRNs with $t_{oh} = 0$ computes as:

$$\mathfrak{I}_i^n(k) = \frac{\Sigma_{j=1}^{i-1}\lambda_j}{\mu_i(k - \Sigma_{t=1}^{i-1}\rho_t)} \tag{11}$$

Theorem 4. C_i's average nested interrupts in M/G/k MP-CRNs with $t_{oh} \neq 0$ computes as:

$$\mathfrak{I}_i^n(t_{oh}, k) = \frac{\Sigma_{j=1}^{i-1}\lambda_j}{\mu_i(k - \Sigma_{t=1}^{i-1}\rho_t) - t_{oh} \times \mu_i \times \Sigma_{j=1}^{i-1}\lambda_j} \tag{12}$$

3.4   Some Properties of Nested Interrupts

As referred to previously, the non-nested interrupts characterize service interruption from a single priority user's point of view; the nested interrupts depicts performance at the system level. Both of them are performance metrics, but emphasize on different aspects. We here give a brief discussion on relationship between them.

Theorem 5. C_i's average nested interrupts satisfies:

$$\mathfrak{I}_i^n = \Sigma_{j=1}^i \mathfrak{I}_j$$
$$\mathfrak{I}_i^n(t_{oh}) = \Sigma_{j=1}^i \mathfrak{I}_j(t_{oh})$$
$$\mathfrak{I}_i^n(k) = \Sigma_{j=1}^i \mathfrak{I}_j(k)$$
$$\mathfrak{I}_i^n(t_{oh}, k) = \Sigma_{j=1}^i \mathfrak{I}_j(t_{oh,k}) \tag{13}$$

Correspondingly, we further have:

Theorem 6. The average non-nested interrupts of C_i satisfies:

$$\mathfrak{I}_i = \mathfrak{I}_i^n - \mathfrak{I}_{i-1}^n$$
$$\mathfrak{I}_i(t_{oh}) = \mathfrak{I}_i^n(t_{oh}) - \mathfrak{I}_{i-1}^n(t_{oh})$$
$$\mathfrak{I}_i(k) = \mathfrak{I}_i^n(k) - \mathfrak{I}_{i-1}^n(k)$$
$$\mathfrak{I}_{t_{oh},k} = \mathfrak{I}_i^n(t_{oh}, k) - \mathfrak{I}_{i-1}^n(t_{oh}, k) \tag{14}$$

Eq.(14) can be simply achieved by one step difference over Eq.(13).

4   Minimization of Nested Interrupts

4.1   The Mutual Minimizing Algorithm

Consider the M/G/1 MP-CRNs with $t_{oh} = 0$, the average nested interrupts of MP-CRNs, $\mathfrak{I}_{MP-CRNs}^n$, can be calculated as:

$$\mathfrak{I}_{MP-CRNs}^n = \frac{\Sigma_{i=2}^n \mathfrak{I}_i^n}{n-1} \tag{15}$$

Expending Eq.(15), we get:

$$\mathfrak{I}^n_{MP-CRNs} = \frac{\frac{\lambda_1}{\mu_2(1-\rho_1)} + \frac{\lambda_1+\lambda_2}{\mu_3(1-\rho_1-\rho_2)} + \cdots + \frac{\Sigma^{n-1}_{j=1}\lambda_j}{\mu_n(1-\Sigma^{n-1}_{t=1}\rho_t)}}{n-1} \quad (16)$$

We examine C_i's $(2 \leq i \leq n)$ contribution to $\mathfrak{I}^n_{MP-CRNs}$. According to Theorem 1, C_i's average nested interrupts can be calculated as:

$$\mathfrak{I}^n_i = \frac{\Sigma^{i-1}_{j=1}\lambda_j}{\mu_i(1-\Sigma^{i-1}_{t=1}\rho_t)} \quad (17)$$

Eq.(17) indicates that the only adjustable parameter for C_i to reduce its nested interrupts is μ_i. To be concrete, by maximizing μ_i, $\mathfrak{I}^n_i$ is minimized. If we apply this strategy (**maximizing μ_i strategy**) to all the $C_j(j \neq 1, j \neq i)$, can we minimize $\mathfrak{I}^n_{MP-CRNs}$? The answer is affirmative.

The key doubt here is that by maximizing μ_i, what is the influence on other users? Considering $C_i, C_j, i < j$, both of them adopt the **maximizing μ_i strategy** to minimize their nested interrupts. By maximizing μ_i, ρ_i will be minimized. This will contribute to the maximization of $1 - \Sigma^{j-1}_{t=1}\rho_t$ in $\mathfrak{I}^n_j$. Because both of the two parts (μ_j and $1 - \Sigma^{j-1}_{t=1}\rho_t$) in the denominator of $\mathfrak{I}^n_j$ are maximized, C_j's nested interrupts is minimized when considering C_i. If $i > j$, then maximization of μ_i has nothing to do with $1 - \Sigma^{j-1}_{t=1}\rho_t$; and by maximizing μ_j, $\mathfrak{I}^n_j$ are minimized. We achieve the same result when the above process is extended to all the $n-1$ priorities. By greedily minimizing oneself's nested interrupts, a mutual minimization phenomenon emerges amazingly! The same results hold in M/G/1 MP-CRNs with $t_{oh} \neq 0$ and M/G/k MP-CRNs. So, in the rest of our paper, we concentrate the discussion on the case of M/G/1 MP-CRNs with $t_{oh} = 0$. The *Mutual Minimizing Algorithm*(Algorithm 1) summarizes as following:

Algorithm 1. Mutual Minimizing Algorithm

Require: $C_i, \lambda_i, \mu_i, i = 2, 3, \cdots, n$
   for each C_i **do**
      increase μ_i as large as possible
   end for

4.2 The Turnaround Time Control Algorithm

According to Algorithm 1, to decrease nested interrupts, each user increases its μ_i as much as possible. Here, we will discuss how this increment affect user's turnaround time. As a matter of fact, in a M/G/1 queue with preemptive resume priority, C_i's turnaround time satisfies:

$$\mathfrak{T}_i = \frac{(1/\mu_i)(1 - \Sigma^i_{j=1}\rho_j) + R_i}{(1 - \Sigma^{i-1}_{j=1}\rho_j)(1 - \Sigma^i_{j=1}\rho_j)} \quad (18)$$

Where

$$\rho_i = \frac{\lambda_i}{\mu_i}, \quad 1 - \Sigma_{j=1}^i \rho_j > 0 \tag{19}$$

$$R_i = \frac{\Sigma_{j=1}^i \lambda_j E[X_j^2]}{2} \tag{20}$$

The average turnaround time of MP-CRNs, $\mathfrak{T}_{MP-CRNs}$, can be calculated as:

$$\mathfrak{T}_{MP-CRNs} = \frac{\Sigma_{i=2}^n \mathfrak{T}_i}{n-1} \tag{21}$$

Our goal is to find an algorithm which limits $\mathfrak{T}_{MP-CRNs}$ as small as possible. Like Algorithm 1, the train of thought is to first find a way to minimize $\mathfrak{T}_i$, and then check whether all $\mathfrak{T}_i$ can be mutually minimized.

For C_i ($2 \le i \le n$), differentiate $\mathfrak{T}_i$ with μ_i, we get:

$$\frac{\partial \mathfrak{T}_i}{\partial \mu_i} = \frac{s-t}{(1-\Sigma_{j=1}^{i-1}\rho_j)^2(1-\Sigma_{j=1}^i\rho_j)^2} \tag{22}$$

Where

$$s = \frac{\partial[(1/\mu_i)(1-\Sigma_{j=1}^i\rho_j)+R_i]}{\partial \mu_i}(1-\Sigma_{j=1}^{i-1}\rho_j)(1-\Sigma_{j=1}^i\rho_j) \tag{23}$$

$$t = \frac{\partial[(1-\Sigma_{j=1}^{i-1}\rho_j)(1-\Sigma_{j=1}^i\rho_j)]}{\partial \mu_i}[(1/\mu_i)(1-\Sigma_{j=1}^i\rho_j)+R_i] \tag{24}$$

Substitute R_i with Eq.(20), we get:

$$\frac{\partial R}{\partial \mu_i} = \lambda_i(\mu_i - \frac{1}{\mu_i} - \frac{1}{\mu_i^3}) \tag{25}$$

Replacing $\frac{\partial R}{\partial \mu_i}$ with Eq.(25) in Eq.(23,24), we get:

$$s - t < \frac{[\lambda_i(\mu_i^3 - \mu_i) - (1-\Sigma_{j=1}^{i-1}\rho_j)](1-\Sigma_{j=1}^{i-1}\rho_j)(1-\Sigma_{j=1}^i\rho_j)}{\mu_i^2} \tag{26}$$

According to function theory, if $\frac{\partial \mathfrak{T}_i}{\partial \mu_i} < 0$, $\mathfrak{T}_i$ is a monotone decreasing function of μ_i. Considering Algorithm 1, to reduce $\mathfrak{T}_{MP-CRNs}^n$, we increase μ_i as much as possible. Combined with the turnaround time, to reduce both $\mathfrak{T}_{MP-CRNs}^n$ and $\mathfrak{T}_i$, we must guarantee that μ_i is located in the area where $\mathfrak{T}_i$ is a monotone decrease. Thus, we expect the following InEq.(27) hold:

$$[\lambda_i(\mu_i^3 - \mu_i) - (1-\Sigma_{j=1}^{i-1}\rho_j)](1-\Sigma_{j=1}^{i-1}\rho_j)(1-\Sigma_{j=1}^i\rho_j) < 0 \tag{27}$$

Considering $1 - \Sigma_{j=1}^{i-1}\rho_j > 0, 1 - \Sigma_{j=1}^i\rho_j > 0$, we only need :

$$\lambda_i(\mu_i^3 - \mu_i) - (1-\Sigma_{j=1}^{i-1}\rho_j) < 0 \tag{28}$$

Define:
$$g(\mu_i) = \lambda_i(\mu_i^3 - \mu_i) - (1 - \Sigma_{j=1}^{i-1}\rho_j) \tag{29}$$

Solving equation (29), we get:

$$\mu_i^* = \cfrac{1}{3\{\frac{1-\Sigma_{j=1}^{i-1}\rho_j}{2\lambda_i} + [\frac{(1-\Sigma_{j=1}^{i-1}\rho_j)^2}{4\lambda_i^2} - \frac{1}{27}]^{\frac{1}{2}}\}^{\frac{1}{3}}}$$
$$+ \{\frac{1-\Sigma_{j=1}^{i-1}\rho_j}{2\lambda_i} + [\frac{(1-\Sigma_{j=1}^{i-1}\rho_j)^2}{4\lambda_i^2} - \frac{1}{27}]^{\frac{1}{2}}\}^{\frac{1}{3}} > 0 \tag{30}$$

Till now, we have controlled C_i's turnaround time, the next step is to minimize the average turnaround time of MP-CRNs ($\mathfrak{T}_{MP-CRNs}$). However, the situation here is a little more complicated than Algorithm 1. Consider $C_i, C_j, j < i$, by increasing μ_j, the denominator of $\mathfrak{T}_i$ increase, which results in a decrease of $\mathfrak{T}_i$. Unfortunately, the numerator of $\mathfrak{T}_i$ also changes, with the first part $(1-\Sigma_{j=1}^i\rho_j)$ increasing and the second part (R_i) decreasing. We have no idea about how the sum of these two parts changes. Thus, the mutual decrease effect is not as apparent as previously.

For C_i ($2 \le i \le n$), differentiate $\mathfrak{T}_i$ with $\mu_j, j < i$, we get:

$$\frac{\partial \mathfrak{T}_i}{\partial \mu_j} = \frac{s' - t'}{(1 - \Sigma_{j=1}^{i-1}\rho_j)^2(1 - \Sigma_{j=1}^i\rho_j)^2} \tag{31}$$

Where

$$s' = \frac{\partial[(1/\mu_i)(1 - \Sigma_{j=1}^i\rho_j) + R_i]}{\partial \mu_j}(1 - \Sigma_{j=1}^{i-1}\rho_j)(1 - \Sigma_{j=1}^i\rho_j) \tag{32}$$

$$t' = \frac{\partial[(1 - \Sigma_{j=1}^{i-1}\rho_j)(1 - \Sigma_{j=1}^i\rho_j)]}{\partial \mu_j}[(1/\mu_i)(1 - \Sigma_{j=1}^i\rho_j) + R_i] \tag{33}$$

According to Eq.(25),

$$\frac{\partial R}{\partial \mu_j} = \lambda_j(\mu_j - \frac{1}{\mu_j} - \frac{1}{\mu_j^3}) \tag{34}$$

Replacing $\frac{\partial R}{\partial \mu_j}$ with Eq.(34) in Eq.(32,33), we get:

$$s' - t' < \frac{\lambda_j}{\mu_j^3}(\mu_j^4 - \mu_j^2 - 1)(1 - \Sigma_{j=1}^{i-1}\rho_j)(1 - \Sigma_{j=1}^i\rho_j) \tag{35}$$

Define:

$$g'(\mu_j) = \mu_j^4 - \mu_j^2 - 1 \tag{36}$$

Solving equation (36), we conclude that in area of $\mathbb{R}^{**} : 0 < u_j^* < \mu_i^{**} = \sqrt{\frac{1+\sqrt{5}}{2}}$, $\mathfrak{T}_i$ is a monotone decreasing function of μ_j. Once again, we have the satisfying conclusion that in the area of $\mathbb{R}^* \cap \mathbb{R}^{**}$, all $C_i(2 \le i \le n)$ can be mutually minimized. The *Turnaround Time Control Algorithm*(Algorithm 2) summarizes as following, which can also be extended to M/G/1 MP-CRNs with $t_{oh} \ne 0$ and M/G/k MP-CRNs.

Algorithm 2. Turnaround Time Control Algorithm

Require: $C_i, \lambda_i, \mu_i, i = 2, 3, \cdots, n$
  for each C_i **do**
    increase μ_i as large as possible within the area of $\mathbb{R}^* \cap \mathbb{R}^{**}$
  end for

---

5 Experimental Simulation

5.1 Validation

Firstly, we verify the formulas given in Section 3 by numerical experiments. The simulation is comprised of four sub-experiments: M/G/1 queue with no time consumption (Exp1); M/G/1 queue with time consumption (Exp2); M/G/k queue with no time consumption (Exp3); M/G/k queue with time consumption (Exp4). The simulated MP-CRNs is comprised of three priority users: C_1, C_2 and C_3 (3MP-CRNs). All the users are Poisson arrived and Poisson served (according to random process theory, the M/M/k queue has almost the same statistical property as M/G/k queue in the limiting case, so we simplify our simulation). A total time of 72 hours is simulated to let our 3MP-CRNs reach its steady state. The time consumption t_{oh} is fixed chosen as $0.01s$ when considering interruption overhead and the system channel k is simply assumed to be 2 when considering the M/G/k model. The detailed parameter settings are shown in Table 2.

Table 1. Parameter Settings of Exp 1~4

	$\lambda_i(users/s)$	$E[X_i](s)$	$Remark$
C_1	0.6	0.5	$fixed$
C_2	0.3	0.01~2.0/0.5	$step{=}0.01s$
C_3	0.3	0.01~1.5	$step{=}0.01s$

In all the four experiments, λ_1 is set to 0.6 *users/s* and $E[X_1]$ is fixed as $0.5s$. In Exp1, λ_2 is set to 0.3 *users/s* and $E[X_2]$ increases from $0.01s$ to $2.0s$ with increasing step of $0.01s$. The simulation *V.S.* theoretical chart of $\mathfrak{I}_2^n$ is depicted in the left side of Figure 1(a). To calculate $\mathfrak{I}_3^n$, $E[X_2]$ is then fixed to be $0.5s$. λ_3 is set to 0.3 *users/s* and $E[X_3]$ increases from $0.01s$ to $1.5s$ with increasing step equals to $0.01s$. The corresponding result is shown in the right side of Figure 1(a). Exp2 $[\mathfrak{I}_2^n(0.01), \mathfrak{I}_3^n(0.01)]$ differs from Exp1 only in that the transition overhead is now set to $0.01s$, whose results are shown in Figure 1(b). For the other two figures, Figure 1(c) shows the results of Exp3 $[\mathfrak{I}_2^n(2), \mathfrak{I}_3^n(2)]$ and Figure 1(d) shows the results of Exp4 $[\mathfrak{I}_2^n(0.01, 2), \mathfrak{I}_3^n(0.01, 2)]$ respectively. The black line, $y = x$, is the measure of our result, which means the simulation coincide perfectly with theory if the dots are plot right upon it. The simulated results in Figure 1 apparently validate our formulas in the previous section.

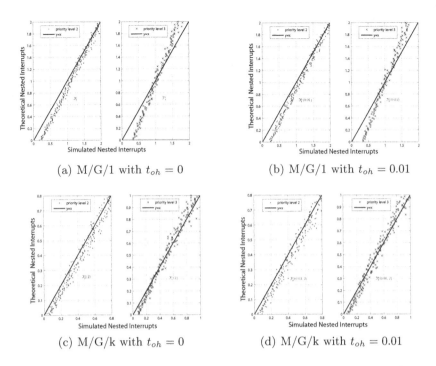

(a) M/G/1 with $t_{oh} = 0$

(b) M/G/1 with $t_{oh} = 0.01$

(c) M/G/k with $t_{oh} = 0$

(d) M/G/k with $t_{oh} = 0.01$

Fig. 1. Simulated V.S. Theoretical Average Nested Interrupts in 3MP-CRNs

5.2   Minimization

Next, we check whether the nested interrupts and turnaround time can be mutually minimized if μ_i increases within the area of $\mathbb{R}^* \cap \mathbb{R}^{**}$ (Exp5). The M/G/1 queue with no time consumption sets up as following: In 3MP-CRNs, C_1, C_2 and C_3 are all Poisson arrived and Poisson served. The detailed parameter settings are shown in Table 3. λ_1 is set to 0.6 *users/s* and μ_1 is fixed as $2s^{-1}$. λ_2 is set to 0.3 *users/s* and μ_2 increases from μ_2^* to μ_2^{**} ($\mathbb{R}^* \cap \mathbb{R}^{**}$) with an increasing step of 0.01 s^{-1}. We also examine the cases of $\mu_2 < \mu_2^*$ ($\mathbb{R}_-^*$) and $\mu_2 > \mu_2^{**}$ ($\mathbb{R}_+^{**}$). To calculate $\mathfrak{I}_3^n$, μ_2 is then fixed to be 2 s^{-1}. λ_3 is set to 0.3 *users/s* and μ_3 increases from μ_3^* to μ_3^{**} with an increasing step of 0.01 s^{-1} as well as the region $\mu_3 < \mu_3^*$ ($\mathbb{R}_-^*$) and $\mu_3 > \mu_3^{**}$ ($\mathbb{R}_+^{**}$).

Table 2. Parameter Settings of Exp 5

	$\lambda_i(users/s)$	$\mu_i(s^{-1})$	Remark
C_1	0.6	2	*fixed*
C_2	0.3	$\{\mathbb{R}_-^*/2, \mathbb{R}^* \cap \mathbb{R}^{**}/2, \mathbb{R}_+^{**}/2\}$	*step*=$0.01s^{-1}$
C_3	0.3	$\{\mathbb{R}_-^*, \mathbb{R}^* \cap \mathbb{R}^{**}, \mathbb{R}_+^{**}\}$	*step*=$0.01s^{-1}$

The simulated results in Figure 2(a) validate our *Mutual Minimizing Algorithm*. All of $\mathfrak{I}_2^n, \mathfrak{I}_3^n$ and $\mathfrak{I}_{3MP-CRNs}^n$ monotone decrease in area $\mathbb{R}_-^* \cup (\mathbb{R}^* \cap \mathbb{R}^{**}) \cup \mathbb{R}_+^{**}$. The average nested interrupts lies under C_3's nested interrupts and above C_2's nested interrupts, indicating the order of $\mathfrak{I}_3^n > \mathfrak{I}_{3MP-CRNs}^n > \mathfrak{I}_2^n$.

The simulated results in Figure 2(b) validate our *Turnaround Time Control Algorithm*. Both of $\mathfrak{T}_2$ and $\mathfrak{T}_3$ monotone decrease in area $(\mathbb{R}^* \cap \mathbb{R}^{**}) \cup \mathbb{R}_+^{**}$. The average turnaround time lies under C_3's turnaround time and above C_2's turnaround time, indicating the order of $\mathfrak{T}_3 > \mathfrak{T}_{3MP-CRNs} > \mathfrak{T}_2$. However, in area $\mathbb{R}_+^{**}$, the average turnaround time has non-simple monotonicity. In area $\mathbb{R}^* \cap \mathbb{R}^{**}$, $\mathfrak{T}_i$ mutually minimizes each other and $\mathfrak{T}_{MP-CRNs}$ is monotone-decreasing.

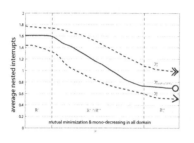   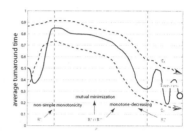

(a) Mutual Minimizing Algorithm   (b) Turnaround Time Control Algorithm

Fig. 2. Minimization of Nested Interrupts

6   Conclusion

We have proposed a general MP-CRNs model. Based on the model, the nested interrupts are derived and proved for the first time, and further validated by simulations. We analyze some properties of nested interrupts. We have designed a *Mutual Minimizing Algorithm* to minimize SU's interrupts and the average number of MP-CRNs's nested interrupts. We have also proposed a novel *Turnaround Time Control Algorithm* to keep SU's turnaround time to an acceptable level. Simulations and experiments demonstrate the efficiency and effectiveness of the proposed algorithms.

Acknowledgments. This work has been supported by the following grants: the Science and Technology Planning Projects of Zhejiang Grants 2011C14024 and 2011C13006-1; the Key Innovation Team of Science and Technology Department of Zhejiang Province, No. 2010R50041. This work was also industrially supported by the National Development and Reform Commission, China under Special Grants "The Operation System of Multimedia Cloud Based on the Integration of Telecommunications Networks, Cable TV Networks and the Internet".

References

1. Mitola, J., Maguire, G.Q.: Cognitive radio:making software radios more personal. IEEE Personal Communications 6(4), 13–18 (1999)
2. Haykin, S.: Cognitive radio: brain-empowered wireless communications. IEEE Journal on Selected Areas in Communications 23(2), 201–220 (2005)
3. Akyildiz, I.F., Lee, W., Vuran, M., Mohanty, S.: Next generation/dynamic spectrum access/cognitive radio wireless networks: A survey. Computer Networks 50(13), 2127–2159 (2006)
4. Tachwali, Y., Lo, B.F., Akyildiz, I.F., Agusti, R.: Multiuser resource allocation optimization using bandwidth-power product in cognitive radio networks. IEEE Journal on Selected Areas in Communications 31(3), 451–463 (2013)
5. Takine, T., Sengupta, B.: A single server queue with service interruptions. Queueing Systems 26(3-4), 285–300 (1997)
6. Lee, D.S.: Analysis of a single server queue with semi-markovian service interruption. Queueing Systems 27(1-2), 153–178 (1997)
7. Núñez Queija, R.: Sojourn times in a processor sharing queue with service interruptions. Queueing Systems 34(1-4), 351–386 (2000)
8. Pang, G.D., Whitt, W.: Heavy-traffic limits for many-server queues with service interruptions. Queueing Systems 61(2-3), 167–202 (2009)
9. Chou, C.T., Sai Shankar, N., Kim, H.: What and how much to gain by spectral agility? IEEE Journal on Selected Areas in Communications 25(3), 576–588 (2007)
10. Gozupek, D., Buhari, S., Alagoz, F.: A spectrum switching delay-aware scheduling algorithm for centralized cognitive radio networks. IEEE Transactions on Mobile Computing 12(7), 1270–1280 (2013)
11. Wang, L.C., Wang, C.W., Chang, C.J.: Modeling and analysis for spectrum handoffs in cognitive radio networks. IEEE Transactions on Mobile Computing 11(9), 1499–1513 (2012)
12. Pan, M., Yue, H., Zhang, C., Fang, Y.G.: Path selection under budget constraints in multihop cognitive radio networkss. IEEE Transactions on Mobile Computing 12(6), 1133–1145 (2013)
13. Irwin, R.E., MacKenzie, A.B., DaSilva, L.A.: Resource-minimized channel assignment for multi-transceiver cognitive radio networkss. IEEE Journal on Selected Areas in Communications 31(3), 442–450 (2013)
14. Zhou, X.W., Li, G.Y., Sun, G.L.: Multiuser spectral precoding for ofdm-based cognitive radio systems. IEEE Journal on Selected Areas in Communications 31(3), 345–352 (2013)
15. Wang, S.W., Zhou, Z.H., Ge, M.Y., Wang, C.G.: Resource allocation for heterogeneous cognitive radio networks with imperfect spectrum sensing. IEEE Journal on Selected Areas in Communications 31(3), 464–475 (2013)
16. Li, H.S., Han, Z.: Socially optimal queuing control in cognitive radio networks subject to service interruptions: To queue or not to queue? IEEE Transactions on Wireless Communications 10(5), 1656–1666 (2011)
17. Gunawardena, S., Zhuang, W.H.: Service response time of elastic data traffic in cognitive radio networks. IEEE Journal on Selected Areas in Communications 31(3), 559–570 (2013)

ContactSim: An Efficient Realistic Trace Driven Contact Simulator for Vehicular Opportunistic Networks

Jianbin Jia, Xu Ming, Chen Yingwen, Wang Chengqian,
Xiao Xiaoqiang, and Xia Geming

School of Computer Science, National University of Defense Technology
410073 Changsha Hunan, China
{jiajianbin.nudt,csywchen,wangchq.wlb}@gmail.com,
{xuming,xqxiao}@nudt.edu.cn, xiageming@126.com

Abstract. Opportunistic networking is an innovative data delivery solution, which leverages the contact opportunities between mobile terminals to exchange messages. The contact events are highly relevant to human behaviours. And thus the contact simulation driven by the realistic mobility trace plays an important role in the research field of opportunistic networking. Making contact simulation based on a large scale of sampled traces has two drawbacks should be taken into account: (1) the simulation output is as good as input, which means the discrete records lead to limited simulation accurate; (2) simulation that scans all the input data simultaneously with time sequence leads to heavy computing cost. In this paper, we proposal an efficient trace driven simulation framework named ContactSim for vehicular opportunistic network. The framework has the functionalities of geographical interpolation to reduce the negative impact of discrete trace records on simulation results. And it uses an asynchronous simulation method to extract contact data from input data, which can not only cut down simulation time, but also relieve memory overhead. The main objective of ContactSim is to provide an efficient platform to assist researchers in validating new concepts and implementations towords vehicular opportunistic networks.

Keywords: opportunistic networks, simulator, inter contact time.

1 Introduction

Opportunistic networking has emerged as an fascinating technique to enable the communication between various wireless mobile terminals. It usually evolves a large scale of nodes and leverages the contact opportunities between them to exchange messages. Vehicular Ad-Hoc Network (VANET) is a typical application scenarios of opportunistic communication [1], particularly in conditions of sparse density or in the remote districts. It can be mentioned as *vehicular opportunistic network*, which has attracted many attentions in the research community [2][3].

M. Pathan, G. Wei, and G. Fortino (Eds.): IDCS 2013, LNCS 8223, pp. 30–40, 2013.
© Springer-Verlag Berlin Heidelberg 2013

But due to the lack of practical deployment in reality, as well as the large scales in vehicle number and networking geographic coverage, performing experimentation on vehicular opportunistic networks is a difficult task. Thereby, researchers usually use the simulation method to study the opportunistic networking characteristics and performance. Conventionally, the synthetic mobility and traffic models are widely used in the simulation [4]. In recent years, because of the fast development of sensor networks, more and more raw data can be collected from realistic environment, for example the GPS trace records collected from Shanghai [5] and San Francisco [6]. As an alternative input to drive simulations, the collected data has the advantage of reflecting scenarios more real against synthetic models. Therefore, the trace records based simulation becomes an important methodology in the research of mobile networks.

In the simulation of vehicular opportunistic network, there are two main characteristics should be considered. First, the number of participant vehicle is usually very large, and so is the scale of trace records to be input. Second, the contact between vehicle pairs don't occur frequently, and the duration is usually very short. Those characteristics may introduce drawbacks in the simulation. For example, after the trajectory records of mobile nodes are fed into the simulator, they are usually scanned with synchronized time slot to engine the interactive between individuals, and finally generates a sequence of global connectivity topologies to depict the dynamic of network. This is important for the link-based network. But for opportunistic network, the prime concern is nodes' contact information, and the global connectivity knowledge is not necessary. In this case, to make synchronized scan is not efficient in the simulation, because it consumes more computing resource but produces less contact information, especially for the vehicular opportunistic network with large scale participants and infrequent contacts. Besides that, due to the fact that the output of simulation is only as good as input, the discrete property of input records brings inaccuracy to the simulation results.

To offset these drawbacks, we propose an asynchronous simulation framework named *ContactSim*, to simulate opportunistic contact between vehicles based on their trace records. It has two features to counter the disadvantages aforementioned: (1) utilizing geography interpolation method to enhance the result accuracy of simulation driven by discrete trace records; (2) employing an asynchronous progress to reduce simulation time as well as computing overhead. This paper describes the design architecture and implementation of the *ContactSim* simulation tool, and also presents the results and conclusions obtained with a first set of simulations performed.

The remainder of the paper is organized as follows. The next section presents related work, followed by a third section that introduces the framework and implementation of *ContactSim*. In section 4, we conduct a first set of simulations based on two realistic vehicular trace datasets and make a first-step analysis of their inter-contact time characteristics. Finally, the conclusion of this paper is made in Section 5.

2   Related Works

Opportunistic networking has attracted a great deal of attentions in the research field of mobile and wireless networks. But performing experimentation is quiet difficult due to the lack of practical deployment and the large scale of heterogeneous participants. The problems are more serious in the vehicular opportunistic networks. Therefore, simulation method is widely used in the community of research.

Opportunistic networking can be simulated with the similar approach as used in mobile ad hoc network. On the one hand, in most of existing such simulator, there are some components that can generate mobility data according to some commonly used synthetic mobility models [7], such as random direction, random waypoint, Gauss-Markow, Manhattan Grid and Reference Point Group Mobility model, and so on. On the other hand, some simulators support feeding trace-file as input, for example the NS-2 [8], Opportunistic Network Environment (ONE) [9] and OMNeT++ [10], etc. All those tools utilize a synchronized simulation method which loads all the input data in once time. This method will lead to severe computing resource exhausting when simulating a large scale system. Moreover, synthetic trace record usually is generated based on a regular road topology, but the realistic trace records collected from physical world usually has a complicated mobility constrain. Additionally, the synthetic mobility framework is mainly targeted at simulating closed systems of wireless mobile nodes. While in vehicular opportunistic networks, nodes may leave or participate in the network from time to time. This characteristic requires the simulated network should be an open system.

Based on the realistic trace data and contact record, a groups of empirical researches have conducted, and provided a lot of new viewpoints to understand the intrinsic characteristics of delay tolerant networks (DTN) and opportunistic networks (ON). Inter-Contact Time (ICT), which is regarded as a critical metric reflecting the average delay level of DTN and ON, has been investigated in a vast range. Specifically, Chaintreau et al. [11] present empirical evidence suggesting that the CCDF (complementary cumulative distribution function) of ICT between mobile devices such as handset follows a power law over a wide range of timescales from a few minutes to half a day. This empirical finding motivates them to draw out the hypothesis that ICT has a CCDF with power law tail. While T. Karagiannis et al. [12] examine a diverse set of mobility traces, and find that the power low tail hypothesis is deficiency, for the CCDF of ICT between mobile devices features dichotomy with a characteristic time separating the distribution to follow power low in beginning part and decays exponentially in tail. H. Zhu [5] investigate the ICT characteristic in a VANET composed by operational taxi in urban area, and obtain an exponential distribution on a large range of timescale. We compare the ICT distribution derived from two different vehicular trace datasets collected from different cities, and find the VANET configurations, in particular the node density, have obvious impact on the ICT characteristics. Those studies are helpful to achieve better understanding of the theoretical limits and routing protocol performance in opportunistic networks, as well as provide implication and guidelines for strategy and protocol design.

3   ContactSim Framework and Implementation

In this section, we introduce the design architecture and implementation of ContactSim in details. The kernel function of the simulator is to extract the contact events of mobile nodes from their trace records. To counter the disadvantages arisen from the discrete and large scales properties of trace records, we devise the simulator with functionalities of preprocessing input data with geographic interpolation and computing the contact events with an asynchronous method.

3.1   Overview

To be more effective, ContactSim is implemented with C language. The architecture and flow chart of the simulator is showed in Figure 1. It is mainly composed of five parts: 1) Data Preparing; 2) Timing Aligning; 3) Spatial Interpolation; 4) Contact Extraction; 5) Contact Trace Output. The input and output data files are organized as plain text format. For the input mobility trace file, it must contain three fields at least, the *latitude, longitude* and *time stamp*. While in the output contact trace file, each contact record is made up by a $< ICT, contact\ time, duration >$ triple fields, in which the first field is the inter contact time from last contact to the current contact, while the second and third field are the contact beginning time and contact duration respectively.

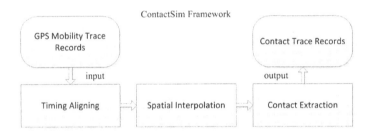

Fig. 1. The architecture and flow chart of ContactSim

3.2   Data Preparing

The simulator feeds on the trace records of all the nodes in the network as input. Specifically, each node has an independent trace records file, which contains the three necessary fields of longitude, latitude and time stamp. To be processed easier, we use the Unix time format to log the location time stamp in a trace record, and the geographic longitude and latitude are represented with the form of decimal value. In practical, the raw trace data file may not only contain information of geographic location-time fields, but also some other mobility information such as speed, ahead direction and so on. Therefore, to be more adaptive, ContactSim examines a configuration file at first to get the field number setting in input files. Actually, some other simulation parameters such as communication range and so on are also indicated in this file.

3.3   Timing Aligning

The function of Timing Aligning is to locate the contact simulation beginning time to a proper point, which is called as an aligned time. This is necessary because the trace records collected from real environment are not as uniform as expected in practical. On the one hand, the record length are not uniform, which means the record start time and end time may be not coincident or even not close. On the other hand, the regular interval between two successive records of some nodes may be longer, and others may be shorter. For example, some nodes make a location record every 60 seconds, and another may record every 30 seconds. Beside this, there are possible temporary breaks in the record list, which will lead to a much longer interval in the trace file.

Specifically, the timing aligning operation is illustrated in Figure 2. It compares the start time in the record lists of a pair of nodes, and finds out the earliest common time-stamp or the nearest one as an aligned time. From this point, the simulator makes geographic interpolation and starts contact extracting. Because the time intervals that has no contact events are skipped by time aligning operation, the efficiency of simulation is improved. It also has the ability to simulate the feature of an open system that allow node to participate in or withdraw from the opportunistic networking. When the trace records are continuous, we can consider the node as joining in the network, while it keep silence or withdraw when the records has a longer interval. For example, if the records time gap exceeds 10 minutes in the trace file, we can treat it as a vehicle that is silence or does't take part in communication in this period.

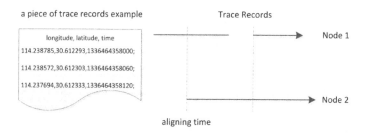

Fig. 2. Timing aligning of the trace records

3.4   Spatial Interpolation

The raw realistic trace records usually has a coarse granularity sampling frequency, for example sampled every 1 minute or even 5 minutes. But the contact duration between vehicles usually continues a relative short period. Therefor, such a record sampling gap will lose many short-duration contact opportunities in the simulation. This drawback can be partially remedied by the method of making geographic interpolation for the raw trace records. In most urban area, the attitude difference usually can be ignored, so that we only consider the surface geographic interpolation in two dimensions of longitude and latitude. The commonly used Linear interpolation algorithm is devised in ContactSim.

Linear interpolation is a method of curve fitting using linear polynomials. If the two sampled geographical points are given by the coordinates (x_1, y_1) and (x_2, y_2) (where x_i is the longitude, and y_i is the latitude), the linear interpolation is the straight line between these points. For a value x in the interval (x_1, x_2), the value $y = f(x)$ along the straight line is given from the equation

$$\frac{y - y_1}{x - x_1} = \frac{y_2 - y_1}{x_2 - x_1} \tag{1}$$

In particular, we sample geographical coordinates according to the trace time stamp. For example, if two successive raw trace records (x_1, y_1) and (x_2, y_2) have the time stamp of t_1 and t_2, and the expected record interval is T, then we sample the coordinates according to the interpolation function $f(x)$ in points of $\{(x, y) \mid x = x_1 + T * i\}$, where i is the integers satisfying $i \leq \frac{t_2 - t_1}{T}$.

3.5   Contact Extracting

To simulate opportunistic networking based on trace record, the primary problem is to extract connection opportunities between each pair of mobile nodes. Suppose the wireless communication distance is r meters. When two nodes move into each other's communication range, a contact is established between them, and the current contact opportunity continues till their distance is larger than the communication range. Since the trace records are discrete, to estimate connection opportunities more accurately, we use a *Contact Window* (CW) to adjust the deviation caused by discrete geographic-time coordinates. The basic idea is as follows.

Given two position record triple <*latitude, longitude, time*>, $P_1 < x_1, y_1, t_1 >$ and $P_2 < x_2, y_2, t_2 >$, corresponding to the positions of vehicles V_1 and V_2 at time instance t_1 and t_2 respectively. Suppose the contact window is W, and the wireless communication range is r. Then we can resolve a contact opportunity between V_1 and V_2, if the following two conditions are satisfied:

$$\textbf{Contact Condition:} \quad \begin{cases} (1)\ \Delta t \leq W; \\ \\ (2)\ d \leq (1 - \Delta t / W) \cdot r \end{cases} \tag{2}$$

where $\Delta t = |t_1 - t_2|$, d is the Euclidean distance of points (x_1, y_1) and (x_2, y_2). To avoid splitting a long contact into small pieces, we assume that if two successive records in the trace of V_1 and V_2 satisfy the contact conditions, then the corresponding successive contacts are merged to a long one for V_1 and V_2.

3.6   Output Contact Trace

Firstly, let's introduce a contact based network model used in ContactSim. The conventional static graph network model is not suitable for opportunistic network, because it can't capture their inherent dynamic connectivity characteristics such as contact duration and the time order of contacts, etc. To reflect the time varying nature of interaction between mobile nodes, the time-varying or temporal graph model is utilized in literatures [14][15]. It splits continuous time into discrete slots, and uses a traditional topology graph to describe the link state between nodes in each time slot. Thus, time-varying graph is represented as a series of time-dependent adjacency matrix $A(t)$, $t = 1, 2, 3, \cdots, T$. Obviously, such a model can reveal the time sequence of connectivity evolution in dynamics network. But it assumes nodes timing are synchronized in network, which is difficult to achieve in practical, especially for a large scale network. Moreover, because the beginning and end time of contact events in the network are asynchronous, contacts are not aligned with time slot. In fact, a contact may be broken down into multiple time slots, or wrapped in a slot. Therefore, the start time and duration of node contact is hardly to be described accurately.

Here, we introduce a contact based opportunistic network model named *Contact Memory networks Model* (CMM). It uses a node-centric way to record contact information, in which every node records its contact events independently, and so that it need no synchronization. Specifically, consider a mobile node set $\mathbf{N}$. Each node $i \in \mathbf{N}$ can be represented by an array $A_i : \{X_1, X_2, X_3, \cdots X_m\}$, where X_j ($j \in [1, m]$, $m \leq |\mathbf{N}| - 1$) is a contact sequence in which each contact event between node i and j is recorded. Each contact event in contact sequence X_j is noted by a quadruple $\langle U_j, I_k, T_k, D_k \rangle$. The quadruple elements' meaning is explained as follow: U_j is the unique identification of a mobile node in the system; T_k indicates the start time of the k-th contact event in current sequence; I_k represents the inter-contact time between the k-th and its previous, i.e. the $(k + 1)$th contact; while the last notation D_k indicates the duration time of the k-th contact.

ContactSim output the results of Contact Extracting into a CMM structure. When a contact is extracted, its information will be appended to the corresponding contact sequence. At last, when the contact simulation process complete, ContactSim write every array A_i into a single plaint file, in which each line is a quadruple $\langle U_j, I_k, T_k, D_k \rangle$ representing a contact event, and the whole file stores the contact trace of node i with all other nodes.

4   Inter-contact Time Characterizing

In this section, we present the first set of simulation results generated by ContactSim, and analyze the temporal characteristic of vehicular opportunistic network described in term of Inter-Contact Time (ICT). The meaning of ICT refers to the wait period between two successive contact events of the same pair of nodes. It is regarded as a critical metric reflecting the delivery delay for opportunistic forwarding and has been studied in a wide range [5][11][12][16].

4.1   Simulation Setting

As the first set of simulation, we use two trace datasets of taxi as input to feed ContactSim simulator. These trace records are collected by the Cabspotting Project [6] and ShanghaiGrid Project [5] respectively. The Cabspotting Project recorded a group of taxi cabs running in San Francisco Bay Area. A released dataset of this project can be found in CRAWDAD [13]. It includes the trace records of 536 cabs from May 17 to June 10 in 2008 (the record periods for each cab are not equal in fact). While the ShanghaiGrid Project collects the driving traces of 2,444 taxis in Shanghai city during the February of 2007.

In our simulation, to examine the impact of communication range on the distribution of ICT, three different distances are examined for both datasets, i.e. 100, 200 and 300 meters. For simplicity, we randomly separate the ShanghaiGrid dataset into three subsets which include 819, 803, 822 vehicles, and running different communication ranges towards them respectively. After the interpolation process, the interval between two adjacent trace records is 20 seconds. The contact window is set to be 5 seconds. In summary, the parameters of our simulation and the statistics of results are summarized in Table 1.

Table 1. Simulation parameters and statistic data of results for two datasets

	Cabspotting	ShanghaiGrid
Node Number	536	819, 803, 822
Node Density ($vehicles/km^2$)	3.8	1.6
Dataset Duration	25 days	28 days
Comm. Range ($meters$)	100, 200, 300	100, 200, 300
Contact Number ($\times 10^6$)	7.86, 17.5, 27.4	7.02, 19.1, 32.8
Contact Pair	279374, 282853, 283457	1053792, 1398878, 1637821
Average Contact	28.1, 61.8, 96.6	6.7, 13.7, 20.1

4.2   Characteristics of Inter-contact Time in VON

Firstly, let's look at Table 1. The *contact number* item means the total number of contact obtained in the corresponding simulation setting. The *contact pair* item means the number of node pairs that have at least one contact. And the *average contact* item means the average number for each contacted node pair, which indicates the contact frequency of them. From this table, we find that the average contact number is approximately linear with the communication range, while it is approximately exponential with the node density. This implies node density has more impact on opportunistic networking performance. Increasing the participated nodes will reduce message delivery latency obviously. While in the scenario with sparse nodes, increasing communication range can also bring benefit for opportunistic communication.

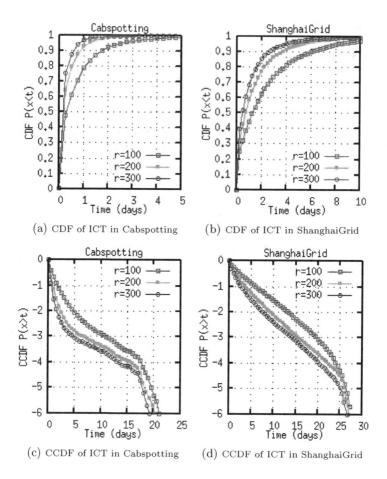

Fig. 3. CDF and CCDF of Aggregated ICT for Cabspotting and ShanghaiGrid. From left to right, (a) and (b) show the CDF curves in Lin-Lin scale. (c) and (d) show the CCDF curves in Lin-Log scale. The horizontal axis is delay time measured by days, and the vertical axis is cumulative probability.

Some previous works have investigated the distribution of ICT in a vast range. However, it is still ambiguous to know which distribution form is more fitting to describe the ICT distribution in a specific real-world scenario. And in the similar scenarios, whether it has the similar ICT characteristics? Specifically, the authors in [5] investigated the ICT distribution in the opportunistic vehicular networking scenario based on ShanghaiGrid trace dataset. They found that the aggregated ICT complementary cumulative distribution function (CCDF) is more likely to decay exponentially. Here, we examine the same type of scenario based on Cabspotting trace data, and make a comparison with ShanghaiGrid. Their aggregated ICT distributions in cases of three different communication ranges (100, 200, and 300 meters respectively) are showed in Fig. 3, in which the CDF curve is plot with Lin-Lin scale, while the CCDF curve is plot with Lin-Log scale. From Fig. 3(a) and

Fig. 3(b), we can find that the front part of CDF increases fast and the tail part increases slowly. This characteristic implies the most of meeting intervals of a pair of nodes are short. Besides, these two plots show that the ICT curve of Cabspotting increases faster than ShanghaiGrid, which indicates that in Cabspotting scenario, contact between vehicles occurred more frequent than it is in ShanghaiGrid.

In the CCDF plots showed in Fig. 3(c) and 3(d), the curves of ShanghaiGrid are almost straight lines with negative slopes in Lin-Log scale. This is in accordance with the result in [5]. But for Cabspotting, the curves are not fitting to linear well. Specifically, at first, it decays faster in the lower ICT value, and then turn to milder decay in the larger. We attribute the reason causing this diversity to the differences in network coverage range and node density. Actually, in the major coverage area, the density of Cabspotting is about 3.8 *vehicles per km^2*, and in ShanghaiGrid it is about 1.6 *vehicles per km^2*. This result suggests that a simplex distribution maybe not enough to describe the similar opportunistic network scenarios with different setting.

5   Conclusions and Future Work

In this paper, we introduce a trace-driven simulator framework to perform experiments on the vehicular opportunistic networks. It uses the geographic interpolation method to relieve the negative impact introduced by the discrete input trace record upon the simulation accuracy, and uses an asynchronous contact extract method to adapt to the characteristic of fast varying opportunistic network. In fact, the proposal simulator framework is not only meaningful for the experiments of vehicular opportunistic networks, but also available for other trace-based networking scenario.

Based on the realistic vehicle trace data collected from two different cities, we carried out simulation with our tools and discussed the inter-contact time (ICT) characteristics. From the simulation result, we find the simplex exponential decay is not enough to describe the ICT CCDF characteristics in similar opportunistic vehicular networking scenario having different setting such as node density. In order to further understand the intrinsic reason leading to such diversity, we will work on the investigation of vehicle trace data with considering other factors, such as vehicles speed and different geographical interpolation methods considering road features in different cities.

Acknowledgments. This research is partially supported by the National Science Foundation of China under Grant No. 61070211, No. 61070201, No. 61003304 and No. 61272485; Hunan Provincial Natural Science Foundation of China under grants No. 09JJ4034.

References

1. Zhao, J., Cao, G.: VADD: Vehicle-Assisted Data Delivery in Vehicular Ad Hoc Networks. IEEE Transactions on Vehicular Technology 57(3), 1910–1922 (2008)
2. Zhu, H., Chang, S., Li, M., Naik, K., Shen, S.: Exploiting temporal dependency for opportunistic forwarding in urban vehicular networks. In: INFOCOM 2011, pp. 2192–2200. IEEE Press, New York (2011)
3. Moghadam, K.R., Badawy, G.H., Todd, T.D.: Opportunistic vehicular ferrying for energy efficient wireless mesh networks. In: 2011 IEEE Wireless Communications and Networking Conference (WCNC 2011). IEEE Press, New York (2011)
4. Skordylis, A., Trigoni, N.: Delay-bounded Routing in Vehicular Ad-hoc Networks. In: MOBIHOC 2008 (2008)
5. Zhu, H., Fu, L., Xue, T., Zhu, Y.M., Li, M.L., Ni, L.M.: Recognizing Exponential Inter-Contact Time in VANETs. In: IEEE INFOCOM 2010 (2010)
6. Piorkowski, M., Djukic, N.S., Grossglauser, M.: A Parsimonious Model of Mobile Partitioned Networks with Clustering. In: The First International Conference on COMmunication Systems and NETworkS, COMSNETS (2009)
7. Khabbaz, M.J., Fawaz, W.F., Assi, C.M.: A Simple Free-Flow Traffic Model for Vehicular Intermittently Connected Networks. IEEE Transactions on Intelligent Transportation Systems 13(3), 1312–1326 (2012)
8. The Network Simulator - ns-2, http://www.isi.edu/nsnam/ns/
9. Keranen, A.: Opportunistic Network Environment simulator. Helsinki University of Technology (2008)
10. OMNeT++, http://www.omnetpp.org/
11. Chaintreau, A., Pan, H., Crowcroft, J., Diot, C., Gass, R., Scott, J.: Impact of Human Mobility on the Design of Opportunistic Forwarding Algorithms. In: IEEE INFOCOM 2006 (2006)
12. Karagiannis, T., Boudec, J.L., Vojnovic, M.: Power Law and Exponential Decay of Inter Contact Times between Mobile Devices. In: ACM Mobicom 2007 (2007)
13. CRAWDAD, http://www.crawdad.cs.dartmouth.edu/
14. Tang, J., Scellato, S., Musolesi, M., Mascolo, C., Latora, V.: Small-world behavior in time-varying graphs. Physical Review E 81(5), 81–84 (2010)
15. Huang, M., Chen, S.Y., Zhu, Y., Wang, Y.: Cost-Efficient Topology Design Problem in Time-Evolving Delay-Tolerant Networks. In: GLOBECOM 2010 (2010)
16. Cai, H., Eun, D.Y.: Crossing Over the Bounded Domain: From Exponential to Power-law Inter-meeting Time in MANET. In: ACM MobiCom 2007, Montreal, Canada (2007)

A Stability-Aware Cooperative Routing Scheme in Multi-rate Mobile Ad-Hoc Wireless Networks

Le The Dung[1] and Beongku An[2]

[1] Dept. of Electronics & Computer Engineering in Graduate School, Hongik University, Korea
thedung_hcmut@yahoo.com
[2] Dept. of Computer & Information Communications Engineering, Hongik University, Korea
beongku@hongik.ac.kr

Abstract. In this paper, we propose a stability-aware cooperative routing scheme in multi-rate mobile ad-hoc wireless networks to provide high data transmission with stable and reliable routes. The main features and contributions of the proposal are as follows: First, we use the cross-layer concept with network layer, MAC layer, and physical layer. Second, a stable routing path is selected as the main routing path. Third, we use the RSSI, PHY delay, and MAC delay for choosing relay and appropriate data rate adaptively. Forth, we derive mathematical models to investigate the tradeoff between point-to-point transmission rates and the corresponding effective transmission ranges. The performance evaluations through analysis and simulation demonstrate that the proposal can adaptively select optimal data rate and outperforms single rate routing protocol in terms of packet delivery ratio and network throughput in all settings of node density and node mobility.

Keywords: mobile ad-hoc wireless networks, route stability, cooperative routing, muli-rate, rate adaption.

1 Introduction

Mobile ad-hoc wireless networks consist of many mobile nodes communicating in decentralized manner. As mobile wireless devices are developed rapidly, consumer demand for communication in mobile ad-hoc wireless networks includes both high speed and reliability. Currently, wireless devices using 802.11a, 802,11b, 802.11g, and HiperLAN2 can operate at many different transmission rates [1].

Due to the physical properties of communication channels, i.e. the signal quality decreases as the distance between two devices increases, there is an inherent tradeoff between transmission rate and effective transmission range to support reliable communication. Both high speed transmission and long range transmission cannot be achieved simultaneously. Researches of multi-rate wireless environment are mostly on MAC layer [2-4] and static ad-hoc networks [5-6]. As far as we know, only the authors in [7] propose a multi-rate aware routing protocol for mobile ad-hoc networks. However, the metric for selecting relay node does not include the transmission time of MAC header and PHY header. Also, there is no mathematical model to show the data rate – transmission range tradeoff, and the performance of that proposed routing protocol with different node density and node mobility is not investigated.

M. Pathan, G. Wei, and G. Fortino (Eds.): IDCS 2013, LNCS 8223, pp. 41–50, 2013.
© Springer-Verlag Berlin Heidelberg 2013

We observe an important fact that in mobile ad-hoc wireless network it is meaningless if mobile nodes are ready to send data at high speed but wireless links do not exist due to node mobility or short effective radio range. Therefore, multi-rate devices must have routing protocols that can adaptively select the appropriate next hop and data rate for each wireless links. This issue is extremely challenging in dynamic network such as mobile ad-hoc wireless networks. The main contributions of this paper are both to derive mathematical models to evaluate network connectivity and to provide stability-aware cooperative routing scheme using our proposed metrics with cross-layer concept for adaptive selecting robust and high speed routes in mobile ad-hoc wireless networks.

The rest of this paper is organized as follows. In Section 2, we define our multi-rate model used for analysis and simulation. We also derive mathematical formulas showing the tradeoff between effective transmission range and network connectivity. In Section 3, we present our proposed stability-aware cooperative routing scheme. The performance of our proposed scheme is intensively evaluated in Section 4. Finally, Section 5 concludes the paper.

2   The Multi-rate Model to Support Stability-Aware Cooperative Routing Scheme

In this section, firstly, we describe the multi-rate model used in our analysis model and stability-aware cooperative routing scheme. Then, from that model we derive mathematical expressions to show the impact of data rate and corresponding effective transmission range on network connectivity and transmission time. Finally, by using those mathematical expressions as routing metrics, we propose stability-aware cooperative routing to provide high data transmission with stable and reliable routes from a source node to a destination node.

2.1   Multi-rate Model

In our multi-rate model, there is a mapping relationship between the distance of two mobile nodes and the corresponding transmission rate that the channel between them can support as in Fig. 1.

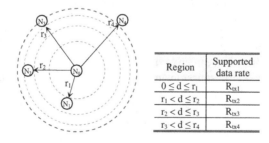

Region	Supported data rate
$0 \leq d \leq r_1$	R_{tx1}
$r_1 < d \leq r_2$	R_{tx2}
$r_2 < d \leq r_3$	R_{tx3}
$r_3 < d \leq r_4$	R_{tx4}

Fig. 1. Data rates and corresponding transmission range in multi-rate wireless networks

That relationship depends on the hardware characteristic of mobile nodes and the environment of considered wireless networks, and is standardized by organizations. In this paper, we use the IEEE 802.11b/g standard showing the data rates and corresponding transmission range in wireless environment [1]. The mapping relationship between the effective transmission ranges and the corresponding data rates of IEEE 802.11b/g is plotted in Fig. 2. As we can see in Fig. 2, effective transmission range does not linearly decrease with the increase of data rate.

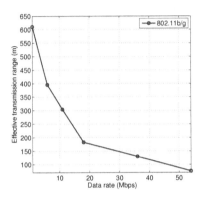

Data Rate	54 Mbps	36 Mbps	18 Mbps	11 Mbps	6 Mbps	1 Mbps
Tx Range	76 m	130 m	183 m	304 m	396 m	610 m

Fig. 2. Data rates and corresponding transmission ranges in wireless environment of IEEE 802.11b/g standard

2.2   Transmission Range versus Network Connectivity

In this section, we will use the above multi-rate model to show the tradeoff between transmission rate and effective transmission range which correlates with network connectivity. We consider a mobile ad-hoc network with N nodes uniformly distributed inside the network area a^2. The probability that a mobile node has m neighbor nodes in half circular area $\pi R^2/2$ can be approximated by Poisson distribution as

$$P_M(m) = \frac{(\rho\gamma)^m}{m!} e^{-\rho\gamma} \tag{1}$$

where $\rho = N/a^2$ is node density, $\gamma = \pi R^2/2$ is half circular area.

A point-to-point wireless link exists if there is at least one node in half circular area with effective transmission rage R. Thus, the connectivity of point-to-point link is

$$p_{p2p} = P(M \geq 1) = 1 - P(0) = 1 - e^{-(N/a^2) \times (\pi R^2/2)} \tag{2}$$

The Eq. (2) is plotted in Fig. 3(a) with $N = 50$ and different effective transmission ranges and network sizes. The cross sections at network size $a = 1000m$, $2000m$, and $3000m$ are shown in Fig. 3(b), respectively. As we can see in Fig. 3, the connectivity of wireless link depends on both node density and effective transmission range.

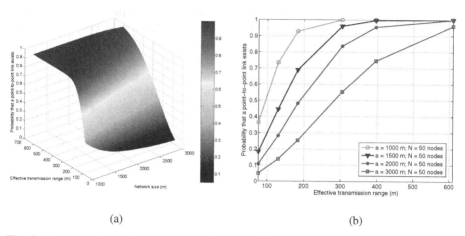

(a)   (b)

Fig. 3. The connectivity of point-to-point link with different effective transmission ranges and network sizes in multi-rate wireless networks.

3   The Proposed Stability-Aware Cooperative Routing Scheme

We apply the cross–layer concept for our proposed stability-aware cooperative routing scheme. The proposed scheme consists of two algorithms. Initially, the first algorithm selects stable routing path. That stable routing path is used as the main routing path from a source node to a destination node. The second algorithm works in adaptive manner to select relay nodes for supporting nodes on main routing path to send data faster. Details of two algorithms are presented in the following parts.

3.1   Selection of Stable Routing Path

Figure 4 illustrates the algorithm for selecting stable routing path in our scheme.

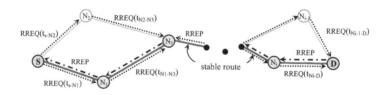

Fig. 4. Selection of stable routing path based on the information of link duration

We extend the idea in our previous work [8] by using optimal mobile node's transmission range calculated from Eq. (2) in Section 2.2. For details of how to calculate link duration and use it to select stable routing path please refer to our previous work [8]. In the following, we present step-by-step the algorithm.

- **Step 1:** At the initial time, all nodes select optimal base data rate and corresponding transmission range that provides network connectivity greater than or equal to 0.99 by using Eq. (2). Then a source node (S) broadcasts its location and waypoint in Route Request (RREQ) packet.
- **Step 2:** When a mobile node receives unduplicated Route Reply (RREP) packet, it uses the location and waypoint information of itself and pre-hop to calculate link duration of the link between it and pre-hop. If this link duration is greater than the one stored in Routing Cache, node updates the information in RREQ then forward it. Otherwise, it does nothing.
- **Step 3:** Upon receiving RREQ packet, a destination node (D) chooses the most stable path from the available routing paths. It copies the route record and route life time (i.e. the link duration of the weakest link) of this path to RREP packet and sends RREP packet back to source node.
- **Step 4:** After receiving RREP packet, the source node sends data packet through this stable path.

3.2   Selection of Relay and Cooperative Data Transmission

Figure 5(a) presents the cooperative process operating on mobile nodes in the cooperative region, while Fig. 5(b) presents the basic concepts of cross-layer stability-aware cooperative routing of multi-hop path, respectively.

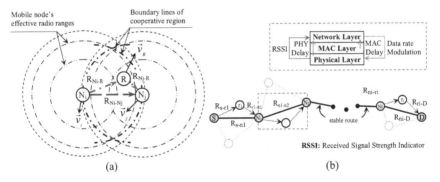

(a)   (b)

Fig. 5. Basic concepts of the proposed stability-aware cooperative routing scheme: (a) Cooperative process of each wireless link. (b) Cross-layer cooperative routing of multi-hop path.

Any node staying in cooperative region is neighbor node of both sender and receiver. When a data packet with length L is transmitted, the transmission time τ using direct transmission and cooperative transmission via relay node will be:

$$\tau = \begin{bmatrix} \tau_d = T_{MAC} + \dfrac{L}{R_{tx-rx}} + T_{PLCP} & \text{direct transmission} \\[3mm] \tau_c = 2T_{MAC} + \dfrac{L}{R_{tx-r}} + \dfrac{L}{R_{rx-r}} + 2T_{PLCP} & \text{cooperative transmission} \end{bmatrix} \qquad (3)$$

where R_{tx-rx}, R_{tx-r}, R_{rx-r} are the data transmission rates of wireless sender-receiver channel, sender-relay channel, receiver-relay channel, and T_{MAC}, T_{PLCP} are additional time associated with transmitting header of MAC layer and physical layer, respectively. According to IEEE 802.11b/g standard, the MAC and PHY header are transmitted with fixed rate; only data unit is transmitted with variable rates. Therefore, the condition for cooperative transmission would be

$$T_{MAC} + \frac{L}{R_{tx-r}} + \frac{L}{R_{rx-r}} + T_{PLCP} < \frac{L}{R_{tx-rx}} \qquad (4)$$

In this paper, the sizes of MAC header and PLCP are 272 bits and 192 bits, respectively. They are all transmitted with 1 Mbps. The length of data packet is 4 Kbits. In the following steps, we describe in detail the relay selection and cooperative data transmission algorithm by using Fig. 5(a) and Fig. 5(b). The format of control overheads Coop-Ack and data frame are in Fig. 6.

- **Step 1:** By overhearing the data forwarding from node N_i to node N_j on the main routing path, mobile node R staying in cooperative region can get the data packets sent from them. From the received signal strength, node R calculates the distance from it to node N_i and node N_j. Then, it will select the appropriate data transmission rate for channel N_i-R and N_j-R using the mapping relationship in Fig. 2. Node R also checks the cooperative condition by using metric in Eq. (4). If the condition is met, it participates in cooperative transmission by sending Coop-Ack packet with Cooperation Valid is set to 1. The data rates for the wireless channels N_i - R and N_j - R are specified in R_{tx-r} and R_{rx-r}, respectively. Then those data rates are set to SIGNAL field of data frame to inform physical layer of sending that data frame at those rates.
- **Step 2:** When the wireless link N_i - R or N_j - R is broken due to node mobility and node N_j cannot receive three data packets sending from relay node R, node N_j will send Coop-Ack to node N_i with Cooperation Valid is set to 0 to inform switching to direct transmission mode. The Coop-Ack does not have packet fields R_{tx-r} and R_{rx-r} if Cooperation Valid is 0.

Step 3: The cooperative transmission process repeats if there is another relay node that can participate in cooperative transmission.

Cooperation Valid 1 bit	Relay ID 8 bits	Sender ID 8 bits	Receiver ID 8 bits	R_{tx-r} 8 bits	R_{rx-r} 8 bits

(a)

SIGNAL 8 bits	SERVICE 8 bits	LENGTH 16 bits	CRC 16 bits

PLCP Preamble 144 bits at 1 Mbps	PLCP Header 48bits at 1 Mbps	MAC Header 272 bits at 1 Mbps	Route Record 8 bits at 1 Mbps	PSDU 4 Kbits variable at 1, 6, 11, 18, 36, 54 Mbps

(b)

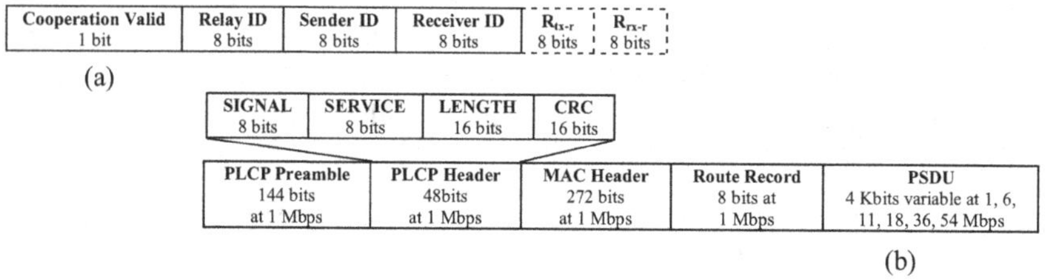

Fig. 6. The format of (a) control overhead Coop-Ack and (b) data frame in our cooperative routing scheme

4   Performance Evaluation

In this section, we evaluate the performance our proposed stability-aware cooperative routing scheme with different node density, and node mobility and data rate in terms of packet delivery ratio and network throughput to compare with DSR routing protocol [9]. For all simulation scenarios, Constant Bit Rate/User Datagram Protocol (CBR/UDP) traffic is used. In order to eliminate the packet loss due to buffer overflow light traffic is generated. Specifically, a source node sends CBR traffic at 80 Kbps, where data packet length is 4 Kbits. There are 50 mobile nodes in the network area. The optimal base transmission ranges of mobile nodes selected by our first algorithm in Section 3.1 are 304m, 396m, 610m, 610m with respect to network size $a = $ 1000m, 1500m, 2000m, 3000m and can be verified in Fig. 3(b). Each simulation is executed 10 times and the average results are plotted in the graphs.

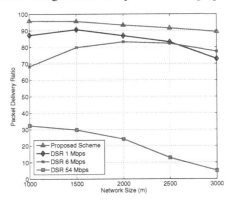

Fig. 7. Packet Delivery Ratio (PDR) vs Network Size (m); Node Mobility = 20km/h

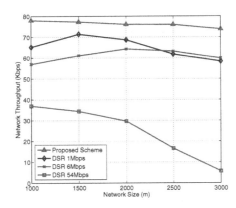

Fig. 8. Network Throughput vs Network Size (m); Node Mobility = 20km/h

Figure 7 and Fig. 8 show the packet delivery ratio (PDR) and network throughput as functions of network size, respectively. We change node density by increasing network size while node mobility is kept at 20 km/h. As we can see in Fig. 7, the PDR obtained from our proposed scheme outperforms the PDR of single-rate DSR routing protocol in all cases because mobile node can adaptively select optimal data rates so that with corresponding effective transmission ranges network connectivity is ensured. Our scheme also selects the most stable route during route discovering process.

The 'side effect' of larger transmission range at lower data rate can be seen in Fig. 7. The PDR of DSR 1Mbps is lower than that of DSR 6Mbps because mobile node has much more neighbor nodes due to larger transmission range and leads to RREP packet storm in the network. This effect is reduced as node density is lower. With DSR 54Mbps, the PDR is very low due to lack of network connections. However, our proposed scheme can adaptively selects optimal node's transmission ranges based on node density. Therefore, there is no 'side effect' or lack of connection due to inappropriate node's transmission ranges, results in higher and stable PDR and network throughput. Since network throughput of CBR data in Fig. 8 closely relates to PDR, it has quite similar pattern with PDR in Fig. 7.

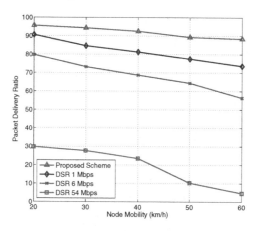

Fig. 9. Packet Delivery Ratio (PDR) vs Node Mobility; Network Size = 1500m × 1500m

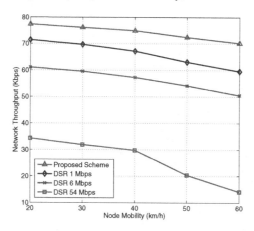

Fig. 10. Network Throughput vs Node Mobility; Network Size = 1500m × 1500m

Figure 9 and Fig. 10 show the packet delivery ratio (PDR) and network throughput as functions of node mobility, respectively. We change node density while network size is kept at 1500m× 1500m. As we can see in Fig. 9, the pattern of PDR is different with that in Fig. 10 because node mobility does not have 'side effect' as node's transmission range. When node mobility increases, link disconnection also increase which results in lower PDR. Since our proposed scheme selects stable routing path as main path, it is more robust against node mobility. Moreover, our scheme performs cooperative transmission with best effort to support the main routing path in sending data at higher rate. Therefore, the PDR and network throughput obtained from our scheme are higher than single rate DRS in all settings of node mobility. Again, network throughput of CBR data in Fig. 10 has quite similar pattern with PDR in Fig. 9.

5   Conclusion

In this paper, with given network density we derive mathematical models used as metrics to adaptively select relay nodes and the optimal data rates with corresponding transmission ranges. Based on those metrics, we propose stability-aware cooperative routing scheme in multi-rate mobile ad-hoc wireless networks adaptively that can select stable routing path and optimal data rate for each wireless link to achieve high data transmission with reliability. Our proposed scheme applies cross-layer concept by using physical layer information and MAC layer information to support selecting relays and data rate efficiently at network layer. The simulation results show that the PDR and network throughput obtained from our scheme outperform those in single-rate DSR routing protocol in all scenarios.

Acknowledgment. This research was supported by Basic Science Research Program through the National Research Foundation of Korea (NRF) funded by the Ministry of Education, Science and Technology (20120007119) and by National Research Foundation of Korea (NRF) funded by Korea government (MEST) (2012046780).

References

1. IEEE Computer Society: Part 11: Wireless LAN Medium Access Control (MAC) and Physical Layer (PHY) Specifications, Amendment 4: Further Higher Data Rate Extension in the 2.4 GHz Band. In: IEEE Std 802.11g – 2003 (2003)
2. Liu, P., Tao, Z., Narayanan, S., Korakis, T., Panwar, S.S.: CoopMAC: A Cooperative MAC for Wireless LAN. IEEE Journal on Selected Areas in Communications 25(2), 340–354 (2007)
3. Jang, J., Yoon, D., Kim, S.: Performance Evaluation of a Cooperative MAC Protocol at Ad Hoc Networks. In: Proc. of IEEE International Conference on Advanced Communication Technology (ICACT), pp. 920–925 (2010)
4. Feng, X., Lei, L., Liu, W., Tao, L.: A Rate Adaptive Scheme for Improving Concurrent MAC protocol performance in Multi-hop Ad hoc Networks. In: Proc. of IEEE ICCSNT 2001, pp. 2164–2168 (2011)

5. Awerbuch, B., Holmer, D., Rubens, H.: High Throughput Route Selection in Multi-Rate Ad Hoc Wireless Networks. In: Battiti, R., Conti, M., Cigno, R.L. (eds.) WONS 2004. LNCS, vol. 2928, pp. 253–270. Springer, Heidelberg (2004)
6. Hieu, C.T., Hong, C.: RAI: A High Throughput Routing Protocol for Multi-hop Multi-rate Ad hoc Networks. In: Proc. of IEEE ICUFN 2010, pp. 39–44 (2010)
7. Seok, Y., Park, J., Choi, Y.: Multi-rate Aware Routing Protocol for Mobile Ad Hoc Networks. In: Proc. of IEEE VTC 2003, vol. 3, pp. 1749–1752 (2003)
8. Dung, L.T., Ha, S.H., An, B.: A Practical Adaptive Scheme for Enhancing Network Stability in Mobile Ad-Hoc Wireless Networks. In: Park, J.J(J.H.), Arabnia, H.R., Kim, C., Shi, W., Gil, J.-M. (eds.) GPC 2013. LNCS, vol. 7861, pp. 886–892. Springer, Heidelberg (2013)
9. Johnson, D., Maltz, D., Broch, J.: DSR: The Dynamic Source Routing Protocol for Mutlti-hop Wireless Ad Hoc Networks. In: Ad Hoc Networking, ch. 5, pp. 139–172. Addison-Wesley (2001)

Using Human-Centric Wireless Sensor Networks to Support Personal Security

Pablo Carreño[1], Francisco Gutierrez[1], Sergio F. Ochoa[1], and Giancarlo Fortino[2]

[1] Computer Science Department, Universidad de Chile
Av. Blanco Encalada 2120, 3rd floor, Santiago, Chile
{pcarreno,frgutier,sochoa}@dcc.uchile.cl
[2] DIMES, Università della Calabria
Via P. Bucci, cubo 41C, 87036 Rende (CS), Italy
g.fortino@unical.it

Abstract. Violence and crime in large urban areas are a worldwide problem that is still open. After several attempts to reduce its occurrence and impact, there seems to be an agreement that crime preventive actions, which can be taken by citizens and security organizations, are the best way to address it. This paper proposes the use of human-centric wireless sensor networks to help address this problem, and the proposed solution is complementary to those already used by security organizations. The architecture and main components of these networks are described in detail. The article also describes a software system that implements most of the components of these networks. Such a system helps people be aware of the risks that appear to exist in a certain place at a certain time. Based on that information, citizens can take appropriate and on-time preventive actions. A preliminary evaluation of the system has been conducted, and the obtained results are also presented and discussed.

Keywords: Personal security, crime prevention, participatory sensing, human-centric wireless sensor networks, crowdsourcing, social computing.

1   Introduction

Everyday more and more applications link their functionality to social networking services (SNS) in some way. SNS capabilities, like crowdsourcing, can contribute to address challenges that were not easy to tackle in the past; particularly those requiring people opinions or observations [16, 19]. One of these problems is crime (e.g. assault, robbery, rape, vandalism, physical aggressions, and also murders) that is still an open issue in most countries around the world. Although government organizations are continually working to improve the personal security of civilians, crime rate does not seem to change too much [1, 11].

Today there seems to be a consensus that crime prevention is the best way to address this problem. Unfortunately most solutions used to try reducing crime, like the use of surveillance cameras or increasing the presence of security agents in the field, are not robust enough in terms of crime prevention for civilians [9, 24, 28]. For

M. Pathan, G. Wei, and G. Fortino (Eds.): IDCS 2013, LNCS 8223, pp. 51–64, 2013.

instance, these types of solutions do not have a good scalability, because it is not feasible to flood a city with surveillance cameras or police personnel that can be active all the time protecting civilians. The cost and complexity of these solutions make them not feasible, even for developed countries.

Conscious of such situation, during the last years government organizations have involved citizens to a greater extent (e.g. through anonymous reports of crimes or suspicious activities) in the process of crime prevention. This has allowed them to increase the coverage area and the monitoring capability of security organizations [6]. However, citizen participation is still bureaucratic (e.g. it requires to do a phone call or fill a denounce form), therefore it tends to be slow and with a low participation rate.

This article proposes the use of a participatory sensing strategy [4, 5], supported by a human-centric wireless sensor network [23], to help tackle the stated problem. The solution empowers ordinary citizens to collect and share security information from their surrounding environments, using their mobile phones in an easy and anonymous way. Considering the information provided by multiple participants, it is possible to perform an online diagnosis that allows civilians being aware of their current risk and personal security level, while they move through urban areas. The article also reports the design, development and evaluation of a mobile application that implements most of the components of this proposal.

Next section presents the related work. Section 3 briefly introduces the concept of human-centric wireless sensor networks. Section 4 discusses the main requirements and design decisions made in the system implementation. Section 5 describes the structure and main components of the solution. Section 6 shows and discusses the preliminary results. Section 7 presents the conclusions and the future work.

2   Related Work

Personal security can be understood as the level of protection of a person from intentional criminal acts [29]. It is considered a core element of the well-being of individuals. The OECD Better Life Index reports that 4.0% of people in OECD countries say they have been assaulted or mugged over the past 12 months, and the average homicide rate in those countries is 2.2 murders per 100,000 inhabitants [27].

Criminologists recognize crime prevention strategies aimed at reducing the criminal opportunities that arise from the routines of everyday life (e.g. improving surveillance of areas that might attract crime by using closed-circuit television). These strategies are conceptualized under the notion of *situational crime prevention* [30]. Situational prevention seeks to reduce opportunities for specific categories of crime, by increasing difficulties to perform those actions and decreasing the associated risks and rewards [7]. This crime prevention strategy requires that the potential victims be conscious of their current risk situation, which seems to be the most unexplored and complex part of the problem.

Typically people do not have supporting information about the personal security in many areas of a city, even while living in that place. This lack of information can be managed in different ways by people. Individuals can use their own experience to quantify the security level of the area in which they are located, or they can use the experience of their contacts (e.g. friends in a SNS) or mainstream media (e.g. newspaper articles). For example, neighborhood programs and patrols can provide friendly, non-invasive support for members in a community, aiming to help these people feel better connected to the neighborhood and help them reduce their risk of becoming victims of frauds and scams as well as other crimes.

Information is also usually managed by official sources from the government and other public agencies, which publish studies and relevant statistics related to homeland security. Even if these latter sources provide good references to estimate the inherent risk of a particular area, users may be confronted to information provided in a complex format (e.g. in confusing long documents), thus being perceived as difficult to understand. Particularly, this is a problem when individuals are faced to quickly and accurately find out the inherent risk of a particular area at a particular time.

Burke et al. [4] introduced the concept of *participatory sensing*. It refers to "task deployed mobile devices to form interactive, participatory sensor networks that enable public and professional users to gather, analyze and share local knowledge". Currently, the growth in mobile devices (e.g. smartphones) has deployed hardware capabilities in the form of multiple sensors (e.g. motion sensor or accelerometer, gyroscope, ambient light sensor). These sensors have made participatory sensing viable in the large-scale. Therefore, individuals and groups of people actively participate in the collection of information for purposes ranging from crime prevention to scientific studies [14].

Naturally, one of the critical factors to drive success in participatory sensing is related to the data collecting from users in order to generate collective intelligence. Lan et al. [18] proposed an incentive scheme for a vehicle-based mobile surveillance system by adopting participatory sensing, under the assumption that video surveillance is commonly used by the police and private security officers to determine and investigate crimes and other incidents. Ballesteros et al. [2] studied a set of techniques for evaluating the people security based on their spatial and temporal dimensions. The authors show that information collected from geo-social networks can be used to prevent crimes. Therefore it seems to be clear that participatory sensing could be a good strategy to address the stated problem; however the way in which we implement the supporting solution can affect its usability and usefulness.

Estrin [10] proposed a layered architecture to support participatory sensing. The data collection performed using that architecture requires a permanent link between the sensors and the server that stores and manages the data. The dependence of particular components (e.g. server or communication links) represents a serious restriction to address personal security evaluation, because the system should be available when required. Duarte et al. [8] go a step forward in the decentralization of the system architecture for participatory sensing, and propose the use of mobile units acting as an intermediary between servers and the sensors, which eventually can support asynchronous communication among the network components. Ochoa and Santos [23] go a step even further proposing a human-centric wireless sensor network

(HWSN), which include all the components of its predecessors, but also witness units that act as a repository of information for users located in a particular area. These units considerably increase the system availability, in terms of information support to make decisions, in any area. Therefore, it is the alternative chosen to support participatory sensing in the described scenario.

3   Human-Centric Wireless Sensor Networks

These networks are heterogeneous in terms of the communication support and the type of nodes that can participate to them. The communication support can be any that allows interaction between two or more nodes. The nodes are also heterogeneous, and they can play up to four roles: *regular sensors*, *human-based sensors*, *mules* and *witness units*. Regular sensors (RS) measure a certain context variable and transmits their value to other units. Examples of these sensors are GPS, temperature sensors, wearable sensors (also used as Body Sensor Networks - BSNs [3, 12]), and also mobile devices able to detect the presence of other devices (i.e. sensors) in the area. The human-based sensors (HBS) are people that use their senses (possibly complemented by regular sensors, especially belonging to BSNs) to capture information about a certain variable of interest (e.g. the delinquency in a particular area), elaborate on it, and then produce knowledge that represents the current value of that variable. HBS use a mobile device and a wireless network to share the generated knowledge with other network nodes. Although the information provided by HBS is not accurate, they represent our best option when the observed variable is not measurable with a regular sensor but by means of virtual/logical sensors [25].

Mules (Mu) are mobile units that connect two or more disconnected networks. Examples of mules are vehicles and passersby having a mobile computing device. These mules usually also act as witness units (WU), i.e. network nodes that store the information shared by other nodes in a certain area. These units are passive repositories of information (e.g. about personal security) that is relevant in the area where the WU is located. These units interact on-demand with the HBS and they can be implemented using almost any computing device with ad hoc communication and storage capability; i.e. from tiny computing devices to servers.

Figure 1 shows the architecture of a HWSN, which is typically composed of four layers: *sensing, communication, information persistence* and *application*. The lower layer is in charge of sensing the variables to be considered in the process that is being supported; in our case, the evaluation of the personal security of people in a certain area at a certain time. The information captured by the sensors is then shared using the services provided by communication units (e.g. WiFi or cellular antennas) or mules. These components are part of the communication layer.

In order to increase the information availability in the area where it is required, the shared information is temporarily or permanently stored in HBS and witness units located in the area, and eventually in remote servers or on Cloud computing infrastructures [13]. These components are part of the information persistence layer.

Fig. 1. Layered architecture of a human-centric wireless sensor network

Finally, the mobile systems are in the application layer, which use the information managed by the lower layers to provide a direct service to the end-users; for instance to inform them their current personal security level. It is important to note that the same network node can play several roles at the same time. For instance, an HBS can act as a sensor when its user shares information through the network, as a Mu while the user move through a certain area, and as a WU when the user is in the neighborhood where he/she lives. The roles of a network node in a certain instant are given by the services it provides to other nodes and also to its user.

4   Main Requirements and Design Decisions

The design of the mobile application that informs the people about their current personal security level should consider several functional (FR) and non-functional requirements (NFR). These requirements were obtained and validated through a focus group with twelve potential users of the system. By addressing these requirements the application has a chance of being usable and useful in a real scenario. Next we describe the main non-functional requirements that were defined, and also the design decisions made to address them.

- *High availability*. The system should be available independently of the possibility to access remote servers (i.e. WUs). For that reason, the geographical information of an area and also its vulnerability information should be managed using a loosely-coupled schema. This means that a mobile device running the system must locally keep all the information of the area where it is located. Periodically the device synchronizes its information with WUs in charge of the information persistence, and eventually downloads information of new areas that are now relevant, if the user moved to other places. If the system does not have access to a WU, it evaluates the user vulnerability based on the local information. Eventually, if it does not have enough information to determine the user vulnerability, it can ask to neighbor devices for additional information or for a complete vulnerability diagnosis. Interactions with other network nodes require counting on access to infrastructure based on ad hoc communication units. Since the system availability also depends on the availability of the device where it runs, the target device should be mobile and be most of the time with the user. Considering these restrictions, a handheld device like a smartphone or a small slate seems to be the most appropriate option for deploying the system.

- *Quick access.* In case that the user wants to get personal security information on-demand, the access to such information should be quick, and the most relevant information must be shown first. In that sense, the use of visual information is usually the best alternative to deliver information to the user. The type of actions for crime prevention that can be taken by the user can depend on it. Moreover, it is important to use a mobile device with fast boot, like a smartphone or a slate. The use of a loosely-coupled data link strategy, which prioritizes the use of locally stored map tiles, also contributes to have a quick access to the supporting information.

- *Proactiveness.* The system should contribute to prevent crime by autonomously informing the user about possible vulnerability situations that it identifies. For that reason the system should be active all the time, monitoring and evaluating the personal security context of the user. Usually this functionality is implemented through an autonomous agent. An alarm should be triggered every time that a vulnerability situation exceeds a certain threshold. Depending on its criticality, more than one alarm can be triggered using awareness mechanisms, e.g. visual messages, ringtones or tactons.

- *Information trustworthiness.* When a service quality depends on the quality of the information that it provides, the information trustworthiness becomes a critical requirement. Although there are several strategies to address this requirement, the recent research in participatory sensing indicates that crowdsourcing and reputation is usually a good combination to deal with this issue [17, 20]. Data held by other network nodes and WUs can also contribute to increase the trustfulness of the information.

- *Understandable information.* The system must notify to its users, as soon as possible, when they are in risk. Therefore, the information that the system provides them should be easy to understand by average users. In that sense, the use of visual information and voice messages seem to be appropriate to address this requirement in most work contexts. In case of messages indicating physical locations, the use of geo-referenced visual information (e.g. a map) is usually the easiest way to provide an effective communication to end-users. Provided that an effective communication requires that input and output channels be aligned, awareness mechanisms are usually required to do that.

- *Interoperability*. The system should be able to exchange data and requests services to other devices, as a way to provide more accurate and on-time advices/alarms to end-users. This interoperability requirement has a well-known solution, which consists on using data and service representations that adhere to standard formats (e.g. XML for data, and Web services to implement functionality). The interaction between nodes will require counting on infrastructure-based or ad hoc communication units.

Moreover, there is a list of FRs that can also be addressed by the system. The services that address those requirements must also deal with the previously presented NFR.

- *Map navigation*. The system must provide geo-referenced visual information, because warnings are typically related to a particular place or area of the city. Therefore the user should be able to navigate the map of the area, using several zoom levels. The use of geo-referenced tiles and GPS positively impact usability and performance of these systems [21].

- *Device positioning*. In order to determine the personal security of people, the system needs to know its users location. Since a risk evaluation requires a coarse-grain position of the user, in most cases the use of GPS is a good option to make a diagnosis of the area. In the case of indoor locations, the use of the last known outdoor position of the user could be enough to determine his/her vulnerability level. Although using only GPS can lead the system to make some error when the user is indoor, this strategy considerably reduces the complexity to implement services that perform device positioning. Devices not having positioning capabilities can request such information to neighbor nodes using ad hoc communication services.

- *Communication*. The information provided by the crowd should be shared as soon as possible to benefit the participants and reduce the feasibility that malicious interventions affect the trustworthiness of the shared data. In both cases, counting on communication among participants is mandatory. Such a communication can be done using ad hoc or infrastructure-based communication systems, or a combination of them. Typically the former helps addressing information sharing in a small area, and it is usually enough to support the diagnosis of pedestrians' personal security. The latter covers larger areas and provides a wider bandwidth that allows supporting properly the crowd activities. This communication modality helps diagnosing the personal security of an ample range of users, from pedestrians to car drivers.

- *Device tracking*. This requirement allows remote users to monitor the movements of a user on a map. Typically it is required when the user is asking for help to someone else, e.g. friends or family. The tracking capability can be implemented using device positioning and communication; and the grants for monitoring the user movements can be implemented using the user's personal contacts from a SNS (like Facebook).

- *Easy feeding.* If we want that many people report vulnerability (in terms of crime) of city areas, the reporting process should be easy and fast. This process can be done using handheld devices that are easy to transport, deploy and use, and most of them have GPS that allows users to geo-reference their vulnerability reports. The information of these reports should be locally stored into the device, and then appropriately transferred to a WU to avoid delays in the feeding process. People reporting information about vulnerability are HBS that use their senses, knowledge and experience to determine that a place or area, under certain conditions, is vulnerable to specific types of crimes. The use of visual information during the feeding process usually contributes to reduce the users error rate.

- *Data sharing.* Data sharing benefits the system users and reduces the impact of malicious interventions. The ad hoc and infrastructure-based communication units play a key role in this process. Moreover, the presence of MUs and WUs typically can contribute to enhance the data sharing among network nodes, which positively impacts on the availability, performance and trustworthiness of the whole system.

- *Warnings/alarms delivery.* The main goal of the system is to deliver notifications to users, in order to make them aware of their current vulnerability situation. The evaluation of users vulnerability requires geo-localization (GPS) to determine the users' position, and awareness mechanisms to inform them about their possible risks. In case that a user asks for external help (e.g. friends or family), the system would require connecting to a social networking service to retrieve the user's personal contact information, and deliver the alarms accordingly.

Figure 2 summarizes the relationship among the main FR, NFR and design decisions involved in the system. The relationship also indicates whether a design element is mandatory, optional or not required to implement a certain requirement.

Requirement / Design Decision	Loosely-coupled data link	Handheld devices	Fast boot devices	Autonomous agents	Context-aware behavior	Crowsourcing	Map tiles	GPS	Infrastructure-based comm. units	Ad hoc communication units	Human-based sensors	Witness units	Mules	Awareness mechanisms	Visual Information	Social networking services	Reputation	Standard formats for data and services
High availability	X	X							O	O		O						
Quick access	X		X			X									X			
Proactiveness				X	X										X			
Information trustwortiness					X				O	O	O	O					X	
Understandable information														X	X			
Interoperability									O	O								X
Map navigation							X	X						X				
Device positioning								X		O	O	O	O					
Communication									O	O			O					
Device tracking								X	X							X		
Easy feeding	X	X	X					X	O	O	X				X			
Data sharing				X				X	X	O	O	O					O	
Warnings/alarms delivery									O	O				X		O		

Note: X - *Mandatory*
         O - *Optional*

Fig. 2. Correspondence matrix: requirements vs. design decisions

5   System Implementation

The current implementation of the system determines the risks of a user to car theft and vandalism, regular delinquency (robbery and assaults), drugs traffic and disturbance (physical violence). Figure 3 describes the technologies and components used in the system implementation. The system architecture adheres to the architecture of a HWSN (see Figure 2).

Fig. 3. Architecture of the implemented system

The sensing layer considers HBS (e.g. passersby or neighbors) that use smartphones and simple GUI forms to add information to the system in a loosely-coupled way. Fig.4.a shows two samples of these forms, through which the HBS indicates what event they saw or suffered, when it happened and how many times they have seen similar situations in that place. The users indicate on a digital map the exact location of the events, and the GPS geo-references that information.

The system considers a 3G connection with a server (WU) and WiFi-based mobile ad hoc network that is implemented using an High Level MANET Protocol (HLMP) infrastructure [26]. Such an infrastructure also allows a network node (e.g. a HBS or WU) to detect other nodes in the area and exchange information among them.

The information persistence layer considers the participation of WU and HBS. Two particular WUs play a key role in the system: the system server and the

Facebook server. The first one stores and makes the fusion of the security information of every area, considering the reports features and the reputation of the users reporting the incidents. The Facebook server is used to authenticate the users and to retrieve the users' contact list, in case that an "ask for help" message is delivered. The HBS (i.e. HLMP network nodes) participating in this layer act as temporal repositories of the security information of the area where they are located. They exchange information with other nodes through the HLMP infrastructure.

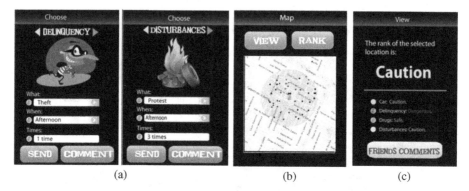

(a)   (b)   (c)

Fig. 4. User interfaces of the implemented system

In the application layer, we can see the information about the user vulnerability. Fig. 4.b. shows the user current location and the records of incidents in an area of 200 meters around him/her. Fig. 4.c. shows the information that the system deliver to the user when a risk overcame a certain threshold. The colors used to represent the risk level of a user follow the same semantics as a semaphore: green means "ok", red means "dangerous situation", and yellow means "caution". The system also allows filtering the incident records and shows only those added by Facebook contacts of the user. Several awareness mechanisms (from ringtones to tactoons) were implemented to notify the user about his/her current risk level.

6 Results

Section 4 highlighted the importance of the usefulness and usability concerns in the design of the system. Therefore, we conducted a usability evaluation with end-users in order to assess at what extent these concerns were considered. As target end-users, we worked with individuals aged between 18 and 35 years old that extensively use smartphones and SNS. As an additional constraint, we limited the evaluation to the city of Santiago, Chile, in order to have a common geographical context within the group of evaluators. The usability attributes considered in the evaluation were: learnability and satisfaction, and the assessment techniques used were: *questionnaire*, and *observation and thinking aloud*.

The sample was formed by following typical recommendations in usability testing [15, 22]. On one hand, the *questionnaire* consisted of items graded in a 5-point Likert scale that intended to assess satisfaction and learnability. It was applied to 20 evaluators once they have used the application. On the other hand, we applied the *observation and thinking aloud* technique to a group of 5 evaluators. We assigned them a set of tasks to be performed by interacting with the application and we noted relevant observations regarding their performance (i.e. task easily completed, completed, completed with difficulty, or not completed) and user experience (i.e. spontaneous reactions indicating frustration and/or ease of use). Fig. 5 shows the median score assigned to each item in the questionnaire.

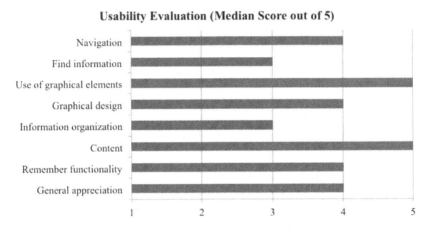

Fig. 5. Usability evaluation results

According to the evaluators, the current design of the application allows an easy navigation. However, the information architecture (at the user interface) can be improved, as the evaluators consider that some elements are difficult to find, as well as the logic behind the organization of some visual elements. A plausible explanation to this latter result may be linked to the lack of familiarity of evaluators with social applications specifically designed to provide awareness in security matters. Regarding the esthetics and graphical design of the application, the evaluators liked this particular point, as the fonts and used colors are sober and try to enhance the value of the information that is presented in the interface. Moreover, the evaluators praised the content of the application, as they consider it to be relevant and useful in the context for what the service is provided.

Next we present the results of the evaluation using the *observation and thinking aloud* technique. Fig. 6 shows the median perceived ease or difficulty for achieving the proposed tasks: (1) voting for a particular place, (2) understanding the presented results, and (3) reading comments.

According to the results, the three proposed tasks were perceived as easy to achieve. Regarding the spontaneous comments stated by the evaluators, there was no difficulty for integrating *Facebook* as a SNS working with the application. However, two users showed frustration when deciding how to cast a vote for a particular spot. This was partly due to a problem when launching the application, since it displayed sometimes a spot that was not known or recognized beforehand by the evaluators.

Perceived Ease or Difficulty for Task Achievement

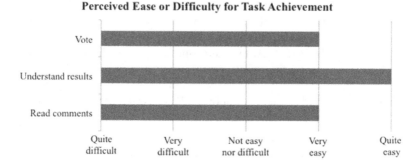

Fig. 6. Perceived ease or difficulty for task achievement

This was improved in the next iteration in the development life cycle of the application.

The system performance was not formally evaluated in this stage, but it was indirectly evaluated through the system usability. No evaluator mentioned this issue, which probably means that the system performance was considered as appropriate.

7   Conclusions and Future Work

The current mechanisms to provide personal security are not particularly focused on helping potential victims easily determine their inherent risk to crimes in real-time; therefore their capability to take appropriate and on-time preventive actions is diminished. Trying to help addressing that problem, this article proposes a participatory sensing system that complements the already used solutions by government organizations. The system is based on a human-centric wireless sensor network. It uses crowdsourcing, human-based sensors and regular sensors to collect information from the field, and several awareness mechanisms to inform the users about their current personal security risks. The information provided by the system can also be used to build a spatiotemporal view of crime (e.g. by incident type) that allows security organizations to understand its evolution and improve the prevention/fight actions.

The usability of the system was evaluated using two different techniques. The obtained results allowed us to identify the need to adjust some components of the user interface, even though they were minor issues. The system performance and the pertinence of the warnings given by the application were not formally evaluated at this stage. However they were indirectly assessed through the activity test performed by the evaluators. Our preliminary feelings indicate that these aspects of the solution are at least between the regular values that a user can expect for these systems.

The next step in this initiative is to evaluate the quality aspects of the solution that were not considered in this first stage. Moreover, we want to evaluate the information flow in the field using different quantities and distribution of WUs. That is a research issue that this initiative wants to explore, because it could indicate that, by increasing the number of witness units and HBS, society could become more resilient to physical delinquency and crime. Such a strategy will be particularly focused on crime prevention.

Acknowledgments. This work has been partially supported by the Fondecyt Project (Chile), grant: 1120207. The work of Francisco Gutierrez has been supported by the Conicyt (Chile) Ph.D. scholarship.

References

1. Aebi, M.F., Linde, M.F.: Conviction Statistics as an Indicator of Crime Trends in Europe from 1990 to 2006. European Journal on Criminal Policy and Research 18, 103–144 (2012)
2. Ballesteros, J., Rahman, M., Carbunar, B., Rishe, N.: Safe Cities. A Participatory Sensing Approach. In: Proceedings of the 37th IEEE Local Computer Networks Conference (LCN 2012), Clearwater Beach, United States (2012)
3. Bellifemine, F., Fortino, G., Giannantonio, R., Gravina, R., Guerrieri, A., Sgroi, M.: SPINE: A domain-specific framework for rapid prototyping of WBSN applications. Software Practice and Experience 41(3), 237–265 (2011)
4. Burke, J., Estrin, D., Hansen, M., Parker, A., Ramanathan, N., Reddy, S., Srivastava, M.B.: Participatory Sensing. In: Proceedings of the World Sensor Web Workshop, in Conjunction with ACM SenSys 2006 (2006)
5. Campbell, A., Eisenman, S., Lane, N., Miluzzo, E., Peterson, R.: People-centric Urban Sensing. In: Proceedings of 2nd Annual Int. Wireless Internet Conference, WICON 2006 (2006)
6. Cattelino, J.R.: The Difference that Citizenship Makes: Civilian Crime Prevention on the Lower East Side. Political and Legal Anthropology Review 27(1), 114–137 (2008)
7. Clarke, R.: Situational Crime Prevention. In: Tonry, M., Farrington, D. (eds.) Building a Safer Society: Strategic Approaches to Crime Prevention, University of Chicago Press, Chicago (1995)
8. Duarte, S., Navalho, D., Ferreira, H., Preguica, N.: Scalable Data Processing for Community Sensing Applications. Mobile Networks and Application 18(3), 357–372 (2013)
9. Dubbeld, L.: Observing Bodies: Camera Surveillance and the Significance of the Body. Ethics and Information Technology 5(3), 151–162 (2003)
10. Estrin, D.: Participatory sensing: applications and architecture (Internet Predictions). IEEE Internet Computing 14(1), 12–42 (2010)
11. Federal Bureau of Investigation. Crime in The United States 2010 - FBI Statistics, http://www.fbi.gov/about-us/cjis/ucr/crime-in-the-u.s/2010/crime-in-the-u.s.-2010/tables/10tbl01.xls (last access: July 12, 2013)
12. Fortino, G., Giannantonio, R., Gravina, R., Kuryloski, P., Jafari, R.: Enabling Effective Programming and Flexible Management of Efficient Body Sensor Network Applications. IEEE Transactions on Human-Machine Systems 43(1), 115–133 (2013)
13. Fortino, G., Parisi, D., Pirrone, V., Di Fatta, G.: BodyCloud: A SaaS Approach for Community Body Sensor Networks. To appear in Future Generation Computer Systems (2014)
14. Hall, D., Chong, C.-Y., Llinas, J., Liggins, M.: Distributed Data Fusion for Network-Centric Operations. CRC Press, Boca Raton (2012)
15. Holzinger, A.: Usability engineering methods for software developers. Communications of the ACM 48(1), 71–74 (2005)

16. Howe, J.: Crowdsourcing: Why the power of the crowd is driving the future of business. Crown Business, New York (2008)
17. Huang, K., Kanhere, S.S., Hu, W.: Are You Contributing Trustworthy Data? The Case for A Reputation Framework in Participatory Sensing. In: Proceedings of ACM MSWiM, Bodrum, Turkey (2010)
18. Lan, K.-C., Chou, C.-M., Wang, H.-Y.: An Incentive-Based Framework for Vehicle-Based Mobile Sensing. Procedia Computer Science, 1–6 (2012)
19. Lim, S.L., Quercia, D., Finkelstein, A.: StakeSource: Harnessing the power of crowdsourcing and social networks in stakeholder analysis. In: Proceedingsof the 32nd ACM/IEEE International Conference on Software Engineering (ICSE 2010), Cape Town, South Africa (2010)
20. Mashhadi, A.J., Capra, L.: Quality control for real-time ubiquitous crowdsourcing. In: Proc. of UbiCrowd 2011, Beijing, China (2011)
21. Monares, A., Ochoa, S.F., Pino, J.A., Herskovic, V., Rodriguez-Covili, J., Neyem, A.: Mobile Computing in Urban Emergency Situations: Improving the Support to Firefighters in the Field. Expert Systems with Applications 38(2), 1255–1267 (2011)
22. Nielsen, J.: Usability Engineering. AP Professional, Cambridge (1993)
23. Ochoa, S.F., Santos, R.: Human-centric Wireless Sensor Networks to Improve Information Availability During Urban Search and Rescue Activities. Information Fusion (in press, to appear, 2014)
24. Posner, R.A.: Privacy, Surveillance, and Law. The University of Chicago Law Review 75(1), 245–260 (2008)
25. Raveendranathan, N., Galzarano, S., Loseu, V., Gravina, R., Giannantonio, R., Sgroi, M., Jafari, R., Fortino, G.: From Modeling to Implementation of Virtual Sensors in Body Sensor Networks. IEEE Sensors Journal 12(3), 583–593 (2012)
26. Rodríguez-Covili, J.F., Ochoa, S.F., Pino, J.A., Messeguer, R., Medina, E., Royo, D.: A Communication Infrastructure to Ease the Development of Mobile Collaborative Applications. Journal of Network and Computer Applications 34(6), 1883–1893 (2011)
27. Safety - OECD Better Life Index,
http://www.oecdbetterlifeindex.org/topics/safety/
(last visit: July 11, 2013)
28. Travis, A.: CCTV Schemes in City and Town Centres Have Little Effect on Crime, says Report, http://www.guardian.co.uk/uk/2009/may/18/
cctv-crime-police (last visit: July 20, 2013)
29. United Nations Development Programme. New Dimensions of Human Security. Human Development Report (1994),
http://hdr.undp.org/en/reports/global/hdr1994/
(last visit: July 12, 2013)
30. Von Hirsch, A., Garland, D., Wakefield, A.: Ethical and Social Perspectives on Situational Crime Prevention. Hart Publishing, Oxford (2004)

Toward Efficient Packet Buffering
and Congestion Control Approaches
for Reliable Data Delivery in Mobile Ad Hoc Network

Mohammad Mehedi Hassan[1], Atif Alamri[1], and Md. Abdur Razzaque[2]

[1] College of Computer and Information Sciences
King Saud University, Riyadh, Saudi Arabia
[2] University of Dhaka, Bangladesh
{mmhassan,atif}@ksu.edu.sa, razzaque@cse.univdhaka.edu

Abstract. In this paper, we address two important problems of mobile ad hoc network (MANET)- route failure and congestion, which reduce the data delivery performance of the network. We propose an efficient and reliable data delivery mechanism that introduces the concept of local packet buffering and multilevel congestion detection and control approaches for improving the reliable delivery of data packets. The nodes on an active route buffer incoming packets at their local transport layer queues, and on finding a new path, resume their transmissions. As a result, packet dropping rate of the network decreases. In addition, we employ a multi-level congestion detection and control mechanism at the source and intermediate nodes that can judiciously take the most appropriate decision for congestion control in the network proactively. Various simulations were carried out based on different traffic loads and route failure rates using NS2 simulator to evaluate the performance of the proposed approaches. The results demonstrate that our approaches outperform a number of state-of-the-art approaches in terms of packet delivery ratio and average end-to-end packet delay.

Keywords: Ad hoc network, data delivery, route failure, packet buffering, and congestion control.

1 Introduction

Mobile ad hoc network (MANET) [1] is a non-infrastructure network having wirelessly connected mobile nodes. The nodes in MANETs are independent of each other and can move frequently and dynamically, causing routes/links to break. Another important problem in MANETs is the dropping of data packets due to congestion in the network. Congestion may occur due to failure of link, queue overflow or channel or media overloading [3]. The congestion leads to packet losses, throughput degradation of networks, and wastage of time and energy for congestion recovery. In addition, since there is no fixed infrastructure, all nodes in a MANET share a single transmission channel; many nodes may contend for the channel simultaneously to transmit data packets, increasing packet collisions in the network.

M. Pathan, G. Wei, and G. Fortino (Eds.): IDCS 2013, LNCS 8223, pp. 65–77, 2013.

In such a situation, the congestion collapse [4] may occur when no node will be able to transmit their data packets. Therefore, achieving reliable and timely data delivery is a challenging problem in mobile ad hoc network.

A significant research effort [2, 4-21] has been observed in recent years on handling route/link failures and congestion in mobile ad hoc networks. For example, in AODV-based backup routing scheme (AODV-BBS) [10], each node maintains two hop neighborhood information for finding alternative routes to handle primary route failure. However, the maintenance of multiple alternative paths is difficult, costly, and time-consuming. Some other researches use multiple routes to balance traffic loads on the event of congestion [4] or route failures and thus improve the network performance. For example, a distributed multipath dynamic source routing (DSR) protocol [11] improves QoS with respect to end-to-end reliability; SMR [5] uses multiple routes to split traffic and mitigate congestion; nodes in CRP [6] use bypass routes to mitigate congestion, etc., but the problem is that multiple oute maintenance overhead affects the network performance significantly.

Several other research works focus on link failure of MANETs using local recovery process. For example, in local repair AODV based on link prediction, LRAODV_LP [2], if a node detects that the signal strength goes below a predefined threshold, it initiates a fresh route discovery rather than sending error message backward. However, packets might be dropped at the intermediate nodes if the local route discovery takes longer period of time. There are some researches on using packet buffering or route caching to handle link failure. For example, Ela Kumar et al. proposed a THR [7] protocol, in which if a node needs to transmit data, it first checks its own routing table which contains route of two hop distance nodes. If any route is found, only then data packets are delivered; otherwise, a fresh route discovery process is initiated. If route failure occurs, the intermediate nodes start packet buffering in a separate physical memory module. However, the requirement of a separate memory module is not only costlier but also not implementable for all devices in the network.

The aforementioned approaches can handle either congestion or link failure. To cope up with both the problems simultaneously, we propose a reliable data delivery mechanism that jointly exploits local packet buffering and multilevel congestion detection and control approaches for increasing the data delivery performance. In our approach, each node is capable of buffering data packets at local transport layer. Later, on finding a new path, the node resumes transmission process from local buffer. Also, we propose an efficient congestion control mechanism, where nodes can detect multiple congestion levels of the network and take proper control actions to reduce the packet dropping. Thus, our approach can handle both congestion and link failures more effectively, and ensures end-to-end reliable and efficient data delivery.

The rest of this paper is organized as follows: we describe related works in Section 2 and network model and assumptions in Section 3. Our proposed mechanism is presented in Section 4, and the simulation results are presented in Section 5 along with discussion. Finally, we conclude the paper in Section 6.

2   Proposed Approaches

To address the problem of reliable delivery of data packets for highly dynamic mobile ad hoc networks, our proposed approach considers both local packet buffering and multilevel congestion detection and control mechanism. In the following sections, we describe these two approaches in more detail.

2.1   Packet Buffering Using Transport Layer Queue

Since a mobile node in MANETs can act both as a router and a host, in our mechanism, all intermediate routing nodes use a separate queue in Transport layer (TQ) to store incoming data packets, when needed. We assume, as long as there is no link failure or the network does not become heavily congested, nodes act like a conventional router and simply forward data packets. However, when the network is heavily congested or link failure occurs, nodes use their TQs for buffering incoming packets.

Now a question arises—why does our approach use separate queue at transport layer for buffering the packets? Many source nodes in a MANET might deliver data packets to many other destination nodes simultaneously. An intermediate node may work as a forwarder of many such source–destination pairs, and it needs to store incoming data packets in the network layer queue for a very small period of time before forwarding the packets from the queue by examining the addresses of corresponding destination nodes. However, in case of link failure or congested state, nodes have to store data packets for relatively longer period of time since they have to wait for a partial path. For this reason, storing data packets into network layer queue during link failure or congestive states might hamper packet forwarding of other good connections and thus cause queue overflow at the node. As a result, packet dropping rate at the node will increase and over- all throughput of the network will decrease. Further- more, storing data packets at the transport layer during link failure may facilitate the intermediate node to ensure the end-to-end reliability from that node, rather than from the source. In this case, the intermediate node does not stamp any new sequence number with the stored packets and takes special care for their delivery. For the aforementioned reasons, an intermediate node uses separate queue in transport layer to buffer incoming data packets, allowing smooth packet forwarding of other connections through the node.

We define a cross-layer interface between network layer and transport layer as shown in Fig. 1. The interface has two components: receive interface "R" and delivery interface "D". The interface "R" receives the packets from network layer queue and puts them into the transport layer queue when a link failure or congestion occurs. Similarly, all the intermediate nodes buffer the packets in their transport layer queues for that corresponding destination using their cross-layer interfaces. Whenever, a partial path is found, the net- work layer of the node informs transport layer through the interface. Then the interface "D" delivers the data packets to network layer and the node resumes data transmission process. Similarly, all the intermediate nodes resume their transmission processes. As a result, the source node does not need to retransmit all the data packets during a link failure, increasing the overall throughput of the network.

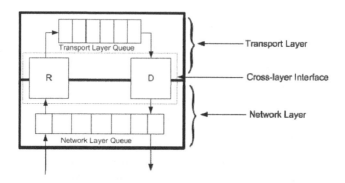

Fig. 1. Interface between network and transport layers

In what follows, we describe the aforementioned buffering mechanism with the help of an example. Consider Fig. 2a, where node B forwards data packets of three sources S1 , S2 , and S3 to three destination nodes D1 , D2 , and D3 , respectively. Fig. 2a shows the normal situation in which all the data packets are queued at network layer queue of node B.

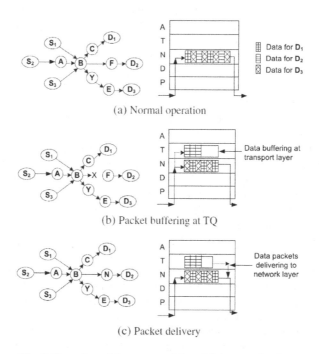

Fig. 2. Operation of the proposed data delviery mechanism

Now, suppose the link between node B and F is broken. As soon as node B detects the link failure, it buffers all the packets for the destination node D2 in its TQ and continues its normal operation for other destinations. Meanwhile, B starts a local query process for destination node D2 and sends a route disconnection notification (RDN) message towards the source node S2. All the intermediate nodes buffer their packets for the destination node D2 in their TQs on receiving RDN message. Node S2 stops its transmission and waits for a reply from node B. Fig. 2b describes this situation. Whenever the node B finds a partial path B → N →D2, it sends route successful notification (RSN) control message toward source node S2 and resumes its transmission process from transport layer queue. All the intermediate nodes also resume their transmission processes same way after getting the (RSN) message. Such a mechanism decreases packet dropping rate and node S2 does not need to transfer all the packets. The source node only retransmits the packets that are dropped during the link failure. Fig. 2c shows node B performs normal operation from network layer as well as resumes transmission process from its TQ for destination node D2.

However, if no partial path is found any link, the intermediate node creates another control message called Route Unsuccessful (RUN) message and sends it back to the source node. The source node, on receiving the RUN message, starts a new route discovery process.

2.2   Congestion Detection and Control Mechanism

Our approach uses congestion-aware data delivery mechanism so that nodes in the network can easily identify the congestion level of the network and take appropriate action. At each intermediate node, we measure the congestion level and piggybacks that information toward the source node with each transmitted packet so that appropriate control actions can be taken in time. We use two bits control flag in both data packets and acknowledgement packets, referred to as congestion notification (CN) flag. Every node in an active route sets this flag when it forwards data packets. The value of the CN flag detects the congestion level of the network according to Table 1. From the value of the CN flag, the neighborhood nodes can easily be informed about the congestion status of the network and they can take proper actions to handle congestion. What follows, we describe how a node detects the congestion level and assigns the value of CN and how the congestion is controlled based on the value of CN flag.

Table 1. Congestion notification

Value of CN	Congestion level
00	Lightly loaded
01	Loaded
10	Heavily loaded
11	Congested

1) Detection of congestion level

Based on queue occupancy, here we use an early congestion detection technique by which a node can detect the current congestion status. We use minimum and maximum thresholds, Q_{min} and Q_{max}, respectively, for queue occupancy at any node as follows:

$$Q_{min} = l \times Q_{size}, \tag{1}$$

$$Q_{max} = h \times Q_{size}, \tag{2}$$

where, l and h are two control parameters; in our simulation, we set $l = 0.5$ and $h = 0.9$, respectively. If the queue length of a node is less than the Q_{min}, then we can say the network is lightly loaded, e.g., queue occupancy is less than 50 %; if the queue length is greater than Q_{min} but less than Q_{max}, then it is operating in the safe region; and, if the queue length is greater than Q_{max}, the node is considered as congested. Even though the above thresholds help to identify congestive or non-congestive states, they don't protect nodes moving from non-congestive state to congestive one. In support of implementing congestion-aware data delivery mechanism, we introduce a warning threshold parameter Q_{warn}, defined as follows:

$$Q_{warn} = w \times Q_{size}, \tag{3}$$

where, w is a weight factor, and in our simulation, we choose $w = 0.8$.

We then calculate average queue occupancy of a node every after a certain interval using exponentially weighted moving average formulae as follows:

$$Q_{avg} = (1 - \alpha) \times Q_{avg} + Q_{curr} \times \alpha, \tag{4}$$

where, α is a weight factor and Q_{curr} is the current queue size. Now, based on the value of Q_{avg}, we determine the value of CN flag as follows:
- if $Q_{avg} < Q_{min}$, then CN = 00
- if $Q_{avg} >= Q_{min}$ and $Q_{avg} < Q_{warn}$, then CN = 01
- if $Q_{avg} >= Q_{warn}$ and $Q_{avg} <= Q_{max}$, then CN = 10
- if $Q_{avg} > Q_{max}$, then CN = 11

1) Congestion Control Mechanism

In our proposed mechanism, a node takes proper actions to control the congestion according to the values of CN bits. If the value of CN flag at a node is '00', it assumes the network is lightly loaded. In such case, the node performs its normal operations. It allows the other nodes of the network to transmit packets through it. So the node accepts new RREQ messages from new source and rebroadcasts to create new routes through it. When the value of CN is '01', it discards new RREQ messages, allowing no new route through it in order to avoid any future congestive states; however, in this case, the sources of the existing routes may increase their traffic rates passing through this node. If the value of the CN is '10', the network becomes heavily loaded. So, further increasing of data arrival rates from source nodes will lead the network to fall into congestive state. In this case, the node generates a new control message called

ALERT message and sends back toward every source node so that they do not increase the data forwarding rates. Thus, our proposed mechanism controls the network in ahead of time and implements a congestion-aware reliable data delivery mechanism. But if a node detects the value of CN is '11', this means the network has already fallen into congestive state and it then starts buffering data packets in TQ and stops forwarding packets afterwards. Table 2 shows the operations taken by a node for different congestive states.

Table 2. Actions taken by a node to control the congestion

Congestion level	Actions
Lightly loaded	Normal operation - no change
Loaded	Stop forwarding any RREQ message
Heavily loaded	Send ALERT message to all sources
Congested	Start buffering packets

3   Performance Evaluation

In this section, we evaluate the performance of our proposed mechanism in network simulator v2.34 [23] and compare the simulation results with that of AODV-BBS [10], SMR [5], IBR-AODV [12], and THR [7]. We did the simulations for various traffic loads and route failure rates, We used two performance metrics for the comparison – packet delivery ratio and average end-to-end packet delay. The results of our simulation state that our approaches outperform the other protocols.

3.1   Simulation Environment

In our simulation, we consider a square area of size 1, 000 × 1, 000 m2, where 100 mobile nodes are deployed randomly. The simulation time is set to 200 s. Each node has the transmission range of 100 m. The source nodes of our network generate constant bit rate data streams at the rate of 1–8 packets per s. This helps to measure performance for various traffic load at each mobile node. The size of each data packet is 512 bytes, link bandwidth is kept at 11 Mbps, and the underlying transport and MAC layer protocols are UDP and IEEE 802.11 DCF, respectively. We have used expanding ring search [19] algorithm for repairing local route failures. Table 3 summarizes the simulation parameters. For each data point in the graphs, we take the average of 10 simulation runs that helps us in studying the steady state behavior of the protocols.

Table 3. Simulation parameters

Parameter	Value
Network area	1,000 m × 1,000 m
Number of nodes	100
Deployment type	Random
Number of sources	20
Node movement model	Random waypoint
Transmission range	100 m
Transport layer protocol	UDP
MAC layer protocol	IEEE 802.11 DCF
Bandwidth	11 Mbps
Data packet size	512 bytes
Data packet generation rate	1 to 8 packets/s
Propagation model	Free space
Weight factor α	0.002
T_I	2 s

3.2   Impact of Varying Traffic Loads

In this section, we study the impact of different traffic loads on the performances of the protocols in terms of packet delivery ratio and average end-to-end delay. The data traffic loads at source nodes are varied from 1 ~ 8 packets per s, i.e., from 0.5 to 4.0 KBps. For this experiment, we fix the mobility speed of each node at 2 m/s within the network. The graphs in Fig. 3 and Fig. 4 shows the comparison results of the studied protocols.

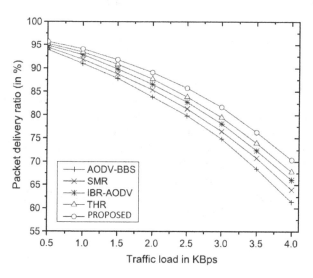

Fig. 3. Packet Delivery Ratio for different traffic loads

As shown in Fig. 3, the packet delivery ratio for all the protocols decreases drastically with increased source traffic loads. This is caused by increased packet drops at the intermediate nodes due to congestion, i.e., the forwarder nodes cannot deliver as many packets as they receive. The simulation results indicate that our proposed mechanism has the higher capability to handle congestion in the network and it outperforms other protocols. Since our proposed mechanism measures the pre-congestive and congestive states more accurately and propagates information along the routes and takes appropriate control actions in time, its congestion control mechanism becomes more efficient than others. Furthermore, the buffering mechanism of the proposed approach reduces the packet drops a lot and thus increases the packet delivery ratio.

Figure 4 shows the average end-to-end packet delay performances of the protocols for various traffic loads. It states that, as expected theoretically, the packet delivery delay increases with the traffic loads. AODVBBS and SMR experience much higher delay than others due to high latency of maintaining multiple alternate routes. IBR-AODV has longer delay than THR and our proposed one since it cannot handle the congestion uses backup nodes only for providing local recovery from route failures. However, our proposed mechanism handles congestion proactively by not allowing an intermediate node to carry additional traffic (1) from new connections when it detects loaded state and (2) from existing connections when it detects heavily loaded state. Our in-depth look into the trace file contents reveals that the above strategy helps nodes to operate in safe mode most of the time and thus it decreases queuing delays of the packets at the intermediate nodes, which in turn decreases the end-to-end packet delivery delay a lot.

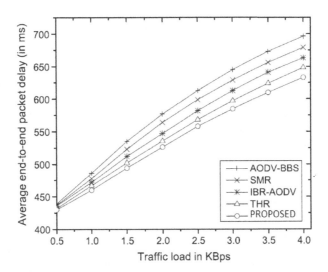

Fig. 4. Average end-to-end delay for different traffic loads

The performance comparisons for per node throughput of the studied protocols have been shown in Fig. 5. The throughputs of the protocols increase as the traffic load increases, but it starts decreasing at around 3.5 KBps traffic load, where the network reaches at saturation condition. The further increase of traffic load makes the network congested and thus the performance decreases. We observe that our proposed mechanism provides high performance than the other protocols since it ensures higher number of packets delivery at the destination within minimum end-to-end delay.

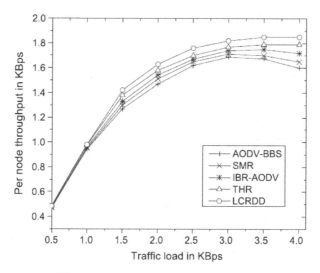

Fig. 5. Throughput for different traffic loads

3.3   Impact of Varying Route Failure Rates

In this section, we evaluate the impact of varying route failure rates on the performances of the studied protocols, keeping the packets generation rate constant at 6 packets per s (i.e., 3 KBps). We vary the route failure rates from 1 to 10 routes/s. The graph in Fig. 6 states that the packet delivery ratio for the all protocols decrease sharply with the increasing route failure rates. This happens because the failure of routes increases the number of packet drops in all the approaches. Since our proposed mechanism jointly exploits the multilevel congestion control and packet buffering schemes on the event of link failures, it is capable to address the route failures more effectively and saves packets from dropping and thus it can increase the packet delivery ratio compared to other protocols.

As expected theoretically, the end-to-end packet delivery delay increases with the route failure rates for all the protocols, as shown in Fig. 7. The SMR experiences the longest end-to-end packet delivery de- lay. The IBR-AODV has lower end-to-end delay than SMR but higher than other protocols. The AODV- BBS uses an alternative route whenever a link failure is detected and thus it decreases the delay than SMR and IBR-AODV. Our proposed local route discovery-assisted packet buffering mechanism helps it to handle route failures more efficiently than others. Also, in our proposed mechanism, the number of retransmissions required on the failure of routes decreases a lot and thus it reduces the traveling time of data packets.

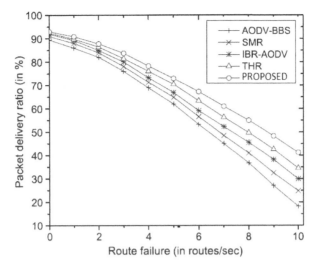

Fig. 6. Packet Delivery Ratio for different route failure rates, data traffic load = 3 KBps

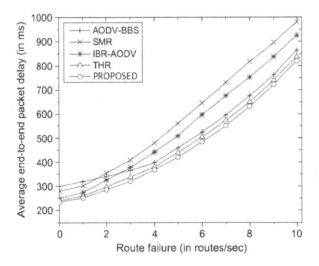

Fig. 7. Average end-to-end delay for different route failure rates, data traffic load = 3 KBps

Figure 8 shows the throughput performances of the studied protocols. The per node throughput decreases for all the protocols as the route failure rate increases. Because of high latency multiple paths, AODV-BBS and SMR provide lower throughput. The IBR-AODV provides better results since it initiates fast recovery. Among all the studied protocols, our proposed mechanism has the highest throughput performance. This result is achieved due to its (1) efficient route failure handling mechanism and (2) congestion-aware data de- livery mechanism.

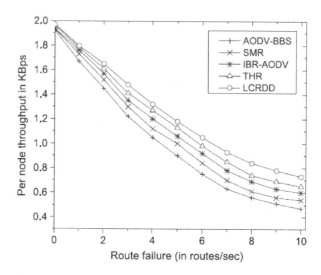

Fig. 8. Throughput for different traffic loads

4   Conclusions

In this paper, we address the problem of reliable delivery of data packets for mobile ad hoc network. Our proposed mechanism introduced the concepts of local buffering a t transport layer and multi- level congestion detection and proactive control actions which improve the network performance significantly. The results of our performance evaluations, carried out for various traffic loads and route failure rates, show that the proposed mechanism outperforms a number of state-of-the-art approaches. Our mechanism is fully distributed and does not depend on network- wide information and thus it reduces the operation overhead as well.

Acknowledgement. This work was supported by the Research Center of College of Computer and Information Sciences, King Saud University, Project No: RC120915. The authors are grateful for this support.

References

[1] Royer, E.M., Toh, C.-K.: A review of current routing protocols for ad hoc mobile wireless networks. IEEE Pers. Commun. 6(2), 46–55 (1999)

[2] Ravindra, E., Kohir, V., Mytri, V.: A local route repair algorithm based on link failure prediction in mobile ad hoc network. World J. Sci. Technol. 1(8), 64–67 (2011)

[3] Wan, C.Y., Eisenman, S.: CODA: congestion detection and avoidance in sensor networks. In: Proceedings of ACM SenSys, pp. 266–279. ACM, Helsinki (2003)

[4] Floyd, S., Jacobson, V.: Random early detection gateways for congestion avoidance. IEEE/ACM Trans. Netw. 1(4), 397–413 (1993)

[5] Lee, S.J., Gerla, M.: Split multipath routing with maximally disjoint paths in ad hoc networks. In: IEEE International Conference on Communications, ICC (2001)

[6] Valarmathi, A., Chandrasekaran, R.: Congestion aware and adaptive dynamic source routing algorithm with load-balancing in MANETs. Int. J. Comput. Appl. 8(5), 6–9 (2010)

[7] Rajotiya, R.N., Kumar, E.T.: a two-hop look ahead with packet buffering protocol for MANETs. Int. J. Inf. Technol. Knowl. Manag. 4, 109–112 (2011)

[8] Toh, C.: Associativity-based routing protocol for mobile ad hoc networks. Wirel. Pers. Commun. 4(2), 103–109 (1997)

[9] Marina, M.K., Das, S.: On-demand multipath distance vector routing in ad hoc networks. In: 26th Annual IEEE International Conference on Local Computer Networks (LCN), November 11-14, pp. 14–23. IEEE (Comput. Soc.), Flordia (2001)

[10] Huang, T.-C., Huang, S.-Y., Tang, L.: AODV-based backup routing scheme in mobile ad hoc networks. In: Proceedings of the 2010 International Conference on Communications and Mobile Computing, CMC 2010, vol. 3, pp. 254–258. IEEE Computer Society, Washington, DC (2010)

[11] Leung, R., Jilei, R.L., Poon, E., Chan, A.-L.C., Li, B.: MPDSR: a QoS-aware multi-path dynamic source routing protocol for wireless ad-hoc networks. In: The IEEE Conference on Local Computer Networks LCN, pp. 132–141 (2001)

[12] Jeon, J., Lee, K., Kim, C.: Fast route recovery scheme for mobile ad hoc networks. In: International Conference on Information Networking (ICOIN), pp. 419–423 (2011)

[13] Natsheh, E., Jantan, A., Khatun, S., Subramaniam, S.: Adaptive optimizing of hello messages in wireless ad-hoc networks. The International Arab Journal of Information Technology (2007)

[14] Johnson, D.B., Maltz, D.A., Broch, J.D.: the dynamic source routing protocol for multi-hop wireless ad hoc networks. In: Perkins, C.E. (ed.) Ad Hoc Networking, ch. 5, pp. 139–172. Addison-Wesley (2001)

[15] Valera, A.C., Seah, W.K.G., Rao, S.: Improving protocol robustness in ad hoc networks through cooperative packet caching and shortest multipath routing. IEEE Trans Mobile Comput. 4, 443–457 (2005)

[16] Castañeda, R., Das, S.R., Marina, M.: Query localization techniques for on-demand routing protocols in ad hoc networks. Wirel. Netw. 8(2-3), 137–151 (2002)

[17] Lee, S.J., Gerla, M.: AODV-BR: Backup routing in ad hoc networks. In: IEEE Wireless Communications and Networking Conference (WCNC 2000), pp. 1311–1316 (2000)

[18] Rachuri, K.K., Siva, R.: On the scalability of expanding ring search for dense wireless sensor networks. J. Parallel Distrib. Comput. 70, 917–929 (2010)

[19] Ramanathan, R., Redi, J.: A brief overview of ad hoc networks: challenges and directions. IEEE Commun. Mag. 40, 20–22 (2002)

[20] Tran, D.A., Raghavendra, H.: Congestion adaptive routing in mobile ad hoc networks. IEEE Trans. Parallel Distrib. Syst. 17, 1294–1305 (2006)

[21] Lee, S.J., Gerla, M.: Dynamic load-aware routing in ad hoc networks. The network simulator NS-2, Helsinki, Finland, vol. 23, pp. 3206–3210 (2011), http://www.isi.edu/nsnam/ns/ (accessed in 2013, 2001)

On Using Bittorrent for File Sharing in Mobile Ad-Hoc Networks

Burkhard Englert and Souroush Pourezza

California State University Long Beach,
Dept. of Comp. Engr. & Comp. Science
Long Beach, CA 90840
burkhard.englert@csulb.edu

Abstract. Many challenges exist in the design of a good distributed file sharing system. Transporting huge files over the network can create latency and sluggish performance. Scalability of a distributed file sharing system is another challenge. There is also no universal software that can transfer files between various platforms and devices and functions in all types of networks. In this paper we focus on the problem of distributed file sharing in the context of Mobile Ad Hoc Networks (MANETs). In such networks nodes may join or leave at any given point in time so that traditional file sharing algorithms are not viable anymore. We present the architecture and implementation of an efficient distributed file sharing system for MANETs. Our system employs the Bittorrent protocol and a new tracker replicating procedure that enables file sharing even with nodes joining or leaving. By removing the tracker as a single point of failure our system outperforms other existing file sharing applications.

Keywords: Bittorrent, Peer to Peer, Mobile Ad Hoc Networks, File Sharing.

1 Introduction

File sharing has always been of paramount importance in all systems, organizations, platforms and networks. Speed, security and reliability are the most critical features of a file sharing system. It is important to know that current file sharing applications and protocols cannot be directly applied to Mobile Ad-hoc Networks (MANETs). In wired networks, we expect high bandwidth, almost no link breakage and no change in the network topology, which is the opposite in wireless networks. For file sharing in the setting of a MANET, node mobility is the most challenging issue. In such a MANET that is a P2P (Peer to Peer) system it is always possible that a node may be cut off from the system, so the file sharing system must work around this issue. Bittorrent is a peer to peer file sharing application. Among all peer-to-peer file sharing protocols, Bittorrent has certain features which make it attractive for MANETs. In a peer-to-peer network in which files are being shared, each end point is called a peer [10]. A Bittorrent tracker is a node that assists in the peer to peer file exchange communication.

M. Pathan, G. Wei, and G. Fortino (Eds.): IDCS 2013, LNCS 8223, pp. 78–91, 2013.

The tracker, in the original version of the protocol, is the only single point of failure, since clients must communicate with the tracker to initiate downloads. Clients that have already begun downloading also communicate with the tracker periodically to negotiate with newer peers and provide statistics; however, after the initial reception of peer data, peer communication can continue without a tracker. Through the tracker clients get information about other nodes and download sources. Trackers never participate in the actual exchange of the file data. In a sense trackers act like servers in a client server interchange. Hence since all other nodes depend on information provided by the tracker trackers can become single points of failure. This is a problem especially in MANETs. Here a tracker may not only crash but it could simply become unavailable for a file requesting node since it moved out of the vicinity of that node. In our file sharing protocol for MANETs we use Bittorrent but eliminate the tracker as a single point of failure. All nodes are now able to share information about other nodes and downloads with each other. There is no more need for centralized control.

Crucially in Bittorrent, the peer overlay is not constructed until a client enters into the P2P network. At this time, the node contacts a tracker to receive the list of peers that are seeding the file. Hence the overhead for Bittorrent does not depend on the distance of the client from the peers, and therefore, the overhead time is constant. This makes Bittorrent very attractive for MANETs. But because of the possibility of node mobility in MANETs, a new paradigm beyond simple peer to peer file sharing is needed in wireless ad-hoc networks. Namely each node should act as a router for other nodes, so they can acquire their desired file [8].

Many applications perform distributed file sharing using various algorithms, with different goals. Our work is motivated by the need to share files between moving vehicles. Any protocol suitable for such an environment must be able to deal with highly mobile nodes. Issues such as exiting the network range and adding new nodes to the network also raise new challenges for a distributed file sharing system. Many existing file sharing applications, such as Bittorrent are restricted by a file manager module which controls pieces of the file that is being downloaded. Not that it is hard to fragment a file into different pieces; but finding, sending, receiving pieces and authenticating the pieces in a highly mobile environment is a very challenging issue. In our work we overcome these challenges.

1.1   Related Work

Kevin C. Lee et al. [8] recently developed CarTorrent, an application for file sharing between cars or nodes with high mobility. The application works on top of AODV (Ad-hoc On-demand Distance Vector Routing) which is a routing algorithm in an Ad-hoc network. Other than AODV, it contains a component called SendGossipThread which sends a message periodically in two forms. The first message is from the client and the second message is in the form of a queue that other clients have sent. The other components of the application contain ReceiveGossipThread, FileManager and ListenThread which all are used to communicate to share and download a file. This file sharing system has some shortcomings. There are no multiple downloads possible at any given point in time. Also a node only can download a file from just one peer. Moreover nodes are not able to recognize corrupted file pieces. Our file sharing protocol overcomes all these shortcomings.

CarTel, introduced in [6], was built for handling traffic information, not file sharing. It also contained a hardware component which runs in Linux. This tool also provided Bluetooth connectivity with a users peripheral devices. The device could connect to the internet to exchange data. The software infrastructure contains a web server, a portal which handles traffic speed and delays, WiFi monitor, camera and OBD-II. In this tool, CarTelDB was used to keep this information in the vehicle device. Most of its usage was only for transferring traffic information and suggesting new routes. The main drawback is that it needs a peripheral device to be run on and that unlike our protocol it cannot be used for file sharing. Authors in [11] suggested a cooperative swarming protocol for file sharing in vehicular networks. Studies showed that gossiping helps peer selection by making location awareness better and more accurate. Their protocol, however, also employs a tracker in a fixed location, namely a central access point. Cars would pass by the access point and receive information about which other cars nearby had pieces of a desired file. In our protocol no central access point is required anymore. Nodes receive information about other nodes directly each other.

Contributions

In this paper, based on Bittorrent, we present a distributed file sharing protocol for MANETs. Our protocol eliminates the file manager, the tracker, as a single point of failure by distributing information about nodes and downloadable files throughout the network. Unlike other distributed file sharing applications our protocol is hence suitable for a mobile environments where nodes may come or leave and where a fixed file manager may become permanently unreachable. With our protocol a node that previously acted as a tracker can leave the network without affecting other nodes as long as the information it owns about other nodes and downloadable files has been replicated.

1.2   Related Terminology

In this section, we explain some terms and definitions that are used later in this paper.

- Leech: Refers to a peer that has not downloaded the whole torrent file. Also it may refer to a peer that downloads much more than it uploads.
- Seed: A peer which has 100% of a file. A leech turns into a seed after it downloads a complete file.
- Announce: An announce is a request sent to a tracker. It is what every client does to any tracker that is hosting a torrent which is loaded into the client.

An announce declares the client to the tracker and requests a list of peers from that tracker [3].

- Swarm: All peers that share the same torrent are called a swarm. This contains all leechers and seeds that work on the same torrent.
- Tracker: A peer that keeps track of other peers and seeds that are in the swarm. Clients connect to the tracker to get information about seeds and download sources. Trackers never participate in the actual exchange of the data. There are two types of trackers; public trackers and private trackers. A public tracker allows anyone to add the tracker address to an existing torrent or they can even be used by new torrents. On the other hand, with a private tracker, the user has to register first in order to be able to add the tracker to the torrent.

2   Bittorrent Architecture and Protocol

2.1   Background

Bittorrent was created by Bram Cohen as a peer to peer file sharing application for the Linux operating system. According to Torrentfreak [4], Bittorrent creates the most traffic for upstream traffic on the internet. One of the features that makes Bittorrent different from other file sharing protocols is that its users cannot search for a specific file to download. Another difference is that unlike other protocols, Bittorrent does not allow other peers to download a file directly; rather they should create a torrent file which is a metadata file that represents a peer to peer session for files. There are two states for a peer. If a peer is downloading and uploading a file, it is called a leecher. If a peer has downloaded a complete file, it turns into a seeder which then just uploads file pieces to other leechers. For a torrent to be alive, it has to have at least one seeder, although it is possible for a torrent to be downloaded just by leechers in a way that a peer downloads each piece from a leecher that has that piece. Peers keep track of all peers they are connected to. These peers are kept in a list called a peer set. By keeping track of which piece is being downloaded, which piece is being uploaded, and which peers have connected to a node, the Bittorrent protocol can manage downloading and uploading of pieces very efficiently. Compared to other P2P protocols, the Bittorrent protocol uses on average only one tenth of the bandwidth for file and peer information overhead. Fast download speeds also require a good, namely fair piece selection algorithm. Fair means that a leecher cannot download too much without uploading a piece. In the following sections, we will explain this algorithm and its architecture [12].

2.2   Bittorrent Architecture

The architecture of Bittorrent is a combination of client-server architecture and peer to peer architecture. There is a centralized server called tracker which is responsible for maintaining torrent sessions. In each torrent session, the tracker keeps track of all peers and nodes participating in the download and upload of a torrent file. Connecting to the tracker will not consume a lot of bandwidth because each peer connects to the tracker for a small period of time, including the time to get the address of a specific torrent. In certain time periods (which is normally 30 minutes), peers will contact the tracker again to find out if there is any new information or if there are any new files available. The IP address or the URL of the tracker is written in the torrent file, which explains how the peer can find the tracker [12] [9]. The torrent file is a metadata file which consists of information about the tracker, file or files to be downloaded, and some other relevant information. It is a binary file, called a bencoding. The bencoding contains nested dictionaries and lists. The bencoded torrent file has a dictionary which contains announce and info keys. The info key is also another dictionary, but announce is simply the address of a tracker.

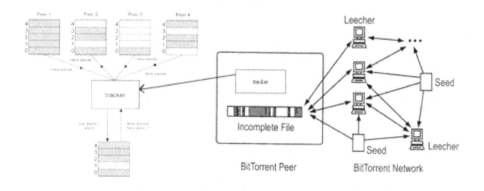

Fig. 1. A Bittorrent peer uses the tracker to download a file

Figure 1 shows how a BitTorrent peer uses the information provided by a tracker to download a file from the Bittorrent network. The info key is a dictionary that includes the pieces, piece lengths, name and one of the files or length keys. Piece length is the length of each piece in bytes. The name key is the name of the torrent. The files or length keys depend on the torrent file. If the torrent file contains only one file, the length key is set. If it contains more than one file, the files key is set. The piece key is basically a hashed value of each piece. The algorithm used for hashing is SHA1. The hashed value is used to verify the downloaded piece so the client application can check for download or transmission errors so that if it did not correctly download a piece, it can download it again. Before a torrent client application starts downloading, it allocates space for the downloaded files, since the downloading process is done in order. Figure 2 shows an example of the interaction between peers that share a piece.

Without the tracker there is simply no way for a client application to find other peers to download pieces from. Essentially a tracker is similar to an HTTP

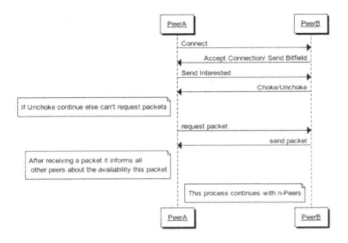

Fig. 2. Interaction between peers using Bittorrent

server. A tracker, in response to the HTTP GET request that it receives, sends a bencoded message containing information about peers and torrent pieces.

The HTTP GET request contains: downloaded, port, uploaded, left, event, info_hash, peer_id and ip keys [7]. The uploaded field represents total uploaded bytes, downloaded indicates total downloaded bytes and left is the amount of bytes left. The IP field is optional indicating the IP of the origin. The port key is the port number where each peer is listening for incoming connections. At the beginning of each download, the client generates a random ID called peer_id. The last key is called info_hash. This is the hash of the bencoded form of the info value from the metadata file. With this the tracker can find out what session the torrent is joining. All this information helps the client application to receive statistics about the available pieces, downloaded or uploaded data. It can also indicate how many leechers and seeders exist in the torrent session (see Figure 1). Finally, the event field shows the status of the client namely either downloading, uploading, seeding or finished. The response of the tracker is a bencoded message that is a dictionary containing key value elements. It contains two keys; interval and peers. Interval represents the number of seconds the peer should wait between sending each request to the tracker. Peers is another dictionary that represents the peers available to download from. This dictionary contains the IP address, port number and peer ID of the peers that are available. Usually the tracker sends about fifty random peers as the response [7] to a GET request.

2.3   Bittorrent Peer Protocol

Two peers can communicate directly through the Bittorrent peer protocol over TCP, in order to exchange data. Before transferring the data, the peers have to connect to each other and the first message for creating the connection starts with a string. After the handshake, peers are connected and they can start transferring data (for an illustration see Figure 2). Before the peers can start downloading data, they should be informed of the state of the other peer. Each connection is either *choked* or *unchoked*, *available* or *unavailable*. Choked means that the peer is not allowed to download anything from the connection. In order to download data from a connection, a peer should be interested and unchoked. All peers must send a message to see what pieces other peers have and whether they are interested in exchange. All peers, initially, start with not interested and in an unchoked state. After a handshake, there are nine other messages that a node can send to other peers:

1. Interested 2. Not interested 3. Choke 4. Unchoke 5. Bitfield 6. Request 7. Have 8. Piece 9. Cancel

To initiate a Bittorrent, peer A sends a request to the tracker and receives a list of peers (Figure 1). Peer A then sends handshaking messages to all peers in the list. After a connection has been established, peer A expects to receive a bitfield from the other peers. A bitfield message is sent from the peer if it has already downloaded at least one distinct piece of the file. The bitfield message is important as the peers have to know what pieces the other peers have. The peer set must change very often so that it can maintain the maximum upload speed [12]. The Choke algorithm takes care of this part. Now that peer A is connected to other peers, it can send the interested message to those peers. Peer A should wait until a peer is unchoked; this implies that the other peer should send an unchoke message to peer A. Once peer A received the unchoke message, it can now send a request message to that peer (Figure 2). This request should contain the index, length and begin parameters. Index tells the other peer which piece peer A needs to download, and the begin and length parameters specify which part of that piece it needs. Each part of a piece is called a block. After sending a request, peer A receives a message containing the actual data. After receiving all the blocks of the piece, peer A checks its integrity using the SHA1 algorithm and compares it with the value stored in the torrent file. If the computed value and the value in the torrent file are the same, peer A sends out a have message to all other peers that it is connected to, so that they know what piece peer A downloaded. Peer A cannot start uploading to other peers until it at least receives all blocks of one piece. Peer A should keep a list of pieces that other peers have when they change their state and should send interested and not interested messages to them. As mentioned earlier, a peer can decide which peer to upload to by using the choke algorithm.

Choke Algorithm

We now briefly explain the choke algorithm. A peer is choked if other peers refuse to send file pieces to it. Several situations may happen in which a peer chokes another peer:

1. When a client is not interested at all, which means it is a seed.
2. If a client is uploading at its full capacity.
3. If other clients find out that a peer is on the black list for being abusive.

The active peer set should be updated very often so that the system can maintain maximum upload and download speeds. In Bittorrent using the choke algorithm, clients offer their fastest speed to the peers that upload to them. This is what makes Bittorrent a fair protocol. Since the choke algorithm is fair, it behaves differently in leecher and seeder states. For example in the leecher state, it should keep the current download speed for the corresponding peer connection. In the choke algorithm unutilized connections are uploaded to on a trial basis to see if better transfer rates could be found using them. A peer always unchokes a fixed number of its peers (with a default of 4). The decision to choke/unchoke is done based on current download rates, which is evaluated on a rolling 20-second average. This means the peer decides whether to continue uploading to this peer (unchoke) based on whether it can download from it too. The evaluation on who to choke/unchoke is performed every 10 seconds. This prevents the waste of resources by too rapidly choking/unchoking peers.

To protect resources the algorithm uses time measurements and makes decisions based on what happens in fixed time intervals. The reason why the decision which peer to choke/unchoke is evaluated every 10 seconds is that TCP connections can get their full capacity in 10 seconds [1]. So the algorithm sorts peers based on their download rate, but only peers that are interested and have already sent a block in the past thirty seconds, will be sorted. A peer is called *snubbed* if it has not sent any message in the past thirty seconds. This allows the algorithm to filter out choked peers and to make sure that active peers are unchoked, so that the snubbed peers will be left out of the peer set. The main loop of the algorithm also selects an unchoked and interested peer randomly every thirty seconds. This specific peer is called a *planned, optimistic, unchoked peer*. This is done to see whether a better (faster) connection can be achieved with this random peer. In other words a peer while downloading or uploading at the same time always tries to optimize its connections. Without an optimistic unchoked peer, peers would have no way of finding a better connection than what they have. If the optimistic unchoked peer is one of the three fastest peers, another peer will be selected randomly. In addition, even if the selected peer is snubbed and interested, it can be selected. The research presented by Bharambe et al. [5] showed that Bittorrent is still unfair in certain situations. For example, if the network is heterogeneous and low bandwidth and high bandwidths peers are connected to each other, the algorithm is not fair. The solution these researchers proposed was to incorporate a bandwidth matching tracker [5]. Yet, even this algorithm is not perfect, but improves the fairness to some extent.

2.4 Piece Selection Algorithm

Bittorrent attempts to have as many equal pieces as possible in all peers. To accomplish this, the diversity of available pieces should be at a maximum. *Rarest first* is the algorithm that Bittorrent uses to figure out what piece a peer should download next. Another benefit of using rarest first is that this algorithm makes it more likely that each peer has always a piece to offer to other peers. Every time a peer leaves the peer set or it receives a have message, the peers set gets updated. Since each peer knows what pieces other peers in its peers set have, it can always compute the number of all replications and ask for the rarest one. In this case, each peer can always download the rarest piece first. A peer should be able to download its first piece so that it can use the choke algorithm. Once a new peer joins the connection, it will first download a random piece. After it downloaded three complete pieces, it uses the rarest piece first strategy [9]. There is another rule saying that a peer cannot download just a block of a rare piece, rather it has to download all blocks in a piece and then move to the next piece. The reason is that a peer cannot eventually just upload a bunch of blocks; it has to be have a whole piece in order to upload that piece.

3   A Bittorrent Based File Sharing Protocol

We now first present our Bittorrent based file sharing protocol and then discuss an implementation using Mono Torrent. Our protocol is based on the Bittorrent protocol.

CarTorrent is an example of a file sharing protocol that can be used in wireless ad hoc networks. It is also the closest application to our work in this paper. CarTorrent has several advantages over other file sharing protocols, for example, using AODV as the routing algorithm, enables the fast finding of a peer or node that has a file. There are, however, some disadvantages of the CarTorrent protocol, which we overcome in this paper through our extension of the Bittorrent protocol. These disadvantages of CarTorrent are:

1. It does not allow for multiple downloads at any given point in time.
2. A node only can download a file from just one peer.
3. The dissemination time for a specific file is longer compared with our protocol.
4. Downloading nodes do not have the ability to detect corrupted file pieces.

3.1   Our MANET File Sharing Protocol

Our protocol has two phases:

1. Phase 1: Sharing and downloading the *torrent metadata file*,
2. Phase 2: Sharing and downloading the *actual torrent file* (the file to be exchanged).

Since our protocol is designed for Mobile Ad Hoc networks it must respond to the challenge of the tracker being unreachable. In traditional bittorrent one node acts as the tracker, essentially a server that provides other nodes with information about files that are available and about where to find fragments of these files. In an ad hoc network this simple solution will not work anymore. The tracker while still being physically nearby may become unreachable for a node. Such a node would then subsequently be unable to share and receive a file. We solve this challenge through our new protocol where now all nodes can become trackers by **sharing torrent metadata files with other nodes**. This also solves the problem of a single point of failure (the tracker) in the traditional bittorrent protocol. In phase one of our protocol a node first looks for information about available files by requesting a bittorrent metadata file from an available tracker. All other nodes in this phase simply act as relays for the transfer of information between a source and destination. In phase 2 the actual file is exchanged. The reason for separating the sharing of the torrent metadata file from sharing of the file itself is that it is much easier and faster to download a torrent metadata file in one piece - instead of downloading it piece by piece like other shared files. We will now explain how both parts work in detail.

Phase 1 - Sharing a torrent metadata file:

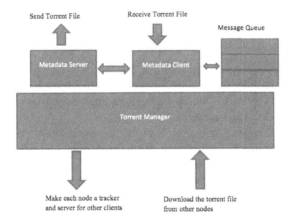

Fig. 3. Metadata file sharing implementation

The process of downloading a shared torrent file starts with sharing a torrent metadata file. In the traditional Bittorrent protocol this is the sole task of the tracker. To allow all nodes to possibly become trackers we need to enable them to share these metadata files. The application for sharing the metadata file - dependent on its current goal - can act as either a server or a client (see Figure 3). As a server (Tracker) it listens for incoming requests asynchronously and as a client it sends requests to a server. In this way the torrent metadata file sharing function is similar to CarTorrent. Each requesting client sends a message to other nodes to find out whether they have a metadata file to share. So a requesting node sends a broadcast message to all other nodes in the reachable subnet to receive the IP address of these nodes (Figure 4).

After receiving the IP address of other clients in the network, the node tries to find a client/server that has information about the sharing of a file within the network. This is done by sending its IP address along with a time to live counter which holds the number of hops it wants the request to pass through to find a shared file. Each hop after receiving a message packet stores it in a queue and

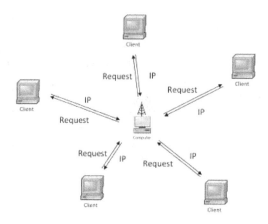

Fig. 4. Initial broadcast message

sends it off along the network. The routing algorithm we use for these requests is DFS (Depth First Search), which guarantees that each message will be seen by each node one and only one time.

After receiving a message from a client, if the node has a torrent metadata file to share, it will push the requesters IP address onto a local queue and send the file name back to the requester node. With this information the client then requests directly to download the metadata file. This torrent metadata file will be downloaded in one piece because its size is not more than couple of hundred Kilo bytes. After downloading the metadata file, the second phase starts.

Figure 5 shows a simple example. There are three nodes where the first node (A) is in the range of the second node (B), the third node (C) is in the range of the second node, and the torrent file exists on the third node. Assume the first node wants to download the torrent file from the third node. In this case, A sends a message to node B and since B has no file to share, it will queue the request message (containing the requesters IP address) and send the original request off to its queue list (a list of reachable nodes it knows). The routing algorithm used in our protocol is just a simple DFS (Depth First Search) algorithm.

Once node C receives the message from node B, which contains the IP address of node A, it will send back the torrent file to node A through hop B. C has become a tracker. Since the file size is usually not more than a couple of hundred kilo bytes, the data would be sent in just one piece.

Phase 2 - File Sharing:
Downloading the actual torrent file is exactly like downloading a torrent file in the original Bittorrent protocol, with a crucial difference: After downloading each torrent file, the client (requester) will also turn into a tracker by sharing - on request - the torrent metadata file for this just downloaded file with others. By so replicating the tracker we eliminate the tracker as a single point of failure, enabling file sharing for environments such as MANETs.

Fig. 5. Torrent Metadata File Sharing example

3.2 Routing Algorithm

As mentioned in the previous section, the routing algorithm for this section of the protocol is a simple DFS algorithm. Before a node starts sending a message, it sends a broadcast message to all reachable nodes in the subnet. Once it receives the IP addresses of the other reachable nodes in the network, it will send the message containing its IP address and time to live parameter to other nodes. After a node that has a torrent file to share receives the message, it will respond to the message. Otherwise, it puts the message in a queue and performs the same procedure as the previous node. This procedure will continue and repeat until the counter becomes zero or a file to share has been found. A stack is being used to implement the DFS routing algorithm. It is important to note that having such a routing algorithm also guarantees the delivery of the message to its destination(s).

3.3 Application Implementation

We use Mono Torrent to implement a distributed file sharing application based on the file sharing protocol described above. MonoTorrent is a cross platform and open source implementation of the Bittorrent protocol. It supports many advanced features such as Encryption, DHT, Peer Exchange, Web Seeding and Magnet Links [2]. One of the best features of the MonoTorrent library is that it is based on the multi-platform mono architecture. The MonoTorrent library is built for .NET and the mono architecture. The C# programming language is used for building the library. We also used the .NET framework and C# to implement the application. There are other Bittorrent libraries such as for example libtorrent (built using C++) which we did not consider.

3.4 Implementation Using Monotorrent and Results

To implement our distributed file sharing protocol, that is to allow for faster dissemination and to take out the single point of failure, we modified the library in a way that each node after downloading the whole torrent file, will turn into a tracker. After downloading a torrent file, each peer becomes a seed and then it changes the torrent metadata file in order to add itself to its tracker lists.

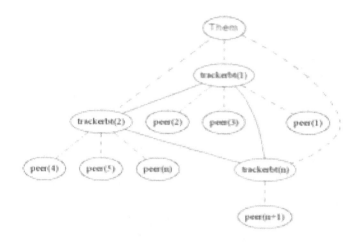

Fig. 6. Multiple trackers with peers contacting them

At this point, it can be observed that the same torrent file can have different metadata files and different seeders. However, it causes the overall download process to speed up. Moreover the single point of failure, the tracker has been distributed across all nodes, hence allowing file sharing to continue even under tracker failure. Assuming a peer downloads two or more torrent metadata files with the same torrent content, it will choose one of the files randomly and start downloading from the associated peer (Figure 6).

Preliminary results show that our protocols performance in a MANET is comparable to the performance of Bittorrent in a fixed network. In our experiments peers are able to download a metadata file and hence initiate a torrent session even if they are not directly connected to the peer owning this metadata file. Our protocol performs especially well in the case of larger files being shared. With smaller files the Bittorrent overhead (requires the sharing of metadata files) overwhelms the actual file sharing protocol.

4   Conclusion and Future Work

In this paper, we presented a distributed file sharing protocol for MANETs that can tolerate node crashes and node unavailability. Our protocol is based on the Bittorrent protocol and takes advantage of the strengths of Bittorrent as data dissemination in a swarm using Bittorrent is very fast. Our protocol sends the torrent metadata file in one piece. This simplifies the metadata file transfer and eliminates the need for file piece management. Moreover each node can now share an available torrent metadata file with other interested nodes, making each node a potential tracker. This eliminates the tracker as a single point of failure from our system and allows us to use our protocol in settings such as MANETs where nodes may become unreachable and where hence the traditional Bittorrent protocol would not suffice. Our algorithm uses the Depth First Search algorithm to find nodes with a torrent file. Messages traverse the network based on a number of counters we define in the algorithm. Thus, the algorithm looks for a torrent file within a range of a given hop count from the source node. In future work we plan to improve the performance of our algorithm and test the scalability of our protocol and its applicability in other contexts. We are also working on a secure file sharing algorithm for MANETs.

References

1. Bittorrent protocol, `http://www.bittorrent.org/protocol.html`
2. Monotorrent overview, `http://www.monotorrent.com`
3. Open bittorrent, `http://openbittorrent.com`
4. Torrentfreak-breaking file-sharing, copyright and privacy news (2012), `http://www.torrentfreak.com`
5. Herley, C., Bharambe, A.R., Padmanabhan, V.N.: Analyzing and improving bittorrent performance. In: Proceedings of the 25th IEEE International Conference on Computer Communications (INFOCOM 2006), pp. 1–12 (2006)
6. Zhang, Y., Chen, K., Goraczko, M., Miu, A., Shih, E., Balakrishnan, H., Hull, B., Bychkovsky, V., Madden, S.: Cartel: a distributed mobile sensor computing system. In: Proceedings of the 4th ACM International Conference on Embedded Networked Sensor Systems, p. 138 (2006)
7. Cohen, B.: Incentives build robustness in bittorrent. In: Proceedings of the International Workshop on Peer-To-Peer Systems, pp. 1–5 (2003)
8. Lee, K.C., Yap, I.Y.: Car torrent: A bittorrent system for vehicular ad-hoc networks. Technical report, University of California Los Angeles (2006)
9. Legout, A.: Understanding bittorrent: An experimental perspective. In: 24th Annual Joint Conference of the IEEE Computer and Communications Societies, INFOCOM 2005, pp. 2235–2245 (2005)
10. Rajagopalan, S., Shen, C.-C.: A cross-layer decentralized bittorrent for mobile ad-hoc networks. In: Proceedings of the 3rd IEEE Annual International Conference on Mobile and Ubiquitous Systems - Workshops, pp. 1–10 (2006)
11. Nandan, A., Das, S., Pau, G.: Spawn: A swarming protocol for vehicular ad-hoc networks. In: Proceedings of the 1st ACM VANET Conference, p. 94 (2004)
12. Toole, R.: Bittorrent architecture and protocol. Technical report, University of Massachusetts Dartmouth (2006)

Self-healing Schemes Suitable for Various WSNs

Atsuko Miyaji and Kazumasa Omote

Japan Advanced Institute of Science and Technology (JAIST)
{miyaji,omote}@jaist.ac.jp

Abstract. Wireless Sensor Networks (WSNs) mainly consist of small, battery-operated, limited memory and limited computational power sensor nodes. It is important to achieve secure communication among WSNs even if some nodes are compromised. In this paper[1], three kinds of self-healing schemes for WSNs are described, a polynomial-based self-healing scheme (RPoK), a proactive co-operative self-healing scheme (POLISH), and a simple random key pre-distribution scheme with self-healing (S-RKP). Comparing three schemes, we clarify each difference and discuss optimal scheme under each different environments.

Keywords: wireless sensor networks, security, resiliency, self-healing.

1 Introduction

Wireless Sensor Networks (WSNs) consist of small, battery-operated, limited memory and limited computational power sensor nodes. Hence most existing schemes in WSNs are based on symmetric key cryptography. One of the most popular schemes, referred to as *RKP* (Random Key Pre-distribution) in this paper, was firstly proposed by Eschenauer and Gligor [6]. In this scheme, each node is configured with a key ring of m sub-keys. These keys are randomly drawn from the large key pool of P sub-keys. Two nodes establish their symmetric key from the sub-keys they have in common in their key ring. However, the security of the whole network in RKP degrades over time in hostile areas. An attacker who corrupts several nodes can partially reconstruct, from key rings of the compromised nodes, the key pool of the system. If the attacker is continuously corrupting nodes, it will eventually learn the whole key pool, and all newly-deployed nodes will establish links that will immediately be compromised. This is a non-desirable quality.

The WSNs are usually deployed to operate for a long period of time. Availability is very important to long-term use of WSNs under the presence of an attacker. Actually, we can find several schemes [2,17,10,7,16,8], which maintain availability of the secure link. We call these schemes *self-healing WSNs*.

Castelluccia and Spognardi [2] have proposed the RKP scheme with self-healing property, named *RoK* scheme, for *multiphase WSNs*, in which a link

---

[1] This study is partly supported by Grant-in-Aid for Scientific Research (A)i21240001) and Grant-in-Aid for Young Scientists (B) (25730083).

M. Pathan, G. Wei, and G. Fortino (Eds.): IDCS 2013, LNCS 8223, pp. 92–105, 2013.

self-heals against node-capture attacks by redeploying a sensor node (with the server's help) when the battery of a sensor is depleted. The RoK scheme improves the resiliency of the RKP scheme by limiting the lifetime of the keys, and by refreshing keys. Some recent schemes improve the resiliency of the RoK scheme. Yilmaz et al. [17] proposed a more resilient scheme than the RoK scheme to speed up the self-healing process. Kalkan et al. [10] proposed a zone-based RKP (Zo-RoK) scheme which combines the best parts of Du et al.'s scheme [5] and the RoK, and improves the resiliency of the RoK.

As for self-healing of the secret key for the purpose of data survival, the POSH scheme [14] and the DISH scheme [12] have been proposed by Pietro et al. and Ma et al., respectively. These schemes use key evolution and sensor cooperation to self-heal the secret key which encrypts the sensed data on a sensor node, for the purpose of data survival. These schemes involve each sensor sharing an initial key with the sink (base station). At any time, sensors are either occupied (red), sick (yellow) or healthy (green). The self-healing of a sensor means that a sick sensor becomes healthy. The POSH and the DISH schemes update a secret key using the random data transmitted from other sensor nodes. That is, if at least one of the sensor nodes that send random data is not corrupted, the compromised secret key is updated and then is self-healed.

In this paper, we summarize the three kinds of self-healing schemes for WSNs, RPOK, S-RKP, and POLISH, and clarify each difference from the point of view of environment for the usage:

1. **RPoK**[8] is a strongly resilient polynomial-based RKP scheme for WSNs. A private sub-key is not directly stored in each sensor node by applying the polynomial-based [11] scheme to the RoK scheme [2]. As a result, RPoK is suitable in situations where higher resiliency is required such as a more hostile area.
2. **S-RKP**[13] is a simple random key pre-distribution (RKP) scheme with self-healing for WSNs, without lightweight operations such as a hash function. S-RKP can enhance the RKP with self-healing property, without changing the functions of sensors. This means that S-RKP is suitable for WSNs that use resource-poor sensors.
3. **POLISH**[9] is the first proactive co-operative link self-healing scheme, without the help of a server. POLISH is suitable for the situations where 100% secure connectivity is required since it is a deterministic key sharing scheme. POLISH can also keep higher resiliency without the help of a server, where the sensor operates independently. Hence, POLISH is suitable for WSNs where the key management is not necessary by a server.

2   Preliminaries

2.1   Notation

We use the following common notations.

Symbol	Explanation
n	total number of sensors (i.e., size of network)
s_A, ID_A	sensor s_A and index of s_A
λ	total sub-key space
P	number of sub-keys in the key pool, which is a set of sub-keys randomly chosen from λ $(P \ll \lambda)$
m	length of key ring on a sensor $(m \ll P)$
r	round index (i.e., fixed-length time slot)
R	number of rounds in one generation
c	number of nodes captured in one round
Gw	generation window (i.e., maximum lifespan of a sensor)
δ	renewal ratio of the key pool at every round
KP^r, KR_A^r	key pool and key ring of s_A which is deployed at round r
k_ℓ^r	ℓ-th sub-key $\in KP^r$
q	large prime number
H	cryptographic hash function which is one-way and collision-resistant, $H : \{0,1\}^* \to \{0,1\}^q$
F	hash function $F : \{0,1\}^* \to \{0,1\}^{log_2(P)}$
$f_s^j(x,y)$	s-th bivariate t-degree polynomial at generation j over a finite field $\mathbb{F}_q$
FKP^j, BKP^j	forward and backward key pool at generation j
PLP^j	polynomial pool at generation j
FKR_X^j	forward key ring of X at generation j
BKR_X^j	backward key ring of X at generation j
PLR_X^j	polynomial ring of X at generation j
fk_s^j, bk_s^j	s-th forward key $\in FKP^j$ and backward key $\in BKP^j$ at generation j
w	number of links with neighboring sensors
$K_{i,j}^r$	pairwise symmetric key (secure link) between s_i and s_j at round r
$S_i^r, c_{i_\ell}^r$	seed of s_i and ℓ-th *contribution* received by s_i at round r
G^r, Y^r, R^r	set of green, yellow and red sensors at round r
GL^r, RL^r	set of green and red links at round r

2.2   Requirements

The following requirements need to be considered when designing a self-healing scheme in WSNs.

Highly-Secure Connectivity. After deployment, two nodes share a key to establish a secure link. A probabilistic key-sharing scheme is required to keep the probability of key-sharing high. This probability is called a secure connectivity. Actually, in the RKP schemes, a secure connectivity becomes almost perfect 100% by adjusting P and m.

Self-healing. Sensor nodes may be deployed in public or hostile locations in many applications. We assume that the adversary can mount a physical attack on a sensor node after it has been deployed, and read secret information from its memory. Therefore, a self-healing property is very important for long-term use of

WSNs. Self-healing means that the compromised links are automatically healed with time even if the adversary corrupts the sensor nodes of the network. The degree of self-healing is measured by *resiliency*. Resiliency is estimated by the ratio of links which have not been compromised by the capture of nodes. Self-healing is achieved by security properties: *forward* and *backward security*. These security properties are defined in [14]. Forward secrecy means that adversary cannot learn any keys used to decrypt and/or authenticate before compromise, and backward secrecy means that adversary cannot learn any keys used to decrypt and/or authenticate after compromise.

Restricted Resources. It is required that WSNs consist of small, battery-operated devices with limited memory and limited computational power. It is also desirable that we do not use even lightweight operations on a sensor, such as a hash function.

2.3   Attacker Model

The main purpose of attacker is to steal as many keys in each node as possible in order to compromise a secure link. We assume two different types of attackers, eager attackers and temporary attackers, in order to consider different environments [2].

- Eager attacker model: This type of attacker regularly corrupts nodes of the network without stopping operations. More concretely, the eager attacker keeps compromising nodes at a constant rate, from the deployment of the first round of sensors to the end of the life of the network.
- Temporary attacker model: This type of attacker is active only during a limited of time. The temporary attacker regularly corrupts nodes within a specific period.

Attacker knows the entire topology of the WSNs, and can create a table of sensor secrets and share it. Attacker does not stay at one local place for stealthy operation and then does not interfere with sensor's behavior, i.e., it does not delete, delay or introduce messages.

2.4   Multiphase WSNs

Multiphase WSNs: A multiphase WSN is a network where a sensor is replaced with the server's help after its battery has been depleted. More concretely, sensor nodes which run out of power will be removed from the network and new sensor nodes need to be periodically deployed to assure network connectivity. Note that a multiphase WSN does not always have self-healing property.

Resilient Multiphase WSNs: A resilient multiphase WSN possesses the feature that the network automatically self-heals against node-capture attack. The key pool refreshes over time in resilient multiphase WSNs, and hence the pre-distributed keys have limited lifetimes. The key ring also refreshes over time. This implies that each sensor gradually stops using the old sub-keys.

2.5   Probability of Pairwise Key Sharing

In the RKP schemes [3,6], a pairwise key is stochastically constructed. The probability that two nodes share i sub-keys is defined as:

$$p_i = \frac{\binom{P}{i}\binom{P-i}{2(m-i)}\binom{2(m-i)}{m-i}}{\binom{P}{m}^2}, \tag{1}$$

where m is the key ring size and P is the key pool size. Therefore the probability that two nodes share at least one sub-key is defined by $1 - p_0$.

3   WSN Protocols

System and Network Assumptions. Time is divided into equal and fixed rounds. In RPoK and POLISH schemes, round synchronization can be implemented, but, in the S-RKP, round synchronization is not necessary to be implemented in a node. The network is connected at all times. Any two sensors can communicate either directly or indirectly, via other sensors. In RPoK and POLISH, each sensor can perform cryptographic hashing and polynomial execution, but, in S-RKP, no sensor performs cryptographic hashing or polynomial execution (same as the RKP schemes).

3.1   RPoK

The primary aim of RPoK is to not only increase secure connectivity between nodes, but also decrease the compromised ratio of nodes against node-capture attacks in multiphase WSNs. Practically, a private sub-key is not directly stored in each sensor node by applying the t-degree polynomial-based scheme to the RoK scheme [2]. As a result, an attacker has to capture $(t + 1)$ sub-keys in order to corrupt a link. Furthermore, we achieve the forward and backward security of the polynomial by linear transformations using forward and backward keys. Therefore, RPoK can dramatically improve the ratio of compromised links compared with the RoK scheme.

Protocol Description. The protocol details of RPoK are as follows:

1. Pool generation. RPoK uses three kinds of pools, i.e., FKP^j, BKP^j and PLP^j, where FKP^j and BKP^j are the same as RoK. PLP^j is defined as $PLP^j = \left\{ f_1^j(x,y), f_2^j(x,y), \ldots, f_{P/2}^j(x,y) \right\}$, where $f_s^j(x,y) = \alpha_{j-1} f_s^{j-1}(x,y) + \beta_{j-1}$, $\alpha_{j-1} = H(fk_s^{j-1} \parallel bk_s^{j-1})$ and $\beta_{j-1} = H(bk_s^{j-1} \parallel fk_s^{j-1})$ $(j = 1, \ldots, N, s = 1, \ldots, P/2)$.

2. Ring assignment. Node A is configured with key rings, defined as: $FKR_A^j = \left\{ fk_s^j \right\}$, $BKR_A^j = \left\{ bk_s^j \right\}$ and $PLR_A^j = \left\{ f_s^j(x,y) \right\}$, such that $s = F(ID_A \parallel i \parallel g_A)$ $(i = 1, 2, \ldots, m/2)$. Note that $g_A = j$ when the node A is deployed at generation j.

3. Establishing a secure link. After deployment, a node A initiates neighbors discovery procedure with node B and both nodes calculate indices, similar to RoK. If there are collisions such that $F(ID_B \parallel y \parallel g_B) = F(ID_A \parallel x \parallel g_A)$, where $x, y \in \{1, 2, \ldots m/2\}$, then it is known that they both have $fk^{g_B}_{F(ID_B \parallel y \parallel g_B)}$, $bk^{g_A + Gw - 1}_{F(ID_B \parallel y \parallel g_B)}$ and $f^{g_B}_{F(ID_B \parallel y \parallel g_B)}(ID_A, ID_B)$ in their memory. In this way, all colluding local indices $a, b, \ldots, z \in \{1, 2, \ldots m/2\}$ are found and the following becomes their pairwise symmetric key:

$$K^{RPoK}_{AB} = H\left(f^{g_B}_{F(ID_B \parallel a \parallel g_B)}(ID_A, ID_B) \parallel \cdots \parallel f^{g_B}_{F(ID_B \parallel z \parallel g_B)}(ID_A, ID_B) \right)$$

Note that $f^{g_B}_s(ID_A, ID_B)$ satisfies both forward and backward security because of linear transformations, as mentioned in the pools generation phase. Furthermore, in the RPoK scheme, K^{RPoK}_{AB} is a session key in each time-slot, while K^{RoK}_{AB} in RoK is a common key in the overlapping generations. We assume that K^{RPoK}_{AB} is updated in each time slot.

3.2   S-RKP

In order to attach self-healing property to the RKP scheme, all the previous RKP schemes with self-healing property had to change the process of each sensor as well as that of a server. On the other hand, the primary aim of S-RKP is to attach self-healing property to the RKP scheme by simply changing only the server process. The S-RKP can attach self-healing property to existing RKP schemes by updating the key pool of a server with time. The most interesting point of this scheme is that processing of each sensor is the same as in the RKP scheme, that is, round synchronization is not necessary to be implemented in a node. We emphasize that the keys which can be assigned to a sensor are not updated, same as the RKP scheme. Nevertheless, the keys have a limited lifetime, similar to the RoK scheme. The S-RKP scheme takes a different approach from the RoK scheme. Thanks to such a server process in the self-healing RKP, a sensor does not use even lightweight operations such as a hash function.

Protocol Description. This protocol is quite simple. Some additional executions by a server are required, while no additional execution on a node is necessary. The procedure on each sensor is the same as in the RKP scheme. The key pool in the RKP scheme is composed of random keys that do not evolve with time. In contrast, the key pool is composed of random keys that the server evolves with time in the S-RKP scheme.

1. Pool generation. A server sets the key pool in this protocol. In order to generate the key pool, the server uses a hash chain using a cryptographic hash function H and a seed s. The key pool is initiated with P random sub-keys. Let k^r_ℓ be the ℓ-th key at round r in the key pool. A server computes the sub-keys $k^0_1 = H(s \parallel 1)$, $k^0_2 = H(s \parallel k^0_1)$, $\ldots$, $k^0_P = H(s \parallel k^0_{P-1})$ in the key pool. Thus, the key pool at round 0 (i.e., when the network is first deployed) is defined as $KP^0 = \{k^0_1, k^0_2, \ldots, k^0_P\}$, where k^0_1 is the oldest sub-key at round 0. KP^0

corresponds to the key pool of the RKP scheme.

2. Pool update. At each round, the key pool is partially updated over time. Let δ be the renewal size of the key pool at every round. For instance, if $\delta = 1$ at round 1, then $k_1^1 \leftarrow k_2^0$, $k_2^1 \leftarrow k_3^0$, ..., $k_{P-1}^1 \leftarrow k_P^0$, $k_P^1 \leftarrow H(s||k_{P-1}^1)$. Generally, the keys are partially renewed at round r as follows:

$$KP^r = \{k_1^r, k_2^r, \ldots, k_{P-\delta}^r, k_{P-\delta+1}^r, \ldots, k_{P-1}^r, k_P^r\}, \tag{2}$$

where $k_1^r = k_{1+\delta}^{r-1}$, $k_2^r \leftarrow k_{2+\delta}^{r-1}$, ..., $k_{P-\delta}^r \leftarrow H(s||k_{P-\delta-1}^r)$, $k_{P-\delta+1}^r \leftarrow H(s||k_{P-\delta}^r)$, ..., $k_{P-1}^r \leftarrow H(k_{P-2}^r)$, $k_P^r \leftarrow H(k_{P-1}^r)$. Since the key pool slides just δ at every round, all the keys in the key pool are replaced after $\lceil P/\delta \rceil$ rounds. A server manages the current P sub-keys in the key pool. The server discards the old sub-keys.

3. Ring assignment. This step is the same as ring assignment in the RKP scheme. For each sensor, m keys are randomly selected from the current key pool and stored in the sensor's memory before deployment. This set of m keys is called the sensor's key ring.

4. Establishing a secure link. This step is also the same as the establishment of a secure link in the RKP scheme. After the sensors are deployed, s_i initiates key-discovery procedure with their neighbors with whom they share a key. Sensors which discover that they contain a shared key in their key rings can then verify that their neighbors actually holds the key through a challenge-response protocol. Of course, this protocol can use "path keys", as used in the RKP scheme.

3.3   POLISH

In this section we describe the POLISH (Proactive co-Operative LInk Self-Healing) scheme. The primary aim of this scheme is to decrease the compromised ratio of links against node-capture attacks without help of a server, that is, links compromised in WSNs automatically self-heal with time. The POLISH updates a link using the random data transmitted from the neighboring sensors, based on the idea of the POSH scheme. Although this protocol is very simple like POSH, more importantly, our security evaluation is not achieved easily, i.e., it is necessary to newly take the security of a link between sensors into consideration in POLISH since such security is not considered in the POSH scheme.

A link self-heals in two steps: first two neighboring sensors are self-healed, and then the link between these sensors is self-healed. A major difference between POSH and POLISH is the security analysis of a link. While the POSH scheme in a sense treats the secure link between a sensor and a powerful sink, the POLISH scheme treats the secure link between sensors. In addition, POLISH uses a bivariate t-degree polynomial, and thus an attacker has to capture $(t+1)$ polynomial shares during a limited period of time (i.e., at round 1) in order to corrupt a link.

An adversary breaks into $k = |R^r|$ sensors to read the pairwise symmetric keys and secret seeds of PRNG in R^r, and to monitor all the communication of

R^r. At any time, we identify three sets of sensors (i.e., green, yellow and red) and two sets of links, as follows:

- *Red links* (RL^r) are those that have been compromised in some round $r' < r$ and the pairwise symmetric key of the link is known to adversary in round r.
- *Green links* (GL^r) are those that have either never been compromised or regained their security in round r.

Note that, in this scheme, a red sensor s_i at round r means that adversary knows a seed S_i^r. If s_i becomes red in round r' and is self-healed at the end of round $r > r'$, then adversary can compute the contributions of s_i from round r' to r.

Protocol Description. The protocol details of POLISH are as follows:

1. Setup. To predistribute pairwise keys, the setup server randomly generates a bivariate t-degree polynomial $f(x, y)$ over a finite field $\mathbb{F}_q$, such that it has the property of $f(x, y) = f(y, x)$. For each sensor s_i, the setup server computes a polynomial share of $f(x, y)$, that is, $f(x, ID_i)$. Each sensor can use a secure hash function, a polynomial and a PRNG with a unique secret seed. Note that the secure degree t of polynomial is dependent on the number of adversary at each round. For instance, if we set $t \geq 10$ as the secure degree of polynomial when we assume $k = 10$, then adversary cannot recover $f(x, y)$.

2. Establishing a secure link. For any two sensors s_i and s_j, the sensor s_i can compute the key $f(ID_j, ID_i)$ by evaluating $f(x, ID_i)$, and the sensor s_j can compute the same key $f(ID_i, ID_j) = f(ID_j, ID_i)$ by evaluating $f(x, ID_j)$. As a result, sensors s_i and s_j can establish a pairwise symmetric key $K_{i,j}^1 = f(ID_i, ID_j)$ in the first round (round 1). After key establishment, s_i deletes all the coefficients of a polynomial.

3. Key and Seed Update. The neighboring sensors s_i and s_j have a pairwise symmetric key $K_{i,j}^1$ (secure link) when they are deployed at the beginning of the first round (round 1). At the beginning of round r, s_i produces w pseudo-random values (contributions) using its PRNG for w neighboring sensors, and sends them to the neighboring sensors using a secure link. Note that all the contributions that s_i sends are different. Then, each sensor receives contributions from the neighboring sensors during round r. The recipient uses two contributions as inputs to the secure hash function used for key update. To update the secure link at the end of round r, s_i computes:

$$K_{i,j}^{r+1} = H(K_{i,j}^r || c_{i_\eta}^r || c_{j_\lambda}^r), \tag{3}$$

where $c_{i_\eta}^r$ is the η-th contribution that s_i received at round r and $c_{j_\lambda}^r$ is the λ-th contribution that s_j received at round r. Both s_i and s_j delete $K_{i,j}^r$ after key updating. Furthermore, each sensor updates a seed of PRNG using w contributions, which are all contributions received by the neighboring sensors. To update the seed S_i^r at the end of round r, s_i computes[2]:

$$S_i^{r+1} = H(S_i^r || c_{i_1}^r || \cdots || c_{i_w}^r) \tag{4}$$

---

[2] The update of a PRNG seed is similar to [15].

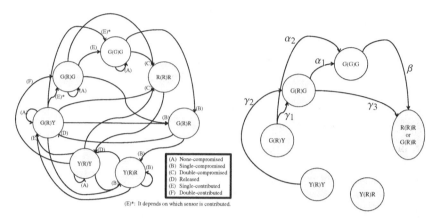

Fig. 1. Link state transition diagram   **Fig. 2.** Partial link state transition diagram

After seed updating, s_i deletes S_i^r. A seed is updated in every round, and then w contributions are generated by PRNG with such new seed.

The Link State. A link self-heals in two steps: first two neighboring sensors are self-healed, and then the link between them is self-healed. We can generate the seven kinds of link states as described in Fig. 1 (i.e., $GL^r = \{G(G)G\}$ and $RL^r = \{G(R)G, G(R)Y, Y(R)Y, Y(R)R, G(R)R, R(R)R\}$). A pair of sensors and their common link constitutes a link state. For example, G(R)Y means that two neighboring sensors of green and yellow are connected by the red link. The conditions of transition are as follows:

1. *Double-compromised* condition means that both of two neighboring sensors are compromised.
2. *Single-compromised* condition means that either of two neighboring sensors is compromised.
3. *None-compromised* condition means that neither of two neighboring sensors is compromised.
4. *Single-contributed* condition means that either of two neighboring sensors receives at least one "secure contribution".
5. *Double-contributed* condition means that both of two neighboring sensors receive at least one secure contribution.

Note that the secure contribution is a green contribution that is not intercepted by adversary.

4 Security Evaluation by Analytical Model

4.1 Secure Connectivity

It is important to raise the secure connectivity, strengthening resiliency. The higher the secure connectivity is, the better the self-healing scheme is. A self-healing scheme can be divided into two schemes, a deterministic and probabilistic

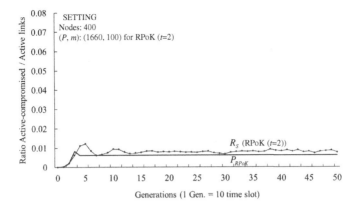

Fig. 3. RPoK: Analytical results and simulation results against eager attackers

key sharing schemes. In this paper, POLISH is a deterministic key sharing scheme but RPoK and S-RKP are probabilistic key sharing scheme.

In a deterministic key-sharing scheme, the POLISH has an advantage that the probability of establishing a secure link is 100%, since a sensor s_i has a polynomial $f(x, ID_i)$ and also shares the pairwise symmetric key $K_{i,j}^r = f(ID_j, ID_i)$ with s_j in the first round (round 1). After that the pairwise symmetric key of each link is updated, and hence the secure connectivity is 100% at every round.

In a probabilistic key-sharing scheme, there is a tradeoff between secure connectivity and resiliency against node capture attacks. The secure connectivity of RPoK is the same as that of the original RKP [6], i.e., the probability that two nodes share i sub-keys is the same as Equation (1). Thus, the probability that two nodes share at least one sub-key is defined by $1 - p_0 = 0.998$ using the parameters in Fig. 3. On the other hand, the secure connectivity of S-RKP is a little inferior to that of the original RKP, RoK and RPoK because of the pool update. However, S-RKP can achieve secure key sharing without using the security executions. The δ sub-keys in the key pool are updated at every round as described in Section 3.2. We can derive p_i which is the expected value of key-sharing probability by [13], as follows:

$$p_i = \frac{\binom{P-\delta E[\alpha]}{i} \cdot \sum_{x=0}^{m-i} \binom{P-\delta E[\alpha]-i}{x}\binom{\delta E[\alpha]}{m-i-x}\binom{P-i-x}{m-i}}{\binom{P}{m}^2} \tag{5}$$

The probability that two nodes share at least one sub-key is defined by $1 - p_0 = 0.992$ using the parameters in Fig. 4.

4.2   Resiliency

The degree of self-healing is measured by resiliency. Resiliency is estimated by the ratio of links that have not been compromised by the capture of nodes.

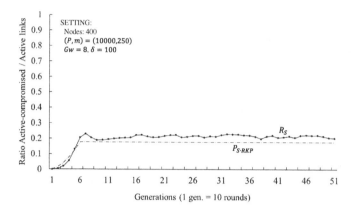

Fig. 4. S-RKP: Analytical results and simulation results against eager attackers

In RPoK, we can measure the resiliency by the following analytical model in [8]. We obtain the analytical model by combining P_{RoK} [2] with the polynomial-based scheme [11], in order to dramatically improve resiliency (i.e., the ratio of compromised links). The ratio P_{RPoK} at generation j in RPoK is defined by:

$$P_{RPoK} = 1 - \sum_{i=0}^{t} {}_{c \cdot E'_c} C_i \left(\frac{m}{P}\right)^i \left(1 - \frac{m}{P}\right)^{c \cdot E'_c - i} \tag{6}$$

Fig. 3 shows a comparison of the analytical result (P_{RPoK}) with simulation result (R_S) ($t = 2$) [8] in RPoK. We found that the resiliency $(1 - R_{RPoK}) = 99.4\%$ by Fig. 3 holds, where $E'_c = 3$ and $c = 10$. We set such parameters in order to fairly compare with other two schemes. As a result, we see that the resiliency is much higher than other two schemes by Table 1.

In S-RKP, we can measure the resiliency by the following analytical model in [13]. The idea of modeling the RoK scheme is to replace the generation j by the constant value. We evaluate this scheme employing the modeling method of RoK, i.e., we estimate a constant value and replace it by j. Then, the ratio $P_{S\text{-}RKP}$ in [13] is defined by:

$$P_{S\text{-}RKP} = \sum_{i=1}^{m} \left(1 - \prod_{r=1}^{E''_c} \left(1 - \frac{m}{P + (r - 1)\delta}\right)\right)^i \frac{p'_i}{1 - p'_0}, \tag{7}$$

where $E''_c = P/2\delta$. We can easily confirm that Equation (7) is the extended form of P_{RoK} by [8]. Fig. 4 shows a comparison of the analytical result ($P_{S\text{-}RKP}$) with simulation result (R_S) [13] in S-RKP. We found that the resiliency $(1 - P_{S\text{-}RKP}) = 90.1\%$ by Fig. 4 holds when $\delta = 100$. This means that S-RKP can achieve resiliency without using the security executions.

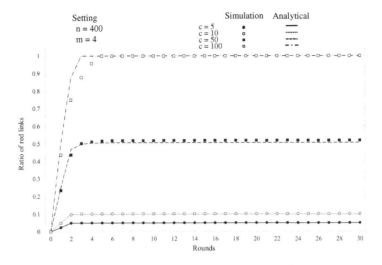

Fig. 5. POLISH: Analytical results and simulation results against eager attackers

To evaluate the resiliency of POLISH, we analyze the number of green links by evaluating the state of sensors in any round, i.e., the number of $G(G)G^3$ in Fig. 2. The partial state transition diagram of a link is shown in Fig. 2, in which only the transition required to analyze the number of green links is depicted. That is, we consider only the input and the output of $G(G)G$ and $G(R)G$. Let α_1, α_2, β, γ_1, γ_2 and γ_3 be the number of link state transition (use not probability but a number.) and let $RL^r_{G(R)G} \subset RL^r$ be a set of the link state $G(R)G$. This figure shows that the expected number of green links in round r is:

$$E[|GL^{r+1}|] = |GL^r| + \alpha_1 + \alpha_2 - \beta \tag{8}$$

On the other hand, the number of red links between two green sensors is estimated in Fig. 2 as follows:

$$P_{POLISH} = E[|RL^{r+1}_{G(R)G}|] = |RL^r_{G(R)G}| - \alpha_1 + \gamma_1 + \gamma_2 - \gamma_3 \tag{9}$$

Resiliency is estimated by the ratio of red links. Fig. 5 shows a comparison of the analytical results (P_{POLISH}) with simulation result [9] in POLISH scheme. We found that the resiliency $(1 - P_{POLISH}) = 82.3\%$ holds when $c = 10$. This means that POLISH can achieve resiliency without the help of a server.

4.3 Discussion

Table 1 shows the comparison of three self-healing schemes for WSNs from the viewpoint of security computation and procedure overhead that sensor/server

---

[3] For example, $G(R)Y$ means that two neighboring sensors of green and yellow are connected by the red link.

Table 1. Comparison of self-healing schemes for WSNs

	Self-healing WSNs		
	RPoK[8]	S-RKP[13]	POLISH[9]
Key management by server	Necessary	Necessary	no
Sever overhead	Hash + Poly	Hash	no
Sensor overhead	Hash + Poly	no	Hash + PRF
Round sync.	Necessary	no	Necessary
Secure connectivity	99.8%	99.2%	100%
Resiliency	99.4%	82.3%	90.1%

execute. Secure connectivity and resiliency are the results of each analytical evaluation based on the same memory size for keys (i.e., 5kB). Furthermore, the number of attackers is the same (i.e., $c = 10$) at each generation (note that we need to consider "round" as "generation" in the POLISH scheme.).

RPoK can dramatically increase resiliency and hence it is suitable for situations that require higher resiliency such as a more hostile area, compared with the other two schemes. On the other hand, S-RKP can enhance the RKP with self-healing property, without changing the functions of the sensors. Thus, S-RKP can increase resiliency under realistic assumptions since a sensor does not have the functions of security executions and round synchronization. This means that S-RKP is suitable for WSNs that use resource-poor sensors although resiliency is somewhat low, compared with the other two schemes. Note that secure connectivity of RPoK and S-RKP is not 100% since they are probabilistic key sharing schemes.

POLISH is suitable for the situations where 100% secure connectivity is required since it is a deterministic key-sharing scheme. Also, POLISH can keep higher resiliency without the help of a server, where the sensor operates independently. Hence, POLISH is suitable for WSNs where the key management is not necessary by a server.

5   Conclusion

We summarize the three kinds of self-healing schemes for WSNs. RPoK is a scheme which emphasizes security (resiliency) and it is suitable in situations that require higher resiliency such as a very hostile area. S-RKP is a scheme which emphasizes efficiency of a sensor and it is suitable for WSNs which use resource-poor sensors. They are probabilistic key sharing schemes and they can attach self-healing property to existing RKP schemes. On the other hand, POLISH is a scheme which emphasizes the sensor operations without the help of a server. Hence, POLISH is suitable for WSNs where the key management is not necessary by a server, and it is also suitable for the situations where 100% secure connectivity is required since it is a deterministic key sharing scheme.

References

1. Blundo, C., De Santis, A., Herzberg, A., Kutten, S., Vaccaro, U., Yung, M.: Perfectly-secure key distribution for dynamic conferences. In: Brickell, E.F. (ed.) CRYPTO 1992. LNCS, vol. 740, pp. 471–486. Springer, Heidelberg (1993)
2. Castelluccia, C., Spognardi, A.: Rok: A robust key pre-distribution protocol for multi-phase wireless sensor networks. In: SecureComm 2007, pp. 351–360 (2007)
3. Chan, H., Perrig, A., Song, D.: Random key predistribution schemes for sensor networks. In: SP 2003, pp. 197–213 (2003)
4. Da, A.K.: A random key establishment scheme for multi-phase deployment in large-scale distributed sensor networks. Int. J. Inf. Sec. 11(3), 189–211 (2012)
5. Du, W., Deng, J., Han, Y.S., Chen, S., Varshney, P.K.: A key management scheme for wireless sensor networks using deployment knowledge. In: INFOCOM 2004, pp. 586–597 (2004)
6. Eschenauer, L., Gligor, V.D.: A key-management scheme for distributed sensor networks. In: CCS 2002, pp. 41–47 (2002)
7. Ergun, M., Levi, A., Savas, E.: Increasing Resiliency in Multi-phase Wireless Sensor Networks: Generationwise Key Predistribution Approach. The Computer Journal 54(4), 602–616 (2011)
8. Ito, H., Miyaji, A., Omote, K.: RPoK: A Strongly Resilient Polynomial-based Random Key Pre-distribution Scheme for Multiphase Wireless Sensor Networks. In: GLOBECOM 2010, pp. 1–5 (2010)
9. Iida, T., Miyaji, A., Omote, K.: POLISH: Proactive Co-operative LInk Self-Healing for Wireless Sensor Networks. In: Défago, X., Petit, F., Villain, V. (eds.) SSS 2011. LNCS, vol. 6976, pp. 253–267. Springer, Heidelberg (2011)
10. Kalkan, K., Yilmaz, S., Yilmaz, O.Z., Levi, A.: A highly resilient and zone-based key predistribution protocol for multiphase wireless sensor networks. In: Q2SWinet 2009, pp. 29–36 (2009)
11. Liu, D., Ning, P., Li, R.: Establishing pairwise keys in distributed sensor networks. ACM Trans. Inf. Syst. Secur. 8(1), 41–77 (2005)
12. Palsberg, J., Tsudik, G.: DISH: Distributed self-healing. In: Kulkarni, S., Schiper, A. (eds.) SSS 2008. LNCS, vol. 5340, pp. 47–62. Springer, Heidelberg (2008)
13. Miyaji, A., Omote, K.: How to Build Random Key Pre-distribution Schemes with Self-Healing for Multiphase WSNs. In: AINA 2013, pp. 205–212 (2013)
14. Pietro, R.D., Ma, D., Soriente, C., Tsudik, G.: POSH: Proactive co-operative self-healing in unattended wireless sensor networks. In: SRDS 2008, pp. 185–194 (2008)
15. Pietro, R.D., Oligeri, G., Soriente, C., Tsudik, G.: Intrusion-Resilience in Mobile Unattended WSNs. In: INFOCOM, pp. 2303–2311 (2010)
16. Tian, W., Han, S., Parvin, S., Dillon, T.S.: A Key Management Protocol for Multiphase Hierarchical Wireless Sensor Networks. In: EUC 2010, pp. 617–623 (2010)
17. Yilmaz, O.Z., Levi, A., Savas, E.: Multiphase deployment models for fast self healing in wireless sensor networks. In: SECRYPT 2008, pp. 136–144 (2008)

RAS: A Task Scheduling Algorithm Based on Resource Attribute Selection in a Task Scheduling Framework

Yong Zhao, Liang Chen, Youfu Li, Peng Liu, Xiaolong Li, and Chenchen Zhu

Department of Computer Science and Engineering,
University of Electronic Science and Technology of China, Chengdu, China
{yongzh04,youfuli.fly}@gmail.com, chen218147@126.com,
{695624471,xiaolong43651}@qq.com, cheryzcc@163.com

Abstract. With the advent of big data and cloud computing era, scheduling and executing large-scale computing tasks effectively and allocating resources to tasks reasonably are becoming a quite challenging problem. And there is theoretical significance to research on efficient scheduling algorithm to improve resource utilization and task execution efficiency. We present a scheduling algorithm based on resource attribute selection (RAS) by sending a set of test tasks to an execution node to determine its resource attributes before a task is scheduled; and then selecting the optimal node to execute a task according to its resource requirements and the fitness between the resource node and the task, which also uses history task data if exists. We (1) give a formal definition of the resource attributes and (2) compute the fitness of the resource nodes and (3) store the information of node selection for next round. We integrate our algorithm into the Gearman scheduling framework, and through comparison with three other scheduling frameworks, we find out there is significant improvement in resource selection and resource utilization using RAS. The throughput of the RAS (with work-stealing, WS) is at least 30% higher than the other frameworks and the resource utilization of RAS (WS) reaches 0.94. The algorithm can make a good model for practical large scale application scheduling.

Keywords: Task Scheduling, Resource Attribute Selection, Resource Management, Work-Stealing.

1 Introduction

Task scheduling has been around for many years and provides essential support for both grid computing and cloud computing to increase the system performance and efficiency. In cloud computing and grid computing environment [3], the computing resources can be varied in many aspects which provide appropriate conditions to execute applications with multiple intrinsic parallelism. The purpose of task scheduling is to minimize the execution time of seeking appropriate resources based on given independent tasks and resources. With the advent

M. Pathan, G. Wei, and G. Fortino (Eds.): IDCS 2013, LNCS 8223, pp. 106–119, 2013.

of big data and cloud computing era, the computing resource, storage resource and even the network bandwidth can be provided as services which allow users to pay-on-demand [1]. Efficient resource distribution and utilization can reduce users cost greatly. However, the task scheduling in cloud is becoming more and more complicated due to the heterogeneous computing environment and task complexity [2]. Scheduling the tasks according to the resource attribute can obviously help to further reduce the cost and improve the efficiency. The overall operating performance of a scheduling system is closely and inseparably related to the efficiency of scheduling algorithm, which has been drawing great attention from researchers and scholars. The goal of scheduling algorithm research is to obtain an optimal value, which can be regarded as the highest performance or the shortest execution time [3], through a series of calculations. An optimization problem can be defined by expressions 1 and 2 as follows:

$$min\sigma = f(x) \tag{1}$$

$$s.t.x \in S = \{x|g_i(x) \leq 0, i = 1, 2, \ldots, n\} \tag{2}$$

$\sigma = f(x)$ can be regarded as the objective function, $g_i(x)$ is the constraint function and there can be multiple of such functions, S is the range of constraint field, x is a n-dimension optimization variable. Then solving the optimization problem can be transformed into a minimization problem of the above equation.

In network systems, resource node malfunction is quite common which may influence the overall structure of the system and cause unpredictable events. In such circumstance, resource management program should be able to monitor and manage the system resources dynamically, figure out the optimal resource configuration among available resources, and furthermore reduce the unnecessary cost caused by changing system conditions. To deal with the above situation, scholars proposed the adaptive scheduling heuristics [22] [23], which can improve the overall dispatching performance of the system through adaptive scheduling based on certain parameters such as computing ability, storage capacity, load level, network status, etc.

The rest of the paper is organized as follows: in Sect. 2, we discuss related work about scientific scheduling frameworks and algorithms. In Sect. 3, we present our resource attribute selection algorithm (RAS). In Sect. 4, we demonstrate and analyze our algorithm by integrating it into Gearman [7] framework. In Sect 5, we draw our conclusions and discuss future work.

2   Related Work

Falkon [4] [5] [6] is a fast and light-weight task execution framework. Falkon uses a three-tier architecture (a first-tier submit host, a group of second-tier dispatchers, and a group of third-tier workers), it tracks task status on a single first-tier submit host, thus the scalability of running short tasks stops growing linearly at some point (which is dependent on system resources).The key design of Falkon is to enable efficient dispatch and execution of large number of small tasks.

Gearman provides a generic application framework to farm out tasks to other machines or processes that are better suited to do the work. A Gearman-powered application consists of three parts: a client, a worker, and a job server. The client is responsible for creating a job to be run and sending it to a job server. The job server will find a suitable worker that can run the job and forwards the job onto the worker. The worker performs the work requested by the client and sends a response to the client through the job server. Gearman has some advantages such as open source, multi-language integration, synchronous and asynchronous queues and natural load balancing [21]. There are also some weak points: ineffective matching upon worker resource, complex installation process and poor visualization.

Sparrow [8] [17] presents a decentralized load balancing approach called batch sampling, based on a generalization of the power of two random choices, that performs within a few percent of an optimal centralized scheduler. Batch sampling takes inspiration from web architectures where multiple frontends balance incoming requests across service nodes. Thus, as task durations continue to decrease, distributed scheduling using batch sampling presents a viable alternative to centralized schedulers.

Mesos [10] and Yarn [11] are similar cluster resource managers and use the same two-level scheduling model, with per-application masters request resource from a global resource manager. Compared to centralized scheduling model, this design can provide support for many computing frameworks and improve resource utilization. But they have some difference in framework deployment and resource request models. Up to now both systems are still in development. Researchers are trying to deploy their frameworks on Yarn and Mesos.

A typical Condor system [12] [13] [14] consists of four components: A Condor pool, the central manager, submitting machine and execution machine. The ClassAd [15] is a flexible representation of the characteristics and constraints of both machines and jobs in the Condor system. HTCondor [16] is a cluster manager whose goal is to implement, deploy, and evaluate mechanisms and policies that support High Throughput Computing (HTC) on large collections of computing resources. HTCondor plays the role of a matchmaker by continuously reading all the job ClassAds and all the machine ClassAds, matching and ranking job ads with machine ads.

Load Sharing Facility (LSF) is a commercial job scheduler sold by Platform Computing. It can be used to execute batch jobs on networked Unix and Windows systems on many different architectures [18]. LSF also has a lot of impressive features, such as managing cluster resources, making several heterogeneous clusters interconnected and improving resource utilization [19] [20].

To deal with different problems and meet various requirements, researchers have proposed a variety of scheduling algorithms, such as simulated annealing [25], load balancing [26], ant colony algorithm [27] and Tabu search [28]. The scheduling algorithms mentioned above all share a common disadvantage that tasks independency is the precondition for scheduling. Nevertheless, many tasks are dependent on each other in practical environment, especially in cloud computing environment which may contain varied tasks, and these interdependent subtasks can be classified into three types: collaborative type, sequence type and parallel type.

In recent years, scholars who focus on scheduling algorithms have taken into consideration the dependency relationship of tasks, and some hypotheses were proposed upon these relationships, such as parallel genetic algorithm and parallel gene expression programming algorithm [9]. To implement the parallel execution between tasks, we not only need to transform the serial scheduling algorithm into parallel execution, but also need to restructure the serial algorithm to form a parallel system model in order to implement parallel resource matching.

3   Resource Attribute Selection Algorithm (RAS)

3.1   Resource Attribute

Resource Definition. Computing resources generally depend on computer mainframe and can be classified into three layers from top to bottom: 1) Application Layer (the operation status of network server, database server and other related servers); 2) Network Layer (routing between hosts, data transmission bandwidth, communication delay, etc.); 3) System Layer (CPU information, memory size, etc.). Meanwhile, computing resources also include operation system, disk space, network communication capabilities, data resources, equipment and other related resources. The resources discussed in this paper consist of computing capability, storage space and network bandwidth, and we can distribute appropriate task to different execution nodes through the definition and analysis of these three kinds of resources.

Resource Attribute Analysis. We consider computing capability, network bandwidth and storage space as the main resources that may influence the task scheduling and execution efficiency.

1) Computing capability

The computing capability is generally determined by CPU performance and memory size, and the CPU performance mainly relies on CPU operating frequency, cache capacity, instruction set and logical structure. If we take all the parameters into consideration and quantize them with value, calculating the computing capability of one execution node may be too complicated and inaccurate. When a new execution node is added into the scheduling network, we perform a set of test tasks to initialize the node and calculate the computing capability *"ComCap"*, shown in formula 3.

$$ComCap = \frac{1}{n} \sum_{i=1}^{n} t_i \tag{3}$$

t_i is the execution time of each test task; n is the number of test tasks.

2) Storage space

Storage space is generally determined by the amount of storage space in an execution node. An execution node needs to perform multiple tasks in parallel instead of performing just one or several tasks, which requires the execution node to confirm the available storage space for task execution before the task is scheduled to execute. We define "StoR' as the storage space of one node, indicated in formula 4:

$$StoR = StoS - StoU \tag{4}$$

$StoR$ represents the available storage space size; $StoS$ represents the initialization storage space size when the node is added into the cluster; $StoU$ indicates the amount of storage space which is already in use.

3) Network bandwidth

Information transmission between execution nodes and communication between scheduling service layers and nodes are determined by network bandwidth. When performing short-time tasks, an execution node with lower computing capability, larger network bandwidth and faster transmission speed may be more efficient than those with higher computing capability, smaller bandwidth and slower transmission speed. And when involving long-time tasks, we should take all the factors into consideration to evaluate the efficiency. The bandwidth can be influenced by network equipment, node number, client and server machines, etc. Bandwidth size "BandW" is mainly represented by the communication time cost between scheduling service layers and execution nodes.

3.2   Algorithm Analysis

Tasks are submitted to a server through a client terminal which is also in charge of initializing the tasks and generating task information table including task number, storage space required, task type, receive time, etc. Along with the tasks, task information table will be delivered to the scheduling server. Then the scheduling server can choose appropriate computing nodes for task execution according to a Resource Attribute Selection (RAS) algorithm. When the tasks are finished, the execution nodes return the results to the scheduling server, and the data including computing result and operation information will be sent back to the client. In our implementation, there is one scheduling server with multiple workers registered and one backup server in case of failure. Fig. 1 illustrates the task scheduling processes.

Task Request Description. Users can write the execution program, which contains the information about task number, at the client and use the submission tool to submit tasks. During task initialization, the client side will also predict the storage space required and record the start time of the task execution. All relevant task information will be integrated into the task information table and sent to the scheduling server. Here we give a sample implementation of execution program using an advanced language.

Sample Implementation

```
$client= new Client();  /*initial client*/
$client->addServer();  /*client is added to the server*/
function sleep-1_function($job)  /*define sleep-1 task*/
{
    return($job->workload(), sleep(1000));
}
$task_num = 100;    /*define the number of taks*/
for ($i=0; $i<task_num; $i++)   /* 100 sleep-1 tasks*/
{
    $job_handle = $client->doBackground("R", "sleep-1_fuction", i,
    task_num, "store", "start_time", "finish_time ");
    /*define task type, task number, the number of tasks,
     storage space, starting time, finished time.*/
if ($client->returnCode() != SUCCESS)  {
    echo "task scheduling fail\n";
     exit;
    }
}
```

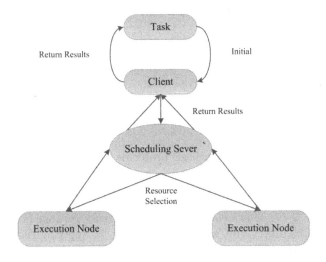

Fig. 1. Task Scheduling Processes

Basic Idea of the Algorithm. An efficient resource attribute selection algorithm could help to execute tasks with relatively shorter time, high resource utilization, resource load balance and adapting to changes in resource status dynamically.

The fundamental principle of RAS is to acquire appropriate nodes for task execution according to the information matching degree between the current tasks and former tasks and the operation performance of execution nodes when executing former tasks. Then the operation status of the current tasks will be recorded by the scheduling server and used to allocate execution nodes when the server receives similar tasks.

1) Data Structure

"Chromosome" is comprised of single or several genes which formed by one linear fixed-length string. The "chromosome" is the basic unit for genetic operation in gene expression programming algorithm. The Data structure used in this paper is similar to chromosome. It uses a string to represent resource attributes and suitable task type of the execution node. And the string can be divided into two parts: head and tail. Head part is used to mark the appropriate task type, and the tail part is used to describe the resource attribute of execution node and average fitness of suitable tasks.

1) Fitness Function

The fitness of an execution node is an evaluation which is given to the executing node by the scheduling server, and can be calculated by sending a group of test tasks to the executing node and collecting the execution information.

Classic Gene Expression Programming algorithm (GEP) contains three kinds of functions for fitness calculation:

(a) Fitness function based on absolute errors

$$f_i = \sum_{j=1}^{n}(M - |C_{(i,j)} - T_j|) \tag{5}$$

(b) Fitness function based on relative errors

$$f_i = \sum_{j=1}^{n}(M - \left|\frac{C_{(i,j)} - T_j}{T_j} \times 100\right|) \tag{6}$$

(c) Fitness functions for logic synthesis problems

$$if \quad n \geq \frac{1}{2}C_i, then \quad f_i = n; else \quad f_i = 1 \tag{7}$$

In expression 5 - 7, M is a constant used to control the range fitness f_i, $C_{(i,j)}$ represents the function result, which is calculated by applying the j-th sample variable into the function expression of the i-th gene. T_j is the target value of the j-th sample variable. In formula 7, C_i is the total number of test samples, and n is the number of the correct instances.

In a practical application, the fitness function based on absolute errors may be unable to fully evaluate the accuracy of approximation. Instead, the fitness function based on relative errors is often referred, but still has some drawbacks [24]. In this paper, we proposed a new fitness function, shown in expression 8 and 9.

$$f_i = 100 \times \frac{1}{1 + U_i} \tag{8}$$

Where,

$$U_i = \frac{1}{n} \sum_{j=1}^{n} (C_{(i,j)} - T_p)^2 \qquad (9)$$

$C_{(i,j)}$ is the execution time of the i-th task running in the j-th executor. T_p is the average execution time of the same task running in all executors, and n represents the executor number. When $C_{(i,j)} = T_p$, the fitness reaches maximum. The fitness function is an important factor that can influence system performance. The fitness function described in expression 8 can perform resource matching according to task execution requirement, which will be proven in the experiments in Sect. 4.

3.3   Work-Stealing Algorithm

Load balance is a key factor for system evaluation. Dispatching the tasks to an idle node is the distribution strategy adopted in Gearman, which may influence the load balance of the overall system when tasks are dispatched to a node with poor efficiency and all the high-performance executors are idle. The scheduling system model introduced in this paper adopts modified task-stealing strategy to ensure fair load balance.

Load balancing strategy: when the system uses the parallel resource attribute selection algorithm described above to generate the pair of task and resource, the most appropriate execution node for the task will be given. Using the dichotomy strategy, half tasks are dispatched to the chosen execution node and the other half will be dispatched to other nodes equally. If one node completes the assigned tasks, it will automatically steal half of remaining tasks from the node which has the most unfinished tasks. The work-stealing procedure will keep repeating until all the tasks are completed.

Applying the load balancing strategy, a number of tasks will be distributed to each node to execute, and when the assigned tasks have been completed, one executor may steal some unfinished tasks from other nodes. This strategy could keep all the executors busy executing tasks and ensure load balance of the system.

4   Experiments

In last section, we present our effort of integrating RAS algorithm into the Gearman scheduling framework and replacing its original scheduling algorithm to verify the functionality and efficiency of our proposed algorithm.

4.1   Environment Configuration

The benchmark environment (illustrated in Fig. 2) is a distributed parallel computing environment consists of 7 desktop computers. One of them is initialized to launch three virtual machines which are configured as clients. We use the clients to submit tasks and establish distributed database to store the information of the resource pool. Four desktop computers are used to launch 8 virtual machines with different CPU performance and memory size. We set these 8 virtual machines as execution nodes which are connected by two kinds of networks: 1Mbps and 100Mbps. Each execution node can be initialized to launch 8 workers. The other 2 computers (servers), configured as the service scheduling layer, are responsible for scheduling tasks and selecting resource attribute, and one of them is set up as a backup server in case of malfunction.

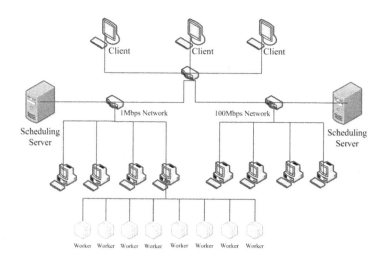

Fig. 2. Experiment Configuration

4.2   Algorithm Input

In order to guarantee the quality of experiment, we select two representative types of tasks: real-time (R) processing and off-line (O) processing.*Real-time task:* Compared to off-line task, R task trends to occupy less storage space and prefers execution nodes with high processing speed, computing capability and wide bandwidth.*Off-line task:* Relatively, O task inclines to occupy more storage space and prefers execution nodes with high processing speed, computing capability and large storage space. We set task sleep-1 and sleep-60 as R-type task and O-type task respectively. The proportion of resource properties is presented in Table 1.

Table 1. Proportion of Resource Attributes

	Computing capability	Storage space	Network bandwidth
Real-time(R)	50%	20%	30%
Offline(O)	30%	35%	35%

We launch 8, 16, 32 and 64 workers to test the throughput and load balance of our algorithm based on Gearman scheduling framework, and the task number is set as 50, 100, 200 and 400. Then we compare the execution time, throughput and resource utilization rate of several scheduling frameworks including Falkon, Gearman, Sparrow and RAS. Table 2 describes the configuration of the 8 execution nodes and the suitable task type for each execution node.

Table 2. Description of Execution Node(STT: Suitable Task Type)

	CPU	GPU	RAM	Storage	Bandwidth	STT
1	1.0GHz	512MB	512MB	20GB	1Mbps	O
2	1.0GHz	512MB	512MB	100GB	100Mbps	R
3	1.8GHz	1GB	512MB	50GB	1Mbps	O
4	1.8GHz	1GB	512MB	100GB	100Mbps	O
5	1.8GHz	512MB	1GB	20GB	100Mbps	R
6	2.0GHz	512MB	2GB	20GB	1Mbps	R
7	2.4GHz	1GB	1GB	50GB	1Mbps	O
8	2.8GHz	1GB	4GB	50GB	100Mbps	R

4.3   Execution Time Comparison

To evaluate the execution time of these five different frameworks, we launch 64 workers to execute tasks. We successively generate 50, 100, 200 and 400 tasks of two types (sleep-1 and sleep-60) and dispatch to the five scheduling frameworks. Then record the time when these tasks complete.

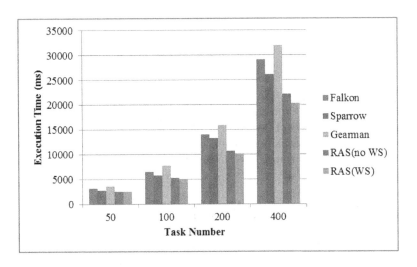

Fig. 3. Execution Time Comparison

As shown in Fig. 3, the execution time of five kinds of scheduling frameworks increases with the number of tasks. When the number of tasks is 50 or 100, except Gearman, the execution times of Falkon, Sparrow and RAS do not show significant difference over each other. As the number of tasks keeps increasing, RAS (WS) seems to be more efficient than other frameworks, nearly 37% faster than Gearman, and 23% faster than Sparrow.

4.4   Throughput Comparison

We randomly generate 1000 of sleep-0 tasks and send them to the five algorithms to execute. We record the number of tasks dispatched by each algorithm per unit time.

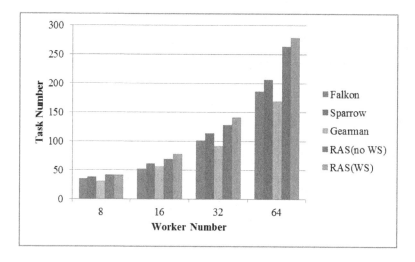

Fig. 4. Throughput Comparison

As shown in Fig. 4, the throughput of the RAS (WS) is higher than the other five frameworks regardless of the number of workers, and the throughput of the RAS (WS) reaches 279 tasks per second when the number of workers increased to 64. Compared to Gearman, the throughput is clearly improved and about 65% higher.

4.5   Resource Utilization Comparison

We randomly generate 200 tasks of two types (sleep-1 and sleep-60) and send them to the five algorithms to execute. We record the proportion of task executing time and the total executing time of all the tasks. In the experiment, the definition of resource utilization is the proportion of task executing time and the total executing time of all the tasks.

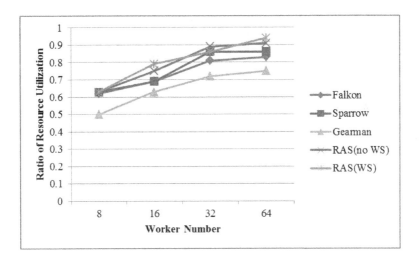

Fig. 5. Resource Utilization Comparison

Resource utilization of the five frameworks are between 0.5 and 0.63 when the number of workers is small, as illustrated in Fig. 5.The rate of the five scheduling frameworks rises with the number of workers. And when the number of workers reaches 64, the utilization rate of RAS (WS) can reach 0.94, higher than all the other frameworks. RAS(no WS) is the second best, which shows that our scheduling algorithm based on resource selection achieves better resource utilization, and work-stealing can further improve load balance across execution nodes.

From the above experiments, we observe that our task scheduling algorithm based on resource attribute selection can improve execution time, throughput and resource utilization compared with other scheduling frameworks such as Falkon, Sparrow and Gearman. Our algorithm can adapt to changing resource conditions dynamically and also better load balance execution nodes with work stealing algorithm.

5   Conclusion

This paper describes an advanced task scheduling algorithm based on resource attribute selection and work-stealing. It can take full advantage of computer resource to schedule tasks faster and more efficient. With the comparison with other scheduling frameworks such as Falkon, Gearman and Sparrow, RAS seems to be more efficient and can achieve higher computing resource utilization rate. Nevertheless, there are still much to improve: the tasks introduced in the experiments did not cover all the possible situations in practical environment, and using dichotomy to realize the task-stealing strategy was not proved to be better than addition, multiplication or exponent method. In future studies, we will focus on how to improve the load balance, increase the efficiency of resource allocation and extend and compare the strategies of task scheduling; we will also look at a broader set of resource attributes, and model the tasks with more realistic requirements such as input/output file sizes.

Acknowledgments. The research was partially supported by National Natural Science Foundation of China Grant 61272528, 61073175, 61035004 and 61150110486.

References

1. Foster, I., Zhao, Y., Raicu, I., et al.: Cloud computing and grid computing 360-degree compared. In: Proceedings of the 2008 Grid Computing Environments Workshop, pp. 1–10. IEEE Computer Society, Washington, DC (2008)
2. Ilavarasan, E., Thambidurai, P., Mahilmannan, R.: Performance effective task scheduling algorithm for heterogeneous computing system. In: Proceedings of the Fourth International Symposium on Parallel and Distributed Computing, Lille, France, pp. 28–38 (2005)
3. Beman, F., Fox, G., Tony, H.: Grid Computing-making the Global Infrastructure a Reality, pp. 65–80. John Wiley and Sons Ltd, USA (2003)
4. Zhao, Y., Raicu, I., Foster, I.: Scientific Workflow Systems for 21st Century e-Science, New Bottle or New Wine?, Invited Paper. In: IEEE Workshop on Scientific Workflows 2008, Co-located with IEEE International Conference on Services Computing, SCC (2008)
5. Zhao, Y., Raicu, I., Foster, I., et al.: Realizing Fast, Scalable and Reliable Scientific Computations in Grid Environments. In: Grid Computing Research Progress. Nova Publisher (2008) ISBN: 978-1-60456-404-4
6. Raicu, I., Zhao, Y., Dumitrescu, C., Foster, I., Wilde, M.: Falkon: A Fast and Light-weight tasK executiON Framework. IEEE/ACM SC (2007)
7. Gearman (2013), http://gearman.org/
8. Ousterhout, K., Wendell, P., Zaharia, M., Stoica, I.: Batch Sampling: Low Overhead Scheduling for Sub-Second Parallel Jobs. Under Submission
9. Zaharia, M., Chowdhury, M., Das, T., Dave, A., Ma, J., McCauley, M., Franklin, M.J., Shenker, S., Stoica, I.: Resilient Distributed Datasets: A Fault-Tolerant Abstraction for In-Memory Cluster Computing. In: Proc. NSDI (2012)
10. Hindman, B., Konwinski, A., Zaharia, M., Ghodsi, A., Joseph, A.D., Katz, R.H., Shenker, S., Stoica, I.: Mesos: A platform for ne-grained resource sharing in the data center. Technical Report UCB/EECS-2010-87, EECS Department, University of California, Berkeley (2010)
11. YARN (2013), http://hadoop.apache.org/docs/current/hadoop-yarn/hadoop-yarn-site/YARN.html
12. Liu, C., Zhao, Z., Liu, F.: An Insight into the Architecture of Condor - A Distributed Scheduler. In: International Symposium on Computer Network and Multimedia Technology, CNMT 2009, pp. 1–4 (2009)
13. Tannenbaum, T., Wright, D., Miller, K., Livny, M.: Condor - A Distributed Job Scheduler. In: Sterling, T. (ed.) Beowulf Cluster Computing with Linux. The MIT Press (2002) ISBN: 0-262-69274-0

14. Thain, D., Tannenbaum, T., Livny, M.: Distributed Computing in Practice: The Condor Experience. Concurrency and Computation: Practice and Experience 17(2-4), 323–356 (2005)
15. Coleman, N.: Distributed Policy Specification and Interpretation with Classified Advertisements. In: Russo, C., Zhou, N.-F. (eds.) PADL 2012. LNCS, vol. 7149, pp. 198–211. Springer, Heidelberg (2012)
16. HTCondor (2013), http://research.cs.wisc.edu/htcondor/
17. Ousterhout, K., Wendell, P., Zaharia, M., Stoica, I.: Sparrow: Scalable Scheduling for Sub-Second Parallel Jobs. Technical Report No. UCB/EECS-2013-29 (2013)
18. LSF (2013), http://en.wikipedia.org/wiki/Platform_LSF
19. Xu, M.Q.: Effective metacomputing using LSF Multicluster. In: Proceedings of the First IEEE/ACM International Symposium on Cluster Computing and the Grid, pp. 100–105 (2001)
20. Costen, F., Brooke, J., Pettipher, M.: Investigation to make best use of LSF with high efficiency. In: Proceedings of the 1st IEEE Computer Society International Workshop on Cluster Computing, Melbourne, Vic, pp. 211–220 (1999)
21. Day, E., Aker, B.: Gearman: Bringing the Power of Map/Reduce to Everyday Applications (Slides). In: OSCON 2009 (2009)
22. Kaya, K., Aykanat, C.: Iterative-Improvement-Based Heuristics for Adaptive Scheduling of Tasks Sharing Files on Heterogeneous Master-Slave Environments. IEEE Transactions on Parallel and Distributed Systems 17(8), 883–896 (2006)
23. He, X., Sun, X., von Laszewski, G.: QoS guided Min-Min heuristic for grid task scheduling. Journal of Computer Science and Technology 18(4), 442–451 (2003)
24. Yanchun, W.: On Gene Expression Programming Algorithm and its Application. Computer Applications and Software 27(6), 23–26 (2010)
25. Abdulal, W., Ramachandram, S.: Reliability-Aware Scheduling Based on a Novel Simulated Annealing in Grid. In: 2012 Fourth International Conference on Computational Intelligence and Communication Networks (CICN), pp. 665–670 (2012)
26. Lu, B., Zhang, H.: Grid Load Balancing Scheduling Algorithm Based on Statistics Thinking. In: The 9th International Conference for Young Computer Scientists, pp. 288–292 (2008)
27. Ku-Mahamud, K.R., Nasir, H.J.A.: Ant Colony Algorithm for Job Scheduling in Grid Computing. In: 2010 Fourth Asia International Conference on Mathematical/Analytical Modelling and Computer Simulation (AMS), pp. 40–45 (2010)
28. Darmawan, I., Kuspriyanto; Priyana, Y., Joseph, M.I.: Grid computing process improvement through computing resource scheduling using genetic algorithm and Tabu Search integration. In: 2012 7th International Conference on Telecommunication Systems, Services, and Applications (TSSA), pp. 330–334 (2012)

A Model-Driven Service Integrated Framework Based on Three-Layer Ontology

Zijia Liu, Hongming Cai, and Lihong Jiang

School of Software, Shanghai Jiao Tong University, Shanghai, China
lleaq@hotmail.com, {cai-hm,jiang-lh}@cs.sjtu.edu.cn

Abstract. The misunderstanding of business models and the inefficiency of service integration impede the business process management and cause inconvenience to enterprise operations, especially in the Internet era. In this paper, a model-driven service integrated framework based on three-layer ontology is proposed to manage the processes and web services in a comprehensive and semantically way. It covers four phases of business process management, including designing, management, execution and feedback. The proposed ontology consists of three layers: the general ontology for business process modeling, the domain ontology for a domain-specific modeling and the scene ontology for a certain business scene. With the ontology's capability of finding correlations and automatic reasoning, the framework unifies the semantics of business process models, supports the transformation from models to services, promotes the service integration, facilitates the automation of process execution and ensures the sustainability.

Keywords: Three-layer Ontology, Model-driven, Business Process Management, Standardization, Automation, Service Integration.

1 Introduction

The growth of the cloud computing has brought significant changes in the field of information technology. Cloud computing is an on-demand pattern for web resources, which involving provider and consumer. It has brought the participants in both business and IT field to a new wide collaborative environment. Business Process Management (BPM) is a "holistic management" approach which makes a great contribution to promoting the effectiveness of an organization [1]. Business Process Modeling focuses on the designing phase of the BPM. It is the foundation of Model-Driven Development (MDD), which establish the link between the business experts and IT developers. Web service is a distributed component for a specific execution task. It is a technology based on Service-oriented Architecture (SOA), which ensures the interoperability among the different Internet-based platforms. Web services are responsible for the execution phase of BPM.

The life-cycle of the enterprise operation includes the proposition, designing, development, deployment and maintenance of strategic objects. With the popularity of cloud computing, more and more operators are involved in enterprise operation, they have different professional backgrounds and may come from different organizations,

M. Pathan, G. Wei, and G. Fortino (Eds.): IDCS 2013, LNCS 8223, pp. 120–133, 2013.
© Springer-Verlag Berlin Heidelberg 2013

including business experts, model designers, managers, developers and customers. It is difficult for them to reach a consensus on the meaning of the business process models without any technical support. Moreover, the trend of collaborative modeling increases the chance of making more mistakes. Since a large number of web services are available on the internet, the loose semantically connection between models and services impedes the effectiveness of service execution. Many problems may occur during the service integration, just like the incompleteness of service discovery, the inaccuracy of service selection and the inflexibility of service composition. The misunderstanding of the business models, the lack of automation and the inefficiency of service integration hinder the progress of MDD, increase the difficulty of enterprise resource management and decrease the effectiveness of enterprise operation.

In this paper, a framework is proposed based on three-layer ontology. It covers four phases in enterprise operation, including business process modeling, business model management, process execution and feedback. The framework uses ontology to provide a specification that covers the whole life cycle of building and managing business models and web services. It also uses the semantic relationships to strengthen the communication among the business models and support the transformation from models to services. In addition, the reasoning technology can make contribution to the discovery, selection, composition and execution of the models and services. Finally, the information feedback can be used to enrich the ontology to ensure the sustainability of our framework.

The paper is organized as follows: the related work is given in section 2; the overview of the framework is presented in section 3; Section 4 describes the three-layer ontology. The integrated management methodology based on the proposed framework for business process management and service integration is discussed in section 5. In order to verify the availability of our framework, a case study in logistics domain is shown in section 6, and we also compare our method with another solution in this section. The conclusion is drawn in section 7.

2   Related Work

Semantic Business Process (SBP) is one of the most important research subjects to cope with the misunderstanding of business models and services. It combines the ontology with business process, to cover semantic relationships and meanings of components more properly [2]. Nicola [3] presents an ontological approach to Business Process Modeling and proposed a Business Process Abstract Language (BPAL) to eliminate the misunderstanding. Rospocher [4] presents a framework that supports business analysts in the collaborative specification and annotation of business processes. [5] constructs an logistics distribution domain ontology and add semantics to business process to cover the gaps between operators.

Ruokolainen [6] presents a domain ontology that provides the knowledge elements needed for service integration. Asuncion [7] separates the business rules from the business process to promote the flexibility of service integration. Heller [8] presents a service integration framework with a pattern-based modeling approach to enhance the extensibility of enterprise systems.

Simply binding semantic and business process is not enough. Without an appropriate architecture and a suitable framework, the BPM can still be difficult and complex. Khalaj [9] presents a style-based semantic framework for business process modeling. He uses the Architecture Styles to structure the concepts and to realize the cooperation of components. His approach can help the service provider to build a more comprehensive and automatic-executable process. As several approaches have been raised to deal with the misunderstanding in the enterprise operation and promote the service integration, some achievements have been reached. However, most of them have not presented a holistic framework that covers the whole life cycle of the BPM yet.

3   The Model-Driven Service Integrated Framework

The framework is shown in Fig. 1. It is based on Three-Layer Ontology and presents a specification for the modeling, management, execution and feedback phase of business process. It can effectively eliminate the misunderstanding among the business process operators and promote the efficiency of service integration.

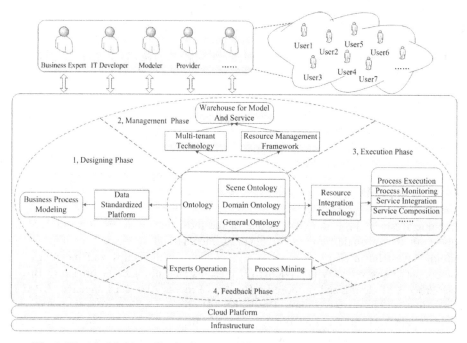

Fig. 1. The Model-driven Service Integrated Framework Based on Three-Layer Ontology

The proposed Three-Layer Ontology consists of three layers: the general ontology for business process modeling, the domain ontology for a domain-specific modeling and the scene ontology for a certain business scene. The details of the Three-Layer Ontology will be discussed in the next section. The framework cover four phase as follows:

Designing Phase: The general ontology covers the four aspects of business process modeling: information entity, organization, functionality and control flow. The domain ontology covers the common concepts and relationships in certain domain. This framework provides a specification for collaborative business modeling, which ensures the comprehensiveness of the business models as well as the comprehensibility and consistency in semantic level.

Management Phase: In this phase, a business process model repository is responsible for the storage and management of business models and services, which is based on the multi-tenant architecture. A multi-view management is presented to ensure the intelligent management for models and services of each tenant. Models and web services in each tenant are assigned to four views: information view, organization view, function view and control view. Basing on the relationship of each view, an intelligent model management can be realized.

Execution Phase: This framework supports process execution, which includes the integration of enterprise resources, the orchestration of complex processes and the selection, mapping, composition, management of services effectively. It also supports the SOA by realizing the transformation from business models to web services. Considering the semantic relationship and reasoning ability of ontology, the consistency and automated execution is ensured.

Feedback Phase: Considering the scalability and sustainability of the framework, the information extracted from the real operation and knowledge obtained by process mining will be used as feedback to enrich the ontology. With the continuous optimization of ontology, our framework will be more suitable for the industry specification and satisfy the rapid changing of enterprise demand.

4   Three-Layer Ontology Model

4.1   General Ontology

After researching several specifications in business modeling, including ARIS, BPMN, EPC, we propose a general ontology for business process modeling, which is shown in Fig. 2. We divide the business model into four views: information view, organization view, function view and control view.

   Information view covers relevant business entities throughout enterprise operations. It is the foundation of business modeling. Information object is the core of information view. Each object contains identifier, attributes and states.

   Organization view defines the hierarchical structures and functional divisions of involved organizations, which includes companies, departments and roles. Root node is company, which is represented by the name of the organization. Department is a fine-grained node, divided by the different functionality. Role is the leaf node of the structure which represents the responsibility assigned to the employee.

   Function view describes the function point related to the business process execution. Each function point represents an atomic operation with some parameters. Input

Object is the input required by the function point. Output Object is the result of the function. Reference Object is limited in the process and invisible externally.

Control view describes the procedure to achieve certain business purpose. Process consists of task, action, event and router. Task is an abstract definition of functional division of a process. Action is an atomic functional operation to complete a task. Event represents a state of information object before or after an action. Router represents the branch structure of process which includes XOR-Split, OR-Split, AND-Split, XOR-Join, OR-Join and AND-Join.

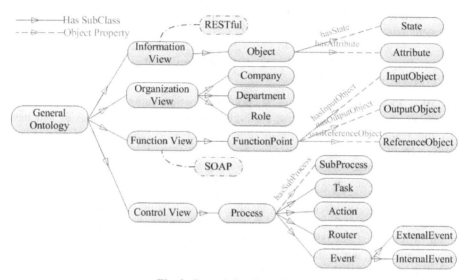

Fig. 2. General Ontology Model

4.2   Domain Ontology

Domain ontology is the ontology for a specified domain which describes the concepts, relationships and constraint. As Fig. 3 shown, we propose the core concepts and relationships related to a domain model.

Basic Information (BI) is the information that used to describe and measure other information in the domain. It consists of attribute, type, state and measure. Attribute is the basic, inalienable character of an object. Type represents classification of the object and the classification method may accord to different standards and patterns. An object must be in a certain state at one point of time, and its state may change under certain circumstance. Measure is used to measure an object in a standard way.

Stakeholder represents groups and people related to the domain. It consists of Organization and Person.

Business Object (BO) is domain-specified entity. It is the most important part of the domain model which distinguishes the domain from others. Real Object is the thing that actually exists in the domain. Abstract Object defines the general characteristics of objects, and it represents a set of objects with common feature, while Real Object represents existing object.

Process represents a procedure in order to achieve a business objective. It consists of Task, Action and Rule. Task is a coarse-grained division of a process. Action is atomic execution step. Rule is the business process logic which defines the selection constraints and operation standards in specific conditions.

Event is a notable occurrence caused by external operation or internal transfer rule.

Environment is a set of characteristic vector used to describe the business objects' context. It includes Natural Environment and Unnatural Environment. The former includes time, location and temperature, and the latter includes social institution, culture, legal norm and so on.

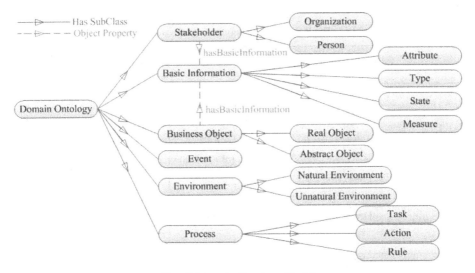

Fig. 3. Domain Ontology Model

4.3   Scene Ontology

Scene is a projection of a real world in specific space-time. It is a combination of a set of information in different dimensions. The scene ontology is shown in Fig. 4.

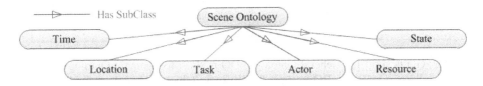

Fig. 4. Scene Ontology Model

Time and **Location** defines when and where that the scene occurs.

Task indicates the process node when the scene occurs.

Actor is the person who is responsible for the task in this scene.

Resource represents all the information objects that related with this scene.

State is the situation of the related resources and task in this scene.

4.4   Relationships between the Three Ontologies

The three ontologies mentioned above focus on the different dimensions of BPM respectively. However, the real enterprise operation is a complex combination which covers many aspects of BPM. The knowledge in a domain is always applied to business process modeling. And a scene projection of process execution is composed of the information extracted from business models, domain knowledge and surroundings. The overall consideration of business modeling technology, domain knowledge and real scene information should be paid attention to ensure the availability and flexibility of business models. The relationships between three ontologies are shown in Table 1.

Table 1. The Relationships between the three ontologies

General Ontology			Domain Ontology			Scene Ontology
Information View	Object		Business Object			Resource
	State		Basic Information	State		State
	Attribute			Attribute		
				Measure		
Organization View	Company		Stakeholder	Organization		
	Department					
	Role			Person		Actor
Function View	Function Point		Process	Action		
Control View	Process	Action				
		Task		Task		Task
		Router		Rule		
		Event	Event			
			Environment		Time	
					Location	

Here, GO is short for General Ontology; DO is short for Domain Ontology; SO is short for Scene Ontology. BO is short for Business Object; BI is short for Basic Information; FP is short for Function Point.

• Relationships between GO and DO

GO_Object ⊆ DO_BO; GO_Attribute ⊆ DO_BI_Attribute ∪ DO_BI_Measure; GO_State ⊆ DO_BI_State; GO_Com ⊆ DO_Stakeholder_Org where Org refers to a company; GO_Dep ⊆ DO_Stakeholder_Org where Org refers to functional division in the company; GO_Role ⊆ DO_Stakeholder_Person where Person refers to the employee in the company; (GO_FP == GO_Pro_Action) $\subseteq$ DO_Pro_Action $\cup$ DO_BO $\cup$ DO_Stakeholder_Person when resources and actors should be taken into consideration; GO_Pro_Task $\subseteq$ DO_Pro_Task; GO_Pro_Router $\subseteq$ DO_Pro_Rule; GO_Pro_Event $\subseteq$ DO_Event $\cup$ DO_Environment when the factors in Environment, just like time and location, should be taken into consideration

- Relationships between GO, DO and SO

A scene is a projection of the real operation. It is composed by the information extracted from GO and DO.

SO_Res $\subseteq$ GO_Object $\cup$ DO_BO; SO_Actor $\subseteq$ GO_Role $\cup$ DO_Person; SO_Task $\subseteq$ GO_Pro_Task $\cup$ DO_Pro_Task; SO_State $\subseteq$ GO_State $\cup$ DO_BI_State; SO_Time $\in$ DO_Environment_Time; SO_Location $\in$ DO_Environment_Location

The general ontology presents a standard for business modeling. The domain ontology gives a specification for the related industry and it is replaceable to ensure the flexibility of our framework. The scene ontology proposes a guidance to extract useful information from an enterprise operation. The reasoning relationship and loose coupling of the three-layer ontology ensures the universality, professionality, usability and flexibility of our framework.

5   A Methodology for BPM and Service Integration

5.1   Collaborative Business Process Modeling

We propose a semi-automatic Collaborative Business Modeling Architecture (CoBMA) based on the three-layer ontology and map the structure of the general ontology into the modules of the CoBMA. The concepts from the domain ontology can be used to build the business models. The CoBMA is an internet-based architecture that people in different places can edit the business models collaboratively through the internet. The modeling approach contains four steps:

Step 1: Building Information View Model
Considering that information object is the base of the business modeling, the information view should be modeled first. According to the ontological definition of the information object, the Identifier, Attribute and State of the information object are modeled. An information object can be used as a complex attribute of another. The relationship between information objects includes aggregation and composition.

The business object defined in domain ontology can be used as a reference to model information view. Some general information objects and their relationships are given automatically and modeling staff can modify the details on-demand.

Step 2: Building Organization View Model
According to the definition of organization view in general ontology, the organization model is structured in tree hierarchy. The root node is company, followed by department, and role is the leaf node. The information about the organization and person in domain ontology is useful in modeling the organization view. User can choose the

elements provided by the system automatically and modify on-demand, instead of building all the elements manually.

Step 3: Building Function View Model

The information of actions defined in domain ontology is extracted and the general function points corresponded to the actions can be provided automatically when we build function model. The input object, output object and reference object related to the function point can be selected from the information model directly.

Step 4: Building Control View Model

The control view model represents the workflow of business process. The Action in the control view model is the function point defined in the function model. The Actor who is responsible for an action corresponds to the role in the organization model. And the event is related to the state of an information object. All the elements in control view model can be selected from other models directly.

Basing on the three-layer ontology, a semi-automatic business process architecture is proposed. The element in each model has a knowledge support and can be built semi-automatically. The completeness and consistency of the models are ensured by the relationship of ontologies and the reduction of manual operation. A collision detection mechanism is presented to avoid the collisions caused by users' behaviors.

5.2   The Transformation from Model to Service

The business models and services belong to the different phase of BPM. The former is focused on the process design and the latter concerns more about the process execution. By transforming business model to service, we can fill the gap between the process design and service execution, and benefit the service integration.

Table 2. The Mapping Rules from Model to Service

	WSDL	Function View
Type	ComplexType	FunctionPoint:Name +"Ele"
	Element	Input:Name
Message	Name	Input:Name + "Input"
		Output:Name + "Output"
	Part	Input:Name + "Request"
		Output:Name + "Response"
PortType	Name	FunctionPoint:Name +"PortType"
	Operation	FunctionPoint:Name
	Input	Input:Name + "Input"
	Output	Output:Name + "Output"
Binding	Name	FunctionPoint:Name +"Binding"
	Operation	FunctionPoint:Name

The Web Services Description Language (WSDL) [10] is an XML-based language that is used for describing the functionality of a web service. The core elements of WSDL include Types, Message, PortType and Binding. The mapping rules from model to service are given in Table 2.

The basic mapping rules are given in Table 2. However, considering the complex relationships between the models, the superficial transformation from the model to service will result in the information loss. How to ensure the completeness and consistency of the information during the transformation is challenge that should be overcome. Fortunately, the framework based on three-layer ontology proposed in this paper can cope with this problem efficiently. A reasoning engine is presented to extract all the related information from different models based on the relationship and reasoning ability of ontology.

5.3   Process Execution and Monitoring

The process execution is based on the collaboration of services. The reasoning engine can be used to support the selection, composition and execution of web services by reasoning the semantic association relationships between the business models and services.

The traditional method of process monitoring is to analyze the process execution log. However, only by parsing the log file, some useful information may be difficult to detect from massive irrelevant information. Therefore, we present the scene ontology to record the information during the process execution. It defines the core information of a real operation in six dimensions: time, location, actor, resource, task and event. It is very helpful to promote the efficiency of process mining by focusing on the core information and ignoring the useless parts.

The knowledge obtained by process mining can be used to eliminate the bottleneck of the process execution and optimize the business process modeling. Additionally, the feedbacks can be used to enrich the three-layer ontology as well.

6   Case Study and Discussion

6.1   Case Study

In this section, we choose a logistics resource integrated platform as an example to represent the usability and availability of our framework.

(1)Collaborative Business Process Modeling

We built a logistics ontology by using the Protégé as shown in Fig. 5(A).

Four object properties are defined to associate the elements of domain ontology with the general ontology :

- hasBelongToInformationView
- hasBelongToOrganizationView
- hasBelongToFunctionView
- hasBelongToControlView

Basing on the general ontology, we developed a Collaborative Multi-View Business Modeling Application (CoMBMA), which is an Internet-based application and supports SOA. The business models are built in four views: information view, organization view, function view and control view. According to the modeling rule presented in the previous section, association relationships are built. The input, output and reference objects in function view are imported from information view. All the elements in control view are imported from other views. The meta-data defined by the logistics ontology is provided to the modelers automatically through the collaborative modeling engine. The business models built by CoMBMA are shown in Fig. 5(B).

Considering semantic relationship and reasoning ability of ontology, the CoMBMA ensures the consistency and comprehensibility of the business models and covers the gaps between the business experts and IT developers.

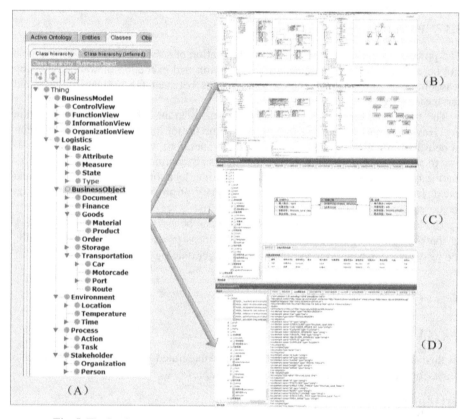

Fig. 5. The Implementation of the Proposed Framework in Logistics Domain

(2)Business Model Repository for Multi-tenant

The Business Model Repository for Multi-tenant (BMRM) provides the capability of storing and managing business models and services in the multi-tenant architecture of cloud platform. The BMRM provides the functionality, including the intelligent management of models and services, version control, modification management and service registering. We present a multi-view management framework which includes information view, organization view, function view and control view. As Fig. 5(C) shown, each tenant's models are placed into four views with a certain version tag.

According to the semantic relationship between models and services, a heterogeneous service integrated searching engine is built to ensure the completeness and accuracy of semantic searching, based on domain ontology and their association relationship based on general ontology,

(3)Service Transformation

By analyzing the information from relevant view models, we extract the information needed to build web service. After some operations and configurations mentioned in previous section, we transform the business models to service. It benefits the subsequent service integration. As Fig. 5(D) shown, the relevant WSDL file is generated automatically. We can also transform the multi-view models into WADL, BPMN and BPEL to satisfy the different business demand.

(4)Service Integration

The enterprise resources scattered in a heterogeneous environment can be integrated effectively by our framework. The semantic association and reasoning ability provided by the three-layer ontology promote the efficiency of process execution and service integration. It benefits the integration of enterprise resources, complex processes choreography and the selection, matching, composition and management of services. By extracting the information of process execution based on scene ontology, the bottleneck of process execution and the imperfection of the ontology can be explored through process mining and data analysis. The feedbacks can be used to optimize the business process design and enrich the ontology. The continuous optimization ensures the sustainability of the framework.

6.2 Discussion

In order to have a better understanding of our framework, we will compare Khalaj's style-based semantic framework [9] with ours in seven dimensions: Applicable scope, Covered aspects, Method, Related Domain, Support for business modeling, Support for service integration and Sustainability. The result is given in Table 3.

The style-based semantic framework is focused on the management of business process, while our approach covers the designing, management, execution and feedback phase of BPM. The semantic framework only concerns the process model, while our framework covers the four aspects of an enterprise. Khalaj's method is based on Architectures Styles and our approach is based on Three-Layer Ontology. Both of the two methods have good flexibility. Khalaj stores and retrieves the domain ontology in a warehouse, while the domain ontology in our framework is replaceable. In addition to adding semantic to business models as Khalaj does, we present a semi-automatic Collaborative Business Modeling Architecture. We use the reasoning ability of ontology to promote the efficiency of service integration, while Khalaj pays little attention to it. In the sustainability aspect, Khalaj's method can discovery new semantic relationships and constraints between business processes, while our method uses the knowledge extracted by process mining as feedbacks to enrich the three-layer ontology.

Table 3. Comparison with Style-based Semantic Framework

Feature	Style-based Semantic Framework	Our Method
Applicable Scope	Focus on the management of business process	Cover the designing, management, execution and feedback phase of BPM
Covered Aspects	Process Model	Information view, Organization view, Function view, Control view
Method	Based on Architecture Styles	Based on Three-Layer Ontology
Related Domain	Store and retrieve the domain ontology in a warehouse	Domain ontology is replaceable
Support for Business Modeling	Add semantic to business process	Present a semi-automatic Collaborative Business Modeling Architecture and add semantic to business models
Support for Service Integration	Pay little attention to service integration	The reasoning ability of three-layer ontology can promote the efficiency of service integration
Sustainability	Can discovery new semantic relationships and constraints between business processes	Use information feedback to enrich the ontology continuously

We can find out that the contributions of our research are obviously. The proposed framework presents a comprehensive, flexible and scalable approach to overcome the ambiguity and lack of automation for the whole life cycle of business process management. We concern the comprehensive aspects of business models, while most approaches only focus on process model. The relationship of three-layer ontology ensure the consensus and automation of business process and eliminate the misunderstandings effectively. The replaceability of domain ontology ensures the flexibility of our framework. The transformation from model to service is presented to fill the gap between the process design and execution. And the reasoning ability of ontology promotes the effectiveness of service integration. Moreover, we ensure the sustainability by using the feedback to enrich the three-layer ontology continuously.

7   Conclusion and Future Work

The misunderstanding of business process models, the lack of automation and the inefficiency of service integration have brought many inconveniences in enterprise operations. This paper presents a framework based on three-layer ontology to manage the business models and promote service integration. It covers four phases of business process management, including designing, management, execution and feedback. The general, domain and scene ontology support the whole lifecycle of BPM in an efficient way. The semantic relationships in ontologies strengthen the relationship between the multi-view models, and ensure the consistency of the models and services. Moreover, along with reasoning ability, they benefit the execution of the business process and the service integration. We also realize the transformation from the business process models to services so as to improve automation. In the feedback phase, the information obtained by process mining can be used to enrich the ontology and achieve the sustainability of the framework.

Our future work will focus on the transformation from the different modeling standards to our framework. One key problem will be how to make sure of the consistency and semantic completeness of the transformation operation. Moreover, the improvement of automation will be taken into consideration.

Acknowledgement. This research is supported by Shanghai Natural Science Foundation (No. 13ZR1419800), the National Natural Science Foundation of China under Grant No.71171132.

References

1. Rosemann, M.: Handbook on Business Process Management 2: Strategic Alignment, Governance, People and Culture. Springer, Heidelberg (2010)
2. Lautenbacher, F., Bauer, B., Seitz, C.: Semantic business process modeling-benefits and capability. In: AAAI 2008 Stanford Spring Symposium-AI Meets Business Rules and Process Management (AIBR). Stanford University, California (2008)
3. De Nicola, A., Lezoche, M., Missikoff, M.: An ontological approach to business process modeling. In: Proceedings of IICAI 2007 (2007)
4. Rospocher, M., Di Francescomarino, C., Ghidini, C., Serafini, L., Tonella, P.: Collaborative specification of semantically annotated business processes. In: Rinderle-Ma, S., Sadiq, S., Leymann, F., et al. (eds.) BPM 2009. LNBIP, vol. 43, pp. 305–317. Springer, Heidelberg (2010)
5. Meng, X.L., He, F., Sun, L.L.: Research on Semantic Business Process Model in Logistics Distribution Field. Applied Mechanics and Materials 198, 899–904 (2012)
6. Ruokolainen, T., Kutvonen, L.: Managing interoperability knowledge in open service ecosystems. In: 13th IEEE Enterprise Distributed Object Computing Conference Workshops, EDOCW 2009, pp. 203–211 (2009)
7. Asuncion, C.H., Iacob, M., van Sinderen, M.J.: Towards a flexible service integration through separation of business rules. In: 2010 14th IEEE International on Enterprise Distributed Object Computing Conference (EDOC), pp. 184–193. IEEE (2010)
8. Heller, M., Allgaier, M.: Model-based service integration for extensible enterprise systems with adaptation patterns. In: Proceedings of the 2010 International Conference on e-Business (ICE-B), pp. 1–6. IEEE (2010)
9. Khalaj, M.E., Moaven, S., Habibi, J., et al.: A Semantic Framework for Business Process Modeling Based on Architecture Styles. In: 2012 IEEE/ACIS 11th International Conference on Computer and Information Science (ICIS), pp. 513–520. IEEE (2012)
10. Christensen, E., Curbera, F., Meredith, G., et al.: Web services description language (WSDL) 1.1 (2001)

An Improved Collaborative Filtering Approach Based on User Ranking and Item Clustering

Wenlong Li[1,2] and Wei He[1,2]

[1] School of Computer Science and Technology Shandong University, Jinan, 250101, China
[2] Shandong Provincial Key Laboratory of Software Engineering, Jinan, 250101, China

Abstract. Collaborative filtering is one of the most successful technologies applied in recommender systems in multiple domains. With the increasing growth of users and items involved in recommender systems, some inherent weaknesses of traditional collaborating filtering such as ratings data sparsity, new user problems become more and more manifest. We believe that one of the most important sources of these problems is the deficiency of user similarities based on all users and items in authenticity and accuracy. In this paper, we propose an improved collaborative filtering method based on user ranking and item clustering, in which the users are classified and ranked in multiple item clusters by computing their rating qualities based on the previous rating records, and items are recommended for target users according to their similar users with high-ranks in different item categories. Experiments on real world data sets have demonstrated the effectiveness of our approach.

Keywords: recommender system, collaborative filtering, user ranking, item clustering.

1 Introduction

With the development of internet applications, information overload problems have become one of the biggest challenges to making good use of mass information. Recommendation systems are approaches for solving this problem, in which collaborative filtering (CF) [1],[2],[2],[14] is one of the most successful technologies. Collaborative filtering works by constructing a preference information database for items and users. For specific target users, their similar users are identified based on their previous selection records and then items are computed and recommended based on the preferences of their similar users.

Collaborative filtering appears in multiple domains including e-commerce, information retrieval etc., and has made a great progress in these fields. Compared with other technologies such as content-based recommender methods [4], [5], CF can improve recommendation qualities and user satisfaction without dependence on item features that may be difficult to be figured out such as music artwork. As collaborative filtering uses the experience of similar users instead of items, it is comprehensive and accurate to the viewpoint of personalized expectations and requirements.

M. Pathan, G. Wei, and G. Fortino (Eds.): IDCS 2013, LNCS 8223, pp. 134–144, 2013.

Nowadays, with the development of internet applications, especially in the domains of e-commerce and information retrieval, the numbers of users and items are much more than before. The disadvantages of collaborative filtering systems has appeared and become more evident than before, including problems of rating sparsity, new users and new items which leads to low accuracy of recommendation problems. How to improve the performance and accuracy has become more important than ever before.

In this paper, we propose an improved collaborative filtering algorithm(ICF) to handle the problems of current recommendation methods. In our approach, the users are classified and ranked according to their previous evaluating records and the actual choosing data. Considering that the professional user can make a accurate judgment about new items, we can make use of professional user to solve the new items problem. Then, an improved user similarity model is constructed based on training data set. Finally, several recommendation methods are proposed and will be applied to different users with different classifications and ranks to figuring out the recommending items for them. According to the experiment results, our method can efficiently solve some inherent problems of current collaborative filtering systems, such as inaccurate recommending results for new users without enough data to computing their similar users.

The rest of this paper is organized as follows. Section 2 introduces the general CF models. Section 3 proposes our improved collaborative filtering algorithm. Section 4 presents the performance of the algorithm based on MovieLens dataset[12]. Section 5 introduces the related work. Section 6 concludes this paper.

2   Related Work

In this section we briefly present some of the research literature related to collaborative filtering, recommender system.

User-Item subgroups [7] propose a unified framework to extend the traditional CF algorithms by utilizing the subgroups information for improving their top-N recommendation performance .Social collaborative filtering [8] recommend items of interest to user in a social network setting. To alleviate the spasity problem, many matrix factorization models are used, such as the Singular Value Decomposition[2], Non-negative Matrix Factorization[9],[10],Maximum Margin Matrix Factorization[11]. These models usually reduce the dimensions of the user-item matrix and smoothing out the noise information, which is also helpful to algorithm scalability. Personality diagnosis [13] is a special kind of hybrid approach which combines memory based and model based CF methods and retains some advantages of both algorithms.

3   The General Collaborative Filtering Model

The computation of user similarity is the basis of any recommendation method based on collaborative filtering ideas. The first step of CF is to construct users' rating matrix based on their previous choosing records. Supposing there are m users and n items, then the users' choosing and rating data for the items is expressed as a $m \times n$ matrix, in which a set with m members denotes the users: $U = \{u_1, u_2, ..., u_m\}$, and similarly the other set $I = \{i_1, i_2, ..., i_n\}$ denotes the items. So we can use $A(m, n)$ to denote the users' rating matrix as following:

Table 1. User rating matrix $A(m, n)$

	$Item_1$	$Item_2$	$Item_3$	......	$Item_n$
$User_1$	R_{11}	R_{12}	R_{13}	......	R_{1n}
$User_2$	R_{21}	R_{22}	R_{23}	......	R_{2n}
$User_3$	R_{31}	R_{32}	R_{33}	......	R_{3n}
......	......	......	......	......	......
$User_m$	R_{m1}	R_{m2}	R_{m3}	......	R_{mn}

In Table 1.user rating matrix, $R_{j,k}$ is the score that u_j rates i_k.

In CF, usually Pearson correlation coefficient [6] is used to compute user similarity. Pearson correlation coefficient is a method which is used to rate the relevance between two vectors. It figures out a digit between -1 and 1. Value 1 represents that two vectors are complete positive correlation, 0 represents they have nothing with each other, and -1 represents that the two vectors are complete negative correlation.

The Pearson function is expressed as :

$$r_{uv} = \frac{\sum_{i \in I_{uv}} (R_{ui} - \overline{R}_u) \times (R_{vi} - \overline{R}_v)}{\sqrt{\sum_{i \in I_{uv}} (R_{ui} - \overline{R}_u)^2} \sqrt{\sum_{i \in I_{uv}} (R_{vi} - \overline{R}_v)^2}} \tag{1}$$

In this function, u, v denote two users, and $u \neq v$; r_{uv} is the similarity between u and v; I_{uv} is the items which both u and v have rated ; R_{ui} is the score user u give item i and R_{vi} is the score user v give item i, $\overline{R}_u$ is the average score about user u in I_{uv}, $\overline{R}_v$ is the average score about user v in I_{uv}.

4   User Ranking and Item Clustering

4.1   Similarity Model

In original CF, user similarity relies on the scores of user rating items, and it can not show out which feature of items a specific user concerns most. That is to say, no matter two users concern on the same features of items or not, if they rate same score for an item, the similarity is the same. Obviously, this is not the expected result. We present a user characteristics based method by classifying users into different ranked clusters according to the user-item matrix, then we use different methods to compute user similarities in different clusters.

4.1.1   The Method of User Classification
First of all, we classify items into different classes by features.

1 : Classifying items method : .

Suppose the items have regular and homogeneous features, and $S = \{s_1, s_2 \dots s_n\}$ is the set of features of items, each property has score, $M = \{m_1, m_2 \dots m_n\}$ is the score set .Each score of the feature ranges in $[0,10]$. We use a threshold h select the items. If most score of features of the item are higher than h, the item is classified into excellent items. Except these items, the other items are classified into class I, If $m_i = MAX\{M\}$.

2 : Classifying users based items method:

We make use of the historical information of user u, considering different classes of items, we count out the times of each class items which user has chosen. The set $N = \{n_1, n_2, \dots n_n\}$ denotes user has chosen class i items n_i times .If a user rating Computing $MAX\{N\}$, then we classify user into the class according to $MAX\{N\}$.

4.1.2   Similarity Based on User Classification
Firstly, we establish user-class matrix, it is a $i \times i$ matrix, we use $B(i,i)$ to represent it:

Table 2. User-class matrix

$user/user$	b_1	b_2	......	b_i
b_1	b_{11}	b_{12}	......	b_{1i}
b_2	b_{21}	b_{22}	......	b_{2i}
......	......	......	......	......
b_i	b_{i1}	b_{i2}	......	b_{ii}

In Table 2 user-class matrix, b_{jk} denotes score between the user of j class and the user of k class. The score between same class users is 1.The score of different users ranges in $[0,1]$.

Computing user similarity :

Based on user rating matrix and user-class matrix computing user similarity

$$r_{uv} = e \times \frac{\sum_{i \in I_{uv}} (R_{ui} - \overline{R}_u) \times (R_{vi} - \overline{R}_v)}{\sqrt{\sum_{i \in I_{uv}} (R_{ui} - \overline{R}_u)^2} \sqrt{\sum_{i \in I_{uv}} (R_{vi} - \overline{R}_v)^2}} \qquad (2)$$

In this function, u and v denote two similar users, e is the score about two users in the user-class matrix. if u is a j class user, v is a k class user, then the value of e is b_{jk}, and $u \neq v$; r_{uv} is the rating similarity between u and v ; I_{uv} is the items which both u and v have rated ; R_{ui} is the score user u gives item i and R_{vi} is the score user v gives item i, $\overline{R}_u$ is the average score about user u in I_{uv}, $\overline{R}_v$ is the average score about user v in I_{uv}.

The method based on user classification can improve the accuracy of user similarity, for example :

Example 1:

We have A, B, C, D 4 items and 4 users, $user_1, user_2, user_3, user_4$. Each item has three features such as brand , quality, price . The value set of the features is (k_1, k_2, k_3). Each value ranges in $[0,10]$. (E.g. Suppose iphone is a perfect phone, every feature of it is good such as brand, quality. So that the value set is (10, 10, 10).) Then we use user rating information to rate the value of item properties.

Assume that the features of A is (10,6,5) (k_1 is 10, k_2 is 6, k_3 is 5).B is (6,10,4). C is (10,10,10). D is (7,4,10). According to classifying items method, the value of k_1 of item A is higher than others. So that item A is k_1 item. B is k_2 item .C is excellent item. D is k_3 item.

User rating matrix is shown in Table 3:

Table 3. User rating matrix

	A	B	C	D
$user_1$	Null	6	10	7
$user_2$	Null	10	10	4
$user_3$	Null	4	10	10
$user_4$	10	Null	10	?

The problem is to compute the score of $user_4$ about item D.

In original method, from user rating matrix, $user_1$, $user_2$, $user_3$, $user_4$ has made same rating to item C, and $user_1$, $user_2$, $user_3$ have only rating the same item C with $user_4$, so that the similarities about $user_1$ and $user_4$, $user_2$ and $user_4$, $user_3$ and $user_4$ are the same.

In our method, according to Table 3, the scores of $user_1$ rating items are same with the scores of k_1 features of items. So we set the $user_1$ is k_1 user. Similarly, $user_2$ is k_2 user, $user_3$ is k_3 user, $user_4$ has only rated item A and C, but C is excellent item, according to the score of $user_4$ rating A, we can make conclusion that $user_4$ is k_1 user, so that $user_4$ is more similar with $user_1$ than others. The score of $user_1$ rating item D is more similar with $user_4$'s. This result is more accurate.

Considering that users may pay more attention to some properties, so that even though two users give same score to an item, they may concern on different properties. In original method, this problem can not be solved. We propose the method based on user characteristics can solve this problem.

4.2   Recommendation Model

New user problem and new item problem exist in original method. And the original method recommend items to the target user only relying on user similarity. But considering that when the target user has little knowledge of those items, his similar users are all the same These users can not make a accurate rating result. So recommendation result based on his similar users will not be satisfied. (E.g. If a user has little knowledge of phones, his similar users may be the same. When he wants to buy a phone, we should make less use of his similar users information).

The method based on excellent user classified users into different level relying on the user historical information. If user is familiar with items in some fields, we will give him a high level in these field. Otherwise we will give him a low level .When recommend items to a low level user, we will make use of more high level users. When recommend items to a high level user, we will make user of more similar users. This method is efficacious to solve new user problem, at the same time, high level user can make a accurate judgment about new items, so new item problem can also be solved. (e.g. if a user has a lot knowledge of mobile phones, he would make a accurate judgment about the new phones) And it can improve the result to low level users.

The method based on excellent user:

We compute the user recommendation success rate and user professional rate in the field to classify users.

4.2.1   Computing User Professional Score

n_j is the total times of u_j recommendation in T field ,if all user recommendation

times in T field is N, The score of u_j rating times is $\dfrac{n_j}{N}$ .We use $\lambda = \dfrac{n_j}{N}$

a_j is the total times of the successful times of u_j recommendation in T .if all

successful times in T field is A .The successful score of u_j is $\dfrac{a_i}{A}$ .We use $\mu = \dfrac{a_i}{A}$.

The user professional score is $p = \lambda \cdot \mu$ 。

4.2.2   User Classification

We classify user into different level dependent on user professional score .The level is proportional to p . The highest level user is excellent user.

The method based on user classification.

Firstly, we need to determine the percentage of the excellent users and similar users for recommending to the target user. The percentage is dependent on p_i ,

The similar user recommendation function:

$$M_{ijk} = r_{ij} \cdot p_j \cdot R_{jk} \tag{3}$$

In this function, r_{ij} is the similarity of u_j and u_i , p_j is the user professional score

of u_j , R_{jk} is the score that u_j rate i_k .

The excellent user recommendation function :

$$M_{ijk} = p_j \cdot R_{jk} \tag{4}$$

$\sum\limits_{j} M_{ijk}$ is the recommendation score for u_i about i_k .

5   Experimental Evaluation

5.1   Data Set

We used data from MovieLens,MovieLens is a web-based research recommender system that debuted in Fall1997. Each week hundreds of users visit MovieLens to rate and receive recommendations for movies. This dataset had 943 rows(i.e., 943 users) and 1682 columns(i.e., 1682 movies that were rated by at least one of the users).

5.2   Evaluation Metrics

Statistical accuracy metrics evaluate the accuracy of a system by comparing the numerical recommendation scores against the actual user ratings for the user-item pairs in the test dataset. Mean Absolute Error (MAE) between ratings and predictions is a widely used metric. $\{p_1, p_2, ..., p_N\}$ is the result of the ratings of N items of recommendation system, and the real user-rating score is $\{r_1, r_2, ..., r_N\}$, MAE is:

$$MAE = \frac{\sum_{i=1}^{N}|p_i - r_i|}{N} \qquad (5)$$

5.3   Experimental Procedure

We stated our experiments by first dividing the data set into a training and a test portion. The training and test sets were randomly choosed. We made 5 training and test sets.

To compare the performance of our system prediction we entered the training ratings set into CF and ICF.

5.4   Experimental on MAE

In Fig. 1, it is evident that the MAE of ICF is lower than CF. In the 5 experimental, ICF had a good performance all the time .In order to know the accurate differences between ICF and CF, we calculate the improved percentage. As we can see in Fig.2, the improved percentage were between 13.94% and 4.75%. The range of the

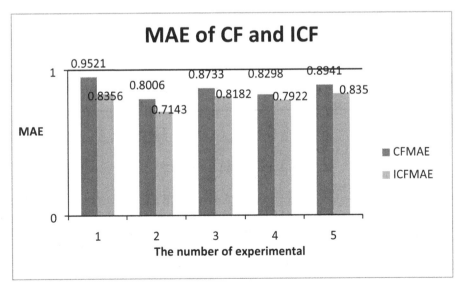

Fig. 1. MAE of CF and ICF

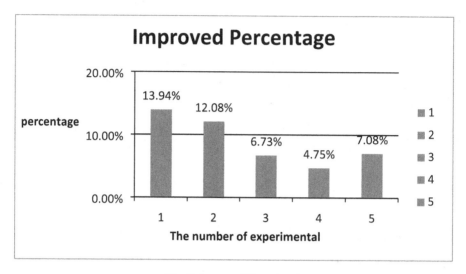

Fig. 2. Improved Percentage

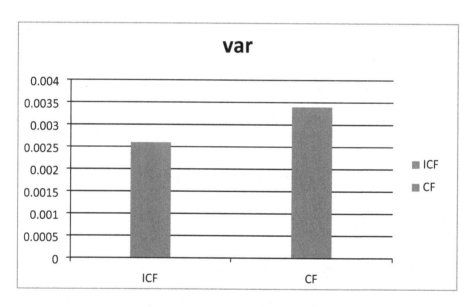

Fig. 3. Variance of ICF and CF

increase percentage is large. We wanted to know if ICF and CF were not stable. We calculate the variances of ICF and CF. In Fig.3, the variance of ICF is lower than CF, we thought the reason was that we made good use of dataset by classify items and users. we made a conclusion that the stability of ICF was better than CF. This is important for a recommendation system.

5.5   Experimental of New User Problem

New user problem is a main problem of collaborative filtering system. Because of the lack of information of new users, recommendation system can hardly make good recommendations for new users. In this experimental, firstly, we need to determine which users were the new users. We chose ten percent users of all which were mostly lack of information .We calculate MAE for ICF and CF.

In Fig. 4, it was obviously that the MAE of both increased, but we can see that the ICF was much better than CF. The difference between ICF and CF was much more than before. For new users, ICF made a better performance; we thought the excellent users we found by our system were important for new users.

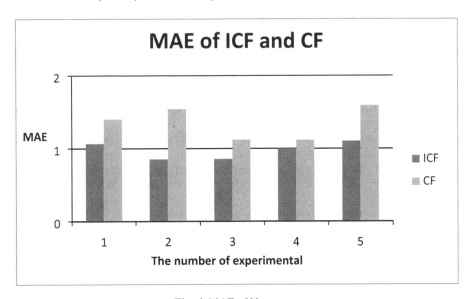

Fig. 4. MAE of New users

6   Conclusion

In this paper, we focused on new user problem and the lack of accuracy problem in CF. We proposed a method via user ranking and item clustering to improve recommendation result. We evaluated CF and our method via Movislens datasets. Results show that our novel algorithm achieves good performance for new user problem and can improve recommendation performance. Such problem as we showed in example 1 can be solved in our algorithm.

Future work can include: alleviating the sparsity problem by user classification, enforcing diversity among recommendations to prevent redundancy.

Acknowledgement. This work is supported by the National Natural Science Foundation of China under Grant No. 61003253 and Shandong Distinguished Middle-aged and Young Scientist Encouragement and Reward Foundation under Grant No. BS2010DX016.

References

1. Resnick, P., Varian, H.R.: Recommender systems. Communications of the ACM 40, 56–58 (1997)
2. Sandvig, J., Mobasher, B., Burke, R.: Robustness of collaborative recommendation based on association rule mining. In: RecSys (2007)
3. Yu, K., Zhu, S., Lafferty, J., Gong, Y.: Fast nonparametric matrix factorization for large-scale collaborative filtering. In: Proceedings of the 32nd International ACM SIGIR Conference on Reseach and Development in Information Retrieval, pp. 211–218 (2009)
4. Basu, C., Hirsh, H., Cohen, W.: Recommendation as Classification: Using Social and Content-based Information in Recommendation. In: Recommender System Workshop 1998, pp. 11–15 (1998)
5. Balabanovic, M., Shoham, Y.: Fab: Content-Based, collaborative recommendation. Communications of the ACM 40(3), 66–72 (1997)
6. Breese, J.S., Heckerman, D., Kadie, C.: Empirical analysis of predictive algorithms for collaborative filtering. Technical Report,MSR-TR-98-12, Redmond:Microsoft Research (1998)
7. Xu, B., Bu, J., Chen, C.: An Exploration of Improving Collaborative Recommender Systems viaUser-ItemSubgroups. In: WWW 2012, April 16-20. ACM, Lyon (2012) 978-1-4503-1229-5/12/04
8. Noel, J., Sanner, S., Tran, K.-N., Christen, P.: New Objective Functions for Social Collaborative Filtering. In: WWW 2012, Lyon, France (2012)
9. Cai, D., He, X., Han, J., Huang, T.S.: Graph regularized non-negative matrix factorization for data representation. IEEE Transactions on Pattern Analysis and Machine Intelligence, 43–52
10. Lee, D., Seung, H.: Algorithms for non-negative matrix factorization. Advances in Neural Information Processing Systems 13 (2001)
11. Rennie, J., Srebro, N.: Fast maximum margin matrix factorization for collaborative prediction. In Proceedings of the 22nd International Conference on Machine Learning, pp. 713–719 (2005)
12. Movielens datasets, http://www.grouplens.org/node/73
13. Pennock, D., Horvitz, E., Lawrence, S., Giles, C.: Collaborative filtering by personality diagnosis: Ahybrid memory-and model-based approach. In: Proceedings of the 16th Conference on Uncertainty in Artificial Intelligence, pp. 473–480 (2000)
14. George, T., Merugu, S.: Ascalable collaborative filtering framework based on-clustering (2005)

Reporting an Experience on Design and Implementation of e-Health Systems on Azure Cloud

Shilin Lu[1], Rajiv Ranjan[2], and Peter Strazdins[1]

[1] Research School of Computer Science, Australian National University, Australia
{s.lu,peter.strazdins}@anu.edu.au
[2] Information Engineering Laboratory, CSIRO ICT Centre, Australia
raj.ranjan@csiro.au

Abstract. Electronic Health (e-Health) technology has brought the world with significant transformation from traditional paper-based medical practice to Information and Communication Technologies (ICT)-based systems for automatic management (storage, processing, and archiving) of information. Traditionally e-Health systems have been designed to operate within stovepipes on dedicated networks, physical computers, and locally managed software platforms that make it susceptible to many serious limitations including: 1) lack of on-demand scalability during critical situations; 2) high administrative overheads and costs; and 3) in-efficient resource utilization and energy consumption due to lack of automation. In this paper, we present an approach to migrate the ICT systems in the e-Health sector from traditional in-house Client/Server (C/S) architecture to the virtualized cloud computing environment. To this end, we developed two cloud-based e-Health applications (Medical Practice Management System and Telemedicine Practice System) for demonstrating how cloud services can be leveraged for developing and deploying such applications. The Windows Azure cloud computing platform is selected as an example public cloud platform for our study. We conducted several performance evaluation experiments to understand the Quality Service (QoS) tradeoffs of our applications under variable workload on Azure.

Keywords: cloud computing, e-Health, energy-efficiency.

1   Introduction

Providing efficient healthcare services is becoming a challenging problem for governments across the world. On one hand, the increasing health-awareness among people has led to soaring demands for the health care services. On the other hand, the governments have limited fund and limited personnel to dedicate to this sector. Recent studies have shown that the health care sector consumes a large of proportion of GDP in many countries. Over the past decades, ICT has been widely adopted within the health care sector, which has significantly improved the work efficiency [1]. This has led to the highly developed e-Health care service sector worldwide. E-Health is a new term where ICT systems are deployed for better management and coordination of information.

M. Pathan, G. Wei, and G. Fortino (Eds.): IDCS 2013, LNCS 8223, pp. 145–159, 2013.

However, the substantial application of ICT systems to healthcare has led to number of serious concerns [2]. Since large number of computing, storage and networking equipment are widely deployed for e-Health applications in the hospitals, the equipment consume huge electrical power or energy, which is becoming an issue. According to Chamara [3], a traditional PC Dell 2350 1.8GHz Pentium 4 (only the host unit) consumes 6 Watts in its sleep state and 60 to 85Watts when fully powered on. Another study by Lawrence Berkeley National Laboratory suggested that 60% of all desktop PCs in commercial buildings remain fully powered-on, 36% were turned off and 4% were asleep during nights and weekends [4] with existing power management utilities of the computing servers or networking equipment almost always disabled. Further, the research has confirmed that even at a very low load, such as 10% CPU utilization, the power consumed is over 50% of the peak power [5]. Similarly, non-consolidated ICT systems also lead to increased cooling costs.

Recent technological advances in e-Health services, such as Medical Body Area Networks (MBAN) are challenging the existing in-house ICT infrastructures. According to the market intelligence company ABI research [6], over the next five years, close to five million disposable wireless MBAN sensors will be shipped. MBANs enable a continuous monitoring of patient's condition by sensing and transmitting measurements such as heart rate, electrocardiogram (ECG), body temperature, respiratory rate, chest sounds, and blood pressure etc. MBANs will allow: (i) real-time and historical monitoring of patient's health; (ii) infection control; (iii) patient identification and tracking; and (iv) geo-fencing and vertical alarming. However, to manage and analyze such massive MBAN data from millions of patients in real-time, healthcare providers will need access to an intelligent and highly scalable ICT infrastructure.

Hence, it is clear that there is an immediate need to leverage efficiency and dynamically scalable ICT infrastructure for deploying current and next-generation e-Health applications. We propose to achieve this by leveraging cloud computing systems. Cloud computing assembles large networks of virtualized ICT services such as hardware resources (such as CPU, storage, and network), software resources (such as databases, application servers, and web servers) and applications. In industry these services are referred to as Infrastructure as a Ser-vice (IaaS), Platform as a Service (PaaS), and Software as a Service (SaaS). Cloud computing services are hosted in large data centers, often referred to as data farms, operated by companies such as Amazon, Apple, Google and Microsoft.

Today, cloud computing presents an immense opportunity for the health care sector. First, it can significantly reduce the initial capital investments in the IT infrastructure in hospitals due to the pay-as-you-go pricing models. Second, it can improve the utilization of IT resources and improve the quality of health care service delivery among the healthcare sector [2]. In addition, sharing and managing large amounts of distributed medical information including EHR and X-Ray images across the e-Health system through cloud environment is the current trend [7]. The cloud storage services provide the good and scalable solution for such massive data management challenges [8].

We note that optimizing energy efficiency [9] of cloud computing data center has also emerged as one of the important research in the past few years. Discussion on how to optimize the energy efficiency of data centers is beyond the scope of this paper. We assume that cloud data center provider implements number of software and hardware-based approaches to perform energy optimizations. Our argument is based on the fact that cloud computing has better energy efficiency than traditional C/S application hosting approaches, as it does better consolidation of application workload via dynamic system scaling and de-scaling (server shutdown, migration, and the like).

In this paper we present two e-Health applications, which are programmed as SaaS applications using Azure cloud services at PaaS and IaaS layers. We developed two practical applications (Cloud-based Medical Practice Management System [10] and Cloud-based Telemedicine Practice System [11]) to demonstrate how cloud computing can be applied for e-Health for overcoming those limitations on traditional ICT architectures and improving the scalability and energy efficiency of healthcare applications. The Windows Azure cloud computing platform is carefully selected as an example of public cloud platform for hosting our applications. On the programming level, ASP.NET MVC programming model, SQL Azure Database and C# programming language are leveraged for developing our applications.

The main contributions of the paper are: (1) we illuminate a concept of migrating the e-Health applications from traditional C/S architecture to cloud computing environment for improved energy-efficiency and salability; (2) we present designs and implementations of two e-Health applications and their deployments in a public (Microsoft Azure) cloud computing environment; and (3) we conduct extensive experiments for evaluating the Quality of Service (QoS) features of our application on Windows Azure.

The rest of the paper is organized as follows. In section 2, the literature review will be given to show the state-of-the-art e-Health and cloud computing research. In section 3, we will discuss details in the e-Heath applications and cloud-based ICT architecture deployed in the hospitals. In section 4, we will demonstrate the outcome of experiments. We end the paper in section 5 with concluding remarks.

2   Literature Review

Computers have been widely used by health practitioners since 1990's. Nowadays, most doctors, nurses and other health practitioners are using personal computers to process the patients' records, prescriptions, and appointments. Some typical computing approaches are widely adopted by the health care sector such as EHRs, e-Prescription, e-Pharmacy and telemedicine. The term Electronic Health Record (EHR) refers to the digital records saved in database to store the patients' personal medical information. The records can contain various types of information, such as patients' personal profile, physiological data, medical history, prescriptions from the medical providers, physiological test results, or even some multimedia data such as digital X-ray films. The EHR data can be used for further verification of patient's condition by the doctors, or provided to the insurance for claim verification. Compared with paper-based medical records used in the past, the EHR system has many advantages, including easy to search and store.

Many countries have initiated high profile EHR programs. For example, in Australia, the government has appointed the National E-Health Transition Authority Limited (NEHTA) to research the EHR system since 2004. In China, the EHR system has been developed for many years it will be deployed by next year. Moreover, in contemporary hospitals and clinics, electronic prescription (e-prescription) has been prevailing as another popular application in e-Health practice, so is the electronic pharmacy (e-Pharmacy). Telemedicine is another contemporary approach for connecting the patient and doctor at distance using high definition video conferencing technologies. It is usually deployed with videoconference device, audio device, scanner and respective data compression algorithm to transfer the data between two points. The benefit of this approach is obvious.

In addition, the cloud computing technique is good for health data exchange, data mining for health science research. In the traditional way, in order to discover new drugs and new medical treatments, scientists need to analyze vast medical data over years where millions of dollars are invested. With cloud computing, investments and time consumption are significantly reduced [12]. Further, the cloud can be used for body sensor network, for example, the patients' physiological data at remote can be accessed and verified by the doctors over the cloud [8] [13] in real time. Obviously, in recent years, more and more sectors including healthcare are adopting cloud computing to replace their own computing infrastructure. A survey indicates that almost three-quarters of health industry respondents are planning or already using cloud-based services [8].

3   Application Architecture

In order to demonstrate the advantages of hosting the health applications in cloud computing environments, we developed two e-Health applications and deployed them on the Windows Azure cloud platform. Though there are several vendors, who provide cloud computing services, including Amazon, IBM, Google and Microsoft. Compared with other cloud platform, Windows Azure has a few unique advantages. The first advantage is that the Visual Studio .Net Development Platform has close integration Windows Azure cloud platform leading to seamless application programming and deployment experience. Therefore, one can develop and debug cloud-based applications within Visual Studio. Microsoft also provides a tool called 'Publish to Windows Azure' for developer to deploy the application to Azure. Another advantage of Windows Azure is that it directly integrates the 'SQL Azure' as the database system into the cloud platform. Developers can move their SQL server database from existing in-house database systems to Azure cloud with minimal programming. The third advantage is that Windows Azure provides very high performance backup mechanism for database, web service, virtual machine and virtual network.

Our first application is called 'Cloud-based Medical Practice Management System' and the second is called 'Cloud-based Telemedicine Practice System'. Figure 1 shows the Windows Azure-based system architecture for deploying the proposed e-Health applications. From the figure, we can see that there are three layers in our cloud-based e-Health application architecture, IaaS, PaaS and SaaS. At the IaaS layer, Windows Azure provides the infrastructure services such as virtual machines, storage unit and high speed network.

Our application components are deployed on the virtual machines to provide web services as well as to store the huge health data on the Azure's Blob storage, which is a service for storing large amounts of unstructured data that can be accessed via HTTP or HTTPS. A single blob can be very big in size (Gigabytes), and a single storage account can contain up to 100TB of blobs which can be used for distributed access [14]. Windows Azure provides two different kinds of blobs; first one is block blob and second one is page blob. Hence, Azure can support different data formats based on type and mix of e-Health applications. Our applications leverage blob storage to save the patients' image files, X-ray data, EHR documents, video and audio data. Assuring security [15] and privacy [16] of e-Health data on public cloud storage services is beyond the scope of this paper. However, in future we intend to integrate our e-Health applications with TrustStore system [15] developed by CSIRO. TrustStore is a service-oriented solution for provisioning hybrid (including both private and public) data center resources with strong guarantees on data security and privacy.

On the user side or client side based on the IaaS layer, all the typical desktop computers in the hospital can be replaced with the thin cloud terminals. In this case, all the healthcare staff can directly access the cloud-hosted applications via remote desktop Utility.

At the PaaS layer, our applications rely on the web services to provide online services, the SQL Azure server to provide SQL queries service and the media server to provide live streaming service for the videoconference communication. Our two e-Health applications operate at SaaS layer for providing the software functionalities for the users or healthcare staff (doctors, nurses, pharmacists, etc.). Our application can be scaled based on the workload demands (e.g., number of users, data size, etc.). Discussion on how our applications can be automatically scaled dynamically based on workload demands is beyond scope of this paper.

3.1   Cloud-Based Medical Practice Management System

The first e-Health application is called 'Cloud-based Medical Practice Management System', which is shown in Figure 2. The application is integrated with the typical health management systems which can be used for the hospitals, clinics and other medical organizations. In this system, most useful medical relevant business processes and data are efficiently managed including EHR, e-Prescription, Personal Health Archives, X-Ray data, e-Pharmacy Management, e-Appointment, Billing, Accounting and Finance management systems.

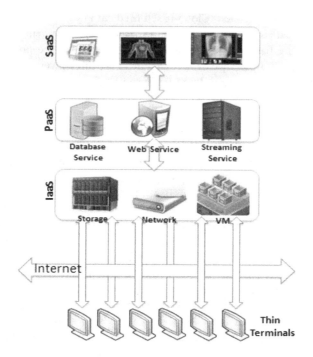

Fig. 1. Windows Azure-based e-Health Application Architecture

In this application, we developed the software components using C# language on the Visual Studio 2012 development platform. We adopt the MVC programming model and SQL Server 2008 as the database. Figure 3 shows a UML (Unified Modeling Language) flow diagram of the Cloud-based Medical Practice Management System. In this flow diagram, the main business processes are described as four models: patient module, doctor module, system administrator module and pharmacy module.

Since the application is designed using MVC model, there several core classes defined in the Controller component. These core 6 classes are shown in the UML diagram in Figure 4. Each class implements a service. In each class, few methods are defined as well based on their relative functionalities.

In the pharmacy service, the 3 core sub-module is defined as DrugInventory, DrugPurchase and DrupSales. For example, in the DrugInventory class, 6 methods are created as Figure 5: (1) DrugInventoryCreate; (2) DrugInventoryDetails; (3) DrugInventoryIndex; (4) DrugStockCreate; (5) DrugStockDetails; (6) DrugStockIndex.

In this application, the database is MS SQL and deployed on the SQL Azure database system of Windows Azure platform. After create a SQL database instance on Azure, users can run the SQL Server scripts which is developed on local machine. The database will be replicated on one SQL Azure instance. Application can connect to the database instance on Azure SQL server through the ADO.NET or ODBC connection strings. In this application, several tables are designed. Figure 6 shows the

UML database diagram of Cloud-based Medical Practice Management System. There are 4 main database tables are designed to support the most functionalities in the e-Health system including 'Patients', 'eAppointments', 'Billings' and 'EHR'.

Fig. 2. Cloud-based Medical Practice Management System

3.2   Cloud-Based Telemedicine Practice System

Another e-Health application applied on the cloud architecture is called 'Cloud-based Telemedicine Practice System'. It is integrated with multi-functions such as e-Appointment, e-Consulting, Telemedicine and e-Prescription. Based on the Azure cloud platform, the patients can see the doctors by remote through internet and consult any health problems. The doctor can check the health records, X-Ray graphics etc. for the patient and even check the patient's live physiologic data by real-time with some body sensor network.

Telemedicine application is a hybrid system. It combines diverse communication techniques and hardware. In this experiment, we adopt web camera as the user front device and Microsoft Expression Encoder 4 as the video compression technique, Windows Azure virtual machine as the live video stream server. In the Azure cloud platform, the live streaming media server is deployed for video/audio processing. Figure 7 shows the diagram of main modules provided in the Cloud-based Telemedicine Practice System. Window Azure offers the scalable video streaming service through the web role media service running in the virtual machine.

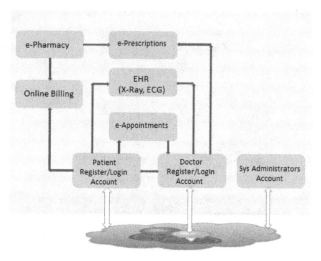

Fig. 3. Cloud-based Medical Practice Management System

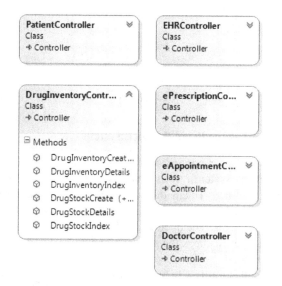

Fig. 4. Classes defined in Controller component

In the telemedicine system, a patient can register and then login to search the appropriate doctor at remote for him/her and then make appointment with the remote doctor on the available date and time. Then at the appointed date and time, the patient

Fig. 5. Methods defined in DrugInventory Class

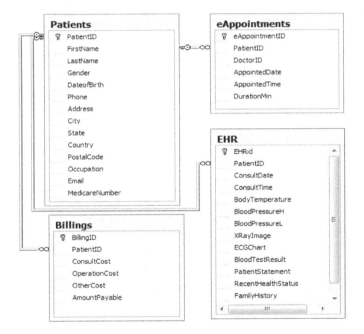

Fig. 6. SQL Azure Database Diagram

login the system to meet with the appointed doctor. The patient is able to see the doctor on the system interface by video and audio and then talk to the doctor with his/her statement. In addition, the patient can present his/her other physiological data to the doctor, such as his/her recent blood test report, X-ray image, and EGG chart or other multimedia data or text descriptions. At the end of consultation, the doctor can give the conclusion and solution or prescription. The prescription will be presented to the patient on his/her system. The patient will follow the advice. Then the consultation ends.

4   Experimental Results

In our experiments, we deploy the aforementioned e-Health applications on Windows Azure cloud [17]. The following services on Windows Azure are leveraged for this deployment: Cloud Web Services, Azure SQL Databases, Virtual Machine, IIS and Live Smooth Streaming Media Services. We assumed unsaturated server availability for these experiments, so that enough capacity could always be allocated to a virtualized web service or SQL database for any service request. At user-end, we simulate large number of users in the hospital, who access the services of two e-Health applications using different workload generation tools. First, we use JMeter [18] for simulating 20 groups of concurrent users to evaluate the scalability of our applications hosted on Windows Azure cloud. In particular, we quantify the Average Response Time of HTTP Request (ARTHR) of the following components related to the Cloud-based Medical Practice Management System: (i) web service and (ii) SQL database.

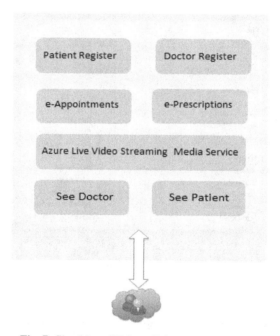

Fig. 7. Cloud-based Telemedicine Practice System

Figure 8 shows the measurement for the ARTHR under different-sized groups of concurrent users. As expected, from the initial results it is clear that the ARTHR degrades as the number of users accessing the service increase. We observed that the ARTHR stayed below 200ms for a user population below 93. However, as the concurrent users' workload was increased to 93 or above, the ARTHR grows beyond 200ms. For example, as we increased the concurrent user population to 1024, the ARTHR rises significantly and finally it soars to 1205ms. The red line on the graph shows the elevated HTTP response latency. A red horizontal line at 200ms shows the threshold of the HTTP response latency of web service on Azure cloud. That means our e-Health applications with its current Azure configuration (single instance) provide the best QoS in terms of ARTHR for the web service and database query when we keep the concurrent user below than 93. We believe that our applications can be scaled for much larger population of users via implementation of an autonomic application provisioning technique, which will adapt to the increase or decrease in workload by dynamically scaling the number of instances of the application components. We intend to investigate this aspect in our future work.

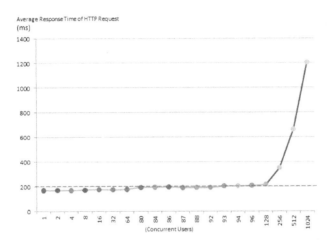

Fig. 8. Average Response Time of HTTP Request to concurrent users

In the second experiment we evaluate the scalability and QoS of the live video streaming service hosted on the virtual machine (an IaaS layer service) of Windows Azure. In the Cloud-based Telemedicine Practice System, we deploy the Live Smooth Streaming Media Services on the virtual machine to enable the patient and doctor to implement an easy to use online medical consultation via the video conferencing system. In this experiment, we use Smooth Stream Performance Testing Tool [19] that generates simulated workload for the streaming media services. This tool simulates the real users, who try to connect to the media stream available from the streaming service. Here we analyses the average video/audio chunk retrieval time for assessing the media streaming QoS of the virtualized media service.

In this experiment, we selected a medium size virtual machine with 2 cores, 3.5GB memory and located at the datacenter in West US for hosting the media service. In our system, the video conferencing involves 2 users, i.e., one patient and other the healthcare provider. Our early results show that the performance of audio stream remains constant and stable around 164ms at 64kbps over different chunks or files. This is understandable as the audio files are not generally network communication heavy if compressed using an efficient encoding technique. However, the video stream shows uncertain QoS in terms of response time for different chunks or file fragments, as shown in Figure 9. We believe that uncertain video QoS is due to the variability of network bandwidth between the two users. In future work, we will work on developing network QoS profiling technique for dynamically learning the congestion and bandwidth between users and cloud-hosted applications. Such a technique will help us in dynamic migration of video content across data centers for improving user's QoS.

Figure 10 and figure 11 show the media stream service's performance with 4 cameras and 2 cameras respectively. We can see the average video chunk response time is 497ms at the scenario of 4 cameras compared with 496ms at the scenario of 2 cameras, while the audio performance is the same 169ms during the two scenarios.

Chunk Type	Bitrate	Fragment Index	Response Time
video	400kbps	2191619705	488ms
video	400kbps	2166821321	489ms
video	400kbps	2142202474	486ms
video	400kbps	2117395074	489ms
video	400kbps	2093106349	658ms
video	400kbps	2068467064	488ms
video	400kbps	2044179014	488ms
video	400kbps	2019691348	490ms
video	400kbps	1995403057	490ms
video	400kbps	1971084462	487ms
video	400kbps	1946445346	164ms
video	400kbps	1921676889	975ms
video	400kbps	1897038189	487ms

Fig. 9. Average Video Chunk Response Time

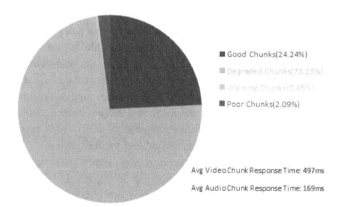

■ Good Chunks(24.24%)
■ Degraded Chunks(73.23%)
■ Warning Chunks(0.45%)
■ Poor Chunks(2.09%)

Avg Video Chunk Response Time: 497ms
Avg Audio Chunk Response Time: 169ms

Fig. 10. Media Stream Services Performance with 4 Cameras

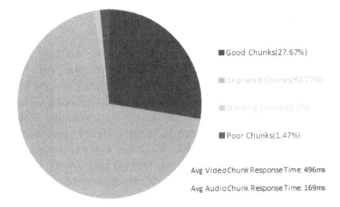

Fig. 11. Media Stream Services Performance with 2 Cameras

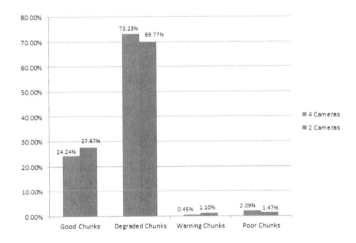

Fig. 12. Comparison of the Media Stream Services Performance

In Figure 12, we compare the overall performance of media stream services for two scenarios. We can see there is no significant difference in the two situations due to different video content delivery workload generated by cameras. As expected for 4 cameras setting the performance of the media stream service degraded to increasing processing and network transfer overload. Overall, we conclude that it is feasible to engineer e-Health applications using public cloud services. However, to guarantee QoS of applications one needs to develop intelligent cloud service and network provisioning technique. Further, one also needs to develop data security and privacy preserving techniques for protecting confidential e-Health data.

5   Conclusion

In this paper, we presented our experience on designing and implementing two e-Health application systems by leveraging Azure cloud platform. We started by analyzing challenges (lack of scalability, energy in-efficiency and the like) healthcare sector faces when using traditional C/S architecture for delivering e-Health services. Our proposed approach addresses these challenges by leveraging cloud computing services. We have implemented the prototype of our e-Health application systems and successfully evaluated its QoS performance on Azure cloud under variable workload settings. As part of our ongoing work, we are working on an intelligent elastic framework for autonomic provisioning of e-Health applications in private or public cloud environments. This framework will allow knowledge-driven optimized resource provisioning where it adapts to uncertain data streams/volumes, the number of users and varying resource and workload unpredictability.

References

1. Hansen, D.P., Gurney, P., Morgan, G., Barraclough, B.: The Australian e-Health Research Centre: enabling the health care information and communication technology revolution. Medical Journal of Australia 194(4), S5 (2011)
2. Maria, A.F., Fenu, G., Surcis, S.: An Approach to Cloud Computing Network. In: Proceedings of the 3rd International Conference on Theory and Practice of Electronic Governance, Bogota, Colombia, November 10-13, pp. 409–410 (2009)
3. Chamara, G., Christensen, K., Nordman, B.: Managing energy consumption costs in desktop PCs and LAN switches with proxying, split TCP connections, and scaling of link speed. International Journal of Network Management 15(5), 297–310 (2005)
4. Roberson, J., Webber, C., McWhinney, M., Brown, R., Pinckard, M., Busch, J.: After-hours power status of office equipment and inventory of miscellaneous plug-load equipment. Technical Report LBNL-53729, Lawrence Berkeley National Laboratory (January 2004)
5. Holzle, L.A.U.: The case for energy-proportional computing. IEEE Computer 40(12), 33–37 (2007)
6. ABI Report on Medical Body Area Networks, http://www.abiresearch.com/press/disposable-wireless-sensor-market-shows-signs-of-1
7. Sukanta, G.: Sharing information and data across heterogeneous e-health systems. Telemedicine and e-Health 15(5), 454–464 (2009)
8. Wan, D., Greenway, A., Harris, J.G., Alter, A.E.: Six questions every health industry executive should ask about cloud computing, http://newsroom.accenture.com/images/20020/HealthcareCloud.pdf
9. Beloglazov, A., Buyya, R., Choon Lee, Y., Zomaya, A.: A Taxonomy and Survey of Energy-Efficient Data Centers and Cloud Computing Systems. Advances in Computers 82, 47–111, ISBN: 978-0-12-385512-1
10. Lu, S., Ranjan, R., Strazdins, P.: Cloud-based Telemedicine Practice System (May 2013), http://telemedicine.cloudapp.net
11. Lu, S., Ranjan, R., Strazdins, P.: Cloud-based Medical Practice Management System (May 2013), http://mhealth.cloudapp.net

12. Kaufman, W.: Cloud Computing Saves Health Care Industry Time And Money, `http://www.npr.org/blogs/alltechconsidered/2012/10/01/162080613/cloud-computing-saves-health-care-industry-time-and-money` (accessed on May 12, 2013)

13. Eman, A., Mohamed, N., Al-Jaroodi, J.: e-Health Cloud: Opportunities and Challenges. Future Internet 4(3), 621–645 (2012)

14. Microsoft, `http://www.windowsazure.com/en-us/develop/net/fundamentals/cloud-storage/` (accessed May 10, 2013)

15. Nepal, S., Friedrich, C., Henry, L., Chen, S.: A Secure Storage Service in the Hybrid Cloud. In: Proceedings of the International Conference on Utility and Cloud Computing (UCC 2011), pp. 334–335. IEEE Computer Society, Washington, DC (2011)

16. Fan, L., Lo, O., Buchanan, W., Ekonomou, E., Sharif, T., Sheridan, C.: SPoC: Protecting Patient Privacy for e-Health Services in the Cloud, `http://www.flexiant.com/wp-content/uploads/2012/09/E-Health-FP7.pdf`

17. Microsoft Azure Cloud Services, `http://www.windows.azure.com`

18. Apache JMeter, `http://jmeter.apache.org/` (accessed June 15, 2013)

19. Smooth Streaming Performance Testing Tool, `http://ssperf.codeplex.com`

Content Delivery Technologies:
A View from ChinaCache

Alexei G. Tumarkin[1,2]

[1] ChinaCache, Silicon Valley R&D Office, California, USA
[2] Beijing University of Posts and Telecommunications, Beijing, China
alexei.tumarkin@chinacache.com

Abstract. The idea of content delivery services was proposed in 1994 by Hans-Werner Braun and kc claffy, who outlined many basic principles, which are still valid today. This paper presents some recent advances in content delivery technologies including client-sensitive DNS redirection, dynamic content acceleration, improved caching techniques and value-added services based on Web usage mining.

Keywords: content delivery, Web mining, caching, Web performance, Web security.

1   Introduction

The idea of content delivery is almost twenty years old. Its basic principles were formulated in a seminal paper by Hans-Werner Braun and kc claffy presented at the Second International World Wide Web (WWW) Conference in October of 1994 [1]. This is how these authors formulated their vision, which is still relevant today:

> "The popularity of information resources on the Internet has already caused an explosion in bandwidth demand, leading to the need for more judicious design of server topology and information distribution mechanisms. A longer term approach may include deploying information servers/caches as well as statistics collectors for them at strategically selected locations (e.g., Network Access Points). Such colocation will offer tighter integration of network functionality and facilitate evaluation and improvement of efficiency of information servers and supporting caches. Statistics collected at cache points could also provide a basis from which to plan future cache locations, and perhaps even hierarchical information systems that can balance efficiencies among the network, the servers, and the users."

In this paper we will discuss several technologies that constitute the foundation of modern content delivery with a special emphasis on the challenges and directions of future research. In many ways we will follow the paper [1] to examine whether the problems posed there have been adequately addressed.

Meanwhile the Web content itself has significantly changed. In particular, Web pages have become increasingly non-cacheable, dynamic and personalized. They are

M. Pathan, G. Wei, and G. Fortino (Eds.): IDCS 2013, LNCS 8223, pp. 160–168, 2013.

now accessed from a wide variety of devices with different processing and displaying capabilities. The networks have become even more ubiquitous and diverse with mobile access driving the increased global adoption rates. Modern content delivery technologies have been able to address many of these new challenges, but even more important and difficult problems remain to be solved.

2   Client-Sensitive Global Load Balancing

The first objective of an efficient and well-distributed content delivery system is to choose the best location from which it can serve an end-user's request. Most of modern content delivery systems have adopted a DNS-based approach proposed in [1]:

"Automating selection of an appropriate cache will require that nameservers provide geographically oriented responses relative to the source of domain name server queries. That is, a modified Domain Name Service (DNS) should resolve an IP address destined for the "virtual" server (NCSA's in this case, although a similar architecture would apply to any cached file depositories, in fact any other distributed information service), and redirecting the source to the server/cache closest to the client. "Closest" may reflect metrics including but not limited to physical distance or number of hops from the query source".

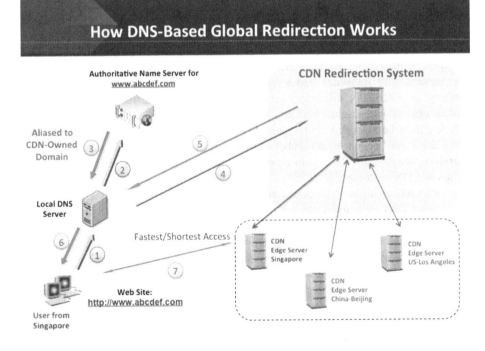

Fig. 1. Steps of DNS resolution in a CDN system

This method assumes that the end-user's local DNS resolver can serve as a good approximation of the end-user's actual location. The owner of the Web property delegates its DNS resolution to the CDN provider by using DNS aliasing as depicted in Fig. 1. When the end-users local DNS server contacts the authoritative server for a domain www.abcdef.com, it receives a response containing a CNAME record which points to another domain, owned by CDN. After contacting special-purpose CDN DNS servers, the local DNS server gets an IP address of the CDN server which is chosen according to its proximity to the end-user, the current load, etc.

However the end-user is not always using the closest DNS resolver. Many big ISPs are assigning central DNS servers to their customers, which are often located in a different region. Also, public DNS services, such as Google's or OpenDNS, are gaining more in popularity [2]. A recent proposed extension to the DNS protocol (called "edns-client-subnet") lets local DNS resolvers include information about the end-user IP address in the request sent to authoritative name servers [2-3]. To preserve the end-user privacy only the first three octets of the IP address are used in this his information. Thus a CDN operator, such as ChinaCache, who has implemented this protocol extension, has the ability to improve the quality of the global redirection at the expense of greatly increasing the database of network measurements not only of local DNS resolvers, but also all IP blocks of end-users.

3   Caching

Caching is the basic technology of any CDN. Original CDNs often used a straightforward approach to caching using a common LRU (Least-Recently Used) cache replacement policy. However LRU is not optimal for many CDN applications [4-5].

Indeed, some CDN customers are looking for reducing the number of requests to their servers. This translates into a caching strategy that optimizes a hit-rate metric resulting in potentially discarding larger objects from cache to free up space for smaller objects with higher hit rate. Many other customers are more interested in reducing their bandwidth requirements. For such customers a byte-hit-rate strategy, which takes into account total number of bytes saved by caching, is more appropriate. Therefore, ideally, a CDN would employ different caching algorithms for different groups of CDN customers.

Another interesting new development in the CDN industry is driven by virtualization. Many new CDNs are being deployed directly in the cloud using an IAAS provider such as Amazon's EC2 [6], or their own cloud infrastructure. Such cloud deployments are much more flexible in terms of meeting elastic capacity requirements and redistributing resources between customers. However every time a new virtual caching server is started with an empty cache, it will experience a very low hit rate. By using a hierarchy of caches, CDNs often can absorb these cache misses and shield the customers. Another possibility is to pre-populate these new caches with an optimally chosen set of objects. An efficient way to do this pre-population can be based on mining the cache hit history obtained from similar active servers and pushing (or pulling) the right objects into the new cache instance from its neighbors.

4   Dynamic and Non-cacheable Content

The observed Web latency is very far from being optimal. It has long been established that a theoretical limit for client-server interaction is directly related the amount of data to be transferred and the capacity of the link [7]:

> "Logically, the minimum possible transaction time is the one roundtrip time delay inherent in communication, plus the time it takes to send the request and receive the reply, and any time spent at the server."

However, in a typical Web communication even a delivery of a single object takes multiple round-trips. If such object is non-cacheable (or is a cache miss), and thus should be retrieved from a remote origin, then the performance suffers.

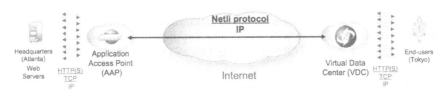

• Maintains standard HTTP(s)/TCP at each end

• Specialized protocols in between

• Total transparency (no changes to HW, SW or Apps)

Fig. 2. Dynamic content acceleration through protocol optimization

A widely used CDN technology to overcome this problem was proposed back in early 2000's by Netli (later acquired by Akamai) [8-9]. It uses a hierarchy of proxies (caches) as shown in Fig. 2. A cache miss (or a request for a non-cacheable content) is relayed by the first proxy located near the end-user, to the second proxy strategically placed near the origin server. These two proxies use either a proprietary non-TCP protocol or specially tuned and pre-warmed TCP links in order to eliminate the overhead of establishing TCP connections and discovering the available bandwidth. By doing so, the whole request-response communication takes just a single round-trip between these two proxies.

5   Prefetching

Since early days of the Web, prefetching was considered to be a promising way to decrease the time to retrieve objects [10-11]. It can be used to eliminate delays due to unavailability objects in the CDN cache, and also to efficiently use browser idle time to pre-position objects into the browser cache. We will refer to the former as the "proxy prefetching", and to the latter as the "browser prefetching". They work quite differently, and we will discuss them separately. We will confine our discussion to prefetching of only cacheable content, because prefetching of non-cacheable content is a more sensitive subject for most CDN customers, and should be usually addressed directly by the content owner.

5.1   Proxy Prefetching

If a CDN is delivering the whole site, including base HTML, then proxy prefetching is usually implemented based on parsing and proactively retrieving the links for embedded objects inside HTML tags on the base page before receiving the end-user's requests for them. This technique is far from being perfect. It can result in excessive requests (if some of these objects are already cached by the browser). Also, in the modern Web, many sites use sophisticated JavaScript technologies, and the links for many (if not all) embedded images are "hidden" inside JavaScript statements. And, obviously, if the CDN is just delivering the static content for the site, then there is no way for it to get access to the rest of the site (such as to base HTML).

A more efficient approach is based on the offline analysis of access logs. CDNs are routinely collecting standard Web logs containing the timing of each request, end-user's IP address, referring URL, etc. These logs can be used to devise an algorithm for proxy prefetching in the following manner. For each end-user session (identified by timing, end-user IP address and other available unique information), we identify all cacheable objects having the same REFERER request header (i.e., having the same referring page). Among those we are especially interested in those, which resulted in a cache miss, so that we can proactively pull them into the proxy cache without incurring more latency penalty.

5.2   Browser Prefetching

For a CDN to support browser prefetching it should be able to handle and modify content of the Web pages. With the consent of the content provider, the CDN determines the candidate objects to be prefetched by the end-user. This is also done based on the log analysis, however the problem is somewhat more complicated. Indeed, ideally we would like to know what pages will be retrieved after the current page is downloaded, and to insert references to the objects from these subsequent pages into the current page. Predicting the end-user behavior with a high degree of certainty is always a nearly impossible task.

Because we are interested not in a perfect prediction of end-user's browsing sequence, but just in the likelihood of retrieval of some static objects, we can obtain a lot of useful information from the logs. First we need to process all end-user sessions in order to construct a "tree map" of the Web site where each page is associated with its most likely followers. This is done through a straightforward analysis of access logs using the REFERER information. For each page we also preserve the list of embedded objects requested by the users. The next step is to aggregate the information about the embedded objects among all pages. Namely, if there were four user sessions that first downloaded Page_0, then we look for the next page downloaded by these four users (say, the first user went to Page_1, the second user to Page_2, the third user to Page_3 and the fourth user also browsed to Page_1). All objects downloaded during these four sessions from Page_1, Page_2 and Page_3 are counted according to their presence in the logs (so if Object_1 from Page_1 was downloaded during accessing all four pages, it will have a rank of 4). Then the algorithm uses a probability threshold (say, 50%) to choose the most likely objects to be requested after the download of Page_1.

After we have determined the list of candidates for prefetching for each page that we want to process, then we can insert into each page certain Ajax directives to prefetch these objects after the rest of the page has been fully loaded, thus using the idle time (while the end-user processes the original information on the page) to pre-warm the browser cache before the next activities.

Of course, as with all prefetching implementations, one needs to monitor closely the excessive resource utilizations as a result of incorrectly predicting the browsing behaviors. The corresponding adjustments to the parameters of the algorithm might make it more accurate, or a decision to stop all prefetching activities might be made based on the ensuing cost-benefit analysis.

6   Adaptive Content Rewriting and Transmission

Acting on behalf of their customers (content providers), content delivery networks can apply various front-end optimization techniques to enhance end-user experience. In particular, many CDNs are actively adopting open-source solutions such as Google's PageSpeed [13]. Content-Aware Network Services (CANS) introduced by ChinaCache in [9], can further improve this approach by adjusting the content adaptation and data transmission steps to better accommodate the vast variety of end-user devices and access methods.

First of all, the delivered content should be tailored to the type of the end-user device, especially taking into account the screen resolution and display size. For example, it does not make sense to deliver a high-definition image, which will be downsized by the mobile device anyway. Therefore, after seeing the User-Agent (UA) HTTP header sent by the browser which each request, the CDN content-adaptation proxy associates this UA with the database of known devices to retrieve the display characteristics. After that the proxy either chooses a pre-stored version of this image with the right characteristics, or resizes the image on the fly before delivering it to the end-user.

The TCP transmission rates can be adjusted too [14]. It does not make sense to try to open TCP windows to exceed the link capacity. For many end-user subnets, the previous TCP sessions provide a stable and reliable set of measurements to determine the maximum capacity of end-user connections. Such information is statistically processed, aggregated and stored at CDN proxy servers for constraining the ranges of TCP parameters to be used for new TCP sessions.

This adaptive behavior can be further enhanced by taking into account the timing of end-user sessions. Indeed, many access methods and ISPs suffer from insufficient capacity during peak hours while delivering a much better performance during less busy periods. Therefore, it is advisable to have different profiles for predicting end-user connectivity parameters (such as RTT, packet loss and maximum throughput) for different days of the week and times of the day. By doing so, CDNs can greatly reduce uncertainty in estimating and aggregating network characteristics of the global end-user population.

7   Value-Added Services

7.1   Mining Access Logs

The approach to prefetching described above can be also used to detect incorrect (or suboptimal) caching directives associated with some objects. Indeed, if the logs contain repeated 304 requests (If-Modified-Since), which result in server responding Not-Modified, then the CDN should report those instances to its customers with recommended changes (based on observed time intervals between the objects actually being changed).

Moreover, even for seemingly non-cacheable objects, the logs can provide useful tips about their cacheability. The most straightforward way is to monitor most popular non-cacheable objects and their sizes. Whenever such object does not change its size, it becomes a candidate for a cacheability check performed, for example, by calculating a checksum of the content.

CDN access logs also contain a lot of information that can be used for reporting a rough estimate of the page download times. This requires a sufficient granularity of the timestamp used by CDN logging (say, up to a millisecond accuracy). Then the steps of the algorithm are as follows (see also [15]):

1.   Identify an end-user session by IP address and other unique features such as User-Agent
2.   Inside each session search for all first page requests determined as a log entry with a request URL which serves as a REFERER for some later objects
3.   For each first page request search for the last page request determined as a log entry with a REFERER being the first page request and not being a REFERER for any other object
4.   Calculate the time difference between the log entries for the last and the first objects.

Of course, this algorithm won't give precise end-user whole-page download results, but it is easy to implement. It can be further improved by correlating with real end-user measurements and then applying empirical calibration adjustments.

Access logs can be also used for various security-related purposes [15] (see also the next Section). In particular, CDNs can identify "valuable" users based on a behavioral analysis of access logs, and aggregate these users' IP addresses. During suspected attacks, the IP blocks of "valuable" users can be treated preferentially to make sure that these users are not blocked by anti-attack measures. Also, requests from such "valuable" users can re-queued during periods of peak traffic to ensure that the customer servers would service them first.

7.2   Security

CDNs have always prided themselves on their ability to protect their customers. In particular, such attacks as SYN floods can be successfully absorbed by CDN's servers. However, there are recent academic studies that have identified vulnerabilities in the CDN architecture that can be potentially explored by malicious parties [16]. Since such exploits can be quite unpredictable in nature, it is very important to efficiently detect "unusual" activities and curb them without disrupting core CDN functionality.

In [9] we have described such detection approach used by ChinaCache in our DNS servers and Web proxies/caches. The detection algorithm is based on comparing specially constructed and optimized short- and long-term averages of inter-arrival times of various types of requests. Let us consider, for example, a so-called "404 storm" distributed denial-of-service (DDoS) attack, where the attackers request a multitude of invalid URLs from a CDN's customer property, generating an avalanche of 404 HTTP response code messages. In order to detect such attack, our algorithm constantly monitors inter-arrival times of end-user requests resulting in 404 responses. If the short-term average exceeds a certain threshold times the long-term average, then an alert is declared. Among mitigating measures during the alert time a CDN can choose not to serve 404 responses to the end-users and ultimately to block all client IP addresses (or IP blocks) that generate an unusual number of 404 requests.

The origin server attack described in [16], when the attacker forces a cache miss by adding a query string to a valid cacheable resource, can be treated similarly. All caching proxies should process inter-arrival times of requests resulting in cache misses. Whenever such an unusual surge in such requests is detected, the proxy should rate-limit (or block) requests from the unusually active clients. If such attack is launched by a malicious botnet, then we can apply some additional processing of the requested URLs to determine common patterns in them, so that the proxy will rate-limit requests matching the attack pattern, and continue to serve other requests in a normal way.

8   Conclusion

Content delivery technologies have evolved into one of the major enabling Web components. Content delivery is a vibrant area of academic research and software development activities. We covered only a handful of topics in this field, which we have dealt most actively in the recent years. Many more interesting problems remain to be solved especially in the areas of mobile content delivery and Web security.

In China bandwidth is still very expensive, therefore bandwidth-saving technologies will remain a major component of CDN strategies for companies like ChinaCache [17]. In particular, WAN optimization techniques that are suitable massive for CDN deployments can be successfully used to optimize traffic within the CDN infrastructure and even to the clients [9].

Another target area of ChinaCache's efforts is working with mobile carriers to improve end-user experience and decrease the peak utilization of wireless networks. Device- and connectivity-sensitive content adaptation can be successfully used to reduce congestion on over-subscribed links. Other technologies, forming the basis of Content-Aware Network Services, were discussed in Sections 6-7 of this paper. Further extending these services to the end-user's devices is a challenging but exciting area of ultimate improvements in mobile Web performance on a global scale.

References

1. Braun, H.W., Claffy, K.: Web Traffic Characterization: An Assessment of the Impact of Caching Documents from NCSA's Web Server. Computer Networks and ISDN Systems 28, 37–51 (1995)
2. Otto, J.S., Sánchez, M.A., Rula, J.R., Bustamante, F.E.: Content delivery and the natural evolution of DNS: remote dns trends, performance issues and alternative solutions. In: Proceedings of 2012 ACM Internet Measurement Conference (IMC 2012), pp. 523–536. ACM, New York (2012)
3. Calder, M., Fan, X., Hu, Z., Katz-Bassett, E., Heidemann, J., Govindan, R.: Mapping the Expansion of Google's Serving Infrastructure. In: Proceedings of 2013 ACM Internet Measurement Conference (IMC 2013). ACM, New York (to appear, 2013)
4. Hosseini-Khayat, S.: Replacement Algorithms for Object Caching. In: Proceedings of the 1998 ACM symposium on Applied Computing, pp. 90–97. ACM, New York (1998)
5. Podlipnig, S., Boszormenyi, L.: A Survey of Web Cache Replacement Strategies. ACM Comput. Surv. 35, 374–398 (2003)
6. Höfer, C.N., Karagiannis, G.: Cloud Computing Services: Taxonomy and Comparison. Journal of Internet Services and Applications 2, 81–94 (2011)
7. Heidemann, J., Obraczka, K., Touch, J.: Modeling the Performance of HTTP Over Several Transport Protocols. ACM/IEEE Transactions on Networking 5, 616–630 (1997)
8. Pathan, M., Buyya, R.: A taxonomy and survey of content delivery networks. Technical Report, GRIDS-TR-2007-4, The University of Melbourne, Australia (2007)
9. Talyansky, M., Tumarkin, A., Xu, H., Zhang, K.: Content Delivery in China: A ChinaCache Perspective. In: Pathan, M., Sitaraman, R., Robinson, D. (eds.) Advanced Content Delivery and Streaming in the Cloud. Wiley, New York (to appear, 2013)
10. Venkataramani, A., Yalagandula, P., Kokku, R., Sharif, S., Dahlin, M.: The Potential Costs and Benefits of Long Term Prefetching for Content Distribution. Computer Communications - COMCOM 25, 367–375 (2002)
11. Sidiropoulos, A., Pallis, G., Katsaros, D., Stamos, K., Vakali, A., Manolopoulos, Y.: Prefetching in Content Distribution Networks via Web Communities Identification and Outsourcing. World Wide Web 11, 39–70 (2008)
12. Padhye, J., Nielsen, H.: A comparison of SPDY and HTTP performance. Microsoft Research Report MSR-TR-2012-102 (2012)
13. Al-Fares, M., Elmeleegy, K., Reed, B., Gashinsky, I.: Overclocking the Yahoo!: CDN for faster web page loads. In: Proceedings of the 2011 ACM SIGCOMM Internet Measurement Conference (IMC 2011), pp. 569–584. ACM, New York (2011)
14. Cherkasova, L., Fu, Y., Tang, W., Vahdat, A.: Measuring and Characterizing End-to-End Internet Service Performance. Journal ACM/IEEE Transactions on Internet Technology 3, 347–391 (2003)
15. Vigna, G., Robertson, W., Kher, V., Kemmerer, R.A.: A Stateful Intrusion Detection System for World-Wide Web Servers. In: Omondi, A.R., Sedukhin, S.G. (eds.) ACSAC 2003. LNCS, vol. 2823, pp. 34–43. Springer, Heidelberg (2003)
16. Triukose, S., Al-Qudah, Z., Rabinovich, M.: Content Delivery Networks: Protection or Threat? In: Backes, M., Ning, P. (eds.) ESORICS 2009. LNCS, vol. 5789, pp. 371–389. Springer, Heidelberg (2009)
17. Li, Y., Wang, H., Dong, J., Li, J., Cheng, S.: Operating Cost Reduction for Distributed Internet Data Centers. In: Proceedings of the 13th IEEE/ACM International Symposium on Cluster, Cloud and Grid Computing (CCGrid 2013), pp. 589–596. IEEE (2013)

Quality Control for Crowdsourcing
with Spatial and Temporal Distribution

Gang Zhang and Haopeng Chen

REINS Group, School of Software
Shanghai Jiao Tong University
Shanghai, P.R. China
{infear,chen-hp}@ sjtu.edu.cn

Abstract. In the past decade, crowdsourcing has become a prospective paradigm for commercial purposes, for it brings a lot of benefits such as low cost and high immediacy, particularly in location-based services (LBS). On the other side, there also exist many problems need to be solved in crowdsourcing. For example, the quality control for crowdsourcing systems has been identified as a significant challenge, which includes how to handle massive data more efficiently, how to discriminate poor quality content in workers' submissions and so on. In this paper, we put forward an approach to control the crowdsourcing quality from spatial and temporal distribution. Our experiments have demonstrated the effectiveness and efficiency of the approach.

Keywords: crowdsourcing, location-based service (LBS), quality control, spatial and temporal distribution.

1   Introduction

The proposal of "Crowdsourcing" paradigm extends back to 2006. It was defined as "a company or organization outsources their tasks to those who are not specific in the form of free voluntary (and usually large public networks)"[1]. As we can see, "crowdsourcing" actually originates from the transformation of innovation mode of enterprises. Nowadays, with the popularity of Internet, It is becoming a trend that consumers generate contents by their enthusiasm on innovation. For instance, BMW [2] found its innovation laboratory in Germany to provide users with online tools which can help them participate in the production design, which would not only promote innovation, but also increase the popularity of enterprise.

In the age of the Internet, the concept of crowdsourcing, that virtually anyone has the potential to plug in valuable information is extended to wiki and other collaboration tools [3]. For example, Amazon's Mechanical Turk [4], one of the most successful commercial crowdsourcing platforms, offers businesses and developers access to an on-demand, scalable work force. Essentially, potential employers post tasks and workers select jobs they would like to perform.

Recently this paradigm has also flourished in location based services (LBS), in which the smart-device users contribute information about their surroundings, thereby

M. Pathan, G. Wei, and G. Fortino (Eds.): IDCS 2013, LNCS 8223, pp. 169–182, 2013.

providing a collective knowledge about the physical world [5]. LBS are typical application scenario of crowdsourcing, since it always need large amounts of resource to collect the information about locations. This would cost a lot without using crowdsourcing. It also requires high immediacy, since the physical world is always changing. So it still faces the challenge of quality control. In some cases, the services rely on mapping software such as Google Maps. For example, CROWDSAFE [6], a novel convergence of Internet crowdsourcing and portable smart devices to enable real time, location based crime incident searching and reporting. In addition, there are also many other indoor LBS based on the Access Points (AP). But no matter which kind of LBS, the quality of service completely depends on the crowdsourcing quality. In this paper, we regard indoor LBS as our research background and discuss about the quality control in crowdsourcing.

In our system, we hope to locate all APs accurately in an area in order to provide people with value-added services later. As long as one's smart-device gets connected to an AP, he could submit the information about it, such as its identification and its possible position to the server. Then, these submitted contents would be aggregated to accurately locate AP on the server side. But since the worker's smart-device may not be precise or there exist workers' cheating behaviors, the aggregation quality would be poor. So here we try to solve such three problems: 1.How to eliminate useless contents that workers submit in order to handle massive data more efficiently. 2. How to aggregate these contents and generate results more accurately. 3. How to evaluate workers' single contribution in each task and overall performance periodically.

The paper is structured as follows. Section 2 gives a quick overview of the concept of crowdsourcing and the research already done in the area. In Section 3, we present our main method on how to solve the questions mentioned above. Detailed implementation would be involved in Section 4 and experience results would be analyzed in Section 5. In Section 6, we would do conclusion and some discussion about our future work.

2   Related Work

In crowdsourcing paradigm, there are two roles, employer and worker as shown in Fig.3. People called employer submit tasks, evaluate worker's submitted results and pay workers, while workers pull and complete tasks, get payment from employers.[7]

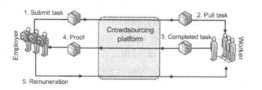

Fig. 1. Crowdsourcing scheme

Generally, crowdsourcing task is simple but needs large amounts of resource to be accomplished. Thanks to global growth in Internet connectivity and bandwidth, we can now harness human resource in near-real time from a vast and ever-growing, distributed population of online Internet users [8]. In this way, crowdsourcing brings low cost and high efficiency. But if exists cheating in workers' accomplishments, the quality of tasks would be influenced. Meanwhile, it costs a lot that validating whether a worker is cheating in the task. For example, on EBay website, everyone could maliciously add good or bad comments on products which would affect their reputation later. So it is essential to have a mechanism to judge workers' overall performance during a period and single contribution in each crowdsourcing task.

Some researches focus on judging whether the contents which workers submit should be accepted or rejected. They consider that inaccurate acceptance or rejection would affect not only current task, but also possibly drive a new wave of fraudsters, because those who have cheated do not receive any punishment. For example, Matthias et al. raise "Majority Decision Approach" [7] to judge whether worker's submission is correct in simple tasks, and using "Control Group Approach" method in complicated cases. Besides, Petros and Hector propose "Gold Standard Performance" to detect one worker's performance before the crowdsourcing task starts [9]. Many other researchers think that workers' characteristics such as demographics or personality traits are related to the quality of their work under specific task conditions [10]. In [11], Winter Mason et al. put forward a data-driven model for quality control in the context of crowdsourcing systems, which aims to assess the quality of individual contribution for parallel distributed tasks. There are also many other discussion on quality control for crowdsourcing in certain fields such as geographic [12] and real-time applications [13] . In addition, it is also a hot topic that to balance the task quality and reward cost [14]. For instance, in 2009, Yahoo's research institute made a quantitative analysis on the relationship between "Financial Incentives" and "Performance of Crowds" [15], and found that higher reward can accelerate the accomplishment of the task, but cannot improve its quality.

In this paper, we discuss about the task quality from a new aspect which is called analysis with spatial and temporal distribution. It has to be noted that the value of contents submitted by workers would attenuate from two prospective: time and space. From the point of space, for example, if one has submitted a piece of record r, his subsequent submissions during a short period, which contain the same contents about the position as the previous one, are less meaningful. It is because that AP's position is fixed during a short period in reality. On the other hand, the submission of one worker's history tasks is not important as that of up-to-date ones, which is a kind of attenuation on value with time. It is assumed one worker's late submission is more persuasive than before, for AP's position may be changed during a long period.

3   Method

As shown in Fig.2, there are three phases in our system design: *Filtering*, *Aggregating*, and *Feedback*. Since the scale of contents submitted may be too large like several TBs every day, we would use some parallel-computing model such as Mapreduce [16] here to improve efficiency of data processing.

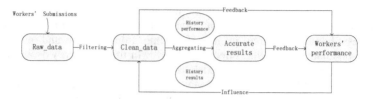

Fig. 2. System design

3.1 Background

In our design, each record submitted by workers contains a key-value pair which is made up of an AP's id (*apid*) and its position (*pos*). The record would also include other information about the worker such as his id (*workerid*) and the time he submits the record (*timestamp*). We use a 16-bit unsigned integer to denote these elements respectively except *timestamp*. In particular, the position is made up as follows:

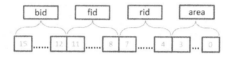

Fig. 3. 16-bit integer denote each AP's position

The position is composed of a building (*bid*), a floor (*fid*), a room (*rid*) and the location in the room (*area*). As shown in Fig.3, there are max 2^16 different positions and each room is partitioned to 2^4 grids. For the sake of simplification, we define the distance *d* between two positions *pos₁* and *pos₂* as follows:

$$d_{pos_1, pos_2} = \left| pos_1 - pos_2 \right| \tag{1}$$

It is assumed that two positions are close as their values are numerically close. For example, the room of rid 1 and that of rid 2 are supposed to be close geographically. So these two positions may be covered by the same signal from one AP. Meanwhile, if two positions are located in different buildings, the distance between them would be very large (at least 2^12).It is almost impossible that they could access to the same AP.

The records set submitted by workers are called "raw data", since it is highly possible that some records among the set are incorrect and meaningless. So it is necessary to filter out these records to obtain the clean data. After that, we try to obtain the accurate results of AP's position from the clean data. It is realistic that the position of AP is comparatively fixed during a short period. Therefore, we regard one day as the minimum unit to do aggregation. However, each worker's performance or credibility is different, so the records in their submission should also have different quality. Here, we define *ar* to describe each worker's overall performance which is summarized from his history task. Last but not least, it is necessary to update each worker's performance according to the latest aggregated result (still regard one day as the minimum unit). It is a kind of feedback on *ar*, which would come into effect in one's next task.

3.2   Spatial Distribution

Since our research is based on LBS, it is natural to utilize spatial distribution to evaluate workers' submission. It was involved in the *Filtering* and *Feedback* phase.

In Filtering phase, we want to find out those meaningless records. But which records are meaningless? It is supposed that AP's position is fix during a short period. So the frequent submissions which contain the same contents are meaningless. It is highly possible since workers would like to get more rewards by more submissions. This is thought of as a kind of cheating like that in "Page Rank" [17]. Therefore, only the records earliest submitted are considered meaningful and the subsequent ones are less valuable. We introduce r_v to describe such value of each record(r) and p_c to denote the short period. For example, if one worker first submits a record which contains the pair $\{apid_1, pos_1\}$, the record would own a value of $1(r_v =1)$. But the records of the same pair in his subsequent submission during p_c would have value smaller than 1 and get lower and lower. A shrink factor on value f is defined to demonstrate the speed of such attenuation on value. The detail is shown in Fig.4. It is supposed that p_c lasts 1 minute here and the shrink factor f_1 is set 0.5:

Workerid	Records={apid, position}	Timestamp	Value(r_v)
10	(1, 32)	12:00:00	1
20	(1, 32)	12:00:00	1
20	(1, 32)	12:00:10	0.5
20	(1, 32)	12:00:40	0.25
20	(1, 32)	12:00:55	0.125

Fig. 4. Records value table with f_1=0.5 and p_c=1 min

On the other hand, we also use spatial distribution to evaluate the accuracy of workers' submissions. It is natural to compare one's submissions and the accurate results to get how many records match. We introduce *hit* to denote the worker's contribution in each task, which can be calculated as follows:

$$hit=mrw/trw \tag{2}$$

Where *mrw* denotes the count of one's matched records, *trw* is the count of all one's records in his submissions. It has to be noted that even if one worker doesn't have any cheating deliberately in the task, it is also highly possible that his submission is not accurate due to device problems or wireless interference. Therefore, if the record in one's submission is different from the aggregated result, which means they contain different positions of the same AP, it would still be retained instead of discarded while the worker's *hit* is calculated. But the weight of this record, which was denoted by w in our definition, is related to the distance between these two positions. As pos_1 and pos_2 denote the positions, the weight w of the record would be:

$$w = \begin{cases} e^{-d_{pos_1,pos_2}}, & d_{pos_1,pos_2} \leq R \\ 0, & d_{pos_1,pos_2} > R \end{cases} \tag{3}$$

If $pos_1=pos_2$, it is considered to be an accurate match. So the weight of the matched record is 1.Otherwise, the weight would get smaller as the position in the record gets farther from the accurate one. When the distance is large than the threshold R in our definition, the record is supposed to have no weight. Suppose that r_i denotes the i_{th} record, the total weights of one's records denotes his mrw each day, and trw is just the number n of all his records.

$$mrw = \sum_{i=1}^{n} w_{r_i} \tag{4}$$

$$trw = n \tag{5}$$

3.3   Temporal Distribution

It is obvious that worker's history performance could determine his later performance to some extent. Here, we define ar to describe each worker's overall performance which initial value is 1. It is also used to judge the credibility (r_c) of the records in one's later submissions. Two arguments s_1 and s_2 are introduced to denote the ar thresholds. For example, if one's ar is more than s_1, all records he submits in next task would be regarded as credibility of 1(r_c=1) and accepted completely. Because he is supposed to be an honest worker without any cheating before. On the other side, if one's ar is lower than s_2, his submissions may also have poor credibility and thus, discarded. Otherwise, one's submissions would be accepted partly and his records would have credibility of his updated ar (r_c=ar). Meanwhile, we generate other four records whose contents are close semantically to the origin one, for these records are also trustable to some extent. But their credibility is lower than the original one. The details are shown in Fig.5.

	Workerid	Ar	Records	Credibility(r_c)
Completely accepted	10	1	(1, 32)	1
Partly accepted	20	0.6	(1, 32)	0.6
	20	0.6	(1, 33)	0.1
	20	0.6	(1, 34)	0.1
Generated records	20	0.6	(1, 31)	0.1
	20	0.6	(1, 30)	0.1
Discarded	30	0.1	(1, 100)	0

Fig. 5. Worker's ar and his records credibility with s_1=0.8 and s_2=0.2

Then, we use one's history ar and his recent contributions c to obtain his up-to-date performance ar'. It is calculated as follows:

$$ar' = (1 - m_1) * ar + m_1 * c \quad 0 < m_1 < 1 \tag{6}$$

An impact factor m_1 is still defined here, which denotes the weight of the worker's latest contribution while update his ar. It has to be noted that the weight of one's initial performance would decrease exponentially and close to zero at last. The later one's contribution is the more weight it would have.

Similarly, although the position of AP is fixed during a short period, it is still of high possibility that AP would be located in any other places during a long period. It is natural to use both the history result and the latest result to obtain the up-to-date location of AP. The details would be involved in the Section 4.

4   Implementation

In this Section, the details, particularly the algorithms, about our system implementation are involved. According to our design, the section would be divided into three parts.

4.1   Filtering with Quality Table

In crowdsourcing, it is essential to discriminate the quality of workers' submissions. Here, we define the *quality* (r_q) of each record (r) in our system to describe how the record is trustable, which is affected by the *credibility* (r_c) and the *value* (r_v) of the record mentioned in Section 3. For the sake of simplification, the product of *credibility* and *value* are used to denote the *quality*:

$$r_q = r_c * r_v \tag{7}$$

For example, if one's *ar* is 0.6, which means that each records except our generated ones in his submissions would have a credibility of $0.6(r_c=0.6)$. Meanwhile, the value of his one record *r* is 1, then this record *r* would have a quality of $0.6*1=0.6(r_q=0.6)$. So we have the Quality table [18] which is extended from Fig.4 and Fig.5 as follows:

WorkerId	Ar	Records	Timestamp	Credibility(r_c)	Value(r_v)	Quality(r_q)
10	1	(1, 32)	12:00:00	1	1	1
10	1	(1, 32)	12:00:10	1	0.5	0.5
10	1	(1, 32)	12:00:20	1	0.25	0.25
20	0.6	(1, 32)	12:00:00	0.6	1	0.6
20	0.6	(1, 33)	12:00:00	0.1	1	0.1
20	0.6	(1, 34)	12:00:00	0.1	1	0.1
20	0.6	(1, 31)	12:00:00	0.1	1	0.1
20	0.6	(1, 30)	12:00:00	0.1	1	0.1
30	0.1	(1, 100)	12:00:00	0	1	0

Fig. 6. Records Quality Table with $s_1=0.8$, $s_2=0.2$, $f_1=0.5$ and $p_c=1$ min.

As shown in Fig.6, the records submitted by the worker 10 whose *ar* is 1 are always of high credibility ($r_c = 1$), but of low value if he try to cheat by repeated submission ($r_v = 0.5$ or 0.25).So his third record of (1, 32) only has a quality of 0.25. On the other hand, since the *ar* of worker 20 is between s_1 and s_2, we generated other four records of low credibility ($r_c=0.1$). Otherwise, the worker's submission would be discarded ($r_c=0$ and $r_q=0$) as his low *ar*.

4.2   Aggregating with Mapreduce Model

Majority Decision Approach (MDA)
Majority Decision Approach could be explained through a simple case. For example, for AP of id 1, there exist 100 records (including the generated ones) that show the position of it is pos_1 and another 60 records that tell pos_2.Then, the first result is

obviously more trustable than the other, since it has more supporters. So pos_1 is considered the position of this AP.

Here, we use the sum of quality instead of the count of each record. For instance, in Fig.6, the total quality of the record (1, 32) would be 1+0.5+0.25+0.6=2.35, while that of the record (1, 34) is only 0.1. Therefore, the AP of id 1 is more likely located at position 32.

As mentioned in the design part, one day is regarded as the minimum unit to do aggregation. It is assumed that there are n workers who involved in the task during the period. Besides, we have the following arguments as input:

- S_r: clean data set derived from workers' submitted records. The format of each record is (*apid, pos, workerid, timestamp*).
- $A = \{ar_1...ar_n\}$: the latest *ar* of each worker.
- S_1, S_2: two *ar* thresholds used to judge how worker's submission would be accepted.

Since the records set may be too large to handle, we use HADOOP [19] framework here to improve performance of data processing. So our algorithm can be divided into mapper part and reducer part. The Mapper procedure is as follows:

```
Algorithm1: MDA Mapper Procedure
Input:  Records Set S_r, Accept Rate (ar) Set A = {ar_1...ar_n},
S_1 and S_2 act as ar thresholds
Output: Record Set S'. Each record owns an extra element
quality describes the accuracy of this record.
For each (apid, pos, workerid, timestamp) in S:
        ar = A [workerid]
        If ar > S_1
// completely accepted, quality=1.
// output format:key= apid:pos, value=quality.
                Output (apid:pos, 1)
        Else if ar > S_2:
//partly accepted, quality=ar.
                Output (apid:pos, ar)
                _quality = (1 - ar) /4
//generate records contain positions around.
                p^1, p^2, p^3, p^4=gen (pos)
                Output (apid: p^1, _quality)
                Output (apid: p^2, _quality)
                Output (apid: p^3, _quality)
                Output (apid: p^4, _quality)
        Else: // omitted
                Continue next loop.
```

Algorithm1: MDA Mapper Procedure

If one's submission is accepted partly, we would generate other four records whose contents are close to the origin one. The implementation of the method *gen ()* is omitted here, since it is not our focus and may involve some knowledge of geography. It has also to be noted that our approach is not limited to the LBS scenario, as long as you generate the data which is semantically close in your scenario context.

Now we do reduce job (Fig.8). Since each record in *S'* contains an *apid*, position information *pos* and a quality r_q, it is natural to count the quality each key (*apid:pos*) appears first and group them by *apid* later. Then, we sort them by the quality each one appears in each group and the max one is our wanted result, for most workers think this position is the accurate one where the AP is located. For example, the total quality of record (1, 100) is 80.0, while the record (1, 200) has a quality of 100.0. Then we consider the second one more trustable and output the result like (1:200,100.0), which means position 200 is a more accurate position.

```
Algorithm2: MDA Reducer Procedure
Input: Set S' consists of the records whose format is
(apid: pos, quality).
Output: Each AP's id, its accurate position and the total
quality.
input = {} //key= (apid:pos), value=total quality.
result_table = {}    // key= apid, value=pos.
quality_table={}   // key= apid, value=quality
For each (apid:pos, quality) in S':
        k, v = (apid:pos),  quality
        If k in the keyset of input:
                Update its value by adding v
        Else:
                Insert (k, v) into input
//find the max quality of each in each AP group.
For each (apid:pos, quality) in input:
        If apid in the keyset of result_table:
                k',v'= apid,quality_table[k']
                If quality>v':
//find more accurate position.
                        Update by set:
                                result_table[k] =pos,
                                quality_table[k]=quality
        Else:
                Insert (apid, pos) into result_table
                Insert (apid, quality) into quality_table
//output results.
For each apid in the keyset of result_table:
        Output apid,
result_table[apid],quality_table[apid]
```

Algorithm2: MDA Reducer Procedure

Aggregating with Temporal Distribution

The position got above is only temporary result, since we need to combine it with the history result as mentioned in Section 3. While both of them are useful in determining the up-to-date position of AP, it is natural that the former would have more weights.

The weight of the history result could be divided into two parts. The first part is its total quality. For instance, if the history position of one AP has a quality of 100.0, which means there exists at least 100 supporter before (because each record has at most 1.0 quality), then it is obviously more trustable than the temporary result of quality 1.0.So,the quality of result plays a role in determining the latest position of AP.

On the other hand, it had s to be noted that the quality would attenuate over time. Suppose that we got the history result of one AP with a timestamp one month ago, the quality of it has decreased dramatically. So it is not accurate as before and may be replaced by the temporary result.

We define f_2 to denote the speed of the attenuation in the quality of history results one day. Given that pos_{apid_h} is the history result of the AP of $apid$ and its quality is q_{apid_h}. Meanwhile, we got the temporary result pos_{apid_t} and its quality q_{apid_t} from the last step. The up-to-date result pos_{apid} is:

$$pos_{apid} = \begin{cases} pos_{apid\_h}, & q_{apid_h} * f_2 > q_{apid\_t} \\ pos_{apid\_t}, & q_{apid_h} * f_2 \leq q_{apid\_t} \end{cases} \tag{8}$$

It has to be noted that the quality of up-to-date result is always higher than or equal the quality of history result which has shrunken. Therefore, our aggregated position of each AP would be more and more accurate.

4.3   Feedback: Sliding Window Analysis

Sliding Window Analysis is a flexible and accurate approach which is used to evaluate each worker's performance periodically. Here, we still regard one day as the minimum unit to calculate each one's hit and also update his ar every day. In addition, we introduce the following definitions:

- SW_i, $i \in N$: A sliding window denotes the i_{th} dynamic period $[t_{i1}, t_{i2}]$. Here the length of SW is p days for example and we mark each day as an integer from 1. So first SW is $[1, p]$ and it would slide to right by increasing both t_{i1} and t_{i2} by 1. For instance, the third SW would be $[3, p+2]$ and the n_{th} SW is $[n, n+p-1]$.
- H_i, $i \in N$:The set contains one's contribution every day during the current SW_i period. Each contribution is a tuple (mrw, trw, hit)
- ar_i, $i \in N$: One worker's ar on the i_{th} day.
- m_1: an impact factor, which denotes the weight of the worker's latest contribution while update his ar

For instance, if given period one week and we want to calculate one's ar_{10} on the 10_{th} day, the 4_{th} sliding window, which denotes the period [4, 10], and H_4 would be used. That is to say, when we want to calculate ar_i, the SW_{i-p+1} would be $[i-p+1, i]$ and all the tuples in H_{i-p+1} are used. The details could be seen in Fig.7.

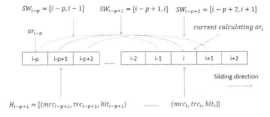

Fig. 7. Sliding Window Analysis

So in the formula (6), worker's recent contribution c would be calculated as:

$$c = \frac{\Sigma_{i-p+1}^{i} mrw_j}{\Sigma_{i-p+1}^{i} trw_j} \qquad (9)$$

And ar would be:

$$ar_i = (1 - m_1) * ar_{i-p} + m_1 * \frac{\Sigma_{i-p+1}^{i} mrw_j}{\Sigma_{i-p+1}^{i} trw_j} \qquad (10)$$

It has to be noted that we take the worker's history performance into account by giving ar_{i-p} a certain weight, regarding that it would influence one's later performance (ar_i) to some extent. Second, instead of the average of one's hits every day, we make use of the weighted average. It is because that the former may not reflect one's contribution accurately. For example, if one submits 10 records and 9 of them match aggregated results, the hit would be 90%. Meanwhile, he submits only 1 record which is also correct in another day, the hit is 100%. But obviously the first hit is more persuasive than the latter, since it contains more records. Last but not least, we also do periodically analysis which would not suffer from the case in which one's contributions vary dramatically from day to day.

With Sliding Window Analysis, one's history performance and his contributions in recent tasks are combined together, which is more persuasive and thoughtful. Meanwhile, it is also not sensitive to one's single contribution each day. But the cost on time is also higher, since each worker's ar need to be updated every day.

5   Experiments and Evaluation

To evaluate the effectiveness of our approach, we generate massive data set to simulate the submitted records under crowdsourcing model. The data set has the characteristics of that in crowdsourcing in reality. For example, while most workers are honest and always submit accurate contents, there exist a group of cheaters who may submit wrong contents. In addition, the data set has a kind of self-learning ability. For instance, if a cheater doesn't get his ar reduced, he would do more and more cheating in subsequent tasks and even drive other honesty workers to cheat, since he doesn't receive any punishment. We would see the improvements as using our approaches. Time cost and the accuracy of aggregated results are our focus.

Given 1000 workers and 1500 Access Points (AP), we generate data of 1GB size to simulate the records that submitted by workers in crowdsourcing every day during a period of 30 days. The other arguments are set as follows:

- Thresholds: $S_1=0.8$, $S_2=0.3$, $R=2^8=256$.
- Impact factor: $m_1=0.3$.
- Shrink factors: $f_1=f_2=0.5$.
- Sliding Window of 5 days length.
- Each worker's initial ar is 1 or 100%.

We pick up a piece of period (5 days) of the results in our experiments to be shown. There are four cases. (1) C_1: without filtering and quality table. (2) C_2: only using filtering procedure. (3) C_3: only aggregate with quality table. (4) C_4: using both filtering procedure and quality table to aggregate.

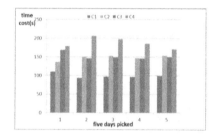 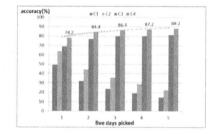

Fig. 8. Time cost and accuracy in different cases

As shown in the Fig.8, without our approach, the accuracy of the aggregated result is lower than 30%, which is an unacceptable value in practical applications. In addition, as time goes on, the accuracy is going down continuously (include the case of C_2), since more and more workers submit records of low quality.

On the other side, although the time cost of aggregating that utilize filtering and quality table is higher (2~3 times more than C_1), its accuracy is very satisfied (more than 80% at last). Since each worker's performance tends to be stable, it would be more and more accuracy to validate one's submission quality. Besides, aggregating with quality table would bring more continuous improvements than filtering.

In conclusion, although time cost is a little higher, our approach, particularly the aggregating procedure with quality table, performs well on quality control of the workers' submission.

6   Conclusion and Future Work

In crowdsourcing, the contents submitted by workers are always large and inaccurate. So as an employer, it is essential to control the quality of the contents. Here, we regard our indoor AP located system as research background and discuss how to qualify these data efficiently and accurately.

First, the meaningless contents in the raw data are eliminated with spatial distribution analysis, since they would only cause interference in our subsequent procedure. After that, we obtain the clean data. Then, we define *ar* to describe one's overall performance and it also determines the probability that one worker's submission would be accepted. There exist three cases, completely or partly accepted and discarded. Last but not least, we utilize HADOOP framework to aggregate the records to get the accurate position of each AP with Majority Decision Approach.

Moreover, the approach Sliding Window Analysis is introduced to update workers' *ar*. It utilizes time distribution analysis to describe one's performance accurately and dynamically. But it would cost high on time, since it need update one's *ar* every day.

It has to be noted that our approach can be applied to many other applications. Our core idea is to utilize spatial and temporal distribution to analyze the submission quality, which is irrelevant to the semantics of the contents in the submission. The detection of malicious grading on E-commerce sites is another suitable scenario. For example, it is treated as malicious behavior that one's frequent commits of the same grading during a short period. Meanwhile, we can still bind one's credibility with the quality of his grading together. If necessary, we could also generate the possible grades which are close to the origin one.

Our next work will focus on further experiments on our idea. For example, the length of the Sliding Window is the point. Although short sliding window could evaluate workers' performance accurate, it also brings high time cost. So it is essential to find a tradeoff between accuracy and cost. On the other hand, data refreshing in crowdsourcing is also a problem need to be solved. As time goes on, the scale of the data would be too massive to retain. So it is necessary to have a mechanism to eliminate those data with low value or freshness.

References

1. Howe, J.: The Rise of Crowdsourcing, Wired (June 2006),
   http://www.wired.com/wired/archive/14.06/crowds.html
2. BMW innovation lab, https://www.bmwgroup-cocreationlab.com/
   cocreation/project/customer-innovation-lab
3. Greengard, S.: Following the crowd. Communications of the ACM 54(2), 20–22 (2011)
4. Amazon Mechanical Turk, http://www.mturk.com
5. Alt, F., Sahami, A., Schmidt, S.A., Kramer, U., Nawaz, Z.: Location-based crowdsourcing: extending crowdsourcing to the real world. In: 6th Nordic Conference on Human-Computer Interaction: Extending Boundaries, pp. 13–22
6. Shah, S., Bao, F., Lu, C.-T., Chen, I.-R.: CROWDSAFE: crowdsourcing of crime incidents and safe routing on mobile devices. In: 19th ACM SIGSPATIAL International Conference on Advances in Geographic Information Systems, pp. 521–524
7. Hirth, M., Hoβfeld, T., Tran-Gia, P.: Cost-Optimal Validation Mechanisms and Cheat-Detection for Crowdsourcing Platforms. In: 5th International Conference on Innovative Mobile and Internet Services in Ubiquitous Computing, pp. 316–321
8. Lease, M., Yilmaz, E.: Crowdsourcing for information retrieval. Newsletter ACM SIGIR Forum Archive 45(2), 66–75 (2011)
9. Venetic, P., Garcia-Molina, H.: Quality control for comparison microtasks. In: The 1st International Workshop on Crowdsourcing and Data Mining, pp. 15–21

10. Kazai, G., Kamps, J., Milic-Frayling, N.: The face of quality in crowdsourcing relevance labels: demographics, personality and labeling accuracy. In: 21st ACM International Conference on Information and Knowledge Management, pp. 2583–2586

11. Zhu, S., Kane, S., Feng, J., Sears, A.: A Crowdsourcing Quality Control Model for Tasks Distributed in Parallel. In: CHI 2012 Extended Abstracts on Human Factors in Computing Systems, pp. 2501–2506 (2012)

12. Andrew, J., Flanagin, M.J.: Metzger. The credibility of volunteered geographic information. Geo Journal, An International Journal on Geography, Published Online (July 24, 2008)

13. Mashhadi, A.J., Capra, L.: Quality control for real-time ubiquitous crowdsourcing. In: 2nd International Workshop on Ubiquitous Crowd Souring, pp. 5–8

14. Kamar, E., Horvitz, E.: Incentives for truthful reporting in crowdsourcing. In: 11th International Conference on Autonomous Agents and Multiagent Systems, vol. 3, pp. 1329–1330

15. Mason, W., Watts, D.J.: Financial incentives and the "performance of crowds". ACM SIGKDD Explorations Newsletter 11(2), 100–108 (2009)

16. Dean, J., Ghemawat, S.: MapReduce: simplified data processing on large clusters. Communications of the ACM - 50th Anniversary Issue: 1958 - 2008 51(1), 107–113 (2008)

17. Chen, Z., Ma, J., Cui, C., Rui, H., Huang, S.: Web page publication time detection and its application for page rank. In: 33rd International ACM SIGIR Conference on Research and Development in Information Retrieval, pp. 859–860

18. Cheng, R., Chen, J., Xie, X.: Cleaning uncertain data with quality guarantees. Journal VLDB Endowment 1(1), 722–735 (2008)

19. Hadoop, http://hadoop.apache.org/

A 2.4-GHz Fractional-N PLL Frequency Synthesizer with a Low Power Full-Modulus-Range Programmable Frequency Divider

Jhin-Fang Huang and Jia-Lun Yang

Department of Electronic Engineering,
National Taiwan University of Science and Technology,
No. 43, Kee-Lung Rd. Sec. 4, Taipei, 10672 Taiwan
{jfhuang,m10002260}@mail.ntust.edu.tw

Abstract. A low-phase noise fractional-N PLL (phase-locked loop) frequency synthesizer operating at 2.4 GHz band is fabricated in TSMC 0.18-um CMOS process. The proposed prototype with a $\Sigma\Delta$ MASH 1-1-1 modulator and a full-modulus-range programmable frequency divider of static D-flip-flop-based (DFF based) divider cells to reduce both power consumption and phase noise features high programmability, full modulus range, smaller area, and good phase noise. At 1.8 V supply voltage, measured results achieve a wide tuning range from 2.11 to 2.42 GHz, corresponding to 13.7%, a phase noise of -107.4 dBc/Hz at 1 MHz offset from 2.36 GHz, a power consumption of 21.3 mW and an output power of -9.93 dBm. Including pads, the chip area only occupies 0.744 mm^2.

Keywords: voltage-controlled oscillator, frequency synthesizer, PLL.

1 Introduction

Numerous designs of 2.4 GHz PLLs are found in standard CMOS process and performed much growth in recent years [1]-[3]. In [1], the authors adopt hybrid technique to achieve a locking time of 20 us, but at the expenses of a high power consumption of 29.6 mW and a chip area of 2.08 mm^2. Literature [2] uses a low power technique to reduce power consumption, but suffers from long locking time of 55 us. A low voltage design to reduce power consumption is published and attractive, but with a bigger chip area of 1.68 mm^2 [3].

Actually, low frequency PLL with low chip area is a big challenge since inductors will consume much chip area. Hence with those factors of supply voltage, power consumption, phase noise and chip area etc, a high performance of PLL under 1.8 V supply voltage is proposed and fabricated in TSMC 0.18 μm CMOS process. The features of the proposed PLL are in four aspects. First, gain-boosting Colpitts LC-tank VCO is used to improve phase noise. Second, since the frequency divider dominates the overall power consumption, a combination of $\Sigma\Delta$ MASH 1-1-1 modulator and TSPC in the frequency divider is adopted to relieve this effect. Third point adopts hybrid technique with combining integer-N and fractional-N advantages to lower

M. Pathan, G. Wei, and G. Fortino (Eds.): IDCS 2013, LNCS 8223, pp. 183–194, 2013.
© Springer-Verlag Berlin Heidelberg 2013

locking time, and using off-chip filter to reduce chip area. Deliberate and compact layout to reduce the problems of process variation after manufacturing and choosing Colpitts VCO to achieve a good phase noise is the forth contribution. Measured results achieve a tuning range of 2.11 GHz to 2.42 GHz, a locked phase noise of - 107.4 dBc/Hz at 1 MHz offset frequency, a power consumption of 21.3 mW at a supply voltage of 1.8 V and a chip area of 0.744 mm^2.

2   Phase-Locked Loop (PLL) Architecture

The proposed fractional-N PLL structure shown in Fig. 1 mainly contains a phase/frequency detector (PFD), a charge pump (CP) working in tandem with an off-chip 3rd low-pass RC filter, a tunable loop filter, and a Gm-boosting Colpitts VCO in the feedforward path and a full-modulus frequency divider (FMFD) and a ΣΔ MASH 1-1-1modulator in the feedback path. However, the integer-N PLL has some limitations. Integer-N PLLs suffer from essential tradeoffs between loop bandwidth and channel spacing and allow alternative tradeoffs among PLL design constraints for phase noise, locking time and reference spurs [4], the fractional-N architecture can decouple the relationship between the loop bandwidth and frequency resolution. Normally fractional-N PLL can achieve a wide loop bandwidth (hence fast locking) and fine frequency resolution at the same time. In additional, it can sustain various reference frequencies.

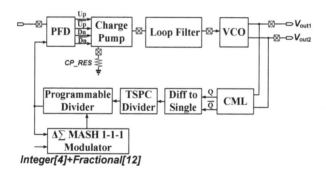

Fig. 1. The proposed PLL frequency synthesizer architecture

3   Phase-Locked Loop Functions

3.1   Voltage-Controlled Oscillator (VCO)

Conventional Colpitts oscillators using Gm-boosting technique contain a tapped inductor and two varactors to form a LC tank VCO as shown in Fig. 2. Two single-ended Colpitts oscillators are connected into a differential Colpitts oscillator. The phase of gate voltage of M_1 and M_2 is as same as the phase of drain voltages of M_2 and M_1 respectively. Connecting them together behaves the effect of Gm-boosting scheme. The small signal transconductance looking from the drain of M_1 or M_2 can be evaluated as follows:

$$Y_{in} = \frac{s^2 C_1 C_2 - g_m s C_2}{g_m + s(C_1 + C_2)}.$$

(1)

The real part and imaginary part of the trans-conductance are:

$$R_e[Y_{in}] = -\frac{g_m \omega^2 C_2 (2C_1 + C_2)}{g_m^2 + \omega^2 (C_1 + C_2)^2},$$

(2a)

and

$$I_m[Y_{in}] = j \frac{\omega^2 C_1 C_2 (C_1 + C_2) - g_m^2 \omega C_2}{g_m^2 + \omega^2 (C_1 + C_2)^2}.$$

(2b)

The real part of the transconductance of the traditional Colpitts oscillator can be evaluated as [4]:

$$R_e[Y_{in}] = -\frac{g_m \omega^2 C_1 C_2}{g_m^2 + \omega^2 (C_1 + C_2)^2}.$$

(3)

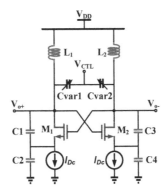

Fig. 2. Traditional Colpitts oscillator by using Gm-boosting technique

Comparing (2a) and (3), the real part of the transconductance of the Colpitts VCO using Gm-boosting technique will increase as $(2+C_2/C_1)$ than the traditional Colpitts oscillator. It explains that the power consumption of the Colpitts VCO by using Gm-boosting technique could reduce a factor of $(1+C_2/C_1)$. The cross-coupled current mirror directly connected to gates of M_1 and M_2 reduce the voltage headroom. Since pMOS has smaller flicker noise than nMOS, so pMOS is chosen. Fig. 3 illustrates the proposed VCO circuit which includes a core circuit and output buffer circuits [4]. The LC-tank consists of a differential high-Q inductor which is a fully symmetric spiral inductor and two nMOS varactors. To have a wide tuning range, metal insulator metal (MIM) capacitors are used.

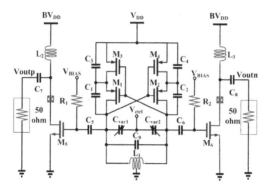

Fig. 3. The proposed Colpitts VCO with output buffer circuits

3.2   Low-Pass Loop Filter Design

The low-pass loop filter is used to suppress the spurs introduced by the reference frequency and CP. To design the 3rd RC low-pass loop filter has to note several important factors, such as reference frequency, frequency divider ratio (N), loop filter bandwidth (K), charge pump current (I_{CP}), VCO tuning range gain (K_{VCO}) and phase margin etc. These factors determine the stability of PLL. After considering mentioned factors, Fig. 4 shows the 3rd low pass filter circuit. The filter's transimpedance ($V_{tune}(s)/I_{cp}(s)$) can be expressed as:

$$Z(s) = \frac{sR_1C_1 + 1}{s^3 R_1R_3C_1C_2C_3 + s^2(R_1C_1C_2 + R_1C_1C_3 + R_3C_2C_3 + R_3C_1C_3) + s(C_1 + C_2 + C_3)}. \quad (4)$$

As illustrated in (4), resistor R_1 and capacitor C_1 in the loop filter generate a pole at the origin and a zero at $1/(R_1C_1)$. Capacitor C_2 combining R_2 and C_3 generates extra poles at frequencies higher than PLL bandwidth to reduce the feedthrough at the reference frequency and to decrease spurious sidebands at harmonics of the reference frequency. The element values used in this 3rd loop filter with considerations of CP current, 100 uA, VCO gain, 300 MHz/V, frequency divider ratio, 96, loop filter bandwidth 250 kHz and phase margin 62°, are listed as R_1=6.3 kΩ, R_2=12.6 kΩ, C_1=402 pF, C_2= 18 pF, and C_3=1.5 pF.

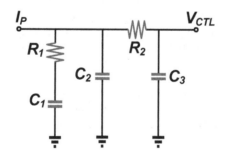

Fig. 4. The proposed 3rd low-pass filter circuit

3.3   Phase Frequency Detector (PFD) Circuit

To design PFD operating at high frequency with minimum dead-zone, minimum phase offset and reduced blind zone, a domino-logic PFD in Fig. 5 is chosen to reach those purposes [5]. The PFD compares the edges of the reference signal F_{REF} and feedback signal F_{DIV}. When the F_{REF} leads the F_{DIV}, U_P outputs pulse signal and D_N outputs reset signal. On the other way, when the F_{DIV} leads the F_{REF}, D_N outputs pulse signal and U_P outputs reset signal. On the reset path, delay cell is inserted to improve the dead zone.

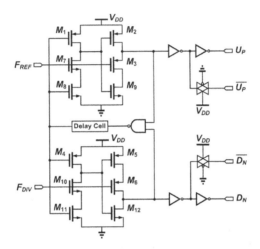

Fig. 5. The proposed PFD circuit with minimum dead-zone

3.4   Charge Pump (CP) Circuit

A CP consists of a bias circuit, a start-up circuit and a current steering charge pump circuit as shown in Fig. 6 [4]. The phase error is converted into a proportional amount of charge at the charge pump output. The switch is put at the drain to have the shortest switch time. The differential U_P and D_N signals from the PFD steer the current one way or the other in the differential pair in the CP. Transistors M_{P1} and M_{N1} are designed to ensure CP current works smoothly and R_b is an off-chip resistor to adjust the bias current. The start-up circuit contains transistors M_{P8}, M_{N8}, M_{N9} and M_{N10} and injects currents into the bias loop which will start up the circuit. Once the loop starts up, M_{N10} sinks all the currents from M_{P8}. The gates of M_{N8} and M_{N9} will be pulled low, and thereby turned them off that they no longer affect the bias circuit. The differential CP employs a rail-to-rail buffer to reduce the charge injection, thus the spur level.

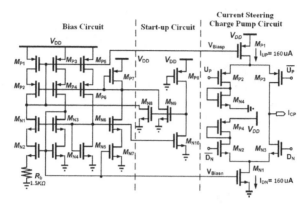

Fig. 6. Schematic of CP with start-up and bias circuits

3.5   Full-Modulus Frequency Divider (FMFD) Circuit

In general design, the logic functions of the conventional (2/3) cell were implemented with the current-mode logic (CML) structure, which requires two accurate resistances and biased current to achieve high speed, low cost and low power. However, the cell area is increased, and the tolerance of integrated resistors due to process and temperature variations is large, typically around 30%. Fig. 7 shows the FMFD architecture, which consists of four asynchronous divided-by-2/1 stages [6]. Using dynamic latch (or DFF) of the divider can be increased the operation frequency but at the cost of higher power consumption and phase noise. Thus, the proposed design implements with the static DFFs to reduce both power consumption and phase noise.

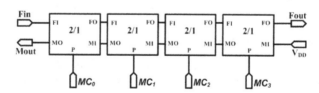

Fig. 7. The proposed full-modulus frequency divider structure

The output frequency of VCO therefore can be tuned by controlling the ports by off-chip codes from MC_0 to MC_3 and then the division number (DN) is varied with full modulus range from 1 to 15. Fig. 8 shows the 2/1 divider architecture consists of the traditional static DFF (D flip-flop) which reduce both power consumption and phase noise. The DN can be programmable and expressed as:

$$DN = 2^4 - 2^3 \times MC_3 - 2^2 \times MC_2 - 2^1 \times MC_1 - 2^0 \times MC_0. \tag{5}$$

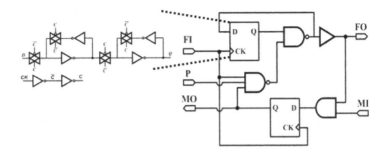

Fig. 8. A 2/1 divider cell structure

3.6   MASH 1-1-1 Σ–Δ Modulator Circuit

The FMFD division ratio is controlled by the $\Sigma\Delta$ MASH 1-1-1 modulator which is preferred in this work. Σ–Δ modulators are useful in the field of communication and extensively used for ADC and DAC conversion applications. A systematic way to remove the fractional spurs is to employ the Σ–Δ modulator. The technique of a Σ–Δ modulator can improve the signal-to noise ratio (SNR) at low frequency. The error resulting from the quantization nonlinearity is filtered by the Σ–Δ modulator.

This proposed fractional-N frequency synthesizer designs a Σ–Δ modulator to reduce bit number necessary to generate fractional division ratio. Since lower-order modulators are prone to generating limit cycle oscillations and tones, a first-order modulator produces significant unwanted spurious components. Higher-order Σ–Δ modulators generate fewer limit cycle oscillations and tones, but they require signal conditioning around the loop for stability control. Under this consideration, a 6-bit Σ–Δ modulator is selected to achieve our purpose.

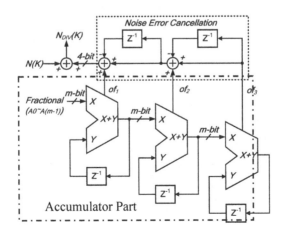

Fig. 9. The proposed $\Sigma\Delta$ MASH 1-1-1 modulator architecture

Since fractional spurs occur at low offset frequency, it is difficult to remove them by the loop filter. A better way for a fractional-N frequency divider is to use an accumulator. The MASH 1-1-1 architecture based on digital accumulators is depicted in Fig. 9 [7]. The overflow from the accumulator is usually one bit, i.e., either 0 or 1. High order $\Sigma-\Delta$ modulator can provide even better noise shaping results, and thus smaller fractional spurs.

The digital realization of m-bit MASH 1-1-1 $\Sigma-\Delta$ modulators can be applied to frequency synthesizer where m is the input of MASH 1-1-1, N(k) is the integer input of the frequency synthesizer and $N_{DIV}(k)$ connects the divider of the frequency synthesizer and is the output to the divider of PLL. The MMFD divide ratio controlled by the MASH 1-1-1 $\Sigma-\Delta$ modulator mainly consists of two parts of accumulator and noise error cancellation and is preferred in this implementation, since it is unconditionally stable, and can accommodate a wide-range input for high resolution frequency synthesizer. With the controlled m-code, the fractional value of the total divide ratio is determined by

$$f_{Fractional} = \frac{2^{(m-1)} \times A(m-1) + 2^{(m-2)} \times A(m-2) + ... + 2^1 \times A1 + 2^0 \times A0}{2^m}, \tag{6}$$

where A(m), m=0, 1, ... (m-1) is the off-chip controlled code, either 0 or 1.

4   Measured Results

The VCO circuit is placed left side and near the pad that can reduce the signal attenuation. The right side blocks are digital circuits that must add the guard ring to isolate the external noise influence. The proposed PLL was implemented in TSMC 0.18 μm CMOS process. The chip microphotograph is shown in Fig. 10. The chip area is 0.744.

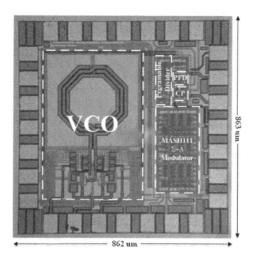

Fig. 10. Chip microphotograph of the proposed frequency synthesizer with a chip area of 0.744 mm^2

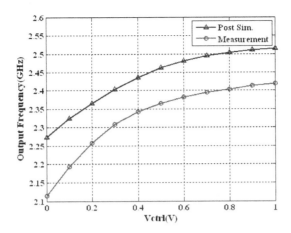

Fig. 11. Measured tuning range of VCO versus the controlled voltage Vctrl varied from 0 to 1.0 V

Fig. 12 shows the measured power spectral density of -9.93 dBm of the proposed PLL with a reference spur of -44 dBc after phase-locking which is locked at 2.361 GHz. Fig. 13 shows the function of measured phase noise versus offset frequency from 2.361 GHz and is about -107.4 dBc/Hz at 1 MHz offset frequency. Fig. 14 shows the pie chart distribution of power with different PLL frequency synthesizer partials. It is obvious that the programmable digital divider consumes much power of 7.63 mW, or 35% and then the $\Sigma\Delta$ modulator is 7.03 mW, or 33%. The VCO and buffer circuits only consume 2.13 mW and 4.69 mW, about 10% and 22%, respectively.

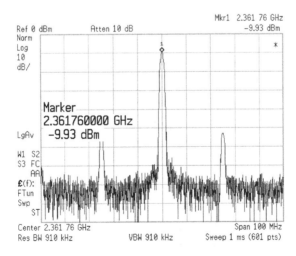

Fig. 12. Measured output spectrum of the proposed PLL with. V_{DD}=1.8 V and V_{ctrl} =0.5 V of VCO

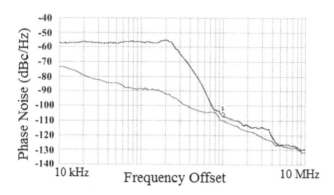

Fig. 13. Measured phase noise versus offset frequency of the proposed PLL

Operating at 2.4 GHz and 1.8 V supply voltage with 300 MHz frequency tuning range, the proposed PLL achieves a FOM of -161.5 dB, defined as [8]

$$\text{FOM}_{pn} = PN(f_{offset}) - 20\log(\frac{f_o}{f_{offset}}) + 10\log(\frac{P_{DC}}{1\,mW}), \tag{7}$$

where $PN\left(f_{offset}\right)$ is measured phase noise, f_o is the oscillating frequency in MHz, $f_{offset} = 1\,MHz$ and P_{DC} is the power consumption in mW. As shown in (7), FOM improves as f_o increases, thus the circuit can benefit from higher f_o. Table 1 summarizes the measured performances of the proposed PLL in comparison with other recently published papers. The proposed prototype achieves the smallest chip area except [10] which uses 90 nm advanced process, almost the best FOM and the best phase noise except [1] which consumes much power of 29.6 mW and high chip area of 2.08 mm^2. The proposed prototype achieves measured phase noise of -107.4 dBc/Hz@1 MHz from 2.36 GHz, but only consumes power of 21.3 mW and chip area of 0.744 mm^2.

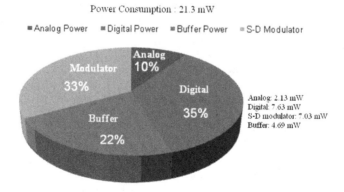

Fig. 14. Simulated power consumption of the proposed prototype devices

Table 1. Comparison of Proposed PLL Frequency Synthesizer with Previously Published Papers

Design	[1] 2008	[10] 2011	[3] 2010	[9] 2009	This Work
Technology (μm)	0.18	90 nm	0.18	0.18	0.18
Supply voltage (V)	1.8	0.5	0.6	1.8	1.8
Tuning range (GHz)	2.36~2.49	0.4~2.24	2.4~2.64	2.2~2.6	2.11~2.42
(%)	(5.36)	(139.4)	(9.5)	(16.7)	(13.7)
Phase noise dBc/Hz @ 1MHz	-113	-87	-104.69	-105.5	-107.4
K_{VCO} (MHz/V)	N/A	NA	400	N/A	300
Loop filter bandwidth (kHz)	50	3000	50	270	250
PLL locking time (μs)	20	NA	N/A	N/A	35*
Power Consump. (mW)	29.6	2.08	14.4	22	21.3
Chip area (mm^2)	2.08	0.074	1.682	2.25	0.744
FOM	-165.9	-150.82	-161.27	-159.96	**-161.5**

* Post-simulation value.

5   Conclusions

This proposed PLL is presented and fabricated in TSMC 0.18-μm CMOS process. To improve the phase noise adopts a Colpitts LC-tank VCO and adopts a static DFF to perform the FMFD circuit which reduce both power consumption and phase noise. The FMFD is used to change the frequency channel by different input digital codes. The locking time can be reduced by carefully designing system parameters, such as CP current, VCO gain and loop bandwidth. Measured results of the prototype illustrate that the proposed PLL is comparable to recently published papers and achieves a wide tuning range from 2.11 GHz to 2.42 GHz corresponding to a frequency tuning range of 13.7%, an almost lowest phase noise of -107.4 dBc/Hz and an almost smallest chip area of 0.744 mm² among the known 2.4 GHz-band reports.

Acknowledgements. The authors would like to thank the National Chip Implementation Center (CIC) for the chip fabrication and technical supports. Prof. Ron-Yi Liu for his valuable suggestions is also appreciated.

References

1. Woo, K., Liu, Y., Nam, E., Ham, D.: Fast-Lock Hybrid PLL Combining Fractional-N and Integer-N Modes of Differing Bandwidths. IEEE J. of Solid-State Circuit 43, 379–389 (2008)

2. Srinivasan, R., Turker, D.Z., Park, S.W., Sinencio, E.S.: A Low-Power Frequency Synthesizer with Quadrature Signal Generation for 2.4 GHz Zigbee Transceiver Applications. IEEE Int. Symp. Circuits and Systems, 429–432 (2007)
3. Lu, C.T., Hsieh, H.H., Lu, L.H.: A Low-Power Quadrature VCO and Its Application to a 0.6 V 2.4 GHz PLL. IEEE Trans. on Circuit and System 57, 793–802 (2010)
4. Huang, J.F., Jiangn, Y.J., Liu, R.Y.: The Gm-boosting VCO Chip Design for 5.8 GHz WiMAX Applications. In: The 21st VLSI Design/CAD Symposium, pp. 443–445 (2010)
5. Young, I.A., Greason, J.K., Wong, K.L.: A PLL Clock Generator with 5 to 110 MHz of Lock Range for Microprocessors. IEEE J. Solid-State Circuits 27, 1599–1607 (1992)
6. Lin, C.S., Chien, T.H., Wey, C.L.: A 5.5 GHz 1-mW Full-Modulus-Range Programmable Frequency Divider in 90-nm CMOS Process. IEEE Trans. Circuits Syst. II, Exp. Briefs 58, 550–554 (2011)
7. Deng, P.Y., Kiang, J.F.: A 5 GHz CMOS Frequency Synthesizer with an Injection Locked Frequency Divider and Differential Switched Capacitors. IEEE Trans on Circuits and Systems 56, 320–326 (2009)
8. Huang, J.F., Mao, C.C., Liu, R.Y.: The 10 GHz Wide Tuning and Low Phase-Noise PLL Chip Design. In: International Conference on Anti-Counterfeiting, Security, and Identification, pp. 1–4 (2011)
9. Lin, T.H., Ti, C.L., Liu, Y.H.: Dynamic Current-Matching Charge Pump and Gated-Offset Linearization Technique for Delta-Sigma Fractional-N PLLs. IEEE Trans. Circuits Syst. I, Reg. 56, 877–885 (2009)
10. Cheng, K.H., Tsai, Y.C., Lo, Y.L.: A 0.5 V 0.4–2.24-GHz Inductorless Phase-Locked Loop in a System-on-Chip. IEEE Trans. Circuits Syst. I, Reg. Papers 58, 793–802 (2011)

Multiple Sources Network Coding Signature in the Standard Model

Jun Shao[1], Jinlin Zhang[1], Yun Ling[1], Min Ji[1], Guiyi Wei[1], and Bishan Ying[2]

[1] School of Computer and Information Engineering
Zhejiang Gongshang University, Hangzhou, Zhejiang, P.R. China, 310018
http://ndc.zjgsu.edu.cn/People.htm
[2] Wasu Media Network Co., Hangzhou, China
billsun_ying@hotmail.com

Abstract. Network coding is a new routing technique that can improve a network's throughput. The key idea is to allow network routers to code the received packets before transmission. However, network coding is vulnerable to pollution attacks where malicious node(s) can flood the network with invalid packets and prevent the receiver from the right decoding. Network coding signature offers a good solution to this problem. Nevertheless, existing network coding signature schemes cannot either be proven-secure in the standard model, or support multiple sources or in-time signing. In this paper, we propose a new network coding signature scheme to solve the above problems.

Keywords: multiple sources, network coding, signature.

1 Introduction

Network coding, proposed by Ahlswede et al.[2], is a novel paradigm to improve a network's throughput. Instead of the traditional "store and forward routing", network coding allows intermediate nodes to code the received packets before transmission. In this paper, we consider the linear network coding as the underlying coding method. In linear network coding, packets are treated as vectors and combined using random and independent coefficients chosen by intermediate nodes. After receiving sufficient correct packets, destination node(s) can be able to recover the original files, even if the destination node does not know the coefficients. Due to its magic transformation, the linear network coding provides robustness, adaptability and good throughput. It has been suggested as an efficient method for file sharing in peer-to-peer networks, and it improves the function of large-scale data content distribution over the Internet.

Unfortunately, network coding suffers from pollution attacks [19][12], where malicious node(s) could inject invalid packets into the network. Once the invalid packets has been coded with valid packets in the rest of transmission, the destination nodes cannot recover the original file. In the linear network coding, even if only an invalid packet has been injected, the pollution attack works.

M. Pathan, G. Wei, and G. Fortino (Eds.): IDCS 2013, LNCS 8223, pp. 195–208, 2013.

To prevent the network from invalid packets, the honest intermediate nodes should have a way to verify the incoming vectors and discard invalid ones. To the best of our knowledge, there exist two main approaches. One is information-theoretic approach [13,14] that introduces redundant information into original packets to defend against malicious packets. However, the redundant information leads inefficiency of communication. The other is cryptographic one, where the main idea is to provide a method to authenticate incoming vectors to alleviate pollution attacks. Unfortunately, standard digital signatures or MACs cannot solve the pollution attack problem well [1]. It is because that the source node(s) should sign the entire file or every transmitted part before transmission, and the destination node(s) can verify the validity only after receiving (revealing) the entire file. To improve the inefficiency, Boneh et al. [6] proposed the concept of network coding signature, which allows signature(s) can be coded, and coded signature(s) can still be verified as un-coded signature(s). The existing network coding signature schemes cannot either be proven-secure in the standard model (i.e., random oracles are required), or support multiple sources or in-time signing. On the one hand, it has been shown that the security obtained in the random oracles cannot guarantee the security in the real world [8,4]. On the other hand, many network situations, such as real-time stock information system (Dow Jones, S&P 500 and Nasdaq in USA), are characterized by continuous data streaming from multiple sources.

In this paper, we would like to propose the first network coding signature scheme supporting multiple sources, in-time signing, and security in the stand model.

Outline of the Paper. In the following, we review the background of linear network coding, single source network coding, multiple sources network coding, and pollution attack. Then we introduce previous works in Section 3.1, and we describe the advantages of our schemes in section 3.2. In Section 4 we present a satisfying security model, and we introduce bilinear pairing and computational assumption. Our proposal and security analysis are described in Sections 5.

2   Background of Network Coding

For a better understanding of the network coding, we would like to introduce the background of network coding, including the concept of network coding, linear network coding with single source and multiple sources, and the pollution attack on the network coding.

2.1   Network Coding

Assume that a network as shown in Fig.1 [18], the source node S sends two packets v_1 and v_2 to both the destination nodes T_1 and T_2. Traditional network as shown in the Fig.1a, the packet(s) received from upstream is/are simply stored and sent out by every forwarder. Thus, the channel from W to X has been used twice. Fig.1b also describes a way used in network coding on the same network.

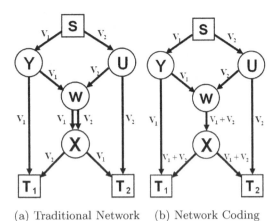

(a) Traditional Network   (b) Network Coding

Fig. 1. Traditional Network and Network Coding

The node W receives packets v_1 and v_2 from upstream and combines them to create the combination $v_1 + v_2$, then send them to T_1 and T_2 via X. On receiving v_1 and $v_1 + v_2$, the node T_1 can obtain v_1 and v_2. The similar situation to T_2. Consequently, all the channels in the network are used once, and the network's throughput is improved.

2.2   Linear Network Coding with Single Source

In this section, we present a brief overview of linear network coding with single source. We model the network as a directed graph $G = (E, V)$, where E, V are sets of edges and vertices in the network, respectively. As usual, the graph G is connected. We assume that a source node $S \subset V$ wishes to transmit one file F to a set of destination nodes through the network. Firstly, the source file F is interpreted as a set of m vectors $\widehat{v}_1, ..., \widehat{v}_m \in \mathbb{F}_p^n$, ($p$ is a big prime). Secondly, the source node S additionally creates m augmented vectors $v_1, ..., v_m$, which have the following format.

$$v_i = (\widehat{v}_i, \overbrace{0, ..., 0, \underbrace{1}_{i}, 0, ..., 0}^{m}) \in \mathbb{F}_p^{n+m}.$$

The first n entries and last m entries of vector v_i are named as the data component and augmentation component, respectively. The vectors $v_1, ..., v_m$ form a basis of the subspace $V \subset \mathbb{F}^{m+n}$. Vectors v_i and the values of $(v_1, ..., v_m)$ are named as properly augmented vectors and augmented basis, respectively. Once an augmented vector is generated, the source node S can send it to its neighbor nodes with the file identifier id.

After receiving $\mu(\geq 1)$ vectors $(v_1, ..., v_\mu)$ with the same file identifier id, the intermediate node computes a linear combination y by $y = \sum_{j=1}^{\mu} \alpha_j v_j$, where the coefficients $(\alpha_1, ..., \alpha_\mu) \in Z_N^\mu$ can be chosen randomly by the intermediate or fixed by the application. At last, the intermediate node sends y to its neighbor nodes.

Upon receiving m linearly independent vectors $(y_1, ..., y_m)$ with the same file identifier id, the destination node(s) can recover the original vector $\hat{v}_j$ as follows. Let y_i^L and y_i^R denote the left-most n positions and the right-most m positions of the vector, respectively. The destination node firstly computes an $m \times m$ matrix M:

$$M = \begin{pmatrix} y_1^R \\ \cdot \\ \cdot \\ \cdot \\ y_m^R \end{pmatrix}^{-1} \tag{1}$$

Then it recovers the original vectors as follows.

$$\begin{pmatrix} \hat{v}_1 \\ \cdot \\ \cdot \\ \cdot \\ \hat{v}_m \end{pmatrix} = M \cdot \begin{pmatrix} y_1^L \\ \cdot \\ \cdot \\ \cdot \\ y_m^L \end{pmatrix} \tag{2}$$

2.3   Linear Network Coding with Multiple Sources

Usually, there exist multiple source nodes in the network, like that in the stock system. While, the network coding with multiple sources is different from that in the single-source case. In particular, they are different on the intermediate node side and destination node side.

The file identifier id has different functionality. In the single source network coding, each file is associated with a file identifier id. The destination nodes group vectors together if packets have the same identifier. But in the multiple sources case, the file identifier id has more crucial functions, and it allows the intermediate nodes to code vectors from different files. The sources may produce vectors at different times, and the vectors between a source-destination pair are subject to random delays or pass different routers. Thus, it will face the problem of confusion in packets and attack is produced by an adversary who injects an old packet into network.

In this paper, we propose a new method to deal with these problems is to group vectors into generation, see the details in Section 5.1.

2.4   Pollution Attack

In network coding, the receivers can reconstruct the original file iff sufficiently correct and linearly independent vectors can be received. However, the basic network coding scheme offers no means of isolating any fault. If destination nodes receive one of vectors w_i is invalid, the error would exist in every block one of the reconstructed file. What's worse, if one malicious node injects one single vector, the error will be propagated by every node downstream.

Now, we take the multiple source network in Fig.2 as an example. Once an invalid packet $v_a^{(2)'}$ is injected into the network, the combination $v_a^{(1)} + v_a^{(2)'}$ is also incorrect. As a result, T_1 receiving $v_a^{(1)}$ and $v_a^{(1)} + v_a^{(2)'}$ cannot decode $v_a^{(1)}$ and $v_a^{(2)}$.

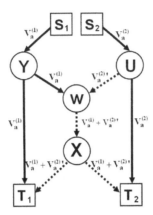

Fig. 2. Threat Model

At the same time, the source nodes may be malicious in the network coding with multiple sources, and they may forge packets [1].

3 Related Works on Network Coding Signatures

3.1 Related Works

There are a lot of network coding signature schemes. Boneh et al. [6] adapted homomorphic signatures (first suggested by Johnson et al. [15] in a general setting) to the network coding, and proposed an efficient homomorphic network coding signature scheme and proved its security based on the CDH assumption in the random oracle model. They also proposed a network coding signature in the standard model but eliminated the homomorphic property.

One year later, Gennaro et al. [16] proposed a homomorphic network coding signature based on the RSA assumption in the random oracle model and showed that it is possible to work with small coefficients in the linear combination even if the signature works over the integers (or a large finite field).

In [3], Attrapadung and Libert gave a homomorphic network coding signature scheme in the standard model, and the scheme is based on the dual encryption techniques of Waters [17]. But the scheme relies on the composite order groups, so the scheme is not so efficient as expected. Furthermore, the efficiency gap is still significant between the resulting construction and those in the random oracle solutions even if the scheme were to be converted to prime order groups.

After that, Catalano, Fiore and Warinschi [10] proposed two efficient network coding signature schemes in the standard model. The one based on the strong Diffie-Hellman assumption and the other based on the RSA assumption.

Besides the above schemes, there are also many other schemes [11,7,9], that can only work in the single source setting. However, we usually have multiple sources and they would send messages simultaneously in the network. But single source signature schemes cannot be applied to the multiple sources setting. The main reason is that the adversary would not only be the intermediate nodes but also the source nodes.

In [1], Agrawal et al. considered the situation of mixing packets from multiple sources. They introduced a security model and proposed a generic construction of multiple sources network coding signature in the standard model. They constructed a generic attack where an intermediate may accept invalid packets as valid one. But their scheme required to sign all the base vectors of a subspace at once. Later, Yan et al. [18] proposed a short signature scheme for multiple sources network coding, and gave the security in the random oracle model. In their scheme, one source just set one packet of the file, which cannot be applied in the real multiple sources setting.

3.2 Our Contribution

In this paper we propose a multiple sources network coding signatures scheme. The construction follows the second signature scheme by Boneh et al. [6] and the first signature scheme by Catalano et al. [10]. The proposal has the following properties:

1. Multiple sources: The proposal supports the real multiple sources, i.e., any source can send out one entire file not only a part of one file like that in [18].
2. In-time signing: The proposal allows the nodes in the network to transmit streaming data, i.e., the source nodes need not know the whole file before transmitting the first corresponding packet. Therefore, the packets can be of in-time transmission and this is more realistic.
3. Security in the stand model: There are two models. and it has been shown that security in the random oracle model does not guarantee the security in the real world. Our scheme is provably secure in the standard model.

4 Preliminaries on Network Coding Signatures

In this section, we briefly introduce some involved parties of our proposal.

4.1 Network Coding Signature

We review the definition of the multiple sources network coding signatures and its security notion.

Definition 1. *(Multiple Sources Network Coding Signatures). A Multiple Sources network coding signature is defined by a triple of probabilistic, polynomial-time algorithms* (**Setup**, **KG**, **Sign**, **Verify**, **Combine**) *such that:*

Setup$(1^\lambda, n, m)$. *Input: a security parameter 1^λ and integers n, m, n is data space dimension and m is subspace dimension. Output: the public parameters.*

KG(u). *Input: the total number u of the source nodes. Output: public keys $\mathbf{pk}_i$ and secret keys $\mathbf{sk}_i$, and $i = 1, ..., u$.*

Sign$(\mathbf{sk}, id, v)$. *Input: a i-th secret key $\mathbf{sk}_i$, identifier id_a that is an element of a randomly samplable set I, and $v_a^{(i)} \in \mathbb{F}_p^{n+m}$ is a properly augmented vector. Output: a signature σ.*

Verify$(\mathbf{pk}, id, v, \sigma)$. *Input: public keys $\mathbf{pk}_i$, an identifier $id_a \in I$, vectors $v_a^{(i)} \in \mathbb{F}_p^{m+n}$, and signatures $\sigma_a^{(i)}$. Output: $\perp$ (reject) or $\top$ (accept).*

Combine$(\{\mathbf{pk}_i, \alpha_i, \sigma_i\}_{i=1}^\mu, id)$. *Input: public keys $\mathbf{pk}_1, ..., \mathbf{pk}_\mu$, an identifier $id_a \in I$, vectors $v_a^{(1)}, ..., v_a^{(\mu)} \in \mathbb{F}_p^{m+n}$, and μ pairs consisting of a weight $\alpha_i \in \mathbb{F}_p$ and signatures $\sigma_a^{(1)}, ..., \sigma_a^{(\mu)}$. Output: a signature σ.*

We require that for each $(p, \mathbf{pk}, \mathbf{sk})$ output by **KG**(u), *the following holds:*

- *For $id_a \in I$ and vectors $v_a^{(i)} \subseteq \mathbb{F}_p^{n+m}$, if $\sigma_a^{(i)} :=$ **Sign**$(\mathbf{sk}_i, id_a, v_a^{(i)})$ then* **Verify**$(\mathbf{pk}_i, id_a, v_a^{(i)}, \sigma_a^{(i)}) = \top$ *for all $v_a^{(i)} \in V$.*
- *For $id_a \in I$, any $\mu > 0$, and all sets of triples $\{\mathbf{pk}_j, v_a^{(j)}, \sigma_a^{(j)}\}_{j=1}^\mu$, if* **Verify** $(\mathbf{pk}_j, v_a^{(j)}, \sigma_a^{(j)}, id_a) = \top$ *for all j, then it must be the case that*

$$\textbf{Verify}\big(\{\mathbf{pk}_j\}_{j=1}^\mu, \sum \alpha_j v_a^{(j)}, id_a, \textbf{Combine}(\{\mathbf{pk}_j, v_a^{(j)}, \alpha_j, \sigma_a^{(j)}\}_{j=1}^\mu, id_a)\big) = \top$$

Definition 2. *(Security of Multiple Sources Network Coding Signatures). A multiple sources network coding signature scheme $S =$ (**Setup**, **KG**, **Sign**, **Verify**, **Combine**) is secure if the advantage of any probabilistic, polynomial-time adversary $\mathcal{A}$ in the following security game is negligible in the security parameter λ:*

Setup. *The adversary $\mathcal{A}$ sends positive integers n, m to the challenger. The challenger runs* **Setup**$(1^\lambda, n, m)$ *to obtain the public parameters, and sends the public parameters to $\mathcal{A}$.*

Queries. *Proceeding adaptively, the adversary $\mathcal{A}$ can request the following queries:*

1. $\mathcal{O}_{pk}$. *The adversary $\mathcal{A}$ sends i to the challenger. The challenger sends the public key $\mathbf{pk}_i$ to $\mathcal{A}$.*
2. $\mathcal{O}_{sk}$. *The adversary $\mathcal{A}$ sends i to the challenger. The challenger sends the secret key $\mathbf{sk}_i$ to $\mathcal{A}$.*
3. $\mathcal{O}_{sign}$. *The adversary $\mathcal{A}$ specifies vector subspaces $V_i^{(j)} \in \mathbb{F}_p^N$. The challenger chooses an identifier id_i uniformly at random from the set of identifiers I, and sends id_i and $\sigma_i^{(j)} :=$ Sign$(sk, id_i, V_i^{(j)})$ to $\mathcal{A}$.*

Output. *The adversary $\mathcal{A}$ outputs $\mathbf{pk}^*$, an identifier id^*, a signature σ^*, and a vector $w^* \in \mathbb{F}_p^N$.*

The adversary wins the security game if **Verify**$(pk^*, id^*, w^*, \sigma^*) = \top$*, and either (1)* $id^* \neq id_i$ *for all* i *and* $w^* \neq 0$*, the adversary outputs vector* $y^* \neq 0$ *and other values are forgeries for honest source node (a type 1 forgery), or (2)* $id^* = id_i$ *for some* i *and* $w^* \notin V_i^{(j)}$ *(a type 2 forgery).*

Note 1. The definition of type 1 forgery is different from other security models proposed in [6,3,10], where it just requires $id^* \neq id_i$ *for all* i *and* $w^* \neq 0$*. It is easy to see that our security model is weaker than those security models, however, our security model is still meaningful.*

The advantage NC-adv$[\mathcal{A}, \mathcal{NS}]$ of $\mathcal{A}$ is defined to be the probability that $\mathcal{A}$ wins the security game.

4.2   Bilinear Pairing

Let $\mathbb{G}$, $\mathbb{G}'$ and $\mathbb{G}_T$ be cyclic groups of order q. Throughout the paper, we view all the groups as multiplicative groups. And $e : \mathbb{G} \times \mathbb{G}' \rightarrow \mathbb{G}_T$ is a bilinear map and they satisfy the following properties:

1. Bilinear: $e(g^a, h^b) = e(g, h)^{ab}$ for all $g \in \mathbb{G}$ and $h \in \mathbb{G}'$ and all $a, b \in \mathbb{Z}$.
2. Non-degenerate: if g is generator of $\mathbb{G}$ and h is generator of $\mathbb{G}'$, then $e(g, h)$ is a generator of $\mathbb{G}_T$, in that way $e(g, h) \neq 1$.
3. Computable: for all $g \in \mathbb{G}$ and $h \in \mathbb{G}'$, the value $e(g, h)$ can be computed.

The q-Strong Diffie-Hellman assumption was introduced by Boneh and Boyen [5]. Let $\mathbb{G}, \mathbb{G}'$ and $\mathbb{G}_T$ be bilinear groups of prime order p such that $e : \mathbb{G} \times \mathbb{G}' \rightarrow \mathbb{G}_T$ is a bilinear map. The assumption is defined as follows [10]:

Definition 3. *(q-SDH Assumption). The prime is* $p > 2^k$*, and* $k \in \mathbb{N}$ *is the security parameter,* g *and* g' *are the generators of* $\mathbb{G}$ *and* $\mathbb{G}'$ *respectively. Then we say that the q-SDH Assumption holds in* $\mathbb{G}, \mathbb{G}', \mathbb{G}_T$ *if for any PPT algorithm $\mathcal{A}$ and any $q = poly(k)$, the following probability (taken over the random choice of x and the random coins of $\mathcal{A}$)*

$$Pr[\mathcal{A}(g, g^x, g^{x^2}, ..., g^{x^q}, g', (g')^x) = (c, g^{\frac{1}{(x+c)}})] = \epsilon,$$

ϵ *is negligible in* k*.*

5   Our Proposal

5.1   The Construction

In the section we construct a multiple sources network coding signature scheme. In our proposal, packets will be combined only with those packets in the same generation. We describe the concept of generation in a simple system model in which there are source nodes S_1 and S_2, and each source node wants to send file to the destination nodes T_1 and T_2, see Fig.3. Similar to single source network coding, the source nodes create augmented vectors and all the first augmented vector with identifier id_1 as a generation whose identifier is id_1:

$$generation_{id_1} = \{v_1^{(1)} \parallel id_1, v_1^{(2)} \parallel id_1\}$$

where $v_1^{(1)} = (\widehat{v}_1^{(1)}, \underbrace{1, 0, ..., 0}_{m})$ is sent by S_1, $v_1^{(2)} = (\widehat{v}_1^{(2)}, \underbrace{0, 1, 0, ..., 0}_{m})$ is sent by S_2, and the id_1 could be generated by a common function at the sources. When the sources send the second generation packets, they generate a new identifier id_2 $(id_2 \neq id_1)$:

$$generation_{id_2} = \{v_2^{(1)} \parallel id_2, v_2^{(2)} \parallel id_2\}$$

where $\{v_2^{(1)}, v_2^{(2)}\}$ is a set of packets of second generation, $v_2^{(1)} = (\widehat{v}_2^{(1)}, \underbrace{0, 1, ..., 0}_{m})$

is sent by S_1, and $v_2^{(2)} = (\widehat{v}_2^{(2)}, \underbrace{0, 0, 1, 0, ..., 0}_{m})$ is sent by S_2. At the intermediate

nodes the packets with the same generation identifier can be encoded together.

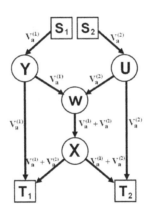

Fig. 3. Network Coding with Multiple Sources

Generally, we suppose that there are u source nodes and each source has file to be sent. As described in Table 1, each source node creates augmented vectors based on the files they send, and assume one file can be interpreted as m packets at most. We group these source packets into m generations: where $v_a^{(i)} \in \mathbb{F}_p^{m+n}$ is the a-th packet from source S_i, and $a = 1, 2, \ldots, m$; $i = 1, 2, \ldots, u$, $u \leq m$.

$$v_a^{(i)} = (\widehat{v}_a^{(i)}, \overbrace{\underbrace{0, ..., 0, 1, 0, ..., 0}_{k}}^{m}),$$

and if $k \leq m$, $k = a + i - 1$; if $k > m$, $k = a + i - m - 1$. The identifiers $id_1, id_2, \ldots, id_m$ could be generated by a common function at the source nodes and they must be different from each other.

Table 1. Our Identity Use in Multiple Sources Network Coding

Generation	S_1	...	S_i	...	S_u
id_1	$v_1^{(1)} \parallel id_1$	...	$v_1^{(i)} \parallel id_1$	...	$v_1^{(u)} \parallel id_1$
id_2	$v_2^{(1)} \parallel id_2$	...	$v_2^{(i)} \parallel id_2$	...	$v_2^{(u)} \parallel id_2$
...	...	...	...	...	...
id_m	$v_m^{(1)} \parallel id_m$	...	$v_m^{(i)} \parallel id_m$	...	$v_m^{(u)} \parallel id_m$

Now we propose our scheme which is based on the q-Strong Diffie-Hellman assumption.

Setup$(1^\lambda, n, m)$. Input a security parameter 1^λ, two integers m and n, where n is data space dimension and m is subspace dimension. Do the following:

1. Let $e : \mathbb{G} \times \mathbb{G}' \to \mathbb{G}_T$ be a bilinear map, $\mathbb{G}, \mathbb{G}', \mathbb{G}_T$ be bilinear groups, $\mathbb{G}, \mathbb{G}', \mathbb{G}_T$ have prime order $p > 2^k$, and $g \in \mathbb{G}$, $g' \in \mathbb{G}'$ are two generators. Choose random elements $h, g_1, ..., g_n, h_1, ..., h_m \xleftarrow{\$} \mathbb{G}$.
2. Output the public parameters $(g, g', h, p, g_1, ..., g_n, h_1, ..., h_m)$.

KG(u). Let u be the total number of the source nodes. Choose $z_j \xleftarrow{\$} \mathbb{Z}_p^*$, $j = 1, ..., u$ and set $Z_j = (g')^{z_j}$. Output the public key $\mathbf{pk}_j = Z_j$ and the secret key $\mathbf{sk}_j = z_j$, $j = 1, ..., u$.

Sign$(\mathbf{sk}_j, id_a, v_a^{(j)})$. Let z_j be j-th source's secret key, $v_a^{(j)} \in \mathbb{F}_p^{m+n}$ is a properly augmented vector, and let an identifier id_a be randomly chosen in $\mathbb{Z}_p^*$. Pick $s_j \xleftarrow{\$} \mathbb{Z}_p^*$. This algorithm computes the hash $X_a^{(j)} = h^{s_j} \cdot \prod_{k=1}^{n} g_k^{v_{ak}^{(j)}} \cdot \prod_{t=1}^{m} h_t^{v_{a(n+t)}^{(j)}}$ and the signature $\tau_a^{(j)} = X_a^{(j)\frac{1}{z_j + id_a}}$. Finally, outputs $\sigma_a^{(j)} = (X_a^{(j)}, \tau_a^{(j)}, s_j)$.

Verify$(\mathbf{pk}_j, v_a^{(j)}, \sigma_a^{(j)}, id_a)$. This algorithm checks whether $\sigma_a^{(j)}$ is a valid signature on a hash $X_a^{(j)}$ for the identifier id_a and $X_a^{(j)}$ is a valid signature on the vector $v_a^{(j)}$, and $\sigma_a^{(j)} = (X_a^{(j)}, \tau_a^{(j)}, s_j)$. If the following two equations hold, this algorithm outputs $\top$; otherwise it outputs $\bot$.

$$e(\tau_j, Z_j \cdot (g')^{id_a}) = e(X_a^{(j)}, g') \quad \text{and} \quad (h^{s_j} \prod_{k=1}^{n} g_k^{v_{ak}^{(j)}} \cdot \prod_{t=1}^{m} h_t^{v_{a(n+t)}^{(j)}}) \overset{?}{=} X_a^{(j)}$$

$\top$ means that $\sigma_a^{(j)}$ is a valid signature on vector $v_a^{(j)}$, where $\bot$ means that $\sigma_a^{(j)}$ is not valid.

Combine$(\{\mathbf{pk}_j, v_a^{(j)}, \alpha_j, \sigma_a^{(j)}\}_{j=1}^{\mu}, id_a)$. Given public keys $\mathbf{pk}_1, ..., \mathbf{pk}_\mu$ and an identifier id_a. The vector $y_a = \sum_{j=1}^{\mu} \alpha_j v_a^{(j)} \in \mathbb{F}_p^{m+n}$, and a randomly chosen coefficient $\alpha_j \in \mathbb{F}_p$ for all $j \in \{1, ..., \mu\}$. The algorithm computes

$$X = \prod_{j=1}^{\mu} X_a^{(j)\alpha_j} \quad \text{and} \quad s = \sum_{j=1}^{\mu} \alpha_j \cdot s_j \bmod p$$

then outputs $\sigma = (X, \tau_1^{(j)}, ..., \tau_\mu^{(j)}, s)$.

5.2   Analysis

Correctness. We demonstrate the correctness requirement of Definition 1.

1. For primitive signatures: Think about the j-th source node has the key pair $(\mathbf{sk}_j, \mathbf{pk}_j) \leftarrow \mathbf{KG}(1^\lambda, n, m)$ and $v_1^{(j)}, ..., v_m^{(j)}$ is a properly augmented basis. Interpret a vector space $V \subset \mathbb{F}_p^{n+m}$ as $V^{(j)} = (v_1^{(j)}, ..., v_m^{(j)})$. Let $\sigma = (X_a^{(j)}, \tau_a^{(j)}, s_j)$ be the output of $\mathbf{Sign}(\mathbf{sk}_j, id_a, v_a^{(j)})$. We check correctness of **Verify** for primitive signature as follow:

   (a) Since $h^{s_j} \cdot \prod_{k=1}^n g_k^{v_{ak}^{(j)}} \cdot \prod_{t=1}^m h_t^{v_{a(n+t)}^{(j)}} = X_a^{(j)}$, we have $h^{s_j} \cdot \prod_{k=1}^n g_k^{v_{ak}^{(j)}} \cdot \prod_{t=1}^m h_t^{v_{a(n+t)}^{(j)}} = X_a^{(j)}$.

   (b) Since $\tau_a^{(j)} = (X_a^{(j)})^{\frac{1}{z_j + id_a}}$, we have $e(\tau_a^{(j)}, Z_j \cdot (g')^{id_a}) = e(X_a^{(j)}, g')$.

   If every augmented basis vector $v_a^{(j)}$ passes the test of signature verify, i.e.,

   $$\mathbf{Verify}(\mathbf{pk}_j, id_a, v_a^{(j)}, \sigma_a^{(j)}) = \top.$$

2. Recursively, we can check correctness of combined signature: Consider μ public keys $\mathbf{pk}_1, ..., \mathbf{pk}_\mu$, μ signatures $\sigma_a^{(1)}, ..., \sigma_a^{(\mu)}$, and $\sigma_a^{(1)}, ..., \sigma_a^{(\mu)}$ are signatures of augmented vector $v_a^{(1)}, ..., v_a^{(\mu)}$, respectively. Then we have:

   $$\mathbf{Verify}(\mathbf{pk}_1, id_a, v_a^{(1)}, \sigma_a^{(1)}) = ... = \mathbf{Verify}(\mathbf{pk}_\mu, id_a, v_a^{(\mu)}, \sigma_a^{(\mu)}) = \top. \quad (3)$$

   Let $y = \sum_{j=1}^\mu \alpha_j v_a^{(j)}$, and let $\alpha_1, ..., \alpha_\mu \in \mathbb{F}_p$ be combination coefficients. The signature $\sigma = (X, \tau_a^{(1)}, ..., \tau_a^{(\mu)}, s)$ is output of the **Combine** algorithm when the algorithm's input is $(v_a^{(1)}, \sigma_a^{(1)}, \mathbf{pk}_1, \alpha_1), ..., (v_a^{(\mu)}, \sigma_a^{(\mu)}, \mathbf{pk}_\mu, \alpha_\mu)$, where the signature $\sigma_a^{(j)} = (X_a^{(j)}, \tau_a^{(j)}, s_j)$, and $j = 1, ..., \mu$.

   $$s = \sum_{j=1}^\mu \alpha_j s_j \bmod p \quad \text{and} \quad X = \prod_{j=1}^\mu (X_a^{(j)})^{\alpha_j}$$

   We check correctness of the **Verify** algorithm:

   (a) According to assumption 3, we have $(h^{s_j} \prod_{k=1}^n g_k^{v_{ak}^{(j)}} \cdot \prod_{t=1}^m h_t^{v_{a(n+t)}^{(j)}}) = X_a^{(j)}$ for $j = 1, ..., \mu$, we can obtain

   $X = \prod_{j=1}^\mu (X_a^{(j)})^{\alpha_j}$

   $= \prod_{j=1}^\mu (h^{s_j} \prod_{k=1}^n g_k^{v_{ak}^{(j)}} \cdot \prod_{t=1}^m h_t^{v_{a(n+t)}^{(j)}})^{\alpha_j}$

   $= h^{\sum_{j=1}^\mu \alpha_j s_j} \prod_{k=1}^n g_k^{\sum_{j=1}^\mu \alpha_j v_{ak}^{(j)}} \cdot \prod_{t=1}^m h_t^{\sum_{j=1}^\mu \alpha_j v_{a(n+t)}^{(j)}}$

   $= h^s \prod_{k=1}^n g_k^{y_k} \cdot \prod_{t=1}^m h_t^{y_{n+t}}.$

   So we have

   $$h^s \prod_{k=1}^n g_k^{y_k} \cdot \prod_{t=1}^m h_t^{y_{n+t}} = X. \quad (4)$$

(b) According to assumption 3, we have $e(\tau_a^{(j)}, Z_j \cdot (g')^{id_a}) = e(X_a^{(j)}, g')$ for $j = 1, ..., \mu$, we obtain

$$e(X, g') = e(\prod_{j=1}^{\mu}(X_a^{(j)})^{\alpha_j}, g')$$
$$= \prod_{j=1}^{\mu} e(X_a^{(j)}, g')^{\alpha_j}$$
$$= \prod_{j=1}^{\mu} e(\tau_a^{(j)}, Z_j \cdot (g')^{id_a})^{\alpha_j}$$
$$= \prod_{j=1}^{\mu} e(\tau_a^{(j)}, Z_j \cdot (g')^{id_a})^{y_{a(n+j)}}.$$

So we have

$$\prod_{j=1}^{\mu} e(\tau_a^{(j)}, Z_j \cdot (g')^{id_a})^{y_{a(n+j)}} = e(X, g'). \tag{5}$$

Thus, according to 4 and 5, we have

$$\mathbf{Verify}\left(\{\mathbf{pk}_j\}_{j=1}^{\mu}, id_a, y, \sigma\right) = \top.$$

Note 2. Agrawal et al. [1] showed that it is impossible to obtain a multiple sources network coding signature scheme from a single source network coding signature scheme by giving an attack, where an intermediate node is fooled into accepting invalid packets and in this attack one of the senders is malicious. In particular, a malicious sender can prepare two different vectors with the same *id* and signs the two vectors using his secret key. These two vectors are both individually valid, but not pairwise valid. Hence, any intermediate node cannot detect this attack, which leads the incorrect decoding on the destination nodes. Although our proposal is built on the single source network coding signature [10], it can resist with this attack. The main reason is that the signatures on different vectors are combined in [6,10], but not in our proposal.

5.3 Security Analysis

Theorem 1. *Our proposal is secure in the standard model based on the q-SDH assumption*

Due to the limited space, we omit the proof, which can be found in the full version of this paper.   □

6 Conclusion and Discussion

In this paper we have proposed a new multiple sources network coding signature scheme, which is provably secure based on the q-SDH assumption in the standard model. In the underlying security model, it allows the adversary to control $u-1$ source nodes at most if there are u sources in the network. Furthermore, the proposal allows sources to transmit streaming data, which supports the real time transmission.

The current version of our proposal only support the combining operation on the vectors from multiple sources, not the ones from the same source. However, with a little modification, our proposal can support two kinds of combining operations. In particular, the source nodes create augmented vectors by appending a coding vector of length $u \cdot m$, assuming $v_a^{(i)} \in \mathbb{F}_p^{u \cdot m + n}$ is the a-th generation packet from the source S_i and $a = 1, 2, \ldots, m;\ i = 1, 2, \ldots, u$.

$$v_a^{(i)} = (\widehat{v}_a^{(i)}, \overbrace{\underbrace{0, \ldots, 0, 1, 0, \ldots, 0}_{(i-1) \cdot m + a}}^{u \cdot m})$$

In this case, the combining operation could be processed on not only the vectors from multiple sources, but also the ones from the same source.

Acknowledgement. Jun Shao, Jinling Zhang was supported by NSFC No. 61003308, QJD1102009, NSFZJ No. LR13F020003, Program for Zhejiang Leading Team of Science and Technology Innovation, and SRF for ROCS, SEM. Guiyi Wei was supported by the Science and Technology Planning Projects of Zhejiang Grants 2011C14024 and 2011C13006-1. Bishan Ying was supported by the National Development and Reform Commission of China under Special Grants "The Operation System of Multimedia Cloud Based on the Integration of Telecommunications Networks, Cable TV Networks and the Internet".

References

1. Agrawal, S., Boneh, D., Boyen, X., Freeman, D.M.: Preventing pollution attacks in multi-source network coding. In: Nguyen, P.Q., Pointcheval, D. (eds.) PKC 2010. LNCS, vol. 6056, pp. 161–176. Springer, Heidelberg (2010)
2. Ahlswede, R., Ning-Cai, Li, S., Yeung, R.W.: Network information flow 46(4), 1204–1216 (2000)
3. Attrapadung, N., Libert, B.: Homomorphic network coding signatures in the standard model. In: Catalano, D., Fazio, N., Gennaro, R., Nicolosi, A. (eds.) PKC 2011. LNCS, vol. 6571, pp. 17–34. Springer, Heidelberg (2011)
4. Bellare, M., Boldyreva, A., Palacio, A.: An uninstantiable random-oracle-model scheme for a hybrid-encryption problem. In: Cachin, C., Camenisch, J.L. (eds.) EUROCRYPT 2004. LNCS, vol. 3027, pp. 171–188. Springer, Heidelberg (2004)
5. Boneh, D., Boyen, X.: Short signatures without random oracles. In: Cachin, C., Camenisch, J.L. (eds.) EUROCRYPT 2004. LNCS, vol. 3027, pp. 56–73. Springer, Heidelberg (2004)
6. Boneh, D., Freeman, D., Katz, J., Waters, B.: Signing a linear subspace: Signature schemes for network coding. In: Jarecki, S., Tsudik, G. (eds.) PKC 2009. LNCS, vol. 5443, pp. 68–87. Springer, Heidelberg (2009)
7. Boneh, D., Freeman, D.M.: Linearly homomorphic signatures over binary fields and new tools for lattice-based signatures. In: Catalano, D., Fazio, N., Gennaro, R., Nicolosi, A. (eds.) PKC 2011. LNCS, vol. 6571, pp. 1–16. Springer, Heidelberg (2011)
8. Canetti, R., Goldreich, O., Halevi, S.: The random oracle methodology, revisited. Journal of the ACM (JACM) 51(4), 557–594 (2004)

9. Catalano, D., Fiore, D., Warinschi, B.: Adaptive pseudo-free groups and applications. In: Paterson, K.G. (ed.) EUROCRYPT 2011. LNCS, vol. 6632, pp. 207–223. Springer, Heidelberg (2011)
10. Catalano, D., Fiore, D., Warinschi, B.: Efficient network coding signatures in the standard model. In: Fischlin, M., Buchmann, J., Manulis, M. (eds.) PKC 2012. LNCS, vol. 7293, pp. 680–696. Springer, Heidelberg (2012)
11. Charles, D., Jain, K., Lauter, K.: Signatures for network coding. In: Proceedings of the Fortieth Annual Conference on Information Sciences and Systems. Citeseer (2006)
12. Han, K., Ho, T., Koetter, R., Medard, M., Zhao, F.: On network coding for security. In: Military Communications Conference, MILCOM 2007, pp. 1–6. IEEE (2007)
13. Ho, T., Leong, B., Koetter, R., Médard, M., Effros, M., Karger, D.R.: Byzantine modification detection in multicast networks with random network coding. IEEE Transactions on Information Theory 54(6), 2798–2803 (2008)
14. Jaggi, S., Langberg, M., Katti, S., Ho, T., Katabi, D., Médard, M., Effros, M.: Resilient network coding in the presence of byzantine adversaries 54(6), 2596–2603 (2008)
15. Johnson, R., Molnar, D., Song, D., Wagner, D.: Homomorphic signature schemes. In: Preneel, B. (ed.) CT-RSA 2002. LNCS, vol. 2271, pp. 244–262. Springer, Heidelberg (2002)
16. Rosario, G., Jonathan, K., Hugo, K., Tal, R.: Secure Network Coding Over the Integers. pp. 142–160 (2010)
17. Waters, B.: Dual system encryption: Realizing fully secure IBE and HIBE under simple assumptions. In: Halevi, S. (ed.) CRYPTO 2009. LNCS, vol. 5677, pp. 619–636. Springer, Heidelberg (2009)
18. Yan, W., Yang, M., Li, L., Fang, H.: Short signature scheme for multi-source network coding. Computer Communications 35(3), 344–351 (2012)
19. Zhao, F., Kalker, T., Médard, M., Han, K.J.: Signatures for content distribution with network coding. In: IEEE International Symposium on Information Theory, ISIT 2007, pp. 556–560. IEEE (2007)

A Study of LDoS Flows Variations
Based on Similarity Measurement

Zhijian Huang, Wei Peng, Yongjun Wang and Ruiyuan Zhao

National Key Laboratory for Parallel and Distributed Processing,
National University of Defense Technology
Changsha, Hunan, 410073, China
{zjhuang,wpeng,wangyongjun,ryzhao}@nudt.edu.cn

Abstract. Variability of end-to-end paths is an important issue which affects the effectiveness of Low-rate Denial-of-Service (LDoS) attacks and the corresponding detection methods. It remains unclear how and to what extent an LDoS flow will be affected by the end-to-end delay in the Internet. In this paper, we investigate the LDoS flow variations using the method of similarity measurement of time series. We establish the LDoS Measuring Model and the Packet Arriving Model to analyze differences in packet sequence pattern, and propose new metrics to measure the similarity of two time series. Using real data sampled on PlanetLab from the Internet, we reveal a neglected but important fact: LDoS flows on PlanetLab perform differently with flows on home networks. Thus, the threat of CXPST attack on the Internet's inter-domain routing system may not be so serious than what has been expected in previous work due to the variation of end-to-end paths.

Keywords: LDoS, Similarity, Measurement, End-to-end delay, PlanetLab.

1 Introduction

Initially proposed by Kuzmanovic and Knightly, Low-rate Denial-of-Service (LDoS) [1] attack has been a hot topic ever since. Unlike traditional Denial-of-Service (DoS) attacks which exhaust network resources of the victims by sending continuous high-rate data flows, only short-term bursts are sent in LDoS attacks to induce victims continuously switching from a state to another state. Classic LDoS flows exhibit periodic ON/OFF activity as illustrated in Fig.1, and with parameter values of period, duration and magnitude, we can define an LDoS flow. Since the average rate of an LDoS attack flow is not significantly greater than that of a normal flow, previous detection mechanisms against DoS attacks seldom work well on LDoS attacks.

Researchers have been engaged in discovering new kinds of LDoS attacks aiming at new vulnerabilities as well as developing more effective detecting and defending mechanisms. But most of them are experimented on simulators or testbeds, and few pay attention to the variations of LDoS flows caused by dynamics of end-to-end paths in the Internet. Our previous work [2] is the first to study the impact of end-to-end delay on LDoS flows. In the paper, we have put forward an algorithm to measure the time series of incoming packets using the triple (*Period, Duration, Magnitude*), and by analyzing the distributions, we have found that end-to-end delay can distort LDoS flows greatly.

M. Pathan, G. Wei, and G. Fortino (Eds.): IDCS 2013, LNCS 8223, pp. 209–222, 2013.

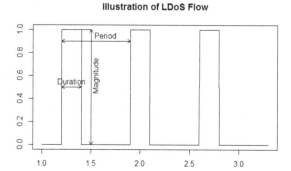

Fig. 1. An illustration of LDoS Flow

Since the triple can not reflect the details of LDoS flows or quantify the variations precisely between a sender and a receiver, we turn to the method of time series analysis and put forward new metrics to measure the variations. Besides, we propose a Packet Arriving Model to study the packet sequence pattern. Most of our experiments are performed on PlanetLab, a well-known platform for network experiments in the Internet. To prevent possible damages, LDoS flows are cultivated from PlanetLab hosts to a specified server with the packet sending rate strictly limited.

We make comparisons of flow variations between PlanetLab and home networks, and find great differences between them. For PlanetLab flows, the end-to-end delay does have impacts, but the impacts are limited on *Period* and *Duration* variations, while the impacts are greater for flows from home networks. Results have shown that the *Period* of a LDoS flow seems to react negatively against the similarity distance, while its *Duration* value reacts positively on PlanetLab, but on home networks that trend doesn't exist. Both flows from PlanetLab and home networks suffer changes in the packet sequence pattern, and the changes are much bigger on home networks. While the success ratio of Coordinated Cross Plane Session Termination (CXPST) attack [5] on the Internet's inter-domain routing system depends greatly on the effectiveness of LDoS flows, the threat of CXPST attack may not be so serious than what has been expected in previous work.

The rest of the paper is organized as follows. Section 2 presents the related work of LDoS attacks and similarity theory of time series. Section 3 and Section 4 introduce the measuring models and methods. Section 5 describes the results, and in section 6, we have a discussion.

2   Related Work

2.1   Low-Rate Denial-of-Service Attack

During the last decade, various new LDoS attacks have been proposed. Based on the different targets, they could be clustered into two kinds: the first kind aims at adaptive congestion control mechanisms and the other aims at disrupting network using the existed LDoS methods.

Other than the first LDoS attack which targets against retransmission timeout mechanism of TCP (Transfer Control Protocol), there have come out many other kinds of LDoS attacks. PDoS (Pulsing DoS attacks) [3] exploits the vulnerability of AIMD (Additive Increase Multiplicative Decrease) mechanism of TCP. LoRDAS (Low-rate DoS Attack against Application Server) uses normal packets to fill up the request queue of the server thus   preventing the server from operating normally. As well, LDoS attacks against the Active Queue Management (AQM)'s Random Early Detection(RED) mechanism have been put forward. ZMW [4] attack represents the other kind of LDoS attacks, which describes a collaborative way to attack the internet routing system. CXPST (Coordinated Cross Plane Session Termination) [5] attack, well known as "digital artillery", simulates a situation in which a large-scale botnet launches distributed LDoS attacks against some inter-domain routers simultaneously, and force the routers to produce an enormous amount of BGP update messages, which are far beyond the computing capability of Internet routers, thus causing the routers to operate abnormally and resulting in losing control of the Internet.

2.2   LDoS Detection and Defence Mechanisms

Though LDoS has a relatively lower rate than DoS, but the rate is high during the pulsing time. Aiming at this high-rate pattern, Kwok [6] proposed a stateful adaptive queue management technique HAWK (Halting Anomalies with Weighted Choking), which monitors the buffer size and justifies LDoS flows by compare it to threshold values. Generally, the algorithms are easy to implement, but there exists high error rate, and also the stateful mechanism could bring in new problems. Sun et. al's Dynamic Detection [7] solution makes use of auto-correlation methods to extract the periodic characteristic, and uses the DTW (Dynamic Time Warping) algorithm to do pattern matching. Also they put forward a collaborative detection mechanism and a back-off method to trace the attacking sources. Fourier transmission and wavelet transmission methods are also popular ways to extract the attack patterns [2,12]. But the accuracy of these methods relies on attack signature database. Apart from the methods listed above, new approaches such as analyzing the behaviours of TCP packets and self-similarity methods have been proposed [13].

Generally, there are two solutions for defence. The fist is to improve the existing AQM mechanisms [6,7,8] to block the LDoS flows. But that could request more computing sources and some stateful solutions could bring new vulnerability to routers. The other and the most radical one is to make modifications on the existing protocols, such as increasing the initial window size parameter and randomizing the minimum retransmission timeout (minRTO) value. Although these methods can make systems robust against LDoS, system performances may be forced to do some sacrifice [1].

2.3   Similarity Analysis of Time Series

Time series analysis methods are widely used in data mining areas, and similarity measurement is a hot topic. Intuitively, researchers use distance to measure similarity. Classic similarity distance definitions include Minowski Distance, Manhattan Distance, Euclidean Distance, Edit Distance, LCS (Longest Common Subseries), Dynamic Time Warping Distance and so on, but there is not a uniform definition for similarity.

Based on previous researches, Liu [9] proposes the concept of the time series similarity, in which he defines similarity by a similarity function and a transformation function:

For time series $X\{x_1,x_2,...,x_n\}$ and $Y\{y_1,y_2,...,y_n\}$, construct a similarity function $sim(X,Y)$. If $sim(X,Y) \leq \xi$, then X and Y are similar under error level ξ. For any time series a,b,c, the similarity function should follow two rules:

1. $sim(a, b) = sim(b, a) \geq 0$, $sim(a, b) = 0$ only when a equals b.
2. $sim(a, c) \leq sim(a, b) + sim(b, c)$.

Usually, raw time series data have long lengths that require great computing resources. Time series representation converts the series to symbolic representations, helping reduce the computing complexity. At present, there are representations like: Discrete Fourier Transformation, Discrete Wavelet Transformation, Singular Value Decomposition (SVD) [10], and Piecewise Linear Approximation (PLR) [11]. Considering the representations, similarity is defined as $sim(F(X),F(Y))$, in which F stands for the representation function.

Different representations have different properties and complexities, so choices of representation method and similarity distance definition are essential for time series data mining.

3   Models

Researchers have proposed a series of LDoS models. The first and most classic one uses the (Period, Duration, Magnitude) triple to represent an ideal LDoS flow [1]. Sun et. al [7] introduce background traffic to the model [1]. Luo et. al [3] divide LDoS flow into pulses and model each pulse separately. In this section, we analyze the possible impacts of end-to-end delay on LDoS flows. Based on the analysis, we put forward our models for measuring the variations.

3.1   Impacts of End-to-End Delay on LDoS Flows

As we know, network is dynamic all the time. Links that are free at present time could be extremely congested or even broken down at the next moment, which would lead to packets rerouting. After being cultivated from the sender, packets spend different time on transmitting over the routine, and finally assemble at the receiver as a flow. Due to end-to-end delay, the assembled flow could probably fail to exhibit strict periodic ON/OFF pattern, the lengths of each pulse (or duration), the interspaces between pulses (or period-duration) may distribute abnormally.

Previous paper [1] has shown that a successful LDoS attack has to be configured with the proper values of *Period*, *Duration* and *Magnitude* according to the state of target link. Each pulse should last enough long time, and simutaneously the rate of each pulse should stay in a high rate to induce the victim into the Retransmission Timeout State. The *Period* should be set as a proper value so that the victim are able to return to the normal state [1,4] against which the DoS flow target.

Shifted values of *Period* and *Duration* on the receiver might not able to induce the victim into an unstable state. At the same time, the packets arriving at the receiver may not keep a steady high rate, that as well helps to alleviate the attack perfomance. So analyzing the varaitions of *Period*, *Duration* and the arriviving pattern is essential for studying the validity of LDoS attack.

3.2   Measuring Models

Luo et. al [3] model the flow as $(T_{Extent}(n), S_{Extent}(n),)T_{Space}(n), j)$, in which $T_{Extent}(n)$ denotes the duration of the nth pulse, $S_{Extent}(n)$ determines the shape of the nth attack pulse. $T_{Space}(n)$ measures the time between the end of the n_{th} attack pulse and the beginning of the $(n+1)_{th}$ attack pulse. N represents the number of pulses in one flow, and n is the sequence of pulse. In the model, the pulse time is separated from rest time by the packet rate differences, but that is not precise enough for measurement, because there may be packets mistaken as background traffic and as well background traffic could be mistaken as LDoS packets.

In fact, PCs for experiments are under absolute control, we can easily and accurately tell the start or end time of a single pulse by resolving the information label added in the cultivated packets. So on the basis of Luo et. al's model, we propose the LDoS Measuring Model (see Fig.2(a)) to measure the variations for parameter *Period* and *Duration*.

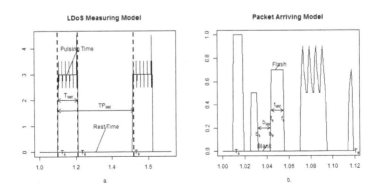

Fig. 2. The measuring Models (a) is used to measure *period* and *duration* values, and (b) for packets arriving in a single pulse

Further, we put forward a Packet Arriving Model (see Fig.2(b)) and some metrics to measure the continuity of the packets receiving rate inside a pulse. In our model, we term a consecutive intervals with packets in the pulse as **flash**, and consecutive intervals with no packets as **blank**. The symbol $f(i,j)$ is used to locate the j_{th} **flash** in the i_{th} pulse of the flow, and $b(i,j)$ for **blanks**.

Table 1 illustrates the terminologies and notations of the model, prefixes 'S_' and 'R_' are used to differentiate the sender from the receiver.

Table 1. Notations and Definitions of the Models

Notation	Definition
$T_s(i)$	The arrival time of the first packet in i_{th} pulse of a flow.
$T_e(i)$	The arrival time of the last packet in i_{th} pulse.
$T_{last}(i)$	The time interval between $T_s(i)$ and $T_e(i)$.
$TP_{last}(i)$	The time interval between $T_s(i)$ and $T_s(i+1)$.
$f_s(i,j)$	The arrival time of the first packet of the j_{th} flash during i_{th} pulse.
$f_e(i,j)$	The arrival time of the last packet of the j_{th} flash during i_{th} pulse.
$f_{last}(i,j)$	The time interval between $f_s(i,j)$ and $f_e(i,j)$.
$b_{last}(i,j)$	The time interval between $f_e(i,j)$ and $f_s(i, j+1)$.

3.3   Metrics

Here, we denote a LDoS flow time series as $X\{x_1,x_2,...,x_n\}$, the values xi represents the number of packets dumped between the$(i-1)_{th}$ and the i_{th} interval. X_i is used to represent the i_{th} pulse time series, or $T_s(i)\sim T_e(i)$, or $\{x_{Ts(i)}, x_{Ts(i)+1}, ..., x_{Te(i)}\}$.

A. Flow Similarity Distance

To save the shape information, we normalize the time series as Eq.1, and then we use

$$x_i = \frac{x_i - \min(x)}{\max(x) - \min(x)} \tag{1}$$

Flow Similarity Distance: Since representation methods could lose some characteristics of the flow, so we apply Euclidean Distance to the raw time series.

$$FD(X,Y) = \sqrt{\sum_{i=1}^{L}(x_i - y_i)^2} \tag{2}$$

When $FD(X,Y)$ equals 0, it means X and Y are exactly same with each other in their wave appearance, ignoring the differences in rates. The bigger $FD(X,Y)$ is, the less similar X and Y are.

B. Packets Arriving Metrics

As analyzed in 3.1, LDoS attacks make use of short-term DoS flow to induce the victim into an unstable state. The DoS flow should keep high enough rate for a sufficiently long time, and we term this as **continuity**. In order to measure continuity, we define two new metrics, **Rate of Blanks (RoB)** which reflects the rate of blanks in a single pulse and **Average Rate (AR)** is related to the packets dropping rate in the router, the higher AR is, the bigger possibility for packet loss.

$$RoB_{pulse}(i) = \frac{\sum_{j=1}^{N'-1} b_{last}(i,j)}{T_{last}(i)} \tag{3}$$

$$RoB_{flow} = \frac{\sum_{i=1}^{N} \sum_{j=1}^{N'-1} b_{last}(i,j)}{\sum_{i=1}^{N} T_{last}(i)} \tag{4}$$

$$AR_{pulse}(i) = \frac{1}{\sum_{j=1}^{N'(i)} b_{last}(j)} \sum_{j=1}^{T_{last}(i)} x_i \tag{5}$$

$$AR_{flow} = \frac{1}{\sum_{i=1}^{N} \sum_{j=1}^{N'(i)} f_{last}(j)} \sum_{i=1}^{L} x_i \tag{6}$$

In Eq. 6, the value of the time series is normalized in the flow scope. $N'(i)$ denotes the number of flashes in i_{th} pulse of a flow.

4 Methods

Since many previous researches on LDoS do simulations on PlanetLab, so we also performed several experiments on that platform to study the variations. At the same time, we carried out experiments on home networks to test if there were differences for PlanetLab and home networks. Though our study aims to test the variations of LDoS flow, we have to limit the magnitude of flow strictly to prevent possible damages.

4.1 Experiment Settings

The experiment topology is shown in Fig. 3. The selected sites on PlanetLab are distributed in European, Asia and North America (see information in Appendix A). A server with an exclusive IPv4 address on the brim of campus network is set up to collect data, the server is unknown to the public so that there is few unknown traffic disrupting the measuring. To prevent ICMP packets generated by the server for packets toward non-existing ports, a receiver program is launched to deal with the LDoS flows. Packets dump tools like wireshark and tcpdump are deployed on both sides to record the raw flow packets for accurate offline analysis.

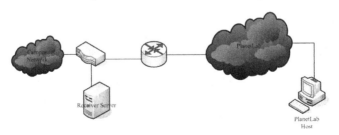

Fig. 3. Experiment Topology

In previous model [1], LDoS flows are recommended for 1000ms period and 100ms duration in most cases. In order to study the variations under different configurations, each host were made to generate 23 flows with the sending rate set as an acceptable rate, and each flow lasts 60 seconds. 11 flows of the 23 flows are configured with constant 1000ms period, with durations varying from 50 to 500ms, separated by 50ms. The other flows are set with 100ms duration, and their periods range from 200 to 1500 by 100ms.

4.2   Data Processing

The packets dump files are converted into time series like $X\{x_1,x_2,...,x_n\}$, in which x_i represents the number of packets dumped between intervals (the interval is set as 1ms in our analysis). Since every packet attaches an information label, we can easily separate pulses of the flow. In this way, the $(T_s(n), T_e(n), T_{last}(n), TP_{last}(n), N)$ tuples are resolved. Each time series begins at the first packet sent or received in the flow, and the first 58 seconds of each flow are truncated for *Flow Similarity Distance* analysis.

5   Results

In this section, we will compare the results on PlanetLab and the home networks. First, we concern on the Measuring Model to test the *Period* and *Duration* variations. Second, we analyze the relationships of *Period vs. Flow Similarity Distance* and *Duration vs. Flow Similarity Distance*. At last, we study the arriving packet pattern variations.

5.1   Period (Duration) Variations

Here we analyze the flows with period 1000ms and duration 100ms, cultivated from site ple2.ipv6.lip6.fr, at local time 22:34 April 7 2013 and home network in Hunan, China, at 10:10 April 10 2013. The home PC connected to the China Telecom 10Mbps optical fiber switch through a 100Mbps wired LAN.

Fig.4 and Fig.5 show the kernel density distribution of period and duration differences ($S\_TP_{last}\text{-}R\_TP_{last}$ and $S\_T_{last}\text{-}R\_T_{last}$). On PlanetLab, the period differences for flows are rather limited, ranging from -4ms to 4ms, in fact only 5 out of the sixty pulses locate outside [-1ms,1ms], and duration differences range from -1 to 4ms. Compared to preconfigured values of period and duration, the variations are rather limited. While on home LAN, the period differences cover a range of -8~12ms, for duration, the range could be even larger, in which most of the values are around -10ms, but the largest one reaches -40ms. Relatively, duration suffers more severe variations than period. We perform sample t tests on the periods of PlanetLab flow, but they all fail, proving end-to-end delay impacts the duration to perform normally and this corresponds to the conclusion in our previous paper [2].

Based on above analysis, we come to the observation that **the impacts that end-to-end delay brings on LDoS flows are limited on durations and periods**. End-to-end delay brings differences between the sender and receiver as well as impacts the triple parameters to distribute abnormally. But in most cases, the differences of PlanetLab flows are rather limited, falling inside an acceptable range (1/10 of the configured value). Relatively, such differences are much bigger on home networks.

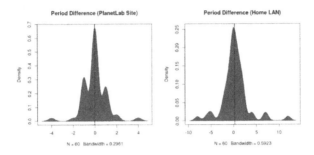

Fig. 4. Period Variations of Single Flow (PlanetLab Site vs. Home LAN)

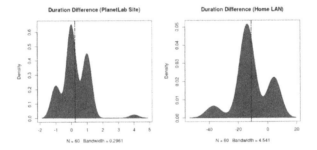

Fig. 5. Duration Variations of Single Flow (PlanetLab Site vs. Home LAN)

5.2 Period (Duration) vs. Flow Similarity Distance

Fig.6 and Fig.7 depict the relationship between period and duration with flow similarity separately; the dotted lines are generated using the linear fitting algorithm. The data are collected from On PlanetLab site ple2.ipv6.lip6.fr and home network described in 5.1.

From the figures, we can see that on PlanetLab the dots are generally scattered around the fitting line, indicating there is a declining trend between *Period* and *Flow Similarity Distance*, as well as an increase trend for *Duration* and *Flow Similarity Distance*. While for Home LAN results, the dots are located far from the fitting line, showing that it does not follow similar trends of PlanetLab sites. Other PlanetLab sites results agree to this trend (Results are shown in Appendix B).

***Period* seems to react negatively against the similarity distance, while *Duration* reacts positively on PlanetLab.** For flows with the same duration and magnitude, the bigger the period value is, the variation gets smaller; and for flows with the same period and magnitude, as the duration grows bigger, the variation gets more severe. Causing that the sender doesn't generate packets during pulses, the pulsing time contributes the biggest part to the similarity distance. So when duration stays in constant, the bigger period is, the smaller duration relatively gets, as well the smaller similarity distance is. In the same way, when duration becomes bigger with period as a constant, similarity distance increases. **But flows generated from home networks don't follow such trend,** indicating that the flows suffered more severe effects of end-to-end delay. This may be explained by that: the hosts of PlanetLab always distribute near the entrances of campus network, which are close to the ISP bone net, while home PCs, which have various accesses to network, optical fiber, wireless and even mobile networks, always locate on the brim of the Internet.

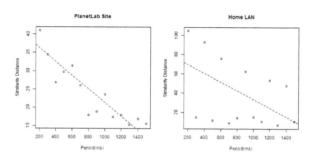

Fig. 6. Period vs. *Flow Similarity Distance* (PlanetLab Site vs. Home LAN)

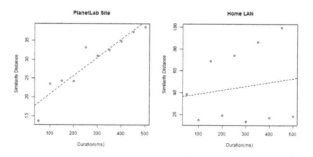

Fig. 7. Duration vs. *Flow Similarity Distance* (PlanetLab Site vs. Home LAN)

5.3   Arriving Packet Pattern Variations

To study the packets arriving pattern variations, we calculate the values of *RoB* and *AR*, the results are shown in the below figures. We can see from Fig.8, the lines of PlanetLab sender and servers are very close to each other, showing that both sides were impacted limitedly by end-to-end delay. Compared to PlanetLab, the variations for home network are much greater. In Fig.9, we can see that the average RoB_{flow} was below 0.1 in the sender, while that's over 0.6 in the receiver side.

End-to-end delay affects the arrival of packet to be non-uniform. In our experiments, we generate flows at a nearly stable rate, but the packets arriving at the receiver failed to keep steady, alternatively appearing like flashes and blanks (As depicted in the packet arriving model). Also the rates of the flashes are not uniform, some rated rather high while some rather low. This non-uniformity is brought in by the various values of time spent in transmitting. Packets sent later but transmit faster merge with the slower packets sent before, forming as flashes. These flash-like flows may not meet the needs to cause TCP packets loss as illustrated in paper [1], thus failing to induce the server switching to unsteady state. Moreover, the dynamic delay could prevent distributed LDoS flows from assembling together at right time. In this sense, distributed LDoS attacks are nearly impossible on the Internet.

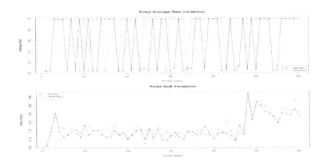

Fig. 8. AR and *RoB* (PlanetLab Site)

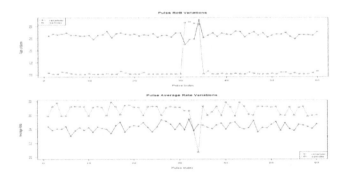

Fig. 9. AR and *RoB* (Home LAN)

6   Discussions and Future Work

Based on our previous work, this paper has gone further and deeper in studying the variations of LDoS flows on the Internet. We provide a novel method to study the variations, including the measuring models and the metrics. With real data sampled from PlanetLab and home networks, we revealed that the flows from PlanetLab and home networks perform differently. Considering that most previous works are done on PlanetLab or other ideal testbeds, our work has the value of revealing the differences of LDoS flows variations on PlanetLab and home networks, and this could give a new prospective on the further studies.

Although the work has gained improvements, but there are still more work to be done in the future. At first, more experiments on both PlanetLab sites and home networks should be done. Experiments concerning locations and time differences are under considerations. Secondly, since the magnitude of the flows in this paper is strictly limited for security concerns, it can not reflect magnitude variations of LDoS attack flows, which is rather an essential factor. Thirdly, this paper throws light on using end-to-end delay for defense, but there would be more research work into how to make this strategy work. For example, the relationships between *RoB* with attack performance, the impacts of end-to-end delay on the synchonization of distributed LDoS attacks, the related defence mechanisms should be studied.

Acknowledgments. This work was partly funded by the National Natural Science Foundation of China under grant No. 61070199 and 61100223, the Specialized Research Fund of the Ministry of Education of China for the Doctoral Program of Higher Education, No.20124307110014, and Higher school specialized research fund for the doctoral program funding issue (863 Program), No.2011AA01A103.

References

1. Kuzmanovic, A., Knightly, E.W.: Low-rate TCP-targeted denial of Service Attacks. In: Proceedings of ACM SIGOMM 2003, Karlsruhe, Germany, pp. 75–86 (2003)
2. Luo, X., Chang, R.K.C.: On a new class of pulsing denial-of-service attacks and the defense. In: Proceedings of the ISOC Symposium on Network and Distributed Systems Security (SNDSS), pp. 61–79 (2005)
3. Zhang, Y., Mao, Z.M., Wang, J.: Low-rate tcp-targeted dos attack disrupts internet routing. In: Proc. 14th Annual Network & Distributed System Security Symposium, pp. 1–15 (2007)
4. Schuchard, M., Mohaisen, A., Foo Kune, D., et al.: Losing control of the internet: using the data plane to attack the control plane. In: Proceedings of the 17th ACM Conference on Computer and Communications Security, pp. 726–728. ACM (2010)
5. Wang, L., Peng, W., Huang, Z., Wang, Y.: An Analysis of Impact of End-to-end Delay on LDoS Flows in the Internet. In: IMCCC 2012, Haerbin, China (2012)
6. Kwok, Y.-K., Tripathi, R., Chen, Y., Hwang, K.: HAWK: Halting anomalies with weighted choking to rescue well-behaved TCP sessions from shrew dDoS attacks. In: Lu, X., Zhao, W. (eds.) ICCNMC 2005. LNCS, vol. 3619, pp. 423–432. Springer, Heidelberg (2005)
7. Sun, H., Lui, J.C.S., Yau, D.K.Y.: Defending against low-rate TCP attacks: Dynamic detection and protection. In: Proceedings of the 12th IEEE International Conference on Network Protocols, ICNP 2004, pp. 196–205. IEEE (2004)
8. Zhang, C., Yin, J., Cai, Z., et al.: RRED: robust RED algorithm to counter low-rate denial-of-service attacks. IEEE Communications Letters 14(5), 489–491 (2010)
9. Shiyuan, L., Hao, J.: Study of the conception of the similarity in time series. Huazhong Univ. of Sci. & Tech. (Nature Science Edition) 32, 75 (2004)
10. Alter, O., Brown, P.O., Botstein, D.: Singular value decomposition for genome-wide expression data processing and modeling. Proceedings of the National Academy of Sciences 97(18), 10101–10106 (2000)
11. Keogh, E., Pazzani, M.: An Enhanced Representation of Time Series Which Allows Fast and Accurate Classification, Clustering and Relevance Feedback. In: Proceedings of the 4th International Conference on Knowledge Discovery and Data Mining, New York, NY, August 27-31, pp. 239–241 (1998)

12. Chen, Y., Hwang, K., Kwok, Y.-K.: Filtering of Shrew DDoS Attacks in Frequency Domain. In: The First IEEE LCN Workshop on Network Security (WoNS 2005), Sydney, Australia, pp. 786–793 (January 2005)
13. Chen, K., Liu, H., Chen, X.: EBDT: A Method for Detecting LDoS Attack. In: Proceeding of the IEEE International Conference on Information and Automation. Shenyang, China, pp. 911–916 (June 2012)

Appendix A: PlanetLab Sites Information

The Table below listed the sites information. In total, we performed experiments on 9 PlanetLab sites, but only 5 of them succeeded to dump the complete flow information of both sides.

Table 2. PlanetLab Sites Information

Site	Country	Local Time	Status
planetlab-1.sysu.edu.cn	China	2013/4/7 08:36	Failed[1] (Server fails to start tcpdump on host)
planetlab2.csg.uzh.ch	Switch	2013/4/7 12:34	Ok
ple2.ipv6.lip6.fr	France	2013/4/7 14:23	Ok
planetlab2.umassd.edu	U.S.A.	2013/4/7 23:13	Failed[2] (Dump file contains broken packets)
ple2.tu.koszalin.pl	Poland	2013/4/8 00:07	Ok
planetlab-1.cs.ucy.ac.cy	Cyprus	2013/4/8 04:15	Failed[3] (Server fails to dump packets)
planetlab1.sics.se	Sweden	2013/4/8 01:08	Ok
planetlab1.lkn.ei.tum.de	German	2013/4/8 01:44	Ok
planetlab-02.kusa.ac.jp	Japan	2013/4/7 08:14	Failed[2]

Appendix B: PlanetLab Sites Results

The Pictures below show relationship between *Period (Duration)* and *Flow Similarity Distance*.

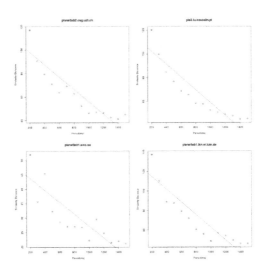

Fig. 10. Period vs. Flow Similarity-Distance(All sites)

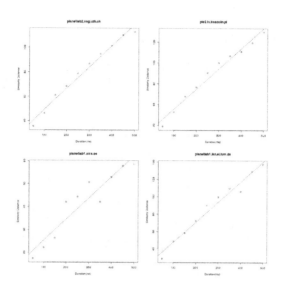

Fig. 11. Duration *vs. Flow Similarity-Distance*(All sites)

Bit Reversal Broadcast Scheduling for Ad Hoc Systems[*]

Marcin Kik, Maciej Gębala, and Mirosław Kutyłowski

Faculty of Fundamental Problems of Technology, Wrocław University of Technology

Abstract. We consider the scenario where a broadcaster sends messages to an ad hoc subset of receivers. We assume that once a receiver becomes active, it must receive all messages directed to it.

The problem considered in this paper is minimization of the energy usage for the receiver. As most of the energy is spent for the receiver's antenna, our goal is to minimize the time period, when this antenna is active.

In this paper we present and analyze RBO broadcast scheduling protocol that attempts to minimize the extra energy usage due to receiving messages that in fact are not meant for the receiver. While RBO scheme enjoys such important properties like correctness in case of transmission failures and ease of implementation, estimating extra energy cost requires a lot of effort.

In this paper we present tight upper bounds for this extra energy together with a rigorous proof. Namely, for a broadcast cycle of length 2^k we show that the overhead is limited to $2k + 3$ extra messages, while there are cases where the overhead is $2k - 1$ extra messages. As it is hard to imagine how to break this upper bound, RBO might be a good choice for broadcast scheduling, when energy efficiency and ease to implementation are concerned.

Keywords: broadcast, ad hoc system, scheduling, energy cost, upper bound.

1   Introduction

In this paper we consider broadcasting systems for ad hoc systems where receivers have limited energy resources. This concerns in particular battery operated devices such as sensors deployed in hardly accessible places. In such a case, battery exhaustion is a major issue due to high costs of battery replacement or recharging. For this reason, particular attention should be paid to optimizing energetic efficiency of these devices. As energy consumption for activating receiver's antenna is by order of magnitude higher than consumption for sensing and internal computations, the main source of optimization is minimizing the time in which the antenna is activated. This is easy, if a device knows exactly the moment in which data will be sent to it. However, we consider ad hoc systems where the receiver has no a priori information whether some data is sent to it by the broadcaster and has to check it by listening to the broadcast channel.

We focus our attention on critical systems where a device *must* receive each message sent to it once it is in the range of the broadcaster. This requirement is self-evident for military applications, traffic control and other systems that have to react without delay.

---

[*] Supported by project "Detectors and sensors for measuring factors hazardous to environment – modeling and monitoring of threats", financed by the European Union via the European Regional Development Fund and the Polish state, Operational Programme Innovative Economy 2007-2013. Ref. No. POIG.01.03.01-02-002/08-00.

M. Pathan, G. Wei, and G. Fortino (Eds.): IDCS 2013, LNCS 8223, pp. 223–237, 2013.
© Springer-Verlag Berlin Heidelberg 2013

Broadcasting model. The system consists of a broadcaster and multiple receivers. Broadcasting transmission consists of *cycles*, each consisting of n *time slots*, where each slot is devoted to one message of a fixed size. We assume that $n = 2^k$, for an integer $k > 0$. The broadcaster has a collection of n messages of a fixed length; the messages are repeatedly transmitted in the same order in each cycle. We can also think about n channels, where a channel corresponds to a time slot position in the cycles.

Further, we assume that each message is preceded by a key identifying the message. Each receiver has its own range of keys, i.e. an interval $[\kappa', \kappa'']$ such that if a message is labeled by a key $\kappa \in [\kappa', \kappa'']$, then the receiver *must* record this message.

The main goal of the broadcasting scheme is to organize the broadcast cycle and the algorithm executed by a receiver. We assume that:

- a receiver may start execution at any moment of a broadcast cycle,
- after activation, a receiver must record all messages from its range and no message can be skipped (e.g. due waiting for the next broadcast cycle),
- a receiver has no prior information on the keys of messages transmitted.

Energy Cost. The receivers must minimize their *energy usage*, which is defined as the number of time slots, when it is listening– the radio antenna of the receiver can be activated and deactivated for any time slot. Since the receiver cannot skip any message with the key from its range, we have to minimize the number of slots, when the receiver listens, but the message's key is outside its range. We call it *extra energy*. A naïve organization of the broadcast cycle is to send the messages according to the order of the keys. However then a receiver must waste a lot of energy, if a it is activated at the beginning of the cycle and its keys appear at the end of the cycle. Some extra energy is inevitable, since when the receiver is activated, it knows nothing and must listen to the next time slot, which may contain a key outside the range of the receiver.

Applications. The model presented above is relevant in many cases of information dissemination and control over a large population of energy constrained devices, e.g.:

- The keys might be the identifiers of database records transmitted in the stream.
- The keys might be the coordinates of objects on the plane encoded by Morton z-ordering [1]. Due to this ordering, a receiver may pay attention only to messages concerning an approximately square region assigned to it.
- The keys may be identifiers of the receiver devices. The broadcaster may send commands or messages to individual receivers.
- The keys may be identifiers of groups of mutually non-interfering sensors. Each frame with such key would contain only the header, while the rest of the time slot can be used for upload transmission by the sensors from this group.

1.1 Outline of the RBO Protocol

RBO protocol has been already described in our technical reports [2],[3], [4].

First let us introduce some notation. Binary representations of numbers are written as bit strings in parentheses: e.g. (0010) stands for a 4-bit binary representation of number 2. For a binary number t, let $\mathrm{rev}_k(t)$ stands for the k-bit number with a binary representation which is the same as the binary representation of $t \bmod 2^k$, but written in the reversed order.

Let $\kappa_0, \ldots, \kappa_{n-1}$ be the sorted sequence of $n = 2^k$ keys of the messages to be sent during a broadcast cycle. The scheduling rule is very simple:

Scheduling Rule

The message with key κ_t is sent during the slot of index $\mathrm{rev}_k(t)$.

Thereby, the first messages have keys $\kappa_{(00\ldots0)}$, $\kappa_{(10\ldots0)}$, $\kappa_{(01\ldots0)}$, $\kappa_{(11\ldots0)}$, $\ldots$, that is κ_0, $\kappa_{n/2}$, $\kappa_{n/4}$, $\kappa_{3n/4}$, $\ldots$.

A receiver, requesting the keys from a range $[\kappa', \kappa'']$, maintains auxiliary variables lb and ub initialized to 0 and $n - 1$, respectively. lb stands for *lower bound* and ub stands for *upper bound*. The receiver may start at an arbitrary time slot s, and executes the following algorithm:

Receiver's Algorithm

In time-slot t, if $\mathrm{lb} \leq \mathrm{rev}_k(t) \leq \mathrm{ub}$, then the receiver activates the antenna and gets a message with key $\kappa = \kappa_{\mathrm{rev}_k(t)}$. Then it updates lb and ub according to the value of κ:

Case 1. if $\kappa < \kappa'$, then $\mathrm{lb} := \mathrm{rev}_k(t) + 1$,
Case 2. if $\kappa'' < \kappa$, then $\mathrm{ub} := \mathrm{rev}_k(t) - 1$,
Case 3. if $\kappa' \leq \kappa \leq \kappa''$, then record the message from this slot,

If after the update $\mathrm{lb} > \mathrm{ub}$, then the receiver concludes that there is no message with a key from $[\kappa', \kappa'']$ in the current broadcast cycle and switches off its antenna.

While correctness of the RBO scheme is self-evident, it turn out to be very hard to estimate the extra energy spent by a receiver.

Recall that each step of the classic *binary search* algorithm actually clips the interval of the possible locations of the searched key in the sorted sequence of keys. The customary presentation is that the keys of the sequence are organized in a balanced *binary search tree*, and the searched key is compared with a sequence of keys from subsequent levels of this tree. RBO permutes the sorted sequence of keys so that the broadcast cycle is a sequence of the subsequent levels of a search tree. Moreover, each level is permuted recursively. However, the most tricky part is that no matter when we start the search, the situation is quite similar and we have a tree organized in almost the same way. This leads to the following main result of this paper:

Theorem 1. *The extra energy of RBO protocol is at most $2k + 3$ for any input configuration.*

The estimation given by Theorem 1 is tight in the sense that there are examples where extra energy is $2k - 1$. This happens if $\kappa_{n/2-1} < \kappa' \leq \kappa'' < \kappa_{n/2}$ and the receiver starts at $s = 2$. Note that tight bounds for RBO do not immediately say that there are no other scheduling permutation with less extra energy (still, it seems to be unlikely). Even if there is such a permutation, it might be useless if computing it is not simple enough (a receiver must immediately decide whether to listen).

1.2   Related Work

Broadcast scheduling for radio receivers with low *access time* (the delay for receiving the required record) and low average *tuning time* (the energy cost) was considered by Imielinski, Viswanathan, and Badrinath (see e.g. [5], [6], [7]). In [6], *hashing* and *flexible indexing* for finding single records in a broadcast cycle have been proposed. In [7], a distributed index based on an ordered balanced tree has been introduced. A broadcast sequence consists of two kinds of *buckets*. Groups of *index buckets*, containing parts of the index tree, are interleaved with the groups of *data buckets* containing proper data and a pointer (i.e. time offset) to the next index bucket. Each group of index buckets consists of a copy of the upper part of the index tree together with a relevant fragment of the lower part of the tree. This mechanism has been applied in more complex scenarios of delivering data to mobile users [8].

Khanna and Zhou [9] proposed a sophisticated version of the index tree aimed at minimizing *mean* access and tuning time, for given probability of each data record being requested. The broadcast cycle contains multiple copies of data items, so that spacing between copies of each item is related to the optimal spacing, minimizing mean access time derived in [10]. However, the key of an item is determined by its probability of being requested. Indexing of broadcast stream for XML documents [11] or for full text search [12] have also been considered.

If a broadcast cycle contains indexing tree structure, then receiving data in current cycle depends on the successful reception of the indexing data. Instead of separate index buckets RBO uses short *headers* of the data frames – the header holds the key assigned to the frame. Consequently, in unreliable transmission conditions a receiver has better chances of efficient navigation towards its frames.

Bit-reversal permutation has been applied in many contexts, e.g. in FFT algorithm, lock-free extensible hash arrays [13] distributed arrays in P2P [14], address mapping in SDRAM [15], scattering of video bursts in transmission scheduling in mobile TV [16].

2   Notation and Preliminaries

Let $\mathbb{Z}$ and $\mathbb{Q}$ denote, respectively, the set of integers and the set of rational numbers. For simplicity, we assume that the keys are from $\mathbb{Q}$. Let $[a, b] = \{x \in \mathbb{Q} | a \leq x \leq b\}$ and $[[a, b]] = [a, b] \cap \mathbb{Z}$. Let $|S|$ denote the number of set S, and $\emptyset$ denote the empty set. We use the convention that $\min \emptyset = +\infty$ and $\max \emptyset = -\infty$.

Binary Strings. For $x \in \mathbb{N}$, let $\mathrm{bin}_i(x)$ denote the i-bit binary representation of $x \bmod 2^i$, e.g. $\mathrm{bin}_4(5) = (0101)$ (a sequence of zeroes and ones in parentheses denotes binary representation). For a binary representation α (a sequence of bits), $(\alpha)_2$ denotes the number represented by α. Let $\mathrm{bin}(x) = \mathrm{bin}_{\lceil \lg_2(x+1) \rceil}(x)$. (Note that $\mathrm{bin}(0) = \mathrm{bin}_0(0)$ is an empty sequence and, hence, for empty sequence α, we have $(\alpha)_2 = 0$.) For a binary representations α, β:

- α^d denotes the concatenation of d copies of α (e.g. $(1)^4 = (1111)$); $\alpha\beta$ stands for the concatenation of α and β (e.g. $(01)(11) = (0111)$),

- $|\alpha|$ denotes the length of α.
- rev α denotes reversal of α (e.g. $\mathrm{rev}(01) = (10)$),
- For $x \in \mathbb{N}$, let $\mathrm{rev}_k(x) = (\mathrm{rev}(\mathrm{bin}_k(x)))_2$.

Note that $\mathrm{rev}_k(x)$ is the number with binary representation that is a reversal of the k-bit binary representation of $x \bmod 2^k$. Thus, $\mathrm{rev}_k(x) \in [[0, 2^k - 1]]$. Note that, if $k > 0$, then $\mathrm{rev}_k(1) = 2^{k-1}$. For a set $S \subseteq \mathbb{Z}$, $\mathrm{rev}_k S$ denotes $\{\mathrm{rev}_k(x) | x \in S\}$.

Key Intervals for RBO Execution. Let $\kappa_0, \ldots, \kappa_{n-1}$ be the sorted sequence of n keys of the messages to be sent during a broadcast cycle. Let $\kappa_{-1} = -\infty$ and $\kappa_n = +\infty$. Let KEYS=$\{\kappa_0, \ldots, \kappa_{n-1}\}$.

We consider a receiver interested for messages from $[\kappa', \kappa'']$. Let s be the time-slot when the receiver starts protocol execution. Let $r' = \min\{r \in [[0, n]] \mid \kappa' \le \kappa_r\}$, and $r'' = \max\{r \in [[-1, n-1]] \mid \kappa_r \le \kappa''\}$. So

$$\kappa_r \in [\kappa', \kappa''] \quad \text{if and only if} \quad r \in [[r', r'']].$$

In particular, if $[\kappa', \kappa''] \cap \mathrm{KEYS} = \emptyset$, then $\kappa_r < \kappa'$ and $\kappa'' < \kappa_{r+1}$, for some $r \in [[-1, n-1]]$, and so $r' = r + 1$, $r'' = r$. If $[\kappa', \kappa''] \cap \mathrm{KEYS} \ne \emptyset$, then $0 \le r' \le r'' \le n - 1$. So in any case $r' \le r'' + 1$. Note that r' and r'' are the ultimate values for the variables lb and ub, respectively. Indeed, as long as lb $< r'$ (respectively, ub $> r''$), the receiver still does not know that $\kappa_{\mathrm{lb}} \notin [\kappa', \kappa'']$ (respectively, $\kappa_{\mathrm{ub}} \notin [\kappa', \kappa'']$).

Time Partition for RBO Execution. Now we introduce several parameters necessary to get insight to what really happens when the messages are sent according to the bit reversal permutation.

Let $t_0 := s$. Then we define inductively the values t_i, l_i and the sets: Y_i, X_i, $Y_{i,j}$, $X_{i,j}$. Namely, for $i \ge 0$:

- $l_i := \max\{l \le k \mid t_i \bmod 2^l = 0\}$ (i.e. l_i is the length of the longest suffix of zeroes in $\mathrm{bin}_k(t_i)$),
- $t_{i+1} := t_i + 2^{l_i}$,
- $Y_i := [[t_i, t_i + 2^{l_i} - 1]]$, and $X_i := \mathrm{rev}_k Y_i$,
- last $:= \min\{i \ge 0 \mid l_i = k\}$.

For $i \ge 0$, for $j \in [[0, l_i]]$ we define:

- $Y_{i,j} := [[t_i + \lfloor 2^{j-1} \rfloor, t_i + 2^j - 1]]$ (so: $Y_{i,0} = \{t_i\}$ and $Y_i = \bigcup_{j=0}^{l_i} Y_{i,j}$,),
- $X_{i,j} := \mathrm{rev}_k Y_{i,j}$.

So $t_0, t_1, t_2, \ldots, t_{\mathrm{last}}$ is a sequence of steps that define partition of a time interval starting at step s into intervals Y_0, Y_1, $\ldots$, Y_{last}. Each of the left endpoints of these intervals has a suffix of zeroes in the binary representation, and this length grows at least by one when we go from Y_i to Y_{i+1}. Note also that all elements in Y_i have the same binary representation except for the last l_i bits that take all possible values. So in $X_k = \mathrm{rev}_k(Y_i)$ we get numbers where l_i most significant positions are arbitrary while the remaining sequence of $k - l_i$ less significant bits is fixed. We call this sequence β_i.

So X_i contains 2^{l_i} numbers evenly distributed within $[[0, n-1]]$. The minimal element in X_i is $\mathrm{rev}_k(t_i) = ((0)^{l_i}\beta_i)_2$ and the maximal is $((1)^{l_i}\beta_i)_2$.

Dividing Y_i into subintervals $Y_{i,j}$ reflects the same recursive structure of Y_i and shows in which order the points of X_i are used by RBO.

W.l.o.g we may assume that $0 \le s < n$. If $s = 0$, then $\mathrm{last} = 0$ and $Y_{\mathrm{last}} = [[0, n-1]]$. If $s \ne 0$, then for $i \in [[0, \mathrm{last}-1]]$, $Y_i \subseteq [[0, n-1]]$, and $Y_{\mathrm{last}} = [[n, 2n-1]]$. So in any case $s + n - 1 \in Y_{\mathrm{last}}$.

For $i \in [[0, \mathrm{last}-2]]$, $t_i + 2^{l_i}$ yields a number with the suffix of l_{i+1} zeroes in the binary representation. So t_i must have the suffix $(0)(1)^{l_{i+1}-l_i}(0)^{l_i}$ and we may represent β_i as $(1)^{l_{i+1}-l_i}(0)\alpha_i$. Then also $\beta_{i+1} = (1)\alpha_i$ for $i + 1 < \mathrm{last}$. On the other hand, $\beta_{\mathrm{last}-1} = (1)^{l_{\mathrm{last}}-l_{\mathrm{last}-1}}$ and $|\beta_{\mathrm{last}}| = 0$. So we get the following property:

Lemma 1. *If* $i \in [[0, \mathrm{last}-1]]$ *and* $\beta_i = \rho\gamma$, *where* $|\gamma| = |\beta_{i+1}|$, *then* $(\gamma)_2 \le (\beta_{i+1})_2$.

Now we take a look at the binary representations of the elements of $X_{i,j}$. For $i \in [[0, \mathrm{last}]]$, for $j \in [[0, l_i]]$, we have $x \in X_{i,j}$ if and only if either $j = 0$ and $\mathrm{bin}_k(x) = (0)^{l_i}\beta_i$ or $j \in [[1, l_i]]$ and $\mathrm{bin}_k(x) = \rho(1)(0)^{l_i-j}\beta_i$, where $(\rho)_2$ is a j-bit number.

For auxiliary purposes we also define the following infinite extensions of the sets of indexes. For $i \in [[0, \mathrm{last}]]$, let $\mathbb{X}_i := \{x \in \mathbb{Z} \mid x \bmod 2^{k-l_i} = (\beta_i)_2\}$. So $\mathbb{X}_i \cap [[0, n-1]] = X_i$. Similarly, for $i \in [[0, \mathrm{last}]]$, $j \in [[0, l_i]]$, let $\mathbb{X}_{i,j} = \{x \in \mathbb{Z} \mid x \bmod 2^{k-j} = ((0)^{l_i-j}\beta_i)_2\}$. Note that $\mathbb{X}_{i,j} \cap [[0, n-1]] = \bigcup_{j' \in [[0,j]]} X_{i,j'}$.

3   Proof of Theorem 1

For the sake of analysis we assume that RBO book keeps its energy cost. Namely, we introduce variables lb_t, ub_t – for the values of lb and ub immediately before time slot t, and and le_t, re_t and ie_t – for energy cost occurred at time slot t. Variable le_t denotes *left energy* - the extra energy due to increasing lb, variable re_t denotes *right energy* - the extra energy due to decreasing ub. Variable ie_t is the *internal energy* due to getting a message from the receiver's range $[\kappa', \kappa'']$. Below find the details of bookkeeping:

a) **if** $\mathrm{lb}_t \le \mathrm{rev}_k(t) < r'$ **then** /* time slot t "on the left side" of $[r', r'']$ */
   i. $\mathrm{lb}_{t+1} \leftarrow \mathrm{rev}_k(t) + 1$, $\mathrm{ub}_{t+1} \leftarrow \mathrm{ub}_t$,
   ii. $\mathrm{le}_t \leftarrow 1$ /* using "left-side" energy in time slot s */
   iii. $\mathrm{re}_t \leftarrow 0$; $\mathrm{ie}_t \leftarrow 0$; /* "internal" and "right-side" energy are not used */
b) **else if** $r'' < \mathrm{rev}_k(t) \le \mathrm{ub}_t$ **then** /* time slot t "on the right side" of $[r', r'']$ */
   i. $\mathrm{ub}_{t+1} \leftarrow \mathrm{rev}_k(t) - 1$, $\mathrm{lb}_{t+1} \leftarrow \mathrm{lb}_t$
   ii. $\mathrm{re}_t \leftarrow 1$ /* using "right-side" energy in time slot s */
   iii. $\mathrm{le}_t \leftarrow 0$; $\mathrm{ie}_t \leftarrow 0$; /* "internal" and "left-side" energy are not used */
c) **else** /* $\mathrm{rev}_k(t)$ is either outside $[\mathrm{lb}, \mathrm{rb}]$ or in $[r', r'']$ */
   i. $\mathrm{lb}_{t+1} \leftarrow \mathrm{lb}_t$; $\mathrm{ub}_{t+1} \leftarrow \mathrm{ub}_t$;
   ii. $\mathrm{le}_t \leftarrow 0$; $\mathrm{re}_t \leftarrow 0$;
   iii. **if** $r' \le \mathrm{rev}_k(t) \le r''$ **then** $\mathrm{ie}_t \leftarrow 1$ **else** $\mathrm{ie}_t \leftarrow 0$

In the following subsections we consider separately left energy and right energy. The proofs are similar, but the right energy cost requires additional subtle observations.

3.1   Left-Side Energy

Preliminary Observations. When time slots from interval Y_i are executed, lb may increase due to the values from X_i that come closer to r'. The final value depends on $p'_i = \max\{x \in \mathbb{X}_i \mid x < r'\}$. Let $x'_i = \lfloor p'_i/2^{k-l_i} \rfloor$, and $p'_{i,j} = \max\{x \in \mathbb{X}_{i,j} \mid x < r'\}$.

The next parameters used below are $m'_{i,j} = \mathrm{lb}_{\max Y_{i,j}+1} - 1$ and $m'_i = m'_{i,l_i}$. They denote the upper bound for a value used to increase lb before leaving time interval, respectively, $Y_{i,j}$ and Y_i. Therefore,

Proposition 1. $p'_{i,j} \leq m'_{i,j}$ and $p'_i \leq m'_i$.

Let L_t denote the set containing the value used to update lb at time slot t or an empty set - if there is no update. That is, $L_t = \{\mathrm{lb}_{t+1} - 1\} \setminus \{\mathrm{lb}_t - 1\}$. Then $L_t \neq \emptyset$ iff $\mathrm{lb}_t < \mathrm{lb}_{t+1}$ and $L_t = \{\mathrm{rev}_k(t)\}$. Obviously, $\sum_{t \in [[t',t'']]} \mathrm{le}_t = |\bigcup_{t \in [[t',t'']]} L_t|$.

Lemma 2. Let $i \in [[0, \mathrm{last}]]$ and $j \in [[0, l_i]]$. If $Y \subseteq \mathbb{Z}$ and $\max Y_{i,j} < \min Y$, then

$$\bigcup_{t \in Y} L_t \subseteq (\mathrm{rev}_k Y) \cap \left[\left[p'_{i,j}+1, r'-1\right]\right] \subseteq (\mathrm{rev}_k Y) \cap \left[\left[p'_{i,j}+1, p'_{i,j}+2^{k-j}-1\right]\right]$$

Proof. Since $\max Y_{i,j} < \min Y$, we have $\bigcup_{t \in Y} L_t \subseteq (\mathrm{rev}_k Y) \cap \left[\left[m'_{i,j}+1, r'-1\right]\right]$ and $p'_{i,j} \leq m'_{i,j}$. The second inclusion follows from the fact that $r' \leq p'_{i,j} + 2^{k-j}$.   □

Outline of the Analysis. We estimate the left energy cost separately for different parts of transmission:

Lemma 3. For $i \in [[0, \mathrm{last}]]$, for $j \in [[0, l_i]]$, within $Y_{i,j}$ only $p'_{i,j}$ can contribute to the change of lb. I.e. $\bigcup_{t \in Y_{i,j}} L_t \subseteq \{p'_{i,j}\}$ and, hence, $\sum_{t \in Y_{i,j}} \mathrm{le}_t \leq 1$.

Lemma 4. $\sum_{t \in Y_0} \mathrm{le}_t \leq l_0 + 1$.

Lemma 5. $\sum_{t \in Y_{i+1}} \mathrm{le}_t \leq l_{i+1} - l_i$, for $i \in [[0, \mathrm{last}-2]]$.

Lemma 6. If $\mathrm{last} > 0$, then $\sum_{t \in Y_{\mathrm{last}}} \mathrm{le}_t \leq l_{\mathrm{last}} - l_{\mathrm{last}-1} = k - l_{\mathrm{last}-1}$.

By Lemma 4, 5 and 6 and the fact that after Y_{last} no extra energy is used we get our final estimation of left energy:

$$\sum_{t \geq s} \mathrm{le}_t \leq k + 1 .   \tag{1}$$

Proofs of Lemmas

Proof (Lemma 3). The proof is by induction on j. The case $j = 0$ is obvious. Namely, $Y_{i,0} = \{t_i\}$, so if $\mathrm{rev}_k(t_i) < r'$, then $\mathrm{rev}_k(t_i) = p'_{i,0}$ as $\mathrm{rev}_k(t_i) + 2^k \geq r'$. If $\mathrm{rev}_k(t_i) \geq r'$, then $\bigcup_{t \in Y_{i,0}} L_t = \emptyset$ and the lemma holds, too.

Now let us consider $j + 1 \in [[1, l_i]]$. Since $\mathbb{X}_{i,j} \cap [[0, n-1]] = \bigcup_{j' \in [[0,j]]} X_{i,j'}$, by Lemma 2 we have $\bigcup_{t \in Y_{i,j+1}} L_t \subseteq A$, where $A = \mathbb{X}_{i,j+1} \cap [[p'_{i,j}+1, p'_{i,j}+2^{k-j} - 1]]$. However, subsequent elements in $\mathbb{X}_{i,j+1}$ are located at distance $2^{k-(j+1)}$, so $A = \{p'_{i,j}+2^{k-j-1}\}$. Further observe that if $p'_{i,j}+2^{k-j-1} < r'$, then $p'_{i,j+1} = p'_{i,j}+2^{k-j-1}$ and so the lemma holds for j. If $p'_{i,j} + 2^{k-j-1} \geq r'$, then left-energy is not spent and $L_{p'_{i,j}+2^{k-j-1}} = \emptyset$. Hence, in either case $\bigcup_{t \in Y_{i,j+1}} L_t \subseteq \{p'_{i,j+1}\}$.   □

Proof (Lemma 4). By Lemma 3, $\sum_{t\in Y_{0,j}} le_t \le 1$ for each j. So

$$\sum_{t\in Y_0} le_t = \sum_{j\in[[0,l_0]]} \left(\sum_{t\in Y_{0,j}} le_t\right) \le l_0 + 1.$$
□

Proof (Lemma 5). First recall that $l_{i+1} - l_i \ge 1$ and

$$p_i' = 2^{k-l_i} \cdot x_i' + (\beta_i)_2 \le m_i' < r',$$
$$(\beta_i)_2 = ((1)^{l_{i+1}-l_i}(0)\alpha_i)_2 < 2^{k-l_i}, \qquad \beta_{i+1} = (1)\alpha_i.$$

Case A: $r' \le 2^{k-l_i} \cdot (x_i' + 1) + ((0)^{l_{i+1}-l_i}\beta_{i+1})_2.$

By Lemma 2, $\bigcup_{t\in Y_{i+1}} L_t \subseteq A$, where $A = \mathbb{X}_{i+1} \cap [[p_i' + 1, r' - 1]]$. On the other hand, $p_i' > 2^{k-l_i} \cdot x_i' + ((1)^{l_{i+1}-l_i-1}(0)\beta_{i+1})_2$ and $r' \le 2^{k-l_i} \cdot (x_i' + 1) + ((0)^{l_{i+1}-l_i}\beta_{i+1})_2$, so the only element of $\mathbb{X}_{i+1}$ that may fall into the range $[[p_i' + 1, r' - 1]]$ is $2^{k-l_i} \cdot x_i' + ((1)^{l_{i+1}-l_i}\beta_{i+1})_2$. Consequently, $|\bigcup_{t\in Y_{i+1}} L_t| \le 1 \le l_{i+1} - l_i.$

Case B: $r' > 2^{k-l_i} \cdot (x_i' + 1) + ((0)^{l_{i+1}-l_i}\beta_{i+1})_2$

We consider separately two phases and inspect energy cost during each phase.

Phase 1: Time slots in $Y_{i+1,0}, \ldots, Y_{i+1,l_i}$

We aim to prove that left energy for this phase it at most 1. Let $Y = \bigcup_{l\in[[0,l_i]]} Y_{i+1,l}$. Then $\text{rev}_k(Y) = \bigcup_{l\in[[0,l_i]]} X_{i+1,l} \subseteq \mathbb{X}_{i+1,l_i}$. So by Lemma 2 we have $\bigcup_{t\in Y} L_t \subseteq A$, where $A = \mathbb{X}_{i+1,l_i} \cap [[p_i' + 1, p_i' + 2^{k-l_i} - 1]]$.
Since

$$p_i' = 2^{k-l_i} \cdot x_i' + ((1)^{l_{i+1}-l_i}(0)\alpha_i)_2 > 2^{k-l_i} \cdot x_i' + ((0)^{l_{i+1}-l_i}\beta_{i+1})_2$$

and

$$p_i' + 2^{k-l_i} = 2^{k-l_i} \cdot (x_i'+1) + ((1)^{l_{i+1}-l_i}(0)\alpha_i)_2 < 2^{k-l_i} \cdot (x_i'+2) + ((0)^{l_{i+1}-l_i}\beta_{i+1})_2,$$

we have

$$A = \{2^{k-l_i} \cdot (x_i' + 1) + ((0)^{l_{i+1}-l_i}\beta_{i+1})_2\}$$

and hence $\sum_{l\in[[0,l_i]]} \left(\sum_{t\in Y_{i+1,l}} le_t\right) \le 1.$

Observe also that since $r' > 2^{k-l_i} \cdot (x_i' + 1) + ((0)^{l_{i+1}-l_i}\beta_{i+1})_2$, the value p_{i+1,l_i}' must be equal to $2^{k-l_i} \cdot (x_i' + 1) + ((0)^{l_{i+1}-l_i}\beta_{i+1})_2.$

Phase 2: Time slots in $Y_{i+1,l_i+1}, \ldots, Y_{i+1,l_{i+1}}$

Since Phase 1 already may costs 1, now we have to prove that the left energy cost is at most $l_{i+1} - l_i - 1$. This requires some care in estimations.

First observe that by Lemma 3 , $\sum_{t\in Y_{i+1,l}} le_t \le 1$ for each $l \in [[l_i + 1, l_{i+1}]]$. So $\sum_{l\in[[l_i+1,l_{i+1}]]} \left(\sum_{t\in Y_{i+1,l}} le_t\right) \le l_{i+1} - l_i$ and the claim of Lemma 5 holds for sure unless equality holds. Let us consider the later case, that is, $\sum_{t\in Y_{i+1,l}} le_t = 1$ for each $l \in [[l_i + 1, l_{i+1}]]$.

Since $m_{i+1,l_i}' \in \bigcup_{l\in[[0,l_i]]} \bigcup_{t\in Y_{i+1,l}} L_t$ it follows from our previous observations that $m_{i+1,l_i}' = p_{i+1,l_i}' = 2^{k-l_i} \cdot (x_i' + 1) + ((0)^{l_{i+1}-l_i}\beta_{i+1})_2.$

Due to our last assumption $m_{i+1,l-1}' \ne m_{i+1,l}' \in \bigcup_{t\in Y_{i+1,l}} L_t$ for each $l \in [[l_i + 1, l_{i+1} - 1]]$. By Lemma 3, for each $l \in [[l_i + 1, l_{i+1} - 1]]$,

$$m_{i+1,l}' = p_{i+1,l}' = 2^{k-l_i} \cdot (x_i' + 1) + ((1)^{l-l_i}(0)^{l_{i+1}-l}\beta_{i+1})_2.$$

Now observe what happens in time interval $Y_{i+1,l_{i+1}}$. The only time slot that may contribute to left energy cost has index $x = 2^{k-l_i} \cdot (x'_i + 1) + ((1)^{l_{i+1}-l_i} \beta_{i+1})_2$. However,

$$x > 2^{k-l_i} \cdot (x'_i + 1) + ((1)^{l_{i+1}-l_i} (0) \alpha_i)_2 = 2^{k-l_i} \cdot (x'_i + 1) + (\beta_i)_2 = p'_i + 2^{k-l_i} \geq r'$$

Hence $\sum_{t \in Y_{i+1,l_{i+1}}} le_t = 0$, contradicting our assumption. □

Proof (Lemma 6). The proof is closely related to the proof of Lemma 5.

Case A: $r' \leq 2^{k-l_{\text{last}}-1} \cdot (x'_{\text{last}-1} + 1) + ((0)^{k-l_{\text{last}}-1})_2$

Since $m'_{\text{last}-1} \geq p'_{\text{last}-1} = 2^{k-l_{\text{last}}-1} \cdot x'_{\text{last}-1} + ((1)^{k-l_{\text{last}}-1})_2$, there is no value left that could contribute to left energy cost and therefore $\sum_{t \in Y_{\text{last}}} le_t = 0$ and the lemma obviously holds.

Case B: $r' > 2^{k-l_{\text{last}}-1} \cdot (x'_{\text{last}-1} + 1) + ((0)^{k-l_{\text{last}}-1})_2$

Note that $r' \leq p'_{\text{last}-1} + 2^{k-l_{\text{last}}-1} = 2^{k-l_{\text{last}}-1} \cdot (x'_{\text{last}-1} + 1) + ((1)^{k-l_{\text{last}}-1})_2 < 2^{k-l_{\text{last}}-1} \cdot (x'_{\text{last}-1} + 2) + ((0)^{k-l_{\text{last}}-1})_2$ and that $p'_{\text{last}-1} > 2^{k-l_{\text{last}}-1} \cdot x'_{\text{last}-1} + ((0)^{l_k-l_{\text{last}}-1})_2$. So $\bigcup_{l \in [[0,l_{\text{last}}-1]]} X_{\text{last},l} \cap [[p'_{\text{last}-1} + 1, r' - 1]] \subseteq \{2^{k-l_{\text{last}}-1} \cdot (x'_{\text{last}-1} + 1) + ((0)^{k-l_{\text{last}}-1})_2\}$. So the left energy cost for $\bigcup_{l \in [[0,l_{\text{last}}-1]]} Y_{\text{last},l}$ is at most 1.

Now consider left energy cost for $\bigcup_{l \in [[l_{\text{last}}-1+1,l_{\text{last}}]]} Y_{\text{last},l}$. As for Lemma 5, we observe that the energy cost for each $Y_{\text{last},l}$ is at most 1 and therefore the total is at most $k - l_{\text{last}}-1$. We have to exclude that it is exactly $k - l_{\text{last}}-1$.

If the energy cost for each $Y_{\text{last},l}$, where $l \in [[l_{\text{last}}-1 + 1, k - 1]]$ is one, then as in the proof of of Lemma 5 we compute that
$m'_{\text{last},k-1} = 2^{k-l_{\text{last}}-1} \cdot (x'_{\text{last}-1} + 1) + ((1)^{k-1-l_{\text{last}}-1} (0))_2$.
But since $2^{k-l_{\text{last}}-1} \cdot (x'_{\text{last}-1} + 1) + ((1)^{k-l_{\text{last}}-1})_2 \geq r'$, we have

$$X_{\text{last},k} \cap [[m'_{\text{last},k-1} + 1, r' - 1]] = \emptyset$$

and the left energy cost for time interval $Y_{\text{last},k}$ is zero.

We conclude that the total left energy cost is at most $1 + (k - l_{\text{last}}-1 - 1) = k - l_{\text{last}}-1$. □

3.2 Right-Side Energy

Notation. We define parameters analogous to those used for left-side energy cost. Namely, let

- $p''_{i,j} = \min\{x \in \mathbb{X}_{i,j} \mid r'' < x\}$, $p''_i = \min\{x \in \mathbb{X}_i \mid r'' < x\}$, and $x''_i = \lfloor p''_i / 2^{k-l_i} \rfloor$.
- $m''_{i,j} = \text{ub}_{\max Y_{i,j}+1} + 1$, $m''_i = m''_{i,l_i}$,
- $U_t = \{\text{ub}_{t+1} - 1\} \setminus \{\text{ub}_t - 1\}$

Note that:

- $p_{i,j}'' \geq m_{i,j}''$ and $p_i'' \geq m_i''$,
- $U_t \neq \emptyset$ if and only if $ub_t > ub_{t+1}$ and $U_t = \{rev_k(t)\}$,
- $\sum_{t \in [[t',t'']]} re_t = |\bigcup_{t \in [[t',t'']]} U_t|$.

Outline of the Analysis. The estimation follows from the following sequence of lemmas. The first one says that each $Y_{i,j}$ is responsible for right energy cost at most 1.

Lemma 7. *For* $i \in [[0, last]]$, $j \in [[0, l_i]]$, *we have* $\bigcup_{t \in Y_{i,j}} U_t \subseteq \{p_{i,j}''\}$. *So in particular* $\sum_{t \in Y_{i,j}} re_t \leq 1$.

The remaining lemmas determine right energy cost for different time intervals:

Lemma 8. $\sum_{t \in Y_0} re_t = l_0 + 1$.

Lemma 9. *For* $i \in [[0, last-2]]$, *we have either* $\sum_{t \in Y_{i+1}} re_t \leq l_{i+1} - l_i$, *or* $\sum_{t \in Y_{i+1}} re_t = 2$, *while* $l_{i+1} - l_i = 1$ *and* $p_{i+1}'' = 2^{k-l_i} \cdot (x_i'' - 1) + ((1)^{l_{i+1}-l_i} \beta_{i+1})_2$ *and* $m_{i+1}'' = p_{i+1}''$.

Lemma 10. *If* $last > 0$, *then* $\sum_{t \in Y_{last}} re_t \leq k - l_{last-1}$.

Note that the bounds from Lemmas 8 , 9 , 10 are similar to those from Sect. 3.2. However, according to Lemma 9 there are cases where the right energy is higher than $l_{i+1} - l_i$. The following two *lemmas* show that this high energy cost is compensated by low cost at different time slots.

Lemma 11. *If, for some* $i \in [[0, last-1]]$,

- $m_i'' = p_i''$, $x_{i+1}'' \geq (bin(x_i'')(0)^{l_{i+1}-l_i-1}(1))_2$,
- $\sum_{t \in Y_{i+1}} re_t \geq l_{i+1} - l_i$,

then

- $\sum_{t \in Y_{i+1}} re_t = l_{i+1} - l_i$,
- $x_{i+1}'' = (bin(x_i'')(0)^{l_{i+1}-l_i-1}(1))_2$,   *and* $m_{i+1}'' = p_{i+1}''$.

Lemma 12. *If, for some* $i \in [[0, last-2]]$,

- $m_{i+1}'' = p_{i+1}''$, $x_{i+1}'' = (bin(x_i''-1)(1))_2$,
- $\sum_{t \in Y_{i+2+c}} re_t \geq l_{i+2+c} - l_{i+1+c}$ *for each* $c \in [[0, d]]$, *where* $i+2+d \leq last$,

then for each $c \in [[0, d]]$, *we have*

- $\sum_{t \in Y_{i+2+c}} re_t = l_{i+2+c} - l_{i+1+c} \leq 2$,
- $x_{i+2+c}'' = (bin(x_{i+1}'')\gamma_{i+1} \cdots \gamma_{i+1+c})_2$,   *and* $m_{i+2+c}'' = p_{i+2+c}''$,
  where $(0)\alpha_i = \gamma_{i+1} \cdots \gamma_{last-1}$, *and* $\gamma_j = (0)(1)^{l_{j+1}-l_j-1}$ *for each* j *in its range.*

Now let us see that the bound $k + 2$ follows from the above lemmas. We have

$$\sum_{t \geq s} \mathrm{re}_t = \sum_{t \in Y_0} \mathrm{re}_t + \sum_{i=1}^{\mathrm{last}-1} \sum_{t \in Y_i} \mathrm{re}_t + \sum_{t \in Y_{\mathrm{last}}} \mathrm{re}_t$$

By Lemma 8 , $\sum_{t \in Y_0} \mathrm{re}_t \leq l_0 + 1$. By Lemma 10 , $\sum_{t \in Y_{\mathrm{last}}} \mathrm{re}_t \leq k - l_{\mathrm{last}-1}$. Hence it suffices to bound the middle sum by $l_{\mathrm{last}-1} - l_0 + 1$. The source of problems for estimating the second sum are those $i \in [[0, \mathrm{last}-1]]$, for which $\sum_{t \in Y_{i+1}} \mathrm{re}_t > l_{i+1} - l_i$. Let V denote the set of all such indexes i.

By Lemma 9 , if $i \in V$, then $l_{i+1} - l_i = 1$, $\sum_{t \in Y_{i+1}} \mathrm{re}_t = 2$ and $(\mathrm{bin}(x_{i+1}''))_2 = (\mathrm{bin}(x_i'' - 1)(1))_2$.

If $|V| \leq 1$, then $\sum_{i=1}^{\mathrm{last}-1} \sum_{t \in Y_i} \mathrm{re}_t \leq \sum_{i=1}^{\mathrm{last}-1} (l_i - l_{i-1}) + 1 = l_{\mathrm{last}-1} - l_0 + 1$, as required. So we have to consider the case $|V| > 1$.

Let $i \in V$, $i \neq \max V$. Let $i' > i$ be the next bigger element of V. Let d be the biggest number in the set $\{c \mid \sum_{t \in Y_{i+2+c}} \mathrm{re}_t \geq l_{i+2+c} - l_{i+1+c}\}$. If $i + 2 + d \geq i' + 1$, then by Lemma 12, we have $\sum_{t \in Y_{i'+1}} \mathrm{re}_t = l_{i'+1} - l_{i'}$ contradicting that $i' \in V$. Thus, there must be i'', $i < i'' < i'$ such that $\sum_{t \in Y_{i''+1}} \mathrm{re}_t < l_{i''+1} - l_{i''}$. Thus to each $i \in V$, $i \neq \max V$ we may assign an index i'', where the right energy is lower than $l_{i''+1} - l_{i''}$ as for i the energy cost is at most $l_{i+1} - l_i + 1$, the low cost at i'' compensates for the higher cost at i. The only element form V where we do not have compensation is $\max V$. Therefore $\sum_{i=1}^{\mathrm{last}-1} \sum_{t \in Y_i} \mathrm{re}_t \leq 1 + \sum_{i=1}^{\mathrm{last}-1} (l_i - l_{i-1}) = l_{\mathrm{last}-1} - l_0 + 1$, as required.

Proofs of Lemmas. Proofs of Lemmas 7 and 8 are analogous to the proofs of Lemma 3 and 4, so we skip it.

Proof (Lemma 9). Recall that

- $p_i'' = 2^{k-l_i} \cdot x_i'' + (\beta_i)_2$ and at the same time $2^{k-l_i} \cdot (x_i'' - 1) + (\beta_i)_2 \leq r''$,
- $(\beta_i)_2 = ((1)^{l_{i+1}-l_i}(0)\alpha_i)_2 < 2^{k-l_i}$ and $\beta_{i+1} = (1)\alpha_i$.

Case A: $r'' < 2^{k-l_i} \cdot x_i'' + ((0)^{l_{i+1}-l_i}\beta_{i+1})_2$

We show that $\bigcup_{t \in Y_{i+1}} U_t \subseteq \{a, b\}$, where $a = 2^{k-l_i} \cdot x_i'' + ((0)^{l_{i+1}-l_i}\beta_{i+1})_2$ and $b = 2^{k-l_i} \cdot (x_i'' - 1) + ((1)^{l_{i+1}-l_i}\beta_{i+1})_2$.

First, note that $a < p_i'' < a + 2^{k-l_i}$ and $\bigcup_{l \in [[0,l_i]]} \bigcup_{t \in Y_{i+1,l}} U_t \subseteq A$, where $A = \mathbb{X}_{i+1,l_i} \cap [[r'' + 1, p_i'' - 1]]$. On the other hand, $\mathbb{X}_{i+1,l_i} \cap [[a - 2^{k-l_i}, a + 2^{k-l_i}]] = \{a - 2^{k-l_i}, a, a + 2^{k-l_i}\}$ while $a - 2^{k-l_i} < p_i'' - 2^{k-l_i} \leq r''$ and $p_i'' < a + 2^{k-l_i}$. Thus $A \subseteq \{a\}$. Note that since $r'' < a$, we also have $m_{i+1,l_i}'' \leq a$.

Now consider the remaining time slots of Y_{i+1}. Then $\bigcup_{l \in [[l_i+1,l_{i+1}]]} \bigcup_{t \in Y_{i+1,l}} U_t \subseteq B$, where $B = \mathbb{X}_{i+1} \cap [[r'' + 1, m_{i+1,l_i}'' - 1]]$. Note that

$$\mathbb{X}_{i+1} \cap [[b - 2^{k-l_{i+1}}, b + 2^{k-l_{i+1}}]] = \{b - 2^{k-l_{i+1}}, b, b + 2^{k-l_{i+1}}\}$$

On the other hand,

$$b - 2^{k-l_{i+1}} = 2^{k-l_i} \cdot (x_i'' - 1) + ((1)^{l_{i+1}-l_i-1}(0)\beta_{i+1})_2$$
$$< 2^{k-l_i} \cdot (x_i'' - 1) + (\beta_i)_2 = p_i'' - 2^{k-l_i} \leq r'',$$

and $m_{i+1,l_i}'' \leq 2^{k-l_i} \cdot x_i'' + ((0)^{l_{i+1}-l_i}\beta_{i+1})_2 = b + 2^{k-l_{i+1}}$, so $B \subseteq \{b\}$.

Case B: $2^{k-l_i} \cdot x_i'' + ((0)^{l_{i+1}-l_i}\beta_{i+1})_2 \leq r''$

We have $\bigcup_{t\in Y_{i+1}} U_t \subseteq C$, where $C = [[r''+1, p_i''-1]]$.

First observe that $2^{k-l_i} \cdot x_i'' + ((0)^{l_{i+1}-l_i}\beta_{i+1})_2 \leq r''$ and $p_i'' = 2^{k-l_i} \cdot x_i'' + ((1)^{l_{i+1}-l_i}(0)\alpha_i)_2 < 2^{k-l_i} \cdot (x_i''+1) + ((0)^{l_{i+1}-l_i}\beta_{i+1})_2$. So $C \cap \mathbb{X}_{i+1,l_i} = \emptyset$, and, hence, $\sum_{l\in[[0,l_i]]}\sum_{t\in Y_{i+1,l}} re_t = 0$.

By Lemma 7, $\sum_{l\in[[l_i+1,l_{i+1}]]}\sum_{t\in Y_{i+1,l}} re_t \leq l_{i+1} - l_i$. Thus, $\sum_{t\in Y_{i+1}} re_t \leq l_{i+1} - l_i$ in this case.

We see that the only case, when $\sum_{t\in Y_{i+1}} re_t > l_{i+1} - l_i$, is Case A. Note that then with $l_{i+1} - l_i = 1$, $\bigcup_{t\in Y_{i+1}} U_t = \{a, b\}$ and $m_{i+1}'' = b$.   □

Proof (Lemma 10). First recall that

- $m_{\text{last}-1}'' \leq p_{\text{last}-1}'' = 2^{k-l_{\text{last}}-1} \cdot x_{\text{last}-1}'' + ((1)^{k-l_{\text{last}}-1})_2$,
- $r'' \geq 2^{k-l_{\text{last}}-1} \cdot (x_{\text{last}-1}'' - 1) + ((1)^{k-l_{\text{last}}-1})_2$.

Case A: $r'' < 2^{k-l_{\text{last}}-1} \cdot x_{\text{last}-1}'' + ((0)^{k-l_{\text{last}}-1})_2$.

Then $r'' = 2^{k-l_{\text{last}}-1} \cdot (x_{\text{last}-1}'' - 1) + ((1)^{k-l_{\text{last}}-1})_2$. Note that for $u = \min\{t \in Y_{\text{last}} \mid r'' < \text{rev}_k(t) < p_{\text{last}-1}''\}$ we have $\text{rev}_k(u) = 2^{k-l_{\text{last}}-1} \cdot x_{\text{last}-1}'' + ((0)^{k-l_{\text{last}}-1})_2 = r'' + 1$. In particular, ub cannot be changed after time slot u and therefore $\bigcup_{t\in Y_{\text{last}}} U_t = \{r''+1\}$ and $\sum_{t\in Y_{\text{last}}} re_t = 1 \leq k - l_{\text{last}}$, in this case.

Case B: $2^{k-l_{\text{last}}-1} \cdot x_{\text{last}-1}'' + ((0)^{k-l_{\text{last}}-1})_2 \leq r''$.

We have $m_{\text{last}-1}'' \leq p_{\text{last}-1}'' = 2^{k-l_{\text{last}}-1} \cdot x_{\text{last}-1}'' + ((1)^{k-l_{\text{last}}-1})_2$. Thus,

$$\bigcup_{t\in Y_{\text{last}}} U_t \subseteq \{2^{k-l_{\text{last}}-1} \cdot x_{\text{last}-1}'' + x \mid x \in [[1, 2^{k-l_{\text{last}}-1} - 2]]\}$$

Hence, $\bigcup_{t\in Y_{\text{last}}} U_t \cap \mathbb{X}_{\text{last},l_{\text{last}}-1} = \emptyset$ and $\sum_{l\in[[0,l_{\text{last}}-1]]}\left(\sum_{t\in Y_{\text{last},l}} re_t\right) = 0$. In turn, by Lemma 7 $\sum_{l\in[[l_{\text{last}}-1+1,l_{\text{last}}]]}\left(\sum_{t\in Y_{i+1,l}} re_t\right) \leq l_{\text{last}} - l_{\text{last}}-1$. Thus, in any case, $\sum_{t\in Y_{\text{last}}} re_t \leq \max\{1, k - l_{\text{last}}-1\} = k - l_{\text{last}}-1$.   □

Proof (Lemma 11). First note that

$$(\text{bin}(x_i'')(0)^{l_{i+1}-l_i}\beta_{i+1})_2 \leq (\text{bin}(x_{i+1}''-1)\beta_{i+1})_2 \leq r'' < p_i'' = (\text{bin}(x_i'')(1)^{l_{i+1}-l_i}\gamma)_2$$

where $|\gamma| = |\beta_{i+1}|$ and, by Lemma 1, $(\gamma)_2 \leq (\beta_{i+1})_2$. (The first inequality is by assumption of Lemma 11, the second one by definition of p_{i+1}''.)

We have $\bigcup_{l\in[[0,l_i]]}\bigcup_{t\in Y_{i+1,l}} U_t \subseteq \mathbb{X}_{i+1,l_i} \cap [[r''+1, p_i''-1]]$. However, the last set is empty, since the elements of $\text{rev}_k(Y_{i+1,l})$ have the form $(\text{bin}(x)(0)^{l_{i+1}-l}\beta_{i+1})_2$, while $(\text{bin}(x_i'')(0)^{l_{i+1}-l}\beta_{i+1})_2 \leq r''$ and $p_i'' < (\text{bin}(x_i''+1)(0)^{l_{i+1}-l_i}\beta_{i+1})_2$. Thus, we have $m_{i+1,l_i}'' = m_i''$.

Assume that $|\bigcup_{l\in[[l_i+1,l_{i+1}]]}\bigcup_{t\in Y_{i+1,l}} U_t| \geq l_{i+1} - l_i$. By Lemma 7, for each $l \in [[l_i + 1, l_{i+1}]]$, $\bigcup_{t\in Y_{i+1,l}} U_t \subseteq \{p_{i+1,l}''\}$. Thus, for each $l \in [[l_i + 1, l_{i+1}]]$, and $\bigcup_{t\in Y_{i+1,l}} U_t = \{p_{i+1,l}''\} = \{m_{i+1,l}''\}$ and, hence, the right energy cost for all $Y_{i+1,l}$,

$l \in [[l_i + 1, l_{i+1}]]$ is $l_{i+1} - l_i$. This implies in particular that for each $l \in [[l_i, l_{i+1} - 1]]$, $m''_{i+1,l} > m''_{i+1,l+1} = p''_{i+1,l+1}$.

It remains to show that $x''_{i+1} = (\mathrm{bin}(x''_i)(0)^{l_{i+1}-l_i-1}(1))_2$. We have

$$m''_{i+1,l_i} = p''_i = (\mathrm{bin}(x''_i)(1)^{l_{i+1}-l_i}\gamma)_2 \leq (\mathrm{bin}(x''_i + 1)(0)^{l_{i+1}-l_i}\beta_{i+1})_2$$

and $(\mathrm{bin}(x''_i)(0)^{l_{i+1}-l_i}\beta_{i+1})_2 \leq r''$. Thus

$$m''_{i+1,l_i+1} = p''_{i+1,l_i+1} = (\mathrm{bin}(x''_i)(1)(0)^{l_{i+1}-l_i-1}\beta_{i+1})_2.$$

Note that, for $l \in [[l_i + 1, l_{i+1} - 1]]$, if $p''_{i+1,l} = (\mathrm{bin}(x''_i)(0)^{l-l_i-1}(1)(0)^{l_{i+1}-l}\beta_{i+1})_2$, then

$$\{p''_{i+1,l+1}\} = \bigcup_{t \in Y_{i+1,l+1}} U_t \subseteq X_{i+1,l+1} \cap [[r'' + 1, p''_{i+1,l} - 1]]$$
$$\subseteq X_{i+1,l+1} \cap [[(\mathrm{bin}(x''_i)(0)^{l_{i+1}-l_i}\beta_{i+1})_2, p''_{i+1,l} - 1]]$$
$$= \{(\mathrm{bin}(x''_i)(0)^{l-l_i}(1)(0)^{l_{i+1}-l-1}\beta_{i+1})_2\}$$

and, hence, $p''_{i+1,l+1} = (\mathrm{bin}(x''_i)(0)^{l-l_i}(1)(0)^{l_{i+1}-l-1}\beta_{i+1})_2$. Thus, by induction, we have $x''_{i+1,l_{i+1}} = x''_{i+1} = (\mathrm{bin}(x''_i)(0)^{l_{i+1}-l_i-1}(1))_2$.   □

Proof (Lemma 12). First recall some facts:

- $p''_i = (\mathrm{bin}(x''_i)\beta_i)_2 = (\mathrm{bin}(x''_i)(1)(0)\alpha_i)_2$,
- $r'' \geq (\mathrm{bin}(x''_i - 1)\beta_i)_2 = (\mathrm{bin}(x''_i - 1)(1)(0)\alpha_i)_2 = (\mathrm{bin}(x''_{i+1})(0)\alpha_i)_2$ (the last equation follows from assumptions of Lemma 12),
- $(0)\alpha_i = \gamma_{i+1} \ldots \gamma_{\mathrm{last}-1}$, where $\gamma_{i+1+c} = (0)(1)^{l_{i+2+c}-l_{i+1+c}-1}$.

For the proof of Lemma 12 we need the following auxiliary technical proposition:

Proposition 2. *If $r'' \geq (\mathrm{bin}(x''_{i+1})(0)\alpha_i)_2$, then $x''_{i+1+c} \geq (\mathrm{bin}(x''_{i+1})\gamma_{i+1} \ldots \gamma_{i+c})_2$ for arbitrary $c \in [[0, \mathrm{last} -1 - i]]$.*

Proof (Proposition 2). We have $\beta_{i+1+c} = (1)^{l_{i+2+c}-l_{i+1+c}}\gamma_{i+2+c} \cdots \gamma_{\mathrm{last}-1}$. Hence, for $x'' = (\mathrm{bin}(x''_{i+1})\gamma_{i+1} \ldots \gamma_{i+c})_2$, we have

$$2^{|\beta_{i+1+c}|} \cdot (x'' - 1) + (\beta_{i+1+c})_2 < 2^{|\beta_{i+1+c}|} \cdot x'' + (\gamma_{i+1+c} \cdots \gamma_{\mathrm{last}-1})_2$$
$$= (\mathrm{bin}(x''_{i+1})\gamma_{i+1} \ldots \gamma_{\mathrm{last}-1})_2 = (\mathrm{bin}(x''_{i+1})(0)\alpha_i)_2.$$

Thus $p''_{i+1+c} = \min\{x \in \mathbb{X}_{i+1+c} | x > r''\} \geq 2^{|\beta_{i+1+c}|} \cdot x'' + (\beta_{i+1+c})_2$ and, hence $x''_{i+1+c} \geq x''$.   □

Now let us return to the proof of Lemma 12. The proof is by induction on c. We start induction with $c = -1$ where the claim for $c = -1$ is limited to the identity $x''_{i+1} = (\mathrm{bin}(x''_{i+1}))_2$.

Now let us make induction step and prove the lemma for $c \in [[0, d]]$. By inductive assumption $x''_{i+1+c} = (\mathrm{bin}(x''_{i+1})\gamma_{i+1} \ldots \gamma_{i+c})_2$.

Case: $l_{i+2+c} - l_{i+1+c} = 1$.

Then $\gamma_{i+1+c} = (0)$. We also have

$$m''_{i+1+c} = p''_{i+1+c} = (\mathrm{bin}(x''_{i+1})\gamma_{i+1} \ldots \gamma_{i+c}\beta_{i+1+c})_2,$$

where $\beta_{i+1+c} = (1)\gamma_{i+2+c} \cdots \gamma_{\mathrm{last}-1}$. Note that by Lemma 1 $((1)\beta_{i+2+c})_2 \geq (\beta_{i+1+c})_2$. Since $\sum_{t \in Y_{i+2+c}} \mathrm{re}_t \geq 1$, we must have

$$m''_{i+1+c} > m''_{i+2+c} \in \mathbb{X}_{i+2+c}.$$

Since $(\mathrm{bin}(x''_{i+1})\gamma_{i+1} \ldots \gamma_{i+c}(1)\beta_{i+2+c})_2 \geq m''_{i+1+c}$, and, by Proposition 2,

$$x''_{i+2+c} \geq (\mathrm{bin}(x''_{i+1})\gamma_{i+1} \ldots \gamma_{i+1+c}) = (\mathrm{bin}(x''_{i+1})\gamma_{i+1} \ldots \gamma_{i+c}(0))_2$$

we must have
$$m''_{i+2+c} = p''_{i+2+c} = (\text{bin}(x''_{i+1})\gamma_{i+1}\ldots\gamma_{i+c}(0)\beta_{i+2+c})_2.$$
Hence $x''_{i+2+c} = (\text{bin}(x''_{i+1})\gamma_{i+1}\ldots\gamma_{i+1+c})_2$, as required.

Since there are no points of $\mathbb{X}_{i+2+c}$ between m''_{i+2+c} and m''_{i+1+c}, we also have $\sum_{t\in Y_{i+1+c}} \text{re}_t = 1$.

Case: $l_{i+2+c} - l_{i+1+c} = 2$.

Then $\gamma_{i+1+c} = (01)$. Since, by Proposition 2, $x''_{i+2+c} \geq (\text{bin}(x''_{i+1+c})(01))_2$, and $\sum_{t\in Y_{i+2+c}} \text{re}_t \geq l_{i+2+c} - l_{i+1+c}$, we have, by Lemma 11
$$x''_{i+2+c} = (\text{bin}(x''_{i+1})\gamma_{i+1}\ldots\gamma_{i+c}(01))_2 = (\text{bin}(x''_{i+1})\gamma_{i+1}\ldots\gamma_{i+1+c})_2,$$
$p''_{i+2+c} = m''_{i+2+c}$, and $\sum_{t\in Y_{i+2+c}} \text{re}_t = l_{i+2+c} - l_{i+1+c}$.

Case: $l_{i+2+c} - l_{i+1+c} > 2$.

Then $\gamma_{i+1+c} = (0)(1)^q$, where $q = l_{i+2+c} - l_{i+1+c} - 1 > 1$. By Proposition 2 , $x''_{i+2+c} \geq (\text{bin}(x''_{i+1+c})(0)^q(1))_2$ and $\sum_{t\in Y_{i+1+c}} \text{re}_t \geq l_{i+2+c} - l_{i+1+c}$. So by Lemma 11 , $x''_{i+2+c} = (\text{bin}(x''_i)\gamma_{i+1}\ldots\gamma_{i+c}(0)^q(1))_2$.

However, by Proposition 2 , we have also

$$x''_{i+2+c} \geq (\text{bin}(x''_{i+1})\gamma_{i+1}\ldots\gamma_{i+1+c})_2$$
$$= (\text{bin}(x''_{i+1})\gamma_{i+1}\ldots\gamma_{i+c}(0)(1)^q)_2 > (\text{bin}(x''_{i+1})\gamma_{i+1}\ldots\gamma_{i+c}(0)^q(1))_2,$$

which is a contradiction. Thus the case $l_{i+2+c} - l_{i+1+c} > 2$ is impossible. $\qquad\square$

4   Final Remarks

Solution Properties. Important advantage of RBO is its simplicity enabling efficient software implementation. The only non-trivial computation of the RBO receiver is determining the next time slot, when the antenna should be activated. Optimized algorithm and code for this computation has been presented in [3, NSI algorithm]. We have also checked feasibility of RBO for devices run with TinyOS.

RBO requires a certain degree of synchronization – the broadcaster and the receiver should share time slot indices. If this is a problem or synchronization is unreliable, then necessary synchronization information can be sent in headers together with message keys. Which solution is more efficient in the sense of communication volume depends on a concrete case - a longer header mean more reliable execution of RBO, but on the other hand loosing a part of bandwidth volume.

Future Work. In practice, due to certain technical problems a receiver may fail to get some of the messages sent by the broadcaster despite of activating the antenna. Both burst errors and errors occurring independently may occur. Moreover, for some important applications such errors might be quite likely.

Fortunately, design of RBO protocol makes it immune against transmission errors in the sense that a receiver may adjust itself to the situation and proceed the search. Simply, if a key is not received correctly, then the receiver simply does not update the variables lb and ub and proceeds executing the code of RBO. In particular, no error will occur in the sense that no message with the key in the range of the receiver will be skipped as a result of the fault. On the other hand, failure to update lb and ub has negative consequences for energy usage: potentially this may increase *extra energy* spent by the receiver. Fortunately, one can prove that if a message can be received with probability $p < 1$, then the expected extra-energy spent for any fixed range $[\kappa', \kappa'']$, is $O\left((1 + p) \cdot k/p + (1 - p)/p^2\right)$, where the constant hidden by big 'Oh' notation is quite small.

The generic RBO algorithm described in Sect. 1.1 uses bit-reversal permutation. However, one can replace it with an arbitrary permutation of keys. The resulting algorithm would be correct, however the energy cost may change a lot. We expect that no permutation can improve the worst case energy cost below $2k$. However, this requires a rigorous proof, but the underlying mathematical problem might be quite hard.

References

1. Morton, G.: A computer oriented geodetic data base and a new technique in file sequencing. IBM technical report Ottawa, Canada (1966)
2. Kik, M.: RBO protocol: Broadcasting huge databases for tiny receivers. CoRR abs/1108.5095 (2011)
3. Kik, M.: Notes on bit-reversal broadcast scheduling. CoRR abs/1201.3318 (2012)
4. Kik, M., Gebala, M., Kutyłowski, M.: One-side energy costs of the RBO receiver. CoRR abs/1209.4605 (2012)
5. Imielinski, T., Viswanathan, S., Badrinath, B.R.: Energy efficient indexing on air. In: Snodgrass, R.T., Winslett, M. (eds.) SIGMOD Conference, pp. 25–36. ACM Press (1994)
6. Imielinski, T., Viswanathan, S., Badrinath, B.R.: Power efficient filtering of data an air. In: Jarke, M., Bubenko, J., Jeffery, K. (eds.) EDBT 1994. LNCS, vol. 779, pp. 245–258. Springer, Heidelberg (1994)
7. Imielinski, T., Viswanathan, S., Badrinath, B.R.: Data on air: Organization and access. IEEE Trans. Knowl. Data Eng. 9(3), 353–372 (1997)
8. Datta, A., VanderMeer, D.E., Celik, A., Kumar, V.: Broadcast protocols to support efficient retrieval from databases by mobile users. ACM Trans. Database Syst. 24(1), 1–79 (1999)
9. Khanna, S., Zhou, S.: On indexed data broadcast. JCSS 60(3), 575–591 (2000)
10. Vaidya, N.H., Hameed, S.: Scheduling data broadcast in asymmetric communication environments. Wireless Networks 5(3), 171–182 (1999)
11. Chung, Y.D., Lee, J.Y.: An indexing method for wireless broadcast xml data. Inf. Sci. 177(9), 1931–1953 (2007)
12. Chung, Y.D., Yoo, S., Kim, M.H.: Energy- and latency-efficient processing of full-text searches on a wireless broadcast stream. IEEE Trans. Knowl. Data Eng. 22(2), 207–218 (2010)
13. Shalev, O., Shavit, N.: Split-ordered lists: Lock-free extensible hash tables. J. ACM 53(3), 379–405 (2006)
14. Fukuchi, D., Sommer, C., Sei, Y., Honiden, S.: Distributed arrays: A P2P data structure for efficient logical arrays. In: IEEE INFOCOM, pp. 1458–1466 (2009)
15. Shao, J., Davis, B.T.: The bit-reversal sdram address mapping. In: Kavi, K.M., Cytron, R. (eds.) SCOPES. ACM International Conference Proceeding Series, vol. 136, pp. 62–71 (2005)
16. Hefeeda, M., Hsu, C.H.: On burst transmission scheduling in mobile tv broadcast networks. IEEE/ACM Trans. Netw. 18(2), 610–623 (2010)

Personal Health Records Integrity Verification Using Attribute Based Proxy Signature in Cloud Computing

Ximeng Liu[1], Jianfeng Ma[2], Jinbo Xiong[2], Tao Zhang[2], and Qi Li[2]

[1] School of Telecommunications Engineering, Xidian University, Xi'an 710071, China
snbnix@gmail.com
[2] School of Computer Science and Technology, Xidian University,
Xi'an, 710071, China

Abstract. Personal health records (PHRs) have been appeared as patient -centric model for health information exchange, which are often outsourced to be stored in cloud services. However, the integrity and privacy of the PHRs are cause for concern that personal health information could be compromised. The principal method to guarantee integrity of PHRs is using signature mechanism when a PHR owner use the PHR to generate signature and a user is able to verify the PHR by using the signature. In some scenario, PHR owner can not sign the PHR by himself/herself, he/her wants to delegate its sign ability to other people to sign the PHR. In order to solve delegation of original signer's capabilities to guarantee integrity of PHR and the anonymity of the signer, attribute based proxy signature scheme(ABPS) for personal health records was first proposed in this paper. We formalize and construct the ABPS. Our scheme is proved to be existentially unforgeable against chosen message attack in the standard model. Analysis shows that our ABPS is more appropriate for cloud computing environment to guarantee integrity of PHRs.

Keywords: Attribute based signature, Proxy signature, PHRs, Cloud computing.

1 Introduction

In recent years, personal health records(PHRs) have emerged as a patient-centric model of health information exchange. A PHRs service allows a patient to create, manage, and control one's personal health data in one place through the Web, which have made the storage, retrieval and sharing of the medical information more efficient. Because it cost highly to build and maintain the data center, PHRs are often outsourced to third party severs (such as cloud data center) to stored. Patients also want to control their sensitive personal information. However, the cloud data center can not always be fully trusted. Recently, some architecture of storing PHRs in cloud computing have be proposed in [13] [10] [5]. Li et al.[11] enforced access control for outsourcing PHRs and attribute based encryption.

M. Pathan, G. Wei, and G. Fortino (Eds.): IDCS 2013, LNCS 8223, pp. 238–251, 2013.

When a doctor takes PHRs from cloud data center to assessed for disease, it should make sure that the PHRs can not modified by the cloud center. Also, patients sometime do not want his/her identify exposures to the doctor and want to flexible control their privacy.

Attribute based signatures(ABS)[19] scheme offers fine-grained access control in anonymity authentication systems which extends identity-based signature where the signer is associate with a set of attributes instead of a single identity string. It provides a powerful way for users to control their privacy: the patient chooses the subset of their attributes relevanting for the specific scenario in signing PHRs. Any doctor who has the attributes set containing all attributes above could issue the signature. Considering the following scenario, a patient signs PHR with access structure { "paediatrician" AND "hospital A" AND "internal medicine"} and uploads it to cloud center. When a doctor has these three attributes could verify the PHR's integrity, that is to say, a internal medicine paediatrician in hospital A could verify the PHR. In some cases, a patient could not sign the PHR by himself/herself(such as go aborad which could not access internet). The patient wants delegate his/her sign ability to proxy signer(such as the patient's relatives). The PHRs could only be signed by the patient, or signed by a proxy signer authorized by the patient. We want a scheme that an original signers with attribute sets can authorize a designated person as proxy signer which could sign PHRs on behalf of him/her.

In this paper, we propose a scheme called attribute based proxy signature (ABPS) scheme in order to solve the problem mentioned above. The ABPS scheme allows a designated proxy signer with its attribute set to sign the message on behalf of the original signer. The proposed scheme allows users to control their privacy flexibly.

1.1 Related Work

This paper constructs cryptographic primitive to keep personal health records integrity for outsourcing data to the cloud severs. In this subsection, we primarily introduce some related work in cryptography.

Attribute Based Signature. In basic ABE, an important application of the fuzzy identity based encryption (FIBE)[18], a user encrypts a message with a set of n attributes such that users whose decryption key have at least t common attributes with the ciphertext attribute set can decrypt the message. We call this scheme threshold attribute-based encryption (t-ABE) for describe simplicity. Yang et al.[24] introduced a new cryptographic primitive called fuzzy identity based signature (FIBS) which the signature analogue of the FIBE. Shahandashti[20] proposed a threshold attribute-based signature construction for both small attribute universe and large attribute universe. Due to FIBS scheme can not control signer's privacy, Maji et al.[14] introduced an ABS scheme can provide strong privacy guarantee for the signer and strong unforgeability guarantee for the verifier. In order to sign messages with any subset of their attributes issued from an attribute center, Li and Kim[8] gave a hidden attribute-based signatures without anonymity revocation scheme which can reach anonymity and unforgeability. Li et al.[7] proposed a new construction of ABS supporting flexible threshold predicate which could compact the signature size and improve the verification time. Liu et al.[12] proposed a new attribute based multi-signature scheme to reduce the bandwidth needed to transmit attribute based signatures which is more appropriate for the wireless nature where bandwidth is a bottleneck.

Proxy Signature. Mambo et al.[15] first proposed a new signature scheme called proxy signature. In this scheme, the original signer authorized a designated proxy signer to sign the message on behalf. After that, proxy signatures have found numerous practical applications, such as mobile communications[17], distributed systems[16], grid computing[3] and mobile agent applications[6]. Boldyreva [1] was first presented the formal definition and security notion for proxy signature. Their work was proved to be security against adaptive chosen-message attack. Huang et al.[4] proposed a proxy signatureschemes which was proved to be existential unforgeable in the stand model. After Boneh and Franklin[2] used bilinear groups to construct identity-based encryption, a lot of identity-based proxy signature schemes were proposed. Xu et al.[23] formalized the notion of security for ID-based proxy signature schemes and proposed a scheme based on the bilinear pairings. But their schemes could not reach the notion of adaptively chosen message and chosen identity attacker in identity based system. Wu et al.[22] redefined the security models of identity based proxy signature to capture the most stringent attacks against adaptively chosen message and chosen identity attacker. Furthermore, many extensions of the basic proxy signature primitive had been considered include threshold proxy signatures [21] and blind proxy signatures [15].

1.2   Our Contributions

In this work, we make the following contributions. (1) We define a scheme called attribute based proxy signature(ABPS) for PHRs. We also formalize the model of ABPS and give security model for ABPS. (2) The concrete construction of the ABPS scheme is proposed in this paper. (3) We prove our ABPS scheme is existential unforgeability in the standard model by using the computational Diffie-Hellman assumption. Analysis shows that our ABPS scheme is more appropriate for cloud computing environment to keep PHRs integrity and keep PHR owners anonymity.

1.3   Organization

The rest of the paper organized as follows: In section 2, we review some concepts about bilinear pairing, complexity assumption and flexible threshold predicate. In section 3, we give the a formal model and its security model of the ABPS scheme for PHRs. The specific construction about the ABPS scheme for PHRs is presented in section 4. In section 5, we give security and performance analysis for the ABPS scheme. And we conclude this paper in section 6.

2 Preliminaries

In this section we introduce bilinear maps, complexity assumptions and flexible threshold predicate which is associated with our construction.

2.1 Bilinear Maps

Let $\mathbb{G}$ and $\mathbb{G}_T$ be two cyclic groups of prime order p with the multiplication. Let g be a generator of $\mathbb{G}$ and e be a bilinear map. Let $e : \mathbb{G} \times \mathbb{G} \to \mathbb{G}_T$ be a bilinear map has the following properties:

1. Bilinearity: for all $u, v \in \mathbb{G}$ and $a, b \in \mathbb{Z}_p$, we have $e(u^a, v^b) = e(u, v)^{ab}$.
2. Non-degeneracy: $e(g, g) \neq 1$.
3. Computability: There is efficient algorithm to compute bilinear map $e : \mathbb{G} \times \mathbb{G} \to \mathbb{G}_T$.

Notice that the map e is symmetric since $e(u^a, v^b) = e(u, v)^{ab} = e(u^b, v^a)$.

2.2 Complexity Assumptions

Definition 1. *The challenger choose $a, b \in \mathbb{Z}_p$ at random and output (g, g^a, g^b). The Computational Diffie-Hellman(CDH) problem is to compute g^{ab}. An adversary $\mathcal{A}$ has at least an ϵ if*

$$\left| \Pr[\mathcal{A}(g, g^a, g^b) = g^{ab}] \right| \geq \epsilon$$

The computational (t, ϵ)-DH assumption holds if no t-time adversary has at least ϵ advantage in solving the above game.

2.3 Flexible Threshold Predicate

In this paper, we use predicates Υ consisting of thresholds gates. All predicates $\Upsilon_{k,\omega^*}(\cdot) \to 0/1$ for ω^* with threshold value k. If the number of attribute in $\omega' \cap \omega^*$ exceeds threshold k, it outputs 1. Otherwise, it outputs 0.

$$\Upsilon_{k,\omega^*}(\omega') = \begin{cases} 1, & |\omega' \cap \omega^*| \geq k \\ 0, & otherwise \end{cases}$$

2.4 Lagrange Interpolation

In this subsection, we describe Lagrange interpolation which is used in the ABMS schemes. Given d points $q(1), \cdots, q(d)$ on a $d-1$ degree polynomial, we can use Lagrange interpolation to compute $q(i)$ for any $i \in \mathbb{Z}_p$. Let S be a d-element set. We define the Lagrange coefficient $\Delta_{j,S}(i)$ of $q(j)$ in the computation of $q(i)$ as:

$$\Delta_{j,S}(i) = \prod_{\eta \in S, \eta \neq j} \frac{i - \eta}{j - \eta}$$

3 Formal Models and Security Model for ABPS

3.1 Formal Models

The attribute based proxy signature can be described as a collection of the following seven algorithms:

Setup: This algorithm runs by the authority which inputs the security parameter and generates the public parameters *params* of the scheme and the master secret key. The authority entity publishes *params* and keeps the master secret to itself.

Extract: This algorithm runs by authority to generate a private key for the entity involve in the PHR system. It inputs an attribute set ω, the master key and *params* and outputs the private key of ω. After generating private keys for all entities participating in the scheme is generated, the authority distributes the private keys to their respective owner through a secure channel.

StandardSign: This algorithm runs by PHR owner on input a message m, an attribute set ω, a private key d and *params*. It generates the signature σ of ω on m. The entity with attribute set ω will use this algorithm for signing.

StandardVerify: This algorithm runs by verifier on input a signature σ, a message m, attribute set and *params*. It outputs *accept* if a valid signature on message for attribute set or outputs *reject* otherwise.

DelegationGen: This algorithm runs by the PHR owner on input system's public parameters *params*, PHR owner's secret key sk_A, the delegation warrant θ which include the restriction on the class of message delegated, the attribute set of the PHR owner, the attribute set of the proxy user and period of delegation, etc. It outputs delegation σ_θ to proxy user on behalf of the PHR owner.

ProxySign: This algorithm runs by proxy user on input public parameters *params*, proxy signature sk_p, a warrant θ and a message m which satisfies θ. The algorithm outputs a proxy signature $p\sigma_p$ on message m.

ProxyVerify: This algorithm runs by verifier on input public parameters *params*, proxy signature $p\sigma_p$, a warrant θ and a message m. If $p\sigma_p$ is a valid proxy signature for m, the algorithm outputs 1 or outputs 0 otherwise.

3.2 Security Models

In the model defined in [4], they divide potential attackers into the three kinds. We also use these three attackers to define security model for ABPS scheme:

1. **Type 1** ($\mathcal{A}_1$): This type of adversary $\mathcal{A}_1$ only has the public key of PHR owner and proxy user.

2. **Type 2** ($\mathcal{A}_2$): This type of adversary $\mathcal{A}_2$ not only has the public key of PHR owner and proxy user but also has the private key of the proxy user.

3. **Type 3** ($\mathcal{A}_3$): This type of adversary $\mathcal{A}_3$ only has the public key of PHR owner and proxy user, he also has the private key of the PHR owner.

It is easy to find that ABPS scheme is secure against Type 2(or Type 3) adversary, the scheme is also secure against Type 1 adversary. Here, we focus on define the existential unforgeability of the ABPS scheme.

Existential Unforgeability against Adaptive $\mathcal{A}_2$ Adversary
In order to define the secure model of ABPS against adaptive $\mathcal{A}_2$ adversary, we define following game between a challenger $\mathcal{B}$ and an adversary $\mathcal{A}_2$.

Setup: The challenger $\mathcal{B}$ runs the *Setup* algorithm and obtains both the public parameters *params* and the master secret key. $\mathcal{B}$ gives the *params* to adversary and keeps the master secret key by itself.

Queries. The adversary $\mathcal{A}_2$ adaptively makes a polynomial bounded number of queries to the challenger. Each query can be one of the following:

-**Extract query:** The adversary $\mathcal{A}_2$ can ask for the private key of any attribute set ω. The challenger responds by running the *Extract* algorithm and gives the private key to adversary.

-**Delegation queries:** $\mathcal{A}_2$ adaptively make request the delegation on the warrant θ. $\mathcal{B}$ runs the *DelegationGen* algorithm to obtain σ_θ and return σ_θ to the adversary $\mathcal{A}_2$.

-**ProxySign queries:** $\mathcal{A}_2$ can adaptively request the proxy signature on message m under the warrant θ. $\mathcal{B}$ first runs *DelegationGen* algorithm to generate the delegation on the warrant θ. Then $\mathcal{B}$ runs the *ProxySign* algorithm to obtain signature $p\sigma_p$ and return $p\sigma_p$ to the adversary $\mathcal{A}_2$.

Output: Eventually, $\mathcal{A}_2$ halts and outputting a forgery such that :

1). θ^* has not been requested as one of the *Delegation* queries.

2). (m^*, θ^*) has not been requested as one of the *ProxySign* queries.

3). σ^* is a valid proxy signaature of the message m^* under the warrant θ^*.

The type 2 adversary $\mathcal{A}_2$ can adaptively submit the *ProxySign* queries under warrant whose delegation is unknow to $\mathcal{A}_2$. The only restrictions are when $\mathcal{A}_2$ outputs the forgery $(m^*, \theta^*, p\sigma_p^*)$ which θ^* can not be submitted as one of the *Delegation* queries or (m^*, θ^*) can not be submitted as one of the *ProxySign* queries.

Definition 2. *The attribute based proxy signature scheme is* $(t, q_e, q_D, q_{PS}, \epsilon)$-*secure against type 2 adversary* $\mathcal{A}_2$ *if no t-time adversary* $\mathcal{A}_2$ *making* q_e *Extract queries,* q_D *Delegation queries,* q_{PS} *ProxySign queries can win the above game with advantage more than* ϵ.

Existential Unforgeability against Adaptive $\mathcal{A}_3$ Adversary
In order to define the secure model of ABPS against adaptive $\mathcal{A}_3$ adversary, we define following game between a challenger $\mathcal{B}$ and an adversary $\mathcal{A}_3$.

Setup: The challenger $\mathcal{B}$ runs the *Setup* algorithm and obtains both the public parameters *params* and the master secret key. $\mathcal{B}$ gives the *params* to adversary and keeps the master secret key by itself.

Queries. The adversary $\mathcal{A}_3$ adaptively makes a polynomial bounded number of queries to $\mathcal{B}$. Each query can be one of the following:

-**Extract query:** The adversary $\mathcal{A}_3$ can ask for the private key of any attribute set ω. $\mathcal{B}$ responds by running the *Extract* algorithm and gives the private key to $\mathcal{A}_3$.

-**Delegation queries:** $\mathcal{A}_3$ adaptively make request the delegation on the warrant θ. $\mathcal{B}$ runs the *DelegationGen* algorithm to obtain σ_θ and return σ_θ to the adversary $\mathcal{A}_3$.

- **ProxySign queries:** $\mathcal{A}_3$ can adaptively request the proxy signature on message m under the warrant θ. $\mathcal{B}$ first runs *DelegationGen* algorithm to generate the delegation on the warrant θ. Then $\mathcal{B}$ runs the *ProxySign* algorithm to obtain signature $p\sigma_p$ and return $p\sigma_p$ to the adversary $\mathcal{A}_2$.

Output: Eventually, $\mathcal{A}_3$ halts and outputting a forgery such that :

1). (m^*, θ^*) has not been requested as one of the *ProxySign* queries.

2). σ^* is a valid proxy signaature of the message m^* under the warrant θ^*.

Definition 3. *The attribute based proxy multi-signature scheme is $(t, q_e, q_D, q_{PS}, \epsilon)$-secure against type 2 adversary $\mathcal{A}_2$ if no t-time adversary $\mathcal{A}_2$ making q_e Extract queries, q_D Delegation queries, q_{PS} ProxySign queries can win the above game with advantage more than ϵ.*

4   Our Constructions

In this section, we give the concrete construction of attribute based proxy signature scheme.

4.1   Overview of the ABPS Scheme for PHRs

The main goal of our attribute based proxy signature scheme guarantees integrity of PHRs and allows patients to flexible control their privacy. Meanwhile, it solves delegation problem when patients can not sign the PHRs by himself/herself which need to delegate his/her signing ability to proxy user on behalf of him/her. As fig. 1 shows, there are PHR owner, proxy user, verifier(Doctor, emergency staff) and authority involved in the system. The authority first generates a master key and defines a common universe of attributes, such as "paediatrician", "hospital A", "internal medicine", "physician". Then, authority uses the master key and attribute sets to generate user's private keys and send them to the corresponding users involve in the system respectively. PHR owner could sign the PHR by himself/herself, or generates a warrant which includes the restrictions on the proxy signer. After that, the PHR owner uses the warrant to generate delegation and sends it to the proxy signer together with the warrant. When the proxy user receives warrant and delegation, he/she can use his/her own private key and attribute set to proxy sign the delegation on behalf of original signer.

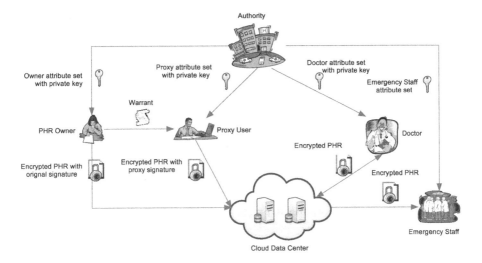

Fig. 1. ABPS for PHRs

The proxy signature combine with the encrypted PHR are sended to cloud data center(third party servers) to stored. When a doctor is requested to diagnose the PHR owner whether has be infected with some diseases or not, he should first retrieval the PHR from cloud data center and then decrypt the the PHR. In order to guarantee the the PHR is not modified by the cloud data center, he must first use the PHR owner's attribute set, proxy user's set and warrant declared by the PHR owner to check the integrity of the PHR. When the PHR passed the verification, it shows that the PHR is not be modified. The doctor can use the information present in the PHR to diagnosed the PHR owner's health condition condition. After that, the doctor uses his own private key to sign the PHR, encrypts the PHR with PHR owner's attribute set and sends back to the cloud data center. When the PHR owner is sent to the hospital in emergency, emergency staff could decrypt the PHR and verify the signature to indicate that the PHR is not falsified by other and believe the authenticity of the PHR. The concrete construction of ABPS will be presented in the next subsection.

4.2   Attribute Based Proxy Signature Scheme

Setup: This algorithm first defines the attributes in the universe U as the element in $\mathbb{Z}_p$. A $d-1$ default attribute set from $\mathbb{Z}_p$ is given as $\Omega = \{\Omega_1, \Omega_2, \cdots, \Omega_{d-1}\}$. It selects a random generator $g \in \mathbb{G}$, a random $\alpha \in \mathbb{Z}_p^*$ and computes $g_1 = g^\alpha \in \mathbb{G}$. Next, it picks a random element g_2 and computes $A = e(g_1, g_2)$. After that it chooses $t_1, \cdots, t_{n+1}$ uniformly at random from $\mathbb{G}$. Let N be the set $\{1, \cdots, n+1\}$ and we define a function T, as:

$$T(x) = g_2^{x^n} \prod_{j=1}^{n+1} t_j^{\Delta_{j,N}(x)}$$

Finally, the algorithm selects random values y' from $\mathbb{Z}_p$, a random vector $\mathbf{y} = (y_1, y_2, \cdots, y_k)$ from $\mathbb{Z}_p^k$ and computes $\mathbf{U} = (u_1, u_2, \cdots, u_k) = (g^{y_1}, g^{y_2}, \cdots, g^{y_k})$. The public parameters are

$$params = (\mathbb{G}, \mathbb{G}_T, e, g, g_1, g_2, t_1, \cdots, t_{n+1}, \mathbf{U}, A)$$

The master key are

$$\text{MSK} = \alpha$$

Extract: This algorithm generates a private key for an attribute set ω related with users involved in the system. It takes the following steps:

1) Firstly, it chooses a $d-1$ degree polynomial at random with $q(0) = \alpha$.

2) It then generates a new attribute set $\hat{\omega} = \omega \cup \Omega$. For each $i \in \hat{\omega}$, the algorithm chooses and computes $d_{i0} = g_2^{q(i)} \cdot T(i)^{r_i}$, $d_{i1} = g^{r_i}$.

3) Finally, it outputs

$$D_i = (d_{i0}, d_{i1})_{i \in \hat{\omega}}$$

as the private key.

StandardSign: This algorithm inputs a private key for the attribute set ω, message m and predicate $\Upsilon_{k, \omega^*}(\cdot)$. In order to sign message m with predicate $\Upsilon_{k, \omega^*}(\cdot)$, i.e., to prove owning at least k attribute among an n-elements ω^*. It selects a k-element form the subset $\omega' \subseteq \omega \cap \omega^*$ and works as follows:

(1) First, it selects a default attribute subset $\Omega' \subseteq \Omega$ with $|\Omega'| = d - k$ and chooses $n + d - k$ random values $r'_i \in Z_p$ for $i \in \omega^* \cup \Omega'$.

(2) It then computes

$$\sigma_0 = [\prod_{i \in \omega' \cup \Omega'} d_{i0}^{\Delta_{i,S}(0)}][\prod_{i \in \omega^* \cup \Omega'} T(i)^{r'_i}](u' \prod_{j \in \mathcal{M}} u_j^{m_j})^{r_s}$$

$$\{\sigma_i = d_{i1}^{\Delta_{i,S}(0)} g^{r'_i}\}_{i \in \omega' \cup \Omega'}, \{\sigma_i = g^{r'_i}\}_{i \in \omega^*/\omega'}, \sigma'_0 = g^{r_s}$$

(3) Finally, the algorithm outputs the signature:

$$\sigma = (\sigma_0, \{\sigma_i\}_{i \in \omega^* \cup \Omega'}, \sigma'_0)$$

StandardVerify: In order to verify the correctness of the signature $\sigma = (\sigma_0, \{\sigma_i\}_{i \in \omega^* \cup \Omega'}, \sigma'_0)$ on m with threshold k for attributes set $\omega^* \cup \Omega'$, it checkes the following equation holds:

$$\frac{e(g, \sigma_0)}{[\prod_{i \in \omega^* \cup \Omega'} e(T(i), \sigma_i)] \, e(u' \prod_{j \in \mathcal{M}} u_j^{m_j}, \sigma'_0)} = A$$

If the equation holds, it indicates that the signature is indeed from some user with k attributes among ω^*. Otherwise, it denotes the signature is not valid.

DelegationGen: In order to delegate the PHR owner's signing capability to the proxy user, the PHR owner first makes a warrant θ which includes the restrictions on the class of messages delegated, the PHR owner's attributess set, proxy user's attribute sets, public parameters and the period of validity, etc. Let

θ be an m-bit message to be signed by the original signer a. θ_j denotes the j-th bit of θ and $W \subseteq \{1, \cdots, m\}$ be the set of all j for which $\theta_j = 1$. The PHR owner's delegation is generated as follows. First, it chooses r_i', r_a randomly in $\mathbb{Z}_p^*$, then the delegation is constructed as

$$\sigma_\theta = (\sigma_{\theta 0}, \{\sigma_{\theta i}\}_{i \in \omega_a^* \cup \Omega_a'}, \sigma_{\theta 2})$$

where

$$\sigma_{\theta 0} = [\textstyle\prod_{i \in \omega_a' \cup \Omega_a'} d_{i0}^{\Delta_{i,S}(0)}][\textstyle\prod_{i \in \omega_a^* \cup \Omega_a'} T(i)^{r'i}](u' \prod_{j \in W} u_j^{\tau_j})^{r_a}$$

$$\{\sigma_{ai} = d_{i1}^{\Delta_{i,S_k}(0)} g^{r'i}\}_{i \in \omega_a' \cup \Omega_a'}, \{\sigma_{ai} = g^{r'i}\}_{i \in \omega_a^* / \omega_a'}, \sigma_{\theta 2} = g^{r_a}.$$

Finally, the PHR owner sends the σ_θ with the warrant θ to the proxy user b.

ProxySign: Let m be an m'-bit message to be signed by PHR owner and m_d denote the d-th bit of m, and $\mathcal{M} \subseteq \{1, 2, \cdots, m'\}$ be the set of all d for which $m_d = 1$. The proxy signature is generated as follows. The proxy user chooses random value $r_i', r_a', r_m \in \mathbb{Z}_p$, then the signature is constructed as:

$$p\sigma_p = (p\sigma_{p0}, \{p\sigma_{ai}\}_{i \in \omega_a^* \cup \Omega_a'}, \{p\sigma_{bi}\}_{i \in \omega_b^* \cup \Omega_b'}, p\sigma_{p2}, p\sigma_{p3}).$$

where

$$p\sigma_p = \sigma_{\theta 0}(u' \prod_{j \in W} u_j^{\tau_j})^{r_a'}[\textstyle\prod_{i \in \omega_b' \cup \Omega_b'} d_{i0}^{\Delta_{i,S}(0)}]$$

$$\cdot [\textstyle\prod_{i \in \omega_b^* \cup \Omega_b'} T(i)^{r'i}](u' \prod_{j \in \mathcal{M}} u_j^{m_j})^{r_m}$$

$$\{p\sigma_{ai}\}_{i \in \omega_a' \cup \Omega_a'} = \{\sigma_{ai}\}_{i \in \omega_a' \cup \Omega_a'}, \{p\sigma_{ai}\}_{i \in \omega_a^* / \omega_a'} = \{\sigma_{ai}\}_{i \in \omega_a^* / \omega_a'}$$

$$\{p\sigma_{bi}\}_{i \in \omega_b' \cup \Omega_b'} = \{\sigma_{bi}\}_{i \in \omega_b' \cup \Omega_b'}, \{p\sigma_{bi}\}_{i \in \omega_b^* / \omega_b'} = \{\sigma_{bi}\}_{i \in \omega_b^* / \omega_b'}$$

$$p\sigma_{p2} = \sigma_{\theta 2} \cdot g^{r_a'}, p\sigma_{p3} = g^{r_m}.$$

ProxyVerify: Given the public parameters, a warrant $\theta \in \{0,1\}^m$, a message $m \in \{0,1\}^{m'}$ and a signature $p\sigma_p$. A verifier accepts $p\sigma_p$ if the following equality holds:

$$e(p\sigma_{p0}, g) = A_a \cdot A_b \left[\prod_{i \in \omega_a^* \cup \Omega_a'} e(T(i), p\sigma_{ai}) \right] e(u' \prod_{j \in \mathcal{M}} u_j^{m_j}, p\sigma_{p3})$$

$$\cdot \left[\prod_{i \in \omega_b^* \cup \Omega_b'} e(T(i), p\sigma_{bi}) \right] e(u' \prod_{j \in W} u_j^{\tau_j}, p\sigma_{p2})$$

5   Security and Performance Analysis

In this section, we first show our ABPS scheme is existentially unforgeable against Type 2 and Type 3 adversary. Then, we give an analysis to show our ABPS is more appropriate for cloud computing environment to keep PHRs integrity.

1. **Type 1** ($\mathcal{A}_1$): This type of adversary $\mathcal{A}_1$ only has the public parameters of the PHR owner (signer) and proxy user.

2. **Type 2** ($\mathcal{A}_2$): This type of adversary $\mathcal{A}_2$ not only has the public parameters of the PHR owner(signer) and proxy user but also has the private key of the proxy user.

3. **Type 3** ($\mathcal{A}_3$): This type of adversary $\mathcal{A}_3$ not only has the public parameters of the PHR owner and proxy user, but also has the private key of the PHR owner(signer).

It is easy to find that ABPS scheme is secure against Type 2(or Type 3) adversary, the scheme is also secure against Type 1 adversary. Here, we focus on define the existential unforgeability of the ABPS scheme.

5.1   Existential Unforgeability against Type 2 Adversary

Theorem 1. *The attribute based proxy signature scheme is $(t, q_e, q_D, q_{PS}, \epsilon)$-unforgeable against type 2 adversary $\mathcal{A}_2$ if the (t', ϵ')-CDH assumption holds in where*

$$\epsilon' \geq \frac{\epsilon}{16 \binom{d-1}{d-k} q_{PS}(q_D + q_{PS})(m+1)^2 p^{2d}}$$

$$t' = t + \mathcal{O}((d(q_e + q_D + q_{PS}) + m(q_D + q_{PS}))\rho + (d(q_e + q_D) + q_{PS})\tau)$$

and ρ and τ are the time for a multiplication and an exponentiation in $\mathbb{G}$ respectively. Where $\mathcal{A}_2$ making q_e Extract queries, q_D Delegation queries, q_{PS} ProxySign queries.

Proof. Due to space limitations, the detailed proof will be shown in the full version of our work.

5.2   Existential Unforgeability against Type 3 Adversary

Theorem 2. *The attribute based proxy signature scheme is $(t, q_e, q_{PS}, \epsilon)$- unforgeable against type 3 adversary $\mathcal{A}_3$ if the (t', ϵ')-CDH assumption holds in where*

$$\epsilon' \geq \frac{\epsilon}{16 \binom{d-1}{d-k} q_{PS}^2 (m+1)^2 p^{2d}}$$

$$t' = t + \mathcal{O}((d(q_e + q_{PS}) + m \cdot q_{PS})\rho + (d \cdot q_e + q_{PS})\tau)$$

and ρ and τ are the time for a multiplication and an exponentiation in $\mathbb{G}$ respectively.

Proof. It is similar to the proof of Theorem 1.

5.3   Performance Analysis

In this subsection, we compare our scheme with existing schemes to indicate our scheme is more suitable for verifying PHRs in cloud computing environment. Huang et al.[4] proposed a proxy signature scheme which has the delegation property. In their scheme, it allows original signer to delegate his/her signing ability to proxy signer on behalf. But this scheme can not reach fine-grained access control and allow user flexible control their privacy. Wu et al.[22] gave a stronger security notion of the proxy signature by allowing the adversaries to behave more adaptively in oracle accessing. But the security of their scheme is proven to be secure under random oracle model. It can neither reach fine-grained access control nor provide user anonymity. Li et al.[9] proposed an attribute based signature scheme which can keep signer anonymity and provide fine-grained access control for user to control their privacy. But this scheme is only proved in the random oracle model and do not have the delegation property which is not appropriate for PHR in the cloud environment to keep the PHR integrity. Our ABPS scheme can ensure anonymity for user to flexible to control the privacy. It can also delegate its signing ability to other person on behalf. Also, the security of ABPS scheme is proved to be existential unforgeability under the standard model. More important, the proposed ABPS is more appropriate for cloud computing environment to keep PHRs integrity which is not modified by the distrust severs.

Table 1. The comparison between ABPS and the existing schemes

Functionality/ Scheme	Huang et al.[4]	Wu et al.[22]	Li et al.[9]	Ours
User's anonymity	No	No	Yes	Yes
Fine-grained access control	No	No	Yes	Yes
Delegation property	Yes	Yes	No	Yes
Standard model	Yes	No	No	Yes
Provable secure	Yes	Yes	Yes	Yes
Data integrity	Yes	Yes	Yes	Yes
Pairing based	Yes	Yes	Yes	Yes
Existential unforgeability	Yes	Yes	Yes	Yes

6   Conclusion

In this paper, we first proposed a scheme called attribute based proxy signature. The ABPS scheme allowed a proxy signer to sign the message on behalf of a original PHR owner. We proved our ABPS scheme secure against existential forgery against Type 2 and Type 3 adversary. More important, we showed our ABPS scheme is appropriate for cloud computing environment to guarantee the integrity of PHR and anonymity of the PHR owners.

Acknowledgment. This research is supported by Changjiang Scholars and Innovative Research Team in University under grant No. IRT1078; The Key Program of NSFC-Guangdong Union Foundation under grant No. U1135002; The National Natural Science Foundation of China under grant No. 61370078; Major national S&T program under grant No. 2011ZX03005-002; The Fundamental Research Funds for the Central Universities under grant No. JY10000903001. We thank the sponsors for their support and the reviewers for helpful comments.

References

1. Boldyreva, A., Palacio, A., Warinschi, B.: Secure proxy signature schemes for delegation of signing rights. J. Cryptology 25(1), 57–115 (2012)
2. Boneh, D., Franklin, M.: Identity-based encryption from the weil pairing. In: Kilian, J. (ed.) CRYPTO 2001. LNCS, vol. 2139, pp. 213–229. Springer, Heidelberg (2001)
3. Foster, I., Kesselman, C., Tsudik, G., Tuecke, S.: A security architecture for computational grids. In: Proceedings of the 5th ACM Conference on Computer and Communications Security, pp. 83–92. ACM (1998)
4. Huang, X., Susilo, W., Mu, Y., Wu, W.: Proxy signature without random oracles. In: Cao, J., Stojmenovic, I., Jia, X., Das, S.K. (eds.) MSN 2006. LNCS, vol. 4325, pp. 473–484. Springer, Heidelberg (2006)
5. Huba, N., Zhang, Y.: Designing patient-centered personal health records (phrs): Health care professionals perspective on patient-generated data. Journal of Medical Systems 36(6), 3893–3905 (2012)
6. Lee, B., Kim, H., Kim, K.: Strong proxy signature and its applications. In: Proc. of SCIS, vol. 1, pp. 603–608 (2001)
7. Li, J., Au, M.H., Susilo, W., Xie, D., Ren, K.: Attribute-based signature and its applications. In: Proceedings of the 5th ACM Symposium on Information, Computer and Communications Security, pp. 60–69. ACM (2010)
8. Li, J., Kim, K.: Hidden attribute-based signatures without anonymity revocation. Information Sciences 180(9), 1681–1689 (2010)
9. Li, J., Wang, Q., Wang, C., Ren, K.: Enhancing attribute-based encryption with attribute hierarchy. Mobile Networks and Applications 16(5), 553–561 (2011)
10. Li, M., Yu, S., Ren, K., Lou, W.: Securing personal health records in cloud computing: Patient-centric and fine-grained data access control in multi-owner settings. In: Jajodia, S., Zhou, J. (eds.) SecureComm 2010. LNICST, vol. 50, pp. 89–106. Springer, Heidelberg (2010)
11. Li, M., Yu, S., Zheng, Y., Ren, K., Lou, W.: Scalable and secure sharing of personal health records in cloud computing using attribute-based encryption. IEEE Trans. Parallel Distrib. Syst. 24(1), 131–143 (2013)
12. Liu, X., Zhang, T., Ma, J., Zhu, H., Cai, F.: Efficient data integrity verification using attribute based multi-signature scheme in wireless network. In: 2013 5th International Conference on Intelligent Networking and Collaborative Systems (INCoS). IEEE (2013)
13. Löhr, H., Sadeghi, A.-R., Winandy, M.: Securing the e-health cloud. In: Proceedings of the 1st ACM International Health Informatics Symposium, pp. 220–229. ACM (2010)
14. Maji, H., Prabhakaran, M., Rosulek, M.: Attribute-based signatures: Achieving attribute-privacy and collusion-resistance. IACR Cryptology ePrint Archive 2008, 328 (2008)

15. Mambo, M., Usuda, K., Okamoto, E.: Proxy signatures: Delegation of the power to sign messages. IEICE Transactions on Fundamentals of Electronics, Communications and Computer Sciences 79(9), 1338–1354 (1996)
16. Neuman, B.: Proxy-based authorization and accounting for distributed systems. In: Proceedings the 13th International Conference on Distributed Computing Systems, pp. 283–291. IEEE (1993)
17. Park, H.-U., Lee, I.-Y.: A digital nominative proxy signature scheme for mobile communication. In: Qing, S., Okamoto, T., Zhou, J. (eds.) ICICS 2001. LNCS, vol. 2229, pp. 451–455. Springer, Heidelberg (2001)
18. Sahai, A., Waters, B.: Fuzzy identity-based encryption. In: Cramer, R. (ed.) EUROCRYPT 2005. LNCS, vol. 3494, pp. 457–473. Springer, Heidelberg (2005)
19. Shahandashti, S.F., Safavi-Naini, R.: Threshold attribute-based signatures and their application to anonymous credential systems. In: Preneel, B. (ed.) AFRICACRYPT 2009. LNCS, vol. 5580, pp. 198–216. Springer, Heidelberg (2009)
20. Shahandashti, S.F., Safavi-Naini, R.: Threshold attribute-based signatures and their application to anonymous credential systems. IACR Cryptology ePrint Archive 2009, 126 (2009)
21. Sun, H.-M., Lee, N.-Y., Hwang, T.: Threshold proxy signatures. In: IEE Proceedings-Computers and Digital Techniques, vol. 146, pp. 259–263. IET (1999)
22. Wu, W., Mu, Y., Susilo, W., Seberry, J., Huang, X.: Identity-based proxy signature from pairings. In: Xiao, B., Yang, L.T., Ma, J., Muller-Schloer, C., Hua, Y. (eds.) ATC 2007. LNCS, vol. 4610, pp. 22–31. Springer, Heidelberg (2007)
23. Xu, J., Zhang, Z., Feng, D.: ID-based proxy signature using bilinear pairings. In: Chen, G., Pan, Y., Guo, M., Lu, J. (eds.) ISPA-WS 2005. LNCS, vol. 3759, pp. 359–367. Springer, Heidelberg (2005)
24. Yang, P., Cao, Z., Dong, X.: Fuzzy identity based signature. IACR Cryptology ePrint Archive 2008, 2 (2008)

Dynamic Scheduling for Usable Service in Network Robot

Jeong-Hwa Lee and Jung-Min Park[*]

Interaction and Robotics Research Center, Korea Institute of Science and Technology (KIST)
Hwarangno 14-gil 5, Seongbuk-gu, Seoul, 136-791, Korea
thankbruna@gmail.com, pjm@kist.re.kr

Abstract. Network robots can provide a variety of services to users of network. Existing service robots not only have been developed for specific purpose with constraint capabilities, but have only focused on how to perform their service efficiently. In order to improve the usefulness of the networked service robot, however, it is necessary to provide services considering the user's needs and service context change. This paper proposes a dynamic service scheduling scheme to provide effective services to multiple users for network robots. The proposed scheme is adaptable to dynamic changes of service type, environment and users by customizing the scheduling policy with both system-centric and user-centric properties in real time. The experimental results show that the proposed scheme enhances the user satisfaction and performance of the robot service compared to other scheduling schemes.

1   Introduction

Robot applications in daily life have been extended so that these applications work in conjunction with the user and provide services directly to the user. A service robot performs various services to help with tasks such as household chores, healthcare, education, and delivery in the home, hospital, and educational environment. Thus far, most service robots have been developed for specific purposes with certain constraint capabilities, and much research has focused only on the functional accuracy of the services.

User satisfaction with the service offered by a service robot is important for the increased activation and availability of service robots. Also, for service robots with high availability, there is a need for robots which run not only a single-purpose service but also a variety of services taking into account the characteristics of the users and the ability to adapt to various environments. In particular, for a network robot connected to network infrastructure which provides various services, it is necessary to perform properly its multi-purpose service. In addition, when a network robot provides a service to a large number of users, the service must be provided considering the needs and characteristics that the user expects from the robot service, as well as information related to the physical environment in which the service is performed.

User satisfaction of service is determined not by how a robot enhances its internal performance, but by how it meets the user expectation. There are several elements

---

[*] Corresponding author.

M. Pathan, G. Wei, and G. Fortino (Eds.): IDCS 2013, LNCS 8223, pp. 252–259, 2013.

such as stability, low power consumption, and autonomy, etc. in user expectation. The most important factor is that the function of a service is fully executed namely, the functional completion. For example, the functional completion of a cleaning robot will be determined by whether user need to clean again or not and the functional completion of a delivery robot will be affected by whether the robot delivered the object at the time user wanted to be served i.e., before the deadline. As in the above cases, user needs and expectation of a service differ depending on the purpose of robot. Existing scheduling schemes in robotic research have mainly focused on the scheduling of the unit operation to perform a single task [1][2] or efficient task allocation among multiple robots when the tasks involve cooperation of robots[3-5].

In this study, we propose a dynamic service scheduling scheme that allows a robot to provide its service effectively to multiple users in various environments. The proposed scheduling scheme is composed of a *user-centric policy designator* and a *persistent monitor*. The user-centric policy designator organizes and updates the scheduling policy according to the service context change as well as user requirements in real time. Based on the scheduling policy, the persistent monitor schedules the execution sequence of requested services considering user requirements as well as the state of robot.

This paper is organized as follow. Section 2 explains the proposed dynamic service scheduling scheme of a network robot. Section 3 defines our evaluation criteria of the study. Section 4 presents the experimental results using a service robot in a simulated office environment and compares the proposed scheme with other schemes. Finally we conclude the paper in Section 5.

2   Dynamic Scheduling Scheme

In this section, we describe a proposed scheduling scheme for the services of a network robot serving multiple users based on both user-centric and system-centric information.

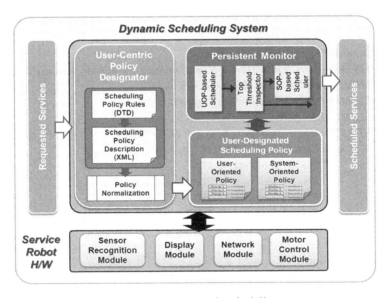

Fig. 1. Diagram of the dynamic scheduling system

To demonstrate the scheme, we designed a dynamic scheduling system composed of a *user-centric policy designator (UCPD)* and a *user-designated scheduling policy* with continuous monitoring of the scheduling by a *persistent monitor (PM)* in real time. The dynamic scheduling system schedules services which are requested by multiple users, as shown in Fig. 1, using the information from the robot hardware and the scheduling policy designated by user.

2.1   User-Centric Policy Designator

The user-centric policy designator converts the user designated scheduling policy to the data format adaptable to persistent monitor through a series of steps in order to generate user-oriented policy automatically. The scheduling properties of user-oriented policy are major requirement of users. Priority and threshold of each property is configured when it is reflected in the scheduling policy.

Policy Description

In order to provide customized services for multiple users, the proposed scheme uses a scheduling policy. The rules for policy are described by the DTD (document type definition) form. The policy consists of the user-oriented policy and the system-oriented policy to consider both system requirements and user preference as scheduling requirements. The policy description represents the properties of each component such as the user, environment and service, as well the relationships among the properties in XML format. The properties are classified into two types, known as picked and related. A property is described as 'picked' if it is not related to any other property. In the case of 'related', a new property is generated from the several requirements to represent relationships among properties. Each property in the scheduling policy has a priority and those properties are used in determining the priority of services during the scheduling.

```
< ?xml version="1.0" encoding="euc-kr"?>
<!ENTITY % PropertyProfile "(Entity, Name, Ordering, Threshold?, Element*)">
<!ELEMENT SchedulingPolicy (UserOrientedPolicy*)>
    <!ELEMENT UserOrientedPolicy (Property*)>
    <!ELEMENT Property %PropertyProfile;>
    <!ATTLIST Property type (picked\related) #REQUIRED>
        <!ELEMENT Entity (#PCDATA)>
        <!ELEMENT Name (#PCDATA)>
        <!ELEMENT Ordering (#PCDATA)>
        <!ELEMENT Threshold (#PCDATA)>
        <!ELEMENT Element (#PCDATA)>
```

Policy Normalization

A policy from the policy description is converted into two types of policy, a user-oriented policy and a system-oriented policy. The policy normalization is conversion process from the text-based policy description to the structure format user-designated scheduling policy. The policy normalization consists of the two phases of syntax verification and scheduling policy generation. Syntax verification checks whether the policy is described by a predefined syntax and can be applied to the scheduling system. After syntax verification, the user designated scheduling policy dataset is generated according to policy rule.

2.2 Persistent Monitor

The persistent monitor performs the scheduling of the requested services with the user-designated scheduling policy dataset. Because the policy dataset is applied according to the service context and states of the user and robot, it is composed of the user-oriented policy (UoP) based scheduler, the system-oriented policy (SoP) based scheduler, and the topmost threshold inspector. The SoP-based scheduler is executed in real-time whenever a service request is newly received, and schedules services based on the state information of robot system. The UoP-based scheduler is only performed scheduling based on the UoP received from user-centric policy designator when it need to decide what is the next request to serve.

Top threshold inspector refers to data of the service database sequentially from the topmost priority service in requested service list which is acquired from the UoP-based scheduler. It execute

There are two modes such as urgent and normal in the state of service according to properties and its threshold in UoP. In normal mode, PM performs services by SoP-based scheduler. In urgent mode i.e. with the excessive designated threshold, PM performs the service firstly. It executes the service if the topmost property information of the service is assigned the highest threshold. In contrast, if the topmost property information does not attain the highest threshold at the service inspection time, the SoP-based scheduler rescheduled and assigns a new priority to the services which were scheduled by UoP-based scheduler. In other words, the result of top threshold inspector determines whether scheduling is performed by user-centric or system-centric manner in real time. When there is no policy designated, FIFO scheduling algorithm, which processes services based on the requested sequence, is applied as a default policy.

The proposed scheduling system typically sets the service sequence of a network robot considering the system performance. However, it performs the service at first if the top property information of the top-priority service has the highest threshold value under the user-oriented policy. Therefore, the system can satisfy user expectations as regards the robot service while fundamentally maintaining the system performance.

3   Evaluation Criteria Definition

In order to verify the effectiveness of the proposed service scheduling scheme, we define several evaluation criteria from a system-oriented and a user-oriented perspective. Fig. 2 shows the timeline from a service request of a user to the service completion of the robot from the perspective of the user, task and robot. The service of a robot always meet three momentous times 'service request', 'service start', and 'service complete' from the user's point of view. Also, from the robot's perspective it has the other set of the momentous times which is 'task start', 'task complete', and 'another task start'.

- Set of requested services : $T = \{T1, \quad T2, \quad T3, \quad \cdots, \quad Tn\}$
- Example of time annotation :
  - $T1_r^1$ - Start time of robot execution of the first requested service
  - Ti_u^3 - Service completion time of the $(1,2,\cdots, n)$-*th* requested service

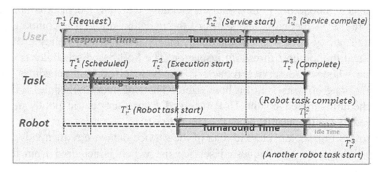

Fig. 2. Timeline of the user, the task and the robot for service in network robot

3.1   System-Oriented Perspective : Performance

The system-oriented measurements are defined as follows:

- Throughput: The average number of the completed task per unit time.

$$\frac{Number\ of\ Completed\ Tasks\ (n)}{ElapsedTime(T1_r^1,\ Tn_r^2)}\ (sec)$$

- Total execution time: The total elapsed time from the start time of the first service to the completion time of the last service.

$$\sum_{i=1}^{n} ElapsedTime\left(Ti_r^1,\ Ti_r^2\right)\ (sec)$$

- Availability: The time rate that it takes to process a service out of the total execution time. It allows a robot to complete more tasks in the same duration.

$$\frac{ElapsedTime(T1_r^1,\ Tn_r^2) - Total\ execution\ time}{ElapsedTime(T1_r^1,\ Tn_r^2)} * 100\ (\%)$$

3.2   User-Oriented Perspective : Satisfaction

There are the three types of times the request time, the complete time and the deadline for a service. Among them, the request time and the deadline are designated by the user. We propose evaluation criteria for user satisfaction as shown below, considering the above time variables:

- Punctuality: The deadline punctuality rate of all requested services.

$$\frac{Number\ of\ Punctual\ Task}{Number\ of\ Completed\ Tasks\ (n)} * 100\ (\%)$$

- Promptness: The average turnaround time between the request and complete time of each service.

$$\frac{\sum_{i=1}^{n} ElapsedTime(Ti_u^1,\ Ti_u^3)}{Number\ of\ Completed\ Tasks\ (n)}\ \ (sec)$$

- User satisfaction: Summation of the time value considering punctuality of each service which has firm or soft deadline by the user's needs. This criterion also implies whether the service is delayed and starvation is occurred.
  - $Ti.w$: The weight on punctuality per each service
  - $Ti.Deadline - Ti_u^3$: The value with punctuality that is time gap between deadline and completion time of the service.

$$\sum_{i=1}^{n}[Ti.w * (Ti.Deadline - Ti_u^3)]\ \ (sec)$$

4   Experiments and Results

4.1   Experimental Setup

The experiment is performed in delivery services using the simulator we implemented. As shown in Fig. 3 the simulated office environment is composed of 10 nodes to service with multiple users. In the simulation, each user requests more than

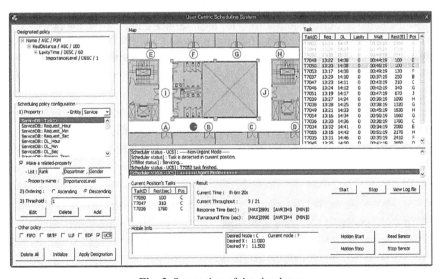

Fig. 3. Screenshot of the simulator

one service and some information for scheduling is set by user when the service is requested. The online UCPD, the left part of the simulator, supports online change of scheduling policy and represents detail configuration of the applied scheduling policy. The simulator also shows the real-time performance of robot service and requested service list in its right part after the scheduling policy is determined. It is possible to monitor the scheduling results carefully because the simulator outputs some decisive attributes organizing the execution order of services.

4.2   Experimental Result

In this simulation, we experimented by applying several conventional 'scheduling schemes such as FIFO[6], SRTF[7], LLF[8], and EDF[9] and the proposed scheme in two situation. In two situations, a robot received and served 20 requests from 10 users and the scheduling schemes are implemented. In the first scenario (scenario 1), each scheduling scheme performs the services considering system-centric information such as deadline, request time, and location of the requested services. In the second scenario (scenario 2), the scheduling schemes take into account user-centric information, for example user rank, as well as system-centric information in scenario 1. Fig. 4 shows comparative experimental results of the proposed scheme with several conventional scheduling schemes with regard to the criteria as mentioned earlier. In scenario 1, the proposed scheme has the highest value compared to the others in 'Throughput' which represents the number of completed services. In the "Total execution time' and 'Availability' graph, the proposed scheme improved 15% compared to SRTF and more than 50% compared to other schemes. Fig. 4 (b) shows the results of the experiment from the user-oriented perspective criteria in scenario 2. From the 'Punctuality' graph, the proposed scheme shows that 95% of the services are completed within the expected deadline, whereas SRTF is completed 75% of the services and others are completed less than half services. It means that all of the service is satisfied by user in the proposed scheme and the others are not satisfied. In the 'Promptness' graph, the proposed scheme has fast response time for each service compared to the others. Lastly, 'User Satisfaction' graph shows that the proposed and SRTF perform within expected deadline. On the contrary, EDF, LLF and FIFO execute the delayed services.

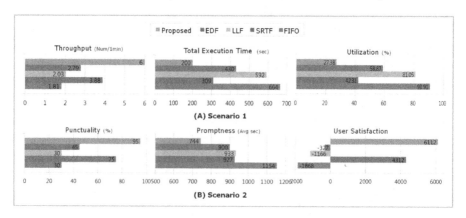

Fig. 4. Experimental results of two scenarios

The experimental results show that the proposed method improves the quality of service as well as maintains good performance. This simulation shows the improvement of user satisfaction by dynamic scheduling considering service properties and user requirements. Therefore, we can see that the proposed scheme improves the usefulness of services and supports effectiveness of services.

5   Conclusion

This paper proposed a method that provides flexible and dynamic service scheduling for a network robot. This work attempted to improve user satisfaction with the service by combining user-centric service scheduling with a traditional approach i.e., system-centric scheduling for the planning of a service. The method was validated in a simulation with several comparative scheduling methods for delivery services in a simulated environment. Simulated experiments with randomly generated services from multiple users were performed with good quality as well as good performance of the services. By applying the user-designated scheduling policy, the availability and usefulness of robot service is enhanced.

Acknowledgment. This work was supported by the KIST Institutional Program (Project No. 2E23840) and by the Global Frontier R&D Program on <Human-centered Interaction for Coexistence> funded by the National Research Foundation of Korea grant funded by the Korean Government (MEST) (2011-0031425).

References

1. Young, G.O.: A faster algorithm for 2-cyclic robotic scheduling with a fixed robot routeand interval processing times. European Journal of Operational Research 209, 51–56 (2011)
2. Dang, Q.V., Nielsen, I.E., Steger-Jensen, K.: Scheduling a Single Mobile Robot for Feeding Tasks in a Manufacturing Cell. In: Proceedings of the International Conference Advances in Production Management Systems, Value Networks: Innovation, Technologies and Management (APMS), Stavanger, Norway (2011)
3. Gerkey, B.P., Mataric, M.J.: A formal analysis and taxonomy of task allocation in multi-robot systems. The International Journal of Robotics Research 23, 939–954 (2004)
4. Labella, T.H., Dorigo, M., Deneubourg, J.-L.: Division of labour in a group of robots inspired by ants' foraging behaviour. Journal ACM Transactions on Autonomous and Adaptive Systems (TAAS) 1, 402 (2006)
5. Alcaide, D., Chu, C., Kats, V., Levner, E., Sierksma, G.: Cyclic multiple-robot scheduling with time-window constraints using a critical path approach. European Journal of Operational Research 177, 147–162 (2007)
6. Jackson, J.J.: Microsoft robotics studio: A technical introduction. IEEE Robotics & Automation Magazine 14, 82–87 (2007)
7. Bansal, N., Harchol-Balter, M.: Analysis of SRPT scheduling: investigating unfairness. In: Proc. ACM SIGMETRICS International Conference on Measurement and Modeling of Computer Systems, pp. 279–290 (2001)
8. Oh, S.H., Yang, S.M.: A modified least-laxity-first scheduling algorithm for real-time tasks. In: Proc. 5th Real-Time Computing Systems and Applications, October 27-29, pp. 31–36 (1998)
9. Andrew, M.: Probabilistic end-to-end delay bounds for earliest deadline first scheduling. This paper appears in Proceedings of the INFOCOM 2000. Nineteenth Annual Joint Conference of the IEEE Computer and Communications Societies, vol. 2, pp. 603–612. IEEE (2000)

Relocation Matching for Multiple Teams in Electric Vehicle Sharing Systems

Junghoon Lee[1], Gyung-Leen Park[1,*], Il-Woo Lee[2], and Wan Ki Park[2]

[1] Dept. of Computer Science and Statistics,
Jeju National University, Republic of Korea
[2] Energy IT Technology Research Section,
ETRI, Republic of Korea
{jhlee,glpark}@jejunu.ac.kr, {ilwoo,wkpark}@etri.re.kr

Abstract. This paper designs a relocation scheduler for electric vehicle sharing systems, aiming at overcoming stock imbalance and enhancing service ratio by evenly distributing relocation load for multiple service teams. To exploit genetic algorithms, a feasible schedule is encoded to an integer-valued vector having ($k+m$-1) elements, where k is the number of vehicles to move and m is the number of service teams. Two indices are built for overflow and underflow stations, making each vector element denote a source and a destination by its position and the value itself. In addition, negative numbers are inserted to separate the subschedules for each team. The maximum of relocation distances is calculated in the cost function while the genetic iterations reduce the cost generation by generation. The performance measurement result, obtained by a prototype implementation, finds out that each addition of a service team reduces the relocation distance to 47.3 %, 32.0 %, and 25.0 %, making it possible to tune the system performance according to the permissible budget and available human resources.

Keywords: Electric vehicle sharing system, relocation schedule, multiple teams, genetic algorithm, relocation distance.

1 Introduction

As an important area of smart grid which pursues energy efficiency from power generation to consumption, smart transportation tries to achieve smart consumption in transportation [1]. Its key component is definitely the electric vehicle, or EV in short, and EVs have many benefits especially in environmental aspects, over legacy gasoline-powered vehicles. These eco-friendly vehicles can reduce air pollutions and greenhouse gas emissions, as they don't need to burn fossil fuels. However, there are several obstacles for them to promptly penetrate into our daily lives. First of all, according to current battery technologies, it takes tens of minutes to fully charge an EV even with fast chargers. A fully charged

---

* Corresponding author.

M. Pathan, G. Wei, and G. Fortino (Eds.): IDCS 2013, LNCS 8223, pp. 260–269, 2013.
© Springer-Verlag Berlin Heidelberg 2013

EV just drives about 100 km practically on average. In addition, their cost is still too high for complete personal ownership.

Considering those problems, carsharing is a reasonable business model in current stage [2]. Here, drivers don't have to look for available charging facilities, worry about complex vehicle maintenance, or buy an expensive EV. The sharing model significantly reduces the number of vehicles especially in urban areas which suffer from heavy traffic load and parking space limitation. Actually, most vehicles are hardly used more than 2 hours a day. Without buying an EV, drivers can ideally share EVs, taking EVs when they want and return after driving. In this intermediary form of a public and private transportation service, a customer rents out an EV, visits his or her destination, sometimes parks for the time being, and returns the EV to a sharing station. However, a sharing request cannot be served if there is no EV available at the sharing station.

Above problem mainly stems from stock imbalance, in which some stations have no EVs while others have too many, irrespective of sharing demand. In one-way rental system, in which a customer does not have to return an EV to the station it has been taken out, this stock imbalance problem can be serious due to temporally and spatially asymmetric travel patterns [3]. [4] points out two stock imbalance patterns. First, the gravitational effect accounts for the tendency a station keeps becoming empty or full. Second, the tide phenomena accounts for the temporal oscillation in demand intensity. To enhance service ratio in sharing systems, EVs must be relocated between stations, possibly considering the current or future sharing demand [5]. Economically, sharing systems can reshape demand patterns by giving benefits to the sharing request starting from an overflow station to an underflow station. Here, a trip of multiple passengers can be split into more than one trip or the renting price can be discounted [4].

However, for better service ratio, explicit relocation is indispensable. Here, unlike bicycle sharing systems [6], the number of vehicles simultaneously relocatable is limited even with towing trucks. Hence, the relocation procedure can be economically carried out by service staffs employed by the sharing company, not purchasing expensive and hard-to-maintain towing vehicles. Basically, two staffs drive to an overflow station in a service vehicle. One drives an EV to an underflow station while the other follows, driving the service vehicle. Then, two go to a next overflow station. Scheduling their relocation operations is a complex optimization problem, which creates a set of pairs consisting of an overflow station and an underflow station, considering the relocation distance. Moreover, if there are two or more teams, the scheduling complexity gets much more serious. Its search space is too vast, suboptimal schemes look promising for reasonable response time even with high-performance computers.

In this regard, this paper designs an efficient relocation scheme for multiple relocation teams in EV sharing systems, taking advantage of intelligent computer algorithms [7]. Specifically, genetic algorithms are exploited to build a relocation schedule as they can yield an efficient suboptimal schedule within a reasonable response time. To run the well-known genetic operations such as selection, reproduction, and mutation, it is necessary to encode a relocation schedule for multiple teams into an integer-valued vector. For (source and destination) station matching, we further define two indices for underflow and overflow stations, respectively. The list of index values can represent the complete set of relocation pairs. In addition, negative numbers are inserted to separate the relocation schedule for different service teams. This relocation scheme then becomes a kind of multiple traveling salesman problem (mTSP) [8].

The rest of this paper is organized as follows: Section 2 reviews some related works. Section 3 describes the proposed scheme in detail, focusing on how to encode a schedule for multiple teams to apply genetic operations. After Section 4 demonstrates and discusses the performance measurement results, Section 5 concludes this paper with a brief introduction of future work.

2   Related Work

Efficient vehicle relocation can essentially enhance the service ratio, cut the cost of hiring service staffs, and reduce the relocation distance and time. As an example, the PICAV (Personal Intelligent City Accessible Vehicle) system develops a fully user-based strategy, which recommends or assigns a return station for each sharing transaction, based on second-by-second microscopic simulation results [9]. Moreover, to overcome the tremendous execution time to investigate the vast search space, its inference engine implements a simulated annealing technique. In addition, [4] regulates the sharing demand by taking different pricing policies. Here, to trace the demand dynamics, the authors develops a fluid approximation from a Markovian formulation of a closed queuing network. However, user-based strategies have limitations in coping with gravitational effect.

Next, as an example of explicit relocation, IntelliShare moves EVs from overflow stations to underflow stations by means of towing trucks [10]. This system also designs trip joining and splitting techniques for user-based relocation. For sophisticated relocation planning, [11] designs a three-phase decision support system consisting of optimizer, trend filter, and simulator phases. Particularly, staff resources and activities are allocated to reduce the relocation cost, mainly considering demand pattern. It combines a linear programming model and a brand-and-bound technique. In addition, [12] presents how to solve a route planning problem for general delivery services for a large number of stations. It divides the stations into a predefined number of groups according to proper decomposition techniques such as k-mean clustering. Then, the optimal or suboptimal routes are found within a cluster and they are modified for intercluster path planning using simulated annealing techniques. This route can be considered as a relocation path for a service team.

For the development of an EV sharing system in Jeju city, which possesses hundreds of EVs and city-wide charging infrastructure, our previous work designs an EV relocation process for different scenarios. To begin with, [13] deals with how to decide the relocation vector, where each element is associated with a sharing station and represents whether the station is an overflow or underflow station. Then, for the primitive service staff operation, matching between an

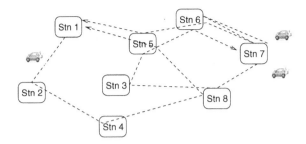

Fig. 1. Relocation by multiple teams

overflow and an underflow station is accomplished by a genetic algorithm [14]. Here, a matching plan is encoded based on two indices for the ordered lists of overflow and underflow stations. In addition, its cost function estimates the relocation distance which is the sum of distances between two stations in all relocation pairs. This approach assumes that a single team works in a cluster, as contrast to this paper scheduling multiple teams in a cluster and focuses on relocation load balancing.

3   Relocation Scheduler

3.1   Problem Definition

The system operator decides to initiate the relocation procedure. Basically, during the nonoperation hours, the relocation must be performed. In addition, if the service ratio is expected to drop shortly, the operator can trigger the relocation process even during the operation hours [11], usually based on current EV distribution and future demand prediction [15]. Anyway, for the given current distribution and target distribution in the station set, $S = \{S_1, S_2, ..., S_n\}$, a relocation vector, $R = \{R_1, R_2, ..., R_n\}$, can be decided, where n is the number of stations. If R_i is positive, S_i is an overflow station, while S_i is an underflow station if R_i is negative. Here, the number of EVs in all overflow stations is equal to that of EVs in all underflow stations. As a single EV can be moved from an overflow station to an underflow station, a relocation schedule is the set of relocation pairs, namely, $\{(S_i, S_j)\}$, where S_i and S_j are overflow and underflow stations, respectively. Here $|\{(S_i, S_j)\}|$ is the number of EVs to be moved.

The efficiency of the relocation schedule is decided by $\sum Dist(S_i, S_j)$, which formally defines the relocation distance. In this set, S_i appears R_i times. With m teams, each of them moves EVs independently. For their operation schedule, the reduction of relocation distance is not enough. It is necessary to evenly assign relocation load to each team. For example, in Figure 1 consisting of 8 stations, 3 teams participate in the relocation procedure. They take different routes and the relocation time is decided by the team taking the longest route. Unless the relocation pairs are elaborately assigned, a relocation team may attempt

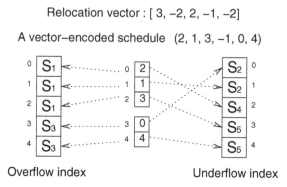

Fig. 2. Encoding scheme

to move an EV from an overflow station whose surplus EV has been already taken by another team. Hence, not total relocation distance reduction but the balanced assignment for multiple teams is more critical to the performance of EV relocation schemes, especially when there are many EVs to move over many sharing stations.

3.2   Encoding and Fitness Function

A relocation schedule, consisting of relocation pairs, must be represented by an integer-valued vector for genetic algorithm application. For relocation pairing, it is efficient to define additional indices [14]. Our encoding scheme can be better described by an example shown in Figure 2. Assume that the given relocation vector is $\{3, -1, 2, -1, -2\}$, and each element is associated with S_1 through S_5 one by one. S_1 and S_3 are overflow stations, while the others are underflow stations. The number of EVs in overflow stations is 5, hence, 5 EVs must be moved to underflow stations. Here, if S_i is an overflow station, S_i is placed to the overflow index as many times as R_i. After all, S_1 appears 3 times from location 0 in Figure 2. Then, two S_3's follows. Likewise, the underflow index is built with the difference that negative R_i's are changed to positive values.

Now, let's further assume that there are 2 relocation teams. Then, our encoding scheme puts $5 + (2-1)$ elements to a chromosome. For m teams, $(m-1)$ elements are added to the number of EVs to be moved. For a vector-encoded schedule of (2, 1, 3, -1, 0, 4), shown in Figure 2, each of 5 positive numbers has discrete values out of 0 to 4. Here, each number has its position in the vector. For example, 2 appears at position 0 and 4 appears at position 6. The negative numbers are used to separate teams. That is, the subvector (2, 1, 3) is for team 1, while (0, 4) is for team 2. If two relocation teams have the equal capability, (2, 1, 3, -1, 0, 4) and (0, 4, -1, 2, 1, 3) are logically same. Inserting negative numbers is originally proposed in mTSP problems [16], but this idea can be exploited also in the relocation schedule. Here, each sequence of numbers from -1 to 4 is mapped to a schedule.

In the schedule for team 1, the position of an element is associated with the overflow index, while the element itself is with the underflow index. For example, the element of location 0 is 2. As there is S_1 in the location 0 of the overflow index and S_4 in the location 2 of the underflow index, this element represents the relocation pair of (S_1, S_4). Likewise, 1 at location 1 denotes (S_1, S_2). Next, in the schedule for team 2, -1 is removed from the vector, and all elements after -1 are shifted forward. Now, 0 is placed at location 3. Hence, this element corresponds to the relocation pair of (S_3, S_2). Finally, the schedule for team 1 is $\{(S_1, S_4), (S_1, S_2), (S_1, S_5)\}$ and that for team 2 is $\{(S_3, S_2), (S_3, S_5)\}$. In this way, for the case of more than 2 teams, the integer vector can be interpreted into respective team schedules.

Relocation matching can be solved in the same way as general TSPs. That is, we can apply genetic operators such as selection, reproduction, and mutation. It must be mentioned that the reproduction operator, which swaps substrings from two parents, may lead to the duplicated entry in a single chromosome. It is necessary to replace the duplicated entries with disappearing ones. The genetic iteration keeps improving the fitness of the solutions in the population. As balanced assignment is important in reducing the relocation time, our scheme defines the cost by the maximum of relocation distances for all teams. In the example of Figure 2, the cost of the given schedule is $max\{Dist(S_1, S_4) + Dist(S_1, S_2) + Dist(S_1, S_5), Dist(S_3, S_2) + Dist(S_3, S_5)\}$. Actually, in the relocation procedure, a relocation team moves each time a relocation pair is completed. How to schedule this service staff operation is another problem and we focus on the reduction of relocation distance.

4   Experiment Result

This section measures the performance of our relocation scheme via a prototype implementation using Microsoft Visual Studio 2012. This implementation takes the Roulette wheel selection method and randomly set the initial population of chromosomes, or feasible solutions encoded by an integer vector. For better population diversity, it does not permit duplicated chromosomes in the contemporary population. They will be replaced by new random ones during mutation operations. Here, the logically equivalent chromosomes, for example, (2, 1, 3, -1, 0, 4) and (0, 4, -1, 2, 1, 3), can coexist in the population, as they can generate different offsprings. The fitness value is calculated when the schedule is first generated for later use for better efficiency. The genetic parameters such as the number of iterations and the population size can be freely selected in experiments. In addition, the experiment fixes the number of stations to 10 by default and inter-station distance exponentially distributes with the average of 3 km.

The performance metric is relocation distance, while performance parameters consist of population size, the number of EVs, the number of moves, and the number of stations, respectively. Underflow and overflow stations are selected randomly. In our configuration setting, 7 out of 10 stations are underflow stations to enlarge the options in selecting relocation pairs. The experiment also randomly sets the number of surplus EVs in overflow stations as well as the number of lacking EVs in underflow stations, respectively. The random numbers are seeded by the system clock for each experiment run. For each parameter setting, 30 different sets of relocation vectors are generated and the results are averaged. In each experiment, the relocation distance will be plotted for the cases of 1, 2, 3, 4, and 5 teams. The same relocation vectors are fed to each case having different number of teams.

The first experiment measures how much relocation distance can be improved by multiple teams according to our relocation schedule, and the result is shown in Figure 3. Here, the population size is set to 30, and the number of iterations is 1,000. The number of moves, namely, the number of EVs in all overflow stations, is set to 10. According to our observation, the relocation distance converges before 100 iterations in most cases, and it is hardly further reduced beyond this point. With 2 teams, the relocation distance is cut down to 47.3 %, this result discovers that not only the relocation load is efficiently distributed to each team but also each schedule intelligently optimizes the relocation distance of subschedules. Hence, the relocation distances for two teams are almost same. With 3, 4, and 5 teams, the reduction ratios are 32.0 %, 25.0 %, and 20.8 %, respectively. Scheduling efficiency is stably maintained even for the case of 5 teams.

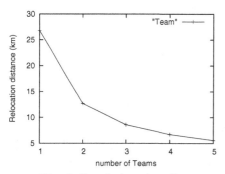

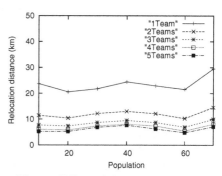

Fig. 3. Population size effect   **Fig. 4.** Effect of the number of EVs

The second experiment measures the effect of population size to the relocation distance, changing it from 10 to 70. Here, the number of EVs is set to 50, 7 out of 10 stations are underflow ones. Generally speaking, large population allows better diversity, but not always leads to a better solution. Even with large population, different initial population can result in a little bit poor quality relocation plans, as shown in the case when the population size is 70 in Figure 4. The relocation distance is more affected by the characteristics of the relocation vectors. In addition, this figure indicates that population size not so much affects the relocation distance. For 1 team, the fluctuation in the relocation distance is worst, reaching 8.9 %. On the contrary, for the 4-team case, the fluctuation is 2.61 %. Anyway, the stable relocation distance reveals that our scheme can obtain an efficient schedule even with small population size, which desirably shortens the response time.

Next, Figure 5 plots the experiment result on the effect of the number of moves, that is, the number of relocation pairs. Here, we assume that the sharing system is closed, so EVs will neither exit nor enter the system. Here, the number of EVs is set to 50, while 7 out 10 stations lack EVs. The performance curves in Figure 5 look quite linear for all cases, indicating the stability of our scheduling scheme. The ratio of relocation distances for 1-team and 5-team cases gets larger according to the increase in the number of moves. In addition, if we compare the relocation distances for the cases of 10 moves and 30 moves for each number of relocation teams, 140 % increase is observed in the 1-team case, while just 115 % in the 5-team case. This result shows that our scheme can find an efficient schedule even when severe grouping is needed for the large number of EVs to be relocated.

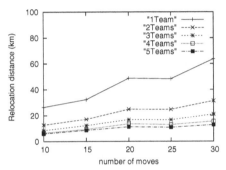
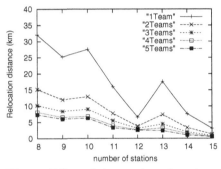

Fig. 5. Effect of the number of moves   **Fig. 6.** Effect of the number of stations

Finally, Figure 6 shows the effect of the number of stations in the sharing system. For each number of stations, different sets of relocation vectors are generated. Hence, the relocation vector effect is added in the relocation distance. Here, on the 12-station case, relocation distance gets abnormally shorter for the cases of 1 to 5 teams. With more stations, our scheme is more likely to find a relocation pair whose inter-station distance is shorter. In this regard, the relocation distance is cut down to around 9.2 % for all cases, when the number of stations changes from 8 to 15. After all, as our scheme shows a predictable performance behavior according to the performance parameters, it is possible to design a sharing system for the given system goal, permissible budget, and available human resources.

5   Conclusions

The modern electricity system pursues energy efficiency in diverse areas, while in the upcoming transport system, EVs will be key elements capable of achieving intelligent energy consumption and reducing greenhouse gas emissions. To cope with long charging time and expensive price, EV sharing is deployed in many cities, but stock imbalance can seriously drop the service ratio. This paper, taking advantage of sophisticated computer algorithms, has designed a relocation scheduler for multiple relocation teams which independently move EVs from overflow stations to underflow stations. To encode a feasible schedule, two indices are built, one for overflow stations and the other for underflow stations. In each encoding, a position of an element is associated with the overflow index and the element itself with the underflow index. Negative numbers are inserted to separate subschedules for respective teams. Then, genetic operators such as selection, reproduction, and mutation keep improving the fitness generation by generation.

The performance has been assessed via a prototype implementation, focusing on the relocation distance according to the number of teams, population size, the number of moves, and the number of stations. The result first shows that each addition of a relocation team predictably reduces the relocation distance and time. Here, relocation pairs having long inter-station distance is discarded in the schedule. Next, with smaller population size, and thus in fast response time, we can obtain a reasonable quality schedule, as the fluctuation according to the population size is less than 8.0 %. Additionally, it works better when there are more stations and more EVs to move, reducing the relocation distance by 9.2%.

As future work, we are planning to extend our scheduler so as to flexibly accommodate diverse options such as the number of service staffs in a relocation team, incremental relocation based on future demand prediction, and so on. The relocation procedure will also integrate charging schedules for better service ratio.

References

1. Goebel, C., Callaway, D.: Using ICT-Controlled Plug-in Electric Vehicles to Supply Grid Regulation in California at Different Renewable Integration Levels. IEEE Transactions on Smart Grid 4(2), 729–740 (2013)
2. Lue, A., Colorni, A., Nocerino, R., Paruscio, V.: Green Move: An Innovative Electric Vehicle-Sharing System. Procedia-Social and Behavioral Sciences 48, 2978–2987 (2012)
3. Correia, G., Antunes, A.: Optimization Approach to Depot Location and Trip Selection in One-Way Carsharing Systems. Transportation Research Part E, 233–247 (2012)
4. Waserhole, A., Jost, V.: Vehicle Sharing System Pricing Regulation: A Fluid Approximation. hal-00727041 (2013)
5. Weikl, S., Bogenberger, K.: Relocation Strategies and Algorithms for Free-Floating Car Sharing Systems. In: IEEE Conference on Intelligent Transportation Systems, pp. 355–360 (2012)
6. Lin, J., Ta-Hui, Y.: Strategic Design of Public Bicycle Sharing Systems with Service Level Constraints. Transportation Research Part E 42(2), 284–294 (2011)
7. Ipakchi, A., Albuyeh, F.: Grid of the Future. IEEE Power & Energy Magazine, 52–62 (2009)

8. Bektas, T.: The Multiple Traveling Salesman Problem: An Overview of Formulations and Solution Procedures. International Journal of Management Science 34, 209–219 (2006)
9. Cepolina, E., Farina, A.: A New Shared Vehicle System for Urban Areas. Transportation Research Part C, 230–243 (2012)
10. Barth, M., Todd, M., Xue, L.: User-based Vehicle Relocation Techniques for Multiple-Station Shared-Use Vehicle Systems. Transportation Research Record 1887, 137–144 (2004)
11. Kek, A., Cheu, R., Meng, Q., Fung, C.: A Decision Support System for Vehicle Relocation Operations in Carsharing Systems. Transportation Research Part E, 149–158 (2009)
12. Lian, L., Castelain, E.: A Decomposition Approach to Solve a General Delivery Problem. Engineering Letters 18(1) (2010)
13. Lee, J., Kim, H.-J., Park, G.-L.: Relocation Action Planning in Electric Vehicle Sharing Systems. In: Sombattheera, C., Loi, N.K., Wankar, R., Quan, T. (eds.) MIWAI 2012. LNCS, vol. 7694, pp. 47–56. Springer, Heidelberg (2012)
14. Lee, J., Park, G.-L.: Design of a Team-Based Relocation Scheme in Electric Vehicle Sharing Systems. In: Murgante, B., Misra, S., Carlini, M., Torre, C.M., Nguyen, H.-Q., Taniar, D., Apduhan, B.O., Gervasi, O. (eds.) ICCSA 2013, Part III. LNCS, vol. 7973, pp. 368–377. Springer, Heidelberg (2013)
15. Wang, H., Cheu, R., Lee, D.: Logistical Inventory Approach in Forecasting and Relocating Share-use Vehicles. In: International Conference on Advanced Computer Control, pp. 314–318 (2010)
16. Shim, V., Tan, K., Tan, K.: A Hybrid Estimation of Distribution Algorithm for Solving the Multi-Objective Multiple Traveling Salesman Problem. In: IEEE World Congress on Computational Intelligence (2012)

A Task Scheduling Algorithm Considering Bandwidth Competition in Cloud Computing

Jie Zhang[1], Xudong Zhu[1], and Bishan Ying[2]

[1] School of Computer Science & Information Engineering
Zhejiang Gongshang University Hangzhou 310018, P.R. China
http://ndc.zjgsu.edu.cn.People.htm
[2] Wasu Media Network Co., Hangzhou, China
billsun_ying@hotmail.com

Abstract. Workflow scheduling in the cloud environment is a challenging and urgent to be solve. Existing studies usually only take the computing power and storage capacity scheduling into consideration, but neglect network bandwidth allocation. In this paper, we present a bandwidth-aware schedule algorithm in cloud computing by using simulated annealing based greedy. We compare the time costs of GSA algorithm with dynamic bandwidth changes situation or not. The result proved that our method is more effective than traditional scheduling without considering bandwidth scheduling strategy.

Keywords: cloud computing, workflow, scheduling.

1 Introduction

The data congestion caused by bandwidth is an important factor which is affects the performance of data-intensive workflow on cloud computing environment. For data-intensive workflow applications, the need to transfer data between tasks is very huge. An example given by Deelman et al [1] shows that the overall run-time is driven by data transfer costs in a data-intensive application. Current distributed computing clusters used the hierarchical network architecture. If the available bandwidth can not provide sufficient input data, the network will become a bottleneck of the whole system. Communication delay is becomes a crucial factor in the impact of computing performance, especially when multiple tasks at the same time need to inter the cluster network transmission data then they will compete bandwidth. The dynamic network congestion model will greatly complicate to forecasts the performance.

A major idea in the data-intensive workflow computing is to send tasks to the computing resources that are close to the input data, in order to reduce the flow of network traffic, to avoid congestion, as well as the waste of unnecessary overhead, after all, for cloud computing is charged as a per-as-you-go pricing. Kavitha ranganathan[2] consider dynamic data replication as a fundamental part of the scheduling problem, use replication of data from primary repositories to other locations .Observe that workflow-base approaches have a potential to work better for data-intensive applications than task-based algorithms[3].

M. Pathan, G. Wei, and G. Fortino (Eds.): IDCS 2013, LNCS 8223, pp. 270–280, 2013.

In general, the problem of mapping tasks on distributed services belongs to a class of problems known as NP-hard problems [4]. For such problems, no known algorithms are able to generate the optimal solution within polynomial time. Even though the workflow scheduling problem can be solved by using exhaustive search, the complexity of the methods for solving it is very high [5]. Traditional scheduling method to reduce the complexity of the problem by simplifying the parameters. To date, there are two major types of workflow scheduling, best-effort based and QoS constraint based scheduling. The best-effort based scheduling attempts to minimize the execution time ignoring other factors such as the monetary cost of accessing resources and various users' QoS satisfaction levels. On the other hand, QoS constraint based scheduling attempts to minimize performance under most important QoS constraints, for example time minimization under budget constraints or cost minimization under deadline constraints [5]. This paper focus on the first type.

The data-intensive workflow in Cloud computing need to transfer large amounts of data between tasks that brings the challenge. Lead to the more dynamic change of network bandwith. A workflow is composed by connecting multiple tasks to their dependencies. Workflow structure, also referred as workflow pattern [6][7][8], indicates the temporal relationship between tasks. In this paper an application workflow is represented as a directed acyclic graph (DAG).The resources of tasks in cloud computing environments has dynamic. Tasks and resources join or leave the system at any time. Current scheduling algorithm basically didn't consider the dynamic change of network bandwidth in cloud. The performance of traditional static scheduling algorithm may be lower in dynamic cloud environment.

This paper we considered the impact of dynamic network bandwidth on the scheduling of workflow in particular on the data-intensive workflow. we proposed a bandwidth-awared schedule algorithm in cloud computing by using simulated annealing based greedy. The simulated annealing algorithm based on greedy selection for the minimized completion time scheduling problem. The objective function is to consider minimizing the makespan of the workflow. We model the network topology of tree structure and consider the link bandwidth competitions in the network.

The rest of the paper is organized as follows. Section 2 describes the problem which we will be solved in this paper. Section 3 presents the bandwidth-awared schedule Algorithm. Section 4 discuss the results of the experimental evaluation. The last section is conclusions and future work.

2   Model Description

In cloud computing environment, bandwidth is a nonnegligible factor in workflow scheduling. For example as shown in Figure 1, we assume a trilaminar network topology containing 8 machines m_1, $m_2 \ldots m_8$. One task node in the DAG is assigned to run on machine m_6 and transmit data to the successor node later. When leaving out link bandwidth competition, there is no difference operating the successor node scheduling on m_5 or m_1. But due to the existing competition, assuming that there is also a transfer operating on m_2, the transmission bandwidth from m_6 to m_1 cannot reach the rated bandwidth thus in this case scheduling on m_5 will be better. Since architecture of the network is generally not considered in traditional scheduling method, the scheduling scheme applied in actual case may not be good, especially in the case with a large quantity of data transfer, a greater impact. Now the data transfer time is a significant factor which affects the overall performance of workflow schedule.

The objective of mapping the tasks of an application workflow to distributed resources in the cloud such that is to minimize the completion time or makespan. One node in the DAG represents one specific data processing operation (operation encapsulating personalized algorithms and concrete realization of end-user). Directed edge in the DAG represents data transferring from one node to another. $G = (V, E)$ usually represents Directed Acyclic Graph (DAG), where V is a set of task nodes (i.e. the node in the DAG) and E is the set of edges between tasks. In other words, E represents the dependencies between two tasks, that is the DAG has the priority constraint task processing sequence—if parent node v_i did not finish, the child node v_j task will not start. We assume that a child task cannot be executed until it receives all inputs from its parent tasks. In the DAG the directed edge on behalf of task dependencies between control and data dependencies. In a DAG, a node without any parent is called an entry node and a node without any child is called an exit node. An example of DAG is shown as Figure 2(a) with 12 tasks.

Let $PRED(v_i)$ be the set of precursor nodes (parent nodes) of v_i. v_i can be scheduled only after all task nodes in $PRED(v_i)$ have been scheduled in container . Container is the physical or virtual machine packaged with resources provided by infrastructure. If node v_i is the entry node, $PRED(v_i)$ is null. Let $SUCC(v_i)$ be the set successor nodes of node v_i. If node v_i is the exit node, $SUCC(v_i)$ is null. Weight of $e_{i,j}$ represents the transmission date size of $e_{i,j}$ edge, which is the amount of data that node v_i transmits to node v_j and it becomes zero when both nodes are scheduled in the same container.

A task (node) in DAG can be modeled as $v(cpu, memory, time)$ where time is the execution time of the task assuming that the computation time of a task is the same on any compute resource. *Cpu* means the average cpu utilization and *memory* means maximum memory capacity needed for execution. In this paper, we assume that one machine can implement only one task at any moment so we can ignore cpu & memory requests. Thus the model can be simplified as $v(time)$. We use $v.time$ to express the execution time.

We use cpu, memory and network bandwidth to represent the container as $cont(cpu, memory, network)$. Same as task, the cpu and memory of the container can generally meet the needs of a task, so they are not important to us and can be assumed the same. The speed at which the container executed can also be ignorable in a task. So we can simplify this model as $cont(network)$.

A schedule S_G of a DAG is an assignment of its tasks into containers. An individual task assignment is modeled as $assgin(v, cont, start, end)$ where *start* and *end* represents respectively the start and end time of the task executed in the corresponding container. Our current distributed computing cluster mostly uses the hierarchical network architecture, just like a tree topology, in which the highest level of the network is the central processor, the lowest level is the terminal and other layers can be multiplexed converters and hubs.

Since the structure of tree is an undirected acyclic graph, we describe the structure as $T = (V_T, E_T)$. $V_T = \{p_1, p_2, ..., p_n\}$ shows a collection of cluster, representing any machine. $n = |V_T|$ is the number of machine. E_T is a collection of links, $e_{p_i, p_j} = (p_i, p_j) = e_{p_j, p_i} \in E_T$, e_{p_i, p_j} indicates that the link p_i to p_j is an undirected link. $M \in V_T$, M is a collection of the containers in V_T.

We layered the tree as $L = \{l_0, l_1 \cdots l_n\}$ as an example shown in Figure 1. We set the size of a communication bandwidth of the link (link belonging to E_T) between two nodes of different layers. $Band(e_{p_i, p_j})$: $e_{p_i, p_j} \in E_T$ indicates nominal bandwidth size of the link between node p_i and node p_j. $Band_f(e_{p_i, p_j})$: $e_{p_i, p_j} \in E_p$ indicates remanent bandwidth size of the link between node p_i and node p_j. We know that there is only one connective path between any two nodes in the tree. So there is only one path between any two nodes in the figure. We describe the bandwidth of the communication path between two nodes as follow:

$Path(p_i, p_j)$: represents a path communicating between node p_i and node p_j; $C(Path(p_i, p_j))$ =Min {respective nominal bandwidth of each edge in the path}, represents the link bandwidth of node p_i and node p_j of this communication path.

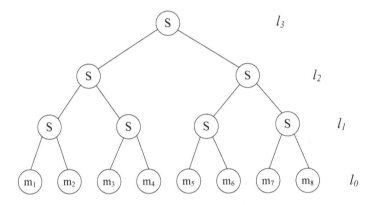

Fig. 1. Network Architecture

Problem: Based on a given DAG and a tree structure cluster T, how to obtain a scheduling allocation scheme which makes the DAG completion time or makespan minimized? The scheduling problem consists of two parts which contains scheduling and execution order information [9].

In our algorithms, task node weight is obtained based on the predictions of task execution time, while edge weight is calculated by predicting data transmission time. In this paper, we assume that the execution speeds of all machines are the same while the transfer speeds between machines are different in cloud computing environment. We traverse workflow DAG from top to bottom, assigning one weight $rank(v_i)$ for each task v_i. Tasks are ordered in our algorithms by their scheduling priorities that are based on upward ranking .Since the rank is computed recursively by traversing the DAG upward, starting from the exit node, it is called upward rank.[10]

The upward rank of a task v_i :

$$rank(v_i) = w_i + \max_{v_j \in SUCC(v_i)} (\overline{c_{i,j}} + rank(v_j)) e_{i,j}$$

$\overline{c_{i,j}}$ is the average communication cost time of $e_{i,j}$, and w_i is the computation cost of task v_i ($w_i = v_i.time$). $c_{i,j} = e_{i,j} / B$, B represents a constant bandwidth size to reflect the general data communication network in the cluster whose specific value is decided by the actual situation. As shown in Figure 2(b), we calculate the rank value of a node of Figure 2(a).

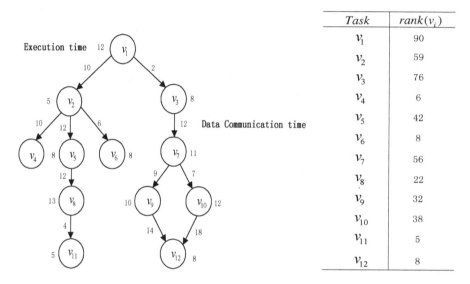

Task	$rank(v_i)$
v_1	90
v_2	59
v_3	76
v_4	6
v_5	42
v_6	8
v_7	56
v_8	22
v_9	32
v_{10}	38
v_{11}	5
v_{12}	8

Fig. 2(a).   Fig. 2(b).

3   Bandwidth-Awared Schedule Algorithm

3.1   Assumptions

ready : indicates readiness task node collection. If $v_i \in ready$ it's means all $PRED(v_i)$ node are assigned to run in the container in addition v_i has not been assigned to run.

Execution v_i operation and the data transfer process operation which has been finished can be separated, in addition, the transfer process and other tasks to perform operations can parallelize to each other. They also do not affect each other .Means the container as long as the completion of the operation do not care about the transmission of data they can be re-assigned to a new task node .while transferring data and while perform on the tasks. Because the CPU and memory overhead when transmission data is very small, so we have simplify this part. (i.e. The data operation is divided into two parts include data processing operations and data transfer operation).

Transfer operation occupied most of the bandwidth, but does not affect the calculation performance of the machine.

Any of the tasks v_i is assigned to the container to perform when the execution time of the task is constituted by two part-time: Setup time + Process time. Setup time=max { $PRED(v_i)$ to v_i data transmission completion time}, Process time= $v_i.time$. (i.e. v_i operation completion time on the container.)So the $assign.v_i.start$ is the start time of the earliest to transmit data to the $assign.v_i.cont$ node in the $PRED(v_i)$ and $assign.v_i.end = setup\ time + v_i.time$.

If a container having a multiple of transfer operations needs to be transmitted, according to the order of these transfer operations, there is no parallel transmission, which means that a container can only do a transfer task. Not transmitted data is stored on the local computer.

3.2   Schedule Time Estimates

Alg. 1 is the core of all algorithms, this algorithm estimates the running time of any scheduling scheme .So estimated the completion time for the whole schedule.

Algorithm 1.Schedule Time Estimates

Input:
  G : a workflow graph
  S_G: a schedule of G
  T : network structure graph
Output:
  S_G : a schedule with *end* and *start* for all tasks in S_G
1: Initial :
2: *ready* ← ∅
3: *time* ← 0
4: *queue* ← {tasks in G that have no dependencies}
5: **for** all tasks in the *queue* **do**
6: *next_event* ← Get(queued)
7: *ready* ← *ready*+ {assign(*next_event*,-,*time*,-)}
8: *queue* ← *queue-next_event*+{tasks in G that have no dependencies}
9: **end for**
10: **while** *ready* ≠ ∅ **do**
11: *time* ← *find_end*(*ready*)
12: *terminate* ← *find_event*(*time*)
13: **for** all tasks T in the *terminate* **do**
14:   S_G ← S_G + {assign(T,-,-, *time*)}
15: **end for**
16: *ready* ← *ready* - *terminate*
17: **for** all tasks in the *queue* **do**
18:   *next_event* ← Get(*queue*)
19:   *ready*← *ready* + {assign(*next_event*,-,*time*,-)}
20:   *queue* ← *queue-next_event*+{tasks in G that have no dependencies}
21: **end for**
22: **end while**
23: **return** S_G

The *Get()* functions is get the node in *queue* that the *rank(v_i)* value is maximum and the allocation of container for the time being there is no task in running. The *find _ end()* function is to find the earliest time of the tasks which will be terminated in *ready* .The *find _ event()* function is to find the tasks which will be terminated at any given time. Finally get the completion time of scheduling program.

3.3   Simulated Annealing Algorithm Based on Greedy Selection

SA is a local search method that finds its inspiration in the physical annealing process studied in statistical mechanics [11]. An SA algorithm repeats an iterative neighbor generation procedure and follows search directions that improve the objective function value. [12] Simulated annealing is also a greedy algorithm, but the search process introduces random factors. Simulated annealing algorithm with a certain probability to accept a solution worse than the current solution, so it is possible to jump out of the local minima to get the globally optimal solution.

The simulated annealing algorithm commonly used Metropolis criterion to accept the transition from the current state S to a candidate new state S' is specified by an acceptance probability function P, that depends on the energies $E(S)$ and $E(S')$ of the two states. ΔE its amount of change. If $\Delta E \leq 0$ accept S' as a new current solution, Otherwise, with probability $\exp(-\Delta E / T)$ to receive S' as new current solution where T is the current temperature.

$$P(\Delta E) = \begin{cases} 1 & (\Delta E \leq 0) \\ \exp(-\Delta E / T) & (\Delta E > 0) \end{cases}$$

In this paper, we propose a simulated annealing algorithm based on greedy selection for the minimized completion time scheduling problem. The objective function is to consider minimizing the makespan.

Algorithm 2:Simulated Annealing
Input:
G: the workflow graph
P:Network Architecture
Output:
S_G:The schedule of G
1: $S_G \leftarrow init()$
2: $T,T_{min},L,N,r \leftarrow$ set the parameters
3: **While** $T>T_{min}$ **do**
4:         **for** L Chains **do**
5:             $S_G' \leftarrow Get\_best(S_G)$
6:             $\triangle \leftarrow f(S_G')$-$f(S_G)$
7:             **if** $\triangle \leq 0$ **then**
8:                 $S_G \leftarrow S_G'$
9:             **else if** $\exp(-\triangle/T)>random()$ **then**
10:                 $S_G \leftarrow S_G'$
11:         **end for**
12:         $T \leftarrow T*r$
13: **end while**
14: **return** S_G

The function *init()* is used to generate an initial solution S_G which is constructed by assigning a container to each task node in the DAG at random. *random()* means randomly generate a number between 0 and 1.Function *Get_best()* it generate N new solution by applying random change on the current solution and selecting the solution with the shortest completion time. The function $f()$ is use Alg.1 to estimate completion time of the schedule S_G of DAG.

4   Experiment

The communication-to-computation-ratio (CCR) of a parallel program is defined as its average communication cost divided by its average computation cost on a given system.[13] We test of random task graphs consists of three subsets of graphs with different CCRs (0.1, 0.5, and 1.0). The random task graphs we tested are made up of three subsets of graphs with different CCRs (0.1, 0.5, 1.0). In each subset, number of nodes changes from 10 to 60 with incrementation of 10 resulting in totally 6 graphs per set.The graphs were randomly generated as follow: First the computation cost of each node in the graph was randomly chosen from a uniform distribution with the mean equal to 40(minimum = 2 and maximum = 78).Then a random number suggesting the number of children was selected from a uniform distribution with the mean equal to v/10 starting with the first node.[14] Besides, another workflow is described A parallel algorithm for Gaussian elimination (GE). Also, the communication cost of each edge with the mean equal to 40 times the specified value of CCR is randomly selected from a uniform distribution.

C-GSA(scheduling scheme which used simulated annealing algorithm with competition network bandwidth) NC-GSA(scheduling scheme which used simulated annealing algorithm with specified network bandwidth in the situation with competition network bandwidth).

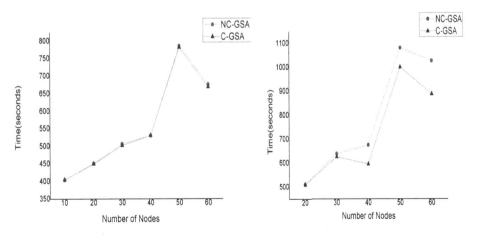

Fig. 3(a). Random Task Graphs CCR=0.1   **Fig. 3(b).** Random Task Graphs CCR=0.5

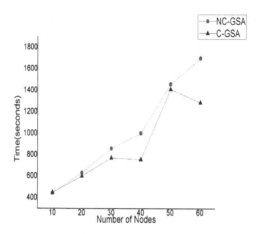

Fig. 3(c). Random Task Graphs CCR=1

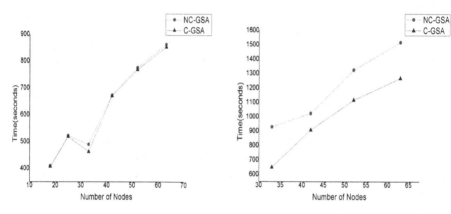

Fig. 4(a). Gaussian Elimination CCR=0.1   **Fig. 4(b).** Gaussian Elimination CCR=0.5

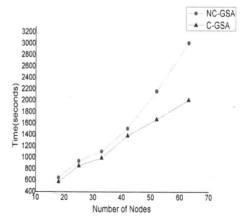

Fig. 4(c). Gaussian Elimination CCR=1

From the fig3 (a) ~4(c), we find out with communication-to-computation-ratio (CCR) become large, in the actual situation the NC-GSA become worse. This indicates in the data-intensive workflow that our algorithm is better than the traditional method.

Since the computational complexity of our algorithm is larger, when the number of nodes in the DAG is relatively less than its scheduled performance is not very good, but when the number of nodes in the DAG is increases then the scheduling algorithms and optimization model has demonstrated good performance.

5   Conclusions

In this paper, we have proposed a bandwidth-awared schedule algorithm in cloud computing by using simulated annealing based greedy. By introducing the simulated annealing algorithm, while at the same time combined with greedy selection policy. This algorithm considered the network bandwidth dynamic changes in computer clusters in the cloud computing environment. The results indicate that our algorithm can be more suitable in cloud computation environment.

As future work, we would like to optimization algorithms to reduce the time complexity, quotes the more parameter consider the case of machine multi-tasks.

Acknowledgements. This work is supported in part by Natural Science Foundation of China "Research on the snapshot data security storage technology for authorization of release.", No. 61100057, and Zhejiang Science and Technology Program No. 2010C33045. The Science and Technology Planning Projects of Zhejiang Grants 2011C14024 and 2011C13006-1. This work was also partially supported by Grant No.2011C14024 from Science and Technology Department of Zhejiang Province Program and Grand No.2010R50041 from Key Innovation Team of Science and Technology Department of Zhejiang Province. This work was industrially supported by the National Development and Reform Commission, China under Special Grants "The Operation System of Multimedia Cloud Based on the Integration of Telecommunications Networks, Cable TV Networks and the Internet".

References

1. Deelman, E., Blythe, J., Gil, Y., Kesselman, C.: Workflow Management in GriPhyN. The Grid Resource Management. Kluwer, Netherlands (2003)
2. Ranganathan, K., Foster, I.: Decoupling Computation and Data Scheduling in Distributed Data-Intensive Applications. In: 11th IEEE International Symposium on High Performance Distributed Computing (2002)
3. Blythe, J., et al.: Task Scheduling Strategies for Workflow-based Applications in Grids. In: IEEE International Symposium on Cluster Computing and Grid, CCGrid (2005)
4. Ullman, J.D.: NP-complete Scheduling Problems. Journal of Computer and System Sciences 10, 384–393 (1975)

5. Jia, Y., Buyya, R., Ramamohanaro, K.: Workflow schdeduling algorithms for Grid computing. Metaheuristics for scheduling in distributed computing environments. Springer, Berlin (2008)
6. van der Aalst, W.M.P., ter Hofstede, A.H.M., Kiepuszewski, B., Barros, A.P.: Workflow Patterns. Technical Report, Eindhoven University of Technology (2000)
7. van der Aalst, W.M.P., ter Hofstede, A.H.M., Kiepuszewski, B., Barros, A.P.: Advanced Workflow Patterns. In: Scheuermann, P., Etzion, O. (eds.) CoopIS 2000. LNCS, vol. 1901, pp. 18–29. Springer, Heidelberg (2000)
8. van der Aalst, W.M.P., ter Hofstede, A.H.M., Kiepuszewski, B., Barros, A.P.: Workflow Patterns (December 2004),
   http://tmitwww.tm.tue.nl/research/patterns/
9. Yang, T., Gerasoulis, A.: aDSC: Scheduling Parallel Tasks on an Unbounded Number of Processors. IEEE Trans. Parallel and Distributed Systems 5(9), 951–967 (1994)
10. Topcuoglu, H., Hariri, S., Wu, M.Y.: Performance-Effective and Low-Complexity Task Scheduling for Heterogeneous Computing. IEEE Transactions on Parallel and Distributed Systems 13(3), 260–274 (2002)
11. Aarts, E.H.L., Korst, J.H.M.: Simulated Annealing and Boltzmann Machines: A Stochastic Approach to Computing. Wiley, Chichester (1989)
12. Bouleimen, K., Lecocq, H.: A new efficient simulated annealing algorithm for the resource-constrained project scheduling problem and its multiple mode version. European Journal of Operational Research 149, 268–281 (2003)
13. Kwok, Y., Ahmad, I.: Dynamic Critical-Path Schduling: An Effective Technique for Allocating Task Graphs to Multiprocessors. IEEE Trans. Parallel and Distributed Systems 7(5), 506–521 (1996)
14. Kwok, Y., Ahmad, I.: Benchmarking and Comparison of the Task Graph Scheduling Algorithms. Joumal of Parallel and Distributed Computing 59(3), 351–422 (1999)

A Discovery Service for Smart Objects over an Agent-Based Middleware

Giancarlo Fortino, Marco Lackovic, Wilma Russo, and Paolo Trunfio

DIMES, University of Calabria
via P. Bucci 41c, 87036 Rende, Italy
{g.fortino,w.russo}@unical.it, {mlackovic,trunfio}@dimes.unical.it

Abstract. This paper proposes a novel discovery framework for smart objects in the Internet of Things (IoT). The discovery service is a fundamental block of the IoT as it allows smart objects and their users to dynamically discover distributed smart objects and, specifically, the services and operations they provide. The proposed framework defines a new metadata model to describe features, services, and operations of network-enabled smart objects, and implements a service-oriented service, accessible through a REST interface, for registering, indexing, and searching smart objects. Thanks to its generic architecture and the use of open Web standards, the proposed discovery service can be easily integrated into any smart object middleware. In particular, we show its integration into an agent-based middleware supported by the JADE platform.

Keywords: Internet of Things, Smart Objects, Web Services, REST, Multi-Agent Systems, JADE.

1 Introduction

The Internet of Things (IoT) usually refers to a world-wide network of interconnected heterogeneous objects (sensors, actuators, smart devices, smart objects, RFID, embedded computers, etc.) uniquely addressable, based on standard communication protocols [1]. In the IoT, all things have their identities, physical attributes, and interfaces. They are seamlessly integrated into the information network such that they become active participants in business, information and social processes wherever and whenever needed and proper.

Hereafter, we will focus on the definition of IoT as a loosely coupled, decentralized system of cooperating smart objects (SOs) [10][7]. An SO is an autonomous, physical digital object augmented with sensing/actuating, processing, storing, and networking capabilities. SOs can interact and communicate each other and with the environment by exchanging data and information "sensed" about the environment, while reacting autonomously to the events by triggering actions and creating services with or without direct human intervention. An SO-oriented IoT raises many in-the-small and in-the-large issues involving low-level communication protocols for SOs, SO programming, IoT system

M. Pathan, G. Wei, and G. Fortino (Eds.): IDCS 2013, LNCS 8223, pp. 281–293, 2013.

architecture/middleware, notably including service discovery and matchmaking, and methods/methodologies for the development of SO-based (large-scale) applications.

A few research efforts can be found in literature about discovery services for SOs. Systems such as Jini[1] and UPnP[2] provide mechanisms for discovering and using arbitrary network services provided by distributed devices. Other discovery services get close to the SO world, although they are more related to smart environments rather than to SOs.

Project Aura [8] manually performs a surrogate discovery: this is based on a small set of service classes for providing contextual information to applications via a particular interface. A component of Aura's architecture called "Environment Manager" [16] embodies the gateway to the environment, it is aware of which service suppliers are available to supply which services, and where they can be deployed.

The Voyager framework [15] includes an Application Manager Interface, which provides "Discovery Management" as one of its key facilities. This component discovers ambient devices by relying on proximity considerations: for devices supporting BlueTooth, discovery at the basic device address level is possible via the built-in "inquiry scan" mechanism of the host control interface implementation. Device discovery is delegated to a single locally running server, which maintains an up-to-date registry of proximate ambient device addresses.

These two services may be used with SOs but are not specifically designed for their context. A discovery service specifically related to SOs has been proposed in [9]: the work describes a framework for building distributed SO systems where one of its primary components, called "Smart object wrapper", has a discovery module that allows service advertisement. SOs are represented by XML documents that provide meta-information regarding the SOs, contain links to the binaries of their services and are also used by the secondary infrastructure *FedNet* to discover the services of the SOs and to associate SOs with applications.

Even though the last system implements some of the functionalities provided by our framework, it lacks a central index registry that makes it difficult to use it to register information about a set of SOs related to each other for a given purpose. In addition, while the system above uses XML to represent SO metadata, in our system we use JSON that offers a more compact metadata representation that in turns results in a more efficient bandwidth utilization. Finally, our system includes a complete API definition and implementation that allow to integrate the discovery service into any existing SO middleware.

This paper proposes a smart object discovery service based on modern Web standards (REST and JSON), designed to be integrated in many infrastructures thanks to its open design. It does not fit only in a specific setting but it is easily adaptable in many scenarios. Our contribution is therefore twofold: we propose a smart object discovery service, and we show its use in the context of an existing middleware to support indexing, discovery and selection of SOs implemented as agents.

---

[1] Sun Microsystems, Jini Specifications: http://www.sun.com/jini/specs ·

[2] UPnP Forum, UPnP Documents: http://www.upnp.org/resources/documents.asp

The remainder of the paper is organized as follows. Section 2 describes the service-oriented discovery framework for SOs. Section 3 describes the agent-oriented middleware for the development of cooperating SOs. Section 4 describes how the discovery framework has been integrated into the middleware. Finally, Section 5 concludes the paper.

2 Service-Oriented Discovery Framework

The proposed framework provides mechanisms for smart objects indexing, discovery and dynamic selection based on their functional characteristics (the provided services) and non-functional features (the quality of service).

Indexing means a document containing the description of a SO is registered, or published, in a registry to facilitate its fast and accurate finding after a search query. *Discovery* means searching for the SOs whose description matches a specified query. *Selection* means finding, among the discovered SOs, those that are closer to preference requisites (for example those with higher computing power, with higher battery life, etc.). The term *dynamic* refers to the need to manage the dynamic environment with SOs that are often turned on and off, and whose characteristics change over time.

We assume that all the SOs are *IP-reachable*, i.e. they are all connected to an IP-based network and can be reached through their IP address [18].

2.1 Metadata Model

In order to represent functional and non functional characteristics of SOs in a structured way, we defined a *metadata model*. The adoption of metadata models in distributed computing systems is fundamental to manage the heterogeneity of resources and to effectively use them [12][11]. The proposed model identifies a set of metadata categories useful to index an SO in the domain of interest, general enough to satisfy most of the application contexts. The metadata represent the SOs static values, the dynamic ones can be obtained by invoking the appropriate operations on their services.

Our metadata model is divided into four main categories:

- **Type:** represents the type of SO (e.g., a smart table, a smart wall). Each SO will have a tag taken from an enumeration of known tags (a taxonomy) through which it will be identified. This category also contains the id of the SO, which allows its unique identification within the system. In case of structured SOs, it will also contain the id of the SO within which it is contained, and the list of identifiers of the SOs contained inside it.
- **Device:** defines the physical characteristics of the device that specify, for example, if the device is running an operating system, what is its name, its version, how many users can use the SO, how many objects it can contain, etc.

- **Services:** contains the list of services provided by the SO. Each service is provided with an id through which it is possible to interact directly with it, without necessarily knowing in advance the SO that exposes it. Every service has a name, a description, the type (sensing or implementation), the return type (boolean, natural number, real number, etc.). A service can be discovered for example by knowing the name or a keyword contained in its description. Each service can also be associated with a quality of service indicator, such as the resolution of the operation performed by the service, its maximum and minimum returned value, and so on. Each service may contain a list of one or more operations that the service can perform. For example, given the "light" service, some operations which may be invoked on the service are "switch on", "switch off" or "invert state";
    - **Operations:** sub-category of Services, it defines the individual operations that may be invoked on a service. As with the SO, and for its services, each operation has an id with which the operation can be can reached and invoked, without necessarily knowing the SO or service for which it is defined. Each operation is equipped with a series of parameters necessary for its invocation, and a description;
- **Location:** represents the position of the device, which can be indicated in absolute terms, specifying the latitude and longitude, or in relative terms through the use of tags, such as "building B", "floor 3", "room 15". If the position of the SO changes over time, then it should be obtained as a service, if it is provided by the SO.

The generation of a metadata description document for a simple SO can be done by the SO creator/manager who, knowing the SO in details, can describe its characteristics following the required formalism. For complex SOs, this procedure could be accomplished by a module installed on the device, called *information provider*, which has the task to generate the metadata.

2.2   Metadata Representation

For the metadata exchange, the JSON text format is used because it is lightweight and easy to read and write manually, as well as to analyze and generate in an automatic way. JSON considerably reduces network traffic compared to XML, which is very important for wireless applications, and is suitable to describe attribute-value pairs. An example of metadata in JSON format, which is the description of a smart projector, is shown in Figure 1.

This JSON has four members associated with each of the four categories of metadata previously described (Type, Device, Services and Location). As it can be easily inferred by reading the JSON, the smart projector is included in another SO (a smart office denoted by the id "office1" specified in the *so-parent* metadata) and provides one sensing service to check the status of the projector (ON/OFF). Two operations are provided to check the status: the former provides the current status of the projector in one-shot mode, whereas the latter provides notifications of the status for a TimeLive period.

```
{
  "type": {
    "id": "projector1",
    "type": "projector",
    "so-parent": "office1"
  },
  "device": {
    "users-number": 1
  },
  "services": [
    {
      "id": "isProjectorOn",
      "name": "isProjectorOn",
      "type": "sensing",
      "return-type": "boolean",
      "description": "TRUE: The device is on; FALSE: The devise is OFF",
      "operations": [
        {
          "id": "isProjectorOn1",
          "description": "one shot request to obtain the projector status"
        },
        {
          "id": "isProjectorOn1",
          "params": "{"timeLive": 3000}",
          "description": "notifies the status of the projector for a time equal to TimeLive"
        }
      ]
    }
  ],
  "location": {
    "place": "Technest",
    "floor": "0",
    "room": "Sensyscal Office",
    "so-nearby": "whiteboard1"
  }
}
```

Fig. 1. JSON representation of a smart projector

2.3   Architecture

The definition of an architectural model tailored to the application scenarios of reference is a key aspect for the implementation of the framework. Between the options initially considered - centralized and peer-to-peer - a centralized solution has been adopted as it appeared to be the most appropriate in view of the projected scenarios. On the other hand, fully decentralized peer-to-peer solutions to resource discovery (as proposed, for instance, in [13] and [17]) could be effectively adopted in larger scale SO scenarios.

In the proposed architecture, there is a central registry, exposed as a service that indexes the information concerning the SOs of a given domain; the search of resources (SOs, services or operations) in that domain can be performed by contacting this central registry. Once the resource has been found, a direct reference to it is given so that it may be controlled/queried directly from a client application.

The centralized architecture model defined, detailed with all its components in Figure 2, is composed of two main parts:

1. **SmartSearch:** A service that contains a central registry where SOs are indexed, and which exposes methods for registering/publishing, searching and selecting SOs;
2. **ClientLibrary:** A module, in the form of software library, which allows the application level to interact effectively with the SmartSearch service using objects and local methods, making the remote methods invocation completely transparent.

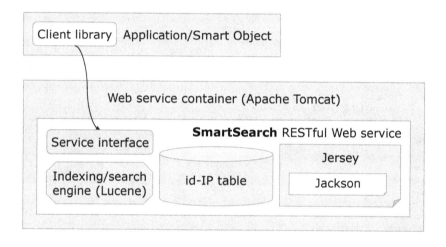

Fig. 2. Discovery framework architecture

2.4 Implementation

The SmartSearch service has been implemented as a RESTful Web service[3] and exposed via the Web service container *Apache Tomcat*[4]. The framework used in our implementation to develop RESTful Web services is *Jersey*[5], an open source framework that implements JAX-RS (Java API for RESTful Web Services) using annotations to map a Java class to a Web resource, and natively supports JSON representations through the integrated library *Jackson*[6].

The core component of the SmartSearch service is the indexing and search engine; this component has been implemented by using the open source library

---

[3] RESTful web services:
   http://www.oracle.com/technetwork/articles/javase/index-137171.html
[4] Apache Tomcat: http://tomcat.apache.org/
[5] Jersey: http://jersey.java.net/
[6] Jackson: http://jackson.codehaus.org/

$Lucene^7$ that provides high performance and feature-rich indexing and searching capability.

Another important component is the *id-IP Table*, a directory service that maps SOs, services and operations to IP addresses. This table, along with the fact that SOs are uniquely identified by their ids and not by their IP addresses, allows for the SOs to change their IP addresses in a transparent way to the client.

The methods exposed by SmartSearch offer the possibility to register an SO (the *register* method), search an SO (*discover*), obtain the IP address of an SO (*resolve*), update the IP address of an SO (*updateIP*), remove an SO from the index (*remove*), and get the metadata of an SO given its IP (*getJSON*).

A Web-based user interface has been implemented to expose all the discovery service methods discussed above. A screenshot of such interface is shown in Figure 3.

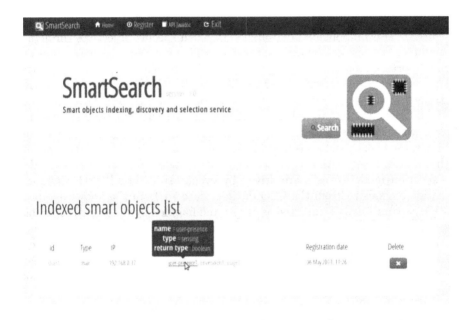

Fig. 3. A JSP Web interface to interact with the discovery service

3   Agent-Based Middleware

The proposed middleware for cooperating smart objects (CSO) is agent-oriented and event-based [7][6]. In particular, CSOs are modelled as agents that can co-operate with each other and with non-agent entities to fulfill specific goals. An ecosystem of CSOs is therefore a multi-agent system (MAS). The implementation of the smart object middleware relies on JADE [2] that provides an effective

---

[7] Apache Lucene: http://lucene.apache.org/

agent management and communication support. In particular, CSOs can be implemented as either JADE or Jadex agents [14] and can cooperate by a direct coordination model based on ACL message passing and/or by a spatio-temporal decoupled coordination model relying on a topic-based publish/subscribe mechanism. In the following subsections, we first overview the architecture of a JADE-based CSO and then provide more details on their communication mechanisms.

3.1 Architecture

The JADE-based CSO architecture is reported in Figure 4. CSOs are agents of the JADE platform so they are managed by the AMS (Agent Management System) and can use the DF (Directory Facilitator) to look up other agents. The communication layer is based both on ACL messages and topic-based Publish/Subscribe.

The main CSO architecture components are:

- *Task Management Subsystem*, which manages the CSO tasks. Tasks are software subcomponents programmed to reach specific objectives through a set of operations, involving computation, communication, sensing/actuation, and storage management. They can be either proactive or reactive. Proactive tasks are able to self-trigger to fulfill specific objectives whereas reactive tasks are only triggered by events sent by other internal or external entities. Tasks have also an internal state and can interact with the CSO subsystems and with other tasks. Tasks are defined as JADE Behaviours or Jadex Plans. Thus, the task execution is based on the mechanisms provided by the specific framework (basic JADE behavioral execution model or plan-oriented Jadex execution model). Tasks are driven by events, so external CSO communication, signals to/from the CSO devices, data to/from the knowledge base (KB) are internally formalized as events and handled by the EventDispatcher component that dispatches them to the interested tasks. In particular, when the EventDispatcher starts its execution, waits for events. When an event arrives, it is inserted into the event queue of the EventDispatcher, which fetches, filters and, if not discarded, forwards the event only to the tasks registered for such event.
- *Communication Management Subsystem*, which provides a common interface for different kinds of communication (local or remote) with other CSOs or different networked entities so as to allow the CSOs to homogeneously manage all their communications. As shown in Figure 4, JADE provides a set of services (TopicManagementService and MessagingService) and an ACL-based communication channel for the agent interaction. In particular, to provide communication among CSOs, an active component, named CommunicationManagerMessageHandler has been introduced (as Behaviour in JADE and as Plan in Jadex), which captures the ACL messages targeting CSOs and translates them into events. Moreover, two other handlers (TCPAdapter and UDPAdapter) have been defined to manage communication with external networked entities based on TCP and UDP.

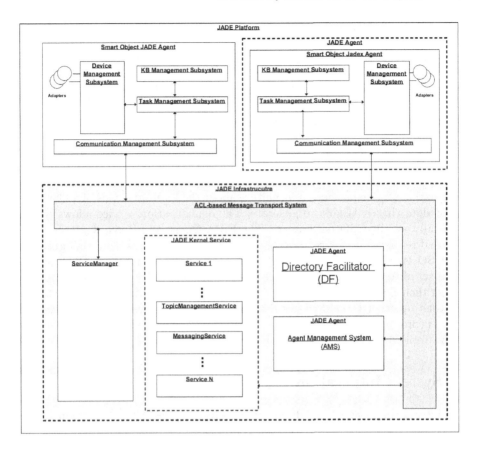

Fig. 4. Jade-based CSO architecture.

– *KB Management Subsystem*, provides CSOs with a knowledge base and consists of a KBManager, which manages and coordinates different KBAdapters, and a KBAdapter, which manages a KB containing the knowledge of the CSO. The KB can be local or remote and stores information that can be shared among tasks.

– *Device Management Subsystem*, manages interactions with internal CSO sensing/actuation devices. The management of (wireless) sensors/actuators is carried out through the DeviceManager that handles several DeviceAdapters. In particular, two DeviceAdapters have been currently implemented: the BMFAdapter, which allows to manage wireless sensor and actuator networks (WSANs) based on the BMF (Building Management Framework) framework [5], and the SPINEAdapter, which allows to manage Body Sensor Networks (BSNs) based on the SPINE (Signal Processing In-Node Environment) framework [4][3]. BMF and SPINE are based on IoT standards protocols such as IEEE 802.15.4, ZigBee, and 6LowPan.

3.2 Communication

CSOs communicate by using two different paradigms: asynchronous message passing and publish/subscribe (P/S). The former is based on the agent communication language (ACL) and allows asynchronous direct communication between pairs or among groups of CSOs; the latter is based on subscription to specific topics and on the notification of the subscribers once information about such topics is produced by publishers, and enables spatio-temporal decoupled interaction between groups of CSOs. Both communication paradigms are fully supported by the JADE platform. According to the ACL-based communication model, a CSO offers two types of services: information and configuration. The information service provides information about the internal status of a CSO and about data that it is able to generate. The configuration service allows to dynamically set the CSO parameters. The FIPA Query and Request protocols [2] are used respectively for requesting information from and setting configuration of a CSO. According to the topic-based P/S communication model, CSOs advertise a set of topics, which are usually specific to data/information they produce during their lifecycle. On the other hand, CSOs subscribe to one or more topics provided by other CSOs and get notified as soon as an event of the subscribed topics is produced by a given CSO. Such model is supported by JADE by means of the TopicManagementService components.

4 System Integration

The integration between the discovery architecture, described in Section 2, and the Agent-based middleware, previously presented, is made by loosely integrating the JADE DF with the discovery service. In particular, the JADE DF is extended with an agent-oriented interface providing the same discovery service offered by the discovery architecture. Thus, the extended JADE DF receives requests from the JADE-based CSOs and fulfill them by using the remote interface of the discovery service (see Section 2). In Figure 5, the structure of the extended JADE DF for cooperating smart objects is shown. The proposed extension follows the pattern of extension of the JADE DF according to which the new DF (SmartObjectDF) should extends the basic DF, the new DF service (SmartObjectDFService) should extend the basic DFService, both of them should implement the new management ontology (SmartObjectManagementOntology), and the new management behavior of requests (SmartObjectManagementBehavior) should extend the basic RequestManagementBehavior. In particular, in the SmartObjectManagementBehavior, the SmartObjectDF interprets the request and invokes the corresponding service provided by the discovery service component (see Section 2).

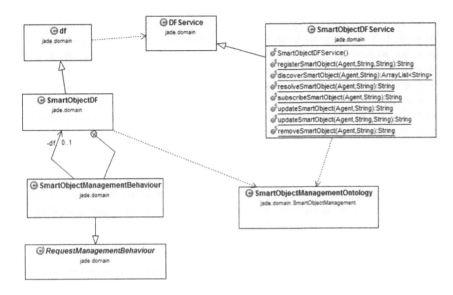

Fig. 5. UML Class Diagram of the SmartObjectDF.

The SmartObjectDFService interface provides the following methods:

- `String registerSmartObject(Agent a, String metadata, String ip)`, which registers a CSO with the SmartObjectDF. `metadata` parameter indicates the metadata of the CSO in JSON format whereas `ip` represents the IP address of the CSO.
- `ArrayList<String> discoverSmartObject(Agent a, String query)`, allows to discover the CSOs that satisfy the `query`.
- `String resolveSmartObject(Agent a, String id)`, returns the IP address associated with the the CSO `id`.
- `String subscribeSmartObject(Agent a, String id)`, registers to notifications related to the change of the status of the CSO with identifier `id`.
- `String updateSmartObject(Agent a, String metadata)`, updates the metadata of the CSO.
- `String updateSmartObject(Agent a, String id, String ip)`, updates the `ip` address of the CSO.
- `String removeSmartObject(Agent a, String id)`, which allows the removal of either a CSO, a specific CSO service or a specific CSO operation (identified by `id`).

5   Conclusions

Indexing and discovery services are fundamental components of any distributed computing system. Providing an effective implementation of such services is particularly important in IoT scenarios, where a large number of heterogeneous

SOs must be dynamically discovered and integrated with each other to satisfy users' and applications' needs, based on the services and operations they provide. We worked in this direction by designing and implementing a service-oriented framework that supports indexing, discovery, and dynamic selection of SOs as a key component to develop complex IoT applications.

The proposed framework includes: *i*) a metadata model to describe network-enabled smart object features, services, and operations; *ii*) a service-oriented system, accessible through a REST interface, for registering, indexing, and searching SOs described using our metadata model; *iii*) a set of APIs to register, search, and select SOs using such system. Thanks to its generic architecture and the use of open Web standards, the proposed discovery service can be easily integrated into any SO middleware. In particular, we described how the proposed discovery service has been integrated into an agent-based middleware supported by the JADE platform.

Acknowledgements. The authors would like to thank Francesco Rango for his implementation efforts. This work has been partially supported by TETRis - TETRA Innovative Open Source Services, funded by the Italian Government (PON 01-00451).

References

1. Bandyopadhyay, D., Sen, J.: Internet of things: Applications and challenges in technology and standardization. Wireless Personal Communications 58(1), 49–69 (2011)
2. Bellifemine, F., Poggi, A., Rimassa, G.: Developing multi-agent systems with a FIPA-compliant agent framework. Softw. Pract. Exper. 31, 103–128 (2001)
3. Bellifemine, F., Fortino, G., Giannantonio, R., Gravina, R., Guerrieri, A., Sgroi, M.: Spine: a domain-specific framework for rapid prototyping of wbsn applications. Software: Practice and Experience 41(3), 237–265 (2011)
4. Fortino, G., Giannantonio, R., Gravina, R., Kuryloski, P., Jafari, R.: Enabling effective programming and flexible management of efficient body sensor network applications. IEEE Transactions on Human-Machine Systems 43(1), 115–133 (2013)
5. Fortino, G., Guerrieri, A., O'Hare, G.M.P., Ruzzelli, A.: A flexible building management framework based on wireless sensor and actuator networks. Journal of Network and Computer Applications 35(6), 1934–1952 (2012)
6. Fortino, G., Guerrieri, A., Lacopo, M., Lucia, M., Russo, W.: An agent-based middleware for cooperating smart objects. In: Corchado, J.M., et al. (eds.) PAAMS 2013. CCIS, vol. 365, pp. 387–398. Springer, Heidelberg (2013)
7. Fortino, G., Guerrieri, A., Russo, W.: Agent-oriented smart objects development. In: IEEE Conference on CSCWD, pp. 907–912 (2012)
8. Garlan, D., Siewiorek, D.P., Steenkiste, P.: Project aura: Toward distraction-free pervasive computing. IEEE Pervasive Computing 1, 22–31 (2002)
9. Kawsar, F., Nakajima, T., Park, J.H., Yeo, S.-S.: Design and implementation of a framework for building distributed smart object systems. J. Supercomput. 54(1), 4–28 (2010)

10. Kortuem, G., Kawsar, F., Fitton, D., Sundramoorthy, V.: Smart objects as building blocks for the internet of things. IEEE Internet Computing 14(1), 44–51 (2010)
11. Mastroianni, C., Talia, D., Trunfio, P.: Managing heterogeneous resources in data mining applications on grids using xml-based metadata. In: Proc. of the 17th International Parallel and Distributed Processing Symposium (IPDPS 2003), Nice, France (April 2003)
12. Mastroianni, C., Talia, D., Trunfio, P.: Metadata for managing grid resources in data mining applications. Journal of Grid Computing 2(1), 85–102 (2004)
13. Pirrò, G., Talia, D., Trunfio, P.: A dht-based semantic overlay network for service discovery. Future Generation Computer Systems 28(4), 689–707 (2012)
14. Pokahr, A., Braubach, L., Lamersdorf, W.: Jadex: A BDI Reasoning Engine, Multiagent Systems. Artificial Societies, and Simulated Organizations, vol. 15. Springer (2005)
15. Savidis, A., Stephanidis, C.: Distributed interface bits: dynamic dialogue composition from ambient computing resources. Personal Ubiquitous Comput. 9(3), 142–168 (2005)
16. Sousa, J.P., Garlan, D.: Aura: an architectural framework for user mobility in ubiquitous computing environments. In: Proceedings of the IFIP 17th World Computer Congress - TC2 Stream / 3rd IEEE/IFIP Conference on Software Architecture: System Design, Development and Maintenance, WICSA 3, pp. 29–43. Kluwer, B.V, Deventer (2002)
17. Talia, D., Trunfio, P., Zeng, J.: Peer-to-peer models for resource discovery in large-scale grids: A scalable architecture. In: Daydé, M., Palma, J.M.L.M., Coutinho, Á.L.G.A., Pacitti, E., Lopes, J.C. (eds.) VECPAR 2006. LNCS, vol. 4395, pp. 66–78. Springer, Heidelberg (2007)
18. Vasseur, J., Dunkels, A.: Interconnecting Smart Objects with IP: The Next Internet. Morgan Kaufmann (2010)

Research on an Adaptive Routing Mechanism of Combination of Packet Forward with Virtual Circuit

Xianming Gao, Xiaozhe Zhang, Zexin Lu, and Shicong Ma

School of Computer Science
National University of Defense Technology
Changsha 410073, China
gxm9000@163.com

Abstract. Virtual circuit transmission mechanism as represented by MPLS has the characteristics of low forwarding overhead and short transmission delay. In contrast, the traditional packet forward mechanism is more flexible than the former in terms of dynamic packet forwarding routing. In this paper, we put forward an adaptation routing mechanism(ARM for short) of combination of packet forward with virtual circuits that is based on combination of the advantages of these transmission mechanisms. It can overcome the shortcomings of static and manual configurations in the MPLS mechanism. The experimental results show that it can not only improve the packet forwarding speed without replacing the router hardware, but also has advantages in reducing load pressure of partial nodes in the network topology and optimizing the partial or entire network transmission performance.

Keywords: transmission mechanism, traditional packet forward, virtual circuit, MPLS, load pressure, network topology.

1 Introduction

At present, internetwork packet exchange is used to convey information, which makes the Internet becoming a channel of developing information service, carrying out mutual communion. And there are two means of datagram transmission and virtual circuit transmission in the Internet [1]. The datagram transmission mechanism can automatically adjust the packet forwarding routing and make the routers modify their forwarding tables in time according to the changes of network link status, which is of strong robusticity on the background disturbance of a single point of failure. In contrast to the datagram transmission mechanism, the virtual circuit transmission only establishes an end-to-end connection that can be kept during mutual communion and make middle nodes forward packets without the need of repeated routing lookup before the ends start to forward packets, which has the advantages of low overhead and short transmission delay.

In order to improve the packet forwarding speed, IETF proposes the Multi-Protocol Label Switching (MPLS) that fully absorbs the characteristics of low overhead and short transmission delay of the virtual circuit transmission [2]. MPLS mainly deriving

M. Pathan, G. Wei, and G. Fortino (Eds.): IDCS 2013, LNCS 8223, pp. 294–306, 2013.
© Springer-Verlag Berlin Heidelberg 2013

from IP switching network was firstly proposed by Lpsilon and developed further by Toshiba and Cisco company, which adopts original IP routing protocols and ATM technologies by combining the existing IP network with the fast ATM network to provide a good service quality [3]. MPLS introduces an independent sub-layer between second data link layer and third network layer of the OSI model proposed by ISO [4]. Compared with the traditional IP network, MPLS can assign labels for the incoming packets into the MPLS network and forward packets based on these labels with a cost-effective and multi-service capabilities, which can overcome the limitations of the traditional IP network and cause more and more attention of research communities and industries. Certainly, there are some limitations of technical aspects in the MPLS mechanism: all of MPLS work concentrates on the additional sub-layer, which introduces many indirect problems; In addition, the MPLS network topology shall be statically configured and the label switch path (LSP) can't be automatically adjusted in accordance with network link status. Especially when the MPLS network is running in an abnormal environment, the performance of MPLS network is relatively poor. At the end, the label edge routers (LER) should have higher hardware requirement needed, which are responsible for dealing with packet header and assigning the labels.

In this paper, we put forward an adaptation routing mechanism of combination of traditional packet forward with virtual circuits transmission based on combination of the advantages of low forwarding overhead and short transmission delay that are the characteristics of the virtual circuit transmission mechanism as represented by MPLS and dynamic packet forwarding routing in the traditional packet forward mechanism. And it has better flexibility in terms of packet forwarding routing that when one packet traffic throughput exceeds a set threshold value of one router, it can "automatically" establish a tunnel to improve the packet forwarding speed. The experimental results show that the ARM mechanism can not only improve the packet forwarding speed and optimize partial or entire network performance, but also it can ease the load pressure of partial nodes in the network topology to enhance network robustness.

The remainder of this paper is organized as follow. Section 2 discusses and illustrates the features and limitations of rerouting mechanism that proposed to support MPLS network better by research communities. Section 3 discusses and describes the ARM mechanism, which presents the algorithms of the ARM mechanism and the tunnel maintenance. Section 4 proves the correctness and usefulness of the ARM mechanism in terms of the changes of network topology and the state of routing loopback. Section 5 presents the results of our experiment to prove the validity of the ARM mechanism proposed by the NS2 simulator. Section 6 concludes this paper with a summary of our study and discusses the next works in the future.

2   Related Works

The MPLS rerouting mechanism has a similar point to reduce the impact of network failures with the ARM mechanism proposed in this paper. In order to protect the MPLS network, the rerouting mechanism creates a bypass tunnel in man-made mode. Once the nodes or links occur a single point of failure, the rerouting mechanism can switch packet forwarding routing to the bypass tunnel by skipping these failure nodes or links. However, the time and location of a single point of failure is often unpredictable, which leads to the inevitable defects by configuring bypass tunnels manually. For this case, MPLS-TE not only provides the bypass tunnel technology, but also uses the fast rerouting technology to provide effective protection for packet forwarding. It can refer to user' strategies and flexibly generate the bypass tunnels in the processing of calculating the best packet forwarding routing. The same method is also applied to RSVP-TE [8-9], which is used to reduce the impact of a single point of failure. But these algorithms are more complex and difficult to be implemented, which also increase the pressure load of partial nodes. Yi [10] creates an adaptive bypass tunnel mechanism that an automatic rerouting scheme can take full advantage of the existing system based on the characteristics of the current network topology.

3   ARM Review

The packet traffic in the Internet has the feature of locality (time locality and spatial locality) as same as other areas that these packets are forwarded to a certain sub-network along the same packet forwarding routing over a period of time. Because the end-to-end connection or session may require multiple packets to finish the task in the Internet, so the packet traffic throughput of partial nodes in the network topology may come up to the higher level. Especially streaming media, VoIP and other chat applications are popular with all over world that may make the session keep for a long time. Meanwhile, 10% hosts in the Internet accounted for 90% network traffics according to the trace information of some core routers in [11].

Although the MPLS technology can effectively improve the packet forwarding speed, it has to encapsulate the packets sent by 100% hosts in the Internet, which not only increases the load pressure of the label edge routers, but also increases the difficulty of tunnel maintenance in the MPLS network. The MPLS technology only can obtain good performance in the core-network, and it does not be suitable for others in the Internet. In this case, we propose an ARM mechanism of combination of traditional packet forward with virtual circuits transmission to overcome the shortcomings of the MPLS technology. The ARM mechanism only may establish tunnels for approximately 10% hosts that account for the vast majority of network traffics without the need of the established tunnels for the remaining hosts in the Internet, which can reduce the cost of the tunnel maintenance and dynamically establish multiple tunnels according to the requirement of network traffics. So the biggest difference between the ARM mechanism and the MPLS technology is that the ARM mechanism can flexibility and dynamically establish multiple tunnels according to the network link status in the Internet, while the MPLS technology is usually adopted in the core-network.

3.1   Algorithms of ARM

The ARM mechanism is no longer confined to the thinking of adopting new technology to improve the packet forwarding performance of the routers, which provides a new way to optimize the packet forwarding routing with the advantages of routing lookup and tunnel management. In the network topology, the routers supporting for the ARM mechanism can count packet traffic throughput. If one packet traffic that is forwarded to a certain sub-network exceeds the set threshold value of one router, this router will send "query" packets to its adjacent routers of the same packet forwarding routing as the packet traffic in order to find the two nearest routers where they are on both sides of this router and the same packet traffic throughput does not exceed their set threshold value. As these two routers are determined in the same packet forwarding routing, the upstream router of these two routers tries to establish a tunnel between these two routers.

The routing table generation algorithm is the core algorithms of the ARM mechanism. This section focuses on this algorithm that its input is a trigger event that the packet traffic that is forwarded to a certain network exceeds a set threshold value and its output is an "establish" packet as follows.

```
Routing table generation algorithm description
Input: a trigger event
Output: an "establish" packet
{
  Router A sends "query" packets;
  Router A waits for the replies of other routers;
  Router A calculates the nearest two routers of the up-
stream router B and the  downstream router C;
  Router A sends one "establish" packet to the router B
to tell that it can establish a tunnel from the router B
and the router C;
  If this tunnel is established by router B
    Router A changes its routing table;
  Return SUCCESS;
}
```

The routing table generation algorithm is relatively easy, which is designed to find these two routers and sends the "establish" packets the upstream routers to establish new tunnels. Once these tunnels are established, the packet forwarding speed will be improved to reduce the load pressure of the router A and optimize the partial network transmission performance.

But a single point of failure (e.g. node failure, operation error, link failure) occurs that can cause the changes of the current network topology in the Internet. If the ARM mechanism can not change the established tunnels in consistent with the network topology, it will be worse in an abnormal environment. So we put forward a routing table update algorithm to make the ARM mechanism can "automatically" adjust the established tunnels in order to be adapt to the changes of the current network topology without the need of administrators' reconfiguration. The routing table update algorithm that its input is trigger event that the routing table is updated by other routing protocols (e.g. OSPF, RIP) and its output is a "change" packet as follows.

```
Routing table update algorithm description
Input: a trigger event
Output: a "change" packet
{
  Router A updates the routing table;
  Router A checks the routing table whether or not af-
fects the established tunnels;
  If it is positive
    Router A sends "change" packets to the upstream rou-
ter of this affected tunnels;
  Return SUCCESS;
}
```

The biggest difference is the sent packet to the upstream router between the routing table update algorithm and the routing table update algorithm. And the routing table update algorithm can make the ARM mechanism have the capacity of the established tunnel maintenance.

3.2   Tunnel Maintenance of ARM

The ARM mechanism uses the tunnel technology to improve the packet forwarding speed that is the challenge for the tunnel maintenance in the ARM mechanism. The established tunnels are one-way virtual links that are established from the upstream router to the downstream router in the same packet forwarding routing. Give the following definitions before we present the tunnel maintenance algorithm of the ARM mechanism in this paper.

1. Tunnel overlap: Two tunnels that are established for the same packet forwarding routing exist partial same nodes and other different nodes, we call it tunnel overlap.
2. Tunnel coverage: Two tunnels that are established for the same packet forwarding routing exist the situation that all of nodes of one tunnel are belong to anther tunnel, we call it tunnel coverage.
3. Tunnel independence: Two tunnels that are established for the same packet forwarding routing exist all of different nodes, we call it tunnel independence.
4. Tunnel accordance: Two tunnels that are established for two different packet forwarding routings exist all of same nodes, we call it tunnel accordance.

In order to avoid the re-establishment of the old tunnels that causes the additional overhead, we give the following policies of tunnel management according to the relationship between two tunnels:

— When the router A establishes the tunnel M of the upstream router B and the downstream router C for a packet forwarding routing, it finds the relationship between the tunnel M and the tunnel N of the upstream router E and the downstream router

F is tunnel overlap. Then the router A will delete the tunnel M and send one "change" packet to the router E in order to tell it that it should delete the tunnel N and re-establish a new tunnel between the router E and the router C.

— When the router A establishes the tunnel M of the upstream router B and the downstream router C for a packet forwarding routing, it finds the relationship of the tunnel M and the tunnel N of the upstream router E and the downstream router F is tunnel coverage. Then the router A will delete the tunnel M.

— When the router A establishes the tunnel M of the upstream router B and the downstream router C for a packet forwarding routing, the router A will send "hello" packets to other routers of the tunnel M over a regular time to ask whether or not the packet traffic throughput exceeds the set threshold value of these routers. If all of responses are negative, the router A will delete the tunnel M. If one of responses is positive, the router A will send "hello" packets over a new regular time that is twice as much as the previous regular time.

— When the router A establishes the tunnel M of the upstream router B and the downstream router C for a packet forwarding routing and the tunnel N of the upstream router B and the downstream router C for anther packet forwarding routing, the router A will delete the tunnel N and change its routing table to make these two packet forwarding routings use the same tunnel M to finish packet forwarding.

The tunnel maintenance algorithm mainly accounts for the established tunnels in the ARM mechanism. This section focuses on this algorithm that its input is control packet of the ARM mechanism, and its output is the tunnels maintenance as follows.

```
Tunnel maintenance algorithm description
Input: a control packet
Output: tunnel maintenance
{
    If the regular time of one tunnel is up {
        Router A sends "hello" packets;
        Router A waits for the responses from others;
        If all of response is negative
            Router A delete this tunnel;
    }
    Switch(packet){
    Case 'hello':
        Router A responses this packet with the status of
the packet traffic.
        Break;
    Case 'query':
        Router A responses this packet with the status of
the packet traffic.
        Break;
    Case 'change':
        Router A deletes an old tunnel and establishes a
new tunnel;
```

```
        Router A issues the configurations.
        Break;
    Case 'establish';
        Router A check the relationship between the new
tunnel and others;
    If the relationship is tunnel coverage
        Router A deletes the shorter tunnel;
    Else if the relationship is tunnel accordance
        Router A deletes one tunnel and modifies the con-
figurations;
    Else {
        Router A establishes a new tunnel;
        Router A issues the configurations.
    }
    Break;
    }
    Return SUCCESS;
}
```

The tunnel maintenance algorithm is used to deal with the different packets to establish or delete tunnels. After the tunnel is successfully established, configuration rules should be issued to data plane of the router. Related configuration rules are as follow: enabling interface can make this interface of the router to support tunnel technology; configuring router ID generally specifies IP address as its router ID to ensure its uniqueness; holding time refers to the running time of the tunnel, which ranges from 160 to 65535 seconds; configuring label allows which router to achieve the establishment of packet forwarding routing.

3.3   Threshold Value K

In the processing of applying the ARM mechanism, the threshold value is not only related to two parameters of link utilization q and packet traffic ratio p, but also considers the frequency of changes of the packet forwarding routing that causes the additional overhead. The threshold value K should satisfy the formula 3.1:

$$K = g(p)*h(q)(f \leq M) \tag{1}$$

We think that when the frequency of changes of the packet forwarding routing is lower than the constant M, the ARM mechanism is more effective. Otherwise, the changes of packet forwarding routing maybe cause the changes of the established tunnels that can induce a higher overhead and cause a larger packet loss rate. These two parameters of link utilization q and traffic ratio p are based on the statistic of packet traffics. At the same time, too many tunnels of one router may cause the decline the performance of the router.

However, the threshold value K has important effect on the performance of the ARM mechanism. For example, if it is too small, the cost of system overhead will be enormous that will cause the decline of the packet forwarding speed; otherwise, you can't achieve the purpose of optimizing the performance of network transmission by adopting the ARM mechanism.

4   Correctness Analysis

In this paper, we analyze the correctness of the ARM mechanism from three aspects as follow:

- Theorem 1: The ARM mechanism does not cause any changes of the current network topology.

Proof. The ARM mechanism can not cause any routers to sent packets to change the network topology that it only establishes tunnels to improve the packet forwarding speed and reduce the load pressure of partial nodes based on the network link status. In other words: the network topology is determined by link layer, but the ARM mechanism is applied between link layer and network layer according to OSI model.

- Theorem 2: The ARM mechanism does not cause the state of routing loopback.

Proof. We prove this theorem in terms of the acquisition of network topology and the generation of routing table.

— The acquisition of network topology.

In the ARM mechanism, it does not affect routers to get the region network topology (Theorem 1) and the network topology is determined by other routing protocols (e.g. OSPF, RIP, BGP). For example, every router generates LSA identified by router ID and others are responsible for the transmission of LSA information without any changes of LSA, which makes any router to have accurate access to region network topology. When nodes or links change, LSA is notified to others that will update link state library after the nodes receive LSA information in OSPF protocol.

— The generation of routing table.

In the ARM mechanism, the tunnels are established based on different packet forwarding routings. So the tunnel is consistent with the packet forwarding routings and its direction is also consistent with the direction of the packet forwarding routing.

It is known that the packet forwarding routing does not generate any routing loopback, so the ARM mechanism will not cause the state of routing loopback as same as the packet forwarding routing.

- Theorem3: The time complexity of ARM is a constant.

In the ARM mechanism, when the packet traffic exceeds the set threshold value of one router, the router will send "query" packets to other routers of the same packet forwarding routing as the router. And the length of the packet forwarding routing is a constant, the time complexity of the ARM mechanism is also a constant that is consistent with the length of the packet forwarding routing.

We conclude that the ARM mechanism is an effective way theoretically without the effect of the current network topology.

5   Performance Analysis of ARM

In this paper, we analyze the advantages of the ARM mechanism in terms of theoretical analysis and simulation by the NS2 simulator. For the sake of analysis simplicity, we only take the two transmission mechanism of the ARM mechanism and the traditional packet forwarding into account. On the other hand, we simulate the performance of the ARM mechanism based on the NS2 simulator that proves its existence superiorities to reduce transmission delay and improve the packet forwarding speed.

5.1   Theoretical Analysis

Before prove the advantages of ARM theoretically, we give the following definitions.

f_{skip} : The number of packets forwarded of the ARM mechanism in a certain time L;

f_{router_i} : The number of packets forwarded by router i of traditional packet forwarding in a certain time L;

T_{tunnel} : The time of a tunnel established of the ARM mechanism;

$T_{transfer}$: The transmission time of two transmission mechanisms;

$T_{disposal\_i}$: The processing time of router i of traditional packet forwarding;

$L_{banwidth}$:   The link bandwidth;

L_{packet} :   The packet length;

The delay time of the ARM mechanism is T_{skip} as shown in formula 2, we can find that T_{tunnel} is a constant value, so T_{skip} is determined by link bandwidth based on $f_{skip} \approx L_{banwidth} / L_{packet}$.

$$T_{skip} = T_{tunnel} + f_{skip} * T_{transfer} \qquad (2)$$

The delay time of the traditional packet forwarding is T_{time} as shown in formula 3,we can find that T_{time} is determined by $\sum f_{router\_i} * T_{disposal\_i}$.

$$T_{time} = \sum f_{router\_i} (T_{transfer} + T_{disposal\_i}) \qquad (3)$$

The minus is mainly determined by T_{tunnel} and $\sum f_{router\_i} * T_{disposal\_i}$ between formula 5.1 and formula 5.2. And the T_{tunnel} is a constant value, so $\sum f_{router\_i} * T_{disposal\_i}$ is the most factor that can reflect the advantages of the ARM mechanism. We can find that the processing time of the traditional packet forwarding is the most important factor that if the greater the factor value, the more obvious of the ARM mechanism.

5.2   Simulation by the NS2 Simulator

We test the processing time of different length sizes on the routers that support the IP network and the tunnel technology as shown in Figure 1. From the experimental data, we can find that the processing time of the IP network is longer than the processing time of the tunnel mechanism, and the processing time will increase both in the IP network and in the tunnel mechanism with the increasing of length of the packets.

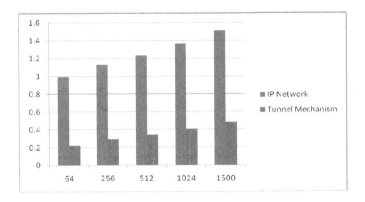

Fig. 1. Processing time with different transmission mechanisms

In this paper, we adopt the NS2 simulator to simulate the ARM mechanism with the assumption that the transmission delay is a constant and the processing delay of all of nodes is the same in test environment. And we configure the processing delay in the NS2 simulator according to the above experimental data of the processing time of the IP network and the tunnel mechanism. More realistic simulation of network environment in the Internet, more advantages highlighted in the terms of optimizing the packet forwarding routing by the ARM mechanism. The diameter of network topology simulated by the NS2 simulator is eight, we test and analyze the experimental results of two different tunnel length (e.g. three and six) as shown in Figure 2. We can clearly find that the longer the tunnel length in the ARM mechanism, the shorter the processing time. At the same time, the shorter packet length, the advantages of the ARM mechanism can be better reflected to improve the packet forwarding speed.

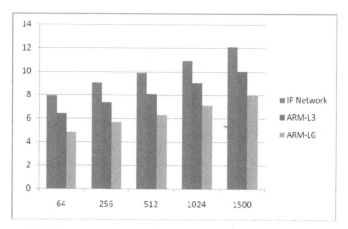

Fig. 2. Processing time with different transmission mechanisms

The ARM mechanism does exist advantages in reducing the packet transmission delay, which can be drawn from the above experimental analysis. In order to further proof the advantages of the mechanism in the terms of reducing the load pressure and optimizing the partial or entire network, we set up a test environment to verify the usefulness of the ARM mechanism by the NS2 simulator as shown in Figure 3. The node C only supports the processing ability of 60Mbps and the link bandwidth of both A-C and B-C is respectively 50Mbps in the network topology. When node A and B try to send 64-bytes packets to node C with the processing ability of 50Mbps, node C will receive 100Mbps packets that exceed the maximum processing capacity supported, which leads to packet loss rate of 40%. And we discuss the advantages of the ARM mechanism in terms of two different scenarios: first, the ARM mechanism only establishes the tunnel of A-C-D-E; on the other hand, it establishes two tunnels of A-C-D-E and B-C-D-F.

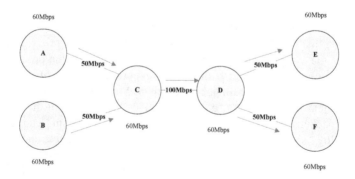

Fig. 3. The network topology of NS2 simulator

The node C gets the packet loss rate of in different scenarios of the NS2 simulator, we can discuss the advantages of the ARM mechanism as shown in Table 1. We can find that the ARM mechanism can effectively reduce the load pressure of partial nodes in the network topology, which is possible to optimize the network performance. Even when we only establish a tunnel, the packet loss rate is very low that fully meet the need of the Internet. At the same time, we can adopt the ARM to meet the requirement of network performance without the upgrade of hardware functions of routers in the Internet. This also provides a reference method for the future optimization of the partial or entire network transmission performance.

Table 1. The statistics of packet loss rate of node C

Scenarios	Packet Loss Rate of Node C
Traditional packet transmission	40%
First scenario of ARM	1.82%
Second scenario of ARM	0%

In addition, the comparative analysis of different transmission mechanisms shows that the ARM mechanism makes it have the characteristics of low forwarding overhead, short transmission delay and flexibility in dynamic forwarding routing. The biggest difference is that the ARM mechanism can quickly establish a tunnel and make adjustments to adapt to the changes of network topology according to the load pressure of network nodes. Meanwhile, the ARM mechanism can alleviate the load pressure of partial nodes (e.g. node C in the Figure 6) and optimize the performance of the current network.

6   Conclusion and Perspective

In this paper, we put forward an ARM mechanism of combination of traditional packet forward with virtual circuits transmission based on combination of the advantages of low forwarding overhead and short transmission delay that are the characteristics of virtual circuit transmission mechanism as represented by MPLS and dynamic forwarding routing in the traditional packet forward mechanism. In the future, we focus on supporting partial reconfiguration and automatic scheduling of dynamic reconfiguration in Internet. The evaluation of transmission mechanism as a power efficient fault injection mechanism for network experimentation is a possibility. Finally, we also plan to evaluate the ARM mechanism that can efficiently allocate abundance bandwidth requirements needed by the most ends.

Acknowledgement. This work is supported by Program for National Basic Research Program of China (973 Program) 'Reconfigurable Network Emulation Testbed for Basic Network Communication'. The National High Technology Research and Development Program of China (2011AA01A103).'Network technology' Aid program for Science and Technology Innovative Research Team in Higher Educational Instituions of Hunan Province and Hunan Provincial Natural Science Foundation of China (11JJ7003).

References

1. Doyle, J., Carroll, J.: Routing TCP/IP, 2nd edn., Beijing, pp. 3–34 (2007)
2. Rosen, E., Viswanathan, A., Callon, R.: Multiprotocol Label Switching Architecture. RFC 3031 (January 2001)
3. He, Z.-M., Wang, H.-B.: The research and Application on the Basis of MPLS technology. Natural Sciences (Quarterly) 2(1), 31–32 (2007)
4. Yang, Z.-Q., He, W.-T., Yang, Y.-X.: Research on MPLS fast reroute multi-failure recovery algorithm. Computer Engineering and Design 33(6), 2133–2140 (2012)
5. Molik, S.U., Srinivasan, S.K., Khan, S.W.: Convergence time Analysis of Open Shortest Path First Protocol in Internet Scale Network. Electronics Letters 48(9), 1188–1190 (2012)
6. Antonio, C., Vincenlo, E., Macro, L., Polverini, et al.: An OSPF –Integrated Routing Strategy for QoS-Aware Engergy Saving in IP Backbone Networks. Network and Service Management 9(3), 254–261 (2013)
7. Goyal, M., Soperi, M., Baccelli, E., Choudlury, et al.: Improving Converygence Speend and Scalahility in OSPF; A Survey. Communication Surveys 14(2), 443–463 (2012)
8. Pan, P., Swallow, G., Atlas, A.: Fast Reroute Extensions to RSCP-TE for LSP Tunnels. RFC4090 (May 2005)
9. Mattews, C.: Prospective Evaluation of Surgical Outcomes of Robot –Assited Sacro colpopexy and sacrocer Vicopexy for the management of Apical pevic Support Defects. Southern Medical Journal 105(5), 271–278 (2012)
10. Ke, Y.: MPLS Traffic Engineering Auto Fast Reroute Arithmetic & Realization (2007)
11. Talbot, B., Sherwood, T., Lin, B.: IP caching for terabit speed routers. In: Proc. of GLOBECOM 1999, pp. 1565–1569. IEEE, Piscataway (1999)

Access-Load-Aware Dynamic Data Balancing
for Cloud Storage Service

Haopeng Chen, Zhenhua Wang, and Yunmeng Ban

School of Software, Shanghai Jiao Tong University
Shanghai, P.R. China
chen-hp@sjtu.edu.cn, aspiration@foxmail.com,
banyunmeng@sjtu.edu.cn

Abstract. Cloud storage is the typical way for storing massive data in Big Data Era. Dynamic data balancing is important for cloud storage since it aims to improve the utilization of computing resource and the performance of data process. However, storage-load-aware data balancing, adopted by almost all existing cloud storage services and systems, is far less effective than access-load-aware one for typical cloud applications with hotspots of data. This paper focuses on the latter and puts forward a mechanism of dynamic data balancing for optimization of resource utilization. The mechanism detects the overloaded and underloaded physical nodes and virtual nodes by monitoring their utilization of resource. Then, it dynamically balances the access load among the nodes by pair, merge, mark, scale up and scale down operations. This mechanism is useful for the applications with hotspots in data. So it is a complementation of storage-load-aware data balancing. The results of experiments on Swift demonstrated the effectiveness of this mechanism.

Keywords: access-load-aware, cloud storage service, data balancing, resource utilization, VM migration.

1 Introduction

With high scalability and reliability, cloud storage has become the dominant technology for both of enterprises and individuals to store their massive structured and unstructured data. According to the report of IDC, the unstructured data has a growth curve substantially greater than that of structured data and its capacity will be shipped to 80EB of storage[1]. To satisfy the growing demand for cloud storage, many providers have offered their public cloud storage services, including Amazon S3[2], Google Cloud Storage[3], Rackspace Cloud Files[4], and so on. Several open source frameworks are also available for building private cloud storage, such as Openstack Swift[5], Eucalyptus Walrus[6] and Nimbu Cumulus[7]. Certainly, we also can store the massive unstructured data with NoSQL database systems, such as Amazon Dynamo[8], Google BigTable[9] and MongoDB[10].

With the diversity of cloud storage services, consumers have to consider over that what an ideal storage service for massive data should be. Firstly, a cloud storage

M. Pathan, G. Wei, and G. Fortino (Eds.): IDCS 2013, LNCS 8223, pp. 307–320, 2013.

service should be high scalable in order to make the extension of its capacity easy and efficient. As a result, it seems more reasonable to build a distributed storage environment with a cluster of storage resources. For example, Google File System (GFS), a scalable distributed file system for large distributed data-intensive applications[11], has been the infrastructure of many cloud storage services. The high scalability means the extension of capacity can be accomplished by simply adding more resources into the storage cluster.

Secondly, a cloud storage service should be able to balance the workload among its storage nodes in order to improve its access performance. For example, in MongoDB[10], the data are grouped into chunks by key ranges, and the chunks are stored on physical nodes, named as shard servers. By specifying the upper bound of the size of a single chunk and the maximal acceptable difference of the numbers of chunks between any two shard servers, it ensures that all the shard servers hold roughly same amount of data. The other example, Swift[5], also provides a hashing mechanism to distribute the data onto its storage nodes. With such a mechanism and a reasonable key generating algorithm, the data can be evenly distributed.

However, we can find that the existing balancing mechanisms are all storage-load-aware. From the view of access performance, unless all the data are accessed with the same possibilities, that is there is not hotspots in data, the effectiveness of storage-load-aware balancing is hardly acceptable. For example, in a news website, the latest news are hotspots since they are accessed much more frequently than other news. In this scenario, the workload of the physical node the latest news stored on is much heavier than other ones though each of these nodes holds almost same amount of data. It is obvious that the heavier the workload of a node is, the lower its performance is. Thus, with a storage-load-aware balancing, the performance of physical nodes are possibly quite different with each other, which is less meaningful for the applications with hotspots in data. Actually, for such applications, access-load-aware data balancing is much more suitable than the storage-load-aware one.

The aim of access-load-aware data balancing is to control the resource utilization of all the physical nodes into a specific range in order to make the performance of data access on each virtual node acceptable. This paper puts forward such a mechanism for optimization of resource utilization. With access-load-aware data balancing, the amount of data stored in a storage node is not forced to be roughly same as other nodes. On the contrary, a node can store much less or more data than other nodes. Moreover, since the storage nodes are virtual nodes hosted on physical nodes, they will be dynamically migrated among physical nodes to ensure the performance of data access.

The remainder of this paper is structured as follows. Section 2 briefly summaries the related works; Section 3 describes a mechanism of access-load-aware data balancing; Section 4 gives the results of experiment performed on Swift to demonstrate the effectiveness of our mechanism; and conclusion is in Section 5.

2   Related Work

Actually, many storage tools have provided the storage-load-aware data balancing. For example, Dynamo supports to evenly distribute the data to all nodes with an improved consistent-hash algorithm[8]; BigTable organizes the nodes into a server farm in which the master server monitors the slave servers and performs the data migration[9]; MongoDB provides auto-sharding to dynamically balance the storage-load by data migration[10]; Swift provides a data balancing based on the key range[5]. However, as discussed in section 1, all the existing data balancing are storage load oriented. It is clear that such data balancing is not suitable for the applications with hotspots in data. So many researchers focus on this area.

The research on data balancing concentrates on three aspects. The first one is the discovery of workload exception, since it is the basis of data balancing. In [12], the nodes of a cluster are grouped into small sets and the central nodes of each set are in charge of monitoring other nodes of its set. This way improves the performance of monitoring, but it doesn't precisely locate the hotspots in data. In [13], for each chunk in MongoDB, its access-load is evaluated by the numbers of various operations on it. However, the weights of different operations are assigned by experience which makes them too subjective. In [14], the exceptions of workload can be found on the base on predicted access load. Predicted workload is much better than real-time access load for data balancing, but it needs much historical records to guarantee the precision of prediction, which makes the monitoring costly. In summary, we need an effective way to monitor the real-time access load and find the exceptions of workload.

The second aspect is the algorithm of workload balancing. In [15], the files are divided into zones according to the foreseen workload in order to balance the access load. This way is a static one since the access load is foreseen and the location of a file will not be changed once it has been stored into a zone. In [16], the data is dynamically re-partitioned to facilitate rapid data balancing by a graph theoretic way. It is noticeable that since a re-partition operations is independent of others, it is time costly in some situations because it is possible that too much data needs to be migrated in a re-partition operation. In [17], an automated control for elastic storage is put forward to improve the efficiency of data balancing. The amount and the distance between the source and target nodes of data to be migrated are not taken account into this mechanism. Actually, we need an algorithm to reduce the cost of data balancing, particularly the cost of data migration, since it has negative impact on the data balancing.

The third aspect is the method of data migration. In [18], a cost-aware method of data migration is designed to minimize the interference between virtual machines. But the amount of data to be migrated is not reduced in the method. In [19] and [20], a location-aware method is proposed to save power when performing data migration in large-scale datacenters. Similarly, the amount of data to be migrated is not optimized in this method. Data migration is a bandwidth-intensive task, so it is costly to balance storage load by data migration. Actually, we need to balance the access load but not storage load. Thus, we can realize this aim to migration virtual machines of process nodes but not storage nodes.

In summary, access-load-aware data balancing is necessary for applications with hotspots in data, but there is not a comprehensive solution has been proposed. Actually, we proposed an approach to dynamic workload balancing in [21], which periodically checks the overloaded and underloaded nodes and then the dynamically balances the access load by VM migration. We also improved this approach in [22] by optimizing the VM migration. However, both the approaches we proposed are potentially costly because data migration is inevitable in them. So this paper tries to put forward a feasible solution to improve the performance of data balancing by reducing its cost.

3   A Mechanism of Access-Load-Aware Data Balancing

In this section, we will give a mechanism of access-load-aware data balancing, including data storage model, resource management flow and algorithms.

3.1   Data Storage Model

In order to improve the access performance, the data are divided into subsets according to some rules, such as key range and consistent hashing. Each of such subsets is stored in a "storage node" and managed by a dedicated "process node" which is running on a dedicated VM (virtual machine). The storage nodes are mapped onto physical nodes by some way, such as hashing. Consequently, there are two maps in a storage service: the first one maps the keys to process nodes, the second one maps the process nodes to physical nodes. It is noticeable that both of them are theoretically dynamic mappings, which means a subset can be divided into more subsets or merged with other subsets and a process node can be migrated among physical nodes. The two maps is stored in proxy node, which is the access entrance of storage service and in charge of routing the requests to storage nodes. Proxy node is also running in VM and multiple proxy nodes can be built as a cluster to support large-scale concurrent clients. Such an architecture is shown in Fig.1.

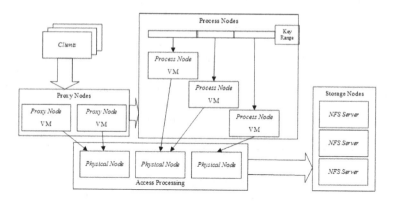

Fig. 1. Architecture of cloud storage service

In Fig.1, each process node processes the access requests to the data it manages. If there are hotspots on a process node, this node will be an overloaded node, and it possibly needs to be migrate to other physical node with more idle resources. If the data are directly stored in process nodes, however, such migration is quite costly since it not only needs to migrate the VM, but also needs to transfer the data, which makes the data balancing non-effective for performance improvement.

Actually, since the data are stored as multiple replicas in cloud storage service, the data can be stored with NFS (Network File System) to avoid the transfer of a large amount of data. With NFS, a process node accesses the NFS servers to fetch and cache the data it manages. When the process node needs to be migrated, only the VM but not the cached data is migrated. After a process node migrated, it needs to fetch the data it manages from the NFS server again, but the fetch is on-demand, so the batch data transfer is not necessary. With such a storage model, the migration of VMs will not be costly any longer and then the data balancing can be accomplished by it.

3.2 Resource Management Flow

In an access load balanced system, the utilization of computing resources of a physical node is roughly same to that of any other physical node. Similarly, the resource utilization of a process node (virtual node) is also roughly equal to that of any other storage node. For a physical node or a process node, if the utilization of any type of resource is too high or too low, we consider it is an overloaded or underloaded node. So we periodically monitor the real-time resource utilization of physical nodes and process nodes and check which nodes are overloaded or underloaded according to the predefined thresholds (upper bounds and lower bounds of resource utilization).

For an overloaded physical node, we should search a paired physical node with more spare resource and choose some process nodes to be migrated to the paired node. After the paired operation, either the overloaded physical node or the paired one is normal. If there is no physical node can be paired, a new physical node is added into the cluster and the process nodes on overloaded physical node can be migrated to it by pair operation.

For an underloaded physical node, we don't process it immediately because it is possible that an overloaded physical node will pair with it later. So we setup a counter, only when it has been underloaded for a specified period, which means there is no overloaded nodes in system, it will search other underloaded node and merge with it. Merging means the physical node with lower resource utilization migrates all the process nodes hosted on it to the physical node with higher resource utilization. After merge operation, the physical node from which the process nodes are migrated out of can be setup as idle.

For an overloaded process node, we allocation more spare resource of its host physical node to it, that is to scale up the process node. If there is no enough spare resource can be allocated to it, we mark the physical node as an overloaded node. Then, the physical node will release more resource by pair operation in order to real-locate them to the overloaded process node.

For an underloaded process node, we simply scale down it by releasing part of its allocated resource. When the allocated resource of a process node is scaled down to the specified lower bound, the scaling down is not executed anymore.

The Fig.2 (a) and (b) respectively shows the resource management flow of physical nodes and process nodes. They are periodically executed and independent with each other.

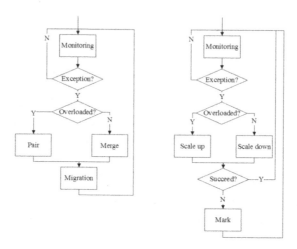

Fig. 2. Resource management flow of (a) physical nodes & (b) process nodes

3.3   Resource Management Algorithms

In the resource management flow, the core is the algorithms for detecting the overloaded and underloaded nodes, finding pair node and merging underloaded nodes.
To describe the algorithms, we define the necessary parameters in Table 1.

Table 1. Parameters for Resource Management

Parameters	Description
U_p	The monitored utilization vector of node p
L_p	The load index of node p
U_{cu}	The upper bound of utilization of CPU
U_{mu}	The upper bound of utilization of memory
U_{bu}	The upper bound of utilization of bandwidth
U_{cl}	The lower bound of utilization of CPU
U_{ml}	The lower bound of utilization of memory
U_{bl}	The lower bound of utilization of memory
w_c	The weight of utilization of CPU
w_m	The weight of utilization of memory
w_b	The weight of utilization of bandwidth
t	The threshold of underloaded utilization of resource
I_m	The interval between two successive monitoring operation
I_r	The interval between two successive exception detection

We used the resource utilization to evaluate the access load of physical nodes and process nodes. Thus, access load balancing is accomplished by controlling the resource utilization into an acceptable range. So we predefine the upper bound and lower bound of the utilization of each type of resources, including CPU, memory and bandwidth. Then we compare the monitored utilization with their upper bounds and lower bounds to detect the overloaded and underloaded nodes.

Actually, the resource utilization of a node p is a vector, since each node has many types of resource, such as CPU, memory, bandwidth, disk and so on. For simplification, we only focus the former three types of resource. So we denote the monitored resource utilization of node p as U_p:

$$U_p = <U_{cp}, U_{mp}, U_{bp}> \tag{1}$$

The utilization is monitored at the interval of I_m. But it is noticeable that the resource utilization is frequently changed in practice. For smoothing the utilization, U_p is the average value of the raw data monitored during I_r.

If any component of U_p is greater than the upper bound of corresponding utilization of resource, such as U_{cp} is greater than U_{cu}, we consider node p is overloaded. However, the process of determining a node whether is underloaded is a little more complex. We calculate the weighted average value of all components of Up as load index L_p, as shown in (2). If L_p is less than t, a predefined threshold, then we consider node p is underloaded. This design makes the responses to overloaded nodes quite rapid and the ones to underloaded nodes prudent. After all, it is the overloaded nodes but not underloaded nodes that are the bottleneck of access performance.

$$L_p = w_c*U_{cp} + w_m*U_{mp} + w_b*U_{bp} \tag{2}$$

The algorithm for determining whether a node is overloaded or underloaded is named as "Exception Detection" shown in Table 2. This algorithm is executed periodically, the interval of between two successive exception detection is I_r, a configurable parameter.

Table 2. Algorithm for Exception Detection

Algorithm: Exception Detection
Input: U_p, L_p
Output: result:enum<NORMAL, OVERLOADED, UNDERLOADED>
1.   **foreach** U_{ip} **in** U_p ($i \in \{c, m, b\}$)
2.   **if** $U_{ip} > U_{iu}$ **then**
3.   result = OVERLOADED
4.   **else if** $L_p < t$
5.   result = UNDERLOADED
6.   **else** result = NORMAL
7.   **endif**
8.   **endif**
9.   **endfor**
10.   **return** result

For the overloaded and underloaded process nodes, we try to scale up and down them. To avoid generating resource fragments, we scale up or down the process nodes by adding or removing certain number of unit resource. The grain of unit resource is dependent on the configuration of physical nodes. For example, a 4-core physical node can define a quarter of its resource as a unit. Suppose an overloaded process node has been allocated with N_p units of resource, we will scale up it by adding N_a units of resource:

$$N_a = \lceil N_p * Max\left(\frac{U_{ip} - U_{iu}}{U_{iu}}\right) \rceil, \ where \ i = c,m,p \tag{3}$$

Here, the maximum of the difference between the monitored utilization and the upper bound of utilization of each type of resource reflects the extent of overloaded. So we use it to determine how many units should be added to the overloaded process node. If the physical node has no enough idle resource to be allocated to the process node, it will be marked as an overloaded physical node.

Similarly, for an underloaded node, we will scale down it by removing N_r units of resource:

$$N_r = \lfloor N_p * \frac{t - L_p}{t} \rfloor \tag{4}$$

Here, the difference between L_p and t denotes the extent of underloaded, which determines how many units should be removed from the underloaded process node. When N_p is 1, even the process node is underloaded, it will not be scaled down yet, since we wouldn't want the resource fragments. However, it is still possible that there are resource fragments inside units if the grain of unit is coarse. Consequently, the grain of unit should be defined carefully.

If a physical node is marked as an overloaded one, it will execute pair operation to find a suitable peer and migrate some process node(s) into it. In the pair operation, the first task is to determine which process nodes should be migrated out. The aim is to ensure that each component of U_p of the physical node is below its upper bound and the number of process nodes to be migrated is minimized in order to improve the efficiency of migration. For the U_{ip} of physical node in (3), we sort the process nodes by their own U_{ip} in ascending order, and choose the one(s) whose U_{ip} or sum of U_{ip} is closest to and greater than the difference between U_{ip} and U_{ic} of the physical node as the target(s) to be migrated.

The second task of pair operation is to find a physical node which can host all the targets chosen in first task and no component of its U_p will be beyond U_{ic} of physical node after migration. Although it possibly exists multiple candidate peers among a large cluster, the pair operation stops when it finds a suitable peer so that its efficiency is guaranteed. If there is no candidate peer is found, a new physical node will be introduced into the cluster for hosting the target process nodes. The algorithm of pair operation is shown in Table 3.

Table 3. Algorithm of Pair Operation

Algorithm: Pair Operation

Input:	P_o: an overloaded physical node
Output:	targets: set of process nodes, peer: paired physical node

1.	targets = Ø
2.	peer = null
3.	max_different = 0
4.	max_comp = null
5.	
6.	**foreach** U_{ip} **in** U_p of P_o
7.	**if** (U_{ip} - U_{iu}) > max_different **then**
8.	max_different = U_{ip} - U_{iu}
9.	max_comp = U_{ip}
10.	**endfor**
11.	
12.	sort(V, max_comp)
13.	// sort all the process nodes V hosted on P_o
14.	// by max_comp in ascending order
15.	
16.	**if** max(U_{ip} of p **in** V) > max_different
17.	**foreach** p_i **in** V
18.	**if** U_{ip} > max_different
19.	targets ←p_i
20.	**break**
21.	**endif**
22.	**endfor**
23.	**else**
24.	**foreach** p_i **in** V // traverse V in reverse order
25.	targets ←p_i
26.	**if** sum(U_{ip} of p **in** targets) > max_different)
27.	**break**
28.	**endif**
29.	**endfor**
30.	**endif**
31.	
32.	**foreach** p_i **in** C
33.	// here, C is the set of all available physical nodes
34.	**if** (U_{ip} + sum(U_{ip} of p **in** targets)) < U_{iu}
35.	peer = p_i
36.	**break**
37.	**endif**
38.	**endfor**
39.	**if** (peer = null)
40.	peer = new PhysicalNode()
41.	**endif**
42.	
43.	To migrate **targets** from P_o to **peer**
44.	
45.	**return** targets and peer

If a physical node is marked as an underloaded one, it will not be merged with other nodes immediately. Instead, it will wait for a specified period to give the overloaded nodes a chance to pair with it. If the waiting period is expired, which means there is no overloaded node at present, an underloaded node will merge with another underloaded one. For the pair of underloaded nodes, the one with lighter load will migrate all of its hosted process nodes to the one with heavier load so that the migration can be efficiently accomplished. After merging, one node is passivated and the other one is remained. Similar to pair operation, no component of U_p of the remained node is beyond U_{ic} of physical node after merging. As a result, merge operation will use the same method as pair operation to find the paired peer.

If an underloaded node cannot find a paired underloaded peer, which means that it is the only underloaded node in the whole system, it will remain underloaded status and no process node needs to be migrated.

The access-load-aware dynamic data balancing we proposed is implemented by the combination of all the above algorithms.

4   Experiments

4.1   Setup and Configuration

We built an experimental environment with 8 physical machines in which 6 machines are used to build a Swift system and 2 machines are setup as clients to generate access load. In the 6 machines of Swift system, 2 of them are setup as an NFS to store the data and support the VM migration, while 4 of them are setup as process servers to host virtual nodes.

On the process servers, we run 17 XenServer[23] VMs to host virtual nodes of Swift, including 2 proxy nodes and 15 process nodes. The locations of these virtual nodes of Swift are not fixed, since they could be migrated among physical nodes. On the client machines, we run 10 XenServer VMs to simulate the customers of Swift and generate access load. All the VMs are installed Ubuntu Server 12.04 as operating systems.

All the machines of Swift are interconnected through LAN, and the client machines access the Swift system through a switch. The configuration of these machines are listed in Table 4.

Each of the VMs is initially provisioned with 1 core, 512MB memory and 25GB disk. All the VMs of Swift has their own preconfigured IPs while the VMs running on client machines are assigned IPs dynamically.

Table 4. Configuration of Physical Machines

Category	Instances	CPU	Memory(GB)	Disk(GB)
Process Server	XenServer1	Intel i5 3.30G Hz	4	500
	XenServer2			
	XenServer3			
	XenServer4			
NFS Server	NFS1	Intel i3 3.30G Hz	4	500
	NFS2			
Client	Client1	Intel i3 3.30G Hz	4	500
	Client2			

Considering all the data and their replicas are stored in NFS servers and each process node can cache at most 25GB data, we generated about 300GB data and stored them into the Swift system. Then, Pylot[24], a free open source tool for testing performance and scalability of web services, is used to generate access load through the cluster of the 10 VMs hosted on client machines.

To simulate the hotspot, Pylot randomly selected several small sets of the data and generated high access load to these sets. In the testing scripts, the maximum of the number of concurrent clients is 100, the ramp up time, that is the time to generate the maximal number of concurrent clients, is 1200 seconds, the interval between two successive access requests sent by the same client is 0 second, that is the agents continuously send requests without any interval, and the duration of testing with the maximal number of concurrent clients is 6000 seconds.

Table 5 shows the configuration of various parameters for resource management of physical machines and VMs used in the experiments.

In Table 5, we assigned rather higher weight to the utilization of memory because we found that in general the data access in Swift is a memory-intensive operation. Meanwhile, we set the upper bound of the utilization of CPU lower than other ones since it has a more significant impact on the access performance. In other implementation of cloud storage services, this configuration is probably not so reasonable and the parameters can be reconfigured with suitable values.

Table 5. Configuration of Parameters for Resource Management of Physical Machine and VM

Parameters		Values for Physical Machine	Values for VM
	U_{cu}	0.6	0.7
	U_{mu}	0.95	0.85
	U_{bu}	0.95	0.95
U_{cl},	U_{ml} & U_{bl}	0.3	0.3
	w_c	0.2	0.2
	w_m	0.7	0.6
	w_b	0.1	0.3
	t	0.7	0.8
	I_m	5 seconds	1 mins
	I_r	15 seconds	5 mins

4.2   Result and Analysis

The result we recorded when the experiment was performed including the following two parts: the first part recorded the utilization of CPU, memory and bandwidth of physical machines and the number of VMs hosted in each physical machines during the experiment, as shown in Fig.3; the second part recorded the utilization of CPU and memory and the allocated memory of all 15 VMs of storage nodes during the experiment.

In Fig.3, we can find that the utilization of CPU, memory and bandwidth of all the 4 physical nodes has never been out of the range specified by the upper bound and lower bound. The sum of the numbers of VMs running on the 4 physical nodes is always 15.

For XenServer1, there are 2 VMs running on it at the beginning and its resource utilization is lower than that of other nodes, so some VMs are migrated from other nodes to it later. After migration, the VM needs to rebuild its cache by reading the data from NFS which results in the increase of utilization of bandwidth. After the number of VMs reaches to 5, the resource utilization is stable, so there is not any more VM migration occurs on XenServer1.

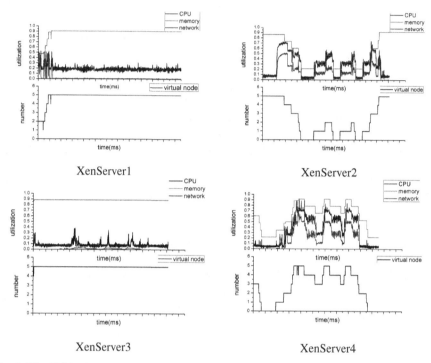

XenServer1   XenServer2

XenServer3   XenServer4

Fig. 3. The Utilization of CPU, memory and network and the numbers of VMs of 4 storage servers

For XenServer2, when the utilization of CPU reaches to the upper bound U_{mu}, the VM migration is executed repeatedly until it becomes lower than U_{mu}. When the utilization of memory is lower than the lower bound U_{mc}, the VM migration is executed again in order to empty the XenServer2 and then passivate it as idle status. When some VM needs to be migrated to an idle server, XenServer2 is activated and hosts the VM.

For XenServer3, its utilization of CPU, memory and bandwidth is rather stable and in the acceptable ranges. Moreover, the utilization of memory is always too high to host any new VM. So the number of VMs running on XenServer3 is unchanged.

The situation of XenServer4 is quite same than XenServer2: VMs are frequently migrated into and out of XenServer4 to ensure the resource utilization is in the acceptable ranges.

We can find that the utilization of CPU and memory of all the 15 VMs has never been out of the range specified by the upper bound and lower bound either. If the utilization of memory of any VM reaches to the upper bound U_{mu}, the VM will be provisioned with more memory. There are 5 VMs got more memory during the experiment.

The Fig.4 shows the number of active physical nodes and the average CPU utilization of all the active physical nodes. We can find that the utilization of CPU is dynamically controlled in an acceptable range to maintain the balance of access load and the number of physical nodes is always the minimum required to guarantee the access performance.

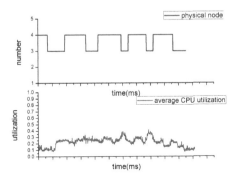

Fig. 4. The number of active physical nodes and the average CPU utilization of all the active physical nodes

In summary, no matter the physical nodes or VMs, their utilization of CPU, memory and bandwidth is always in acceptable ranges, which demonstrates that the access load is indeed dynamically balanced.

5   Conclusion

Aiming to the typical cloud applications with hotspots inside their massive data, we put forward a mechanism of dynamic data balancing by which the access load but not storage load is balanced and therefore the resource utilization is optimized and the performance of accessing data is improved. The mechanism detects the overloaded and underloaded physical nodes and virtual nodes by monitoring their utilization of resource. Then, it dynamically balances the access load among the nodes by pair, merge, mark, scale up and scale down operations. This mechanism is a complementation of storage-load-aware data balancing. At present, our mechanism is only applied in Swift. Although Swift is a popular object storage system widely adopted by many cloud storage services, there are many other storage systems in use. In future, we will apply the mechanism onto other systems to demonstrate its ubiquitous effectiveness.

References

1. Structured vs. Unstructured Data, http://www.robertprimmer.com/blog/structured-vs-unstructured.html
2. Amazon, Amazon S3, http://aws.amazon.com/s3
3. Google Cloud Storage, http://www.google.com/enterprise/cloud

4. Cloud Files, Cloud CDN, and Unlimited Online Storage, http://www.rackspace.com/cloud/public/files/
5. Openstack, http://www.openstack.org
6. Eucalyptus, http://www.eucalyptus.com
7. Nimbus, http://www.nimbusproject.org
8. DeCanadia, G., Hastorun, D., Jampani, M., et al.: Dynamo: Amazon's Highly Available Key-value Store. In: 21st ACM SIGOPS Symposium on Operating Systems Principles, pp. 205–220. ACM Press, New York (2007)
9. Chang, F., Dean, J., Ghemawat, S., et al.: Bigtable: A Distributed Storage System for Structured Data. J. ACM Transaction on Comput. Syst. 26, 1–26 (2008)
10. MongoDB, http://www.mongodb.org/
11. Ghemawat, S., Gobioff, H., Leung, S.: The Google File System. In: 19th ACM SIGOPS Symposium on Operating Systems Principles, pp. 29–43. ACM Press, New York (2003)
12. Deng, Y., Lau, R.: Heat Diffusion Based Dynamic Load Balancing for Distributed Virtual Environments. In: 17th ACM Symposium on Virtual Reality Software and Technology, pp. 203–210. ACM Press, New York (2010)
13. Liu, Y., Wan, Y., Jin, Y.: Research on The Improvement of MongoDB Auto-Sharding in Cloud Environment. In: 7th International Conference on Computer Science & Education, Melbourne, VIC, Australia, pp. 851–854 (2012)
14. Pearce, O., Gambliny, T., Supinskiy, B., et al.: Quantifying the Effectiveness of Load Balance Algorithms. In: 26th ACM International Conference on Supercomputing, pp. 185–194. ACM Press, New York (2012)
15. Zhu, Y., Yu, Y., Wang, W., et al.: A Balanced Allocation Strategy for File Assignment in Parallel I/O Systems. In: 5th IEEE International Conference on Networking, Architecture and Storage, pp. 257–266. IEEE Press, New York (2010)
16. Bui, T.N., Deng, X., Zrncic, C.M.: An Improved Ant-Based Algorithm for the Degree-Constrained Minimum Spanning Tree Problem. J. IEEE Transactions on Evolutionary Computation 16, 266–278 (2012)
17. Lim, H.C., Babu, S., Chase, J.S.: Automated control for elastic storage. In: 7th International Conference on Autonomic Computing, Washington, DC, USA, pp. 1–10 (2010)
18. Qin, X., Zhang, W., Wang, W., et al.: Towards a Cost-Aware Data Migration Approach for Key-Value Stores. In: 2012 IEEE International Conference on Cluster Computing, pp. 551–556. IEEE Press, New York (2012)
19. Liu, Z., Lin, M., Wierman, A., et al.: Greening Geographical Load Balancing. In: Liu, Z., Lin, M., Wierman, A., et al. (eds.) 2011 ACM SIGMETRICS Joint International Conference on Measurement and Modeling of Computer Systems, pp. 233–244. ACM Press, New York (2011)
20. Lin, M., Wierman, A., Andrew, L.L.H., et al.: Dynamic Right-sizing for Power-proportional Data Centers. In: 2011 IEEE INFOCOM, pp. 1098–1106. IEEE Press, New York (2011)
21. Zhang, C., Chen, H., Gao, S.: ALARM: Autonomic Load-Aware Resource Management for P2P Key-value Stores in Cloud. In: 9th IEEE International Conference on Dependable, Autonomic and Secure Computing, pp. 404–410. IEEE Press, New York (2011)
22. Ban, Y., Chen, H., Wang, Z.: EALARM: An Enhanced Autonomic Load-Aware Resource Management. In: 7th IEEE International Symposium on Service-Oriented System Engineering, pp. 150–155. IEEE Press, New York (2013)
23. XenServer, http://www.citrix.com/products/xenserver/resources-and-support.html
24. Pylot, http://www.pylot.org/

Two MRJs for Multi-way Theta-Join in MapReduce

Ke Yan and Hong Zhu

School of Computer Science and Technology, Huazhong University of Science and Technology,
Wuhan, China
{gina2009yan,whzhuhong}@gmail.com

Abstract. MapReduce is the most popular platform used in cloud computing for large-scale data processing. Generally, data processing involves multi-way Theta-joins join operations. Although multi-way Theta-joins could be processed in MapReduce by using a sequence of MRJs (MapReduce Jobs), it would lead to high cost of I/O due to the storage of intermediate results between two sequential MRJs. Thus, we focus on the performance improvement of multi-way Theta-joins by reducing the number of MRJs. In this paper, a multi-way Theta-join is processed in only two MRJs, since it is decomposed into a non-Equi-join and a multi-way Equi-join and each join operation is processed in one MRJ. Our experiments show the good performance of our method.

Keywords: Cloud Computing, MapReduce, Equi-join, Theta-join.

1   Introduction

Efficient large-scale data processing becomes one of the most important challenges. MapReduce is a prevalent programming model for processing large-scale data in cloud computing [1]. It enables to process a massive volume of data in parallel with many low-end computing nodes.

Multi-way Theta-join operations are commonly involved in data analytical queries. A Theta-join means the join condition is defined as a binary function $\theta \in \{=, \neq, <, >, \leq, \geq\}$. Although MapReduce could naturally support the implementation of Equi-join operations [3, 12], which joined datasets with a key-equality condition, and could obtain high performance, it has inherent limitations on multi-way Theta-join.

There are three kinds of multi-way Theta-join: star pattern, chain pattern and hybrid pattern. It is significant for MapReduce to support all kinds of multi-way Theta-join. A straightforward way to implement a multi-way Theta-join is using a sequence of several MRJs (MapReduce jobs). Each MRJ completes a single Theta-join using 1-Bucket-Theta[2]. Each MRJ has to read the results from the previous MRJ and write its own results into a distributed file system (e.g. DFS). That is, n-1 MRJs are needed, which leads to n-1 disk I/O operations, for a multi-way Theta-join with n datasets. The high costs of I/O degrade the performance of multi-way Theta-join. Additionally, because a NameNode is in charge of task scheduling in MapReduce framework, it has to maintain various meta-information for the intermediate results of each MRJ. More

M. Pathan, G. Wei, and G. Fortino (Eds.): IDCS 2013, LNCS 8223, pp. 321–332, 2013.

MRJs lead to more workload for NameNode. Thus, the sequence of several MRJs introduces heavy workload to the NameNode, which impact the performance of multi-way Theta-join as well.

Recently, there are a few works focused on multi-way Theta-join in MapReduce framework. In literature [8], a chain-typed Theta-join is processed in one MRJ using Hilbert curve. However, the datasets in the chain-typed Theta-join need to be the same scale, since Hilbert curve is suitable for hypercube. The method proposed in literature [9] only supports star-typed Theta-join operations.

In this paper, we propose a two-MRJ method to implement all kinds of multi-way Theta-join in MapReduce by using two MRJs. In this method, a multi-way Theta-join is decomposed into non-Equi-joins and a multi-way Equi-join. Each join is implemented in one MRJ. We conduct extensive experiments to evaluate the performance of two-MRJ method. By reducing the number of MRJs, the cost of I/O is reduced. The results show the better performance of two-MRJ method than a sequence of several MRJs.

2   Preliminaries and Related Works

2.1   Equi-Join in MapReduce

Several single Equi-join algorithms [3, 4, 5, 6] are proposed for MapReduce, since the key-value based programming model implies a natural implementation of single Equi-join by making the join attribute (or join key, abbreviated as JK) as the key and other attributes (which are called non-JK) as the value.

Multi-way Equi-join operator is an Equi-join operation on more than two datasets. Intuitively, multi-way Equi-join operations could be processed via a sequence of MRJs and each MRJ completes a single Equi-join. However, it is not desirable due to the storing of the intermediate results between two consecutive jobs. Thus, there are some methods [11, 12, 13] proposed to address this challenge. Especially in [12], a multi-way Equi-join operation is processed using only one MRJ. Different from single Equi-join, records are shuffled from the mappers to the reducers in a one-to-many manner, instead of in a one-to-one manner.

In the instance of a multi-way Equi-join: $R(A, B) \bowtie S(B, C) \bowtie T(C, D)$, B and C are JKs. Supposing k reducers are used to process the multi-way Equi-join, a hash function can be customized to map values of B and C into m and n buckets respectively. Notice that k=m*n. For the one-to-many shuffle manner, each tuple (b_i, c_i) in S is shuffled to the reducer numbered $(h(b_i), h(c_i))$; each tuple (a_i, b_i) in R is shuffled to all the reducers numbered $(h(b_i), x)$, where $1 \leq x \leq n$; and each tuple (c_i, d_i) in T is shuffled to all the reducers numbered $(x, h(c_i))$, where $1 \leq x \leq m$.

In some situations, it is more efficient to implement a multi-way join as a single MRJ than as a cascade of 2-way joins, due to avoiding I/O cost of massive intermediate results.

2.2   Single Theta-Join in MapReduce

Different from Equi-join, Theta-join could not be answered by using JK as the key. Considering a single Theta-join: $R(A, B) \bowtie_{R.B>S.B} S(B, C)$, B cannot be used as key, because each tuple (a, b) in R has to be joined not only with the tuples (b, c) in S, but also all tuples (b_x, c_x) in S, where $b_x<b$. Thus, it is inherently difficult for MapReduce to implement Theta-join.

A method, called 1-bucket-theta [2], is used to evaluate a single Theta-join query in one MRJ. Essentially, it partitions the cross-product results space with rectangle regions of bounded size, which guarantees the output correctness and the workload balance among reducers. Fig. 1 illustrates the partition of cross-product.

Two dataset that will be joined have r and s records respectively. The cross-product has r*s records. k reducers are used to process the Theta-join. Thus, the cross-product is partitioned to k squares. The side length of the square is:

$$\sqrt{r \times s/k}. \tag{1}$$

One square corresponds to a reducer. Thus, the records included in the square are shuffled to the corresponding reducer. Once a reducer received the results from mappers, it joins the records with the join condition. In Fig. 1, the reducer numbered 1 receives 6 records in all, three from R and three from S. The reducer joins these records and filter the joined records using the condition of R.B<S.B.

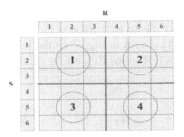

Fig. 1. 1-bucket-theta method

2.3   Multi-way Theta-Join Using a Sequence of MRJs

Multi-way Theta-join is an essential operation in data analytic workload. It is the Theta-join operated on more than 2 datasets and could be processed in a sequence of several MRJs. However, each join has to write the intermediate results into DFS. Thus, this approach not only incurs very high I/O cost, but also introduces heavy workload to the NameNode.

For example, a 3-way Theta-join $R(A, B) \bowtie_{\theta_1} S(B, C) \bowtie_{\theta_2} T(C, D)$ includes 3 datasets and two join conditions. It could be implemented in two MRJs: the first MRJ is used to process the single Theta-join $R(A, B) \bowtie_{\theta_1} S(B, C)$; results of the first MRJ are joined with T (C, D) in the second MRJ. The first MRJ has to write its results into DFS and the second MRJ reads the results from DFS, which leads to high cost of I/O and heavy workload of NameNode.

Recently, some works focus on the multi-way Theta-join. However, there are some limitations on these works. The method proposed in literature [9] supports the star-typed Theta-join. However, it could not support other two types of Theta-join. In work [14], 1-bucket-Theta is extended to process a multi-way Theta-join in only one MRJ by partitioning the cross-product of multiple datasets using the hypercube with fixed length of side. Unfortunately, it is hard to be implemented in real application. A parallel MRJs method is proposed in literature [8]. A MRJ implement a chain-typed Theta-join by using Hilbert curve. Due to the features of Hilbert curve, the datasets in a chain-typed Theta-join need to be the same scale. Actually, in data analytic work-load, the scales of datasets are very different.

3   Two-MRJs Method for Multi-way Theta-Join

In this work, we mainly focus on the efficient processing of multi-way Theta-joins by reducing MRJs. The main idea of our method is: a multi-way Theta-join is decomposed to non-Equi-joins and multi-way Equi-join; each join is processed in one MRJ.

3.1   Decomposition of Multi-way Theta-Join

Definition 1: (join graph) A multi-way Theta-join is presented as an undirected graph G (V, E). Each dataset in the join is a vertex, and V is a set of vertexes. Each join condition is an edge, and E is a set of edges. G is called join graph.

For example, a multi-way Theta-join $R_5 \bowtie_{\theta_3} R_1 \bowtie_{\theta_2} R_2 \bowtie R_3 \bowtie_{\theta_1} R_4$ could be presented as the join graph G shown in Fig. 2. In the join graph G, V = {R_5, R_4, R_3, R_2, R_1}, and E = {θ_1, θ_2, θ_3, =}. R_5 joins R_1 with the condition θ_3, and R_2 joins R_3 with equal condition.

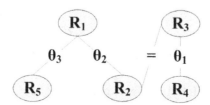

Fig. 2. A join graph G

In order to break a multi-way Theta-join into non-Equi-joins and Equi-join, we remove all the edges presented as equal conditions. Then, if there is a loop in G, an edge tagged as θ_i is removed. θ_i is the edge between two datasets. These two datasets have the largest scales in the loop.

Definition 2: (decomposition graph) G' is a sub graph of a join graph G, in which, there is no loops and no edges tagged as =. G' is called the decomposition graph of join graph G.

Fig.3 shows how to transform a join graph G into the decomposed graph G'. In the graph G, there are an edge tagged as = and a loop that consists of θ_1, θ_4 and θ_5. Firstly, the edge tagged as = is removed. Then, one of the edges θ_1, θ_4 and θ_5 needs to be removed to break the loop. If R_4 and R_6 have larger scales than R_3, θ_5 will be chosen to be removed.

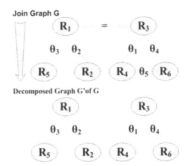

Fig. 3. Transform join graph G into decomposed graph G'

We use one MRJ to process non-equal-joins in G', and the results are joined with equal condition in next MRJ. Notice that, the removed edges from G are also implemented in the second MRJ. In G' shown in Fig.3, four non-equal-joins $R_{12} = R_1 \bowtie_{\theta_2} R_2$, $R_{15} = R_1 \bowtie_{\theta_3} R_5$, $R_{34} = R_3 \bowtie_{\theta_1} R_4$ and $R_{36} = R_3 \bowtie_{\theta_4} R_6$ are implement in the first MRJ. In the second MRJ, the removed edge tagged = between R_1 and R_3 is used to join R_1 and R_3. Thus, a multi-way Equi-join $R_{12} \bowtie R_{15} \bowtie R_{34} \bowtie R_{36}$ is processed in the second MRJ. The removed edge θ_5 is used as a filter condition on the results of the multi-way Equi-join.

3.2   Three Patterns in G'

Obviously, join graph G is a connected graph, while decomposition graph G' is either an unconnected graph or a connected graph. Connected components in G' are independent of each other. Thus, we just need to consider how to implement the non-Equi-joins in one connected component using one MRJ. There are three kinds of connected component: star pattern, chain pattern and hybrid pattern, which are illustrated in Fig.4. Different patterns will be processed using different methods.

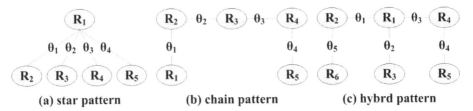

Fig. 4. Three patterns of connected component

Star Pattern

In a star pattern, a dataset (called fact table) is joined with all of the other datasets (called dimension tables). Considering a star-typed connected component with n dimension tables $D_1, D_2, ..., D_n$ and a fact table F, there are n non-Equi-joins will be processed in one MRJ and the join conditions are $\theta_1, \theta_2, ..., \theta_n$ respectively. The solution is: D_1, $D_2, ..., D_n$ are treated as one dimension table (called combination table, abbreviated as CT); a single non-Equi-join between CT and F is implemented using 1-bucket-Theta algorithm.

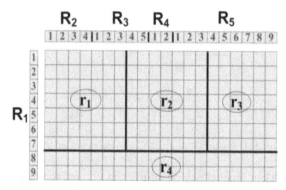

Fig. 5. Partition of star pattern

Taking the star pattern in Fig.4 (a) as an example, R_1 is fact table; R_2, R_3, R_4 and R_5 are dimension tables; $\theta_1, \theta_2, \theta_3$ and θ_4 are join conditions. Thus, four non-Equi-joins need to be implemented in one MRJ. Four dimension tables are combined into CT sequentially and joined with R_1 using 1-bucket-Theta method. Notice that, dimension tables are not combined in physical; they are treated as parts of CT logically.

Assuming that, R_1, R_2, R_3, R_4 and R_5 have 9, 4, 5, 2 and 9 records respectively and 4 reducers are used. Thus, CT has 4+5+2+9=20 records. Each record from dimension tables and fact table are partitioned from mappers to reducers. In Fig.5, the partition process is shown. According to the equation (1), the cross-product of CT and R_1 is partitioned by the square with side length of $\sqrt{20 \times 9/4} \approx 7$. Then, records in the rectangle are shuffled to corresponding reducers. For example, record 1 in R_2 will be shuffle to reducer 1 and 4; record 1 in R_1 will be shuffle to reducer 1, 2 and 3. After receiving records, reducers will process different records from different dimension tables using different join conditions.

Chain Pattern

A chain pattern with n tables is described as $R_1 \bowtie_{\theta_1} R_2 \bowtie_{\theta_2} R_3 \bowtie_{\theta_3} ...... \bowtie_{\theta_{n-1}} R_n$. In order to implement each non-Equi-join condition θ_i in one MRJ, cross product between R_1 and R_2 is partitioned using 1-bucket-theta algorithm at first; then R_i is partitioned as R_{i-2}. For example, R_3 is partitioned as R_1 and R_4 is partitioned as R_2. In the chain pattern shown in Fig.4 (b), we assume R_1, R_2, R_3, R_4 and R_5 have 9, 4, 5, 2 and 9 records respectively and 4 reducers are used. Fig.6 illustrates how to partition these tables.

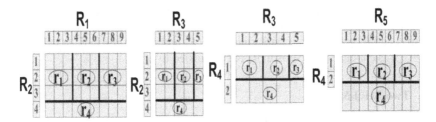

Fig. 6. Partition method of chain pattern

Because R_1 has 9 records and R_2 has 4 records, cross product between these two tables is partitioned by a square with side length of $\sqrt{9 \times 4/4} = 3$. Thus, R_1 is partitioned into 3 parts and R_2 is partitioned into 2 parts. R_3 is partitioned as R_1; R_4 is partitioned as R_2; R_5 is partitioned as R_3.

Hybrid Pattern

A hybrid pattern is composed of star patterns and chain patterns. Fortunately, we observe that a hybrid pattern could be simplified to a chain pattern, because the dimension tables in a star pattern are combined to a CT. We start by the table with the largest degree. Then, we combine its dimension tables to a CT. All the tables joined with these dimension tables are considered to be joined with CT.

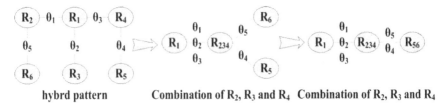

hybrd pattern   Combination of R_2, R_3 and R_4 Combination of R_2, R_3 and R_4

Fig. 7. Simplification of hybrid pattern

Fig.7 illustrated the simplification of the hybrid pattern shown in Fig.4 (c). R_1 has the largest degree 3. Thus, R_2, R_3 and R_4 are combined to a CT (denoted as R_{234}) at first. Because R_5 and R_6 are joined with R_4 and R_2 respectively, they are considered to be joined with R_{234}. Then, R_5 and R_6 are combined to a CT R_{56}, since R_{234} has the largest degree.

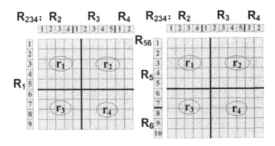

Fig. 8. Partition method of hybrid pattern

After a hybrid pattern being simplified to a chain pattern, join tables are partitioned as chain pattern, which are shown in Fig.8. Notice that, it is unnecessary to shuffle records in R_6 to r_3 and r_4, because R_6 is only joined with R_2 and all records in R_2 are shuffled to r_1 and r_3. It is enough for records in R_6 to be shuffled to r_3.

3.3   Two-MRJ Method

Instead of using a sequence of MRJs, we use two MRJs to implement a multi-way Theta-join. The first MRJ is in charge of non-Equi-joins. Results of the first MRJ are joined together using equal condition and filtered using removed non-equal conditions.

The First MRJ

In map phase, mappers transform records into key-value pairs. Key is the identifier of the reducer where a record will be shuffled to. How to obtain the identifiers of reducers according to the pattern of the connected component is described in section 3.2. Thus, for a record x belongs to component i, a function $pattern_i(x)$ will calculate the identifiers of the reducers where the record t will be shuffled to. Notice that, a record will be shuffled to more than one reducer. We use $identifier\text{-}list_x$ to denote the identifiers of the reducers. Value is the record itself and its table tag. Table tag identifies which table the record is from. The map phase is described in algorithm 1.

```
Algorithm 1: MAP (the first MRJ)
Input: input records x ∈ R₁ U R₂ U······U Rₙ
/* during the initialization of mapper, the mapping from
tables to connected components is loaded into a lookup table;
the mapping from records in the iᵗʰ connected component to
reducers is calculated by patternᵢ() function*/
1: if x∈Rₓ
2:    i = lookup (Rₓ)
3:    identifier-listₓ = patternᵢ(x)
4:    for all identifiers t in identifier-listₓ
5:       Output (t, (x, Rₓ))
```

Before shuffling the key-value pairs produced by mappers to reducers, all pairs with the same key t will be merged as (t, list (x, R_x)). In reduce phase, values will be buffered and separated to several sets according to the table tag. Records from different sets are joined using different join conditions. The reduce phase is described in algorithm 2.

```
Algorithm 2: REDUCE (the first MRJ)
Input: input key-value pairs (t, list(x, Rₓ))
1: for all (x, Rₓ) /*values are separated to several sets
2:    setᵣₓ=setᵣₓ U x      according to the table tag*/
3: for all condition θᵢⱼ /*setᵢ and setⱼ are joined with condition
                        θᵢⱼ*/
4:    for all records x and y in setᵢ and setⱼ
5:       if x and y satisfy the condition θᵢⱼ
6:          Output (i, j, x, y) /*output the records x and y and
                                 their table tag i and j*/
```

The Second MRJ

The results of the first MRJ are joined together with equal condition in the second MRJ. We use the one-to-many shuffle manner proposed in [12] to implement the multi-way Equi-join.

Notice that, some equal conditions and non-equal conditions are removed when transforming join graph G into decomposition graph G', which are described in section 3.1. These conditions need to be processed in the second MRJ to guarantee the correctness of the final results. Equal conditions will be involved in the multi-way Equi-join directly. And the non-equal conditions will be as filter conditions to process the join results.

4   Experiments

Hadoop [12] is a free open-source implementation of MapReduce. Our experiments were performed on a 4-machines cluster running Hadoop 1.0.4. One machine served as NameNode, and the other 3 were DataNodes. Each machine has a four-core 2.13GHz processor, 8GB RAM and 1T hard disks.

To verify the effectiveness of our solution, we conduct two experiments: one uses TPC-H [15] datasets at different scales and the other uses the synthetic datasets.

4.1   TPC-H Datasets

A data generator called dbgen is used to generate an instance of the TPC-H [15] datasets at different scales. Because the queries in TPC-H benchmark are Equi-join, we design a multi-way Theta- join L $\bowtie_{L.orderkey<O.orderkey}$ O $\bowtie_{L.custkey<C.custkey}$ C, where L, O and C are the datasets in TPC-H, which are named Lineitem, Order and Customer respectively. The three datasets are shown in Table1 (a). For example, in the first datasets D_1, three tables L, O and C have 6000, 1500 and 150 records respectively, and the join result have 332678582 records.

Table 1. Results of TPC-H datasets

(a)Scales of three datasets (the number of records)

(b) Execution time (in seconds)

	L	O	C	join results		Map-join	Hive	two-MRJ
D_1	6000	1500	150	332678582	D_1	311	358	225
D_2	12000	3000	300	2697226079	D_2	1838	2221	1706
D_3	24000	6000	600	21125940671	D_3	13808	17014	13558

We compare two-MRJ method with Hive [7] and map-join in this experiment. Hive could not support Theta-join directly, thus we have to process the join by using cross product in two MRJ. In map-join [3], join operations are implemented in mappers and reducers do nothing. The execute time for three methods are shown in Table 1 (b). Two-MRJ method is more efficient than other two methods. There are two reasons: firstly, the second MRJ in two-MRJ method is an Equi-join, which needs less time than Theta-join; second, the cross product is inefficient in Hive.

4.2   Synthetic Datasets

In this experiment, we evaluate two multi-way Theta-joins: one joins three datasets and one joins four datasets. The datasets are synthetize in different scales

Three Datasets
Three datasets, R_1, R_2 and R_3, are joined together. The scales of the datasets are shown in Table 2 (a). Three datasets can be treated as either chain pattern or star pattern. In this experiments, we treat it as star pattern.

Table 2. Results of three datasets

(a) Scales of three datasets (in: million)

	R1	R2	R3	$R_1 \bowtie_\theta R_2$	$R_1 \bowtie_\theta R_2 \bowtie_\theta R_3$
D_1	0.1	0.5	1	0.1	0.4
D_2	0.5	1	2	0.8	0.8
D_3	1	1	2	2	2
D_4	2	2	2	3.6	0.8
D_5	1	1	3	0.4	0.8

(b)Execution time (in seconds)

	A sequence	Two-MRJ
D_1	107	109
D_2	124	121
D_3	144	126
D_4	181	148
D_5	126	133

We compare two-MRJ method with a sequence of MRJs method, which are listed in table 2 (b). For D_1 and D_5, our method is a little slower than a sequence of MRJs method. The main reason is that the scale of the intermediate result is small. Less intermediate results lead to less I/O.

Four Datasets
Four datasets, R1, R2, R3 and R4 are joined together in a star pattern. The scales of these four datasets are shown in Table 3 (a) and the execute time for sequence method and two-MRJ method are presented in Table 3 (b).

More datasets lead to more intermediate results for sequence method and heavier workload for NameNode. Thus, two-MRJ method shows much better performance than sequence method on this kind of join.

Table 3. Results of four datasets in star pattern

(a) Scales of three datasets (in: million)

	R1	R2	R3	R₄	results
D₁	0.5	1	1.5	3	1.6
D₂	1	1	1	3	1.6
D₃	2	2	2	2	1.6

(b)Execution time (in seconds)

	A sequence	Two-MRJ
D₁	198	134
D₂	222	153
D₃	285	185

5 Conclusion

In this paper, we proposed a two-MRJ method to implement all kinds of multi-way Theta-join. Multi-way Theta-join is decomposed into non-Equi-join and Equi-join. Each join could be implemented using one MRJ. In the first MRJ, we extended 1-bucket-theta algorithm to process several single non-Equi-joins using one MRJ. In the second MRJ, the results of non-Equi-joins are joined with equal condition using one-to-many shuffle method. Two-MRJ method reduces the MRJs in processing of multi-way Theta-join without much tuples duplication. Thus, it obtains good performance. There is more work to do along these lines. We suggest the following:

— Since we join several single non-Equi-joins in one MRJ, the high degree of replication of records is necessary. Thus, it would be interesting to implement these joins in several paralleled MRJs.
— For a chain pattern, the partition mode is determined by the first two tables. However, it will introduce serious data skew and high degree of replication of records. Thus, a partition method designed for more efficient chain pattern join is necessary.
— For the second MRJ, which is in charge of multi-way Equi-join, more efficient algorithms will be used, such as concurrent join proposed in [11].

References

1. Dean, J., Ghemawat, S.: Mapreduce: Simplified Data Processing on Large Clusters. In: 6th Symposium on Opearting Systems Design & Implementation, pp. 137–150. USENIX Symposium, San Francisco (2004)
2. Okcan, A., Riedewald, M.: Processing Theta-joins Using MapReduce. In: 31st SIGMOD, pp. 949–960. ACM Press, Athens (2011)
3. Blanas, S., Patel, J.M., Ercegovac, V., Rao, J., Shekita, E.J., Tian, Y.: A Comparison of Join Algorithms for Log Processing in Map Reduce. In: 30th SIGMOD, pp. 975–986. ACM Press, Indianapolis (2010)
4. Jiang, D., Anthony, K.H., Tung, Chen, G.: Map-join-reduce: Towards Scalable and Efficient Data Analysison Large Clusters. J. IEEE Transactions on Knowledge and Data Engineering 23(9), 1299–1311 (2010)

5. Yang, H.C., Dasdan, A., Hsiao, R.L., Parker, D.S.: Map-reduce-merge: Simplified Relational Data Processing on Large Clusters. In: 27th SIGMOD, pp. 1029–1040. ACM Press, Beijing (2007)
6. Lee, T., Kim, K., Kim, H.J.: Join Processing Using Bloom Filter in Map Reduce. In: Proceedings of Applied Computation Symposium, pp. 100–105. ACM Research, NewYork (2012)
7. Hive, `http://hive.apache.org`
8. Zhang, X.F., Chen, L., Wang, M.: Efficient Multi-way Theta-Join Processing Using Map Reduce. PVLDB 5(11), 1184–1195 (2012)
9. Chen, S.Y., Chang, T.P., Chang, Z.H.: An Efficient Theta-Join Query Processing Algorithm on Map Reduce Framework. In: International Symposium on Computer, Consumer and Control, pp. 686–689. IEEE sponsored, Taichung (2012)
10. Hadoop, `http://hadoop.apache.org`
11. Lin, Y.T., Agrawal, D., Chen, C., Ooi, B.C., Wu, S.: Llama: Leveraging Columnar Storage for Scalable Join Processing in the Map Reduce Framework. In: 31th SIGMOD, pp. 961–972. ACM Press, Athens (2011)
12. Afrati, F.N., Ullman, J.D.: Optimizing joins in a map-reduce environment. In: 13rd EDBT, Lausanne, pp. 99–110 (2010)
13. Han, H., Jung, H., Eom, H., Yeom, H.Y.: Scatter-Gather-Merge: An Efficient Star-Join Query Processing Algorithm for Data-Parallel Frameworks. J. Cluster Computing 14(2), 183–197 (2010)
14. Zhang, C., Li, J., Wu, L., Lin, M., Liu, W.: SEJ: An Even Approach to Multi-way Theta-Joins using Map Reduce. In: 2nd Proceedings of the International Conferenceon Cloud and Green Computing, pp. 73–80. XiangTan (2012)
15. TPC-H, `http://www.tpc.org/tpch/`

Dependability Modeling and Certification of Cloud-Based Distributed Systems

Kaliappa Ravindran

City University of New York (CUNY - City College & Graduate Center),
Department of Computer Science,
160 Convent Avenue,
New York, NY 10031, USA
ravi@cs.ccny.cuny.edu

Abstract. A system that is highly dependable under hostile conditions but whose dependability cannot be easily evaluated prior to the deployment of applications is less desirable than a system with lower but predictable dependability. This is because a decision-making on the deployment of high assurance systems is often based on a risk analysis of application failures. For system services implemented on a cloud, the problem of system certification assumes added importance because of third-party control of cloud resources and the attendant problems of faults, QoS degradations, and security violations. Our paper treats system dependability as an application-level QoS for management purposes, and advocates a probabilistic evaluation of dependability. Our approach is corroborated by measurements on system-level prototypes and simulation analysis of system models in the face of hostile environment conditions. A case study of content-distribution networks anchored on cloud infrastructures is also described.

1 Introduction

We consider an application running on top of the computational and communication services realized over one or more cloud infrastructures. The system as a whole implements a core functionality, with augmentations from the service provider to support a variety of para-functional behaviors. For instance, data replication and content distribution may be offered as core services that are often associated with, say, performance, security, and timeliness attributes. Here, the problem of system certification (i.e., reasoning about whether a system behaves in the way it is supposed to) has become important because of the third-party control of cloud resources and the attendant issues of fault-handling, security, maintenance, availability, and the like [1].

The dependability of a cloud-based application system S is a measure of how good S meets its intended QoS objectives under uncontrolled external environment conditions incident on S. Say, for example, S is a content distribution system that advertises content delivery to clients within 5 *sec* of a request (e.g., news). Suppose S achieves the best QoS of 5 *sec* guarantee only with a probability of 0.4, and achieves a latency uniformly distributed between 5 and 15 *sec*

M. Pathan, G. Wei, and G. Fortino (Eds.): IDCS 2013, LNCS 8223, pp. 333–350, 2013.

in other cases: with the client abort of session when the latency exceeds 12 *sec*. Assuming an exponential utility decay beyond 5 *sec* latency, the dependability of S in meeting the latency specs is:

$$0.4 \times 1 + [0.6 \times \frac{1}{(15 - 5)} \times \int_5^{12} \exp(-\overline{x - 5}).dx],$$

which is 0.46 on a normalized scale $[0, 1]$. If the content storage/delivery backlog becomes severe, the 5 *sec* latency is less sustainable (assuming that other parameters of storage/delivery mechanism do not change) — and hence S is now much less than 46%-capable in meeting the latency specs. The system capability may however be enhanced by installing additional proxy server nodes along the content distribution topology. Concomitant with this notion of system dependability is a safety aspect, namely, S should not traverse into unsafe situations while meeting its objectives: say, in this example, the client connectivity to a content getting disrupted.

The goal of our paper is to design the software engineering methods and tools to quantify dependability, and identify the system-level techniques therein to assess the dependability of S. Analyzing the dependability of S involves verifying that the safety requirements are met as S strives to meet its QoS objectives under various external environment conditions incident on the underlying cloud services.

Our notion of dependability of S is at the confluence of QoS, timeliness, and fault-tolerance attributes of S. It is divorced from a traditional view where the dependability of S is rigidly tied to the fault-tolerance of S. The QoS feature depicts an ability of S to control its performance in response to an underlying infrastructure resource allocation or a change in the external environment conditions. The QoS-to-resource mapping relationship should be established in a quantitative manner under specific environment conditions, in order to meet the performance objectives in predictable way. An example is the determination of content delivery latency over a distribution network set up on a geographically spread-out cloud of content storage nodes, in the presence of node failures. Virtualization, which allows realizing the distribution network as a core service from the cloud provider, does not by itself prevent fluctuations in the latency behavior (e.g., jitter) induced by node failures and outages. Here, a para-functional goal is to reduce the latency jitter by resorting to content caching techniques, thereby assuring a stable behavior of applications. The mapping between the output of S and platform resources should be known with reasonable accuracy: either as a closed-form model of S or through a series of incremental allocate-and-observe invocations on S [2].

The domain-specific core adaptation function in a cloud-based application system S is viewed as a control-theoretic feedback loop acting on a reference input P_{ref}: say, for cloud resource management (such a view is also advocated in [3]). Figure 1 concretizes this view . The controller C generates its actions I based on a computational model of S, denoted as: $g(I, O, s, E)$ — where O is the plant output in response to the trigger I, s is the plant state prior to the

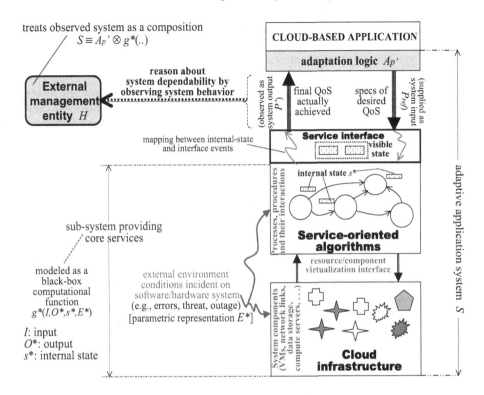

Fig. 1. Structure of adaptation processes in a network application system

incidence of I, and E depicts the environment condition. Since the true plant model $g^*(I, O^*, s^*, E^*)$ is not completely known, C refines its input action in a next iteration based on the deviation in observed output O^* from the expected output O when action I occurs. Upon S reaching a steady-state (over multiple control iterations) with output P', the output tracking error $|P_{ref} - P'|$ is analyzed to reason about the system dependability. Our approach is guided by the concepts and taxonomy of dependable computing presented in [4].

We treat the *dependability as a management attribute* of cloud-based adaptive systems. An external management entity H views the system S as made up of adaptation processes A'_p wrapped around a core system $g^*(\cdots)$, i.e., $S \equiv A'_p \otimes g^*(\cdots)$ — where '$\otimes$' denotes the composition in an object-oriented software view. A'_p is embodied in a distributed agent-based software module that forms the building-block to structure S ([5] provides an architecture for distributed realization of the adaptation logic of A'_p). S interacts with its (hidden) external environment through the core elements $g^*(\cdots)$: e.g., responding to client queries on a web server, and delivering content over a network transport connection. Here, the meta-level signal flows between A'_p and $g^*(\cdots)$ are visible to H. The layered software structure of S intrinsic to cloud-based systems: viz., the infrastructure, service-oriented algorithms, and adaptive application, stacked in that hierarchy and separated across well-defined interfaces[1], lends itself well for the dependability analysis by H. Here, the service attribute exported by the computational algorithm to its applications rests upon the quality of lower-level service received from the underlying infrastructure (e.g., resource allocation, failure detection). These core layers together constitute $g^*(\cdots)$, with A'_p housed in the application layer for behavior monitoring & control. The latter involves exercising the underlying algorithm layer (and in turn, the infrastructure layer) via signaling points defined in the service interfaces. The dependability of S may be quantified, with suitable metrics (for certification and control purposes), by analyzing the external state-machine level signal flows by H. Basically, H reasons about the output tracking error $|P_{ref} - P'|$ under various environment conditions, and maps it onto a measure of the dependability of S. Say, H is a cloud management station, employing a dashboard-based supervisory controller. The paper embarks on a case study of cloud-based content distribution networks, with a focus on system-level dependability.

The paper is organized as follows. Section 2 treats system dependability as compliance to the stated non-functional attributes (e.g., QoS). Section 3 describes a sample application: CDN, from a standpoint of the QoS compliance issues in cloud-based realizations. Section 4 presents our model-based approach to assess the dependability of cloud-based systems, with an assessment of the adaptation capability of CDNs. Section 5 discusses the relationship to existing system management frameworks. Section 6 concludes the paper.

2   Dependability of Cloud-Based Systems

Suppose $\mathcal{G}$ depicts the goal to be met by a cloud-based application system S. The goal $\mathcal{G}$ may include a prescription of one or more *non-functional attributes* associated with the QoS delivered by S to an application: such as resilience to external disturbances, stability against resource fluctuations, responsiveness to user-triggered requirements, and the like. The dependability of S is prescribed in terms of such non-functional attributes — and is hence distinct from the correctness goal of S which is a functional attribute (yielding a YES/NO result). This section provides a non-functional characterization of system dependability. Here, the dependability of S is a measure of how well the adaptation functions programmed into S adjust to the changing external environment conditions in meeting an application-level goal G specified for S.

2.1   Dependability as Application-Level QoS

We treat the dependability of a cloud-based system S as a meta-attribute of application-level QoS achievable under the current operating conditions. An example is how stable is the content delivery latency achieved on a distribution link in the face of bursty demands and resource costs. Another example is how

---

[1] The system layers correspond to IaaS, PaaS, and SaaS, in the cloud computing arena [6].

good is a web service availability in the presence of failures of one or more server replicas. Dependability assessment is anchored on three interwoven properties associated with the behavior of S: measurability, predictability, and adaptability of system output. These properties depict that S is *programmable*, i.e., an external management entity H can exercise control over the behavior of S in a concrete manner. For instance, even if S is 100% fault-tolerant, an inability to reason about this property in various fault scenarios reduces the dependability of S from an application standpoint. In the earlier example of replicated web service, a 95%-availability depicts a verifiable assurance, over a suitable time-scale, that no more than 5% of the client queries incur a latency higher than a set limit, say, 12 *sec*, even in the presence of server crashes. Thus, a characterization of S in terms of behavioral properties improves the reasoning about how dependable S is.

The adaptation processes in system S embody two main functionalities: i) core components and resources set up over the cloud infrastructure that collectively export a service to the application, and ii) a controller C that exercises the core components/resources to meet the application needs P_{ref}. An application interacts with the system core through a service-oriented interface (made up of APIs), with a certain trust on the service delivery vis-a-vis its quality. A model of S captures the following elements — c.f. Figure 1:

- Plant $g^*(I, O^*, E^*, s^*)$ made up of computational algorithms that map the infrastructure resources and components onto a unified service delivered to applications;
- Controller C that decides on an input I to $g^*(.)$: say, resource allocation and/or component assignment in the infrastructure, based on the currently observed service state $s \approx s^*$ and environment condition $e \in E^*$, with[2] a goal of making the output $M(O)$ reach close to P_{ref};
- Sensor that maps the service state s onto the observed service output O to report back to C;
- Actuator to realize a resource/component allocation decision I as domain-specific actions on the infrastructure.

The service interface basically wraps around the physical system $g^*(\cdots)$. A function $g(\cdots)$ that approximates $g^*(\cdots)$ and the errors in sensing/actuation processes are factored in a system model programmed into the controller C.

A dependability metric, denoted as $D_S(e, G)$, is a measure of how good the system S meets its goal G under the environment condition $e \in E^*$. Here, G is prescribed as a behavior of S that moves the physical plant to a desired state. Note that a certification authority quantifying $D_S(e, G)$ may be external to the cloud provider and the application-level user. The external events E^* incident on S can emanate from the application, service-layer algorithms, and cloud infrastructure. E^* includes the errors in QoS specification (e.g., incomplete specs), algorithm formulation (e.g., unspecified events), and resources/components (e.g., a node crash) respectively.

---

[2] Observed service interface state is mapped from service-internal state s^*.

We cast the notion of system dependability in a broader context, as advocated in [4], than the currently prevalent approaches that rigidly tie to the system-level mechanisms for recovery from component-level faults occurring in a system.

2.2 System Dependability, Trust, and Fault-Tolerance

[4] characterizes dependability as a form of trust bestowed on a system S by its users across the service interface to S — where a user may be a human entity or a physical world process or a computational sub-system that acts as the client of S. It depicts how trustable is the service exported by S, as perceived by those who depend on S (i.e., the users of S).

We project the output tracking error $\epsilon = |P_{ref} - P'|$ onto a dependability measure (note: P' is the final converged O^*). The following correspondences can be readily established:

- $\epsilon > \epsilon_m$ depicts a service failure (i.e., S is of no value);
- $\delta < \epsilon \leq \epsilon_m$ depicts a service degradation (but S may still be usable, al beit, in a degraded form);
- s^* depicts the service-external state (s is a computational representation of s^* in the model programmed into C).

The environment E^* covers anything outside the control regime of S but which impacts the operations of S: e.g., the abrupt shut-down of a business unit in an enterprise system causing delays in the servicing of customer demands (or, even scaling down system operations).

Under the above framework, the conventional system-level faults (e.g., node crashes) can be subsumed as part of an uncontrolled external event space E^*. QoS degradations can also be viewed as faults that constitute a part of E^* (e.g., packet loss along a network path). How S reacts to the hostility of an external event $e \in E^*$ and shields the application from the effects e allows us to delineate the hitherto qualitative notions of system robustness and resilience.

Robustness depicts the ability of S to present a service behavior to applications as if there are no failures or hostile events. Here, the application does not see the impact of hostile events, as captured by: $P' \approx P_{ref}$. This is enabled by strong service-layer guarantees provided by S using, say, resource reservations and/or redundant component deployments in the infrastructure, and the underlying algorithms to correctly manage these system-level mechanisms. The signaling interaction between the application and service layers occurs only when an application starts and when it terminates.

In contrast, resilience depicts the ability of S to reconfigure its internal functions and/or parameters, in a way to continue operations in a degraded mode. Here, the application does see the impact of hostile events, al beit, indirectly, by scaling down its operations to a reduced level, which is captured as: $0 \ll (P_{ref} - P') \leq \epsilon_m$. The service-layer is programmable, with S employing parameterizable system-level mechanisms that are invoked by the application at various time-scales during run-time as part of its reconfiguration strategies. Accordingly, a richer API is required to support the signaling interaction needed between the application and service layers: namely, notifying the quality degradation $|P_{ref} - P'|$ to the application and controlling the parametric and/or algorithm changes needed in the service-layer.

We project the management-oriented view of adaptive applications through a prism of *model-based system assessment*, and characterize therein the notion of system dependability.

2.3   Tracking Error Based Dependability Specification

Consider an application system $S \equiv A'_p \otimes g^*(I, s^*, E^*, O^*)$ — c.f. Figure 1. A controller C embodied in A'_p operates on the physical plant $g^*(\cdots)$ to generate to an output close to P_{ref}. E^* depicts the external environment, modeled as a set of parameters, incident on $g^*(\cdots)$ to disturb the output behavior of S ($|E^*| \gg 1$). C is programmed with a plant model $g(I, s, E, O)$ that is an approximate representation of the true model $g^*(\cdots)$, where $E \subset E^*$. C uses the model $g(\cdots)$ to compute the plant input I. If P' is the output sustainable by A'_p (i.e., stable converged value of O^*) in response to a trigger input P_{ref}, then $\epsilon = |P_{ref} - P'|$ denotes the output tracking error of S under the current environment conditions E^* incident on the plant $g^*(\cdots)$ — e.g., failures and outages[3].

For adaptive QoS management systems, P' depicts the stable QoS sustainable by S when attempting to achieve a desired QoS P_{ref}. In an example of content delivery over a geographically spread-out distribution network, S attempts to keep the content latency L' less than a prescribed limit L, as determined by various factors: such as the capacity of content proxy nodes, the bandwidth available on the path leading to clients, and algorithm employed to move content from a node to its downstream clients. The output behavior of S may be associated with non-functional attributes, such as boundedness and jitter. The above attributes capture the ability of S to provide a sustainable output behavior in the presence of changes in user-requirements and/or fluctuations in external environment incident on the physical plant — and even under modifications to the plant itself (e.g., changes in proxy node placement in a CDN). Figure 2 empirically shows how the tracking error of S varies relative to the hostility of an environment condition $e \in E^*$. The system S is deemed as highly risky to be trusted upon (i.e., dependability ≈ 0) when $|P_{ref} - P'| > \epsilon_m$. The convex behavior depicts the increased additional effort (or, cost) incurred by A'_p to counter the disruption caused by an environment change from e to $e + \delta e$: say, extra resource allocation in the infrastructure, deployment of robust infrastructure components, and/or service-layer algorithm reconfigurations [7]. A dependability analysis is thus tied to which of the algorithms is actually employed in the system.

---

[3] The tracking error ϵ depicts the ability of system S to generate a desired output P_{ref}. Whereas, the parameter: $\gamma = |O - O^*|$ depicts the modeling error, i.e., how accurate the computational model $g(I, O, s, E)$, embodied in the controller C of S, is in predicting the actual behavior generated by the physical processes: $g(I, O^*, s^*, E^*)$.

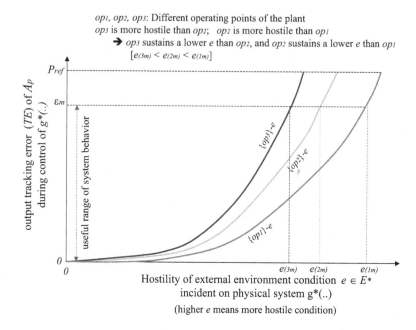

Fig. 2. Output tracking error relative to external environment conditions

3   Sample Application: Latency Control in CDN

Latency in delivery of a content to the clients, L, is a QoS parameter prescribed by clients through the CDN service interface. A service-layer algorithm places proxy nodes in the distribution tree to store contents, whereupon a 'push' or 'pull' strategy is employed to deliver content to the clients [8]. Figure 3 shows our management view of a sample CDN realized on a cloud infrastructure.

3.1   Support of User-Level QoS in CDNs

How stable is the delivery latency L' in the face of changes in the infrastructure resources r and/or the environment conditions e is a para-functional attribute — which may be measured as $\frac{dL'}{dr}$ and $\frac{dL'}{de}$ by a management entity H. To[4] reason about this attribute, H may employ agents to monitor:

– Content delivery latency incurred L' vis-a-vis a latency specs L from client (observable at CDN service interface);

---

[4] From adaptation standpoint, the actual content delivery to clients does not by itself constitute the output of CDN (we assume that L is the only QoS parameter). In a OAM sense, the content delivery to clients is simply a 'data-plane' action. Whereas, taking steps to keep $\frac{dL'}{dr}$ and $\frac{dL'}{de}$ low (say, by increasing the bandwidth of content distribution paths) is a 'control-plane' action. And, charging a price for content delivery to clients is a 'management-plane' action.

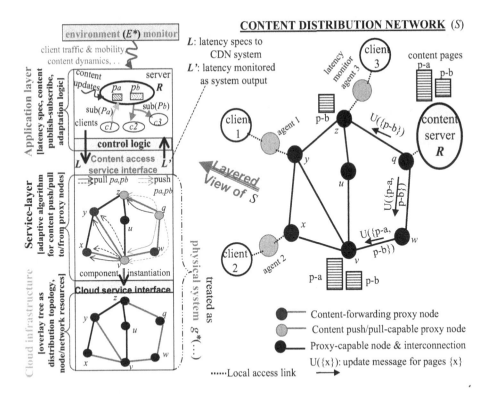

Fig. 3. Functional elements of a CDN and its management view

- System-internal resource allocation r exercised by CDN algorithms on the infrastructure (namely, topological placement of proxy nodes).

In addition, the system-external environment, e, as incident from the CDN application (e.g., content request workload), the CDN algorithms (e.g., excess delay to reconfigure a tree), and the CDN infrastructure (e.g., crash of a proxy node) is also monitored. The monitor agents are equipped with the domain-knowledge to handle the parameters L/L', r, and e in a CDN-specific context.

Referring to Figure 3, the base topology created in the infrastructure is: $\{(x \wr y), (x \wr v), (y \wr z), (z \wr u), (u \wr v), (y \wr v), (v \wr w), (w \wr q), (q \wr z)\}$ — where $(x \wr y)$ denotes the interconnection of nodes x and y over a transport network. The overlay distribution tree on the topology is: $T = \{(x \wr v), (y \wr v), (v \wr w), (w \wr q), (q \wr z)\}$. The proxy placement is given by the tuples: $r(p_a) = [T, (v, q), (x, y, z), q]$ and $r(p_b) = [T, (v, z), (x, y, z), q]$ — indicating the distribution tree, the nodes hosting proxy content p_a/p_b, the nodes to which clients are attached, and the node where master server is attached. When page p_a is updated, the content is pushed to the proxy nodes v, q; for p_b, the push occurs at nodes v, z — with the push to v

occurring via node w. The clients C_1 and C_2 pull p_a, p_b from node v; whereas, client C_3 pulls p_a from q and p_b from node z. A crash of link $(v \wr y)$ will trigger a tree reconfiguration to have C_1 pull p_a and p_b through node z instead of v. Likewise, if node v cannot provide content storage any longer, node w may be upgraded from forwarder to a distributor role by leasing storage in w.

Assuming d units of system overhead (storage, processing, and communication) to move content over a single hop, the push overhead for p_a and p_b are $2d$ and $3d$ respectively. The pull overhead incurred by C_1 and C_2 for p_a/p_b are $(c+d)$ each, while C_3 incurs $(c + d)$ for p_a and none for P_b — where c is the control overhead incurred per node. It is however likely that a client pull at a proxy node finds the requested page as not up-to-date, because of the asynchrony in client requests relative to the page updates. In a push-on-demand (CL) algorithm, the server R sends the logical time-stamp (LTS) associated with each update on a page p_a/p_b to the various proxy nodes hosting p_a/p_b as a control message (but not the page data itself). The LTS information allows a client request reaching a proxy node x' determine if the LTS of the page currently stored at x' matches the last LTS sent by R to x'. A mismatch in the LTS indicates that the page at x' is not up-to-date, thereby triggering a request to R to push the updated page to x'. Whereas, a push-on-update (SR) algorithm sends the page data to x' whenever an update occurs.

3.2   Modeling of CDN Behavior

A traffic-related environment parameter is $e \equiv \frac{\lambda_{s(a)}}{\lambda_{c(1,a)}}$: the ratio of the frequency of updates on page p_a at server R to the frequency of read requests on p_a from client C_1 ($\lambda_{s(a)}, \lambda_{c(1,a)} > 0$). Without loss of generality, the occurrence of updates on p_a and the arrival of read requests on p_a from C_1 and C_2 are modeled as Poisson processes with the rates $\lambda_{s(a)}$, $\lambda_{c(1,a)}$ and $\lambda_{c(2,a)}$ respectively. Each operation: client read or server update, spawns multiple sub-tasks at a proxy node for content indexing, retrieval/write, and forwarding — which involve the processing, storage, and network elements respectively in that sequence (the task flows are additive, because of the M/M/G/1 property).

Taking into account the sharing of node v between clients C_1 and C_2, the probability that a request from C_1 sent through the CL algorithm finds an out-of-date p_a at node v may be shown as:

$$u_{1a} = \frac{\lambda_{c1}^2 . \lambda_s}{(\lambda_{c1} + \lambda_s)^2 . (\lambda_{c1} + \lambda_{c2})}. \tag{1}$$

How often a request from C_1 traverses up the tree from v to pull the up-to-date content from R, instead of pulling from v, is determined by u_{1a}. This in turn determines the message overhead and latency incurred for the content access[5].

---

[5] Equation (1) is based on the statistical independence of task queuing effects across various proxy nodes that arises from the M/M/G/1 property. We also ignore the content transfer delays/overhead incurred on the access links of client devices and server.

The LTS(p_a) at v is synchronized with that at R (with an update of p_a, if needed). This incurs a page update overhead of $2(c + d)$, with the LTS synchronization overhead of $2c$/update amortized across various pulls by the factor $\frac{\lambda_s}{\lambda_{c1}+\lambda_{c2}}$. Whereas, the SR algorithm amortizes only the push overhead of $2d$/update across various pulls, because p_a is always up-to-date at v and hence the minimal overhead of $(c + d)$ is incurred for each pull by C_1. So, the average per-pull overhead and latency incurred by C_1 via the CL and SR algorithms are:

$$O_{\mathrm{CL}}(1a) = (1 - u_{1a}) \times (c + d) + u_{1a} \times 3(c + d) + \frac{\lambda_{c1}}{\lambda_{c1} + \lambda_{c2}} \times 2c$$

$$L_{\mathrm{CL}}^{(\mathrm{min})}(1a) = (1 - u_{1a}) \times \frac{(c + d)}{B} + u_{1a} \times \frac{3(c + d)}{B} \qquad (2)$$

$$O_{\mathrm{SR}}(1a) = (c + d) + \frac{\lambda_s}{\lambda_{c1} + \lambda_{c2}} \times 2d$$

$$L_{\mathrm{SR}}^{(\mathrm{min})}(1a) = \frac{(c + d)}{B}; \qquad (3)$$

where $L_{...}^{(\mathrm{min})}$ depicts the minimum latency incurred for content access (i.e., with no queuing/processing delays at the proxy & server nodes: v, x, q, and R) and B is the bandwidth available on the node interconnect segments. In comparison, the per-pull overhead and latency incurred in a CDN with no proxy-based mechanism, i.e., when p_a (and p_b) are always pulled from R, are $3(c + d)$ and $\frac{3(c+d)}{B}$ respectively. For small values of $\frac{\lambda_s}{\lambda_{c1}}$, $O_{\mathrm{SR}}(1a) < O_{\mathrm{CL}}(1a)$. For $\frac{\lambda_s}{\lambda_{c1}} > e_l$, $O_{\mathrm{SR}}(1a) > O_{\mathrm{CL}}(1a)$ — and hence the CL algorithm may be chosen for content access. When $\frac{\lambda_s}{\lambda_{c1}} > e_h$ for $e_h > e_l$, u_{1a} becomes higher — thereby incurring redundant levels of LTS synchronization. So, an extended form of CL, denoted as CL$'$, is employed that avoids the LTS synchronization — and hence incurs lower overhead than the CL algorithm with LTS support, i.e., $O_{\mathrm{CL}}(1a) > O_{\mathrm{CL}'}(1a)$. The choice of algorithm: SR or CL or CL$'$, is determined by $\frac{\lambda_s}{\lambda_{c1}}$. For requests originating from C_1 on page p_b and from client C_2 on pages p_a/p_b, the Equations (2)-(3) also hold — albeit, with a re-mapping of appropriate parameters (say, the size of p_a/p_b) and the ensuing choice of CL/SR/CL$'$ algorithm[6].

For requests from client C_3 on the other hand, that node z exclusively serves C_3 is factored in the overhead and latency estimates (which is unlike the sharing of p_a at node v by C_1 and C_2). Accordingly the probability of a request from C_3 seeing an out-of-date copy of p_b at node z is:

$$u_{3b} = \frac{\frac{\lambda_s}{\lambda_{c3}}}{1 + \frac{\lambda_s}{\lambda_{c3}}}. \qquad (4)$$

In the simplistic case of no queuing/processing delays at z, q and R, the per-pull overheads and latency incurred by C_3 are:

$$O_{\mathrm{CL}}(3b) = u_{3b} \times (c + d) + \frac{\lambda_s}{\lambda_{c3}} \times c$$

---

[6] Our earlier work on dynamic event dissemination over wide-area distributed networks [9] gives the details of CL/CL$'$ and SR algorithms.

$$L_{\text{CL}}^{(\min)}(3b) = u_{3b} \times \frac{(c+d)}{B} \tag{5}$$

$$O_{\text{SR}}(3b) = \frac{\lambda_s}{\lambda_{c3}} \times d; \ L_{\text{SR}}^{(\min)}(3b) = 0. \tag{6}$$

In a case where the proxy for p_b is removed from node z, the per-pull overhead and latency are simply $(c+d)$ and $\frac{(c+d)}{B}$ respectively, because C_3 always needs to pull p_b from R — as is the case with p_a.

Equations (1)-(6) capture the (normalized) per-pull overhead and latency of CL, CL$'$, and SR algorithms — as incurred by clients C_1 and C_3 relative to the content read and update behavior on pages p_a and p_b, for the sample case shown in Figure 3 (the case of C_1 also holds for client C_2 vis-a-vis the pages p_a and p_b). This operational analysis of CDN performance can be generalized for an arbitrary case of shared and non-shared proxy nodes in a distribution tree, with each client pulling various pages via its serving proxy node (for brevity, we omit the generalization of the analysis).

3.3   Model-Theoretic View of CDN Performance

Intuitively, the SR algorithm incurs the least overhead and latency when the ratio of update-to-read frequency is low. When the update-to-read frequency ratio exceeds e_l, the CL algorithm provides a better performance. And beyond e_h, the CL$'$ algorithm offers the best performance.

The per-pull overhead and latency: $O...$ and $L_{...}^{(\min)}$, depict the quality metrics ascribed to various clients, i.e., a client perceives the utility of CDN system through these metrics. The cost assigned to a client per-pull by the cloud provider of a CDN is tied to the amount of resources r allocated for the CDN operations. An adaptation manager may monitor the environment parameter $e \equiv \frac{\lambda_s}{\lambda_c}$ and system-level parameters $[O..., L'..., r]$ at run-time (using distributed agents). Our studies show that the CDN overhead and latency exhibit a monotonic convex behavior with respect to the environment parameter $e \equiv \frac{\lambda_s}{\lambda_c}$. How convex is a behavior depends on which of the delivery algorithms: CL, CL', and SR, is employed by the system. The optimal performance/cost benefits perceived by a CDN client is thus in the context of a specific delivery algorithm employed: CL, CL' or SR, as the case may be (refer to the meta-view of control algorithm behaviors in Figure 2).

The latency equations for $L_{...}^{(\min)}$ however provide only partial information about the actual latency L' incurred by a client request. Because, L' is also determined by the query processing and content storage/processing overheads, the queue lengths of client queries, and the request task scheduling, at various proxy nodes in the distribution tree. Incorporating an accurate model of L' thus requires another level of stochastic or operational analysis of a CDN system vis-a-vis its node-level processing and storage capacity and the content processing/transfer activities generated by client requests. In this light, our latency equations can be used as building-blocks for higher-level system models to determine the CDN initial conditions and its dynamic operations.

A low-level measure of the total system overhead incurred by various clients served over the access link connecting to C_1 over an observation interval T_{obs} may be given as:

$$tso = T_{obs} \times \sum_{\forall i} [\lambda_{ci,a} \times O..._{(1a,i)} + \lambda_{ci,b} \times O..._{(1b,i)}].$$

This formulation considers the entire clientele supported across the CDN application[7]. The *tso* is of less concern to individual clients however — because a client X worries only about the latency L' experienced by X and the per-pull overhead assigned to X (as a usage cost)[8].

Aided by a systemic mapping of the algorithms onto their output behaviors, we believe that high-level system models can then be formulated by incorporating the composite effects of node storage & processing and queuing delays. Such a comprehensive performance study falls under the ambit of a control-theoretic analysis of CDN performance with the aid of model-based engineering elements.

From a modeling standpoint, we consider a CDN system with fixed resources in the infrastructure to support the client operations: namely, a CDN interconnect topology of proxy-capable nodes. A reconfiguration triggered by control actions programmed in A'_p involves adjusting the distribution tree set up over the infrastructure topology, and select the needed proxy placements therein to meet the client-level QoS requirements and cost perceptions.

4   Evaluating Adaptation in Cloud-Based Systems

We employ model-based analysis of the control-theoretic adaptation loops in a complex system S [10] to reason about system dependability in a cloud setting. Recall the system compositional view: $S \equiv A'_p \otimes g^*(I, O^*, s^*, E^*)$, where A'_p and $g^*(I, O^*, s^*, E^*)$ depict the adaptation and raw physical processes respectively. The reasoning is carried out by the management module H — c.f. Figure 1.

4.1   Cost Considerations for Application Services

In a cloud-based setting, a distributed application involves the use of infrastructure resources, viz., compute nodes and node interconnects, and the running of

---

[7] The formula can be extended to factor in the load-dependent queuing effects at the network, storage, and processing elements of a proxy node, and the statistical inter-dependency of task arrivals at various proxy nodes.

[8] An analogy is the total costs incurred by an Insurance company to provide service to its customers (e.g., auto, medical), versus, the insurance premium paid by individual customers. Though a customer worries about only by his/her premium payment, the total company-wide costs indirectly impact the per-customer premium assignment.

a domain-specific distributed algorithm software on them. This incurs costs that arise from two distinct aspects:

1. Leasing of K nodes and multiple node-interconnects from the infrastructure provider, out of which N nodes and their interconnects provide the service needed by applications, where $2 \leq N < K$;
2. Software development effort in a service-layer algorithm running on the N-out-of-K nodes and their interconnects, with the remaining $(K - N)$ nodes and interconnects functioning as redundant units.

The component redundancy in algorithm layer purports to minimize the occurrence of service degradations and failures. In the example of Figure 3, the number of nodes and links used by CDN algorithm are: $K = [7, 9]$ and $N = [6, 5]$ — with the ability to tolerate up to 2 node and 4 link failures. The redundancy however incurs a cost for the service provider.

The total leasing cost may increase either linearly or monotonically concave with K — which means a constant or a decreasing per-node cost with an increase in K, as negotiated with the infrastructure provider (e.g., pay-by-use pricing) [6]. The service layer cost is tied to the development and running of distributed algorithm software, and hence is domain-specific. In the CDN push/pull algorithm, N proxy nodes in a distribution tree requires $(N - 1)$ content forwarding interconnects and N' content storages (where $1 \leq N' \leq N$) — besides the base software itself to infuse the proxy capability in the N nodes. In a replicated web service layer, the needed software diversity among N servlet replicas (to deter failures) incurs $\mathcal{O}(N^2)$ cost — besides the base software itself running on the $(N+1)$ nodes and N interconnects. The service layer cost often exhibits a monotonic convex behavior with respect to N, and it dominates over the infrastructure costs because of the specialized software development efforts involved.

The combined cost incurred at the infrastructure and service layers gets assigned to the applications in some form. The incurrence of per-node costs may compel a service provider to limit the number of nodes N participating in algorithm execution, thereby lowering the attainable QoS. The resulting loss of some service value to the application may itself manifest as a cost for the service provider that possibly out-weighs the cost savings arising from a lower N or K.

Since our focus is on the assessment of system dependability, we consider only the QoS aspects arising from the changes in N exercised system-wide to deal with a hostile condition e (we ignore the cost considerations).

4.2   Revisiting CDN: Model-Based Control Schema

The traffic generated by content read requests from various clients is random and bursty, making its resource demand on the CDN infrastructure unpredictable. This lack of knowledge about traffic demand is compounded by the variability in the processing/storage capacity of proxy nodes and the network bandwidth of interconnect path segments over the cloud infrastructure. Though the information about placement of proxy nodes in a distribution tree is made known to the

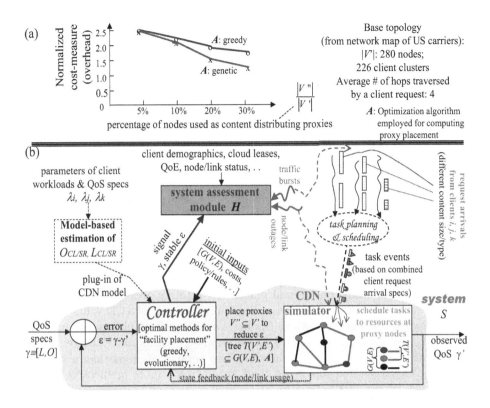

Fig. 4. Adaptive proxy placement in a CDN and its control-theoretic model

service-layer algorithm for content push/pull, the effects of a proxy placement Z on the delay/overhead experienced by clients are not known to the algorithm.

Let $G(V, E)$ is a connected graph representing the topology set up in the infrastructure, where the vertices V are the proxy-capable compute-nodes and the edges E are the node interconnects. Given a set of clients $\{C_i\}_{i=1,2,\cdots,M}$, each client C_i is attached to a node $v_i \in V$ that is located in its geographic proximity to access the remote content X hosted by a server R. The service-layer algorithm creates an overlay tree $T(\hat{V}, \hat{E})$ on the topology $G(V, E)$, where $\hat{V} \subseteq V$ and $\hat{E} \subseteq E$ with one or nodes $V'' \subseteq \hat{V}$ hosting a content distributing proxy server. The QoS specs is denoted as: $\gamma \equiv [O_i, L_i]_{i=1,2,\cdots,M}$, where O_i and L_i indicate the overhead and latency respectively tolerated by C_i. Due to the modeling complexity of CDN system, the actual output QoS γ' in a control round may be different from a model-estimated QoS: $\gamma'' = [O_{\mathcal{A},i}, L_{\mathcal{A},i}]_{i=1,2,\cdots,M}$. C_i may execute a machine-intelligence procedure to reduce the modeling error: $(\gamma'' - \gamma')$ over multiple rounds of proxy placement, with the observed output QoS γ' in each round refining the proxy placement in a next round. The model-based proxy-placement schema, embodied in the controller C_i, is shown in Figure 4-(b). The observe-and-adapt cycle continues over multiple control rounds until the desired QoS is achieved, i.e., $(\gamma - \gamma')$ falls below an acceptable level.

The on-line control schema allows an exhaustive search of the solution space to determine an optimal distribution tree with an appropriate choice of proxy placement and $CL/CL'/SR$ algorithm therein. The model-based determination of optimal solution however may possibly not match with the actual CDN output performance due to inaccuracies in the modeling process itself. The modeling error is factored into the algorithm for revising the optimal placements in subsequent iterations of the solution search. Given this cycle of computing a tree, actual instantiation of the on-tree nodes, and observing the user-level QoS therein during on-line control of the CDN, the quality of adaptation may itself suffer: such as output convergence and stability. Though a final output may be optimal, an algorithmic process of reaching the optimal point that makes the effect of search jitter visible to the clients is not desirable. This is because the user-level QoS may also be affected by how many placements that are actually tried out on the CDN system during the process of determining the optimal proxy placement at the end. Thus, a heuristics-aided search of the solution space that determines a reasonable placement in less number of cycles is desirable.

In an earlier work [11], we studied the use of genetic algorithms and greedy algorithms to determine an optimal placement of proxy nodes in a distribution tree. The study did not consider the on-line control aspects of a CDN, but focused on the algorithmic performance in finding a (sub-)optimal placement: namely, the number of search steps needed to determine the solution. Expectedly, we found that the greedy algorithm incurs a less number of steps than a genetic algorithm for large-sized topologies (and also incurs a more predictable search behavior). But, the cost optimality of a proxy placement as determined by the greedy algorithm is less than that determined by the genetic algorithm. Figure 4-(a) shows the simulation results on content distribution cost (normalized) as determined by these algorithms over a large network consisting of 286 nodes and 226 client clusters (the topology is generated from a network map of US carriers). The choice between the greedy versus genetic algorithms is based on the achievable cost-optimality of a final placement and the search jitter and convergence time in reaching the solution. For model-based CDN assessment by H, the latency and overhead difference of greedy versus genetic algorithms manifests as a quantifiable difference in the robustness of corresponding CDN instances against fluctuating client workloads.

5   Related Works on Adaptive Cloud Systems

Today's distributed systems embody both adaptation and functional behaviors. The former deals with adjusting the system operations according to the environment conditions (e.g., increasing the number of server replicas to improve web service performance). Whereas, the latter deals with requirements such as network robustness and security. In this light, we broadly categorize the existing works as dealing with: (i) Systems engineering for the control-theoretic aspects of adaptation (such as stability and convergence) [2,12]; (ii) Software engineering for the verification of application requirements (including para-functional ones)

[13,14]. There have also been system-level tools developed to aid these studies: such as probabilistic monitoring and analysis [15]. In contrast, our work is on model-based assessment of the dependability of cloud-based systems.

Chisel [16] provides an adaptation framework by separating the core functionality of a system from those dealing with non-functional behaviors. This allows a seamless and transparent infusion of new behaviors at run-time to deal with unanticipated external events $e \in E^*$, and a removal of those behaviors when the conditions causing e cease. This dynamic framework is applicable to cloud-based systems, given the uncontrolled nature of third-party administered cloud resources. It is hard to provide 100%-assured behavior of such systems due to their complexity [17]. Along this line, [18] advocates dependability differentiation as a means to identify distinct classes of cloud-based applications. A system assessment in such settings is feasible with our probabilistic measurement of the service errors vis-a-vis their impact on system dependability.

6   Conclusions

We treat system dependability as application-level QoS at a meta-level (regardless of the system complexity). Dependability assessment of a cloud-based system involves three aspects: measurability, predictability, and adaptability of system behavior — which are enabled by the programmability of cloud-based infrastructures and services. Guided by the concepts provided in [4], the paper studied model-based engineering techniques to quantify system dependability, and certify cloud-based systems therein. System-level fault-tolerance mechanisms, hitherto treated separately, are subsumed in the broader notion of system dependability.

Certifying a cloud-based system S involves determining how good S is in meeting the application-level QoS under uncontrolled environment conditions incident on S (such as attacks and failures in the cloud infrastructure). We employ model-based engineering techniques to analyze the system output behavior relative to what is expected of S. The paper studied a compositional management structure for the assessment of system dependability.

In our management view, the core domain-specific functions of S are embodied in an adaptation module A'_p that interacts with the raw physical processes $g^*(\cdots)$ realized on the system infrastructure by service-layer algorithms. A management entity H incorporates the observation logic to reason about system capability by quantification of control errors and probabilistic QoS assessment. An advantage of our management structure is the reduction in development cost of distributed control software via model reuse and service-level programming.

References

1. Joshi, K.R., Bunker, G., Jahanian, F., Moorsel, A.V., Weinman, J.: (Panel Discussion) Dependability in the Cloud: Challenges and Opportunities. In: IEEE/IFIP Intl. Conf. on Dependable Systems and Networks (June 2009)

2. Li, B., Nahrstedt, K.: A Control-based Middleware Framework for Quality of Service Adaptations. IEEE JSAC 17(9) (September 1999)
3. Lamb, C.C., Jamkhedkar, P.A., Heileman, G.L., Abdallah, C.T.: Managed Control of Composite Cloud Systems. In: Proc. IEEE Intl. Symp. on Service-Oriented System Engineering, Irvine, CA (December 2011)
4. Avizienis, A., Laprie, J.C., Randell, B., Landwehr, C.: Basic Concepts and Taxonomy of Dependable and Secure Computing. IEEE Transactions on Dependable and Secure Computing 1(1), 11–33 (2004)
5. Bridges, P.G., Hiltunen, M., Schlichting, R.D.: Cholla: A Framework for Composing and Coordinating Adaptations in Networked Systems. IEEE Transactions on Computers 58(11), 1456–1469 (2009)
6. Sun Microsys. Introd. to Cloud Computing architecture. White Paper (June 2009)
7. Ravindran, K.: Dynamic Protocol-level Adaptations for Performance and Availability of Distributed Network Services. In: Modeling Autonomic Communication Environments. Multicon Lecture Notes (October 2007)
8. Chen, Y., Katz, R.H., Kubiatowicz, J.D.: Dynamic Replica Placement for Scalable Content Delivery. In: Druschel, P., Kaashoek, M.F., Rowstron, A. (eds.) IPTPS 2002. LNCS, vol. 2429, pp. 306–318. Springer, Heidelberg (2002)
9. Ravindran, K., Rabby, M., Macker, J.P., Adamson, B.: Group Communication for Event Dissemination in Dynamic Distributed Networks. IEEE Comsnets (2013)
10. Cordier, M., Dague, P., Dumas, M., Levy, F., Montmain, A., Staroswiecki, M., Trave-massuyes, L.: A comparative analysis of AI and control theory approaches to model-based diagnosis. In: Proc. 14th European Conf. on AI (2000)
11. Wu, J.: Optimization Algorithms for Proxy Placement in Content Distribution Network. Ph.D. Thesis, Dept. of Computer Science, City University of New York, Advisor: K. Ravindran (April 2011)
12. Lu, C., Lu, Y., Abdelzaher, T.F., Stankovic, J.A., Son, S.H.: Feedback Control Architecture and Design Methodology for Service Delay Guarantees in Web Servers. IEEE Trans. on Parallel and Distributed Systems 17(7) (September 2006)
13. Schaefer, I., Heffter, A.P.: Slicing for Model Reduction in Adaptive Embedded Systems Development. In: Workshop on Software Engineering for Adaptive and Self-Managing Systems, SEAMS 2008 (May 2008)
14. Yi, J., Woo, H., Browne, J.C., Mok, A.K., Xie, F., Atkins, E., Lee, C.G.: Incorporating Resource Safety Verification to Executable Model-based Development for Embedded Systems. In: Proc. IEEE RTAS, pp. 137–146 (2008)
15. Brunner, M., Dudkowski, D., Mingardi, C., Nunzi, G.: Probabilistic Decentralized Network Management. In: Proc. IM 2009 (June 2009)
16. Keeney, J., Cahill, V.: Chisel: A Policy-Driven, Context-Aware, Dynamic Adaptation Framework. In: Proc. IEEE Intl. Workshop on Policies for Distributed Systems and Networks (POLICY 2003), pp. 3–14 (June 2003)
17. Ravindran, K.: Managing Robustness of Distributed Applications Under Uncertainties: An Information Assurance Perspective. In: Proc. Annual Cyber Security and Information Intelligence Workshop. ACM, Oak-Ridge (2010)
18. Chilwan, A.: Dependability Differentiation in Cloud Services. Master's Thesis, Dept. of Telematics, Norwegian University of Science and Technology. P.E. Heegaard (July 2011)

Design of a Transmission-Aware Fault-Tolerant CAN Network

Mi Zhou[1], Renfu Li[1], Lihong Shang[2], and Lei Zhang[3]

[1] School of Energy and Power Engineering, Huazhong University of Science and Technology
Wuhan 430074, China
zoooome@gmail.com
[2] School of Computer Science and Engineering, Beihang University
Beijing 100191, China
shanglh@buaa.edu.cn
[3] AVIC Computing Technique Research Institute
Xian 710068, China
bluedward8457@163.com

Abstract. This paper proposes the design of a fault-tolerant controller area network (CAN). Several candidate redundancy strategies are introduced to improve the reliability. To choose a suitable one wisely, it is meaningful to make comparison on the reliability between the candidates. However, as there are redundant channels, the reliability of the network depends on the transmission requirements, which is difficult to evaluate. In this paper, a general approach based on minimal path set is proposed to model the reliability of complex fault-tolerant systems. With the proposed approach, the transmission-aware reliability of the redundant CAN network is evaluated. Comparisons on the reliability are carried out between the candidate strategies. In addition, comparisons on the cost, complexity and latency are also carried out. The results show the channel redundancy is superior to other strategies due to its high reliability, low latency and acceptable cost.

Keywords: fault-tolerant, transmission-aware reliability, CAN.

1 Introduction

CAN is nowadays used in a wide range of applications due to its reliability, real-time transmission, adaptability and low cost. In particular, its application fields are still significantly increasing [1]. However, CAN shows drawbacks with respect to its reliability in the safe-critical applications. There exist some software failure modes such as the jabber frames, the babble errors and the priority inversion problems, which may disrupt the communication. On the other hand, as the media is shared, a single hardware failure may bring the total loss of the bus [2].

To address the issue of reliability, various redundancy strategies were applied in CAN-based applications, such as the controller redundancy [3], the bus driver redundancy [4], the channel redundancy [5,6,7,8] and the system redundancy [9,10].

M. Pathan, G. Wei, and G. Fortino (Eds.): IDCS 2013, LNCS 8223, pp. 351–361, 2013.
© Springer-Verlag Berlin Heidelberg 2013

To trade off between cost and reliability so that to choose a suitable redundancy strategy, it is meaningful to make comparison among various redundancy strategies on the reliability. However, as there are redundant channels, the reliability of the network is difficult to evaluate since it may change with the transmission requirements. The above issue is seldom concerned in previous researches on reliability analysis. Fortunately, in many fieldbus-based systems, especially in most real-time embedded systems, the transmission requirements are usually determined during the design phase so that the messages can be scheduled statically to ensure real time communication [2]. The above fact enables the designers to take the transmission requirements into account when modeling the reliability in the design phase.

As will be mentioned in Section 2, the transmission-aware reliability is too complex to be modeled with the classic series-parallel model. In this paper, a general approach is presented to model the reliability of complex fault-tolerant systems. With the proposed approach, the transmission-aware reliability of the fault-tolerant CAN network is evaluated. Comparisons are carried out between various candidate redundant solutions. The results show the channel redundancy is superior to other strategies due to its high reliability, low latency and acceptable cost.

The following section describes relative work on redundancy strategies and reliability modeling of CAN-based systems. Section 3 introduces the baseline design and the candidate redundant solutions. Section 4 introduces an approach to evaluate the transmission-aware reliability of a fault-tolerant CAN network. Comparisons among various candidate redundant solutions come in Section 5. The final section concludes with a summary.

2   Related Work

A fault-tolerant approach based on triplex CAN controllers was proposed in [3]. The triplex controllers should come to agreement before issuing the "transmit" (Tx) signal to the bus driver. A dedicated circuit named redundant manager (RM) was introduced to coordinate the CAN controllers in the case of discrepancy by injecting the "receive" (Rx) signal with an error flag. Such an approach is transparent to the application, i.e. the designers need not modify their software to take advantage from the redundancy. A shortage of the approach is the increased latency. A single transient error on any controller will cause all controllers to issue an error flag and break current transmission. Thus the triplex controllers lead to higher probability of retransmission and increased average latency for each message when contrasted with the non-redundant design.

A bus driver redundancy strategy was proposed in [4]. In each node, the CAN controller was connecting with duple transceivers, which were connected with different CAN channels. The Tx signal from the CAN controller was directly connected to the transceivers so that they could transmits data simultaneously. An arbiter circuit was proposed to forward the firstly arriving signals from the corresponding transceiver to the CAN controller, while signals from the other transceiver would be ignored. The approach is also transparent to the application. However, there exists the risk of violating the CAN protocol since the bus controller cannot monitor the Rx signal from the later-arriving transceiver during transmitting. In addition, the experimental results in [4] show the message throughput is very low.

Examples of channel redundancy strategies can be find in [5,6,7,8]. In the channel redundant designs, the node contains separated bus interfaces, each of which contains a bus controller and a transceiver. The redundant channels may work either simultaneously as in [5,6] or alternatively as in [7,8]. Application software needs to be modified to take advantage of the channel redundancy strategies. Contrasting with controller redundancy strategies and driver redundancy strategies, channel redundancy strategies provide higher reliability with higher cost.

System redundancy strategies were applied in [9,10]. In a system redundant design, all functional nodes in the network are duplicated. System redundancy strategies overwhelm other redundancy strategies in reliability, while the hardware cost is much higher.

To trade off between cost and reliability and decide a suitable redundancy strategy, it is meaningful to evaluate the reliability under different redundancy strategies. The classic series-parallel model was used to formulate the reliability under various redundancy strategies in [11,12]. However, the transmission requirement is not concerned in the model, and it may lead to inaccurate estimation as shown below in the example in Fig. 1.

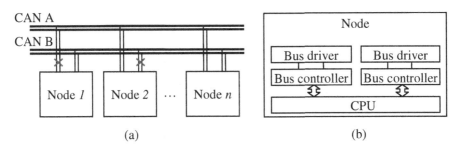

(a)   (b)

Fig. 1. (a) A dual-channel CAN network with two faulty nodes, (b) A dual-channel CAN node

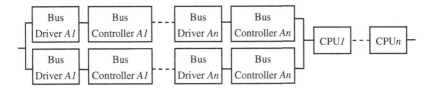

Fig. 2. Series-parallel model of a dual-channel CAN network

As shown in Fig. 1, Node *1* and Node *2* each has a failed CAN controller on different CAN channel. Such a case will be recognized as failure in the series-parallel model shown in Fig. 2 [11,12]. However, if there is no need to transmit message between the two faulty nodes, the above case should be recognized as fail-safe since both Node *1* and Node *2* can communicate with other nodes with the healthy channel.

Thus the reliability will be underestimated without considering the transmission requirements. To take the transmission requirements into account, a new approach is proposed to evaluate the reliability, which will be introduced in Section 4.

3   The Fault-Tolerant Design

The objective of the design is an automatic control system which contains an electronic control unit (ECU), a monitor unit (MU), two sensors and two actuators. The non-fault-tolerant baseline design is shown in Fig. 3. The transmission requirement of the application is modeled as a star topology undirected graph (UG) shown in Fig. 4. As in the UG, a vertex denotes a network node, and an edge between two vertexes denotes that there are data transmissions between the two nodes.

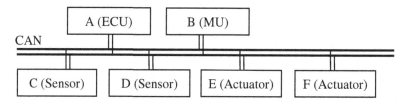

Fig. 3. Baseline design of an automatic control system

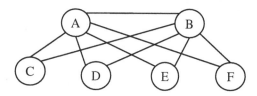

Fig. 4. Data transmission requirement of the objective system

To address the issue of fault tolerance, three candidate solutions with different redundancy strategies were considered, which include controller redundancy (CR), driver redundancy (DR) and channel redundancy (ChnR). The system redundancy was not considered as a candidate strategy due to the high cost.

The CR solution is derived from [3], and the DR solution is derived from [4].

In the ChnR solution, the redundant channels work simultaneously to decrease the latency. The driver-level software is designed to make redundant copies of each message and transmit them simultaneously on the redundant channels. Since the probability of undetected corrupted messages in CAN is 4.7×10^{-11} [2], which is much lower than the hardware failure rate, there is no need to compare the received copies. Thus the firstly arriving copy of each message will be submitted to the application and the later arriving one will be dropped.

The module structures of the CAN node with different redundancy strategies are shown in Fig. 5. The modules of each node can be generally classified into two categories, i.e. the series part which is shown as long-dashed line and the channel interface which is shown as short-dashed line. The series part of a node is necessary to the system since there is no spare for it. The reliability of the series parts of all nodes in a network can be simply multiplied to contribute to the reliability of the whole system. The channel interface modules contribute to the reliability of the network, which should be modeled depending on the transmission requirements.

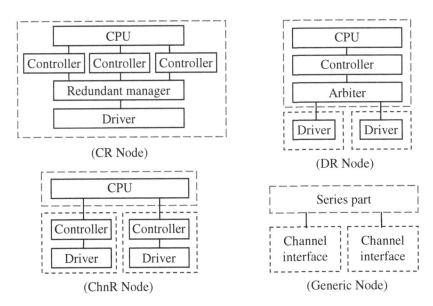

Fig. 5. Module structures of fault-tolerant CAN nodes

Thus the reliability of the whole system can be generally modeled as:

$$R(\text{system}) = R(\text{network}) \cdot \prod R(\text{series parts}).$$

As mentioned in Section 2, when the data transmission requirements are taken into account, the reliability of a redundant network becomes too complex to be formulated using the classic "series-parallel" model since it will contains too many possible cases in which the system works. A new approach will be introduced to evaluate the transmission-aware reliability before we make comparisons among the candidate solutions.

4   Model the Transmission-Aware Reliability

4.1   Minimal Path Set Model

The minimal path set model is a general model for any fault-tolerant systems.

Let $W = \{w_1, w_2, \ldots, w_n\}$ be the universe of discourse, where n is the number of components in W, w_i is the i-th component. It is supposed that faults in W occur probabilistically and independently.

Let S be a fault-tolerant system in W. A minimal path C_i of S is defined as a necessary and satisfactory part of the system S. Even if all elements except C_i are faulty, S still works. However, if another fault occurs in C_i, S fails.

The minimal path set (MPS) model of S is defined as a set of vectors, that is:

$$S = \{C_1, C_2, \ldots, C_p\}, C_i = [c_{i1} \ c_{i2} \ \cdots \ c_{in}], c_{ij} \in \{0,1\}, 1 \le i \le p, 1 \le j \le n,$$

where p is the number of minimal paths, C_i is a n-dimensional vector corresponding with the i-th minimal path. c_{ij} is the j-th element of C_i. $c_{ij}=1$ denotes that component w_j is involved in minimal path C_i, while $c_{ij}=0$ denotes that w_j is not involved in C_i.

The minterm set $M(S)$ of system S is defined as:

$$M(S) = \{v \in \{0,1\}^n \mid \exists i \ \forall j \ v_j \ge c_{ij}, 1 \le i \le p, 1 \le j \le n\},$$

where v_i denotes the i-th element of vector v.

Each vector v in $M(S)$ corresponds to a minterm, which denotes a possible case that S works. The element $v_i=1$ denotes component w_i still works in this case and $v_i=0$ denotes w_i has failed.

The reliability $R(S)$ of system S is formulated as:

$$R(S) = \sum_{v \in M(S)} \prod_{i=1}^{n} \left(e^{-\lambda_i t} v_i + (1 - e^{-\lambda_i t})(1 - v_i) \right), \tag{1}$$

where λ_i is the failure rate of component w_i.

4.2   Deduce the MPS

As shown in Section 4.1, we need to find the MPS of a fault-tolerant system S before evaluating the reliability with (1). However, it is usually difficult to find all minimal paths manually in a complex fault-tolerant system. Some operations are introduced to deduce the MPS of a system from the MPS of its components as follows:

The "Minimize" operation of a set S is defined as:

$$\text{Min}(S) = S - \{v \in S \mid \exists u \ \forall i \ u_i \le v_i, u \in S, u \ne v, 1 \le i \le n\}. \tag{2}$$

To minimize a set S means to remove the non-minimal path vectors from S. According to the definition of minimal path, a non-minimal path contains all components involved in a certain minimal path and contains at least another component. Thus, we can find the subset of non-minimal path vectors by checking each vector v in S literately. For a certain v, if there exists a vector u which satisfies that v contains all components involved in u, there must exists at least one component in v which is not contained in u since $u \ne v$, in other words, the vector v can be recognized as a non-minimal path vector. When we find the subset of non-minimal path vectors of S, we can get $\text{Min}(S)$ as its complementary set.

The logic "OR" operation on the set $\{0, 1\}$ is defined as:

$$0 \vee 0 = 0, \quad 0 \vee 1 = 1, \quad 1 \vee 0 = 1, \quad 1 \vee 1 = 1.$$

The logic "OR" operation of two vectors v and u which are of same dimension n is defined as:

$$v \vee u = \left[v_i \vee u_1 \quad v_2 \vee u_2 \quad \cdots \quad v_n \vee u_n \right].$$

The logic "AND" operation of two sets S_1 and S_2 is defined as:

$$S_1 \wedge S_2 = \mathrm{Min}\left(\{ k = v \vee u \mid v \in S_1, u \in S_2 \} \right). \tag{3}$$

The logic "OR" operation of two sets S_1 and S_2 is defined as:

$$S_1 \vee S_2 = \mathrm{Min}\left(S_1 \cup S_2 \right). \tag{4}$$

By means of composing the MPSs of the components with the logic "OR" operation and logic "AND" operation, the MPS of a fault-tolerant system can be deduced in a natural way.

4.3   Model the Reliability of the Candidate Solutions

As introduced in Section 3, the reliability of the system can be evaluated by multiplying the reliability of the network and the reliability of all series parts. In the CR solution, there is no need to consider the transmission requirements since there is no redundant channel. In the DR solution and the ChnR solution, the reliability of the network can be evaluated as below.

The universe $W = \{ A_1, A_2, B_1, B_2, C_1, C_2, D_1, D_2, E_1, E_2, F_1, F_2 \}$, where each element of W denotes a channel interface module. For example, A_1 denotes the first channel interface of node A. For instance, in the DR solution, A_1 denotes the bus driver of the ECU on the first CAN channel.

The MPS model of the channel interface modules are as follows: $A_1 = \{ [1\ 0\ 0\ 0\ 0\ 0\ 0\ 0\ 0\ 0\ 0\ 0] \}$, $A_2 = \{ [0\ 1\ 0\ 0\ 0\ 0\ 0\ 0\ 0\ 0\ 0\ 0] \}$, $B_1 = \{ [0\ 0\ 1\ 0\ 0\ 0\ 0\ 0\ 0\ 0\ 0\ 0] \}$, $B_2 = \{ [0\ 0\ 0\ 1\ 0\ 0\ 0\ 0\ 0\ 0\ 0\ 0] \}$, et al.

Since the condition that the communication between node A and node B is available can be described as "(both A_1 and B_1 work) or (both A_2 and B_2 work)", the MPS model of the edge AB in the UG shown in Fig. 4 can be deduced as follows:

$$AB = (A_1 \wedge B_1) \vee (A_2 \wedge B_2)$$
$$= \left\{ [1\ 0\ 1\ 0\ 0\ 0\ 0\ 0\ 0\ 0\ 0\ 0], [0\ 1\ 0\ 1\ 0\ 0\ 0\ 0\ 0\ 0\ 0\ 0] \right\}.$$

The MPS model of other edges can also be deduced similar as AB. For instance, the MPS model of the edge AC is as follows:

$$AC = (A_1 \wedge C_1) \vee (A_2 \wedge C_2)$$
$$= \left\{ [1\ 0\ 0\ 0\ 1\ 0\ 0\ 0\ 0\ 0\ 0\ 0], [0\ 1\ 0\ 0\ 0\ 1\ 0\ 0\ 0\ 0\ 0\ 0] \right\}.$$

The MPS model of the condition that both AB and AC work is as follows:

$$AB \wedge AC = \{[1\ 0\ 1\ 0\ 1\ 0\ 0\ 0\ 0\ 0\ 0\ 0], [1\ 1\ 1\ 0\ 0\ 1\ 0\ 0\ 0\ 0\ 0\ 0],$$
$$[1\ 1\ 0\ 1\ 1\ 0\ 0\ 0\ 0\ 0\ 0\ 0], [0\ 1\ 0\ 1\ 0\ 1\ 0\ 0\ 0\ 0\ 0\ 0]\}$$

The condition that the network works can be described as "each edge works". Thus the MPS model of the network (*N*) can be deduced as follows:

$$N = AB \wedge AC \wedge BC \wedge AD \wedge BD \wedge AE \wedge BE \wedge AF \wedge BF .$$

There are 16 vectors in the MPS model of *N*, thus the formulation is not expanded due to page limit. Once we get the MPS model of *N*, the reliability *R(N)* can be evaluated with (1).

5   Comparisons among the Candidate Solutions

To find a suitable redundancy strategy, comparison on the transmission-aware reliability was carried out. In the calculation, we took into account the data presented in [13], and set the failure rate of the modules as shown in Table 1.

Table 1. Failure rate of basic modules

Module	Failure rate (h^{-1})
CPU	10^{-6}
Bus Controller	10^{-6}
Bus driver	10^{-6}
Arbiter circuit	10^{-7}
Redundant manager	10^{-7}
Connector	10^{-8}
Termination	10^{-8}

The comparison on the reliability under various candidate redundant strategies is shown in Fig. 6. As shown in Fig. 6, the curve of the CR solution is very close to that of the DR solution, while the ChnR solution is superior to other solutions in the reliability.

The comparisons on the Mean Time to Failure (MTTF) of different solutions are shown in Table 2, where the MTTF of system *S* is evaluated as:

$$MTTF(S) = \int_0^{+\infty} R(S)dt$$

Table 2. Comparison on the MTTF of the candidate solutions

	Baseline	CR	DR	ChnR
MTTF (h)	5.53×10^4	6.91×10^4	6.90×10^4	8.44×10^4

As shown in Table 2, the CR solution has slightly long life than the DR solution. The ChnR solution has the longest MTTF, which is 52.62% longer than that of the baseline solution.

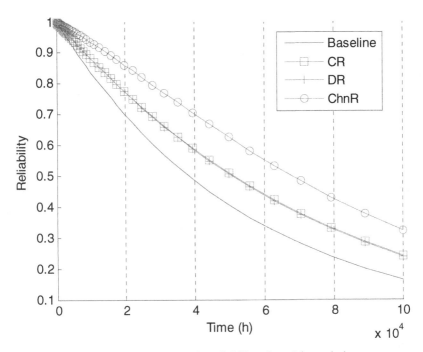

Fig. 6. Comparison on the reliability of candidate solutions

A general comparison on the reliability, complexity and cost is shown in Table 3. As shown in Table 3, in the CR solution and the DR solution, the hardware complexity is high since dedicated circuit must be involved to coordinate the redundant modules. In the DR solution and the ChnR solution, the hardware cost is high due to the spare CAN channel which costs additional cable, connectors and terminations.

Table 3. General comparison of the candidate solutions

	Baseline	CR	DR	ChnR
Reliability	low	medium	medium	high
Hardware complexity	low	high	high	medium
Hardware cost	low	medium	high	high
Software complexity	low	low	low	high
Average latency	medium	high	medium	low

In the ChnR solution, it is left to the software to transmit copies of each message on the redundant channels and to filter received redundant messages, thus the software complexity is higher than in other solutions.

In the CR solution, a single transient error on any controller will cause all controllers to break current transmission, thus the average latency of each message is high. For comparison, in the ChnR solution, a single transient error may lead to retransmission on a channel while it has no effect on the other channel, thus the average latency is reduced since the firstly arriving copy will be received on time.

6   Conclusions and Future Work

In this paper, several candidate redundancy strategies of a fault-tolerant CAN network is introduced. A general approach is presented to model the reliability of complex fault-tolerant systems. With the proposed approach, the transmission-aware reliability of the fault-tolerant CAN network is evaluated. Comparisons on the reliability, cost, complexity and latency are carried out between various candidate redundant strategies. The results show the channel redundancy is superior to other strategies due to its high reliability, low latency and acceptable cost.

A drawback of the proposed MPS model is that the time cost to evaluate the reliability will grow rapidly with the number of nodes. For instance, since there are only 6 nodes in the target design, the time cost is currently less than one second. However, when the number of nodes grows to 15, it will take tens of minutes to evaluate the reliability. It may be helpful to replace M(S) with an approximated minterm set to accelerate the evaluation. We will address this issue in our future work.

References

1. Hu, H.S., Qin, G.: H.: Online Fault Diagnosis for Controller Area Networks. In: 2011 Fourth International Conference on Intelligent Computation Technology and Automation, pp. 452–455 (2011)
2. ARINC Specification 825-2: General Standardization of CAN (Controller Area Network) Bus Protocol for Airborne Use (2011)
3. Guerrero, C., Rodriguez-Navas, G., Proenza, J.: Design and implementation of a redundancy manager for triple redundant CAN controllers. In: IEEE 2002 28th Annual Conference of the Industrial Electronics Society, pp. 2294–2299 (2002)
4. Yang, J., Zhang, T., Song, J.Y., Sun, H.X., Shi, G.Z., Chen, Y.: Redundant design of a CAN bus testing and communication system for space robot arm. In: 10th International Conference on Control, Automation, Robotics and Vision, pp. 1894–1898 (2008)
5. Bertoluzzo, M., Buja, G.: A high-performance application protocol for fault-tolerant CAN networks. In: 2010 IEEE International Symposium on Industrial Electronics, pp. 1705–1710 (2010)
6. Fu, L.L., Li, Z.J.: The application and reliability analysis of excitation equipment with dual redundant CAN network. Large Electric Machine and Hydraulic Turbine (5), 60–62 (2010)
7. Ni, F.L., Jin, M.H., Wang, H.L., Liu, H., Hirzinger, G.: Joint fault-tolerant design of the Chinese space robotic arm. In: 2006 IEEE International Conference on Information Acquisition, pp. 528–533 (2006)
8. Zhai, X.H., Li, J., Qian, K., Tao, J.N.: Design of double redundant interface based on CAN bus for nodes of FCS. In: 2010 Second WRI Global Congress on Intelligent Systems, pp. 394–396 (2010)
9. Pimentel, J.R.: Safety-reliability of distributed embedded system fault tolerant units. In: The 29th Annual Conference of the IEEE Industrial Electronics Society, pp. 945–950 (2003)

10. Sun, X.F., Zheng, L.: Reliability analysis of a novel structure in an automatic sorting system. In: 2010 IEEE 17th International Conference on Industrial Engineering and Engineering Management, pp. 955–957 (2010)
11. Tang, Y.Y., Wang, C.D.: Research of redundant system based on CAN bus and its reliability analysis. Journal of Zhong Yuan University of Technology 21(5), 73–75 (2010)
12. Xia, J.Q., Zhang, C.S., Bai, R.G., Xue, L.Q.: Real-time and reliability analysis of time-triggered CAN-bus. Chinese Journal of Aeronautics 26(1), 171–178 (2013)
13. Barranco, M., Proenza, J., Almeida, L.: Quantitative Comparison of the Error-Containment Capabilities of a Bus and a Star Topology in CAN Networks. IEEE Transactions on Industrial Electronics 58(3), 802–813 (2011)

Quantitative Model of Personnel Allocation Based on Information Entropy

Zhenli He, Hua Zhou, Zhihong Liang, and Junhui Liu

School of Software, Yunnan University,
Key Laboratory of Software Engineering of Yunnan Province Kunming,
Yunnan, 650091, China

Abstract. In the field of the software project management, the distribution and organization of developers has always been a research focus. In a software project, it is of great importance to divide the modules and personnel allocation, which, however, still mainly depends on the project manager's rich experience, lack of quantitative analysis method. To solve these problems, this paper presents two quantitative models based on information entropy, used in the quantitative analysis of the quality of overall division structure of the project and of the personnel allocation structure in the module with more detailed. Finally, based on the above, this article conducts the example analysis to verify the effectiveness and practicability of the method.

Keywords: information entropy, quantitative, personnel allocation, module division.

1 Introduction

With the rapid development of informationization, it has become an indispensable part of people in various areas of work even in daily life to use software. Nowadays, much software development is no longer what a few programmers can do, the scale of much software development is very large, needing a very large development team. A large software project requires a lot of people, spending a year or several years to complete. In order to improve the work efficiency and guarantee the quality of work, the overall division structure of the project as well as the organization and distribution of software developers is the work with great significance and complexity.

Software engineering productivity studies show substantial differences between individual developers. Getting the right people on your project team greatly improves the chances of success[1]. In addition, there are still many investigations recognize that major contributors to the outcome of software projects are personnel allocation decisions[2-5]. However, people continue to be the least formalized factor in process modeling, which tends to focus more on the technical side[6].Defective people assignment and problems among project team members have been identified as two of the main human factor-related issues affecting software project success[7].

In summary, the problem of module partition of whole project and the personnel allocation are closely related to the results of the software project development, which

M. Pathan, G. Wei, and G. Fortino (Eds.): IDCS 2013, LNCS 8223, pp. 362–372, 2013.
© Springer-Verlag Berlin Heidelberg 2013

is very important. For a project, if we can do the quantitative analysis of the module partition and the personnel allocation, evaluating various solutions, we will be able to choose a better solution to increase the success rate of software projects, which shows obviously great significance. This article uses these for the research background, investigating two types of quantitative models based on the information entropy.

2　The Methodology

2.1　Recommendations to Model of Personal Assignment from Otero

In the area of software project management, the problem of the module partition of whole project and the personnel allocation has gained more and more attention from scholars, including Otero, a representative scholar and others. Otero and others proposed a methodology to assign resources to tasks when optimum skill sets are not available. The methodology takes into account existing capabilities of candidates, required levels of expertise, and priorities of required skills for the task. They thought the most important part in study of the personnel allocation was to take two problems into consideration[8]:

- The tasks are usually not expedited by adding extra resources, since there is significant overhead training and communication time required for resources to get familiarized with tasks.
- Estimates of how long it will take to complete tasks are very imprecise, since they depend on a set of hard-to-estimate factors, like developer capabilities.

Because of this, this paper will consider the adding pay expenses incurred from additional personnel as well as different developers with different ability when modeling.

2.2　Brooks's Law

Brooks' law is a principle in software development which says that "adding manpower to a late software project makes it later"[9]. It was coined by Fred Brooks in his 1975 book The Mythical Man-Month[10]. The corollary of Brooks's Law is that there is an incremental person who, when added to a project, makes it take more, not less time. This is mainly because "time and personnel do not swap". When developers grew as arithmetical series, the personnel communication overhead also will be with geometric ratio growth[11].

In order to better illustrate this law, let's do an assumption. There are N groups of programmers, and we are going to achieve the same scale procedure, then the number of each communication is:

$$C = N(N-1)/2$$

Assume that the workload of each communication and exchange of views on an average is μ, then the increase communication overhead is:

$$E_C = \mu N(N-1)/2 \tag{1}$$

When N = 3, into (1)

$$E_C = \mu 3(3-1)/2 = 3\mu \tag{2}$$

When N = 8, into (1)

$$E_C = \mu 8(8-1)/2 = 28\mu \tag{3}$$

Comparing (2) (3)we can find that, despite an increase of only five people, but the communication overhead increases nearly tenfold. Further inference shows that if we increase the number of team members blindly, the productivity of programmers' team will decline.

2.3   Information Entropy Model

Entropy theory is a science theory with very wide range of application. Entropy is a physics concept as well as a mathematical function or a kind of natural law. In statistical physics, entropy is a measure of the number of microscopic state of the system. In information theory, entropy is a measure of the uncertainty of random events. For a generalized system, entropy can be used to measure the state of confusion or disorder.

The concept of information entropy is on the basis of the entropy, making up for the blank of the measurement in the information theory. Founder of information theory, Shannon, in his book "The Mathematical Theory of Communication," proposes the concept of information entropy. Now the information entropy has become the most successful and popular information measurement. Shannon defines information as "something to eliminate" which is natural to describe uncertainty with a probability function[12].

Assume the probability of occurrence of the event A is P(A). Shannon used (4) to measure information content provided by event A, which is called self-information.

$$I(A) = -\log P(A) \tag{4}$$

In (4) it shows that the greater the probability of occurrence of event A is, the less the information it provides. And information content is of dditivity.

$$I(AB) = I(A) + I(B) \tag{5}$$

Assume a random event has N possible results or a message has N possible values. If the probabilities of their occurrences are $p_1, p_2, \cdots, p_N$, the average information content of this event is (6).

$$H = -\sum_{i=1}^{N} p_i \log p_i \tag{6}$$

The result of (6) is known as information entropy (in bit).

3   Quantitative Models for Module Partition and Personnel Allocation

According to the content of Chapter I and Chapter II, this chapter will try to build two models based on information entropy to quantify module partition and personnel allocation. When building the quantitative models, we will focus on considering the communicative overhead of personnel and their various development abilities.

3.1   Quantitative Models of Module Partition

In order to quantify the merit of the overall division scheme, here according to the information entropy model, we have further defined the demand entropy, supply entropy and the partition entropy, and assume that following conditions are fulfilled.

- Assume we want to develop a system with clear user demand. Task amount of the system is clear and divisible.
- Take account of neither architecture style nor model, assume the system is done designing and be divided into corresponding module.
- To complete the project, the main work is divided into several major parts, the interaction relationship between various parts is clear.

Assume we want to develop a software project which has a certain function, the quota of the project is Q, development of the system can follow the responsibilities and functions into N parts, the quota of each part is Qi, So there is.

$$Q = \sum_{i=1}^{N} Q_i \tag{7}$$

In Fig. 1, it shows the module partition of the project.

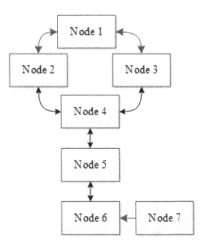

Fig. 1. Module partition of the project

According to Fig. 1, projects have been divided into 7 parts, the relationships of them have been shown above, Node1$\rightarrow$ Node2 represents Node1 communicate to Node2, the arrow represents the communication generated by a support to Node2. In addition, the bidirectional arrows represent two single arrows.

Definition 1. According to Fig. 1, assume the abstract structure is $G =< V, E >$, including:

1. $|V|$ indicates the total number of nodes in Fig. 1.
2. $|E|$ indicates the total number of edges in Fig. 1.
3. i represents a node in the set of nodes V.
4. $\deg^-(i)$ represents the in-degree of node i.
5. $\deg^+(i)$ represents the out-degree of node i.

Demand entropy is defined as follows:

$$H_D = -\sum_{i=1}^{|V|} \frac{\deg^-(i)}{|E|} \log \frac{\deg^-(i)}{|E|} \tag{8}$$

Supply entropy is defined as follows:

$$H_S = -\sum_{i=1}^{|V|} \frac{\deg^+(i)}{|E|} \log \frac{\deg^+(i)}{|E|} \tag{9}$$

Obviously, there is:

$$\sum_{i=1}^{|V|} \deg^-(i) = \sum_{i=1}^{|V|} \deg^+(i) = |E|$$

So, we can find that

$$\sum_{i=1}^{|V|} \frac{\deg^-(i)}{|E|} = \sum_{i=1}^{|V|} \frac{\deg^+(i)}{|E|} = 1$$

In(8)(9) we take no account of the different traffic amount of each module. Assume module i require support from other parts and offer support to other parts at the same time. Thus the larger its task burden is the more supportive traffic amount it requires. So is that it generates to support other module. We may use weighting entropy to improve the module with large task burden.

Demand entropy improved to

$$H_D' = -\sum_{i=1}^{|V|} Q_i \frac{\deg^-(i)}{|E|} \log \frac{\deg^-(i)}{|E|} \tag{10}$$

Supply entropy improved to

$$H_S' = -\sum_{i=1}^{|V|} Q_i \frac{\deg^+(i)}{|E|} \log \frac{\deg^+(i)}{|E|} \tag{11}$$

Definition 2. According to (10)(11), define the partition entropy as follows:

$$H_P = H_D' + H_S'$$ (12)

According to partition entropy, we can use it to measure the rationality of division of labor. It can also employed to the choice of the overall module. (It will be discussed further in chapter IV), and test the correctness of the module.

3.2 Quantitative Models of Personnel Allocation

In order to quantify the merits of the personnel allocation scheme, according to the information entropy model, we have further defined the allocation entropy. to quantify the personnel allocation, we also need the following conditions can be fulfilled.

- Assume the project module partition is clear.
- Take no account of main responsibilities of the module, assume a certain amount of personnel have put into the module to carry out the relative work.
- Each developer's personal capacity differently. Assume that each person i has a capability value for this module is C_i.
- In order to differentiate duty amount of each one, each person i have a workload ratio W_i. It represents how much a person is responsible for the work, it can be a line of code rates, etc.

Choose a module for detailed analysis. For this module, assume five designated staff responsible for the development work; these five individuals have different personal abilities.

Assume the personnel allocation of the module as shown in the figure below:

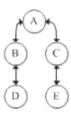

Fig. 2. Personnel allocation of the module

According to Fig. 2, there are A, B, C, D, E five people assigned to the module; and the arrow in this picture represents communication exchanges between personnel. A→B represents A to B communicative amount, different from the quantitative models of module partition, the communication between people is mutual, therefore, the arrow is always double-direction, we can continue to simplify it.

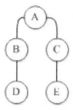

Fig. 3. Simplified Personnel allocation of the module

According to Fig. 3, the undirected arrows represent the mutual communication.

Definition 3: According to Fig. 3, assume the abstract structure is $G =< V, E >$, including:

1. $|V|$ indicates the total number of nodes in Fig. 3.
2. $|E|$ indicates the total number of edges in Fig. 3.
3. i represents a node in the set of nodes V.
4. $\deg(i)$ represents the number of nodes which related to node i.

Allocation entropy is defined as follows:

$$H_A = -\sum_{i=1}^{|V|} \frac{\deg(i)}{2|E|} \log \frac{\deg(i)}{2|E|} \tag{13}$$

Obviously, there is:

$$\sum_{i=1}^{|V|} \deg(i) = 2|E|$$

So, we can find that

$$\sum_{i=1}^{|V|} \frac{\deg(i)}{2|E|} = 1$$

Obviously, in(13) it did not consider the communication amount and the corresponding cost. Assume the larger the ability value of person i is, the stronger his ability is, so is his allocation work proportion in total. Also are the times he communicates with others. Assume the heavier the work that people i has, the more it will cost him to communicate, as he had to take on more development work. We can use the weighted entropy to improve.

Allocation entropy improved to

$$H'_A = -\sum_{i=1}^{|V|} W_i C_i \frac{\deg(i)}{2|E|} \log \frac{\deg(i)}{2|E|} \tag{14}$$

According to the allocation entropy, it can be used to measure the rationality of personnel allocation. We can choose from different people assignment scheme to settle on a best choice. In the next chapter, we will validate the model and test the correctness of the module.

4   Case Studies

4.1   Validation of the Module Partition Models

To verify the quantitative model proposed in the previous chapter, now we use a real-life software projects to be calculated.

Assume we want to develop an online examination system based on B/S architecture, the function of the system and architecture design is not in the scope of consideration of this paper. In order to facilitate calculation, here we only consider the system development process, and complete the workload of normalized processing of system development. That is to say, the total quantity $Q = 1$, each module quota for Q_i.

Assume that the system development were divided into web design, front-end web development, back-end web development, system services development, data persistence development, database scripts development and database design, a total of seven parts, its quota Q_i were 0.1, 0.1, 0.1, 0.4, 0.1, 0.1, 0.1. The relationship between each module as shown in Fig. 4: (the number on the side of the module represents quota of normalized results)

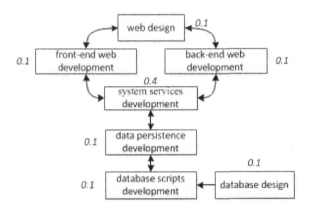

Fig. 4. Module partition of the online examination system

According to (10)(11)(12), the partition entropy can be calculated:

$$H_P = H'_D + H'_S \approx 0.24726198 \qquad (15)$$

Assume another solution for the development process is divided into six parts, we merge the front-end web development and the back-end web development. The relationship between each module as shown in Fig. 5:

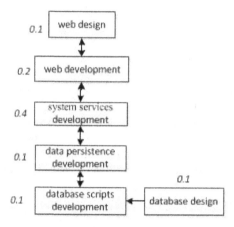

Fig. 5. The other module partition of the online examination system

According to (10)(11)(12), the partition entropy can be calculated:

$$H_P = H_D' + H_S' \approx 0.2601475 \tag{16}$$

According to (15)(16), merging the two identified modules will lead the increase of partition entropy, which corresponds with the actual situation, and the division of labor will not lead to increase the difficulty of project development. In view of the different schemes, according to the partition entropy we can evaluate the module partition of software project in order to choose a better solution and for better completion of the project development.

4.2   Validation of the Personnel Allocation Models

According to the examples of previous section, this section will conduct further analysis to verify the accuracy of quantitative model of personnel allocation. We choose the service programming module with the largest workload for refined analysis. Assume we have A, B, C, D, E five people, whose work is in charge of the development of the module. In order to calculate conveniently, here we only consider the workload of development process, and all the work is to develop (though in fact this is not possible). At the same time, the C_i and W_i are normalized processing in order to calculate the allocation entropy, $C = 1, W = 1$.

Assume that A, B, C, D, E five people of C_i were 0.5, 0.2, 0.2, 0.05, 0.2, and the workload W_i were 0.1, 0.25, 0.25, 0.2, 0.2.

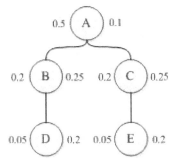

Fig. 6. Personnel allocation of services development

According to Fig. 6, person A is the leader of the module, he has strong technical strength, writing less code, mainly taking charge of commanding. And people B, C are senior programmers, mainly taking charge of the two different tasks of development work, serving as the main force. Person D, E are B, C's assistants respectively, inexperienced ordinary programmers, mainly taking charge of the development of a number of work simple but tedious, assisting B, C to complete the development tasks. In Fig. 6, the left of the numbers represent the staff's ability C_i, and the right of the numbers represents the staff's workload W_i.

According to (14), the allocation entropy can be calculated:

$$H_A \approx 0.024835 \tag{17}$$

Then, assume that the A and E two people exchange their duty, as shown below:

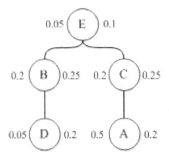

Fig. 7. The other personnel allocation of services development

According to (14), the allocation entropy can be calculated:

$$H_A \approx 0.028222 \tag{18}$$

According to (17)(18), it will cause huge impact to the development of software project if placing the incompetent person in work distribution as a whole, which is consistent with the facts. In the actual development, based on the allocation entropy we are able to measure the pros and cons of different personnel allocation projects, thereby placing the right person at the right position to increase the success rate of projects.

5   Conclusion

This article discusses the quantitative methods towards evaluating the module partition of whole project in the software project development as well as the pros and cons of the development of a program module for personnel allocation, in circumstances with certain workload. It shows two quantitative models based on information entropy and uses practical examples to verify them. The results show that the results of these two models coincide with the facts, which can effectively verify the pros and cons of the module partition of whole project and the personnel allocation. Besides, it is capable to facilitate project management staff in the selection of specific programs with quantifiable basis for reference. However, the model above is also of defection. In this paper, the numerical values of the task and the personnel capacity are estimated values, so the future research will focus on how to obtain more precise numerical values of the task and the personnel capacity.

Acknowledgment. This work is funded by the Open Foundation of Key Laboratory of Software Engineering of Yunnan Province under Grant No. 2011SE13.

References

1. Howard, A.: Software engineering project management. Commun. ACM 44(5), 23–24 (2001)
2. Gorla, N., Lam, Y.W.: Who should work with whom?: building effective software project teams. Communications of the ACM 47(6), 79–82 (2004)
3. e. Silva, L.C., Costa, A.P.C.S.: Decision model for allocating human resources in information system projects. International Journal of Project Management 31(1), 100–108 (2013)
4. Kuchař, Š., Martinovič, J.: Human Resource Allocation in Process Simulations Based on Competency Vectors. In: Snasel, V., Abraham, A., Corchado, E.S. (eds.) SOCO Models in Industrial & Environmental Appl. AISC, vol. 188, pp. 231–240. Springer, Heidelberg (2013)
5. Acuña, S.T., Gómez, M., Juristo, N.: Towards understanding the relationship between team climate and software quality—a quasi-experimental study. Empirical Software Engineering 13(4), 401–434 (2008)
6. Acuna, S.T., Juristo, N., Moreno, A.M.: Emphasizing human capabilities in software development. IEEE Software 23(2), 94–101 (2006)
7. Charette, R.N.: Why software fails. IEEE Spectrum 42(9), 36 (2005)
8. Otero, L.D., et al.: A systematic approach for resource allocation in software projects. Computers & Industrial Engineering 56(4), 1333–1339 (2009)
9. McConnell, S.: Brooks' Law Repealed. IEEE Software 16(6), 6–8 (1999)
10. Brooks, F.P.: The mythical man-month, vol. 1995. Addison-Wesley, Reading (1975)
11. Taylor, J.: A survival guide for project managers. AMACOM Div. American Mgmt. Assn. (2006)
12. Zhang, Y., et al.: Quantitative analysis of system coupling. In: 2011 Eighth International Conference on Fuzzy Systems and Knowledge Discovery (FSKD), vol. 4. IEEE (2011)

An Intelligent Complex Event Processing with D-S Evidence Theory in IT Centralized Monitoring

Bin Cao and Jiyun Li

School of Computer Science and Technology
Donghua University
Shanghai, China
2111453@mail.dhu.edu.cn, jyli@dhu.edu.cn

Abstract. For the mass events monitored from IT infrastructures, it is critical that how to use them effectively to get more valuable information is critical, especially for the large-scale enterprises, application performance issues have an immediate impact on customers' experience and satisfaction. The challenge is that the systems are under uncertain and dynamic operating conditions, so it is difficult to identify the complex critical situations from the large numbers of various events. The existing complex event processing (CEP) systems cannot solve the problem efficiently, in this paper, we propose an intelligent approach to solve the complex event correlation. Combining the CEP with Dempster-Shafer (D-S) evidence theory method, we can find the anomalies timely and locate the root cause automatically. It offers leverage by considering the real-time and accuracy in detecting events.

Keywords: event correlation, complex event processing, uncertain, application performance signature, Dempster-Shafer theory.

1   Introduction

In recent years, with the rapid development of the internet and the increasing of the network size, the management is becoming more and more difficult, but vast amounts of data also becomes important information that people can use. Whether it is the potential threat or opportunity, it is necessary to monitor the network timely. As the IT facilities and resources in all walks of life are deployed perfectly, business is increasingly dependents on highly information-oriented integration. To ensure the whole network running well, it is essential to monitore these devices in real time. A sudden slowdown of application can affect large numbers of customers, which will lead to delay projects and ultimately it can result in the company financial loss. In the existing solutions, CEP is an efficient method for surveillance applications in IT Resource Monitoring System.

CEP is used for analyzing the events coming from multiple sources over a specific period of time by detecting complex patterns between events and by making correlations. It can detect meaningful events or pattern of events which signifies either threats or opportunities from the series of events received continuously, and send

M. Pathan, G. Wei, and G. Fortino (Eds.): IDCS 2013, LNCS 8223, pp. 373–384, 2013.

alerts for the same to responsible entity to respond as quickly as possible. Diagnosis or prediction of system failure has been a hot research topic, people have proposed different solutions, but most of the CEP systems are dealing with the flow of events, and the basic premise underlying the design of the CEP queries proposed is that the associated rules of events are predefined. For the uncertain or unexpected events, the root cause is difficult to diagnose. Moreover, many of predefined rules are based on subjective experience, it's not necessarily accurate in practice. Coupled with the impact of environment, the derived common sets of rules are very difficult to apply for the failure analysis. While rule-based reasoning system structure looks simple, the acquisition of knowledge is a big bottleneck in the system, the rules come from experts, so there are not self-learning function. Even in the process of deductive reasoning, there is no full use of the past experience and lack of memory.

In this paper, we propose an intelligent solution to solve the mass integrated data, which is difficult to define the rules in general and detect the failure automatically. It can output the specific events defined by the rules and classify the uncertain events. For the uncertain events, we use the D-S theory based on rule and application performance signature to analyze the root causes of failure. According to the established rules, we can get the judgment quickly.Our main contribution is that: combining the CEP with D-S techniques, we can quickly locate the anomaly for the uncertain events. As many alarm events related to the detected root cause will not send to the user, it will reduce lots of storage space and decrease the detection time compared to artificial screening. For the event whose detection conditions are inaccurate or inadequate that results in the root cause cannot be detected or analyzed timely, we offer leverage by considering the real-time and accuracy in detecting events.

Next, we will do a brief statement on the related work in the section 2, the section 3 introduces the system's architecture and details on how the CEP classify collected events and how to use the D-S theory to determine the root cause for uncertain events. The section 4 is the experiment evaluation. Finally, a summary for the paper is given.

2   Related Work

Modern event processing is fast becoming a foundation of today's information society. This is a technology that emerged in the late 1990s, but event processing is nothing new. In the 1990s, there were one or two university research projects dedicated to developing new principles of event processing, called CEP. After 2000, CEP began to appear in commercial IT applications, and more recently, starting around 2006, the number of event processing applications and products in the market place has grown rapidly[1].It mainly includes two parts: the commercial products , such as Esper[2],STREAM[3], WebSphere[4] etc., and the research-based projects, such as Cayuga[5],Gigascop[6]. These applications have demonstrated their own advantages, but they are almost for the specific application, and there is no uniform language and rule to define events. Moreover, the premise is proposed based on the predefined rules, even the scalability is well, in practical use, many of the rules are difficult to be defined artificially and most of them are dynamic, and they will vary with the change of environment.

So far, CEP systems are almost used in event-driven architectures, business activity monitoring, business process management, enterprise application integration, network and business level security etc. Network management monitoring and related application monitoring are presented, but the research putting them together is quite a few. Among the appeared centralized monitoring tools, the defined rules are simple, it cannot automatically find all the root cause cascading the failure. For event correlation and its root causes analysis, the main methods are the associated rules, Codebook correlation and artificial intelligence[7]. However, these methods have some short comings, they do not have an appropriate combination of the time with the occured correlation and the accuracy of the data returned by a correlation.

Then [8] suggested integrating events generated across different monitoring tools and putting them together to do analysis, which is a valuable research. The different monitoring tools capture certain information to a data center, by using CEP system to associate events automatically, it generates alarm event or potential trend. Some even proposes detecting the root cause of system anomaly automatically. The automated tools are essential for many performance analysis and applications to understand the application behaviors and changes during the application lifecycle. However, the traditional reactive approach is to set thresholds for observed performance metrics and to raise alarms when these thresholds are violated. This approach is not adequate for understanding the performance changes between application updates. Instead, a proactive approach based on the continuous application performance evaluation may help enterprises reduce loss of productivity. By collecting performance data and correlated event logs and environment variables to detect the essential performance changes in applications, many root cause of the anomaly can be captured in real-time. So information integration is necessary, there are mutual effects between different applications. For example, network failure is likely to pose a threat to service application, also may influence the storage. If they are analyzed separately, many root causes will not be detected. Therefore, in order to accurately determine the root cause of failure, we need not only the certain rules definitions, but the machine learning. Adopting the method of artificial intelligence to train the history data set, we can give out the possibility of different events as root cause. It can be obtained the root cause quickly from the least possible event failure information.

In this paper, we will focus on our specific application, namely the centralized monitoring in IT infrastructure. Event correlation is no longer confined to a single application, we collect the different sources through certain rules, such as filtering, aggregation and so on. From the associated event set, we can find out more potential rules and applications. Some alarm events are hard to find the root cause from a single application, combined application is more accurate to locate. For the failure events, we adopt the method of combining rules associated with D-S theory to obtain the root cause by the probability, which can not only solve the randomness and volatility of the event correlation, but also a substantial reduction in manual. Next we will introduce the related work in details.

3   Integrated Monitoring and Correlation Architecture

Before introducing the associated event, we first have a clear understanding of the event. The event is divided into basic event and composite event. Basic event, also known as simple event, atomic event or single-event, is abstract and predefined by the system, embedded in system to be detected or generated by a fixed mechanism. Composite event is composed of other abstraction events which can be basic events or mixed events. They are defined by the uniform rules attributes. The event is expressed by event id, type, operator, value, timestamp and some additional information. The operator includes unary, binary and customized.

3.1   System Architecture

The whole centralized monitoring system architecture is shown as Fig.1, event correlation mainly involves three blocks: event collector engine, CEP engine and D-S evidence theory. First, the event collector engine, collecting events from different monitoring tools by filtering, conversion, aggregation etc., generates a unified formal definition of the event flow. Followed by the CEP engine, the core of the entire system, processing the collected events through the rule definitions, the generated events is sent out directly to particular users, or reused as input events, or used to do further analysis. Finally, the D-S evidence theory method, which is the addition to the CEP results, in view of the detected uncertainty event set, is used to do further analysis. On one hand, it can detect the root cause from the many alarm events, and reduce large numbers of alarm events to produce, on the other hand, the possible root cause is judged automatically, saving time and manpower.

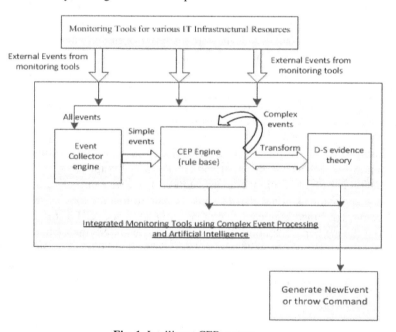

Fig. 1. Intelligent CEP system

Next, we will introduce the key part of the CEP engine, the query model. Then we will focus on the D-S evidence theory method.

3.2   The Query Model

Our event processing system with the modified Cayuga system, which adopts the method of stream processing and event processing, allows the information integration from different monitoring tools. [9] has relevant event model, and made a detailed query engine. Here, we don't do extra statement on event expressions and rule definitions description.We mainly use their framework to process the events, but for the specific rule definition, we do some modification and use the following form:

SELECT [attributes]
FROM [expression]
DO generate New Event or throw Command
Here, the [expression] is constructed as follows:
TYPE Rule content
DECLARE EventClass virtual events list
ON Event Pattern
WHERE Constraints satisfied

TYPE describes the function of the rule. In the rule, we describe the type of detection made. DECLARE lists the virtual events and their classes that are taken as input and the name of the variable representing that class (it is necessary if we have two events of the same class in a rule).ON describes the expected pattern, the declared events are used in the pattern that describes their relationships and the contextual constraints are defined separately. WHERE states the contextual constraints of the rule.

DO describes the actions to be triggered if the rule is activated, 'generate' indicates a new complex event, it will be reused or to be send out, 'throw' indicates a command to do the further analysis.

For different events, we take different rules to process them. We mainly divide them into three cases. For a single application, such as monitoring the service performance, the load of CPU can be detected by stream processing in a certain time interval, output the average CPU utilization. It also can be checked by the rule engine, setting the initial value, an alarm event is generated when a certain threshold is reached. For the complex event from different sources, some rules are very explicit, and it can be obtained by rule matching. For example, all of the applications of network, services and storage send out alarm events. If the network fails, it will cause that the service cannot get request, the store content is empty, so we can define rules to discover automatically the root cause.

For some other events, its root cause is difficult to define, may be the same events in different situations are caused by different events. For example, the server is down, the cause may be: 1. hardware failure; 2. software with a bug; 3. network failure, such as DNS server is down; 4. power outages caused by natural disasters; 5. the fallibility caused by humans. They are all likely to be the cause, and what we can do is to find out all the possible causes and store them. Then we can do the further analysis. The algorithm for selecting uncertain event set is as follows:

```
1. Initialize HS //HS-Hypothesis Set
2. While Constraints satisfied
Do
3. Select h from HS
4. Use inference rule r∈ R
5. Apply r to h to yield h₁,h₂,...,hₙ
6. Add h₁, h₂,...,hₙ to HS
7. Del h from HS
8. Upon cd // cd-correlation description
9. Adjust HS
10. End
```

3.3   D-S Evidence Theory

The Motivation for Application of the D-S Theory. D-S theory is a generalization of the Bayesian theory of subjective probability [10], a transferable belief model, but unlike Bayesian theory, the D-S theory has the ability to represent uncertainties and lack of knowledge. [11] combined different classifiers' results to get a better result, this application inspired us to apply the D-S theory based on the result of CEP in the monitoring IT infrastructure. For the alarm event and these associated with it at the same time, how to determine the root cause, we adopt epistemic event-based correlation approach to solve it, that is the D-S theory based on rule and application performance signature. By giving the probability of events associated with each other and the decision rules, the root cause can be given out by its reliability. Then choosing the root cause from the given events by their degree of belief, so a lot of manual work is saved and more accurate to locate the root cause. [12] verified the feasibility of the method in the use of network management.

Related Concepts and Definitions. In the D-S based on rule and application performance signature, we use some related concepts and theories, referencing[11, 13].

Definition 1. The frame of discernment: a finite set of all possible hypotheses, expressed in Θ, $\Theta=\{\theta_1,\theta_2,...,\theta_K\}$. Its power set is denoted by 2^Θ.

Definition 2. Basic probability assignment (BPA): a basic belief assignment m is a function that assigns a value in [0, 1] to every subset A of Θ and satisfies the following cont:

$$m(\phi) = 0, and \sum_{A\subseteq\Theta} m(A) = 1 \tag{1}$$

Definition 3. Belief function: the belief function $bel(.)$, associated with the BPA $m(.)$, is a function that assigns a value in [0, 1] to every nonempty subset B of Θ. It is called "degree of belief in B" and is defined by

$$bel(B) = \sum_{A\subseteq B} m(A) \tag{2}$$

Definition 4. Plausibility measure: the plausibility (Pls) is a function that the sum of all the basic probability that overlaps with certain set. The formula is:

$$Pls(A) = \sum_{B \cap A \neq \phi} m(B), \quad \forall A \subseteq \Theta \tag{3}$$

It can be shown that the plausibility of an event equals one minus the belief of the complement of that event, and vice versa. That is $Bel(A) = 1 - Pls(A^c)$.

Definition 5. For $\forall A \subseteq \Theta$, the interval $[Bel(A), pls(A)]$ is referred as the reliability interval in A. The Fig.2 describes the uncertainty of the hypothesis.

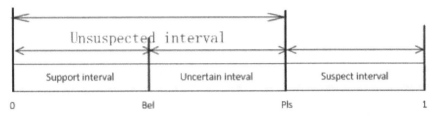

Fig. 2. Uncertainty expression of hypothesis

Definition 6. Focal element: any subset x of the frame of discernment Θ, for which m(x) is non-zero, is called a focal element and represents the exact belief in the proposition depicted by x.

Combination Rule of D-S. Combination rule is a union of different symptom parameters. Given several belief functions based on different rule parameters from unified frame of discernment, and consider the conflicts between the rule parameters. As follows, considering two BPAs m1 (.) and m2 (.) for belief function bel1 (.) and bel2 (.) respectively. Let Aj and Bk denote the focal elements of bel1 (.) and bel2 (.) respectively. Then m1 (.) and m2 (.) can be combined to obtain the belief mass committed to $C \subset \Theta$ according to the following combination or orthogonal sum formula:

$$m(C) = \begin{cases} 0, C = \phi \\ m_1 \oplus m_2(C) = \dfrac{\sum\limits_{j,k,A_j \cap B_k = C} m_1(A_j)m_2(B_k)}{1 - \sum\limits_{j,k,A_j \cap B_k = \phi} m_1(A_j)m_2(B_k)}, C \neq \phi \end{cases} \tag{4}$$

So is the combination of the belief function, that is,

$$((bel_1 \oplus bel_2) \oplus bel_3) \oplus ... \oplus bel_n = \overset{n}{\underset{i=1}{\oplus}} bel_i \tag{5}$$

The Method for Failure Diagnosis. First of all, we will estimate the values of $m_n(\theta_k)$ and $m_n(\Theta)$, which represent the belief in hypothesis k that is produced by condition rule for symptom en and the ignorance associated with condition rule for symptom en. Adopting the method of distance measure, we compute the BPA. Then $m_n(\theta_k)$ and $m_n(\Theta)$ will be estimated according to the following formulas:

$$d_n(\theta_k) = \exp(-\|w_k^n - y^n\|^2) \qquad (6)$$

$d_n(\theta_k)$ is the distance measure used to estimate the BPAs. y^n is the output hypothesis vector produced by condition rule for symptom, w_k^n is a reference vector.

$$m_n(\theta_k) = \frac{d_n(\theta_k)}{\sum_{k=1}^{K} d_n(\theta_k) + g_n} \qquad (7)$$

$$m_n(\Theta) = \frac{g_n}{\sum_{k=1}^{K} d_n(\theta_k) + g_n} \qquad (8)$$

Where $m_n(\theta_k)$ and $m_n(\Theta)$ are the normalized values of $d_n(\theta_k)$ and g_n respectively.

To minimize the mean square error (MSE) between the output vector M which represents the combined confidence in each hypothesis and the target vector T, we adjust the values of w_k^n and g_n through the training set. The metric is denoted by Err, that is $Err = \|M - T\|^2$.

w_k^n and g_n are initialized randomly, their values will be adjusted according to the following formulas:

$$w_k^n[new] = w_k^n[old] - \alpha \frac{\partial Err}{\partial w_k^n[old]} \qquad (9)$$

$$g_n[new] = g_n[old] - \beta \frac{\partial Err}{\partial g_n[old]} \qquad (10)$$

Where α and β are the learning rates, they are set according to the requirements of precision.

Then we design decision rules to obtain the final result. According to the belief interval $[Bel(A), Pls(A)]$ of all the hypotheses and the uncertain probability $m_1(\Theta)$, we choose the hypothesis having the max belief value as the root cause when satisfying the following rules:

Rule 1: $m(\theta_i) = \max_j \{m(\theta_j)\}$;

$m(\theta_i) - \max_{j \neq i} \{m(\theta_j)\} > \varepsilon$,

Rule 2: $m(\theta_i) - m(\Theta) > \varepsilon$,

$\varepsilon \in R \wedge \varepsilon > 0$;

Rule 3: $m(\Theta) < \gamma, \gamma \in R \wedge \gamma > 0$.

The whole algorithm steps are as follows:

```
1.  Θ ← HS ;// the hypothesis set of probably root cause
    E ← cd ;// the correlation descriptions for condition
              rule of symptom
2.  initialize wₖⁿ, gₙ, T, and Ite_no_max ;
    initialize i=0, α=5×10⁻⁴, β=10⁻⁶ , MSE;
3.  While (i< ite_no_max || α >10⁻⁴)
4.    For each pattern
5.      computer mₙ(θₖ) and mₙ(Θ) ;
6.    computer M and Err_new ;
7.    adjust wₖⁿ and gₙ ;
8.    If Err_old − Err_new > MSE
9.    α = α×1.03 ;
10.   else
         α = α×0.7 ;
11.   i++;
12. End while
13. If the condition rule satisfied then
14.   create composite event CE
         CE ← θᵢ ;
15. end if
```

4   Experiment Evaluation

Our experiments are conducted on a machine with Intel(R) Core(TM) i5-2400 cpu @ 3.10 GHz processor and 4 GB main memory, running MyEclipse 8.6 on Windows7. The algorithms were implemented in Java on standard datasets which come from [14]. Assuming the network congestion, we give several kinds of root causes, here is the teardrop attack, smurf attack and udpstorm attack, because the symptoms they show are alike. Then we classify the information for three segments: 1. network connection based on the content features; 2. the basic characteristics of network connection; 3.network traffic features. Depending on the training data, the BPAs for each possible root cause under different symptoms will be calculated. Finally, based on the diagnosis rule, the possible root cause can be judged. To reduce experimental variance, we perform each experiment for several times, and report the average result we measured.

Our evaluation had two main goals: assessing the validity of the method and evaluating the degree of accuracy. Consequently, we separate the two aspects by first measuring the query result and then analyzing the accuracy rate compared to the fact.

The experiment contains three aspects of the content features used to detect the root cause, the probable hypotheses are three. We select all the hypotheses from the dataset, 280790 records for smurf attack, 979 records for teardrop, and 2 records for udpstorm. The original database is split into two parts--while conserving the proportions of detection failures-one is used for model construction, and the other for model evaluation. The final result is shown below, in Fig.3, r1, r2 and r3 denotes the possible cause, u denotes an unknown cause, the horizontal axis denotes the symptom information for failure.

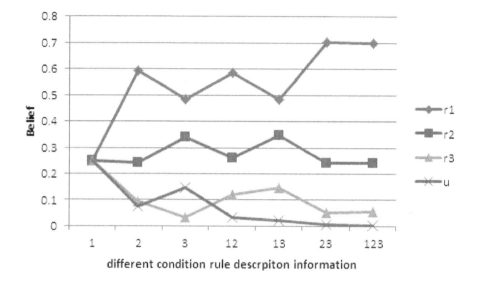

Fig. 3. Changing belief in probable cause with different symptom information

As it can be seen from the graph Fig.3, it is difficult to diagnose failure only using single description information, low belief cannot accurately identify the fault type, and the multi-source information infusion can improve the correct rate for failure detection.

Then we verify the accuracy of the results, using different numbers of training sets to count. The below fig. 4 shows the average accuracy rate. Obviously, the more experimental data, the more accurate the results are. But when it reaches a level, the rate remains the same. This shows that in the practical application, there should be more representative feature selection and rich experience accumulation. It depends on a lot of professional knowledge experience and lots of history records.

Last, it is obvious that the automated detection time and response time are faster than the manual, and because of the further analyses, many alarm events with root event occurred simultaneously will not be generated. A small fault could be a sign of big problem, only trying to avoid it, can the big fault occurrence rate be reduced. We must record all the anomalies and their solutions. So that it can be done the further research.

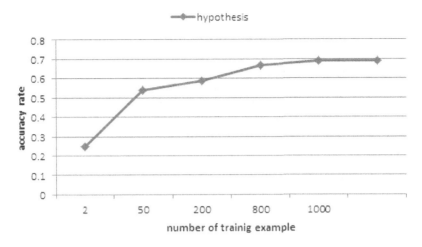

Fig. 4. Detection precision under different training sets

5   Conclusion

In this paper, we propose an intelligent approach for event correlation, particularly in uncertain or unknown events. It reduces large numbers of alarm events to generate finally. The experiments verified theoretically the rationality and validity of the scheme. While this paper also has its shortcoming, namely, when the anomaly or alarm events happen, the fault symptoms are known to us. The further study will focus on the selection of representative and useful performance variables. So far, there is no clear rule features for a lot of anomaly, the efficiency of probability calculation is still a problem to solve, depending on lots of training data.   We believe that this will be solved with the in-depth study and the accumulation of a large number of historical record data. In practice, we don't want big failure to happen, but rather to keep timely inspection of every link to ensure the overall work well. So with the rapid expansion of the network, stronger fault self-healing ability has become an important research topic in the next generation of data center platform.

References

1. Etzion, O., Niblett, P.: Event processing in action. Manning Publications Co. (2010)
2. http://esper.codehaus.org/
3. Arasu, A., Babu, S., Widom, J.: The CQL continuous query language: semantic foundations and query execution. The VLDB Journal—The International Journal on Very Large Data Bases 15(2), 121–142 (2006)
4. Leymann, F., Roller, D., Schmidt, M.-T.: Web services and business process management. IBM Systems Journal 41(2), 198–211 (2002)
5. Demers, A., et al.: Cayuga: A general purpose event monitoring system. CIDR (2007)

6. Cranor, C., et al.: Gigascope: a stream database for network applications. In: Proceedings of the 2003 ACM SIGMOD International Conference on Management of Data. ACM (2003)

7. Tiffany, M., A survey of event correlation techniques and related topics. Research paper. Georgia Institute of Technology (2002)

8. Narayanan, K., Bose, S.K., Rao, S.: Towards' integrated'monitoring and management of DataCenters using complex event processing techniques. In: Proceedings of the Fourth Annual ACM Bangalore Conference. ACM (2011)

9. Hong, M., et al.: Rule-based multi-query optimization. In: Proceedings of the 12th International Conference on Extending Database Technology: Advances in Database Technology. ACM (2009)

10. http://en.wikipedia.org/wiki/Dempster%E2%80%93Shafer_theory

11. Al-Ani, A., Deriche, M.: A new technique for combining multiple classifiers using the Dempster-Shafer theory of evidence. arXiv preprint arXiv:1107.0018 (2011)

12. Ganapathy, V., et al.: An epistemic event-based correlation approach for managing pervasive networks. International Journal of Network Management 22(1), 81–94 (2012)

13. Mordeson, J.N., Wierman, M.J., Clark, T.D., Pham, A., Redmond, M.: Evidence theory. In: Mordeson, J.N., Wierman, M.J., Clark, T.D., Pham, A., Redmond, M. (eds.) Linear Models in the Mathematics of Uncertainty. SCI, vol. 463, pp. 41–56. Springer, Heidelberg (2013)

14. http://kdd.ics.uci.edu/databases/kddcup99/

Quantitative Dependability Assessment of Distributed Systems Subject to Variable Conditions

Salvatore Distefano[1], Dario Bruneo[2], Francesco Longo[2], and Marco Scarpa[2]

[1] Dip. di Elettronica, Informazione e Bioingegneria, Politecnico di Milano, 20133 Milano, Italy
salvatore.distefano@polimi.it
[2] Dip. di Ingegneria (DICIEAMA), Università di Messina, 98166 Messina, Italy
{dbruneo,flongo,mscarpa}@unime.it

Abstract. Dependability evaluation plays a key role in the design of a broad range of systems, where related properties have to be carefully analyzed in order to meet the requirements. This is particularly challenging in distributed contexts, where several entities may interact influencing each other. In this paper, we present an analytical framework that allows the study of a class of phenomena where different working conditions alternate, changing the stochastic behavior of the system. The proposed solution technique, based on phase type distributions and on ad-hoc fitting algorithms, can be applied in dependability evaluation of a wide class of distributed systems. Examples are provided to show the usefulness and the applicability of the framework, characterizing and investigating different dependability aspects of two distributed computing systems, i.e., connection-oriented networks and Internet of Things.

1 Introduction

ICT aims at automating, enhancing, and improving processes and systems towards higher quality standards, significantly impacting in everyone and everyday life. In practical terms this requires, on the one hand, more and more powerful systems able to deal with the issues arising from such an automation process, and, on the other one, pervasive devices able to involve everything and everyone into the game, implementing new degrees of freedom for improving the accuracy of corresponding methodologies and techniques. Distributed systems play a significant role on this trend supporting and implementing aims and goals at the basis of this innovation process.

Functional and non-functional properties such as performance, reliability, availability, security, and safety, usually grouped under the umbrella of *dependability*, are of strategic importance in distributed systems. Indeed, higher quality standards imply tighter constraints and requirements, calling for adequate metrics, policies, and solutions for measuring, monitoring, evaluating, and controlling them. With specific regards to dependability assessments, the fact that the accuracy required in the evaluation is increasing drives to recur to quantitative techniques as well as to consider aspects and behaviors before roughly approximated or neglected at all, e.g., interferences, interdependencies among components, parts, or subsystems, changing environments, especially in distributed contexts. A way to manage all these issues is to study the system under exam by developing a stochastic model where some relevant system quantities

M. Pathan, G. Wei, and G. Fortino (Eds.): IDCS 2013, LNCS 8223, pp. 385–398, 2013.

can *change* their behavior according to internal or external conditions. The notion of change we consider in this work takes into account both the interdependencies among internal quantities and the external environment interactions.

Workload fluctuations, energy variations, environmental phenomena, user-related changing behaviors are only few examples of such aspects that can no longer be neglected in dependability analysis of distributed systems [1,2]. Since phenomena subject to changes are generic, e.g., system reliability or evolution of physical quantities, the timed events describing them cannot be always modeled by using negative exponential distributions. For example, in the reliability context, the Weibull distribution is very often used. When non-exponentially distributed events change in time, the stochastic model has to reflect this behavior by preserving the reached level of the associated quantity and adequate techniques to manage this kind of *memory* have to be considered. More complex and powerful stochastic processes than Markov chains are necessary, such as *semi-Markov processes* [3] or those deriving from *renewal theory* [4], even if these techniques are sometimes not able to cover some specific aspects, such as the presence of different quantities that need to be preserved at the same time.

In this work, we propose an analytical framework to deal with the above discussed aspects and phenomena typical of dependability models of distributed systems, due to the interactions and interferences among components and the external environment. In such cases, an observed quantity may change its behavior due to working condition changes, preserving, under specific assumptions, its continuity. In order to implement such a continuity constraint, we propose a solution technique based on phase type (PH) distributions discussed in Section 2, and we provide ad-hoc fitting algorithms that allow a simple theoretical foundation as well as an easy implementation of the approach in Section 3. To demonstrate the effectiveness and the applicability of the proposed technique, two dependability models of distributed systems have been investigated, i.e., connection-oriented networks and Internet of Things in Section 4. Finally, Section 5 concludes the paper.

2   The Proposed Technique

2.1   The Overall Approach

The problem we consider in this work is the dependability evaluation of distributed systems. Due to the increasing quality standards, the importance of having accurate dependability models of distributed systems becomes a strict requirement. Thus more and more often stochastic techniques have to be used, stochastically characterizing the dependability quantities under exam through probability distribution functions. Furthermore, in distributed systems, components or subsystems may interfere, interact, or depend on each other or even on the external environment influencing the dependability quantities investigated. These complex interactions imply that, on the one hand, the underlying phenomena cannot be approximated by memory-less distributions, since they have to keep memory of such interactions, and, on the other one, the system *operating conditions* should be identified and characterized as well as the process triggering the switching among these conditions.

In previous work [5,6], we characterized this problem by associating to each operating condition of a component a specific cumulative distribution function (CDF) of the observed quantity in *isolation*, i.e., assuming the component is always operating in the same condition. Then, we stochastically characterized the switching process through a specific CDF, moving the problem to the representation and management of the memory conservation and the aging process.

Thus, to deal with the dependability evaluation of distributed systems taking into account complex phenomena and changing conditions, we propose to adopt a three step approach based on state space models. The first phase is related to the *State Space Modeling*: in this step the distributed system components should be identified and the phenomena affecting them characterized as specific operating conditions, together with the metrics of interest requested by the modeler. Then, once the system has been entirely specified, its state space should be characterized accordingly, also taking into account dependencies, interferences, and the influence of the environment triggering operating condition changes.

The state space model thus obtained is not trivial to manage since it includes complex phenomena that should be dealt with specific techniques. The aging process and related memory management issues should be adequately addressed, taking into account the system operating condition changes. More specifically, this means keeping memory of the quantity level reached at a changing point and starting from this value in the new condition. In analytical terms, this implements the continuity of the function describing the whole system, thus preserving the codomain value. To this end, in the *Model Processing* step the state space model is translated into a simpler one, by applying the phase type expansion approach [7]. This way a Markov model is obtained through a first *Markovianisation* sub-step. But the problem of this approach is the *state space explosion*: to deal with such an issue we adopt symbolic techniques based on Kronecker algebra in the next *Symbolic encoding* sub-step.

Finally, the symbolically encoded Markovian model thus obtained is analyzed to evaluate the dependability metrics required by the user into the *Evaluation* step.

2.2   Phase Type Characterization

In this section we characterize the problem above described in the PH domain. Neuts [8,7] popularized the class of PH distributions which correspond to the time until absorption in a finite state Markov chain with n transient states and a single absorbing state labeled $(n+1)$. Thus, a non negative random variable T (or its distribution function) is said to be a PH if T is the time to absorption of a finite-state Markov chain [7]. In the case of continuous time Markov chains (CTMCs), *continuous PH* (CPH) distributions are characterized. According to this definition, T follows a CPH distribution with representation $(\alpha, \mathbf{G})$ and order n. α and $\mathbf{G}$ are formally specified as: let $\pi(0) = [\alpha, \alpha_{n+1}]$ be the $n+1$ *initial probability vector* so that $\alpha_{n+1} = 1 - \sum_{i=1}^{n} \alpha_i$, and $\hat{\mathbf{G}} \in \mathbb{R}^{n+1} \times \mathbb{R}^{n+1}$ be the *infinitesimal generator matrix* of the underlying CTMC

$$\hat{\mathbf{G}} = \left[\begin{array}{c|c} \mathbf{G} & \mathbf{U} \\ \hline \mathbf{0} & 0 \end{array}\right]$$

where $\mathbf{G} \in \mathbb{R}^n \times \mathbb{R}^n$ describes the transient behavior of the CTMC and $\mathbf{U} \in \mathbb{R}^n$ is a vector grouping the transition rates to the absorbing state. Since $\hat{\mathbf{G}}$ is a stochastic matrix, $\mathbf{U} = -\mathbf{G} \cdot \mathbf{1}$ holds, where $\mathbf{1} \in \mathbb{R}^n$ is a column vector of 1. This implies the CDF of T, $F_T(t)$, i.e., the probability to reach the absorbing state of the CPH, can be written as:

$$F(t) = 1 - \boldsymbol{\alpha} e^{\mathbf{G}t} \mathbf{1}, \quad t \geq 0 \tag{1}$$

In order to provide a compact representation of CTMCs resulting from PH expansion, a well-know and effective technique used in literature [7,9,10] is the Kronecker algebra. There are several reasons under this choice: i) the expanded state space have not to be physically generated nor stored; ii) the cost of storing the expanded state space grows linearly with the PH distributions dimensions instead of geometrically; iii) the solution can benefit from specific algorithms developed for similar cases [11,12].

However, the method of stages is used for coding memory through Markov models. A phase could therefore represent a particular condition reached by the underlying stochastic process during its evolution. This condition could be associated to the time. This way, CPHs are specified with the aim of saving the time instant in which a specific event occurs, by just saving the phase reached, in order to continue their evolution from the saved point. Such a mechanism works if the observed events are not changing their nature or condition, since the memory is on the time domain. Indeed, in case of variable conditions, preserving the time domain memory could not be enough due to the changes in the function characterizing the observed event. In such cases, as discussed above, since the distribution or the function describing the observed phenomenon changes according to some events into different conditions, the overall function becomes a multi-variate function of both the observed event and the external events triggering the condition switching.

For the sake of simplicity and without loss of generality, let us consider a specific context, in which the quantity to observe is a CDF. A good one, in the context of reliability, is a component lifetime CDF in changing environments. In such a context, a way for adequately face the problem could be to know the lifetime CDFs of the observed system both in isolation or in the initial working condition (without dependencies or in the *baseline environment*), and in the new environments or after the application of a dependency. In such a way, by representing the lifetime CDFs as CPHs, it is necessary to specify how the system jumps from one of such CPHs to the others by preserving, in the transition between two conditions, the lifetime or the reliability. Such a quantity is usually expressed as a monotonic non increasing function of the time.

In [5,6,13,14], we presented a method based on CPHs and Kronecker algebra able to manage such a kind of memory, without incurring in the complexity of the problem described above. The proposed method is able to manage the condition changing impacting on the system reliability during its evolution.

The method is based on the characterization of the conservation of the work done in terms of CPHs to model the behavior of the system subject to changing conditions. According to such a technique, we start from a simple example just identifying two conditions and a change among them. The two conditions are characterized by the F_X^1 and F_X^2 CDFs of the observed event X and they are represented by two CPHs of order

n_1 and n_2 respectively. If the continuity wants to be imposed at the changing time point y, a time shift τ has to be applied to F_X^2 such that:

$$F_X^1(y) = F_X^2(y + \tau) \Rightarrow \alpha_1 \cdot e^{\mathbf{G_1} \cdot y} \cdot \mathbf{1}_1 = \alpha_2 \cdot e^{\mathbf{G_2} \cdot (y+\tau)} \cdot \mathbf{1}_2 \tag{2}$$

where $\mathbf{1}_1$ ($\mathbf{1}_2$) is a column vector with n_1 (n_2) elements all equal to 1. $\tau \in \mathbb{R}$ represents the memory effect at changing point. In [13], in the context of CPHs, a *memory matrix* $\mathbf{M}^{1 \to 2}(y)$ has been introduced to store switching probabilities from the two CPHs able to satisfies the continuity constraint instead of τ. This way, the overall behavior is represented by a CTMC where the two CPHs are connected through probabilities in $\mathbf{M}^{1 \to 2}(y)$ among their phases in correspondence of a changing event.

Given the two CPHs, the memory matrix satisfying eq. (2) can be computed by solving the following equation:

$$\alpha_1 \cdot e^{\mathbf{G_1} \cdot y} \cdot \mathbf{M}^{1 \to 2}(y) = \alpha_2 \cdot e^{\mathbf{G_2} \cdot (y+\tau)} \tag{3}$$

that is a not straightforward problem in general, especially considering the dependency on switching time y. The problem of obtaining $\mathbf{M}^{1 \to 2}(y)$ is simpler when $\alpha_1 = \alpha_2$ and $\mathbf{G}_1 = k \cdot \mathbf{G}_2$ (thus $n_1 = n_2$) since the memory matrix is an identity matrix $\mathbf{I}$ of dimensions $n_1 \times n_1$.

In the present work, we take advantage of this property to derive appropriate CPHs able to represent the memory conservation principle in different contexts. The basic idea is to associate to each stage of a CPH a specific meaning depending on the problem. Thus, in order to jump from a CPH representing the behavior of the system under a specific condition to the one representing the system in a different condition, it is only necessary to save the reached phase. In other terms, a phase encodes the value reached by the observed quantity. By modeling the functions representing the system in different conditions as CPHs with the same number of phases n, the ith phase of all the CPHs encodes and represents the same value of the observed quantity. As a consequence, the memory matrix is always an identity matrix thus driving to a simpler approach both from the theoretical and the implementation point of view. In the next section, we propose the algorithms implementing such an idea.

3 Dealing with Changing Conditions through CPH

In this section, we propose and discuss two possible solutions for evaluating distributed systems affected by non-Markovian behaviors in changing conditions. We exploit the PH approach taking into account the nature of the changing quantities as well as the way they are represented. The distribution codomain fitting (Section 3.1) can be applied if the CDFs of the observed quantity in the different conditions are known. The underlying phenomena function codomain fitting can be applied if the functions related to the underlying phenomena in the different conditions are provided (Section 3.2) and the model is on the quantity level.

3.1 Cumulative Distribution Functions

The main aim of the proposed fitting technique is to best fit the starting function. Moreover, we want to associate a meaning to the phases. More specifically, we characterize the phases of the CPH with specific information related to the probability codomain. In other words, each phase represents a specific value of probability and, as a consequence, corresponds to a specific sub-interval in $[0, 1]$.

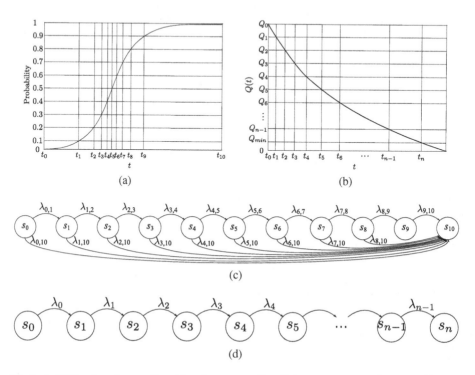

Fig. 1. A CDF codomain sampling (a) and corresponding CPH (c); a generic function $Q(t)$ with its discretized codomain (b) and corresponding CPH (d)

According to this approach, we have to firstly make discrete the codomain of the CDF to be approximated. As an example, the codomain of the CDF shown in Fig. 1a, has been split into $n = 10$ contiguous intervals of equal range $[i/n, (i+1)/n) \in [0, 1] \subset \mathbb{R}$, with $i = 0, \ldots, n - 1$. This way, we identify $n + 1$ endpoints in total. The proposed technique associates to each of such endpoints a phase of the corresponding CPH as shown in Fig. 1c. Thus, referring to the considered example, phase s_0 corresponds to the values in $[0.0, 0.1[$ of the probability codomain, s_1 corresponds to $[0.1, 0.2[$, s_2 to $[0.2, 0.3[$, and so on. Generalizing the jth phase corresponds to the $[\frac{j}{n}, \frac{j+1}{n}[$ probability interval, with $j = 0, \ldots, n - 1$. The dynamic of the model, i.e., the transition between the generic states s_i and s_j, is regulated by the event characterizing the underlying process: it can occur in the i-th interval, and therefore a transition between the i-th and the last n-th phase is possible; otherwise, if the event does not occur in the i-th interval, the CPH transits from phase s_i to phase s_{i+1}. No other transitions are possible among the phases as shown in Fig. 1c. Thus we have $\lambda_{i,i+1} = (1 - \frac{1}{n-i})\frac{1}{t_{i+1}-t_i}$ and

$\lambda_{i,n} = \frac{1}{(t_{i+1}-t_i)(n-i)}$, where t_i is the time instant corresponding to the ith codomain sample. In Section 4.1 an example on how the algorithm can be applied is discussed.

3.2 Generic Functions

An approach similar to that described in the previous section can be adopted for generating CPHs approximating a generic function with codomain $\mathcal{S} \subset \mathbb{R}$ with $\mathcal{S} \neq [0,1] \subset \mathbb{R}$, representing the behavior of a quantity, when a modeler is interested in events occurring if a specific level of the quantity is reached. We assume the observed quantity is described by a continuous and strictly monotonic (thus invertible) function on time $Q(t) : \mathbb{R}^+ \to \mathcal{S}$. An example of a strictly decreasing $Q(t)$ is depicted in Fig. 1b.

Let us assume the initial value of the considered quantity is Q_0 and the event of interest occurs when $Q(t)$ reaches the level Q_{min} thus identifying the codomain range $[Q_0, Q_{min}]$ that we split into n contiguous intervals $[Q_i, Q_{i+1}]$ of equal size $\frac{Q_0 - Q_{min}}{n}$, with $i = 0, \ldots, n-1$. This way, we divide the quantity into $n+1$ levels with generic value Q_i ($i = 0, \ldots, n$), where $Q_n = Q_{min}$. Since $Q(t)$ is invertible, the time instants t_i such that $Q(t_i) = Q_i$, with $i = 0, \ldots, n$, can be unequivocally identified. Let $\tau_i = t_{i+1} - t_i$, with $i = 0, \ldots, n-1$, be the duration of the i-th time interval, where the quantity assumes some value in the range $[Q_i, Q_{i+1}]$. By associating the values assumed in $[t_i, t_{i+1}]$ with Q_i, we represent the evolution of Q through a CTMC by encoding that values in the states. An example of such a representation is the $n+1$-state CTMC shown in Fig. 1d where the state s_i represents the i-th interval of the range $[Q_0, Q_{min}]$. Since $\forall t \in [t_i, t_{i+1}] \Rightarrow Q(t) \in [Q_i, Q_{i+1}]$, τ_i can be considered as the sojourn time into the state s_i and, as a consequence, the transition rate between states s_i and s_{i+1} has to be set to $\lambda_i = \frac{1}{\tau_i}$.

The model is a CTMC with an absorbing state which absorption time represents the time to event {*The level Q_{min} is reached*}. According to the above definition, it represents a CPH of order n and $\boldsymbol{\alpha} = [1, 0, \cdots, 0]$. The CPH thus specified describes the behavior corresponding to a particular environment condition; if different conditions are considered, as many CPHs as the specified conditions have to be defined. Anyway, all of them are characterized by the same number of states if the fitting discretization level is the same (n). Also in this case the set of CPHs thus obtained is compliant with the method described in Section 2. In Section 4.2 we provide an example showing the quality and the effectiveness of the approximation technique here proposed.

4 Examples

In this section, we aim at highlighting the generality of the proposed framework in modeling dependability in distributed system. To this purpose, three examples are proposed focusing on IoT and connection-oriented networks, showing how the proposed approach can be exploited to derive useful dependability analyses. The following examples allow us to give also a practical demonstration of the fitting algorithms described in Section 3 by covering all the two highlighted cases of known CDFs and generic functions. A comparison with pure exponential systems (not affected by memory conservation issues) is given in order to highlight the accuracy of the proposed technique.

4.1   Network Data Dependability

In this example we investigate some dependability attributes such as reliability and performability of data transferred through a connection-oriented virtual-circuit network at datalink or network layer such as X.25, ATM, Frame Relay, GPRS, MPLS or similar. In order to send data in a layer 2/3 virtual-circuit network, it is first necessary to establish a virtual circuit between the two endpoints. This means that communications between two nodes always follow the same network path. Although this implies several benefits in network management (bandwidth reservation, low overhead, simple switching) the main drawback of such an approach is the virtual channel reliability, especially in case of wireless networks, since a channel failure may break the virtual circuit.

   Through this example we are interested in evaluating both the reliability and the performance of sending a packet in a virtual-circuit network taking into account different traffic conditions. We therefore identified two events characterizing the packet transmission: delivery and failure, associated to the time-to-delivery T and time-to-failure X random variables, respectively. The packet lifetime X includes all the causes driving to a sending failure (corrupted/loss data, channel failure, congestion, hardware and software faults, etc.). Furthermore, as discussed above, we assume that both T and X depend on the traffic and also on the bandwidth available for transmission. More specifically, we assume a traffic threshold there exists above which the connection service is no longer able to provide the required performability and reliability levels on the packet sending. This way, we characterize two traffic conditions, *average* below and *high* above the threshold, also assuming to know the CDFs characterizing the packet lifetime and time-to-delivery in such conditions, namely $F_X^A(t)$, $F_T^A(t)$, $F_X^H(t)$ and $F_T^H(t)$, respectively.

   Thus, the trigger events, related to traffic fluctuations, are characterized by two CDFs $F^I(t)$ and $F^D(t)$ corresponding to the switching from average to high traffic (traffic increase - I) and vice versa (traffic decrease - D), respectively. Assuming periodic fluctuations between the two types of traffic following a bursty traffic pattern, we can represent that through a Markov modulated Poisson process, where $F^I(t)$ and $F^D(t)$ are exponentially distributed with rates λ^I and λ^D, respectively, the former related to the average-high traffic switching, the latter representing the inverse transition from high to average traffic.

   The state space model of the system thus characterized is depicted in Fig. 2a. It is composed of 4 main states identifying the reliable channel both in the average (S_{T_A}) and in high (S_{T_H}) traffic conditions, the successful packet delivery (S_{P_D}), and the failed transmission (S_{P_F}). Assuming the channel is initially available, according to the traffic condition, the system starts from either state S_{T_A} or S_{T_H}. Transitions between the latter states represent traffic condition switching triggered by events e_{T_I} (increasing - from average to high traffic) and e_{T_D} (decreasing - from high to average traffic) and characterized by the corresponding CDFs $F^I(t)$ and $F^D(t)$ as discussed above.

   From such states, in case a failure occurs during sending, the state S_{P_F} is reached through transitions labelled e_{F_A} or e_{F_H} depending on the traffic condition and the corresponding CDFs $F_X^A(t)$ or $F_X^H(t)$, respectively. Otherwise, in case of successful delivery, state S_{P_D} is reached through events e_{D_A} or e_{D_H}, according to the traffic and related distribution $F_T^A(t)$ and $F_T^H(t)$, respectively. We use the model to evaluate the CDFs of the

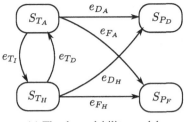

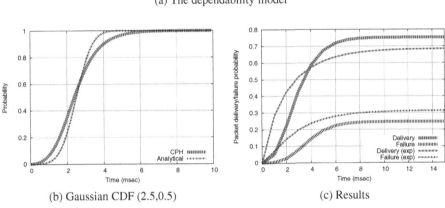

(a) The dependability model

(b) Gaussian CDF (2.5,0.5)

(c) Results

Fig. 2. Network state space model (a), quality of the CDF approximations through the codomain fitting algorithm (b) and results (c)

packet delivery time, i.e., the probability of reaching state S_{P_D}, and the packet sending failure time, i.e., the probability of reaching state S_{P_F}, $F_R(t)$ and $F_F(t)$, respectively. Since states S_{P_D} and S_{P_F} are both absorbing the two CDFs are defective, with steady state probabilities of packet delivery and failure $F_R(\infty)$ and $F_F(\infty)$, respectively. $F_R(\infty)$ is also known as packet/data *delivery ratio*, with $F_R(\infty) + F_F(\infty) = 1$.

In order to evaluate the model, we start from metrics, parameters and real values taken from the specific literature. Several work investigates packet delivery performance and failure, mainly characterizing such quantities through the *time to delivery* or *round trip time* and the delivery ratio. To the best of our knowledge, in literature such parameters have been usually quantified by their statistical moments, i.e., the mean value and sometimes the variance. Thus, we have to obtain the packet time to delivery and the time to failure CDFs by such values. With regards to the time to delivery, we used the data published in [15,16], providing statistics of two workload conditions. Therefore, we stochastically characterized the time to delivery by Gaussian CDFs, the average traffic one with mean value 2.5 ms and variance 0.5 ms, while the high traffic CDF has higher mean value of 11 ms and variance 3 ms.

The packet sending time to failure CDF has been obtained by the delivery ratio taken from [17], i.e., 0.9 in the average traffic case and 0.6 in the high one. To obtain the time to failure CDF further manipulations are required: as stated above the delivery ratio is the steady state probability the packet is delivered in the above model. Thus, by knowing the delivery steady state probability in each traffic condition, the problem is to find a failure CDF such that the steady state probability of delivery in the model of Fig. 2a is equal to the delivery ratio. Assuming the sending lifetime are represented by Weibull CDFs $(1 - e^{-(\frac{t}{\alpha})^\beta})$ commonly and widely used to characterize lifetime distributions, fixing $\beta = 5$, we identified $\alpha_A = 22\ ms$ for the average traffic and $\alpha_H = 22\ ms$ for the high one through the model. Finally, the traffic switching rate is $\lambda_I = \lambda_D = 0.5kHz$, i.e., a switch every $2\ ms$.

Given that in such a case the model parameters are available in the form of CDFs, it is possible to apply the fitting algorithm described in Section 3.1. In fact, we exploited 100 phases and we obtained four CPHs approximating the above described distributions. One of them is depicted in Fig. 2b to show the quality of the CPH approximation. Then, by using such CPHs in the state space model of Fig. 2a we are able to evaluate the packet delivery and failure probability, obtaining the results shown in Fig. 2c. It reports the two defective distributions characterizing states S_{P_D} and S_{P_F} and representing the time to delivery and the lifetime of the packet. In order to evaluate the effectiveness of our technique we compared the results thus obtained against those obtained by evaluating a pure exponential model, i.e., considering all the events associated to the transitions in the model of Fig. 2a as exponentially distributed with the reciprocal of the mean time of the corresponding distributions as rates, i.e., $\lambda^{D_A} = 0.4kHz$, $\lambda^{D_H} = 0.091kHz$, $\lambda^{F_A} = 0.0495kHz$ and $\lambda^{F_H} = 0.272kHz$. The model thus obtained is a Markov chain.

In both cases the steady state is reached at approximately $12\ ms$, with a delivery ratio of about 0.75 through the CPH model while about 0.68 for the Markov model. From a quick rough calculation, since the system spends exact half time each traffic condition, we can estimate the delivery ratio could be close to the mean value between the two starting conditions (0.9 average and 0.6 high), i.e., 0.75. Thus, based on such a consideration, we can assume the results obtained through the CPH state space model to be more reliable than the Markovian model one.

Furthermore, with regards to the transient part, the trends corresponding to the two models are quite different. Indeed, the Markovian model is always convex, meaning that the packets start to be delivered immediately. This is not really true since in the actual system, as shown in Fig. 2b, they start to be delivered after about $0.7\ ms$ in case of average traffic, while after about $3\ ms$ in the other case. The CPH-based model catches this behavior as shown by the first knee on the curves that identifies a changing in probability following the underlying CDFs due to the fact that initially the probability to deliver the packet is very low but then it suddenly increases. The second knee is the gate to the steady state, describing a condition in which very likely either the packet has been already delivered or its sending is failed.

4.2   Longevity of IoT Mobile Devices

A typical IoT scenario consists of a multitude of mobile devices (e.g., in the order of hundreds or thousands) employed in a mobile crowdsensing (MCS) [18] application, where environmental information being collected is augmented with user-generated patterns in order to analyze and forecast crowd behavior and attitude. Such mobile devices (usually smart phones) are used to measure various individual as well as community trends. Such a large scale, collective trends monitoring is possible when a (loosely knit) community of individuals share their resources, mobile devices in our case, usually with certain processing duties involved. MCS refers to a broad range of community-powered sensing approaches of both participatory and opportunistic kind. Participatory scenarios are characterized by individuals that are actively involved in contributing by mean of devices or (meta-)data (e.g., taking a picture, reporting a road bump), while in opportunistic scenarios sensing is more autonomous and user involvement is minimal (e.g., continuous sampling of geo-localized data).

As discussed above, one of the main issues in such a context is certainly the availability since mobile devices are usually equipped with low voltage batteries that limit their lifetime [19,20]. For such a reason, both in participatory and opportunistic scenarios, users are usually allowed to fully control their devices and choose when and how they want to contribute to the IoT mobile crowdsensing service. The exploited policies usually refers to the device energy status in terms of battery charge. Longevity, reliability, and energy consumption of a mobile device depends on the load the device is subjected to, i.e., on the specific tasks and operations the device is performing at a particular time instant. Several tasks and operations request a higher energy consumption with respect to others. Moreover, suspend, idle, or other minimum energy consumption statuses can be forced in order to maximize lifetime.

Let us consider, as an example, a user that accepts to contribute to the IoT mobile crowdsensing service only if the battery remaining power percentage is above 20%. Moreover, getting inspired by work in [21], let us suppose that the main high-level tasks that affect the smart phone energy consumption are: i) making phone calls, and ii) browsing the Web. The smart phone is maintained in a minimum energy consumption (suspend) mode while such tasks are not performed. Finally, let us suppose that the battery duration T_d is approximately equal to 43 hours in suspend mode, 10 hours while making phone calls, and 5 hours while browsing the Web.

Our technique allows us to predict the smart phone longevity, i.e., its battery duration and, accordingly, its reliability with respect to the IoT MCS service. From such an information, the amount of contribution that the mobile device provide to the service, accordingly to a certain usage scenario, i.e, knowing the device usage pattern, can be obtained. Let us consider, as an example, three different usage patterns: generic, student and business. The three patterns are characterized by the percentage of time the user spends in making phone calls and browsing the Web. While in the generic scenario, the user spends about 20% of time making phone calls and 10% of time browsing the Web, over a single day, in the student scenario such percentages change to 10% and 40%, respectively. In the business usage pattern, such percentages are swapped (i.e., 40% making phone calls and 10% browsing the Web).

Fig. 3a, depicts the state space of the model that can be used to represent such a scenario. States S_S, S_C, and S_B represent the suspend, calling, and web browsing modes, respectively. Events e_{S_C} and e_{C_S} represent the switching between suspend and calling modes while events e_{S_B} and e_{B_S} model the switching between suspend and browsing mode. They can be characterized with exponential distributions and their rates have to be fixed so that the mean permanence times in states S_S, S_C, and S_B during a day is set accordingly to the above reported usage patterns. State S_D represents the fully discharged battery situation while events e_{D_C}, e_{D_S}, and e_{D_B} represent the battery discharge process.

As described in [13,22], the non-linear discharge process of a lithium-ion battery (typically employed in modern mobile phones) can be represented through the Peukert's law in the form of a charge vs. time chart. As a consequence, the technique described in Section 3.2 can be applied, thus modeling the discharge process through a hypo-exponential distribution with a sufficient number of phases. In our case, we considered a battery with capacity $c = 2500\ mAh$ and Peukert constant $\eta = 1.08$. Fig. 3b depicts the real discharge function (given by the Peukert's law) and the approximation obtained by using $n = 100$ and $n = 1000$ phases in the case of suspend mode where the battery discharge function is considered to be equal to 61 mA. The case $n = 1000$ gives an excellent approximation and the results shown in the following have been obtained by exploiting such a number of phases.

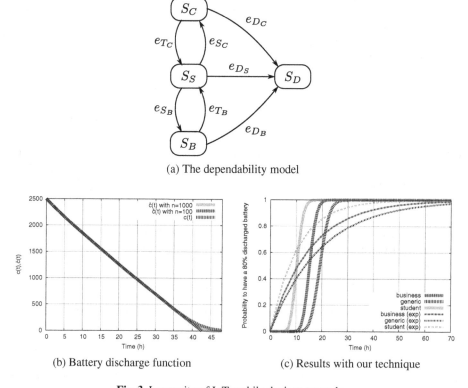

(a) The dependability model

(b) Battery discharge function   (c) Results with our technique

Fig. 3. Longevity of IoT mobile devices example

In such a case, the phases of the CPH assume the physical meaning of the battery charge level, as discussed in Section 3.2. The discharge time is different in the three states as described above. However, the battery charge level should be kept while switching among them. Thanks to the physical meaning of the CPH phases resulting from our fitting algorithm, our technique allows us to compute the probability to have a 80% discharged battery and, as a consequence, the probability for the mobile device to stop contributing to the IoT mobile crowdsensing service, i.e., its unreliability. Fig. 3c shows the mobile phone unreliability in the three considered usage scenarios.

We compared such results with the ones obtained by analyzing a purely exponential model. In such a model, exponential distributions have been associated to events e_{D_C}, e_{D_S}, and e_{D_B} with a rate equal to the inverse of the discharge time in the corresponding usage mode. As the results are self-explanatory, they do not require any comment on the quality of an exponential approximation.

5 Conclusions

Distributed system dependability is often affected by a class of phenomena where different working conditions alternate among themselves by changing the stochastic behavior of the system but still preserving the continuity of the dependability quantities. In this paper, we proposed an analytical framework able to represent such phenomena, based on PH distributions and on ad-hoc fitting algorithms. The framework is general enough to model a wide range of systems and, to demonstrate its usefulness, three examples have been proposed modeling IoT and connection-oriented networks. Different quantitative analyses of dependability quantities have been conducted in order to give an overview of the proposed modeling tools. Future research will move toward further extending our work by introducing a formal characterization of the technique that can drive to the definition of a new high-level formalism and to the implementation of a software tool able to automate the modeling steps and the dependability analysis of distributed systems.

References

1. Finkelstein, M.S.: Wearing-out of components in a variable environment. Reliability Engineering & System Safety 66(3), 235–242 (1999)
2. Sedyakin, N.: On one physical principle in reliability theory. Tekhn. Kibernetika (in Russian - Technical Cybernetics) 3, 80–87 (1966)
3. Limnios, N., Oprisan, G.: Semi-Markov Processes and Reliability. Statistics for Industry and Technology. Birkhäuser, Boston (2001)
4. Cox, D.R.: Renewal Theory. Methuen, London (1962)
5. Distefano, S., Longo, F., Scarpa, M.: Availability assessment of ha standby redundant clusters. In: SRDS 2010 Proceedings of the 2010 29th IEEE Symposium on Reliable Distributed Systems, pp. 265–274 (2010)
6. Distefano, S., Longo, F., Scarpa, M.: Symbolic representation techniques in dynamic reliability evaluation. In: 2010 IEEE 12th International Symposium on High-Assurance Systems Engineering (HASE), pp. 45–53 (2010)
7. Neuts, M.F.: Matrix-geometric solutions in stochastic models: an algorithmic approach. Johns Hopkins University Press, Baltimore (1981)
8. Neuts, M.F., Meier, K.S.: On the use of phase type distributions in reliability modelling of systems with two components. OR Spectrum 2(4), 227–234 (1981)
9. Bobbio, A., Scarpa, M.: Kronecker representation of stochastic petri nets with discrete ph distributions. In: Proc. Third IEEE Ann. Int'l Computer Performance and Dependability Symp, IPDS 1998 (1998)

10. Pérez-Ocón, R., Montoro-Cazorla, D.: A multiple system governed by a quasi-birth-and-death process. Reliability Engineering & System Safety 84(2), 187–196 (2004)
11. Longo, F., Scarpa, M.: Applying symbolic techniques to the representation of non-markovian models with continuous PH distributions. In: Bradley, J.T. (ed.) EPEW 2009. LNCS, vol. 5652, pp. 44–58. Springer, Heidelberg (2009)
12. Scarpa, M., Longo, F.: Two layer symbolic representation for stochastic models with phase type distributed events. International Journal of Systems Science (2013)
13. Bruneo, D., Distefano, S., Longo, F., Puliafito, A., Scarpa, M.: Evaluating wireless sensor node longevity through markovian techniques. Computer Networks 56(2), 521–532 (2012)
14. Bruneo, D., Distefano, S., Longo, F., Puliafito, A., Scarpa, M.: Workload-based software rejuvenation in cloud systems. IEEE Transactions on Computers 62(6), 1072–1085 (2013)
15. Franz, R., Gradischnig, K.D., Huber, M.N., Stiefel, R.: Atm-based signaling network topics on reliability and performance. IEEE Journal on Selected Areas in Communications 12(3), 517–525 (1994)
16. Herrmann, C., Lott, M., Du, Y., Hettich, A.: A wireless atm lan prototype: Test bed implementation and first performance results. In: Proc. of MTT-S Wireless 1998 Symposium, pp. 145–150 (1998)
17. Liu, H.L., Shooman, M.: Reliability computation of an ip/atm network with congestion. In: Annual. Reliability and Maintainability Symposium, pp. 581–586 (2003)
18. Ganti, R., Ye, F., Lei, H.: Mobile crowdsensing: current state and future challenges. IEEE Communications Magazine 49(11), 32–39 (2011)
19. Bruneo, D., Puliafito, A., Scarpa, M.: Energy control in dependable wireless sensor networks: a modelling perspective. Proceedings of the Institution of Mechanical Engineers, Part O: Journal of Risk and Reliability 225(4), 424–434 (2011)
20. Distefano, S.: Evaluating reliability of wsn with sleep/wake-up interfering nodes. International Journal of Systems Science 44(10), 1793–1806 (2013)
21. Carroll, A., Heiser, G.: An analysis of power consumption in a smartphone. In: Proceedings of the 2010 USENIX Conference on USENIX Annual Technical Conference, USENIXATC 2010, p. 21. USENIX Association, Berkeley (2010)
22. Bruneo, D., Distefano, S., Longo, F., Puliafito, A., Scarpa, M.: Reliability assessment of wireless sensor nodes with non-linear battery discharge. In: 2010 IFIP Wireless Days (WD), pp. 1–5. IEEE Press (2010)

Author Index